Volume C:
The Modern Era

The Western Experience

VOLUME C:
THE MODERN ERA

THE WESTERN EXPERIENCE

SEVENTH EDITION

—◆—

MORTIMER CHAMBERS
University of California, Los Angeles

BARBARA HANAWALT
The Ohio State University

DAVID HERLIHY
Late Professor of History
Brown University

THEODORE K. RABB
Princeton University

ISSER WOLOCH
Columbia University

RAYMOND GREW
University of Michigan

Boston   Burr Ridge, IL   Dubuque, IA   Madison, WI   New York   San Francisco   St. Louis
Bangkok   Bogotá   Caracas   Lisbon   London   Madrid
Mexico City   Milan   New Delhi   Seoul   Singapore   Sydney   Taipei   Toronto

McGraw-Hill College

A Division of The McGraw·Hill Companies

THE WESTERN EXPERIENCE, VOLUME C: THE MODERN ERA, SEVENTH EDITION

This book is printed on acid-free paper.

3 4 5 6 7 8 9 0 VNH/VNH 9 3 2 1 0

ISBN 0–07–013069–8

Editorial director: *Jane E. Vaicunas*
Senior sponsoring editor: *Lyn Uhl*
Developmental editor: *Margaret Manos*
Senior marketing manager: *Suzanne Daghlian*
Project manager: *Vicki Krug*
Production supervisor: *Sandy Ludovissy*
Designer: *Ellen Pettengell/Michael Warrell*
Photo research coordinator: *Lori Hancock*
Art editor: *Brenda A. Ernzen*
Supplement coordinator: *Audrey A. Reiter*
Compositor: *York Graphic Services, Inc.*
Typeface: *10/12 Palatino*
Printer: *Von Hoffmann Press, Inc.*

Cover image: *Erich Lessing/Art Resource, NY. Cailebotte, Gustave (1848–94).* Street in Paris, Rain. 1877. *Oil Sketch. Musee Marmottan, Paris, France.*
Photo research: *Deborah Bull/PhotoSearch, Inc.*
Revisions and new art prepared by David Lindroth.

The credits section for this book begins on page C1 and is considered an extension of the copyright page.

Library of Congress Cataloging-in-Publication Data

The western experience / Mortimer Chambers . . . [et al.].— 7th ed.
    p.   cm.
  Includes bibliographical references and index.
  ISBN 0–07–012954–1
  1. Civilization—History. 2. Civilization, Western—History.
 I. Chambers, Mortimer.
 CB59.W38   1999
 909—dc21   98–18172
                                     CIP

About the Authors

Mortimer Chambers is Professor of History at the University of California at Los Angeles. He was a Rhodes scholar from 1949 to 1952 and received an M.A. from Wadham College, Oxford, in 1955 after obtaining his doctorate from Harvard University in 1954. He has taught at Harvard University (1954–1955) and the University of Chicago (1955–1958). He was Visiting Professor at the University of British Columbia in 1958, the State University of New York at Buffalo in 1971, the University of Freiburg (Germany) in 1974 and Vassar College in 1988. A specialist in Greek and Roman history, he is coauthor of *Aristotle's History of Athenian Democracy* (1962), editor of a series of essays entitled *The Fall of Rome* (1963), and author of *Georg Busolt: His Career in His Letters* (1990) and of *Staat der Athener,* a German translation and commentary to Aristotle's *Constitution of the Athenians* (1990). He has edited Greek texts of the latter work (1986) and of the *Hellenica Oxyrhynchia* (1993). He has contributed articles to the *American Historical Review and Classical Philology* as well as to other journals, both in America and in Europe.

Barbara Hanawalt is George III Chair of British History at The Ohio State University and the author of numerous books and articles on the social and cultural history of the Middle Ages. Her publications include *'Of Good and Ill Repute:' Gender and Social Control in Medieval England* (1998), *Growing Up in Medieval London: The Experience of*

Childhood in History (1993), *The Ties That Bound: Peasant Life in Medieval England* (1986), and *Crime and Conflict in English Communities, 1300–1348* (1979). She received her M.A. in 1964 and her Ph.D. in 1970, both from the University of Michigan. She has served as president of the Social Science History Association and has been on the Council of the American Historical Association and the Medieval Academy of America. As Director of the Center for Medieval Studies at the University of Minnesota (1990–1997), she edited five volumes on the intersection of history and literature. She was an NEH fellow (1997–1998), a fellow of the Guggenheim Foundation (1988–1989), an ACLS fellow (1975–1976), a fellow at the National Humanities Center (1997–1998), a fellow at the Wissenschaftskolleg in Berlin (1990–1991), a member of the School of Historical Research at the Institute for Advanced Study (1982–1983), and senior research fellow at the Newberry Library (1979–1980).

David Herlihy was the Mary Critchfield and Barnaby Keeney Professor of History at Brown University and the author of numerous books and studies on the social history of the Middle Ages. His most recent publications were *Opera Muliebria: Woman and Work in Medieval Europe* (1990); *Medieval Households* (1985); and, in collaboration with Christiane Klapisch-Zuber, *Tuscans and Their Families: A Study of the Florentine Catasto* *of 1427* (1985). He received his M.A. from the Catholic University of America in 1952, his Ph.D. from Yale University in 1956, and an honorary Doctor of Humanities from the University of San Francisco in 1983. He was a former president of several historical associations, and in 1990 served as president of the American History Association, the largest historical society in America. He was a fellow of the Guggenheim Foundation (1961–1962), the American Council of Learned Societies (1966–1967), the Center for Advanced Study in the Behavioral Sciences (1972–1973), and the National Endowment for the Humanities (1976). He was a fellow of the American Academy of Arts and Sciences and the American Philosophical Society. His articles and reviews have appeared in numerous professional journals, both here and abroad.

Theodore K. Rabb is Professor of History at Princeton University. He received his Ph.D. from Princeton, and subsequently taught at Stanford, Northwestern, Harvard, and Johns Hopkins universities. He is the author of numerous articles and reviews and has been editor of *The Journal of Interdisciplinary History* since its foundation. Among his books are *The Struggle for Stability in Early Modern Europe* (1975) and *Renaissance Lives* (1993). Professor Rabb has held offices in various national organizations, including the American Historical Association and The National Council for Historical Education. He was the principal historian for the PBS series, *Renaissance.*

Isser Woloch is Moore Collegiate Professor of History at Columbia University. He received his Ph.D. (1965) from Princeton University in the field of eighteenth- and nineteenth-century European history. He has taught at Indiana University and at the University of California at Los Angeles where, in 1967, he received a Distinguished Teaching Citation. He has been a fellow of the ACLS, the National Endowment for the Humanities, the Guggenheim Foundation, and the Institute for Advanced Study at Princeton. His publications include *Jacobin Legacy: The Democratic Movement under the Directory* (1970), *The Peasantry in the Old Regime: Conditions and Protests* (1970), *The French Veteran from the Revolution to the Restoration* (1979), *Eighteenth-Century Europe: Tradition and Progress, 1715–1789* (1982), *The New Regime: Transformations of the French Civic Order, 1789–1820s* (1994), and *Revolution and the Meanings of Freedom in the Nineteenth Century* (1996).

Raymond Grew is Professor of History at the University of Michigan. He earned both his M.A. (1952) and Ph.D. (1957) from Harvard University in the field of modern European history. He was a Fulbright Fellow to Italy (1954–1955), and Fulbright Travelling Fellow to France (1976, 1990), Guggenheim Fellow (1968–1969), Director of Studies at the Écoles des Hautes Études en Sciences Sociales in Paris (1976, 1987, 1990), and a Fellow of the National Endowment for the Humanities (1979). In 1962 he received the Chester Higby Prize from the American Historical Association, and in 1963 the Italian government awarded him the Unita d'Italia Prize; in 1992 he received the David Pinkney Prize of the Society for French Historical Studies. He is an active member of the A.H.A.; the Society for French Historical Studies; the Society for Italian Historical Studies, of which he has been president; and the Council for European Studies, of which he has twice served as national chair. He has authored *A Sterner Plan for Italian Unity* (1963), edited *Crises of Development in Europe and the United States* (1978), and, with Patrick J. Harrigan, authored *School, State, and Society: The Growth of Elementary Schooling in Nineteenth-Century France* (1991); he is also the editor of *Comparative Studies in Society and History* and its book series. He has written on global history and is one of the directors of the Global History Group. His articles and reviews have appeared in a number of European and American journals.

This book is dedicated
to the memory of David Herlihy
whose erudition and judgment
were central to its creation
and whose friendship and example
continue to inspire
his coauthors

Brief Contents

Contents

Chapter 19

THE AGE OF ENLIGHTENMENT 656

Chapter 20

THE FRENCH REVOLUTION 688

Chapter 21

THE AGE OF NAPOLEON 726

Chapter 22

FOUNDATIONS OF THE NINETEENTH CENTURY: POLITICS AND SOCIAL CHANGE 760

Chapter 23

LEARNING TO LIVE WITH CHANGE 794

Chapter 24

NATIONAL STATES AND NATIONAL CULTURES 834

Chapter 25

EUROPEAN POWER: WEALTH, KNOWLEDGE, AND IMPERIALISM 870

Chapter 26

THE AGE OF PROGRESS 908

Chapter 27

WORLD WAR AND DEMOCRACY 942

Chapter 28

THE GREAT TWENTIETH-CENTURY CRISIS 982

Chapter 29

THE NIGHTMARE: WORLD WAR II 1036

Chapter 30

THE NEW EUROPE 1084

EPILOGUE 1135

Maps

Boxes

PRIMARY SOURCE BOXES

Historical Issues Boxes

Chronological Boxes

Preface

The Western Experience was designed to provide an analytical and reasonably comprehensive account of the various contexts within which, and the processes by which, European society and civilization evolved. This edition is the book's seventh, evidence of a long life sustained with the help of many prior revisions. The sixth edition was more extensively rewritten and recast than any of its predecessors—our response to changes in students and in historical study—except in its treatment of the Middle Ages. That section, too, was revised; but its distinguished author was unable to redo his entire section in the way his coauthors could, often with his advice. David Herlihy lived just long enough to give his Presidential Address to the American Historical Association.

For this seventh edition, the discussion of the Middle Ages is in the hands of another distinguished scholar, Barbara Hanawalt. She has built on Dr. Herlihy's impressive work where she could, but her chapters are essentially new, the result of a different intellectual odyssey, a different experience as a teacher, and a record of research in other areas of medieval history. Some of the major changes to the medieval chapters in this edition include covering the historical concepts of feudalism and manorialism in the same chapter; describing the daily lives of medieval nobles, peasants, and townspeople; treating popular religion and culture in great depth; discussing the Crusades chronologically in the text; and offering a more detailed discussion of Islam and the West's interaction with the East during the Middle Ages.

Features of *The Western Experience*, Seventh Edition

Each generation of students brings different experiences, interests, and training into the classroom. These changes can be exaggerated, but they are important to the process of learning; and the students we teach have taught us enough about what currently engages or confuses them, about the impression of European history that they bring to college, and about what they can be expected to take from a survey course to make us want to reconsider the way that this book presents its material. For the previous edition and now again for this edition, our experience as teachers and the helpful comments of scores of other teachers has led to a rewriting and reordering throughout the book as we have sought to make it clearer and more accessible without sacrificing our initial goal of writing a reasonably sophisticated, interpretive, and analytic history.

INCORPORATION OF RECENT HISTORIOGRAPHY

For us the greatest pleasure in a revision lies in the challenge of absorbing and then incorporating the latest developments in historical understanding. From its first edition, this book included more of the results of quantitative and social history than general textbooks of European history usually did, an obvious reflection of our own research. Each subsequent edition provided an occasion to incorporate current methods and new knowledge, a challenge that required reconsidering paragraphs, sections, and whole chapters in the light of new theories and new research, sometimes literally reconceiving part of the past. That evolution has continued with this edition.

Recent work in all aspects of history needs to be taken into account, including economic, intellectual, cultural, demographic, and diplomatic history as well as social and political history. In the last decade, new work in gender studies and cultural studies has been the most striking of all, and we have sought to incorporate these fresh perspectives and new findings in this text.

A BALANCED, INTERPRETIVE, AND FLEXIBLE APPROACH

At the same time, the professional scholar's preference for new perspectives over familiar ones makes a distinction that lay readers may not share. For them, the latest interpretations need to be integrated with established understandings and controversies, with the history of people and events that are part of our cultural lore. We recognize that a textbook should provide a coherent presentation of the basic information from which students can begin to form their historical understanding. We believe this information must be an interpretive history but also that its readers—teachers, students, and general readers—should be free to use it in many different ways and in conjunction with their own areas of special knowledge and their own interests and curiosity.

OVERARCHING THEMES

Throughout this book, from the treatment of the earliest civilizations to the discussion of the present, certain themes are pursued. These seven themes constitute a set of categories by which societies and historical change can be analyzed.

(1) Social structure is one theme. In early chapters, social structure requires consideration of how the land was settled, divided among its inhabitants, and put to use. Later discussions of how property is held must include corporate, communal, and individual ownership, then investment banking and companies that sell shares. Similarly, we treat the division of labor in each era, noting whether workers are slave or free and when there are recognized specialists in fighting or crafts or trade. The chapters covering the Middle Ages and the early modern period explore the distinctions between nobles, commoners, and clergy; analyses of modern social classes accompany the treatment of the French Revolution and industrialization and twentieth-century societies.

(2) What used to be called the body politic is also followed throughout this book. Each era contains discussions of how political power is acquired and used and of the political structures that result. Students are shown the role of law from ancient codes to the present, and they learn about problems of order and the formation of the state, why its functions have increased and how the forms of political participation have changed.

(3) From cultivation in the plains of the Tigris and Euphrates to the global economy, we follow changes in the organization of production and in the impact of technology. We note how goods are distributed, and we observe patterns of trade as avenues of culture in addition to wealth. We look at the changing economic role of governments and the impact of economic theories.

(4) The evolution of the family and changing gender roles are topics fundamental to every period. Families give form to daily life and kinship structures. The history of demography, migration, and work is also a history of the family. The basis of social organization, the family has always been a central focus of religion and the principal instrument by which society assigns specific practices, roles, and values to women and men. These roles, and even more their practical impact, have changed from era to era, differing according to social class and between rural and urban societies. Observing gender roles across time, the student discovers that social, political, economic, and cultural history are

always interrelated; that the present is related to the past; and that social change brings gains and losses rather than evolution in a straight line—three lessons all history courses teach.

(5) No history of Europe could fail to pay attention to war, which, for most polities, has been their most demanding activity. Warfare has strained whatever resources were available from ancient times to the present, leading governments to invent new ways of extracting wealth and mobilizing support. War has built and undermined states, stimulated science and consumed technology, made heroes and restructured nobility, schooling, and social services. Glorified in European culture and often condemned, war in every era has affected the lives of ordinary people. This historical significance, more than specific battles, is one of the themes of *The Western Experience.*

(6) All histories of Europe attend to religion at certain well-established points, and this book does, too. We want as well to establish in the reader's mind that religion is important in all periods of history and that it affects and is affected by all the themes we address, creating community and causing conflict, shaping intellectual and daily life, providing the experiences that bind individual lives and society within a common system of meaning.

(7) For authors of a general history, no decision is more persistently difficult, chapter by chapter, than how much space to devote to cultural expression. In this respect, as elsewhere, we have consciously sought a particular kind of balance. We mean to present the most important formal ideas, philosophies, and ideologies of each era and to do so as clearly and concisely as possible. That presentation obviously requires some principle of inclusion. We emphasize concepts of recognized importance in the general history of ideas and those concepts that illuminate behavior and discourse in a given period. We pay particular attention to developments in science when we believe they are related to important intellectual, economic, and social trends. We write about popular culture in specific sections but also throughout the book, wanting its place in social history to be apparent and concerned not to exaggerate the distance between popular and high or formal culture. Finally, we write about many of the great works

of literature, art, and music, which involves formidable problems of selection; we have tried to emphasize works that are cultural expressions of their time and that have continued to create communities of experience reaching across space and time.

Attending to specific themes occasions heightened problems of organization in addition to issues of selection. It would be possible to structure this book around a series of topical essays, perhaps repeating the series of themes for each of the standard chronological divisions of European history. We have chosen instead to aim for a narrative flow that emphasizes interrelationships and historical context. From the first, we wanted each chapter to stand as an interpretive historical essay, with a beginning and conclusion; we have kept that goal in this edition. Sometimes, then, any one of these themes may reemerge within a discussion of something else—a significant event, an influential institution, an individual life, or a whole period of time. Often, several of these themes intersect in a single institution or historical trend. A reader can nevertheless follow any one of these themes across time and use that theme as a measure of change and a way to assess the differences and similarities between societies.

STRONG COVERAGE OF SOCIAL HISTORY

To discuss history in this way is to think comparatively and to employ categories of social history that in the last generation has greatly affected historical understanding. The impulse behind social history was not new. As early as the eighteenth century many historians (of whom Voltaire was one) called for a history that was more than chronology, more than an account of kings and battles. Although in the nineteenth century historical studies gave primary place to past politics, diplomacy, and war (using evidence from official documents newly accessible in state archives), there was even then important new work in economic history and in the history of ideas, culture, law, and religion. Social history, as a field of study, emerged as a further effort at broader coverage. For some it was primarily the history of the working class and of labor movements. For others it was the history of daily life—daily life in ancient

Rome or Renaissance Florence or old New York as reflected in styles of dress, housing, diet, and so on. Historical museums and popular magazines featured this "pots and pans history," which was appealing in its concreteness but tended (like the collections of interesting objects that it resembled) to lack a theoretical basis.

Modern social history seeks to compensate for the fact that most historical writing has been about the tiny minority who were the powerful, rich, and educated (and who left behind the fullest and most accessible records of their activities) but also to place its findings within a larger interpretive framework, borrowing from the social sciences, especially anthropology, sociology, economics, and political science. Still an arena of active and significant research, social history has also expanded, strengthened by new work on the history of women. With the development of a stronger theoretical sense, these interests have grown into gender studies that have given a whole new dimension to familiar historical issues. Social history has changed in another way, too, shifting away from explanations that gave priority to social structure and material factors and toward cultural studies.

CHRONOLOGICAL/CONCEPTUAL ORGANIZATION AND PERIODIZATION

These developments, which have greatly expanded the range of evidence and issues that historians must consider, make periodization more complex. The mainstay for organizing historical knowledge has been the rise and fall of dynasties, the formation of states, and the occurrence of wars and revolutions. The periodization most appropriate for describing changes in culture and ideas, economic production, or science and technology is often quite different, and changes in everyday life and popular culture often occur on a still different scale. We have sought a compromise. *The Western Experience* maintains the tradition of the introductory course in European history in that the chapters are essentially in chronological sequence. At the same time, insofar as each chapter is an interpretive essay, the information it contains serves to illustrate arguments as well as to

describe a period of European history. Major controversies over historical interpretations are discussed so that students can see how historical understanding is constructed, and some of those are sampled in historiographical boxes to encourage students to participate in these debates and formulate their own positions. For all these reasons, chapters also have topical emphases, and sometimes a cluster of chapters is required to treat a given era.

Pedagogical Features of the Seventh Edition
◄●►

The sixth edition of *The Western Experience* was more attractively produced than its predecessors, with more color, clearer maps, and a more accessible format. This new edition keeps all these changes while improving on them. The seventh edition offers more than 100 maps and 400 illustrations, each with an explanatory caption that enhances the coverage in the text. All the pedagogical devices listed here are designed to help students find their way without sacrificing subtlety of interpretation or trying to hide the fact that history is complex.

PRIMARY SOURCE BOXES

These excerpts from primary sources are designed to illustrate or supplement points made in the text, to provide some flavor of the issues under discussion, and to allow even the beginning student some of that independence of judgment that comes from a careful reading of historical sources.

HISTORICAL ISSUES BOXES

The seventh edition of *The Western Experience* has expanded the number of boxes presenting the contrasting historical interpretations that proved so popular in the sixth edition. These boxes, such as "The Debate over Feudalism" in chapter 8, and "On the Origins of the French Revolution" in chapter 20, provide samples from significant historiographical controversies.

MORE HEADING LEVELS

We have given particular attention to adding more helpful guides, such as the consistent use of the three levels of headings to give a clear outline of a chapter's argument, with much more frequent use of the third-level heading that quickly identifies specific topics.

CHRONOLOGICAL CHARTS

Nearly every chapter employs charts and chronological tables that outline the unfolding of major events and social processes and serve as a convenient reference for students.

Available Formats

In order to provide an alternative to the hardcover edition, *The Western Experience* is being made available in two-volume and three-volume paperbound editions. Volume I includes chapters 1 through 17 and covers material through the eighteenth century. Volume II includes chapters 15 through 30 and the epilogue, and covers material since the sixteenth century. Volume A includes chapters 1 through 12, Antiquity and the Middle Ages; Volume B includes chapters 11 through 21, The Early Modern Era; and Volume C includes chapters 19 through 30 and the epilogue, The Modern Era. The page numbering and cross-references in these editions remain the same as in the hardcover text.

Ancillary Instructional Materials

McGraw-Hill offers instructors and students a wide variety of ancillary materials to accompany *The Western Experience*. These supplements listed here may accompany *The Western Experience*. Please contact your local McGraw-Hill representative for details concerning policies, prices, and availability, as some restrictions may apply.

FOR THE STUDENT

Student Study Guide/Workbook with Map Exercises, Volumes I and II   The Student Study Guide includes the following features for each chapter: chapter outlines, chronological diagrams, four kinds of exercises—map exercises, exercises in document analysis, exercises that reinforce the book's important overarching themes, exercises in matching important terms with significant individuals—and essay topics requiring analysis and speculation. The pages of the workbook are perforated to allow students to hand in exercises as professors may require.

New Multimedia Supplements for the Student: Student Interactive CD-ROM Study Guide   This student CD incorporates the exercises included in the study guide in an augmented, more engaging interactive format.

- Chapter outlines are connected through hyperlinks to self-tests.
- Interactive "drag and drop" exercises ask students to match up significant individuals and key terms with the correct identifications.
- An audio function helps students pronounce difficult terms.
- Self-tests offer students a chance to find out in what areas they need more study.
- Essay questions are available with print capability from the CD-ROM.
- Map exercises are also included.

Web Site   A fully interactive, book-specific Web site features links to chapter- and topic-appropriate sites on the World Wide Web, a guide to using the Internet, and practice midterm and final exams written by the study guide author that will be posted at the appropriate times during the semester. These quizzes will offer students content-specific feedback and will be self-scoring.

FOR THE INSTRUCTOR

An integrated instructional package is available in either print or electronic format.

Instructor's Manual/Test Bank   This fully revised and expanded manual includes chapter summaries, lecture and discussion topics, and lists of additional teaching resources such as recommended films, novels, and Web sites. In addition, the test bank for the seventh edition of *The Western Experience* includes more questions than ever before. Types of questions include multiple choice, identification, sentence completion, essay (both factual and interpretive), and critical thinking exercises (such as map analysis or source analysis questions).

Computerized Test Bank A computerized test bank is available in Windows or Mac formats.

Overhead Transparency Acetates This expanded full-color transparency package includes all the maps and chronological charts in the text.

New Multimedia Supplement for the Instructor: Presentation Manager CD-ROM This CD allows instructors to create their own classroom presentation using resources provided by McGraw-Hill. Instructors may also customize their presentations by adding slides or other electronic resources. In addition, this CD allows instructors access to all their instructional materials (including the test bank) in one integrated instructional package. The Presentation Manager includes the following resources: a Power Point slide show, electronic overhead transparencies (maps and chronological charts from the text), the instructor's manual (with hyperlinks to appropriate maps and timelines to help the instructor build lecture presentations), and the test bank.

Acknowledgments
◀◉▶

Manuscript Reviewers and Consultants, seventh edition Frank Baglione, *Tallahassee Community College;* Paul Goodwin, *University of Connecticut;* Robert Herzstein, *University of South Carolina;*

Carla M. Joy, *Red Rocks Community College;* Kathleen Kamerick, *University of Iowa;* Carol Bresnahan Menning, *University of Toledo;* Eileen Moore, *University of Alabama at Birmingham;* Frederick Murphy, *Western Kentucky University;* Michael Myers, *University of Notre Dame;* Robert B. Patterson, *University of South Carolina at Columbia;* Peter Pierson, *Santa Clara University;* Alan Schaffer, *Clemson University;* Marc Schwarz, *University of New Hampshire;* Charles R. Sullivan, *University of Dallas;* Jack Thacker, *Western Kentucky University;* Bruce L. Venarde, *University of Pittsburgh*

Manuscript Reviewers and Consultants, sixth edition S. Scott Bartchy, *University of California, Los Angeles;* Thomas Blomquist, *Northern Illinois University;* Nancy Ellenberger, *United States Naval Academy;* Steven Epstein, *University of Colorado at Boulder;* Laura Gellott, *University of Wisconsin at Parkside;* Barbara Hanawalt, *University of Minnesota;* Drew Harrington, *Western Kentucky University;* Lisa Lane, *Mira Costa College;* William Matthews, *S.U.N.Y. at Potsdam;* Carol Bresnahan Menning, *University of Toledo;* Sandra Norman, *Florida Atlantic University;* Peter Pierson, *Santa Clara University;* Linda Piper, *University of Georgia;* Philip Racine, *Wofford College;* Eileen Soldwedel, *Edmonds Community College;* John Sweets, *University of Kansas;* Richard Wagner, *Des Moines Area Community College*

Focus Group Reviewers from Spring 1992 Michael DeMichele, *University of Scranton;* Nancy Ellenberger, *United States Naval Academy;* Drew Harrington, *Western Kentucky University;* William Matthews, *S.U.N.Y. at Potsdam*

We would like to thank Leslye Jackson and Amy Mack of McGraw-Hill for their considerable efforts in bringing this edition to fruition.

Introduction

Everyone uses history. We use it to define who we are and to connect our personal experience to the collective memory of the groups to which we belong, including a particular region, nation, and culture. We invoke the past to explain our hopes and ambitions and to justify our fears and conflicts. The Charter of the United Nations, like the American Declaration of Independence, is based on a view of history. When workers strike or armies march, they cite the lessons of their history. Because history is so important to us psychologically and intellectually, historical understanding is always shifting and often controversial.

Some questions must be asked repeatedly, some issues arise again and again; but much of this knowledge is cumulative, for while asking new questions, historians integrate the answers that have been learned from previous studies, and historical knowledge grows. History is not merely a subjective exercise in which all opinions are equally valid. No matter what motivated a particular historical question, the answer to it stands until overturned by better evidence. We now know more about the past than ever before, and we understand it as the people we study could not. Unlike them, we know how their history came out; we can apply methods they did not have, and often we have evidence they never saw. This knowledge and the ways of interpreting it are the collective achievement of thousands of historians.

We also use history for pleasure—as a cultivated entertainment. The biographies of great men and women, dramatic accounts of important events, colorful tales of earlier times can be fascinating in themselves. Through these encounters with history, we experience the common concerns of all people; and through the study of European history, we come to appreciate the ideals and conflicts, the failures and accidents, the social needs and human choices that formed the Western world in which we live. Knowing the historical context also enriches our appreciation for the achievements of European culture, enabling us to see its art, science, ideas, and politics in relationship to real people, specific interests, and burning issues.

We think of Europe's history as the history of Western civilization, but the very concept of a Western civilization is itself the result of history. The Greeks gave the names *east* and *west* to the points on the horizon at which the sun rises and sets. Because the Persian Empire and India lay to their east, the Greeks labeled their own continent, which they called Europe, the west. The distinction between Western civilization and others—ethnocentric, often arbitrary, and frequently exaggerated—continued even as that civilization changed and expanded with the Roman Empire, Christianity, and the European conquest of the New World. The view that the Western civilization is all one, that America is tied more closely to ancient Greece than Greece is to Egypt or Spain to Islam can be easily challenged in every respect save cultural tradition.

The Western Experience gives primary attention to a small part of the world and thus honors that cultural tradition. The concentration on Europe nevertheless includes important examples of city and of rural life; of empires and monarchies and republics; of life before and after industrialization; of societies in which labor was organized through markets, serfdom, and slavery; of cultures little concerned with science and of ones that used changing scientific knowledge; of non-Christian religions and of all the major forms of Christianity in action.

Throughout this book, from the treatment of the earliest civilizations to the discussion of the present, certain themes are pursued. These seven themes constitute a set of categories by which societies and historical change can be analyzed: social structure, the body politic, changes in the organization of production and in the impact of technology, the evolution of the family and changing gender roles, war, religion, and cultural expression.

Attending to specific themes occasions heightened problems of organization, in addition to issues of selection. It would be possible to structure this book around a series of topical essays, perhaps repeating the series of themes for each of the standard chronological divisions of European history. We have chosen instead to aim for a narrative flow that emphasizes interrelationships and historical context. From the first we wanted each chapter to stand as an interpretive historical essay, with a beginning and conclusion; we have kept that goal in this edition. Sometimes, then, any one of these themes may reemerge within a discussion of something else—a significant event, an influential institution, an individual life, or a whole period of time. Often, several of these themes intersect in a single institution or historical trend. A reader can nevertheless follow any one of these themes across time and use them as a measure of change and a way to assess the differences and similarities between societies. To aid students undertaking such an exercise—especially useful in review or when preparing an essay—the index indicates places where each theme is treated.

Readers of this book may thus use it as an introduction to historical method, find within it a framework to which they can attach whatever else they know about Western society, and discover here some challenges to their preconceptions—about the past, about how societies are organized, and about how people behave. Historical study is an integrative enterprise in which long-term trends and specific moments, in which social structure and individual actions, are all brought together. It gives the student training in how to analyze society and assess social issues and provides experience in decision making and argumentation.

A college course is not the only way to build a personal culture. Nor is history the only path to integrated knowledge. Western history is not the only history a person should know, nor is an introductory survey necessarily the best way to learn it. Still, as readers consider and then challenge interpretations offered in this text, they will exercise critical and analytical skills. They can begin to overcome the parochialism that thinks only the present matters. They can acknowledge the greatness of their Western heritage and its distinctiveness, which includes injustice, cruelty, and failure.

To do these things is to experience the study of history as one of the vital intellectual activities by which we come to know who and where we are.

Mortimer Chambers
Barbara Hanawalt
Theodore K. Rabb
Isser Woloch
Raymond Grew

THE WESTERN EXPERIENCE

THE AGE OF ENLIGHTENMENT

*S*harp breaks have been rare in Europe's intellectual and religious life—two of the defining themes in the Western experience—but we are about to witness one. During the eighteenth century the great scientific and philosophical innovations of the previous century evolved into a naturalistic worldview divorced from religion. Scientific knowledge and religious skepticism, previously the concerns of an extremely narrow group of learned people, entered the consciousness of Europe's elites in a way that would have startled Descartes or Newton. Displacing the authority of religion with that of reason, the new outlook offered an optimistic vision of future progress in human affairs. Known as the Enlightenment, this movement formed the intellectual foundation for a new sense of modernity.

Never since pagan times, certainly not during the Renaissance, was religious belief so directly challenged. Many important eighteenth-century intellectuals no longer believed in Christianity and wished to reduce its influence in society. They argued that there was no divine standard of morality, no afterlife to divert humanity from worldly concerns. These writers developed a strong, sometimes arrogant, sense of their own capacity to ignore traditional authority and guide society toward change.

The evolution of cultural institutions and the media of the day gave these writers an increasingly wide forum. While aristocratic patronage and classical culture remained influential, a new kind of middle-class culture was developing alongside a much wider reading public and an expanding sphere of public discussion.

Yet, as we turn to consider the Enlightenment within the varied cultural environments of the eighteenth century, we should not exaggerate. Although they were critics of their society, most eighteenth-century intellectuals lived comfortably amid Europe's high culture. They had scant interest in or understanding of the vibrant popular culture around them. On the contrary, their growing belief in "public opinion" referred solely to the educated elites of the aristocracy and the middle classes.

I. The Enlightenment

Building on seventeenth-century science, on skepticism in matters of religion, and on a heightened appreciation of the culture of classical antiquity, eighteenth-century intellectuals approached their role in a new spirit. They believed that human behavior and institutions could be studied rationally, like Newton's universe, and that their faults could be corrected. They saw themselves as participants in a movement—which they called the Enlightenment—that could make educated men and women more understanding, tolerant, and virtuous.

THE BROADENING REVERBERATIONS OF SCIENCE

It is hard to think of two men less revolutionary in temperament than the seventeenth century's René Descartes and Isaac Newton. Both were conservative on matters outside the confines of science, had relatively little concern for social institutions, remained practicing Christians, and wrote only for small learned audiences. Yet their legacy of insight into the world of nature produced in succeeding generations what has been described as "a permanent intellectual insurrection," which unfolded in a spirit undreamed of by either man.

The Popularization of Science While eighteenth-century scientists pondered the cosmologies of Descartes and Newton, nonscientists in England and on the continent applied the methodologies of Descartes, Newton, and the philosopher John Locke to other realms of human thought. They fused the notion of methodical doubt and naturalistic explanations of phenomena into a scientific or mathematical spirit, which at bottom simply meant confidence in reason and a skeptical attitude toward accepted dogmas. They attempted to popularize scientific method, with the aim of transforming the values of Western civilization. Writers translated the discoveries of scientists into clear and even amusing general reading. The literary talents of these enthusiasts helped make household words of Newton and Descartes among educated Europeans.

A more calculating and ambitious propagandist of the scientific spirit was the Frenchman François-Marie Arouet, who wrote under the pen name of Voltaire and is virtually synonymous with the Enlightenment. While his chief talents lay in literature and criticism, Voltaire also spent some time studying Newton's work. In 1738 he published a widely read popularization called *Elements of the Philosophy of Newton*. However dry the study of physics, Voltaire argued, it frees the mind from dogma, and its experimental methods provide a model for the liberation of human thought. Moreover, Voltaire related Newton's achievement to the environment of a liberal England that also produced Francis Bacon and Locke, the three of whom Voltaire adopted as his personal Trinity. In his *Philosophical Letters on the English* (1734)—a celebration of English toleration and an indirect attack on religious bigotry, censorship, and social snobbery in France—Voltaire had already noted the respect enjoyed in England by its writers and scientists. He saw this recognition of talent as a crucial component of a free society and as a condition for the achievements of a man like Newton.

Popularizations of scientific method stimulated public interest in science, as mathematicians, cartographers, and astronomers made notable advances in their fields. But further scientific progress was far from automatic. In chemistry, for example, the traditions of alchemy persisted, and phenomena such as fire long escaped objective analysis. At the end of the century, however, a major breakthrough occurred when the Englishman Joseph Priestley isolated oxygen and the Frenchman Antoine Lavoisier analyzed the components of air and water and came close to explaining the process of combustion.

The vogue for science also had a dubious side, apparent, for example, in the great popularity of mesmerism. This pseudoscience of magnetic fields purported to offer its wealthy devotees relief from a variety of ailments by the use of special "electrical" baths and treatments. Although repeatedly condemned by the Academy of Sciences in Paris, mesmerism continued to attract educated followers.

Natural History The most widely followed scientific enterprise in the eighteenth century was

▲ French chemist Lavoisier conducts an experiment in his laboratory to study the composition of air during the process of respiration.
Bettmann.

natural history, the science of the earth's development—a combination of geology, zoology, and botany. This field of study was easy for the non-scientist to appreciate. Its foremost practitioner was G. L. Buffon, keeper of the French Botanical Gardens—a patronage position that allowed him to produce a multivolume *Natural History of the Earth* between 1749 and 1778. Drawing on a vast knowledge of phenomena such as fossils, Buffon went beyond previous attempts to classify the data of nature and provided both a description and a theory of the earth's development.

Although he was a nonbeliever, Buffon did not explicitly attack religious versions of such events as the Creation; he simply ignored them, an omission of obvious significance to his readers. Similarly, while he did not specifically contend that human beings have evolved from beasts, he implied it. "It is possible," he wrote, "to descend by almost insensible degrees from the most perfect creature to the most formless matter." Buffon's

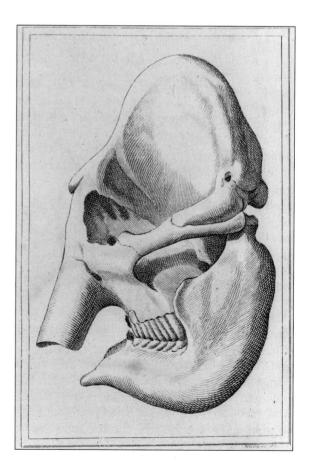

▶ A plate from the section on fossil remains in Buffon's *Natural History* illustrating the skull of an elephant from India.
From "Natural History General and Particular" by George Buffon. Courtesy Brooklyn Public Library.

earth did not derive from a singular act of divine creation that would explain the origins of human beings. The readers of his *Natural History* or its numerous popularizations in several languages thus encountered a universe that had developed through evolution.

BEYOND CHRISTIANITY

The erosion of biblical revelation as a source of authority is one hallmark of the Enlightenment. This shift derived some of its impetus from seventeenth-century scientists and liberal theologians who were themselves believing Christians but who opposed religious superstition or "enthusiasm," as they called it. They had hoped to accommodate religion to new philosophical standards and scientific formulations by eliminating the superstitious imagery that could make religion seem ridiculous and by treating the world of nature as a form of revelation in which God's majesty could be seen. The devil, for example, could be considered as a category of moral evil rather than as a specific horned creature with a pitchfork. They hoped to bolster the Christian religion by deemphasizing miracles and focusing on reverence for the Creator and on the moral teachings of the Bible. Their approach did indeed help educated people adhere to Christianity during the eighteenth century. In the final analysis, however, this kind of thinking diminished the authority of religion in society.

Toleration   One current of thought that encouraged a more secular outlook was the idea of toleration, as propounded by the respected French critic Pierre Bayle. Consciously applying methodical doubt to subjects that Descartes had excluded from such treatment, Bayle's *Critical and Historical Dictionary* (1697) put the claims of religion to the test of critical reason. Certain Christian traditions emerged from this scrutiny as the equivalent of myth and fairy tale, and the history of Christianity appeared as a record of fanaticism and persecution. Bayle's chief target was Christianity's attempts to impose orthodoxy at any cost (for example, the Spanish Inquisition and Louis XIV's revocation of the Edict of Nantes and persecution of French Protestants). Though a devout Calvinist himself, Bayle advocated complete toleration, which would allow any person to practice any religion or none at all. An individual's moral behavior rather than his or her creed is what mattered, according to Bayle. Ethics, he argued, do not depend on the Bible; a Muslim, a Confucian, a Jew, even an atheist can be moral.

The most striking success of the eighteenth-century campaign for toleration came with the Edict of Toleration issued by the Habsburg emperor Joseph II on his ascendancy to the throne in 1781. For the first time a Catholic Habsburg ruler recognized the right of Protestants and Jews in his realm to worship freely and to hold property and public office (see "Joseph II on Religious Toleration," p. 662). Joseph also tried to reduce the influence of the Catholic Church by ordering the dissolution of numerous monasteries on the grounds that they were useless and corrupt. Part of their confiscated wealth was used to support the medical school at the University of Vienna.

Deism   Voltaire became the Enlightenment's most vigorous antireligious polemicist. This prolific writer was one of the century's most brilliant literary stylists, historians, and poets. Those talents alone would have assured his fame. But Voltaire was also a dedicated antagonist of Christianity. For tactical reasons, much of his attack against *l'infame* ("the infamous thing"), as he called Christianity, targeted such practices as monasticism or the behavior of priests. His ultimate target, though, was Christianity itself, which, he declared, "every sensible man, every honorable man must hold in horror."

Voltaire's masterpiece, a best-seller called *The Philosophical Dictionary* (1764), had to be published anonymously and was burned by the authorities in Switzerland, France, and the Netherlands. Modeled after Bayle's dictionary, it was far blunter. Of theology, he wrote, "We find man's insanity in all its plenitude." Organized religion is not simply false but pernicious, he argued. Voltaire believed that religious superstition inevitably bred fanaticism and predictably resulted in bloody episodes like the Saint Bartholomew's Day Massacre.

Voltaire hoped that educated Europeans would abandon Christianity in favor of deism, a belief that recognized God as the Creator but held that the world, once created, functions ac-

▲ In 1745, the Habsburg monarchy expelled an estimated 70,000 Jews from Prague to appease antisemitic sentiment.

cording to natural laws without interference by God. Humanity thus lives essentially on its own in an ordered universe, without hope or fear of divine intervention and without the threat of damnation or the hope of eternal salvation. For deists, religion should be a matter of private contemplation rather than public worship and mythic creeds. Although certain figures in the Enlightenment went beyond deism to a philosophical atheism, which rejected any concept of God as unprovable, Voltaire's mild deism remained a characteristic view of eighteenth-century writers. At bottom, however, this form of spirituality was essentially secular. Broad-minded clergy could accept many of the arguments of eighteenth-century science and philosophy, but they could not accept deism.

THE PHILOSOPHES

Science and secularism became the rallying points of a group of French intellectuals known as the *philosophes*. Their traditionalist opponents employed this term to mock the group's pretensions, but the philosophes themselves used that label with pride. They saw themselves as a vanguard, the men who raised the Enlightenment to the status of a self-conscious movement. The leaders of this influential coterie of writers were Voltaire and Denis Diderot. Its ranks included mathematicians Jean d'Alembert and the marquis de Condorcet, the magistrate baron de Montesquieu, the government official Jacques Turgot, and the atheist philosopher baron d'Holbach. Thus, the French philosophes came from both the aristocracy and the middle class. Outside of France their kinship extended to a group of brilliant Scottish philosophers, including David Hume and Adam Smith; to the German playwright Gotthold Lessing and the philosopher Immanuel Kant; to the Italian economist and penal reformer the marquis of Beccaria; and to such founders of the American Philosophical Society as Benjamin Franklin and Thomas Jefferson.

JOSEPH II ON RELIGIOUS TOLERATION

Between 1765 and 1781 Joseph II was joint ruler of the Habsburg Empire with his pious mother, Empress Maria Theresa. Joseph advocated a utilitarian approach to religious toleration (Document I) but made little headway against Maria Theresa's traditional insistence that the state must actively combat religious dissent. Soon after Maria Theresa's death Joseph promulgated a series of decrees on religion, including a landmark Toleration Edict for Protestants (Document II) and even a special, if somewhat less sweeping, edict of toleration for the Jews of his domains.

(I) LETTER TO MARIA THERESA, JULY 1777

"The word *toleration* has caused misunderstanding.... God preserve me from thinking it a matter of indifference whether the citizens turn Protestant or remain Catholics.... I would give all I possess if all the Protestants of your States would go over to Catholicism. The word *toleration* as I understand it, means only that I would employ any persons, without distinction of religion, in purely temporal matters, allow them to own property, practice trades, be citizens if they were qualified and if this would be of advantage to the State and its industry.... The undisturbed practice of their religion makes them far better subjects and causes them to avoid irreligion, which is a far greater danger to our Catholics."

(II) TOLERATION EDICT OF OCTOBER 1781

"We have found Ourselves moved to grant to the adherents of the Lutheran and Calvinist religions, and also to the non Uniat Greek religion, everywhere, the appropriate private practice of their faith. ... The Catholic religion alone shall continue to enjoy the prerogative of the public practice of its faith. ... Non-Catholics are in future admitted under dispensation to buy houses and real property, to acquire municipal domicile and practice as master craftsmen, to take up academic appointments and posts in the public service, and are not to be required to take the oath in any form contrary to their religious tenets. ... In all choices or appointments to official posts ... difference of religion is to be disregarded."

From C. A. Macartney (ed.), *The Habsburg and Hohenzollern Dynasties in the 17th and 18th Centuries*, HarperCollins, 1970, pp. 151 and 155–157.

Intellectual Freedom The philosophes shared above all else a critical spirit, the desire to reexamine the assumptions and institutions of their societies and expose them to the tests of reason, experience, and utility. Today this might sound banal, but it was not so at a time when almost everywhere religion permeated society. Asserting the primacy of reason meant turning away from faith, the essence of religion. It meant a decisive break with the Christian worldview, which placed religious doctrine at the center of society's values. The philosophes invoked the paganism of ancient Greece and Rome, where the spirit of rational inquiry prevailed among educated people. They ridiculed the Middle Ages as the "Dark Ages" and contrasted the religious spirit of that era to their own sense of liberation and modernity. In *The Decline and Fall of the Roman Empire* (1776–1788), the historian Edward Gibbon declared that Christianity had eclipsed a Roman civilization that had sought to live according to reason rather than myths.

The inspiration of antiquity was matched by the stimulus of modern science and philosophy. The philosophes laid claim to Newton, who made the universe intelligible without the aid of revelation, and Locke, who uncovered the workings of the human mind. From Locke they went on to argue that human personality is malleable: Its nature is not fixed, let alone corrupted by original sin. People are therefore ultimately responsible to themselves for what they do with their lives. Existing arrangements are no more nor less sacred than experience has proved them to be. As the humanists had several centuries before, the philosophes placed human beings at the center of thought. Unlike most humanists, however, philosophes placed thought in the service of change and launched a noisy public movement.

WHAT IS ENLIGHTENMENT?

◆◉◆

The most concise formulation of the Enlightenment's spirit is conveyed in an essay of the 1780s by the German philosopher Immanuel Kant. As Kant makes clear, intellectual freedom and the role of public opinion refer not so much to the average person in the street as to the educated classes— serious writers (whom he calls "scholars") and their public. Note that in drawing the distinction between the public realm (where freedom is vital) and the private realm (where obedience is rightly expected), Kant reverses the labels that we would likely assign to the two realms today.

"Enlightenment is man's emergence from his self-imposed nonage. Nonage is the inability to use one's own understanding without another's guidance. This nonage is self-imposed if its cause lies not in lack of understanding but in indecision and lack of courage to use one's own mind without another's guidance. Dare to know. (*Sapere aude*). 'Have the courage to use your own understanding,' is therefore the motto of the Enlightenment.

"Laziness and cowardice are the reasons why such a large part of mankind gladly remain minors all their lives, long after nature has freed them from external guidance. They are the reasons why it is so easy for others to set themselves up as guardians. It is so comfortable to be a minor. If I have a book that thinks for me, a pastor who acts as my conscience, then I have no need to exert myself. . . .

"This enlightenment requires nothing but freedom: freedom to make public use of one's reason in all matters. . . . On the other hand, the private use of reason may frequently be narrowly restricted without especially hindering the progress of enlightenment. By 'public use of reason' I mean that use which man, as a scholar, makes of it before the reading public. I call 'private use' that use which a man makes of his reason in a civic post that has been entrusted to him . . . and where arguing is not permitted: one must obey. . . . Thus it would be very unfortunate if an officer on duty and under orders from his superiors should want to criticize the appropriateness or utility of his orders. He must obey. But as a scholar he could not rightfully be prevented from taking notice of the mistakes in the military service and from submitting his views to his public for its judgement."

Persecution and Triumph   Philosophes appeared clamorous to their contemporaries because they had to battle entrenched authority. Religious traditionalists and the apparatus of censorship in almost all countries threatened the intellectual freedom demanded by the philosophes. They often had to publish their works clandestinely and anonymously. Sometimes they were pressured into withholding manuscripts from publication altogether or into making humiliating public apologies for controversial books. Even with such caution, almost all philosophes saw some of their publications confiscated and burned. A few were forced into exile or sent to jail: Voltaire spent several decades across the French border in Switzerland, and Voltaire and Diderot both spent time in prison. Although the notoriety produced by these persecutions stimulated the sale of their works, the anxiety took its toll.

By the 1770s, however, the philosophes had survived their running war with the authorities.

Some of them lived to see their ideas widely accepted and their works acclaimed. Thus, even if they had contributed little else to the Western experience, their struggle for freedom of expression would merit them a significant place in its history.

Social Science   But the philosophes achieved far more. In their scholarly and polemical writings, they investigated a wide range of subjects and pioneered in several new disciplines. Some philosophes—Voltaire, for example—were path-breaking historians. Moving beyond traditional chronicles of battles and rulers' biographies, they studied culture, social institutions, and government structures in an effort to understand past societies as well as describe major events. Practically inventing the notion of social science, they investigated the theoretical foundations of social organization (sociology) and the workings of the human mind (psychology). On a more practical

▲ In 1778, the last year of his life, Voltaire returned triumphantly to Paris. When he attended a performance of one of his plays at the national theater (known as the *Comédie Française*), the audience greeted him with tumultuous enthusiasm. To this day a statue of Voltaire holds pride of place in that renowned theater, where he first made his reputation.
Giraudon/Art Resource, NY.

level, they proposed fundamental reforms in such areas as the penal system and education.

The philosophes embedded their study of social science in questions of morality and the study of ethics. Enlightenment ethics were generally utilitarian. Such philosophers as David Hume tried to define good and evil in pragmatic terms; they argued that social utility should become the standard for public morality. This approach to moral philosophy in turn raised the question of whether any human values were absolute and eternal. Among the philosophers who grappled with this challenge, Kant tried to harmonize the notion of absolute moral values with practical reason.

Political Liberty   The most influential work of social science produced by the Enlightenment was probably *The Spirit of the Laws* (1748) by the French magistrate Montesquieu. The book offered a comparative study of governments and societies. On the one hand, Montesquieu introduced the perspective of relativism: He tried to analyze the institutions of government in relation to the special customs, climate, religion, and commerce of various countries. He thus argued that no single, ideal model of government existed. On the other hand, he deeply admired his own idealized version of the British system of government; he thereby implied that all societies could learn from the British about liberty.

Montesquieu's sections on liberty won a wide readership in Europe and in America, where the book was influential among the drafters of the U.S. Constitution. Political liberty, said Montesquieu, requires checks on those who hold power in a state, whether that power is exercised by a king, an aristocracy, or the people. Liberty can thrive only with a balance of powers, preferably by the separation of the executive, the legislative, and the judicial branches of government. Montesquieu ascribed a central role to aristocracies as checks on royal despotism. Indeed, many eighteenth-century writers on politics considered strong privileged groups, independent from both the crown and the people, as the only effective bulwarks against tyranny. To put it another way, Montesquieu's followers thought that the price for a society free from despotism was privilege for some of its members.

Liberal Economics French and British thinkers of the Enlightenment transformed economic theory with attacks against mercantilism and government regulation. We noted in chapter 18 Adam Smith's critique of artificial restraints on individual economic initiative. In France, the Physiocrats similarly argued that economic progress depended on freeing agriculture and trade from restrictions. Since in their view land was the only real source of wealth, they also called for reforms in the tax structure with a uniform and equitable land tax. In opposition to a traditional popular insistence on government intervention to maintain supplies of grain and flour at fair prices, the Physiocrats advocated freedom for the grain trade to operate according to the dictates of supply and demand. The incentive of higher prices would encourage growers to expand productivity, they believed, and in this way the grain shortages that plagued Europe could eventually be eliminated,

although at the cost of temporary hardship for most consumers.

DIDEROT AND THE *ENCYCLOPEDIA*

The Enlightenment thus produced not only a new intellectual spirit but also a wide range of critical writings on various subjects. In addition, the French philosophes collectively generated a single work that exemplified their notion of how knowledge could be useful: Diderot's *Encyclopédie* (*Encyclopedia*).

Diderot Denis Diderot never achieved the celebrity of his friend Voltaire, but his career proved equally central to the Enlightenment. The son of a provincial knife maker, Diderot was educated in Jesuit schools, but at the first opportunity he headed for Paris. Continuing to educate himself while living a bohemian existence, Diderot developed an unshakable sense of purpose: to make himself into an independent and influential intellectual.

Within a few years, he had published a remarkable succession of writings—novels and plays, mathematical treatises, an attack on inept medical practices, and several works on religion and moral philosophy. His most original writings examined the role of passion in human personality and in any system of values derived from an understanding of human nature. Specifically, Diderot affirmed the role of sexuality, arguing against artificial taboos and repression. As an advocate of what was sometimes called "the natural man," Diderot belies the charge leveled against the philosophes that they overemphasized reason to the neglect of feeling. The thread of religious criticism in these works was also notable. Starting from a position of mild skepticism, Diderot soon passed to deism and ended up in the atheist camp.

Diderot's unusual boldness in getting his works published brought him a considerable reputation but also some real trouble. Two of his books were condemned by the authorities as contrary to religion, the state, and morals. In 1749 he spent 100 days in prison and was released only after making a humiliating apology. At about that time, Diderot was approached by a publisher to translate a British encyclopedic reference work into French. After a number of false starts, he persuaded the publisher to sponsor instead an entirely new and more comprehensive work that would reflect the interests of the philosophes.

The Encyclopedia The *Encyclopedia, or Classified Dictionary of the Sciences, Arts, and Occupations,* an inventory of all fields of knowledge from the most theoretical to the most mundane, constituted an arsenal of critical concepts. As the preface stated: "Our Encyclopedia is a work that could only be carried out in a philosophic century. . . . All things must be examined without sparing anyone's sensibilities. . . . The arts and sciences must regain their freedom." The ultimate purpose of the *Encyclopedia,* wrote its editors, was "to change the general way of thinking." Written in this spirit by an array of talented collaborators, the expensive twenty-eight-volume *Encyclopedia* (1752–1772) fulfilled the fondest hopes of its editors and four thousand initial subscribers.

In such a work, religion could scarcely be ignored, but neither could it be openly attacked. Instead, the editors treated religion with artful satire or else relegated it to a philosophical or historical plane. Demystified and subordinated, religion was probed and questioned like any other subject, much to the discomfort of learned but orthodox critics.

Science stood at the core of the *Encyclopedia,* but the editors emphasized the technological or practical side of science with numerous articles and plates illustrating machines, tools, and manufacturing processes. They praised the roles of mechanics, engineers, and artisans in society and stressed the benefits of efficient production in the advance of civilization. Such emphasis implied that technology and artisanal skills constituted valuable realms of knowledge comparable to theoretical sciences such as physics and mathematics.

On economic topics the encyclopedists tended to echo the Physiocratic crusade against restrictions on trade and agriculture. But the opinions and aspirations expressed were those of the elites, whose prerogatives, especially in matters of property, were not being threatened. Articles that might reflect the concerns of the popular masses on such issues as wages or affordable food prices

▼ Diderot's *Encyclopedia* focused much of its attention on technology. Illustrations of mechanical processes, such as the one shown here for making plate glass, filled eleven folio volumes.
Plate from "L'Encyclopédie," Denis Diderot.

were notably absent. Nor did the *Encyclopedia* take a novel line on questions of government. The authors generally endorsed absolute monarchy, provided it was reasonably efficient and just. The major political concerns of the editors were civil rights, freedom of expression, and the rule of law.

The **Encyclopedia's** *Impact*   In retrospect, after the French Revolution, the *Encyclopedia* does not seem very revolutionary. Yet in the context of the times, it assuredly was. The revolution that Diderot sought was intellectual. As he wrote in a letter to a friend, the encyclopedists were promoting "a revolution in the minds of men to free them from prejudice." Judging by the reaction of religious and government authorities, they were eminently successful. "Up till now," commented one French bishop, "hell has vomited its venom drop by drop." Now, he concluded, it could be found assembled between the *Encyclopedia*'s covers.

After allowing the first three volumes to appear, the French government banned the *Encyclopedia* in 1759 and revoked the bookseller's license to issue the remaining volumes. As the attorney general of France put it: "There is a project formed, a society organized to propagate materialism, to destroy religion, to inspire a spirit of independence, and to nourish the corruption of morals." Most of the *Encyclopedia*'s contributors prudently withdrew from the project, but Diderot went underground and continued the herculean task until the subscribers received every promised volume, including eleven magnificent folios of illustrations. By the time these appeared, the persecutions had receded. Indeed, the *Encyclopedia* was reprinted in cheaper editions (both legal and pirated) that sold out rapidly, earning fortunes for their publishers. This turn of events ensured the status of Diderot's project as the landmark of its age.

JEAN-JACQUES ROUSSEAU

Arguably the most original and influential eighteenth-century thinker, Jean-Jacques Rousseau stood close to but self-consciously outside the coterie of the philosophes. For Rousseau provided in his life and writing a critique not only of the status quo but of the Enlightenment itself. Obsessed with the issue of moral freedom, Rousseau found society far more oppressive than most philosophes would admit, and he considered the philosophes themselves to be part of the problem.

Young Rousseau won instant fame when he submitted a prize-winning essay in a contest sponsored by a provincial academy on the topic, "Has the restoration of the arts and sciences had a purifying effect upon morals?" Unlike most respondents, Rousseau answered that it had not. He argued that the lustrous cultural and scientific achievements of recent decades were producing pretension, conformity, and useless luxury. Most scientific pursuits, he wrote, "are the effect of idleness which generate idleness in their turn." The system of rewards in the arts produces "a servile and deceptive conformity . . . the dissolution of morals . . . and the corruption of taste." Against the decadence of high culture, he advocated a return "to the simplicity which prevailed in earliest times"—manly physical pastimes, self-reliance, independent citizens instead of fawning courtiers.

Rousseau's Moral Vision   Rousseau had no wish to return to a state of nature, a condition of anarchy in which force ruled and people were slaves of appetite. But the basis of morality, he argued, was conscience, not reason. "Virtue, sublime science of simple minds: are not your principles graven on every heart?" This became one of his basic themes in two popular works of fiction, *Julie, or the New Héloise* (1761), and *Emile, or Treatise on Education* (1762).

In the first novel Julie is educated in virtue by her tutor St. Preux but allows herself to fall in love with and be seduced by him. In the second half of the novel, Julie breaks away from St. Preux and marries Monsieur de Wolmar, her father's wealthy friend. She maintains a distant friendship with her old lover and rears her children in exemplary fashion, overseeing their education. In the end she overcomes her past moral lapse and sacrifices her own life to save one of her children. Wolmar then brings in the chastened St. Preux to continue the children's education. This tale of love, virtue, and motherhood won an adoring audience of male and female readers who identified with the characters, shed tears over their moral dilemmas, and applauded Rousseau for this superb lesson in the new sensibility.

Mary Wollstonecraft on the Education of Women

◆

The sharpest challenge to Rousseau's widely shared attitude toward women came only in 1792, with the publication of Mary Wollstonecraft's A Vindication of the Rights of Woman. *Inspired by the French Revolution's doctrine of natural rights, this spirited writer deplored the fact that society kept women (in her words) frivolous, artificial, weak, and in a perpetual state of childhood. While men praised women for their beauty and grace, they hypocritically condemned them for a concern with vanity, fashion, and trivial matters, yet refused to treat them as rational human beings who could contribute to society as much as men. Her book emphasized the need for educational reform that would allow women to develop agile bodies and strong minds. Along the way Wollstonecraft took particular aim at Rousseau's* Emile.

"The conduct and manners of women, in fact, evidently prove that their minds are not in a healthy state; for, like the flowers which are planted in too rich a soil, strength and usefulness are sacrificed to beauty. . . . One cause of this barren blooming I attribute to a false system of education, gathered from the books written on this subject by men who, considering females rather as women than human creatures, have been more anxious to make them alluring mistresses than affectionate wives and rational mothers. The understanding of the sex has been so bubbled by this specious homage, that the civilized women of the present century, with a few exceptions, are only anxious to inspire love, when they ought to cherish a nobler ambition, and by their abilities and virtues exact respect.

"[T]he most perfect education, in my opinion, is such an exercise of the understanding as is best calculated to strengthen the body and form the heart. Or, in other words, to enable the individual to attain such habits of virtue as will render it independent. In fact, it is a farce to call any being virtuous whose virtues do not result from the exercise of its own reason. This was Rousseau's opinion respecting men: I extend it to women, and confidently assert that they have been drawn out of their sphere by false refinement, and not by an endeavor to acquire masculine qualities. Still the regal homage which they receive is so intoxicating, that till the manners of the times are changed, and formed on more reasonable principles, it may be impossible to convince them that the illegitimate power, which they obtain by degrading themselves, is a curse, and that they must return to nature and equality."

From Sandra M. Gilbert and Susan Gubar (eds.), *The Norton Anthology of Literature by Women:* The Tradition in English, W. W. Norton Co, 1985.

Emile recounts the story of a young boy raised to be a moral adult by a tutor who emphasized experience over book learning and who considered education a matter of individual self-development. This new kind of man of course required a comparably sensitive wife, attuned to practical matters and without vain aristocratic pretenses. Sophie, the girl in question, received a very different type of education, however, one concerned with virtue but far more limited in its scope. Rousseau depicted men and women liberating themselves from stultifying traditional values, yet in the new relationships he portrayed in these novels, women held a decidedly subordinate position. Their virtues were to be exclusively domestic in character, while the men would be prepared for public roles—a distinction that deeply troubled feminist thinkers in the future (see "Mary Wollstonecraft on the Education of Women").

The Rebel as Cultural Hero Rousseau himself was by no means a saint. His personal weaknesses—including the illegitimate child that he fathered and abandoned—doubtless contributed to his preoccupation with morality and conscience. Nonetheless, his rebellious life as well as his writings greatly impressed the generation of readers and writers coming of age in the 1770s and 1780s. Not only did he quarrel with the repressive authorities of Church and state—who repeatedly banned his books—but he also attacked the pretensions of his fellow philosophes, whom he considered arrogant, cynical, and lacking in spirituality.

By the 1770s the commanding figures of the Enlightenment, such as Voltaire and Diderot, had won their battles and had become masters of the most prestigious academies and channels of patronage. In a sense, they had themselves become the establishment. For younger writers frustrated by the existing distribution of influence and patronage, Rousseau became the inspiration.

Rousseau's Concept of Freedom   What proved to be Rousseau's most enduring work, *The Social Contract,* published in 1762, became famous only after the French Revolution dramatized the issues that the book had raised. (The Revolution, it could be said, did more for the book than Rousseau did for the Revolution, which he neither prophesied nor advocated.) *The Social Contract* was not meant as a blueprint for revolution but rather as an ideal standard against which readers might measure their own society. Rousseau did not expect that this standard could be achieved in practice, since existing states were too large and complex to allow the kind of participation that he considered essential.

For Rousseau, a government distinct from the individuals over whom it claims to exercise authority has no validity. Rousseau denied the almost universal idea that some people are meant to govern and others to obey. In the ideal polity, Rousseau said, individuals have a role in making the law to which they submit. By obeying it, they are thus obeying themselves as well as their fellow citizens. For this reason, they are free from arbitrary power. To found such an ideal society, each citizen would have to take part in creating a social contract laying out the society's ground rules. By doing so, these citizens would establish themselves as "the sovereign." This sovereign—the people—then creates a government that will carry on the day-to-day business of applying the laws.

Rousseau was not advocating simple majority rule but rather a quest for consensus as to the best interests of all citizens. Even if it *appears* contrary to the welfare of some or even many citizens,

▲ The French revolutionaries acclaimed both Voltaire and Rousseau and transferred their remains to a new Pantheon. But Rousseau was the man considered by many French people to be the Revolution's spiritual father, as suggested by his position in this allegorical painting of 1793, filled with the new symbolism of liberty and equality.
Nicholas H. Jeurat de Bertry, "Allegory of the Revolution with a Portrait Medallion of J. J. Rousseau." Giraudon/Art Resource.

Rousseau believed, the best interest of the community must be every individual's best interest as well, since that individual is a member of the community. Rousseau called this difficult concept "the general will." Deferring to the general will means that an individual ultimately must do what one *ought,* not simply what one *wants.* This commitment derives from conscience, which must do battle within the individual against passion, appetite, and mere self-interest. Under the social contract,

ROUSSEAU'S CONCEPT OF THE GENERAL WILL

"The essence of the social compact reduces itself to the following terms: Each of us puts his person and all his power in common under the supreme direction of the general will, and, in our collective capacity, we receive each member as an indivisible part of the whole. . . .

"In fact, each individual, as a man, may have a particular will contrary or dissimilar to the general will which he has as a citizen. His particular interest may speak to him quite differently from the common interest: his absolute and naturally independent existence may make him look upon what he owes to the common cause as a gratuitous contribution, the loss of which will do less harm to others than the payment of it is burdensome to himself. . . . He may wish to enjoy the rights of citizenship with-

out being ready to fulfill the duties of a subject. The continuance of such an injustice could not but prove the undoing of the body politic.

"In order then that the social compact may not be an empty formula, it tacitly includes the undertaking, which alone can give force to the rest, that whoever refuses to obey the general will shall be compelled to do so by the whole body. This means nothing less than that he will be forced to be free; for this is the condition which, by giving each citizen to his country, secures him against all personal dependence. In this lies the key to the working of the political machine."

From Jean-Jacques Rousseau, *The Social Contract*, Book 1, David Campbell Publishers.

---

to use Rousseau's most striking phrase, the individual "will be forced to be free" (see "Rousseau's Concept of the General Will"). Thus for Rousseau, individual freedom depends on a political framework involving consent and participation as well as subordination of individual self-interest to the commonweal. More than any of the philosophes, Rousseau argued that individual freedom depends on the arrangements governing the collectivity.

II. Eighteenth-Century Elite Culture

The Enlightenment was merely one dimension of Europe's cultural life. Europe's economic expansion and relative prosperity, discussed in the previous chapter, were matched by a marked increase in publishing activity that served diverse audiences and by the creation of new cultural forms and institutions. Although the aristocracy still dominated society, men and women of lesser social status participated prominently in cultural life. Eighteenth-century elite culture was cosmopolitan, spilling across national borders as well as certain social class lines.

COSMOPOLITAN HIGH CULTURE

As the expansive, cosmopolitan aspects of European high culture are described here, it must be remembered that the mass of Europe's peasants and workers remained virtually untouched by these developments, insulated within their local environments and traditions. But the educated and wealthy, the numerically small and influential elites, enjoyed a sense of belonging to a common European civilization. French was the international language of this culture; even King Frederick II of Prussia favored French over German. Whatever the effects of Frederick's attitude might have been—the German dramatist Lessing, for one, considered it a deplorable cultural prejudice—the widespread knowledge of French meant that ideas and literature could circulate easily past language barriers.

Travel Europeans sharpened their sense of common identity through travel literature and by their appetite for visiting foreign places. Although transportation was slow and uncomfortable, many embarked on a "grand tour," whose highlights included visits to Europe's large cities (such as London, Paris, Rome, and Vienna) and to the ruins of antiquity—to the glories of the modern and the ancient worlds.

Kings, princes, and municipal authorities were embellishing their towns with plazas, public gardens, theaters, and opera houses. Toward the end of the century, amenities such as street lighting and public transportation began to appear in a few cities, with London leading the way. From the private sector came two notable additions to the urban scene: the coffeehouse and the storefront window display. Coffeehouses, where customers could chat or read, and enticing shop windows, which added to the pleasures of city walking (and stimulated consumer demand), enhanced the rhythms of urban life for tourists and residents alike. When a man is tired of London, Samuel Johnson remarked, he is tired of life.

Travelers on tour invariably passed from the attractions of bustling city life to the silent monuments of antiquity. As the philosophes recalled the virtues of pagan philosophers like Cicero, interest grew in surviving examples of Greek and Roman architecture and sculpture. Many would have agreed with the German art historian Johann Winckelmann that Greek sculpture was the most worthy standard of aesthetic beauty in all the world.

The Republic of Letters

Among writers, intellectuals, and scientists, the sense of a cosmopolitan European culture devolved into the concept of a "republic of letters." The phrase, introduced by sixteenth-century French humanists, was popularized by Pierre Bayle (noted earlier as a proponent of religious toleration), who published a critical journal that he called *News of the Republic of Letters*. The title implied that the realm of culture and ideas stretched across Europe's political borders. In one sense it was an exclusive republic, limited to the educated; but it was also an open society to which people of talent could belong regardless of their social origins. For this reason, European intellectuals felt that their republic of letters was a model for a public sphere in which political and social issues could be debated freely as well.

Aside from the medium of the printed word, the republic of letters was organized around the salons and the academies. Both institutions encouraged social interchange by bringing together socially prominent men and women with talented writers. The philosophes themselves exemplified

this social mixture, for their "family" was composed in almost equal measures of nobles (Montesquieu, Holbach, Condorcet) and commoners (Voltaire, Diderot, d'Alembert). Voltaire, while insisting that he was as good as any aristocrat, had no desire to topple the aristocracy from its position; rather he sought amalgamation. As d'Alembert put it, talent on the one hand and birth and eminence on the other both deserve recognition.

The Salons

Usually organized and led by women of wealthy bourgeois or noble families, the salons sought to bring together important writers with the influential persons they needed for favors and patronage. The salon of Madame Tencin, for example, helped launch Montesquieu's *Spirit of the Laws* in the 1740s, while the salon of Madame du Deffand in the 1760s became a forum in which the philosophes could test their ideas (see figure, p. 672). The salons also helped to enlarge the audience and contacts of the philosophes by introducing them to a flow of foreign visitors, ranging from German princes to Benjamin Franklin. Private newsletters kept interested foreigners and provincials abreast of activities in the Parisian salons when they could not attend personally, but salons also operated in Vienna, London, and Berlin.

The salons placed a premium on elegant conversation and wit. The women who ran them insisted that intellectuals make their ideas lucid and comprehensible to laypeople, which increased the likelihood that their thought and writings would have some impact. The salons were also a forum in which men learned to take women seriously, and they constituted a unique cultural space for women between the domestic and public spheres. But the salons' emphasis on style over substance led Rousseau to denounce them as artificial rituals that prevented the display of genuine feeling and sincerity.

Freemasonry

Throughout Europe, freemasonry was another important form of cultural sociability that often crossed the lines of class and (less commonly) of gender. Operating in an aura of secretiveness and symbolism, the masonic lodges fostered a curious mixture of spirituality and rationalism. Originating as clubs or fraternities dedicated to humane values, they attracted a wide

▲ **This 1814 painting of Mme. Geoffrin's Salon in 1755 reflects the artist Lemonnier's imagination rather than historical reality. His canvas depicts an assemblage of all the major philosophes and their patrons that never actually took place. Yet it does accurately convey the social atmosphere and serious purpose of the Parisian salons. At the center is a bust of Voltaire, who lived in exile at the time.**
Lemonnier, "Salon of Mme. Geoffrin, 1725." Giraudon/Art Resource.

range of educated nobles, commoners, and liberal clergy, while some lodges accepted women as well. But toward the end of the century, freemasonry was torn by sectarian controversies and its influence seemed to be diminishing.

The Learned Academies As important for the dissemination of ideas in the eighteenth century as the salons were the learned academies. These ranged from the Lunar Society in Birmingham, a forum for innovative British industrialists and engineers, to state-sponsored academies in almost every capital of southern and central Europe, which served as conduits for advanced scientific and philosophical ideas coming from Western Europe. In France, moreover, academies were established in more than thirty provincial cities, most of which became strongholds of advanced thinking outside the capital.

These provincial academies were founded after the death of Louis XIV in 1715, as if in testimony to the liberating effect of his demise. Most began as literary institutes, concerned with upholding traditional values such as purity of literary style. A few academies adhered to such goals well into midcentury, but most gradually shifted their interests from literary matters to scientific and practical questions in such areas as commerce, agriculture, and local administration. They became offshoots, so to speak, of the *Encyclopedia*'s spirit. Indeed, when a Jesuit launched an attack against the *Encyclopedia* in the Lyons Academy, many members threatened to resign unless he retracted his remarks.

By the 1770s the essay contests sponsored by the provincial academies and the papers published by their members had turned to such topics as population growth, capital punishment and penology, education, poverty and welfare, the grain trade, the guilds, and the origins of sovereignty. A parallel shift in membership occurred. The local academies began as privileged corporations, dominated by the nobility of the region. Associate membership was extended to commoners from the ranks of civil servants, doctors, and professionals. Gradually, the distinction between regular and associate participants crumbled. The academies admitted more commoners to full membership, and a fragile social fusion took place.

PUBLISHING AND READING

The eighteenth century saw a notable rise in publishing that was geared to several kinds of readers. Traveling circulating libraries originated in England around 1740 and opened untapped markets for reading material; by the end of the century almost one thousand traveling libraries had been established. "Booksellers," or publishers—the intermediary between author and reader—combined the functions of a modern editor, printer, salesperson, and (if need be) smuggler. Their judgment and marketing techniques helped create as well as fill the demand for books, since they conceived and financed a variety of works. The *Encyclopedia* originated as a bookseller's project; so, too, did such enduring masterpieces as Samuel Johnson's *Dictionary*, a monumental lexicon that helped purify and standardize the English language. Booksellers commissioned talented stylists to write popular versions of serious scientific, historical, and philosophical works. Recognizing a specialized demand among women readers, they increased the output of fictional romances and fashion magazines and also began to publish more fiction and poetry by women. In general, the entertainment and instruction of a diverse but educated audience became the focus of most publishers.

Journals and Newspapers Eighteenth-century publishing was notable for the proliferation of periodicals. In England, which pioneered in this domain, the number of periodicals increased from 25 to 158 between 1700 and 1780. In one successful model, Addison and Steele's *Spectator* (1711), each issue consisted of a single essay that sought in elegant but clear prose to raise the reader's

standards of morality and taste. Their goal was "to enliven Morality with Wit, and to temper Wit with Morality. . . . To bring Philosophy . . . to dwell in clubs and assemblies, at tea-tables and coffeehouses." Eliza Haywood adapted this format in her journal, *The Female Spectator* (1744–1756), in which she advocated improvement in the treatment of women and greater "opportunities of enlarging our minds." (A comparable periodical in France, the *Journal des Dames*, which appeared in 1759, propagated the writings of the

▼ The title page of Samuel Johnson's pioneering *Dictionary of the English Language* (1755 edition), one of the masterpieces of eighteenth-century literature.
Mary Evans Picture Library.

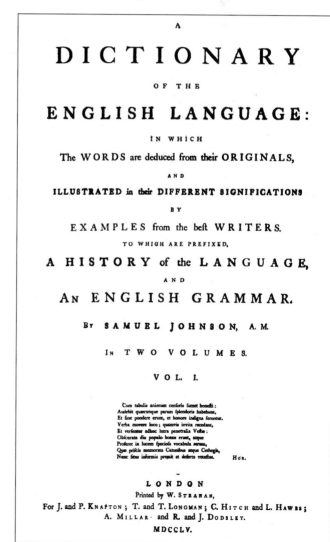

A

DICTIONARY

OF THE

ENGLISH LANGUAGE:

IN WHICH

The WORDS are deduced from their ORIGINALS,

AND

ILLUSTRATED in their DIFFERENT SIGNIFICATIONS

BY

EXAMPLES from the beſt WRITERS.

TO WHICH ARE PREFIXED,

A HISTORY of the LANGUAGE,

AND

AN ENGLISH GRAMMAR.

BY SAMUEL JOHNSON, A. M.

IN TWO VOLUMES.

VOL. I.

Cum tabulis animum cenſoris ſumet honeſti:
Audebit quæcunque parum ſplendoris habebunt,
Et ſine pondere erunt, et honore indigna ferentur,
Verba movere loco; quamvis invita recedant,
Et verſentur adhuc intra penetralia Veſtæ:
Obſcurata diu populo bonus eruet, atque
Proferet in lucem ſpecioſa vocabula rerum,
Quæ priſcis memorata Catonibus atque Cethegis,
Nunc ſitus informis premit et deſerta vetuſtas.   HOR.

LONDON

Printed by W. STRAHAN,

For J. and P. KNAPTON; T. and T. LONGMAN; C. HITCH and L. HAWES; A. MILLAR· and R. and J. DODSLEY.

MDCCLV.

Enlightenment but also raised the question of women's place in society.) Another type of journal published extracts and summaries of books and covered current events and entertainment; one such journal, the *Gentleman's Magazine*, reached the impressive circulation of fifteen thousand in 1740. More learned periodicals specialized in book reviews and serious articles on science and philosophy.

Most important for the future of reading habits in Europe was the daily newspaper, which originated in England. Papers like the *London Chronicle* at first provided family entertainment and then took on classified advertisements (thereby spurring consumerism and the notion of fashion). English newspapers of course published news of current events, but only after strenuous battles for permission from a reluctant government did they win the right to report directly on parliamentary debates. In France, a handful of major Parisian newspapers enjoyed privileged monopolies in exchange for full compliance with government censorship. This arrangement severely restricted their ability to discuss government and politics, although other periodicals published outside France's borders helped satisfy the demand for such coverage in France. With the Revolution of 1789, however, a politically aroused French citizenry provided unimagined opportunities for the growth of political journalism.

"Bad Books" The demand for books and the dynamism of the publishing industry created new employment opportunities for men and women. Although the number of would-be writers swelled, relatively few could develop their talents without constraint or achieve financial independence without patronage. Many remained poverty-stricken and frustrated.

Publishers thus could hire legions of otherwise unemployed writers to turn out the kinds of books for which they sensed a great demand: potboilers, romances, salacious pamphlets, and gossip sheets, which pandered to low tastes. Paid for quantity and speed rather than quality, these hack writers led a precarious, humiliating existence. Booksellers and desperate writers saw money to be made in sensational pamphlets assailing the character of notorious aristocrats, in partisan pamphlets attacking a particular faction in court pol-

itics, and in pornography. Sometimes they combined character assassination and pornography in pamphlets dwelling on the alleged perversions of rulers or courtiers. For all its wild exaggeration, such material helped "desacralize" monarchy and created a vivid image of a decadent aristocracy.

To satisfy the public's demand for gossip, character assassination, and pornography in violation of laws regulating the book trade in France, publishers located just across the French border marketed such books and pamphlets clandestinely. They smuggled this material into France, along with banned books by writers like Voltaire and Rousseau, using networks of couriers and distributors. In their sales lists of what they called Philosophic Books, the clandestine publishers lumped together banned books by serious writers along with such illicit publications as *The Scandalous Chronicles, The Private Life of Louis XV,* and *Venus in the Cloister* (a pornographic account of the alleged perversions of the clergy). The police made the same judgment. In attempting to stop the flow of "bad books," they scarcely distinguished between a banned work by Voltaire assaulting religious bigotry and a libelous pamphlet depicting the queen as a corrupt pervert.

LITERATURE, MUSIC, AND ART

Unlike the artistic style of the seventeenth century, generally classified as baroque, the artistic style of the eighteenth century cannot be given a single stylistic label. The nature of the audience and the sources of support for writers and composers also varied considerably. But several trends proved to be of lasting importance: the rise of the novel in England, the birth of romantic poetry, the development of the symphony in Austria, and the changing social context of French painting late in the century.

The Rise of the Novel The modern novel had its strongest development in England, where writers and booksellers cultivated a growing middle-class reading public. The acknowledged pioneer of this new genre was Samuel Richardson, a bookseller as well as a writer. With a series of letters telling the story, Richardson's *Pamela, or Virtue Rewarded* (1740) recounted the trials and tribulations of an honest if somewhat hypocritical servant girl.

Pamela's sexual virtue is repeatedly challenged but never conquered by her wealthy employer, Mr. B., who finally agrees to marry her. An instant success, this melodrama broke from the standard forms and heroic subjects of most narrative fiction. Richardson dealt with recognizable types of people.

Pamela's apparent hypocrisy, however, prompted a playwright and lawyer named Henry Fielding to pen a short satire called *Shamela,* which he followed with his own novel *Joseph Andrews.* Here comedy and adventure replaced melodrama; Fielding prefaced *Joseph Andrews* with a manifesto claiming that the novel was to be "a comic epic in prose." Fielding realized the full potential of his bold experimentation with literary forms in *Tom Jones* (1749), a colorful, robust, comic panorama of English society featuring a gallery of brilliantly developed characters and vivid depictions of varied social environments.

The novel was thus emerging as a form of fiction that told its story and treated the development of personality in a realistic social context. It seemed to mirror its times better than other forms of fiction, and like the dramas that filled the stage in the second half of the century, most novels focused on family life and everyday problems of love, marriage, and social relations. Novelists could use broad comedy, or they could be totally serious; they could experiment endlessly with forms and techniques and could deal with a wide range of social settings.

Fanny Burney In *Evelina or A Young Lady's Entrance into the World* (1778), the writer Fanny Burney used the flexibility of the novel to give a woman's perspective on eighteenth-century English social life. In the form of letters, like *Pamela* and Rousseau's *Julie, Evelina* traces a provincial girl's adventures in London as she discovers her true father and finds a suitable husband. While falling back on conventional melodrama, in which marriage is the only happy ending for a young woman, Burney also uses social satire to suggest how society restricts, and even endangers, an independent woman's life. If Burney was ambivalent about the possibilities for female independence in the social world, her own writing, together with other women writers of the period, demonstrated the opportunities for female artistic achievement.

▲ **One of the leading French portrait painters, and the most successful female artist of the era anywhere, was Élisabeth Vigée-Lebrun, who enjoyed the patronage of Queen Marie Antoinette. Shown here is one of several portraits that Vigée-Lebrun painted of the French queen.**
Giraudon/Art Resource.

Satire Meanwhile, writers with more didactic objectives perfected a satiric genre called the philosophical tale, as exemplified by the great Irish satirist Jonathan Swift in his *Gulliver's Travels* (1726). The French philosophes favored this form of satire because it allowed them to criticize their society covertly and avoid open clashes with the censors. Thus Montesquieu created a range of mythical foreign settings and travelers from the Levant to ridicule contemporary European morality in *The Persian Letters* (1721). Voltaire similarly achieved great success in his tale *Candide* (1759), a critique of the notion that this was the best of all possible worlds. His exotic characters and incidents disguised an Enlightenment tract against the idiocy and cruelty that he saw in European society.

The Birth of Romantic Poetry During most of this century of innovation in prose fiction, poetry retained its traditional qualities. Still the most prized form of literary expression, poetry followed unchanging rules on what made good literature. Each poetic form had its particular essence and rules; but in all types of poems diction was supposed to be elegant and the sentiments refined. Poets were expected to transform the raw materials of emotion into delicate language and references that only the highly educated could appreciate. In this neoclassical tradition, art was meant to echo eternal standards of truth and beauty. Poets were not permitted to unburden their souls or hold forth on their own experiences. The audience for poetry was the narrowest segment of the reading public— "the wealthy few," in the phrase of William Wordsworth, who criticized eighteenth-century poets for pandering exclusively to that group.

By the end of the century, however, the restraints of neoclassicism finally provoked rebellion in the ranks of English and German poets. Men like Friedrich von Schiller and Wordsworth defiantly raised the celebration of individual feeling and inner passion to the level of a creed, which came to be known as romanticism. These young poets generally prized Rousseau's writings, seeing the Genevan rebel as someone who had forged a personal idiom of expression and who valued inner feeling, moral passion, and the wonders of nature. Hoping to appeal to a much broader audience, these poets decisively changed the nature of poetic composition and made this literary form, like the novel, a flexible and more accessible vehicle of artistic expression.

Goethe The writer who came to embody the new ambitions of poets, novelists, and dramatists was Johann von Goethe, whose long life (1749–1832) spanned the beginnings and the high point of the romantic movement. A friend of Schiller and many of the German writers and philosophers of the day, he soon came to tower over all of them. Goethe first inspired a literary movement known as Sturm und Drang (Storm and Stress), which emphasized strong artistic emotions and

gave early intimations of the romantic temperament. The best-known work of Sturm und Drang was young Goethe's *The Sorrows of Young Werther* (1774), a novel about a young man driven to despair and suicide by an impossible love.

Courted by many of the princes and monarchs of Germany, Goethe soon joined the circle of the duke who ruled the small city-state of Weimar, where he remained for the rest of his life. There flowed from his pen an astonishing stream of works—lyrical love poetry, powerful dramas, art and literary criticism, translations, philosophic reflections, an account of his travels in Italy, and studies of optics, botany, anatomy, and mathematics. Even though he held official posts in the duke's court, Goethe's literary output never flagged. His masterpiece, *Faust*, occupied him for nearly fifty years and revealed the progress of his art. The first part (published in 1808) imbued with romantic longing the somewhat autobiographical story of a man who yearns to master all of knowledge and who makes a pact with the devil to achieve his goal. But the second part (1831) emphasized the renunciation and determination that came to be Goethe's credo. The final lines are:

> He only earns his freedom and existence
> Who daily conquers them anew.

What had begun in the youthful exuberance and energy of romanticism ended in an almost classical mood of discipline. No wonder that Goethe seemed to his contemporaries to be the last "universal man," the embodiment of conflicting cultural values and Western civilization's struggle to resolve them.

The Symphony For Europe's elites, music offered the supreme form of entertainment, and the development of the symphony in music paralleled the rise of the novel in literature. It must be noted at once, however, that a great deal of eighteenth-century music was routine and undistinguished. For much of the century, composers still served under royal, ecclesiastical, or aristocratic patronage. They were bound by rigid formulas of composition and by prevailing tastes tyrannically insistent on conventions. Most listeners wanted little more than pleasant melodies in familiar forms; instrumental music was often commissioned as background fare for balls or other social occasions.

The heartland of Europe's music tradition shifted during the eighteenth century from Italy and France to Austria. Here a trio of geniuses transformed the routines of eighteenth-century composition into original and enduring masterpieces. True, the early symphonies of Franz Joseph Haydn and young Wolfgang Amadeus Mozart were conventional exercises. As light and tuneful as its audience could wish, their early music had little emotional impact. By the end of their careers, however, these two composers had altered the symphonic form from three to four movements, had achieved extraordinary harmonic virtuosity, and had brought a deep if restrained emotionalism to their music. Haydn and Mozart had changed the symphony radically from the elegant trifles of earlier years.

Beethoven   Ludwig van Beethoven consummated this development and ensured that the symphony, like the novel and romantic poetry, would be an adaptable vehicle for the expression of creative genius. In each of his nine symphonies as well as in his five piano concertos, Beethoven progressively modified the standard formulas, enlarged the orchestra, and wrote movements of increasing intricacy. His last symphony burst the bonds of the form altogether. Beethoven introduced a large chorus singing one of Schiller's odes to conclude his Ninth Symphony (1824), making it a celebration in music of freedom and human kinship. Laden with passion, the music is nevertheless recognizable as an advanced form of the classical symphony. Thus it provides a bridge between the music of two periods: eighteenth-century classicism and nineteenth-century romanticism.

Aristocratic and court patronage remained the surest foundation for a career in music during the eighteenth century. Haydn, for example, worked with mutual satisfaction as the court composer for one prince from 1761 to 1790. At the end of his long life, however, Haydn moved out on his own, having won enough international recognition to sign a lucrative contract with a London music publisher who underwrote performances of his last twelve symphonies. In contrast, Mozart had an unhappy experience trying to earn his living by composing. After a few miserable years as court composer for the Archbishop of Salzburg, Mozart escaped to Vienna but could not find a permanent employer. He

was obliged to eke out an inadequate living by teaching, filling private commissions, and giving public concerts. Beethoven did much better at freeing himself from dependence on a single patron through individual commissions and public concerts.

The Social Context of Art   Unlike the situation in literature and music, there were no notable innovations in the field of painting during most of the eighteenth century. With the exception of the Frenchman Jacques-Louis David, eighteenth-century painters were overshadowed by their predecessors. Neoclassicism remained a popular style in the late eighteenth century, with its themes

▼ *J.-H. Fragonard*
The Swing **(1767)**
The kind of art held in high esteem in eighteenth-century France included the sensuous and ornate scenes of aristocratic life in the so-called rococo style painted by Jean-Honore Fragonard, such as shown here (detail).
The Wallace Collection, London/The Bridgeman Art Library, London.

inspired by antiquity and its timeless conceptions of form and beauty, comparable to the rules of neoclassical poetry.

The social context of painting, however, was changing. Most commissions and patronage still depended on aristocrats and princes, but the public was beginning to claim a role as the judge of talent in the visual arts. Public opinion found its voice in a new breed of art critics, unaffiliated with official sources of patronage, who reached their new audience through the press in the second half of the century. The Royal Academy of Art in France created the opening for this new voice by sponsoring an annual public exhibition, or "salon," starting in 1737. People could view the canvases chosen by the Academy for these exhibitions and could reach their own judgments about the painters. In this way a public sphere of cultural discourse came into being, where once the official word of the Academy had determined the matter of taste and reputation in painting.

David and Greuze   David, a brilliant painter in the neoclassical style, won the greatest renown in this arena of public opinion during the 1780s. He skillfully celebrated the values of the ancient world in such historical paintings as *The Oath of the Horatii* (see figure, p. 679), *The Death of Socrates,* and *Brutus.* Discarding many of the standard conventions for history painting (and thereby drawing criticism from the Academy), David overwhelmed the public with his vivid imagery and the emotional force of his compositions. His paintings of the 1780s unmistakably conveyed a yearning for civic virtue and patriotism that had yet to find its political outlet in France. Not surprisingly, David became the most engaged and triumphant painter of the French Revolution.

In an entirely different vein, a few eighteenth-century artists chose more mundane and "realistic" subjects or themes for their canvases, parallel in some respects to what novelists and playwrights were doing. Jean-Baptiste Greuze, for ex-

▼ *Jean-Baptiste Greuze*
THE FATHER'S CURSE
Instead of the aristocrats or classical figures that most artists chose for their subjects, Jean-Baptiste Greuze painted ordinary French people. His portraits and dramatic scenes (such as *The Father's Curse*) seemed to echo Rousseau's call for honest, "natural" feeling.
Jean-Baptiste Greuze, "The Paternal Curse." Giraudon/Arts Resource.

▲ *Jacques-Louis David*
THE OATH OF THE HORATII

The greatest innovation in French painting came in reaction to the artificiality of baroque and rococo styles and subject matter, with a return to favor of "noble simplicity and calm grandeur." This neoclassical style found its supreme expression in the work of Jacques-Louis David. Such history paintings as *The Oath of the Horatii* evoked the ideal of civic virtue in ancient Greek and Roman civilization.

Jacques Louis David, "The Oath of the Horatii." Scala/Art Resource.

ample, made a hit in the Parisian exhibitions of the 1770s with his sentimentalized paintings of ordinary people in family settings caught in a dramatic situation, such as the death of a father or the banishment of a disobedient son. William Hogarth, a superb London engraver who worked through the medium of prints and book illustrations, went further down the social pyramid with his remarkable scenes of life among the working classes and the poor.

III. Popular Culture

While the cultural world of aristocratic and middle-class elites has been extensively studied, the cultures of artisans, peasants, and the urban poor remain more dimly illuminated. In those sectors of society, culture primarily meant recreation and was essentially public and collective. Popular culture had its written forms, but they were relatively unimportant compared to the oral tradition of songs, folktales, and sayings, which have left fewer firsthand traces in the historical record. Nonetheless, it is possible to suggest the rich variety of cultural and recreational practice among working people.

POPULAR LITERATURE

Far removed from the markets for Voltaire and the *Gentleman's Magazine,* existed a distinct world of popular literature—the reading matter consumed by journeymen and peasants, the poor and the almost poor, those who could barely read and those who could not read at all. From the seventeenth through the early nineteenth century, but particularly in the eighteenth century, publishers produced for this audience small booklets written anonymously, printed on cheap paper, and costing only a few pennies. These brochures were sold by itinerant peddlers who knew the tastes of their customers; presumably the booklets were often read aloud by those who could read to those who could not.

This popular literature took three major forms. Religious material included devotional tracts, saints' lives, catechisms, manuals of penitence, and Bible stories, all written simply and generously laced with miracles. Readers who were preoccupied with fears of death and damnation sought reassurance in these works that a virtuous life would end in salvation. Almanacs constituted a second type of popular literature, which appealed to the readers' concern for getting along in this life. Almanacs and how-to-live-successfully pamphlets discussed things like the kinds of potions to take for illnesses and featured astrology—how to read the stars and other signs for clues about the future. The third type of popular literature provided entertainment: tales and fables, burlesques and crude satires, mixtures of fiction and history in which miraculous events frequently helped bring the story to a satisfactory conclusion.

Although useful information may have trickled down through these booklets, most of them were escapist. The religiosity and supernatural events of popular literature separate it from the growing rationalism and secularism of elite culture. Moreover, it could be argued that by ignoring such problems as food shortages, high taxes, and material insecurity, popular writings fostered submissiveness, a fatalistic acceptance of a dismal status quo. Glimpsing the content of this popular literature helps us understand why Voltaire had no hope of extending his ideas on religion to the masses.

▼ **A page from an English almanac of 1769 on the month of July includes saints' days, information about likely weather patterns, and advice about agricultural matters and health care.**
New York Public Library, General Research Division, Astor, Lenox, and Tilden Foundations.

Oral Tradition Almanacs and pamphlets for working people were produced by outsiders, printers and writers who were themselves well educated. Oral tradition encompassed more authentic forms of popular culture: folktales told at the fireside on long winter nights, songs passed on from generation to generation, sayings that embodied the conventional wisdom of the people.

Themes touching on hunger, sex, or oppression were more likely to turn up in songs or oral tales than in booklets. Songs and tales expressed the joyful bawdiness of ordinary men and women but also the ever-present hardships and dangers of daily life: the endless drudgery of work in the fields, the gnawing ache of an empty stomach, the cruelty of parental neglect or mean stepparents, the desperation of beggars on the road. The most fantastic tales evoked a threatening world in which strangers might turn out to be princes or good fairies but might just as well turn into wolves or witches. Oral tradition also celebrated the shrewdness and cunning of ordinary people struggling for survival, in the spirit of the saying: "Better a knave than a fool." Often rendered in local dialects, these tales or songs would have been incomprehensible to an educated Parisian, Londoner, or Viennese.

LITERACY AND PRIMARY SCHOOLING

The Wars of Religion had spurred the spread of literacy and elementary schooling in Europe. Protestantism explicitly promoted literacy so that Christians could read their Bibles directly; strongly Protestant societies such as Scotland, Switzerland, and Sweden had unusually high rates of literacy by the eighteenth century. The Catholic Church, as well, believed that the spread of literacy would serve its cause in the battle against heresy. While teaching reading, Catholic schoolmasters could provide religious instruction and could socialize children into the beliefs and behavior of a Catholic way of life.

A unique study of literacy in France carried out in the late nineteenth century, based on signatures versus Xs on parish marriage registers all across the country, indicates a national literacy rate (meaning the ability to read) in 1686 of about 21 percent, which reached 37 percent a century later. These national averages, however, conceal striking regional and social disparities. The south of France had much lower rates than the north/northeast, and rural literacy rates lagged significantly behind those of the towns. While agricultural laborers rarely could read, urban artisans were generally literate. The widest gap of all, however, separated men from women, the rates in 1786 being 47 and 27 percent, respectively. Similarly, estimates for England suggest a male literacy rate of slightly under 60 percent and a female rate of about 40 percent.

Primary Education Schooling was not intended to transform society or lift the mass of people out of the situations into which they were born. On the contrary, it was supposed to maintain the social order and reinforce the family in promoting piety and decent behavior among the young. Many among the elites (including Voltaire) were skeptical about the value of education for peasants and laborers. Might it not confuse them, or make it more difficult for them to accept the drudgery to which they seemed destined? Peasant or laboring parents might well have shared such skepticism about educating their young. Education could seem a waste of time when their children could be contributing to the family's livelihood; they might especially begrudge spending the money on tuition that most elementary schooling required.

A village usually hired a schoolmaster in consultation with the pastor or priest; schools usually straddled community and church, since the schoolmaster often served as the pastor's aide. Except in towns that had charitable endowments to support schooling, the parents, the village, or some combination of the two paid the schoolmaster, and for that reason numerous villages did without any schooling. Even a modest tuition could deter impoverished parents from hiring a master, enrolling their children, or keeping them in school for a sufficient time. Since schoolmasters taught reading first and writing separately and later, many pupils, especially girls, were not kept in school long enough to learn how to write anything but their names. Schooling, in other words, was largely demand-driven, the product of a community's level of wealth and interest. When a region achieved a critical mass of literacy, however, interest in schooling generally became

▲ Most eighteenth-century elementary school teachers used the extremely inefficient individual method of instruction in which pupils read to the teacher from whatever book they happened to bring from home, while the other pupils occupied themselves as best they could.
Bibliotheque des Art Decoratif, Paris. Photo Jean-Loup Charmet. Tallandier.

more widespread and gradually reached lower down the social scale.

Schooling in Central Europe While England and France left primary schooling entirely to the chance of local initiative, the Habsburg Monarchy seriously promoted primary education and thereby became the first Catholic realm to do so. The Habsburg General School Ordinance of 1774 authorized state subsidies, in combination with local funds, for the support of a school in almost every parish. Attendance was supposed to be compulsory, though the state had no way to enforce it. The state also intended to train future teachers at institutions called normal schools. A similar two-pronged strategy was adopted in Prussia under Frederick II at about the same time, although little was done to implement it.

In Prussia, as in most of Europe, schoolmasters remained barely competent and poorly paid. Frederick II indeed had a limiting vision of popular education: "It is enough for the country people to learn only a little reading and writing. . . . Instruction must be planned so that they receive only what is most essential for them but which is designed to keep them in the villages and not influence them to leave." As elsewhere in Europe, the goals of elementary schooling were to inculcate religion and morality, propagate the virtues of hard work, and promote sobriety and deference to one's superiors.

SOCIABILITY AND RECREATION

If the educated elites had their salons, masonic lodges, and learned academies, the common people also formed organized cultural groups. Many artisans, for example, belonged to secret societies that combined fraternal and trade-union functions. Young unmarried artisans frequently traveled the country, stopping periodically to work with comrades in other towns in order to hone their skills. Artisans also relied on their associations for camaraderie and ritual celebrations. Rivalries among federations of artisan associations occasionally led to pitched battles, however—a far cry from the nineteenth-century ideal of labor solidarity. Married artisans often joined religious confraternities, which honored a patron saint and ensured a dignified funeral when they died, or mutual aid societies to which they contributed small monthly dues to pay for assistance if illness or accident should strike.

Taverns and Festivals Corresponding to the coffeehouses of the urban middle classes were the taverns in working-class neighborhoods. These noisy, crowded places catered to a poor clientele, especially on Sunday and on Monday, which working people often took as a day off, honoring (as they put it) "Saint Monday." The urban common people were first beginning to consume wine in the eighteenth century, still something of a luxury except in its cheapest watered form. In England gin was the poor person's drink, cheap and plentiful until the government levied a hefty excise tax after realizing that too many people were drinking themselves into disability and death—a concern depicted in Hogarth's etchings.

▼ In his *Gin Lane* etching of 1750, Hogarth depicted the results of excessive gin drinking by the English common people as death, apathy, and moral decay. A cheerful companion piece called *Beer Street*, however, suggested that drinking in moderation was an acceptable practice.
Hogarth's "Gin Lane" & "Beer Street." The Metropolitan Museum of Art, Harris Brisbane Dick Fund, 1932.

More commonly, drinking was not done in morbid fashion but as part of a healthy and vibrant outdoor life. In England, before the spread of industrialization changed the cultural as well as physical landscape, popular pastimes followed a calendar of holidays that provided occasions for group merrymaking, eating, drinking, dressing-up, contests, and games. Local festivals were particularly comfortable settings for single young men and women to meet each other. The highlight of a country year usually came in early autumn after the summer harvest was in, when most villages held a public feast that lasted several days. In Catholic countries similar festivities were often linked with church rituals. Popular observances included the commemoration of local patron saints, pilgrimages to holy places, and the period of Carnival before Lent.

Sports A growing "commercialization of leisure" in the eighteenth century supported new spectator sports, such as horse racing and boxing matches. Blood sports constituted a more prevalent popular recreation. Bullbaiting, for example, involved setting loose a pack of dogs on a tethered steer. These events were usually collaborations between a butcher (who provided the steer, its meat to be sold later) and an innkeeper (whose yard served as the arena and who sold refreshments to the spectators). Cockfighting, similar in its gory results, attracted gentlemen and commoners alike, who enjoyed wagering on the outcome.

In early modern Europe, gentlefolk and commoners had been accustomed to mixing in recreational and religious settings: fairs and markets, sporting events, village or town festivals, Carnival in Catholic countries. But in the eighteenth century, as aristocrats and bourgeois alike became more concerned with good manners and refinement, these elite groups began to distance themselves from the bawdy and vulgar behavior of ordinary people. With growing intolerance they censured popular recreational culture in the hope of "reforming" the people into a more sober and orderly lifestyle. Social status was based on birth or wealth, but cultural taste was becoming its behavioral marker.

The philosophes, celebrated members of Europe's cultural establishment by the 1770s, hoped that their society would gradually reform itself under their inspiration. Although these writers criticized their society, they were not its subverters. Distrustful of the uneducated masses and afraid of popular emotion, superstition, and disorder, the philosophes were anything but democrats. Nonetheless, the Enlightenment challenged basic traditional values of European society: from Voltaire's polemics against Christianity through the sober social science of Diderot's *Encyclopedia* to the impassioned writings of Rousseau. Along with a flood of "bad books"—the pornography and scandal sheets of the clandestine publishers—booksellers, writers, and journalists disseminated critical ideas among Europe's educated men and women. The philosophes challenged the automatic respect for convention and authority, promoted the habit of independent reflection, and implanted the conviction that the reform of institutions was both necessary and possible. They promoted a climate which put the status quo on the defensive and in which revolution—when provoked under particular circumstances—would not be unthinkable.

Recommended Reading

Sources

Crocker, Lester (ed.). *The Age of Enlightenment.* 1969.

Gay, Peter (ed.). *The Enlightenment: a Comprehensive Anthology.* 1973.

Gendzier, Stephen (ed.). *Denis Diderot: The Encyclopedia: Selections.* 1967.

Mohl, Mary R., and Helene Koon (eds.). *The Female Spectator: English Women Writers Before 1800.* 1977.

*Rousseau, Jean-Jacques. *The Social Contract and Discourses.* 1950.

Vigée-Lebrun, Marie-Louise Élisabeth. *Memoirs.* S. Evans (ed.). 1989. Memoirs of the most notable female painter in eighteenth-century France.

*Voltaire. *The Portable Voltaire.* 1949, 1977.

*Wollstonecraft, Mary. *A Vindication of the Rights of Woman* [1792]. 1992. The preeminent early feminist text.

Studies

Bernard, Paul. *Jesuits and Jacobins: Enlightenment and Enlightened Despotism in Austria.* 1971. Liberalization and conflict in the Habsburg domain.

Brewer, John. *The Pleasures of the Imagination: English Culture in the Eighteenth Century.* 1997. A lively, panoramic survey of the production and consumption of high culture in all its forms.

Bruford, W. H. *Germany in the Eighteenth Century: The Social Background of the Literary Revival.* 1952. A useful survey.

Capp, Bernard. *English Almanacs, 1500–1800: Astrology and the Popular Press.* 1979. A probing study of the most important genre of popular literature.

*Cassirer, Ernst. *The Question of Jean-Jacques Rousseau.* 1963. Brief and reliable.

Censer, Jack, and Jeremy Popkin (eds.). *Press and Politics in Pre-Revolutionary France.* 1987. The limitations but also the impact of newspapers and journals.

*Chartier, Roger. *The Cultural Origins of the French Revolution.* 1991. A synthesis of recent research on publishing, the public sphere, and the emergence of a new political culture.

*Cragg, G. R. *The Church and the Age of Reason, 1648–1789.* 1966.

Cranston, Maurice. *Jean-Jacques, The Noble Savage,* and *The Solitary Self.* 1982, 1991, and 1995. A three vol-

ume study of the life and work of Rousseau, critical but sympathetic.

*Crow, Thomas. *Painters and Public Life in Eighteenth-Century Paris.* 1985. A pioneering work on the development of a public sphere of critical discourse about art.

Darnton, Robert. *The Business of Enlightenment: A Publishing History of the Encyclopedia.* 1979. The "biography of a book" and of the century's most influential publishing venture.

*———. *The Forbidden Best Sellers of Pre-Revolutionary France.* 1995. A pathbreaking work on the circulation, content, and impact of banned books.

*———. *The Great Cat Massacre and Other Essays in French Cultural History.* 1984. A notable collection of essays on "the social history of ideas" and on the "mentalities" of peasants and workers.

Furet, Francois, and Jacques Ozouf. *Reading and Writing: Literacy in France from Calvin to Jules Ferry.* 1982. An overview of literacy and primary schooling based on quantitative sources.

*Gay, Peter. *The Enlightenment: An Interpretation.* 2 vols. 1966 and 1969. A masterly, full-bodied exposition of Enlightenment thought.

*———. *Voltaire's Politics: The Poet as Realist.* 1959. A lively and sympathetic portrait.

*Goodman, Dena. *The Republic of Letters: a Cultural History of the French Enlightenment.* 1994. Focuses on the salons and the roles of women in cultural and intellectual life.

Hahn, Roger. *The Anatomy of a Scientific Institution: The Paris Academy of Sciences, 1666–1803.* 1971. The rise and problems of a scientific "establishment."

*Hampson, Norman. *A Cultural History of the Enlightenment.* 1969. A good general introduction to Enlightenment ideas.

Herr, Richard. *The Eighteenth-Century Revolution in Spain.* 1958. The reverberations of the Enlightenment in Spain—a case study not discussed in the present text.

*Isherwood, Robert. *Farce and Fantasy: Popular Entertainment in Eighteenth-Century Paris.* 1986. A cultural and institutional history of fairs and popular theater.

Joeres, Ruth-Ellen, and Mary Jo Maynes (eds.). *German Women in the Eighteenth and Nineteenth*

Centuries. 1986. Essays on women's writings and women's roles.

Malcolmson, R. W. *Popular Recreations in English Society, 1700–1850.* 1973. A good survey of a neglected subject.

Marker, Gary. *Publishing, Printing and the Origins of Intellectual Life in Russia, 1700–1800.* 1985.

*Maza, Sarah. *Private Lives and Public Affairs: the Causes Célèbres of Pre-Revolutionary France.* 1993. An original analysis of scandals and lawsuits that raised social consciousness in the later eighteenth century.

McClellan, James. *Science Reorganized: Scientific Societies in the Eighteenth Century.* 1985.

Melton, James Van Horn. *Absolutism and the Eighteenth-Century Origins of Compulsory Schooling in Prussia and Austria.* 1988. An excellent comparative study.

Palmer, Robert R. *Catholics and Unbelievers in Eighteenth-Century France.* 1939. The response of Catholic intellectuals to the century's philosophic thought.

*Paulson, Ronald. *Hogarth: His Life, Art, and Times.* Abridged ed. 1974.

Payne, Harry. *The Philosophes and the People.* 1976. An analysis of the Enlightenment's liberal elitism.

Porter, Roy, and Mikulas Teich (eds.). *The Enlightenment in National Context.* 1981. A comprehensive geographic overview.

*Roche, Daniel. *The People of Paris: An Essay on Popular Culture in the Eighteenth Century.* 1987. On the material culture and aspirations of ordinary Parisians.

Schackleton, Robert. *Montesquieu.* 1961. A biography of the French thinker with influence on both sides of the Atlantic.

*Spencer, Samia (ed.). *French Women and the Age of Enlightenment.* 1984. A pioneering collection of essays on a variety of literary and historical themes.

Venturi, Franco. *Italy and the Enlightenment.* 1972. Essays on important Italian philosophes by a leading historian.

*Watt, Ian. *The Rise of the Novel: Studies of Defoe, Richardson, and Fielding.* 1957. The view from England.

Wilson, Arthur. *Diderot.* 1972. An exhaustive, reliable biography of the consummate French philosophe.

* Available in paperback.

▲ **THE STORMING OF THE BASTILLE.**
Houet, "The Storming of the Bastille." Musée Carnavalet/Photo Bulloz.

THE FRENCH REVOLUTION

Well into the eighteenth century, the long-standing social structures and political institutions of Europe were securely entrenched. Most monarchs still claimed to hold their authority directly from God. In cooperation with their aristocracies, they presided over realms composed of distinct orders of citizens, or *estates* as they were sometimes known. Each order had its particular rights, privileges, and obligations. But pressures for change were building during the century. In France, the force of public opinion grew increasingly potent by the 1780s. A financial or political crisis that could normally be managed by the monarchy threatened to snowball in this new environment. This vulnerability was less evident in Austria, Prussia, and Russia, however, where strong monarchs instituted reforms to streamline their governments. Similarly, in Britain the political system proved resilient despite explosions of discontent at home and across the Atlantic.

Unquestionably, then, the French Revolution constituted the pivotal event of European history in the late eighteenth century. From its outbreak in 1789, the Revolution transformed the nature of sovereignty and law in France. Under its impetus, civic and social institutions were renewed, from local government and schooling to family relations and assistance for the poor. Soon its ideals of liberty, equality, and fraternity resonated across the borders of other European states, especially after war broke out in 1792 and French armies took the offensive.

The French Revolution's innovations defined the foundations of a liberal society and polity. Both at home and abroad, however, the new regime faced formidable opposition, and its struggle for survival propelled it in unanticipated directions. Some unforeseen turns, such as democracy and republicanism, became durable precedents for the future even if they soon aborted. Other developments, such as the reign of terror, seemed to nullify the original liberal values of 1789. The bloody struggles of the Revolution thus cast a shadow over this transformative event as they dramatized the brutal dilemma of means versus ends.

I. Reform and Political Crisis

"ENLIGHTENED ABSOLUTISM" IN CENTRAL AND EASTERN EUROPE

During the late nineteenth century, German historians invented the concept of "enlightened absolutism" to describe the Prussian and Habsburg monarchies of the eighteenth century. Critical of the ineptitude and weakness of French monarchs in that period, these historians argued that the strength of an enlightened ruler had been the surest basis for progress in early modern Europe. A king who ruled in his subjects' interest, they implied, avoided violent conflicts like those of the French Revolution. Earlier strong monarchs such as Philip II of Spain and France's Louis XIV (who had once declared: "I am the state") had been irresponsible; in contrast, these German historians argued, Frederick II of Prussia symbolized the enlightened phase of absolutism with his comment that the ruler is merely the "first servant of the state."

Previous chapters, however, have demonstrated that monarchs dealt with the same fundamental issues during all stages of absolutism. They always strove to assert their authority over their subjects and to maximize the power of their state in relation to other realms, principally by means of territorial expansion. Any notion that Enlightenment thinking caused monarchs to desist from these efforts is misleading. Still, several eighteenth-century monarchs did initiate reforms from above and did modify their styles of ruling in order to appear more modern or enlightened. Frederick II of Prussia and Catherine II of Russia, for example, lavished praise on Voltaire and Diderot, and those philosophes returned the compliment. These rulers may simply have been engaging in public relations. Yet the fact that they seemed supportive of such controversial writers suggests that absolutism had indeed adopted a new image.

Catherine the Great (r. 1762–1796) played this game to its limit. In 1767 she announced a new experiment in the direction of representative government—a policy hailed as a landmark by her philosophe admirers, who were too remote from St. Petersburg to see its insincerity. Catherine convened a Legislative Commission, a body of delegates from various strata of Russian society who were invited to present grievances, propose reforms, and then debate the proposals. In the end, however, she sent the delegates home under the pretext of having to turn her attention to a war with Turkey. Little came of the Legislative Commission except some good publicity for Catherine. In fact, she later promulgated a Charter of the Nobility, which, instead of limiting the nobility's privileges, strengthened their corporate status and increased their control over their serfs in exchange for their loyalty to the throne.

Conceptions of Enlightened Rule in Germany In justification of absolute monarchy, eighteenth-century German writers depicted the state as a machine and the ruler as its mainspring. Progress came from sound administration, through an enlightened monarch and well-trained officials. In keeping with this notion, German universities began to train government bureaucrats, and professors offered courses in the science of public finance and administration called *cameralism.* Before long the governments of Prussia and Austria introduced the rudiments of a civil service system.

The orders for the bureaucracy came from the monarchs, who were expected to dedicate themselves to the welfare of their subjects in return for their subjects' obedience. The framework for this command-obedience chain was to be a coherent body of public law, fairly administered by state officials. According to its advocates, this system would produce the rule of law, a *Rechtsstaat*, without the need for a written constitution or a representative parliament. The ruler and his or her officials, following their sense of public responsibility and rational analysis, would ensure the citizen's rights and well-being.

JOSEPH II AND THE LIMITS OF ABSOLUTISM

Joseph II, coruler of the Habsburg Empire with his mother, Maria Theresa, from 1765 and sole ruler in the 1780s, vigorously promoted reform from above. Unlike Frederick or Catherine, he did not openly identify with the philosophes, and he maintained his own Catholic faith. But Joseph proved to be the most innovative of the century's major rulers as well as one of its most autocratic personalities. It was a problematic combination.

Sound rule for Emperor Joseph involved far more than the customary administrative and financial modernization necessary for survival in the competitive state system. With startling boldness he implemented several reforms long advocated by Enlightenment thinkers: freedom of expression, religious toleration, greater state control over the Catholic Church, and legal reform. A new criminal code, for example, reduced the use of the death penalty, ended judicial torture, and allowed for no class differences in the application of the laws. By greatly reducing royal censorship, Joseph made it possible for Vienna to become a major center of literary activity. And we have already noted Joseph's remarkable Edicts of Religious Toleration for Protestants and for Jews. But Joseph's religious policies did not stop there. To make the Catholic Church serve its parishioners better, Joseph forced the clergy to modernize its rituals and services. Most of his Catholic subjects, however, preferred their traditional ways to Joseph's streamlined brand of Catholicism. These "reforms" proved extremely unpopular.

Agrarian Reform Joseph's most ambitious policies aimed to transform the economic and social position of the peasants. In this respect the Habsburg emperor acted far more boldly than any other eighteenth-century sovereign. Agrarian reform was generally the weak side of "enlightened absolutism," since Frederick II and Catherine II did little to improve the lot of the peasants or serfs in their realms. Joseph, however, set out to eradicate serfdom and to convert Habsburg peasants into free individuals in command of their persons and of the land they cultivated.

By royal decree Joseph abolished personal servitude and gave peasants the right to move, marry, and enter any trade they wished. He then promulgated laws to secure peasants' control over the land they worked. Finally and most remarkably, he sought to limit the financial obligations of peasant tenants to their lords and to the state. All land was to be surveyed and subject to a uniform tax. Twelve percent of the land's annual yield would go to the state and a maximum of 18 percent would go to the lord. This tax replaced previous seigneurial obligations in which

▼ **Joseph II, shown here visiting a peasant's field, actually promulgated his momentous agrarian reform edicts without any significant consultation with the peasants before or after the fact.**
Austrian Press & Information Service.

peasants owed service to their lord that could consume more than 100 days of labor a year.

Joseph ordered these reforms in an authoritarian fashion, with little consultation and no consent from any quarter. Predictably, these reforms provoked fierce opposition among the landowning nobles. But they also perplexed most peasants, who already distrusted the government because of its arbitrary religious policies. Joseph made no effort to build support among the peasants by carefully explaining the reforms, let alone by modifying their details after getting feedback from the grass roots. As a sympathetic chronicler of Joseph's reign observed, "He brought in his beneficial measures in an arbitrary manner."

His arbitrary manner, however, was not incidental. Joseph acknowledged no other way of doing things, no limitation on his own sovereignty. In reaction to the opposition that his reforms aroused he moved to suppress dissent in the firmest possible way. Not only did he restore censorship in his last years, but he elevated the police department to the status of an imperial ministry and gave it unprecedented powers. By the time he died, in 1790, Joseph was a disillusioned man. His realm resembled less a *Rechtsstaat* than a police state, and his successors quickly restored serfdom.

CONSTITUTIONAL CRISES IN THE WEST

While "enlightened absolutists" reigned in Austria, Prussia, and Russia, political tension and spirited debate over the institutions of government erupted in several Western European countries. To understand these crises we must recall the role of estates in European history. The term is both a social and a political signifier. Socially, every person belonged to one legally distinct order or another. The clergy usually constituted the First Estate of the realm, the nobles formed the Second Estate, and both maintained a common aristocratic viewpoint. The remainder of the population constituted the Third Estate. In the past the estates had sent representatives to national and provincial assemblies or diets, which shared in making government decisions. But absolutism had drastically curtailed the political role of the estates, as we have seen in previous chapters. It was the Third Estate's new bid for prominence and power in several countries at the expense of

the dominant aristocratic orders that made the late eighteenth century, as historian R. R. Palmer calls it, "the age of the democratic revolution."

Monarchs and Aristocrats On one level monarchs and the privileged orders were perennial and natural rivals. The rights and privileges of various groups, especially but not solely the aristocratic orders, reduced the fiscal resources of kings and princes and hampered their ability to pursue internal reform. The privileges and monopolies enjoyed by provinces, towns, and guilds restrained trade, hampered economic growth, and militated against the common welfare. Eighteenth-century struggles over political power often began when rulers initiated changes in traditional political or economic arrangements. While monarchs might wish to allocate a smaller place to nobles in the business of government, nobles would not willingly cede the privileges they held and might demand an even larger share in the exercise of power.

Aristocracies all over Europe thus sought to advance their fortunes and consolidate their roles in their country's traditional or unwritten constitutions. Armed perhaps with the ideas of the French philosophe Montesquieu, who held that privilege is the bulwark of liberty, nobles claimed that they had the exclusive right to serve as ministers of the king as well as the obligation to lead the community in the conduct of its important affairs. In the last decades of the century, the nobility continued to enjoy a near monopoly over high offices in the state, the army, and the Church. In 1781, for example, officers' commissions in the French army were limited almost exclusively to those who could prove descent from four generations of nobility. Aristocrats in several countries demanded that local assemblies of estates, which they expected to dominate, be granted a larger share of political power.

Upheavals over such issues erupted in the Austrian Netherlands (Belgium) and in the Dutch Netherlands, where provincial oligarchies rebelled against the centralizing reforms of their princes: Joseph II in Belgium and the Prince of Orange in the Dutch Netherlands. In each case a more democratic element of unprivileged commoners, including urban artisans, turned these conflicts into triangular struggles as they took up arms to oppose both princely tyranny and oligarchic privilege. To a certain extent, these Dutch and Belgian "patriots," as they called themselves, provided a foretaste of the French Revolution. Their suppression, in turn, suggested that counterrevolution was a force to be reckoned with.

UPHEAVALS IN THE BRITISH EMPIRE

An aggressive monarch, George III, helped ignite political unrest in Great Britain. Unlike his Hanoverian predecessors George I and George II, this king had been born in England and knew its language and its political system well. He was intent on advancing royal authority, but rather than bypass Parliament altogether he simply tried, as Whig ministers had before him, to control its members through patronage and influence. The Whig aristocrats saw this operation as a threat to their own traditional power. Not only did they oppose the king and his ministers in Parliament, but they enlisted the support of citizens' groups outside of Parliament as well. These organizations were calling for political reform, including representation in Parliament proportionate to population, stricter laws against political corruption, and greater freedom of the press.

"Wilkes and Liberty" John Wilkes, a member of Parliament and a journalist, became the center of this rising storm. Wilkes viciously attacked the king's prime minister, and by implication the king himself, over the terms of the Treaty of Paris, which ended the Seven Years' War in 1763. The government arrested him for seditious libel on a general warrant. When the courts quashed the indictment, the government then accused Wilkes of having authored a libelous pornographic poem, and this time he fled to France to avoid prison. He stayed in France for four years; but in 1768, still under indictment, he returned to stand once more for Parliament. Three times he was reelected, and three times the House of Commons refused to seat him. With the ardent support of radicals and to the acclaim of crowds in London, who marched to the chant of "Wilkes and Liberty," Wilkes finally took his seat in 1774.

Agitation for parliamentary reform drew support primarily from shopkeepers, artisans, and property owners who had the franchise in a few districts but were denied it in most others. Thus even without a right to vote, English citizens could engage in politics and mobilize the power of public opinion, in this case by rallying to Wilkes. Most radicals called only for political reform, not for the overthrow of the British political system. They retained a measure of respect for the nation's political traditions, which ideally guaranteed the rights of "freeborn Englishmen."

Rebellion in America Great Britain did face revolutionary action in the thirteen North American colonies. George III and his prime minister, Lord North, attempted to force the colonies to pay the costs, past and present, of their own defense. The policy would have meant an increase in taxes and a centralization of authority in the governance of the British empire. Colonial landowners, merchants, and artisans of the eastern seaboard organized petitions and boycotts in opposition to the proposed fiscal and constitutional changes.

The resistance in North America differed fundamentally from comparable movements in Europe. American political leaders did not appeal to a body of privileges that the actions of the monarchy were allegedly violating. Instead they appealed to traditional rights supposedly enjoyed by all British subjects, regardless of status, and to theories of popular sovereignty and natural rights advanced by John Locke and other English libertarian writers. When conciliation and compromise with the British government failed, the American Declaration of Independence in 1776 gave eloquent expression to those concepts. The lack of a rigid system of estates and hereditary privileges in American society, the fluid boundaries that separated the social strata, and the traditions of local government in the colonies—from town meetings in New England to the elected legislatures that had advised colonial governors—blunted the kinds of conflicts between aristocrats and commoners that derailed incipient revolutionary movements in Ireland, Belgium, and the Dutch Netherlands.

These differences help to explain the unique character of the American rebellion, which was simultaneously a war for independence and a political revolution. The theories that supported the rebellion, and the continuing alliance between social strata, made it the most democratic revolution of the eighteenth century before 1789. The American Revolution created the first state governments, and ultimately a national government,

▲ **The committee that drafted the American Declaration of Independence included John Adams, Thomas Jefferson, and Benjamin Franklin, all shown here standing at the desk.**
John Trumball, "The Declaration of Independence, 4 July 1776." Yale University Art Gallery, Trumball Collection.

in which the exercise of power was grounded not on royal sovereignty or traditional privilege but on the participation and consent of male citizens (apart from the numerous black slaves, whose status did not change). Even more important as a historical precedent, perhaps, it was the first successful rebellion by overseas colonies against their European masters.

II. 1789: The French Revolution

Although the rebellion in America stirred sympathy and interest across the Atlantic, it seemed remote from the realities of Europe. The French Revolution of 1789 proved to be the turning point in European history. Its sheer radicalism, creativity,

and claims of universalism made it unique. Its ultimate slogan—"Liberty, Equality, Fraternity"—expressed social and civic ideals that became the foundations of modern Western civilization. In the name of individual liberty, French revolutionaries swept away the institutionalized constraints of the old regime: seigneurial charges upon the land, vestiges of feudalism, tax privileges, guild monopolies on commerce, and even (in 1794) black slavery overseas. The revolutionaries held that legitimate governments required written constitutions, elections, and powerful legislatures. They demanded equality before the law for all persons and uniformity of institutions for all regions of the country, denying the claims to special treatment of privileged groups, provinces, towns, or religions. The term *fraternity* expressed a different kind of revolutionary goal. Rousseauist in inspiration, it meant that all citizens regardless of social class or region shared a common fate in society and that the nation's well-being could override the interests of individual citizens.

ORIGINS OF THE REVOLUTION

Those who made the Revolution believed they were rising against despotic government, in which citizens had no voice, and against inequality and privilege. Yet the government of France at that time was no more tyrannical or unjust than it had been in the past. On the contrary, a process of modest reform had been under way for several decades. What, then, set off the revolutionary upheaval? What had failed in France's long-standing political system?

An easy answer would be to point to the incompetence of King Louis XVI (r. 1774–1792) and his queen, Marie Antoinette. Louis was good-natured but weak and indecisive, a man of limited intelligence who lacked self-confidence and who preferred hunting deer to supervising the business of government. By no stretch of the imagination was he an enlightened absolutist. Worse yet, his young queen, a Habsburg princess, was frivolous, meddlesome, and tactless. But even the most capable French ruler could not have escaped challenge and unrest in the 1780s. It is the roots of the political crisis, not its mismanagement, that claim the historian's attention.

The Cultural Climate In eighteenth-century France, as we have seen, intellectual ferment preceded political revolt. For decades the philosophes had questioned accepted political and religious beliefs. They undermined confidence that traditional ways were the best ways. But the philosophes harbored deep-seated fears of the uneducated masses and did not question the notion that educated and propertied elites should rule society; they wished only that the elites should be more enlightened and more open to new ideas. Indeed, the Enlightenment had become respectable by the 1770s, a kind of intellectual establishment. Rousseau damned that establishment and wrote of the need for simplicity, sincerity, and virtue, but the word *revolution* never flowed from his pen either.

More subversive perhaps than the writings of Enlightenment intellectuals were several sensational lawsuits centered on the scandalous doings of high aristocrats. The melodramatic legal briefs published by the lawyers in such cases were eagerly snatched up by the reading public along with the prohibited "bad books"—the clandestine gossip sheets, libels, exposés, and pornography—discussed earlier. All this material indirectly, at least, portrayed the French aristocracy as decadent and the monarchy as a ridiculous despotism. Royal officials and philosophes alike regarded the authors of this material as "the excrement of literature," as Voltaire put it. And writers forced to earn their living by turning out such stuff were no doubt embittered at being stuck on the bottom rung in the world of letters. Their resentment would explode once the Revolution began in 1789, and many became radical journalists either for or against the new regime. In itself, however, the "literary underground" of the old regime did not advocate, foresee, or directly cause the Revolution.

Class Conflict? Did the structure of French society, then, provoke the Revolution? Karl Marx, and the many historians inspired by him, certainly believed so. Marx saw the French Revolution as the necessary break marking the transition from the aristocratic feudalism of the Middle Ages to the era of middle-class capitalism. In this view, the French bourgeoisie, or middle classes, had been gaining in wealth during the eighteenth century and resented the privileges of the nobility, which placed obstacles in the path of their ambition. Though they framed their ideology in universal terms in 1789, the middle classes led the Revolution in order to change the political and social systems in their own interests.

Three decades of research have rendered this theory of the Revolution's origins untenable. Whether a sizable and coherent capitalist middle class actually existed in eighteenth-century France is questionable. In any case, the leaders of the Revolution in 1789 were lawyers, administrators, and liberal nobles, and rarely merchants or industrialists. Moreover, the barrier between the nobility of the Second Estate and the wealthy and educated members of the Third Estate was porous, the lines of social division frequently (though not always) blurred. Many members of the middle class identified themselves on official documents as "living nobly," as substantial property owners who did not work for a living. Conversely, wealthy nobles often invested in mining, overseas trade, and finance—activities usually associated with the middle classes. Even more important, the gap between the nobility and the middle classes was nothing compared with the gulf that separated both from the working people of town and country. In this revisionist historiography, the bourgeoisie did not make the Revolution so much as the Revolution made the bourgeoisie (see "On the Origins of the French Revolution," p. 697).

Yet numerous disruptive pressures were at work in French society. A growing population left large numbers of young people in town and country struggling to attain a stable place in society. New images and attitudes rippled through the media of the day, despite the state's efforts to censor material it deemed subversive. The nobility, long since banished by Louis XIV from an independent role in monarchical government, chafed at its exclusion, while the prosperous middle classes too aspired to a more active role. The monarchy struggled to contain these forces within the established social and political systems. Until the 1780s it succeeded, but then its troubles began in earnest.

FISCAL CRISIS AND POLITICAL DEADLOCK

When he took the throne in 1774, Louis XVI tried to conciliate elite opinion by recalling the Parlements, or sovereign law courts, that his grandfather had banished in 1770 for their opposition to his policies. This concession to France's traditional "unwritten constitution" did not suffice to smooth the new sovereign's road. Louis' new controller-general of finances, Jacques Turgot, encountered a storm of opposition from privileged groups to the modest reforms he proposed.

The Failure of Reform Turgot, an ally of the philosophes and an experienced administrator, hoped to encourage economic growth by a policy of nonintervention, or laissez-faire, that would give free play to economic markets and allow individuals maximum freedom to pursue their own economic interests. He proposed to remove all restrictions on commerce in grain and to abolish the guilds. In addition, he tried to cut down on expenses at court and to replace the obligation of peasants to work on the royal roads (the corvée) with a small new tax on all landholders. Privately, he also considered establishing elected advisory assemblies of landowners to assist in local administration. Vested interests, however, viewed Turgot as a dangerous innovator. When agitation against him mounted in the king's court at Versailles and in the Paris Parlement, Louis took the easy way out and dismissed his contentious minister. With Turgot went perhaps the last hope for significant reform in France under royal leadership.

Deficit Financing The king then turned to Jacques Necker, a banker from Geneva who had a reputation for financial wizardry. Necker had a shrewd sense of public relations. To finance the heavy costs of France's aid to the rebellious British colonies in North America, Necker avoided new taxes, which gained him wide popularity, and instead floated a series of large loans at exorbitant interest rates as high as 10 percent. (England, through sound management of its public finances and public confidence in the government, financed its war effort with loans at only 3 or 4 percent interest.)

By the 1780s royal finances hovered in a state of permanent crisis. Direct taxes on land, borne mainly by the peasants, were extremely high but were levied inequitably. The great variations in taxation from province to province and the numerous exemptions for privileged groups were regarded by those who benefited from them as traditional liberties. Any attempt to revoke these privileges therefore appeared to be tyrannical. Meanwhile indirect taxes on commercial activity (customs duties, excise or sales taxes, and royal monopolies on salt and tobacco) hit regressively at consumers, especially in the towns. Any tax increases or new taxes imposed by the monarchy at this point would be bitterly resented. At the same time, the cycle of borrowing—the alternative to increased taxes—had reached its limits. New loans would only raise the huge interest payments already being paid out. By the 1780s those payments accounted for about half the royal budget and created additional budget deficits of perhaps 150,000,000 livres each year.

On the Origins of the French Revolution

◆

A long-held view of the French Revolution's origins attributed the starring role to the middle class, "the rising bourgeoisie." Liberal historians of the nineteenth century regarded the middle class as the carrier of liberal ideals—individual freedom, civil equality, representative government—that finally came to fruition in the French Revolution. Marxists considered the triumph of capitalism to be the pivotal issue in modern history and linked it to the political ascendancy of the middle class in the French Revolution. In a sense, both versions of this "social interpretation" of the French Revolution read its causes back from its results. In his classic synthesis of 1939 embodying the social interpretation, for example, Georges Lefebvre begins with these observations:

"The ultimate cause of the French Revolution of 1789 goes deep into the history of France and of the western world. At the end of the eighteenth century the social structure of France was aristocratic. It showed the traces of having originated at a time when land was almost the only form of wealth, and when the possessors of land were the masters of those who needed it to work and to live. It is true that in the course of age-old struggles the king had been able gradually to deprive the lords of their political powers and subject nobles and clergy to his authority. But he had left them the first place in the social hierarchy.

"Meanwhile the growth of commerce and industry had created, step by step, a new form of wealth, mobile or commercial wealth, and a new class, called in France the bourgeoisie. . . . In the eighteenth cen-

tury commerce, industry and finance occupied an increasingly important place in the national economy. It was the bourgeoisie that rescued the royal treasury in moments of crisis. . . . The role of the nobility had correspondingly declined; and the clergy, as the ideal which it proclaimed lost prestige, found its authority growing weaker. These groups preserved the highest rank in the legal structure of the country, but in reality economic power, personal abilities and confidence in the future had passed largely to the bourgeoisie. Such a discrepancy never lasts forever. The Revolution of 1789 restored the harmony between fact and law."

From Georges Lefebvre, R. R. Palmer (trans.), *The Coming of the French Revolution*, Princeton University Press, 1989, pp. 1–2.

Since the 1950s, revisionist historians have challenged this "social interpretation" of the French Revolution. In his new synthesis, William Doyle summarizes some of their research and arguments.

"Money, not privilege, was the key to pre-revolutionary society in France. Wealth transcended all social barriers and bound great nobles and upper bourgeois together into an upper class unified by money. . . . Eighteenth-century capitalism was far from a bourgeois monopoly. One of its basic features was the heavy involvement of nobles. . . . [On the other hand,] the wealth of all social groups in pre-revolutionary France was overwhelmingly non-capitalist in nature. Capitalism had not become the dominant mode of production in the French economy before 1789. . . . there was between most of the nobility and the proprietary sectors of the middle class, a continuity of investment forms and socio-economic values that made them, economically, a single group.

"If the nobility and the bourgeoisie had so much in common, why did they become such implacable enemies in 1789? [Since] the Revolution could not be explained in economic terms as a clash of opposed interests. . . . it was time to revert to a political explanation of the Revolution's outbreak. The radical reforms of 1789 were products of a political crisis, and not the outcome of long-maturing social and economic trends. [As historian George Taylor concluded:] 'It was essentially a political revolution with social consequences and not a social revolution with political consequences.'"

From William Doyle, *Origins of the French Revolution* Oxford University Press, 1988, pp. 16–21.

Calonne and the Assembly of Notables   When the king's new controller-general, Charles Calonne, pieced all this information together in 1787, he warned that, contrary to Necker's rosy projections, the monarchy was facing outright bankruptcy. Though no way had yet been found to win public confidence and forge a consensus for fiscal reform, the monarchy had to act and could no longer rely on old expedients. Bold innovations were essential. Calonne accordingly proposed to establish a new tax, called the *territorial subvention,* to be levied on the yield of all landed property without exemptions. At the same time, he proposed to convene *provincial assemblies* elected by large landowners to advise royal officials on the collection and allocation of revenues.

Certain that the Parlements would reject this scheme, Calonne convinced the king to convene an Assembly of Notables, comprising about 150 influential men, mainly but not exclusively from the aristocracy, who might more easily be persuaded to support the reforms. To Calonne's shock, the Assembly of Notables refused to endorse the proposed decrees. Instead, they denounced the lavish spending of the court and insisted on auditing the monarchy's financial accounts. To save the day, Louis dismissed Calonne and appointed one of the notables, Archbishop Brienne, in his place. Brienne now submitted Calonne's proposals to the Parlement, which not only rejected them but also demanded that Louis convene the Estates General, a body representing the clergy, nobility, and Third Estate, which had not met since 1614. Louis responded by sending the members of the Parlements into exile. But a huge outcry in Paris and in the provinces against this arbitrary act forced the king to back down: After all, the whole purpose of Calonne's proposals had been to build public confidence in the government.

Facing bankruptcy and unable to float new loans in this atmosphere, the King recalled the Parlements, reappointed Necker, and agreed to convene the Estates General in May 1789. In the opinion of the English writer Arthur Young, who was visiting France, the kingdom was "on the verge of a revolution, but one likely to add to the scale of the nobility and clergy." The aristocracy's determined opposition was putting an end to absolutism in France. But it was not clear what would take its place.

FROM THE ESTATES GENERAL TO THE NATIONAL ASSEMBLY

The calling of the Estates General in 1789 created extraordinary excitement across the land. The king invited his subjects to express their opinions about this great event, and thousands did so in pamphlet form. Here the "patriot," or liberal, ideology first took shape. Self-styled patriots came from the ranks of the nobility and clergy as well as from the middle classes; they opposed traditionalists, whom they labeled as "aristocrats." Their top priority was the method of voting to be used in the Estates General. While the king accorded the Third Estate twice as many delegates as the two higher orders, he refused to promise that the deputies would all vote together (by head) rather than separately in three chambers (by order). Voting by order would mean that the two upper chambers would outweigh the Third Estate no matter how many deputies it had. Patriots had hoped that the lines dividing the nobility from the middle class would crumble in a common effort by France's elites at reform. Instead, it appeared as if the Estates General might sharpen the lines of separation between the orders.

The Critique of Privilege   It did not matter that the nobility had led the fight against absolutism. Even if they endorsed new constitutional checks on absolutism and accepted equality in the allocation of taxes, nobles would still hold vastly disproportionate powers if the Estates General voted by order. In the most influential pamphlet about the Estates General, Emmanuel Sieyès posed the question, "What is the Third Estate?" and answered flatly, "Everything." "And what has it been until now in the political order?" he asked. Answer: "Nothing." The nobility, he claimed, monopolized all the lucrative positions in society while doing little of its productive work. In the manifestos of Sieyès and other patriots, the enemy was no longer simply absolutism but privilege as well.

Unlike reformers in England or the Belgian rebels against Joseph II or even the American revolutionaries of 1776, the French patriots did not simply claim that the king had violated historic traditions of liberty. Rather, they contemplated a complete break with a discredited past. As a basis for reform, they would substitute reason for

▲ Thousands of pamphlets were published to discuss the calling of the Estates General in 1789, but the grievances and claims of the Third Estate translated most readily into vivid imagery and caricature; this print was titled "The Awakening of the Third Estate."
Roger-Viollet, Bibliothéque Nationale, Paris.

tradition. It is this frame of mind that made the French Revolution so radical.

Cahiers and Elections For the moment, however, the patriot spokesmen stood far in advance of opinion at the grass roots. The king had invited all citizens to meet in their local parishes to elect delegates to district electoral assemblies and to draft grievance petitions (*cahiers*) setting forth their views. The great majority of rural cahiers were highly traditional in tone and complained only of particular local ills or high taxes, expressing confidence that the king would redress them. Only a few cahiers from cities like Paris invoked concepts of natural rights and popular sovereignty or demanded that France must have a written constitution, that sovereignty belonged to the

nation or that feudalism and regional privileges should be abolished. It is impossible, in other words, to read in the cahiers the future course of the Revolution. Still, these gatherings of citizens promoted reflection on France's problems and encouraged expectations for change. They thereby helped raise the nation's political consciousness.

So too did the local elections, whose royal ground rules were remarkably democratic. Virtually every adult male taxpayer was eligible to vote for electors, who, in turn, met in district assemblies to choose representatives of the Third Estate to the Estates General. The electoral assemblies were a kind of political seminar, where articulate local leaders emerged to be sent by their fellow citizens as deputies to Versailles. Most of these deputies were lawyers or officials, without a single peasant or artisan among them. In the elections for the First Estate, meanwhile, parish priests rather than Church notables formed a majority of the deputies. And in the elections for the Second Estate, about one-third of the deputies could be described as liberal nobles or patriots, the rest traditionalists.

Deadlock and Revolution Popular expectation that the monarchy would provide leadership in reform proved to be ill-founded. When the deputies to the Estates General met on May 5, Necker and Louis XVI spoke to them only in generalities and left unsettled whether the estates would vote by order or by head. The upper two estates proceeded to organize their own chambers, but the deputies of the Third Estate balked. Vainly inviting the others to join them, the Third Estate took a decisive revolutionary step on June 17 by proclaiming that it formed a "National Assembly." A few days later more than a third of the

deputies from the clergy joined them. The king, on the other hand, decided to cast his lot with the nobility and locked the Third Estate out of its meeting hall until he could present his own program. But the deputies moved to an indoor tennis court and swore that they would not separate until they had given France a constitution.

The king ignored this act of defiance and addressed the delegates of all three orders on June 23. He promised equality in taxation, civil liberties, and regular meetings of the Estates General at which, however, voting would be by order. France would be provided with a constitution, he pledged, "but the ancient distinction of the three orders will be conserved in its entirety." He then ordered the three estates to retire to their individual meeting halls, but the Third Estate refused to move. "The assembled nation cannot receive orders," declared its spokesman. Startled by the determination of the patriots, the king backed down. For the time being, he recognized the Na-

▼ **When the king opened the meeting of the Estates General, the deputies for each estate were directed to sit in three separate sections of the hall.**
Bibliothéque Nationale/Photo Bulloz.

▲ Jacques-Louis David's depiction of the Tennis Court Oath, one of the great historical paintings, captures the deputies' sense of idealism and purpose.
Jacques-Louis David, detail from "Oath of the Tennis Court at Versailles, June 20, 1789." Giraudon/Art Resource.

tional Assembly and ordered deputies from all three estates to join it.

Thus the French Revolution began as a nonviolent, "legal" revolution. By their own will, delegates elected by France's three estates to represent their own districts to the king became instead the representatives of the entire nation. As such, they claimed to be the sovereign power in France—a claim that the king now seemed powerless to contest. In fact, however, he was merely biding his time until he could deploy his army to subdue the capital and overwhelm the deputies at Versailles. Twenty thousand royal troops were ordered into the Paris region, due to arrive sometime in July.

THE CONVERGENCE OF REVOLUTIONS

The political struggle at Versailles was not occurring in isolation. The mass of French citizens, politically aroused by elections to the Estates Gen-

eral, was also mobilizing over subsistence issues. The winter and spring of 1788–1789 had brought severe economic difficulties, as crop failures and grain shortages almost doubled the price of flour and bread on which the population depended for subsistence. Unemployed vagrants filled the roads, angry consumers stormed grain convoys and marketplaces, and relations between town and country grew tense. Economic anxieties merged with rage over the obstructive behavior of aristocrats in Versailles. Parisians believed that food shortages and royal troops would be used to intimidate the people into submission. They feared an "aristocratic plot" against the National Assembly and the patriot cause.

The Fall of the Bastille　When the King dismissed the popular Necker on July 11, Parisians correctly assumed that a counterrevolution was about to begin. They prepared to resist, and most

▲ **The fall of the Bastille was understood at the time to be a great turning point in history, and July 14 eventually became the French national holiday. Numerous prints and paintings evoke the daunting qualities of the fortress, the determination of the besieging crowd, and the heroism of individuals in that crowd.** Houet, "The Storming of the Bastille." Musée Carnavalet/Photo Bulloz.

of the king's military units pulled back. On July 14 Parisian crowds searching for weapons and ammunition laid siege to the Bastille, an old fortress that had served as a royal prison and in which gunpowder was stored. The small garrison resisted, and a fierce firefight erupted. Although the troops soon capitulated, dozens of citizens were hit, providing the first martyrs of the Revolution, and the infuriated crowd massacred several soldiers as they left the fortress. Meanwhile, patriot electors ousted royal officials of the Paris city government, replaced them with a revolutionary municipality, and organized a citizens'

militia to patrol the city. Similar municipal revolutions occurred in twenty-six of the thirty largest French cities, thus ensuring that the defiance in the capital would not be an isolated act.

The Parisian insurrection of July 14 not only saved the National Assembly but altered the Revolution's course by giving it a far more popular dimension. Again the king capitulated. He traveled to Paris on July 17 and, to please the people, donned a ribbon bearing three colors: white for the monarchy and blue and red for the capital. This *tricolor* would become the emblem of the new regime.

Peasant Revolts and the August 4 Decree
These events did not pacify the anxious and hungry people of the countryside. Peasants had numerous and long-standing grievances. Population growth and the parceling of holdings reduced the margin of subsistence for many families, while the purchase of land by rich townspeople further shrank their opportunities for economic advancement. Seigneurial dues and church tithes weighed heavily on many peasants. Now, in addition, suspicions were rampant that nobles were hoarding grain in order to stymie the patriotic cause. In July peasants in several regions sacked the castles of the nobles and burned the documents that recorded their feudal obligations.

This peasant insurgency blended into a vast movement known to historians as "the Great Fear." Rumors abounded that the vagrants who swarmed through the countryside were actually "brigands" in the pay of nobles, who were marching on villages to destroy the new harvest and cow the peasants into submission. The fear was baseless, but it stirred up the peasants' hatred and suspicion of the nobles, prompted armed mobilizations in hundreds of villages, and set off new attacks on manor houses.

Peasant revolts worried the deputies of the National Assembly, but they decided to appease the peasants rather than simply denounce their violence. On the night of August 4, therefore, certain deputies of the nobility and clergy dramatically renounced their ancient privileges. This action set the stage for the Assembly to decree "the abolition of feudalism" as well as the end of the church tithe, the sale of royal offices, regional tax privileges, and social privilege of all kinds. Later, it is true, the Assembly clarified the August 4 decree to ensure that property rights were maintained. While personal servitudes such as hunting rights, manorial justice, and labor services were suppressed outright, the Assembly decreed that most seigneurial dues would end only after the peasants had paid compensation to their lords. Peasants resented this onerous requirement, and most simply refused to pay the dues; pressure built until all seigneurial dues were finally abolished without compensation by a more radical government in 1793.

The Declaration of the Rights of Man and Citizen By sweeping away the old web of privileges, the August 4 decree permitted the Assembly to construct a new regime. Since it would take months to draft a constitution, the Assembly drew up a Declaration of the Rights of Man and Citizen to indicate its intentions (see "Two Views of the Rights of Man," p. 704). The Declaration was the death certificate of the old regime and a rallying point for the future. It affirmed individual liberties but also set forth the basic obligation of citizenship: obedience to legitimate law. The Declaration enumerated natural rights such as freedom of expression and freedom of religious conscience but stipulated that even these rights could be circumscribed by law. It proclaimed the sovereignty of the nation and sketched the basic criteria for a legitimate government, which the constitution would eventually amplify, such as representation and the separation of powers. The Declaration's concept of natural rights meant that the new regime would be based on the principles of reason rather than history or tradition.

In his *Reflections on the Revolution in France,* published in 1790, the Anglo-Irish statesman Edmund Burke condemned this attitude, as well as the violence of 1789. In this influential counterrevolutionary tract, Burke argued that France had passed from despotism to anarchy in the name of misguided, abstract principles. Burke distrusted the simplicity of reason that the Assembly celebrated. In his view the complexity of traditional institutions served the public interest. Burke attacked the belief in natural rights that guided the revolutionaries; something was natural, he believed, only if it resulted from long historical development and habit. Trying to wipe the slate of history clean was a grievous error, he wrote, since society "is a contract between the dead, the living, and the unborn." Society's main right, in Burke's view, was the right to be well-governed by its rulers. Naturally this argument did not go unchallenged, even in England. Mary Wollstonecraft countered with *A Vindication of the Rights of Man,* followed shortly by her seminal *Vindication of the Rights of Woman,* while Thomas Paine published *The Rights of Man* in 1792 to refute Burke.

TWO VIEWS OF THE RIGHTS OF MAN

◀◆▶

The radical theoretical and practical implications of French revolutionary ideology are suggested in a comparison of two essentially contemporaneous documents. The Prussian General Code, a codification initiated by Frederick the Great and issued in its final form in 1791 after his death, reinforced the traditional prerogatives of the nobility under an umbrella of public law. The French National Assembly's Declaration of the Rights of Man and Citizen (1789) established the principle of civil equality alongside the doctrines of national sovereignty, representation, and the rule of law. While the Prussian General Code exemplifies the old order against which French revolutionary ideology took aim, the Declaration became a foundational document of the liberal tradition.

Excerpts From the Prussian General Code, 1791

• This general code contains the provisions by which the rights and obligations of inhabitants of the state, so far as they are not determined by particular laws, are to be judged.

• The rights of a man arise from his birth, from his estate, and from actions and arrangements with which the laws have associated a certain determinate effect.

• The general rights of man are grounded on the natural liberty to seek and further his own welfare, without injury to the rights of another.

• Persons to whom, by their birth, destination or principal occupation, equal rights are ascribed in civil society, make up together an *estate* of the state.

• The nobility, as the first estate in the state, most especially bears the obligation, by its distinctive destination, to maintain the defense of the state. . . .

• The nobleman has an especial right to places of honor in the state for which he has made himself fit.

• Only the nobleman has the right to possess noble property.

• Persons of the burgher [middle-class] estate cannot own noble property except by permission of the sovereign.

• Noblemen shall normally engage in no burgher livelihood or occupation.

From R. R. Palmer (trans.), *The Age of Democratic Revolution*, Princeton University Press, 1959, pp. 510–511.

Excerpts From the French Declaration of the Rights of Man and Citizen, 1789

1. Men are born and remain free and equal in rights. Social distinctions may be based only on common utility.

3. The principle of all sovereignty rests essentially in the nation. No body and no individual may exercise authority which does not emanate expressly from the nation.

4. Liberty consists in the ability to do whatever does not harm another; hence the exercise of the natural rights of each man has no limits except those which assure to other members of society the enjoyment of the same rights. These limits can only be determined by law.

6. Law is the expression of the general will. All citizens have the right to take part, in person or by their representatives, in its formation. It must be the same for all whether it protects or penalizes. All citizens being equal in its eyes are equally admissible to all public dignities, offices and employments, according to their capacity, and with no other distinction than that of their virtues and talents.

13. For maintenance of public forces and for expenses of administration common taxation is necessary. It should be apportioned equally among all citizens according to their capacity to pay.

14. All citizens have the right, by themselves or through their representatives, to have demonstrated to them the necessity of public taxes, to consent to them freely, to follow the use made of the proceeds, and to determine the shares to be paid, the means of assessment and collection and the duration.

III. The Reconstruction of France

THE NEW CONSTITUTION

Representative Government From 1789 to 1791, the National Assembly acted as a Constituent Assembly to produce a constitution for France. While proclaiming equal civil rights for all French citizens, it effectively transferred political power from the monarchy and the privileged estates to the body of propertied citizens; in 1790 nobles lost their titles and became indistinguishable from other citizens. The new constitution created a limited monarchy with a clear separation of powers. Sovereignty effectively resided in the representatives of the people, a single-house legislature to be elected by a system of indirect voting. The king was to name and dismiss his ministers, but he was given only a suspensive or delaying veto over legislation; if a bill passed the Assembly in three successive years, it would become law even without royal approval.

Under the French Constitution of 1791, every adult male of settled domicile who satisfied minimal tax-paying requirements (roughly two-thirds of all adult males) gained the right to vote, with a higher qualification needed to serve as an elector. Although it favored the propertied, France's new political system was vastly more democratic than Britain's. Still, the National Assembly considered the vote to be a civic function rather than a natural right. "Those who contribute nothing to the public establishment should have no direct influence on government," declared Sieyès. In the same frame of mind the Assembly excluded all women from voting.

Women in the Revolution That the question of political rights for women was even debated testifies to the potential universalism of the Revolution's principles. A brief but spirited drive for women's suffrage advanced through pamphlets, petitions, and deputations to the Assembly—most notably the "Declaration of the Rights of Women" (1791) drafted by the playwright Olympe de Gouges. But the notion of gender difference and separate spheres, popularized by Rousseau, easily prevailed. The great majority of deputies believed women to be emotional, vain, and frivolous. Too easily influenced to be independent, they must be excluded from the new public sphere—the more so because of the deputies' belief that elite women had used their sexual powers nefariously behind the scenes during the old regime to influence public policy. Now public life would be virtuous and transparent, uninfluenced by feminine wiles. Instead, women would devote themselves to their crucial nurturing and maternal roles in the domestic sphere.

This type of discourse has prompted some feminist scholars to claim that the revolutionary public sphere "was constructed not merely without women but against them." This attitude was especially strong, they argue, after the establishment of the Republic. With the execution of the king in 1793, the arena of politics belonged, metaphorically, to the fraternal band of brothers who had dared to topple their corrupt father, the king.

Balanced against this powerful imagery, however, is an offsetting consideration. Male revolutionaries may have distrusted women, and some were overt misogynists, yet their own ideology and political culture created unprecedented public space for women. True, women could not vote or hold office, but otherwise *citoyennes* had extensive opportunity for political participation. Women actively engaged in local conflicts over the Assembly's religious policy (discussed later in this chapter). In the towns they agitated over food prices, and in October 1789 Parisian women led a mass demonstration to Versailles that forcibly returned the king and queen to Paris. Combining traditional concerns over food scarcities with antiaristocratic revolutionary ideology, women frequently goaded authorities like the national guard into action.

In unprecedented numbers women also took up the pen to publish pamphlets and journals, having gained the right after 1789 to sign their names publicly without permission from their husbands. Their physical presence in public spaces was even more important. Women helped fill the galleries of the Assembly, of the Paris Jacobin Club, and later of the Revolutionary Tribunal—shouting approval or disapproval and in general monitoring their officials. In at least sixty

▲ In October 1789 Parisian women were furious over the high cost of bread and suspicious of the king and queen. In concert with the National Guard, they set out on an armed march to confront the royal couple in Versailles. To appease the menacing crowd, Louis XVI agreed to return to Paris and to cooperate with revolutionary authorities.
Giraudon/Art Resource, NY.

towns women formed auxiliaries to the local Jacobin club, where they read newspapers, debated political issues, and participated in revolutionary festivals.

Nor did Rousseauian antifeminism prevent the revolutionaries from enacting dramatic advances in the civil status of women. Legislation between 1789 and 1794 created a more equitable family life by curbing paternal powers over children, lowering the age of majority, and equalizing the status of husbands and wives in regard to property. Viewing marriage as a contract between a free man and a free woman, the revolutionaries provided the right of divorce to either spouse should the marriage go sour. A remarkably egalitarian inheritance law stipulated that daughters as well as sons were entitled to an equal share of a family's estate. Finally, in the domain of education—central to the feminist vision of Mary Wollstonecraft that the French Revolution had crystalized—an unprecedented system of universal and free primary schooling in 1794 extended to girls as well as boys and provided for state-salaried teachers of both sexes.

Race and Slavery As the Assembly excluded women from voting citizenship without much debate, other groups posed challenges on how to apply "the rights of man" to French society. In eastern France, where most of France's forty thousand Jews resided amid discrimination, public opinion scorned them as an alien race not entitled to citizenship. Eventually, however, the Assembly rejected that argument and extended civil and political equality to Jews. A similar debate raged over the status of the free Negroes and mulattoes in France's Caribbean colonies. White planters, in alliance with the merchants who traded with the islands, were intent on preserving slavery and demanded local control over the islands' racial policy as their best defense. The planters argued that they could not maintain slavery, which was manifestly based on race, unless free people of color were disenfranchised.

When the Assembly accepted this view, the mulattoes rebelled. But their abortive uprising had the unintended consequence of helping ignite a slave rebellion. Led by Toussaint-L'Ouverture, the blacks turned violently on their white masters and proclaimed the independence of the colony, which became known as Haiti. In 1794 the French revolutionary government belatedly abolished slavery in all French colonies.

Unifying the Nation Within France the Assembly obliterated the political identities of the country's historic provinces and instead divided the nation's territory into eighty-three departments of roughly equal size (see map 20.1). Unlike the old provinces, each new department was to have exactly the same institutions. The departments were, in turn, subdivided into districts, cantons, and communes (the common designation for a village or town). On the one hand, this administrative transformation promoted local autonomy: The citizens of each department, district, and commune elected their own local officials, and in that sense political power was decentralized. On the other hand, these local governments were subordinated to the national legislature in Paris and became instruments for promoting national integration and uniformity.

The new administrative map also created the boundaries for a new judicial system. Sweeping away the parlements and law courts of the old regime, the revolutionaries established a justice of the peace in each canton, a civil court in each district, and a criminal court in each department.

▼ MAP 20.1 REDIVIDING THE NATION'S TERRITORY IN 1789: FROM HISTORIC PROVINCES (*RIGHT*) TO REVOLUTIONARY DEPARTMENTS (*LEFT*)

The judges on all tribunals were to be elected. The Assembly rejected the use of juries in civil cases but decreed that felonies would be tried by juries; also, criminal defendants for the first time gained the right to counsel. In civil law, the Assembly encouraged arbitration and mediation to avoid the time-consuming and expensive processes of formal litigation. In general, the revolutionaries hoped to make the administration of justice faster and more accessible.

Individualism The Assembly's clearing operations extended to economic institutions as well. Guided by the dogmas of laissez-faire theory and by its uncompromising hostility to privileged corporations, the Assembly sought to open up economic life to individual initiative, much as Turgot had attempted in the 1770s. Besides dismantling internal tariffs and chartered trading monopolies, it abolished merchants' and artisans' guilds and proclaimed the right of every citizen to enter any trade and conduct it freely. The government would no longer concern itself with regulating wages or the quality of goods. The Assembly also insisted that workers bargain in the economic marketplace as individuals, and it therefore banned workers' associations and strikes. The precepts of economic individualism extended to the countryside as well. At least in theory, peasants and landlords were free to cultivate their fields as they saw fit, regardless of traditional collective practices. In fact, those deep-rooted communal restraints proved to be extremely resistant to change.

THE REVOLUTION AND THE CHURCH

To address the state's financial problems, the National Assembly acted in a way that the monarchy had never dared contemplate. Under revolutionary ideology, the French Catholic Church could no longer exist as an independent corporation—as a separate estate within the state. The Assembly therefore nationalized Church property, placing it "at the disposition of the nation," and made the state responsible for the upkeep of the Church. It then issued paper notes called *assignats,* which were backed by the value of these "national lands." The property was to be sold by auction at the district capitals to the highest bidders. This plan favored the bourgeois and rich peasants with ready capital and made it difficult for needy peasants to acquire the land, though some pooled their resources to do so.

The sale of Church lands and the issuance of assignats had several consequences. In the short run, they eliminated the need for new borrowing. Second, the hundreds of thousands of purchasers gained a strong vested interest in the Revolution, since a successful counterrevolution was likely to reclaim their properties for the Church. Finally, after war broke out with an Austrian-Prussian coalition in 1792, the government made the assignats a national currency and printed a volume of assignats way beyond their underlying value in land, thereby touching off severe inflation and new political turmoil.

Religious Schism The issue of church reform produced the Revolution's first and most fateful crisis. The Assembly intended to rid the Church of inequities that enriched the aristocratic prelates of the old regime. Many Catholics looked forward to such healthy changes that might bring the clergy closer to the people. In the Civil Constitution of the Clergy (1790), the Assembly reduced the number of bishops from 130 to 83 and reshaped diocesan boundaries to conform exactly with those of the new departments. Bishops and parish priests were to be chosen by the electoral assemblies in the departments and districts and were to be paid according to a uniform salary scale that favored those currently at the lower end. Like all other public officials, the clergy was to take an oath of loyalty to the constitution.

The clergy generally opposed the Civil Constitution because it had been dictated to them by the National Assembly; they argued that such questions as the selection of bishops and priests should be negotiated either with the Pope or with a National Church Council. But the Assembly asserted that it had the sovereign power to order such reforms, since they affected temporal rather than spiritual matters. In November 1790 the Assembly demanded that all clergy take the loyalty oath forthwith; those who refused would lose their positions and be pensioned off. In all of France only seven bishops and about 54 percent of the parish clergy swore the oath; but in the west of France only 15 percent of the priests complied. A schism tore through French Catholicism, since the laity had to take a position as well: Should parishioners remain loyal to their priests who had refused to take the oath (the nonjuring, or refractory, clergy) and thus be at odds with the state? Or should they accept the unfamiliar "constitutional clergy" designated by the districts to replace their own priests?

The Assembly's effort to impose reform in defiance of religious sensibilities and Church autonomy was a grave tactical error. The oath crisis polarized the nation. It seemed to link the Revolution with impiety and the Church with counterrevolution. In local communities, refractory clergy began to preach against the entire Revolution. Local officials fought back by arresting them and demanding repressive laws. Civil strife rocked hundreds of communities.

COUNTERREVOLUTION, RADICALISM, AND WAR

Opposition to the Revolution had actually begun much earlier. After July 14 some of the king's relatives had left the country in disgust, thus becoming the first émigrés, or political exiles, of the Revolution. During the next three years thousands of nobles, including two-thirds of the royal army's officer corps, joined the emigration. Across the Rhine River in Coblenz, émigrés formed an army that threatened to overthrow the new regime at the first opportunity. The king himself publicly submitted to the Revolution, but privately he smoldered in resentment. Finally, in June 1791, Louis and his family fled in secret from Paris, hoping to cross the Belgian frontier and enlist the aid of Austria. But Louis was stopped at the French village of Varennes and was forcibly returned to Paris.

Moderates hoped that this aborted escape would finally end the king's opposition to the Revolution. The Assembly, after all, needed his cooperation to make its constitutional monarchy viable. It did not wish to open the door to a republic or to further unrest. Radicals such as the journalist Jean-Paul Marat, on the other hand, had long thundered against the treachery of the king and the émigrés and against the Assembly itself for not acting vigorously against aristocrats and

counterrevolutionaries. But the Assembly was determined to maintain the status quo and adopted the fiction that the king had been kidnapped. The Assembly reaffirmed the king's place in the new regime, but Louis' treasonous flight to Varennes ensured that radical agitation would continue.

The Outbreak of War When the newly elected Legislative Assembly convened on October 1, 1791, the questions of counterrevolution at home and the prospect of war abroad dominated its stormy sessions. Both the right and the left saw advantages to be gained in a war between France and Austria. The king and his court hoped that a military defeat would discredit the new regime and restore full power to the monarchy. Most members of the Jacobin Club—the leading radical political club in Paris—wanted war to strike down the foreign supporters of the émigrés and domestic counterrevolutionaries.

When Francis II ascended the throne of the Habsburg monarchy in March 1792, the stage was set for war. Unlike his father, Leopold, who had rejected intervention in France's affairs, Francis fell under the influence of émigrés and bellicose advisers. He was determined to assist the French queen, his aunt, and he also expected to make territorial gains. With both sides thus eager for battle, France went to war in April 1792 against a coalition of Austria, Prussia, and the émigrés.

Each camp expected rapid victory, but both were deceived. The French offensive quickly faltered, and invading armies soon crossed France's borders. The Legislative Assembly ordered the arrest of refractory clergy and called for a special corps of twenty thousand national guardsmen to protect Paris. Louis vetoed both measures and held to his decisions in spite of demonstrations against them in the capital. For all practical purposes, these vetoes were his last acts as king. The legislature also called for 100,000 volunteers to bolster the French army and defend the homeland.

The Fall of the Monarchy As Prussian forces began a drive toward Paris, their commander, the Duke of Brunswick, rashly threatened to level the city if it resisted or if it harmed the royal family. When Louis XVI published this Brunswick Manifesto, it seemed proof that he was in league with

▲ **The assault on the Tuileries of August 10, 1792 led to a brief battle with numerous casualties among the besiegers and infuriated reprisals against the garrison after it surrendered. The event brought an end to the constitutional monarchy and led directly to the founding of the first French Republic.**
Jean Duplessi Bertaux, "Storming of the Tuileries, August 10, 1792." Giraudon/Art Resource.

the enemy. Far from intimidating the revolutionaries, the threat drove them forward. Since a divided Legislative Assembly refused to act decisively in the face of royal obstructionism, Parisian militants, spurred on by the Jacobin Club, organized an insurrection.

On August 10, 1792, a crowd of armed Parisians stormed the royal palace at the Tuileries, literally driving the king from the throne. The Assembly then had no choice but to declare Louis XVI suspended. That night more than half the Assembly's members themselves fled Paris, making it clear that the Assembly too had lost its legitimacy. The deputies who remained ordered elections for a National Convention to decide the king's fate, to draft a republican constitution, and to govern France during the current emergency. What the events of 1789 in Versailles and Paris had begun, the insur-

rection of August 10, 1792 completed. The old regime in France had truly been destroyed.

IV. The Second Revolution

By 1792—just three years after the fall of the Bastille—the Revolution had profoundly altered the foundations of government and society in France. The National Assembly swept away absolutism and introduced constitutional government, legislative representation, and local self-government. It repudiated aristocratic and corporate privilege and established civil equality and uniform institutions across the country. Peasants were freed from the seigneurial system, religious minorities from persecution. Yet the Revolution was far from over, and in the short view, one might say that it was only beginning. True, these changes ultimately proved to be the most significant. But they had been won at the price of great opposition, and the old order was far from vanquished. European monarchs and aristocrats encouraged refractory priests, émigrés, and royalists in France to resist, while many ordinary French citizens turned against the revolutionaries for a variety of reasons.

The patriots, threatened in 1792 by military defeat and counterrevolution, were themselves divided. Some became radicalized, while others grew alienated from the Revolution's increasingly radical course and joined its opponents. Each spasm of change produced new opponents at home and abroad, but each increment of opposition stiffened the resolve of the Revolution's partisans. Building on the momentum of August 1792, the Jacobins forged a coalition with urban militants known as the *sans-culottes* (literally, men who wore trousers rather than fashionable knee breeches). The sans-culottes sought to revolutionize the Revolution, to create a democratic republic based on a broadening definition of equality. But the government's responses to the crisis distorted this second revolution. To establish liberty, the Jacobins argued, coercion was required. The ideals of equality became confused with problems of national defense and with the impulse to repress opposition.

THE NATIONAL CONVENTION

The insurrection of August 10, 1792 created a vacuum of authority until the election of a National Convention was completed. A revolutionary Paris Commune, or city government, became one power center, but that bastion of radicalism could not control events even within its own domain. As thousands of volunteers left for the battlefront, Parisians nervously eyed the capital's jails, which overflowed with political prisoners and common criminals. Radical journalists like Jean-Paul Marat saw these prisoners as a counterrevolutionary striking force and feared a plot to open the prisons. A

▼ **Beset by invasion jitters and fearing a plot to force open the capital's overcrowded jails, mobs of Parisians invaded the prisons and over the course of three days in September 1792 slaughtered more than two thousand prisoners.**
Musée Carnavalet/Photo Bulloz.

growing sense of alarm finally exploded early in September. For three days groups of Parisians invaded the prisons, set up "popular tribunals," and slaughtered more than two thousand prisoners. No official dared intervene to stop the carnage, known since as the September massacres.

The sense of panic eased, however, with the success of the French armies. Bolstered by units of volunteers, the army finally halted the invaders at the Battle of Valmy on September 20. Two months later it defeated the allies at Jemappes in the Austrian Netherlands, which the French now occupied. Meanwhile, the Convention convened and promptly declared France a republic.

Settling Louis XVI's fate proved to be extremely contentious. While the deputies unanimously found the former king guilty of treason, they divided sharply over the question of his punishment. Some argued for clemency, while others insisted that his execution was a necessary symbolic gesture as well as a fitting punishment for his betrayal. Finally, by a vote of 387 to 334, the Convention sentenced Louis to death and voted down efforts to reprieve this sentence or delay it for a popular referendum. On January 21, 1793, Louis was guillotined, put to death like an ordinary citizen. The deputies to the Convention had become regicides (king killers) and would make no compromise with the counterrevolution.

Factional Conflict From the Convention's opening day, two bitterly hostile groups of deputies vied for leadership and almost immobilized it with their rancorous conflict. One group became known as the *Girondins*, since several of its spokesmen were elected as deputies from the Gironde department. The Girondins were fiery orators and ambitious politicians who advocated provincial liberty and laissez-faire economics. They reacted hostilely to the growing radicalism of Paris and broke with or were expelled by the Jacobin Club, to which some had originally belonged. Mean-

▼ **After the National Convention concluded its trial of former King Louis XVI and voted to impose the death penalty without reprieve, "Louis Capet" was guillotined and the leaders of the Republic became regicides, king killers.**
Musée Carnavalet/Photo Bulloz.

while Parisian electors chose as their deputies leading members of the Jacobin Club such as Danton, Robespierre, and Marat. The Parisian deputation to the Convention became the nucleus of a group known as the *Mountain,* so-called because it occupied the upper benches of the Convention's hall. The Mountain attracted the more militant provincial deputies and attacked the Girondins as treacherous compromisers unwilling to adopt bold measures in the face of crisis. The Girondins, in turn, denounced the Mountain as would-be tyrants and captives of Parisian radicalism and held them responsible for the September prison massacres.

Several hundred deputies stood between these two factions. These centrists (known as the *Plain*) were committed to the Revolution but were uncertain which path to follow. The Plain detested popular agitation, but they were reluctant to turn against the sans-culottes, who so fervently supported the Revolution. In the end they would support men or policies that promised to consolidate the Revolution.

THE REVOLUTIONARY CRISIS

By the spring of 1793 the National Convention faced a perilous convergence of invasion, civil war, and economic crises that demanded imaginative responses. Austria and Prussia had mounted a new offensive in 1793, their alliance strengthened by the addition of Spain, Piedmont, and Britain. Between March and September military reversals occurred on every front. The Convention reacted by introducing a military draft, which in turn touched off a rebellion in western France by peasants and rural weavers, who had long resented the patriot middle class in the towns for monopolizing local political power and for persecuting their priests. In the isolated towns of the Vendée region, south of the Loire River, the rebels attacked the Republic's supporters. Priests and nobles offered leadership to the insurgents, who first organized into guerrilla bands and finally into a "Catholic and Royalist Army." The Vendée rebels briefly occupied several towns, massacred local patriots, and even threatened the port of Nantes, where British troops could have landed.

Meanwhile, economic troubles were provoking the Parisian sans-culottes. By early 1793 the Revolution's paper money, the assignat, had declined to 50 percent of its face value. Inflation was compounded by a poor harvest, food shortages, hoarding, and profiteering. Municipal authorities fixed the price of bread but could not always secure adequate supplies. Under these conditions the government could not even supply its armies.

The Purge of the Girondins   Spokesmen for the sans-culottes declared that even the Convention and the Paris Commune were insufficiently responsive to popular opinion. They demanded that the Convention purge the Girondins and adopt a program of "public safety," including price controls for basic commodities, execution of hoarders and speculators, and forced requisitions of grain. Behind these demands lay the threat of armed insurrection. This pressure from the sans-culottes aided the Mountain in their struggle against the Girondins, but it could easily have degenerated

▼ MAP 20.2 CONFLICTS IN REVOLUTIONARY FRANCE

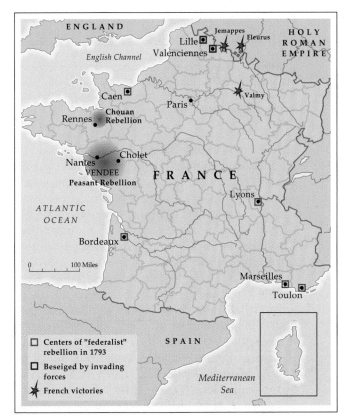

▲ Bitter fighting in the Vendée between counterrevolutionaries and republicans caused a profound split in the loyalties of western France, which endured for at least the next hundred years. Each side cultivated its own memories of the event and honored its own martyrs.
Jules Benoit-Levy, "Battle of Cholet" 1794. Giraudon/Art Resource.

into anarchy. In a sense, all elements of the revolutionary crisis hinged on one problem: the lack of an effective government that would not simply respond to popular pressures but would organize and master them. When the sans-culottes mounted a massive armed demonstration for a purge of the Girondins on June 2, centrist deputies reluctantly agreed to go along. The Convention expelled twenty-three Girondin deputies, who were subsequently tried and executed for treason.

Factionalism in the Convention reflected conflict in the provinces. Moderate republicans in several cities struggled with local Jacobin radicals and sympathized with the Girondin deputies in their campaign against the Parisian sans-culottes. In the south, local Jacobins lost control of Marseilles, Bordeaux, and Lyons to their rivals, who

then repudiated the Convention. As in the Vendée revolt, royalists soon took over the resistance in Lyons, France's second largest city. This act was an intolerable challenge to the Convention. Labeling the anti-Jacobin rebels in Lyons and elsewhere as "federalists," the Convention dispatched armed forces to suppress them (see map 20.2). In the eyes of the Jacobins, to defy the Convention's authority was to betray France itself.

THE JACOBIN DICTATORSHIP

Popular radicalism in Paris had helped bring the Mountain to power in the Convention. The question now was: Which side of this coalition between the Mountain and the sans-culottes would dominate the other? The sans-culottes seemed to believe that the sovereign people could dictate their will to the Convention. Popular agitation peaked on September 5, when a mass demonstration in Paris demanded new policies to ensure food supplies. To give force to the law, urged the sans-culottes, "Let terror be placed on the order of the day." The Convention responded with the Law of the Maximum, which imposed general price controls, and with the Law of Suspects, which empowered local revolutionary committees to imprison citizens whose loyalty they suspected.

Revolutionary Government In June the triumphant Mountain had drafted a new democratic constitution for the French Republic and had submitted it to an unprecedented referendum, in which almost 2 million citizens had overwhelmingly voted yes. But the Convention formally laid the constitution aside and proclaimed the government "revolutionary until the peace." Elections, local self-government, and guarantees of individual liberty were to be suspended until the Republic had defeated its enemies within and without. The Convention placed responsibility for military, economic, and political policy, as well as control over local officials, in the hands of a twelve-man Committee of Public Safety. Spontaneous popular action was about to give way to revolutionary centralization.

Maximilien Robespierre emerged as the Committee's leading personality and tactician. An austere bachelor in his mid-thirties, Robespierre had been a provincial lawyer before the Revolution. As a deputy to the National Assembly he had ardently advocated greater democracy. His main political forum was the Paris Jacobin Club, which by 1793 he more or less dominated. In the Convention, Robespierre was inflexible and self-righteous in his dedication to the Revolution. He sought to

▼ **The Paris Jacobin Club began as a caucus for a group of liberal deputies to the National Assembly. During the Convention it became a bastion of democratic deputies and middle-class Parisian radicals while continuing to serve as a "mother club" for affiliated clubs in the provinces.**
Masquelier, "A Session of the Jacobin Club." Giraudon/Art Resource.

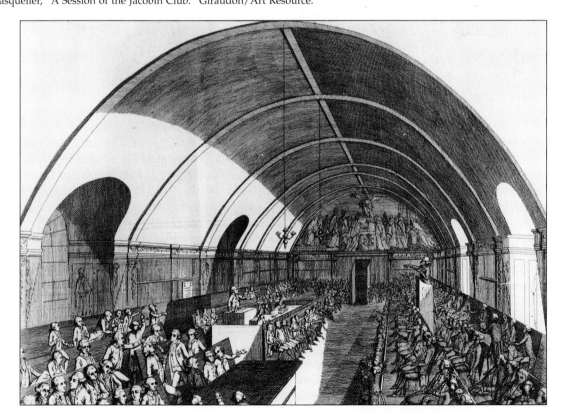

ROBESPIERRE'S JUSTIFICATION OF THE TERROR

"If the spring of popular government in time of peace is virtue, the springs of popular government in revolution are at once *virtue and terror:* virtue, without which terror is fatal; terror, without which virtue is powerless. Terror is nothing other than justice, prompt, severe, inflexible; it is therefore an emanation of virtue. . . . It is a consequence of the general principle of democracy applied to our country's most urgent needs.

"It has been said that terror is the principle of despotic government. Does your government therefore resemble despotism? Yes, as the sword that gleams in the hands of the heroes of liberty resembles that with which the henchman of tyranny are armed. Let the despot govern his brutalized subjects by terror; he is right, as a despot. Subdue by terror the enemies of liberty, and you will be right, as founders of the Republic. The government of the revolution is liberty's despotism against tyranny. Is force made only to protect crime?

"Society owes protection only to peaceable citizens; the only citizens in the Republic are the re-publicans. For it, the royalists, the conspirators are only strangers or, rather, enemies. This terrible war waged by liberty against tyranny—is it not indivisible? Are the enemies within not the allies of the enemies without? The assassins who tear our country apart, the intriguers who buy the consciences that hold the people's mandate; the traitors who sell them; the mercenary pamphleteers hired to dishonor the people's cause, to kill public virtue, to stir up the fire of civil discord, and to prepare political counter-revolution—are all those men less guilty or less dangerous than the tyrants [abroad] whom they serve?

"We try to control revolutions with the quibbles of the courtroom; we treat conspiracies against the Republic like lawsuits between individuals. Tyranny kills, and liberty argues."

From Robespierre's speech to the Convention on "The Moral and Political Principles of Domestic Policy," February 1794.

---

appease the sans-culottes but also to control them, for he placed the Revolution's survival above any one viewpoint (see "Robespierre's Justification of the Terror").

Local political clubs (numbering more than five thousand by 1794) formed crucial links in the chain of revolutionary government. The clubs nominated citizens for posts on local revolutionary institutions, exercised surveillance over those officials, and served as "arsenals of public opinion." The clubs fostered the egalitarian ideals of the second revolution and supported the war effort. They also saw it as their civic duty to denounce fellow citizens for unpatriotic behavior and thereby sowed fear and recrimination across the land.

For the Jacobins tolerated no serious dissent. The government's demand for unity during the emergency nullified the right to freedom of expression. Among those to fall were a group of ultrarevolutionaries led by Jacques-René Hébert, a leading radical journalist and Paris official. The extremists were accused of a plot against the Republic and were guillotined. In reality, Hébert had questioned what he deemed the Convention's leniency toward "enemies of the people." Next came the so-called indulgents. Headed by Georges-Jacques Danton, a leading member of the Jacobin Club, they publicly argued for a relaxation of rigorous measures. For this dissent they were indicted on trumped-up charges of treason and were sentenced to death by the revolutionary tribunal. This succession of purges, which started with the Girondins and later ended with Robespierre himself, suggested, as one victim put it, that "revolutions devour their own children."

The Reign of Terror Most of those devoured by the French Revolution, however, were not its own children but a variety of armed rebels, counterrevolutionaries, and unfortunate citizens swept into the vortex of war and internal strife. As an official policy, the Reign of Terror sought to organize repression so as to avoid anarchic violence

Chronology

TURNING POINTS IN THE FRENCH REVOLUTION

June 17, 1789	Third Estate declares itself a National Assembly.
July 14, 1789	Storming of the Bastille and triumph of the patriots.
August 10, 1792	Storming of the Tuileries and the end of the monarchy (followed by the September prison massacres).
January 21, 1793	Execution of Louis XVI.
March 1793	Vendée rebellion begins.
June 2, 1793	*Sans-culottes* intimidate the Convention into purging the Girondin deputies. "Federalist" rebellion begins in Lyons.
September 5, 1793	*Sans-culottes* demonstrate for the enactment of economic controls and Terror.
October 1793	The Jacobin dictatorship and the Terror begin: The Convention declares that "the government is revolutionary until the peace."
9 Thermidor year II (July 27, 1794)	Fall of Robespierre.
1–2 Prairial year III (May 20–21, 1795)	Failed insurrection by Parisian *sans-culottes* for "Bread and the Constitution of 1793."
18 Brumaire year VIII (November 9, 1799)	Coup d'état by General Bonaparte and the "revisionists."

like the September massacres. It reflected a state of mind that saw threats and plots everywhere (some real, most imagined). The laws of the Terror struck most directly at the people perceived to be enemies of the Revolution: Refractory priests and émigrés, for instance, were banned from the Republic upon threat of death. But the Law of Suspects also led to the incarceration of as many as 300,000 ordinary citizens for their opinions, past behavior, or social status.

The Terror produced its own atrocities: the brutal drowning of imprisoned priests at Nantes; the execution of thousands of noncombatants during the military campaigns of the Vendée; and the summary executions of about two thousand citizens of Lyons, more than two-thirds of them from the wealthy classes. ("Lyons has made war against liberty," declared the Convention, "thus Lyons no longer exists.") But except in the two zones of intense civil war—western France and the area of "federalist" rebellion in the south (see map 20.2)—the Terror struck by examples, not by the execution of entire social groups.

THE SANS-CULOTTES: REVOLUTION FROM BELOW

The Parisian sans-culottes formed the crowds and demonstrations that produced the Revolution's dramatic turning points (see chart), but they also threw themselves into a daily routine of political activism during the second revolution of 1792–1794. The sans-culottes were mainly artisans, shopkeepers, and workers—building contractors, carpenters, shoemakers, wine sellers, clerks, tailors, cafe keepers. Many owned their own businesses; others were wage earners. But they shared a strong sense of local community in the capital's varied neighborhoods.

Popular Attitudes The supply and price of bread obsessed the sans-culottes. As consumers, they faced inflation and scarcities with fear and rage and demanded forceful government intervention to ensure the basic necessities of life. Sansculotte militants believed in property rights, but they insisted that people did not have the right to misuse property by hoarding food or speculating. As one petition put it, "What is the meaning of freedom, when one class of men can starve

▲ **At the height of the "dechristianization" movement (which lasted for about eight months in the period 1793–1794), more than eighteen thousand priests renounced their vocations. About a third were also pressured into marrying as a way of proving the sincerity of their resignations. ("They shave me in the morning and have me married by evening.")**
Bibliothéque Nationale.

another? What is the meaning of equality, when the rich, by their monopolies, can exercise the right of life and death over their equals?" The sans-culotte call for price controls clashed dramatically with the dogma of laissez-faire. By 1793, however, the Jacobins had acknowledged "the right to subsistence" in their new constitution and had instituted price controls under the Law of the Maximum to regulate the economy during the emergency.

Bitterly antiaristocratic, the sans-culottes displayed their social attitudes in everyday behavior. They advocated simplicity in dress and manners and attacked opulence and pretension wherever they found or imagined them to be. Under the sans-culottes' disapproving eye, high society and fancy dress generally disappeared from view. Vices like prostitution and gambling were attributed to aristocrats and were denounced in the virtuous society of the Revolution; drinking, the common people's vice, was tolerated.

The revolutionaries symbolized their break with the past by changing the names of streets and public places to eliminate signs of royalism, religion, or aristocracy. The Palais Royal thus became the Palais d'Egalité (Equality Palace). Some citizens exchanged their Christian names for the names of secular heroes from antiquity, like Brutus. And all citizens were expected to drop honorifics like *monsieur* and *madame* in favor of the simple, uniform designation of *citizen*. Even the measurement of time changed when the Convention decreed a new republican calendar that renamed the months and replaced the seven-day week with a symmetrical ten-day *décadi*. The Year I dated from the establishment of the Republic in 1792.

Popular Politics The Convention believed in representative democracy with an active political life at the grass roots, but during the emergency it decreed a centralized revolutionary dictatorship. The sans-culottes preferred a more decentralized style of participatory democracy. They believed that the local assembly of citizens was the ultimate sovereign body. At the beginning of the year II (1793–1794), the forty-eight sections of Paris functioned almost as autonomous republics in which local activists ran their own affairs. Political life in Paris and elsewhere had a naive, breathless quality and made thousands of ordinary citizens feel that they held real political power (see "A Portrait of the Parisian Sans-Culotte," p. 720).

Within this upsurge of activism, the Society of Revolutionary-Republican Women, founded in Paris in the spring of 1793, constituted a vanguard of feminist radicals. The members of this club were undeterred by their exclusion from the vote, which did not much concern them at this point. Even without voting rights women considered themselves citizens in revolutionary France.

In agitating for severe enforcement of price controls and the compulsory use of republican symbols, however, these women irritated the revolutionary government. Before long the ruling Jacobins perceived them as part of an irresponsible ultra-left opposition, whom they denounced as *enragés*, rabid ones. In October the government arrested the most prominent *enragés,* male and female, closed down the Society of Revolutionary-Republican Women, and forbade the formation of female political clubs in the future. The government's spokesman derided these activists as "denatured women," viragos who neglected their maternal duties. Behind this bitter antifeminist rhetoric can be discerned a sense of anxiety. In the virile and punitive world of radical republicanism (see the illustration of Hercules on p. 720), the Jacobins yearned for an offsetting feminine virtue to soothe exalted male citizens when they returned home, to soften the severity required in the public sphere.

To Robespierre, in any case, the notion of direct democracy appeared unworkable and akin to anarchy. The Convention watched the sans-

▲ The radical activists of the Paris sections—the sans-culottes and their female counterparts—made a point of their plebeian forms of dress, their freedom to bear arms, and their egalitarian insignias, such as the red liberty cap.
Photo Bulloz.

culottes with concern, supportive of their democratic egalitarianism but fearful of the unpredictability, disorder, and inefficiency of this popular movement. The Mountain attempted to encourage civic participation yet control it. From the forty-eight sections of Paris, however, came an endless stream of petitions, denunciations, and veiled threats to the government. In the spring of 1794 the Convention finally curbed the power of the sections by drastically restricting their rights and activities. But in forcibly cooling down the ardor of the sans-culottes, the revolutionary government necessarily weakened its own base of support.

A PORTRAIT OF THE PARISIAN SANS-CULOTTE

"A Sans-Culotte is a man who goes everywhere on his own two feet, who has none of the millions you're all after, no mansions, no lackeys to wait on him, and who lives quite simply with his wife and children, if he has any, on the fourth or fifth floor. He is useful, because he knows how to plough a field, handle a forge, a saw, or a file, how to cover a roof or how to make shoes and to shed his blood to the last drop to save the Republic. And since he is a working man, you will never find him in the Cafe de Chartres where they plot and gamble. . . . In the evening, he is at his Section, not powdered and perfumed and all dolled up to catch the eyes of the *citoyennes* in the galleries, but to support sound resolutions with all his power and to pulverize the vile faction [of moderates]. For the rest, a Sans-Culotte always keeps his sword with a sharp edge, to clip the ears of the malevolent. Sometimes he carries his pike and at the first roll of the drum, off he goes to the Vendée, to the Army of the Alps or the Army of the North."

From a pamphlet attributed to the Parisian militant Vingternier: "A Reply to the Impertinent Question: But What Is a Sans-Culotte?" (1794).

▼ Amidst elaborate arrays of symbolism, revolutionary iconography generally used the figure of a woman to represent its ideals. Briefly in the period 1793–1794, however, the Jacobins introduced the more aggressive masculine figure of Hercules to represent the Republic.
(left) Photo Bulloz. (right) Collection Viollet.

THE REVOLUTIONARY WARS

Ultimately, the Revolution's fate rested in the hands of its armies, although no one had thought in such terms in 1789. France's revolutionary ideology had initially posed no direct threat to the European state system. Indeed, the orators of the National Assembly had argued that the best foreign policy for a free society was peace, neutrality, and isolation from the diplomatic intrigues of monarchs. But peaceful intentions did not imply pacifism. When counterrevolution at home coalesced with threats from abroad, the revolutionaries vigorously confronted both. As in most major wars, however, the initial objectives were soon forgotten. As the war expanded, it brought revolution to other states.

The revolutionary wars involved standard considerations of international relations as well as new and explosive purposes. On the one hand, France pursued the traditional aim of extending and rounding off its frontiers. On the other hand, France now espoused revolutionary principles such as the right of a people to self-determination. As early as September 1791, the National Assembly had declared that "the rights of peoples are not determined by the treaties of princes."

Foreign Revolutionaries and French Armies

Even before 1789 "patriots" in Geneva, the Dutch Netherlands, and the Austrian Netherlands (Belgium) had unsuccessfully challenged the traditional arrangements that governed their societies, and the French Revolution rekindled those rebellious sentiments. Foreign revolutionaries were eager to challenge their governments again, and they looked to revolutionary France for assistance. Refugees from these struggles had fled to France and now formed pressure groups to lobby French

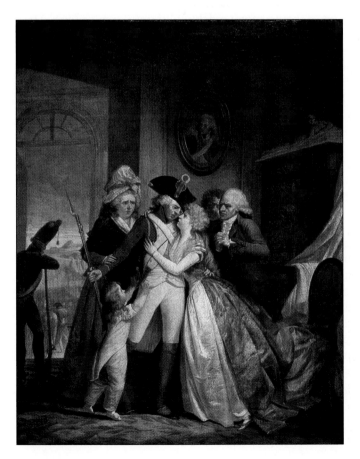

◄ To bolster the professional troops of the line army in 1791 and again in 1792 after the war began, the government called for volunteers, one of whom is shown in this sentimental and patriotic portrait bidding farewell to his family. By 1793, the National Convention had to go further and draft all able-bodied young men.
F. L. J. Walteau, "The Departure of the Volunteers." Musée Carnavalet, Paris, France/Giraudon/Bridgeman Art Library, London/New York.

leaders for help in liberating their own countries during France's war against Austria and Prussia. Some revolutionaries from areas contiguous to France (Belgium, Savoy, and the Rhineland) hoped that the French Republic might simply annex those territories. Elsewhere—in the Dutch Netherlands, Lombardy, Ireland, and the Swiss Confederation—insurgents hoped that France would help establish independent republics by overthrowing the ruling princes or oligarchies.

Few French leaders were interested in leading a European crusade for liberty, but practical considerations led them to intervention. As the war spilled over into Belgium and the Rhineland, the French sought to establish support abroad by incorporating the principles of the Revolution into their foreign policy. Thus in December 1792 the Convention decided that feudal practices and hereditary privileges would be abolished wherever French armies prevailed. The people thus liberated, however, would have to pay for their liberation with special taxes and requisitions of supplies for French troops. By 1794 France had a permanent foothold in Belgium and soon annexed that territory to the Republic. Yet Robespierre was dubious about foreign entanglements; he believed that liberty had to be secured in France before it could be exported abroad. The Committee of Public Safety thus declined to support a distant Polish revolutionary movement, refused to invade Holland, and attempted to avoid any involvements in Italy.

Citizen-Soldiers The fighting men who defended France and carried its revolution abroad were a far different body from the old royal army. The National Assembly of 1789 retained the notion of a professional army but opened officers' careers to ordinary soldiers, especially after most of the royal officer corps emigrated or resigned. At the same time, the concept of the citizen-soldier was introduced in the newly organized national guard, which had elected officers. When the war against the coalition began in 1792 the government enrolled more than 100,000 volunteers for short-term service at the front. But when the coalition launched its second offensive in 1793, the inadequacy of the French army demanded drastic innovations.

The Convention responded with the mass levy of August 1793 (*levée en masse*). All able-bodied unmarried men between the ages of eighteen and twenty-five were drafted for military service, without the option of buying themselves a replacement. About 300,000 new recruits poured into the armies, while perhaps 200,000 draftees fled to avoid service. By the end of 1794 the French had almost 750,000 men under arms. With elected officers at their head, the citizen-soldiers marched off to the front under banners that read "The French people risen against the tyrants." The Convention merged these recruits with the regulars of the line army into units called demibrigades, so that the professionals could impart their military skills to the new troops.

Revolutionary Warfare Military tactics in the field reflected a combination of revolutionary spirit and pragmatism. The new demibrigades did not have the training to be deployed in the well-drilled line formations of old-regime armies. Commanders instead favored mass columns that could move quickly without much drilling. Mass and mobility characterized the armies of the French Revolution. The Committee of Public Safety advised its commanders, "Act offensively and in masses. Use the bayonet at every opportunity. Fight great battles and pursue the enemy until he is destroyed."

The revolutionary government fostered new attitudes toward military life. The military was under civilian control. Discipline applied equally to officers and men, and wounded soldiers received generous veterans benefits. The Convention insisted that generals show not only military talent but the will to win. Many young officers rose quickly to command positions, but some generals fared badly. The commander of the defeated Rhine army in early 1793, for example, was branded a traitor, tried, and guillotined. Meanwhile, economic mobilization at home produced the weapons, ammunition, clothing, and food necessary to support this mass army.

In late 1793 and early 1794 the armies of the Republic won a string of victories, culminating in the Battle of Fleurus in June 1794, which liberated Belgium for the second time. French armies also triumphed at the Pyrénées and the Rhine and forced their enemies one by one to the peace table—first Spain and Prussia, then Piedmont. An army crippled at the outset by treason and desertion, defeat, lack of training and discipline, and collapsing morale had been forged into a potent force in less than two years. Militarily, at least, the revolutionary government had succeeded brilliantly.

To its most dedicated supporters, the revolutionary government had two major purposes: first, to surmount a crisis and steer the Republic to victory; and second, to democratize France's political and social fabric. Only the first objective, however, won widespread adherence. The National Convention held a polarized nation together, consolidated the Republic, and defeated its foreign enemies, but only at enormous and questionable costs. Moderates and ultrarevolutionaries alike resented the stifling political conformity imposed by the revolutionary government. Wealthy peasants and businesspeople chafed under the economic regimentation, and Catholics bitterly resented local "dechristianization" campaigns. The Jacobins increasingly isolated themselves, making enemies on every side. It is not surprising, then, that the security provided by the military victories of 1793–1794 would permit the Convention to end the Jacobin dictatorship and abandon its rhetoric of radical egalitarianism. But the question remained: What would take its place?

Recommended Reading

Sources

*Beik, Paul H. (ed.). *The French Revolution*. 1971. A comprehensive anthology.

*Blanc, Olivier (ed.). *Last Letters: Prisons and Prisoners of the French Revolution, 1793–1794*. 1987. The Terror seen through the eyes of its individual victims.

*Burke, Edmund. *Reflections on the Revolution in France* [1790]. 1969. An influential antirevolutionary tract and a foundational work in the conservative tradition.

*Hunt, Lynn (ed.). *The French Revolution and Human Rights: A Brief Documentary History*. 1996. Excerpts from revolutionary debates on the rights of the poor, free blacks and slaves, Jews, and women.

Kirchberger, Joe H. (ed.). *The French Revolution and Napoleon: An Eyewitness History*. 1989. Key documents and contemporary accounts of the principal events.

*Levy, Darlene, H. Applewhite, and M. Johnson (eds.). *Women in Revolutionary Paris, 1789–1795*. 1979. A documentary history of women activists.

Stewart, J. H. *A Documentary Survey of the French Revolution*. 1951. A compendium of important official documents.

*Walzer, Michael (ed.). *Regicide and Revolution: Speeches at the Trial of Louis XVI*. 1992. Documents and penetrating analysis.

Studies

*Bailyn, Bernard. *The Ideological Origins of the American Revolution*. 1967. A classic account of the impact of British libertarian thought on the American colonies.

Baker, Keith (ed.). *The French Revolution and the Creation of Modern Political Culture: IV: The Terror*. 1994. Original and stimulating essays on a wide range of issues.

Bertaud, Jean-Paul. *The Army of the French Revolution*. 1988. A pioneering political and social study of the soldiers and officers of the Republic's armies.

*Blanning, T. C. W. *The French Revolutionary Wars, 1787–1802*. 1996. A brief but comprehensive synthesis.

———. *Joseph II and Enlightened Despotism.* 1970. A convenient synthesis on a fundamental subject.

*Chartier, Roger. *The Cultural Origins of the French Revolution.* 1990. On the emergence of a public sphere of political discourse in the old regime.

*Christie, Ian. *Wars and Revolutions: Britain, 1760–1815.* 1982. Focuses on British government policy in the age of revolutions.

Cobb, Richard. *The Police and the People: French Popular Protest.* 1970. A study of peasants and sans-culottes that should be compared to Soboul's treatment.

*De Tocqueville, Alexis. *The Old Regime and the French Revolution.* Stuart Gilbert (tr.). 1955. A classic interpretation of the Revolution's genesis, first published in the 1850s.

*Doyle, William. *Origins of the French Revolution.* 1980. A reliable synthesis of revisionist historiography. Should be compared to Lefebvre's interpretation.

*———. *The Oxford History of the French Revolution.* 1989. A readable, detailed narrative.

*Draper, Theodore. *A Struggle for Power: The American Revolution.* 1996. A vigorously argued popular history.

Egret, Jean. *The French Pre-Revolution, 1787–1788.* 1978. A masterly account of the unraveling of the old regime.

Forrest, Alan. *The French Revolution and the Poor.* 1982. A history of good intentions and disappointing results.

*———. *Soldiers of the French Revolution.* 1990. A deft synthesis of recent research.

Furet, Francois, and Mona Ozouf (eds.). *A Critical Dictionary of the French Revolution.* 1989. A collection of essays, some brilliant and some idiosyncratic, on selected events, actors, institutions, ideas, and historians of the French Revolution.

Gershoy, Leo. *Bertrand Barère, a Reluctant Terrorist.* 1962. Perhaps the best available biography of a revolutionary figure.

*Hampson, Norman. *A Social History of the French Revolution.* 1963. A clear, concise history of the Revolution through 1795.

*Hobsbawm, Eric. *Echoes of the Marseillaise: Two Centuries Look Back on the French Revolution.* 1990. An interpretive survey of revolutionary historiography by a renowned partisan of the classical or Marxist tradition.

Hufton, Olwen. *Women and the Limits of Citizenship in the French Revolution.* 1992. A critical view of the subject.

*Hunt, Lynn. *Politics, Culture, and Class in the French Revolution.* 1984. A pioneering analysis of the imagery and sociology of revolutionary politics.

*Jones, Peter. *The Peasantry in the French Revolution.* 1988. A comprehensive study of the impact of the Revolution on rural society.

*Kennedy, Emmet. *A Cultural History of the French Revolution.* 1989. The Revolution's impact on cultural institutions and artistic activity.

Kennedy, Michael. *The Jacobin Clubs in the French Revolution.* 2 vols. 1982 and 1988. A thematic synthesis on the activities of the provincial Jacobin clubs through mid-1793, with a third volume to follow.

*Landes, Joan. *Women and the Public Sphere in the Age of the French Revolution.* 1988. A discussion of eighteenth-century thought on women and of the "gendered republic" of the 1790s.

*Lefebvre, Georges. *The Coming of the French Revolution.* 1967. A classic interpretation dating from 1939 by a major French historian; should be compared to Doyle's revisionist account.

McManners, John. *The French Revolution and the Church.* 1970. A superb synthesis on a major issue.

*Middlekauff, Robert. *The Glorious Cause: the American Revolution 1763–1789.* 1982. A comprehensive and balanced synthesis.

*Palmer, Robert R. *The Age of the Democratic Revolution: A Political History of Europe and America, 1760–1800.* 2 vols. 1959 and 1962. A magisterial comparative survey of the origins and course of revolutionary movements in the eighteenth century, from America to Poland.

———. *The Improvement of Humanity: Education and the French Revolution.* 1985. A history of good intentions and mixed results.

*———. *Twelve Who Ruled: The Year of the Terror in the French Revolution.* 1941. A modern classic, by far the best book on the subject.

*Popkin, Jeremy. *Revolutionary News: The Press in France 1789–1799.* 1990. An excellent analysis of journalism and the impact of journalists in the revolutionary decade.

*Rudé, George. *The Crowd in the French Revolution.* 1959. Description and analysis of popular participation in the Revolution's crucial turning points.

———. *Robespierre: Portrait of a Revolutionary Democrat.* 1975. An extremely admiring portrait.

———. *Wilkes and Liberty.* 1962. On popular movements for parliamentary reform in England.

Schama, Simon. *Patriots and Liberators: Revolution in the Netherlands 1780–1813.* 1977. An exhaustive but lively account.

Scott, H. M. (ed.). *Enlightened Absolutism: Reforms and Reformers in Later Eighteenth-Century Europe.* 1990. The latest and most comprehensive assessment.

*Soboul, Albert. *The Parisian Sans-Culottes and the French Revolution.* 1964. An abridgement of a landmark French thesis; should be compared to Cobb's study.

*Sutherland, Donald. *France 1789–1815: Revolution and Counter-revolution.* 1985. A fine general history of the period.

Tackett, Timothy. *Becoming a Revolutionary: The Deputies of the French National Assembly and the Emergence of a Revolutionary Culture (1789-1790).* 1996. A sensitive collective biography and interpretation of the Revolution's initial course.

———. *Religion, Revolution, and Regional Culture in Eighteenth-Century France: The Ecclesiastical Oath of 1791.* 1986. An exhaustive study of the Revolution's first and most fateful crisis.

Venturi, Franco. *The End of the Old Regime in Europe, 1768–1789.* 3 vols. 1989–1995. Like Palmer's work, a panoramic, comparative survey of Europe during those decades.

*Vovelle, Michel. *The Fall of the French Monarchy, 1787–1792.* 1984. A good synthesis.

*Woloch, Isser. *The New Regime: Transformations of the French Civic Order, 1789–1820s.* 1994. A thematic study of new civic institutions and how they fared, from the beginning of the Revolution to the Restoration of the Bourbons.

*Available in paperback.

▲ **General Bonaparte, in an uncompleted portrait by Jacques-Louis David.**
Jacques Louis David, "Napoleon Bonaparte" sketch. Giraudon/Art Resource.

THE AGE OF NAPOLEON

*T*he second phase of the French Revolution (1792–1794) left a stark legacy of contradictions. On the one hand, the National Convention moved for the first time since ancient Athens to institute a democratic republic: a government without kings, based on universal male suffrage and affirming such popular rights as the right to subsistence and to education for all. On the other hand, the Convention responded to foreign military threats, internal rebellion, and intense factionalism by establishing a revolutionary dictatorship. Individual liberties disappeared, and terror against "enemies of the people" became the order of the day. With the crisis finally surmounted by repression and military victories in 1794, most members of the Convention wearied of those repressive policies and wished to terminate the Revolution as quickly as possible.

Ending the Terror while preserving the Revolution's positive gains, however, proved extremely difficult. By 1794 too much blood had been spilled, too much social hatred and recrimination had accumulated. The new regime could not easily be steered toward the safe harbor of republican liberty in such a polarized atmosphere. In the end General Napoleon Bonaparte replaced the Republic with a personal dictatorship—an outcome that the men of 1789 (schooled in the history of the Roman Republic) had feared from the start.

Would Bonaparte betray the Revolution or consolidate it, as he transformed the Republic's political institutions and social policies? And, since the struggle for and against revolution had long since spilled across France's borders, what would be the consequences for Europe of Napoleon's ascendancy? After 1800 the public life of both France and Europe hinged to an unparalleled degree on the will of a single man. Gradually his designs became clear: a strong centralized state ruled from the top down in France, and an imperial reorganization of Europe totally dominated by France. Undergirding both developments was arguably the most significant priority of Napoleon: the implementation of mass conscription and the consequent militarization of European society. On a vast new scale, war had once again become the central motif of the Western experience.

I. From Robespierre to Bonaparte

Relatively secure after the military victories of the year II (1793–1794), the National Convention repudiated the Terror and turned against the leading terrorists. Jacobinism, however, was now a permanent part of the French political experience, along with antirevolutionary royalism. The political spectrum of modern European history had been created. The surviving revolutionaries attempted to command a centrist or moderate position within this range of opinions, but they proved inadequate to the task. During the four unsteady years of the Directory regime (1795–1799), however, French armies helped bring revolution to other parts of Western Europe, only to provoke a second anti-French coalition. This new challenge brought the weaknesses of the Republic to a head and opened the way to the seizure of power by an ambitious general.

▼ With its field of guillotines, this Thermidorian caricature ("Robespierre Guillotining the Executioner") portrays Robespierre as a murderous tyrant who had depopulated France.
Giraudon/Art Resource.

THE THERMIDORIAN REACTION (1794–1795)

When the military victories over the coalition and the Vendée rebels in the year II eased the need for patriotic unity, long-standing clashes over personalities and policies exploded in the Convention. Robespierre prepared to denounce yet another group of unspecified intriguers, presumably to send them to the guillotine as he had Hébert and Danton. But his enemies made a preemptive strike and denounced Robespierre to the Convention as a tyrant. The Convention no longer needed Robespierre's uncompromising style of leadership. Moderate deputies now repudiated him along with his policies of terror. The Parisian sans-culottes might have intervened to keep Robespierre in power, but the Jacobins had alienated their one-time allies when they curbed the sans-culottes' political autonomy several months earlier. On July 27, 1794 (9 Thermidor year II in the revolutionary calendar), the Convention declared Robespierre an outlaw and he was guillotined the following day, along with several loyal associates.

Anti-Jacobinism Robespierre's fall broke the Revolution's momentum. As the Convention dismantled the apparatus of the Terror, suspects were released from jail, the revolutionary committees that had spearheaded the Terror were abolished, and some of their former members were arrested in turn. The Convention closed the Paris Jacobin Club, once the main forum for Robespierre's influence, while the political clubs in the provinces gradually withered away. The Convention also extended an amnesty to the surviving Girondins and arrested a few leading deputies of the Mountain. Those who had taken responsibility for the

▲ **The Parisian sans-culottes launched a futile rebellion in the spring of 1795 for "Bread and the Constitution of 1793" in response to hyperinflation and severe food shortages.**
LeSeure, lack of bread in Paris 1795. Photothèque des Musées de la Ville de Paris, lcw/Spadem 1995.

Terror in the year II now found themselves under attack. The anti-Jacobin thirst for retribution eventually produced a "white terror" against the Jacobins and the sans-culottes that resulted in arrests, assassinations, and, in the south of France, wholesale massacres.

Thermidor also released France from the social austerity of the year II. The Jacobins' insistence on public virtue gave way to the toleration of luxury, fancy dress, and self-indulgence among the wealthy. The titles *monsieur* and *madame* reappeared, replacing the republican designation of *citizen*. In keeping with laissez-faire ideology, the Thermidorians rescinded economic controls. With the marketplace again ruled by supply and demand, skyrocketing inflation reignited. Worse yet, the harvest of 1795 proved mediocre, and many consumers suffered worse privations than those they had dreaded during the shortages of 1793. In near-famine conditions, mortality rates rose markedly; police reports spoke of little but popular misery.

The Last Revolutionary Uprising Former militants attempted to spark a political reversal and halt the Thermidorian reaction. In the spring of 1795 sans-culottes began to demonstrate in Paris with the slogan "Bread and the Constitution of 1793." The Thermidorians, however, were moving in the opposite direction. They viewed the Jacobin Constitution of 1793 as far too democratic and looked for an excuse to scrap it altogether. In May sans-culottes launched a poorly organized insurrection (the revolt of Prairial year III). In a grim and desperate gamble they invaded the Convention's hall, where they won the sympathy of only a handful of deputies. Their hours were numbered. In two days of street fighting, government forces overwhelmed the insurgents. Afterward, thirty-six sans-culottes were executed, and twelve hundred more were imprisoned for their activism during the Terror. This event proved to be the last mobilization of the Parisian revolutionary crowd and the final eclipse of the egalitarian movement.

THE DIRECTORY (1795–1799)

By the end of 1795, the remaining members of the Convention considered the Revolution over. The extremes had been vanquished, and the time for the "peaceable enjoyment of liberty" seemed at hand. The Thermidorians drafted a new constitution—the constitution of the year III (1795)—proclaimed a general amnesty, and hoped to turn a new page. The revolutionary government, which had replaced the fallen constitutional monarchy in 1793, gave way to a constitutional republic, known as the Directory after its five-man executive.

The Directory's proponents declared that the Republic should "be governed by the best citizens, who are found among the property-owning class." The new constitution said little about the popular rights proclaimed by the Constitution of 1793, like the right to subsistence, public assistance, or free education. The constitution also abandoned the universal male suffrage promised in 1793 and restored the propertied franchise of 1791 and the system of indirect elections. The regime's two-house legislature was designed to moderate the political process, while its five-man executive was meant to prevent the rise of a dictator. The Directory also feared a royalist resurgence. Since genuinely free elections at this point might be carried by the antirepublicans of the right, the outgoing Convention decided to coopt two-thirds of its members into the new legislature, thereby ensuring a substantial degree of political continuity. A royalist revolt against this power grab was easily crushed by government troops led by a young officer named Napoleon Bonaparte.

The Directory wished to command the center of the political spectrum, which one historian has aptly called "the mirage of the moderates." To maintain themselves in power, however, the directorials violated the liberties pledged in their own constitution. They repeatedly purged elected officials and periodically suppressed political clubs and newspapers on the left and right. In general they refused to acknowledge the legitimacy of organized opposition of any kind. This attitude explains the succession of coups and purges that marked the Directory's four years. Although the repressive measures were mild compared with those of the Terror—deportation usually being the harshest punishment meted out—they ultimately undermined the regime's viability. In the end many moderate republicans walked away from their own creation.

The Political Spectrum For all its repressive qualities, however, the Directory regime was democratic enough to allow most shades of the political spectrum some visibility. The full range of opinions in France, obscured previously by the Terror, was evident during the years of the Directory and would persist with some modifications into the twentieth century. The most important legacy of all, no doubt, was the apathy born of exhaustion or cynicism. Most citizens, especially peasants, had wearied of politics and distrusted all officials whatever government they served. Participation in the Directory regime's annual elections was extremely low.

Within this context of massive apathy, politically conscious minorities showed fierce partisanship. On the right, ultraroyalists (including émigrés, refractory priests, and armed rebels in western France) hoped to overthrow the Republic altogether. Some worked with the exiled Bourbon princes and with British secret agents. More moderate royalists hoped to win control of the Republic's political institutions lawfully and then bring back the émigrés and refractory priests while stamping out the last vestiges of Jacobinism. (Since Napoleon later effected such changes on his own terms, former royalists would form one base of his support.)

On the left of the spectrum stood the Neo-Jacobins—democrats in their own eyes, anarchists to their opponents. The Neo-Jacobins adhered to the moderate Republic of 1795 but identified positively with the experience of 1793. They did not advocate a return to the Terror or the use of force to regain power. Instead, the Neo-Jacobins promoted grassroots activism through local political clubs, petition drives, newspapers, and electoral campaigns to keep alive the egalitarian ideals of the year II, such as free public education and progressive taxation.

At the far end of the spectrum stood a tiny group of radicals whose significance would loom larger in the next century than it did in 1796. Their leader was François-Noël Babeuf, who had changed his name to Gracchus Babeuf in 1793. The

Babeuvists viewed the revolutionary government of the year II as a promising stage that had to be followed by a final revolution in the name of the masses. The Babeuvists advocated a vaguely defined material equality, or communism, for all citizens—a "community of goods," as they called it. They also assigned a key role to a small revolutionary vanguard in carrying out this final revolution. Regarding the present Republic as simply a new form of oppression by the elites, they conspired to overthrow it.

The Elusive Center The Directory's adherents stood somewhere in the center of this broad spectrum, hostile to royalists and Neo-Jacobins alike and ready to shift their ground with any change in the political balance. Thus, although the Neo-Jacobins had spurned Babeuf's calls for insurrection, after Babeuf's plot was exposed the Directory joined forces with the right. But when the first regular elections in the year V (1797) produced a royalist victory, the Directory reversed field. Backed by influential generals, the government purged newly elected royalist deputies, suppressed royalist newspapers, and allowed the Neo-Jacobins to open new clubs.

After a few months, however, the Directory grew fearful of the revived left. During the elections of the year VI (1798), Neo-Jacobins and Directorial moderates vied for influence in what almost amounted to party rivalry. But in the end the Directory would not risk the results of free elections. Again it intervened: It closed down clubs and newspapers, manipulated electoral assemblies, and purged those Neo-Jacobins who were elected anyway. Interestingly, at almost the same moment that France's government was quashing its political rivals, leaders of the American republic were reluctantly coming to accept opposition parties as legitimate. In France, however, the Directory would not tolerate organized opposition, and that rigidity contributed to the Republic's demise.

THE RISE OF BONAPARTE

Meanwhile, the Directory years provided unexpected impetus for revolutionary expansion in Europe, which brought into being a half-dozen "sister republics" (see map 21.1), including the

▲ **"The Directory Falls between Two Stools" is a caricature depicting the political dilemma of the Directory, which vainly sought a centrist position between the left and right.**
Musée Carnavalet/Photo Bulloz.

Batavian Republic in the Netherlands and the Helvetic Republic in the Swiss Confederation. Revolutionary change also spread through the entire Italian peninsula, as French commanders in the field began to make their own diplomacy. Among them was a young brigadier general named Napoleon Bonaparte.

Bonaparte personifies the world-historic individual—the rare person whose life decisively dominates the course of historical events. Born in 1769 of an impoverished but well-connected family on the French-controlled island of Corsica, Napoleon scarcely seemed destined to play such a historic role. His youthful ambitions and fantasies involved

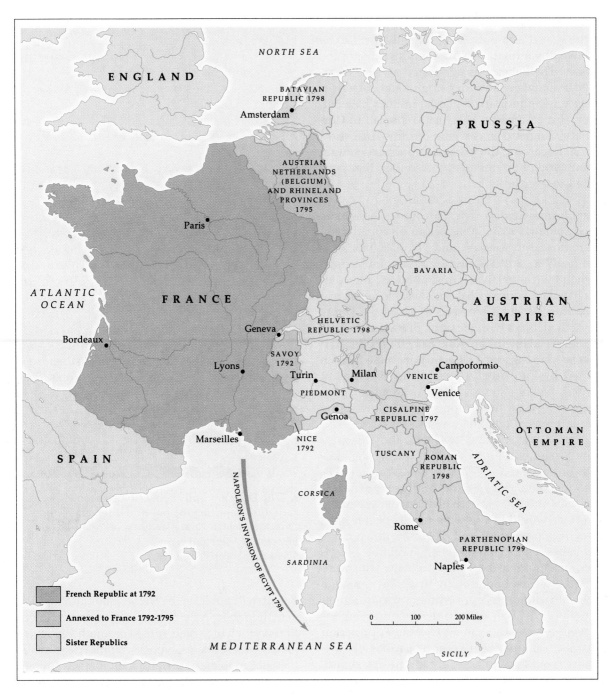

NORTH SEA

ENGLAND

BATAVIAN
REPUBLIC 1798

Amsterdam

PRUSSIA

AUSTRIAN
NETHERLANDS
(BELGIUM)
AND RHINELAND
PROVINCES
1795

Paris

BAVARIA

ATLANTIC
OCEAN

FRANCE

AUSTRIAN
EMPIRE

HELVETIC
REPUBLIC 1798

Geneva

Bordeaux

SAVOY
1792

Lyons

Turin

Milan

Campoformio

VENICE

PIEDMONT

Venice

Genoa

CISALPINE
REPUBLIC 1797

SPAIN

Marseilles

NICE
1792

TUSCANY

ROMAN
REPUBLIC
1798

OTTOMAN
EMPIRE

CORSICA

Rome

ADRIATIC SEA

SARDINIA

PARTHENOPIAN
REPUBLIC 1799

Naples

French Republic at 1792

Annexed to France 1792-1795

Sister Republics

0   100   200 Miles

MEDITERRANEAN SEA

SICILY

▲ MAP 21.1 FRANCE AND ITS SISTER REPUBLICS, 1798

little more than leading Corsica to independence from France. Sent to French military academies, he proved a diligent student, adept at mathematics. Aloof from his aristocratic classmates, whose pretensions he resented, self-reliant and energetic, Bonaparte became an expert on artillery.

After 1789 the young officer returned to Corsica, but his ambitions ran up against more conservative forces on the island. Eventually, local factional conflict drove him and his family off Corsica altogether. Bonaparte then moved onto a much larger stage. He rose steadily and rapidly through the military ranks, based in part on the luck of opportunities but equally on his ability to act decisively and effectively. While on leave in Paris in 1795, Bonaparte was assigned to the planning bureau of the war ministry. There he advocated a new strategy—the opening of a front in Italy to strike at Austrian forces and push into Germany from the south, while French armies on the Rhine pushed as usual from the west. The strategy was approved, and Bonaparte gained command of the Army of Italy in 1796.

The Making of a Hero   Austria's forces outnumbered the French in Italy, but Bonaparte moved his troops rapidly to achieve surprise and numerical superiority in specific encounters. The end result was a major victory that brought the French into the Habsburg domain of Lombardy and its capital, Milan. Bonaparte's overall plan almost miscarried, since the Army of the Rhine did not advance as planned. But this mishap made his own triumphs all the more important to the Directory. And Bonaparte ensured his popularity with the government by making his campaign self-supporting through organized levies on the Italians.

Bonaparte brought a great sense of excitement and drama to the French occupation of Lombardy. His personal magnetism and his talent in manipulating people attracted many Italians. The general encouraged the Italians to organize their own revolutionary movement; the liberation of northern Italy, he believed, would solidify support for his army and enhance his own reputation. This policy distressed the Directory, since it had intended to trade back conquests in Italy in exchange

for security on the Rhine frontier. But in the end the Directory endorsed the Treaty of Campo Formio, in which Bonaparte personally negotiated a peace settlement with Austria in October 1797. Austria recognized a new, independent state in northern Italy, the Cisalpine Republic, and left the Rhine question to future negotiations. The Directory regime had found the hero it so desperately needed.

The French now focused their patriotic aspirations on defeating the last member of the first coalition: the hated British enemy. Bonaparte naturally yearned for the glory of accomplishing this feat, and he was authorized to prepare an invasion force. Previous seaborne landings directed at Ireland had failed, however, and Bonaparte too finally had to abandon the scheme because of France's insufficient naval force.

Instead, in the spring of 1798 Bonaparte launched an expedition to Egypt intended to strike at Britain's colonial interests, including the approaches to India. But British naval superiority, in the form of Admiral Horatio Nelson's fleet, turned the expedition into a debacle. The British destroyed the French fleet at the Battle of the Nile, thereby marooning a French army in North Africa. Worse yet, the French were beaten back in several engagements with Turkish forces. Only cynical news management prevented the full story of this defeat from reaching France; instead, the expedition's exotic details and scientific explorations held the attention of the French public. Bonaparte extricated himself from this mess by slipping off through the British blockade, in effect abandoning his army as he returned to France.

THE BRUMAIRE COUP

While Bonaparte floundered in Egypt, the Directory was faltering under political pressures at home. Charges of tyranny and ineptitude accumulated against the directors. Further French expansion into Italy, which produced new sister republics centered in Rome and Naples, precipitated a new coalition against France, consisting of Britain, Russia, and Austria. In June 1799 ill-supplied French forces were driven out of most of Italy and Switzerland.

Widespread discontent with the Directory led to the defeat of many government-sponsored candidates in the spring elections of 1799. The legislature then ousted four of the five directors and named Sieyès, a respected leader of the patriots in 1789, among the replacements. Sieyès and his supporters secretly wished to alter the constitution itself, for they had lost confidence in the regime's institutions, especially its annual elections. These "revisionists" wanted to redesign the Republic along more oligarchic lines, as opposed to the Neo-Jacobins, who wished to democratize the Republic. The centrist position had virtually disappeared. The revisionists blocked emergency measures proposed by the Neo-Jacobins in reaction to the new war crisis and breathed a sigh of relief as French armies rallied and repulsed Anglo-Russian forces in the Batavian Republic and Switzerland. Most of Italy was lost for the time being, but the threat to France itself had passed. Sieyès and the revisionists moved against the Neo-Jacobins by closing their clubs and newspapers and prepared for a coup.

A General Comes to Power   Although no dire military threat remained to propel the country into the arms of a general, the revisionists wished to establish a more centralized, oligarchic republic, and they needed a general's support. Generals were the only national heroes in France, and only a general could organize the force necessary to ensure the coup's success. Bonaparte's return to France from Egypt thus seemed most timely. Bonaparte was not the revisionists' first choice, but he proved to be the best available one. On his trip up from the Mediterranean, people had cheered him warmly, since they knew little of the Egyptian fiasco and saw him in his role as victor of the Italian campaign.

Contrary to the intentions of Sieyès and his fellow conspirators, Bonaparte became the tail that wagged the dog. Once the coup began, he proved to be far more ambitious and energetic than the other conspirators and thrust himself into the most prominent position. Bonaparte addressed the legislature to denounce a mythical Jacobin plot and to demand emergency powers for a new provisional government. Along with two former directors, he was empowered to draft a new constitution; a cooperative rump of the legislature subsequently approved the new arrangements. Thus unfolded the coup of 18 Brumaire year VIII (November 9, 1799).

The Brumaire coup had not been intended to install a dictatorship, but that was its eventual result. In the maneuvering among the revisionists, Bonaparte's ideas and personality prevailed. The plotters agreed to eliminate meaningful elections, which they saw as promoting political instability. They agreed also to enshrine the social ideals of 1789, such as civil equality, and to bury those of the year II, such as popular democracy. The vague notion of popular sovereignty gave way to concentrated authority. The general came out of the coup as the regime's strongman, and Sieyès' elaborate plans for a republican oligarchy ended up in the wastebasket. On one other point, the plotters were particularly deceived. With General Bonaparte's leadership they hoped to achieve durable peace through military victory. Instead, the Napoleonic regime promoted unbounded expansion and endless warfare.

II. The Napoleonic Settlement in France

Bonaparte's prime asset in his rapid takeover of France was the resignation of its citizens. Most French people were so weary politically that they saw in Bonaparte what they wished to see.[1] The Committee of Public Safety had won grudging submission through its terroristic policies; Bonaparte achieved that result almost by default. As an effective propagandist for himself and a man of great personal appeal, he soothed a divided France. Ultraroyalists and dedicated Jacobins never warmed to his regime, but most citizens fell between those positions and could find comfort in the prospect of a return to order and stability.

---

[1] It is customary to refer to him as Bonaparte until 1804, when the general crowned himself Emperor Napoleon I.

THE NAPOLEONIC STYLE

Napoleon Bonaparte was not a royalist or a Jacobin, not a conservative or a liberal, though his attitudes were flavored by a touch of each viewpoint. Authority, not ideology, was his great concern, and he justified his actions by their results. The revolutionaries of 1789 could consider Napoleon one of theirs because of his hostility toward the unjust and ineffective institutions of the old regime. He had little use for seigneurialism, the cumbersome institutions of Bourbon absolutism, or the congealed structures of aristocratic privilege, which the Revolution had destroyed. Napoleon valued the Revolution's commitment to equality of opportunity and continued to espouse that liberal premise. Other rights and liberties of 1789 he curtailed or disdained.

Ten years of upheaval had produced a grim paradox: The French Revolution had proceeded in the name of liberty, yet successive forms of repression had been mounted to defend it. Napoleon fit comfortably into this history; unlike the Directory, he made no pretense about it. The social gains of the Revolution would be preserved through political centralization and authoritarian control. Napoleon's field of action was in fact far greater than that of the most powerful eighteenth-century monarch, for no entrenched aristocracy existed to resist him. Thanks to the clearing operations of the Revolution, he could reconstruct at will.

Tragically, however, Napoleon drifted away from his own rational ideals. Increasingly absorbed in his personal power, he began to force domestic and foreign policies on France that were geared to his imperial ambitions. Increasingly he concentrated his government on raising men and money for his armies and turned his back on revolutionary liberties.

POLITICAL AND RELIGIOUS SETTLEMENTS

Bonaparte gave France a constitution, approved in a plebiscite, that placed almost unchecked authority in the hands of a First Consul (himself) for ten years. Two later constitutional revisions, also approved overwhelmingly in plebiscites, increased executive power and diminished the legislative

▲ **Napoleon Bonaparte as First Consul, at the height of his popularity, painted by his admirer J.-B. Gros.** Musée Légion d' Honneur/Photo Bulloz.

branch until it became simply a rubber stamp. The first revision, in 1802, converted the consulship into a lifetime post; the second, in 1804, proclaimed Napoleon hereditary emperor. The task of proposing new laws passed from elected representatives to appointed experts in the Council of State. This new body advised the ruler, drafted legislation under his direction, and monitored public officials. Such government by experts stood as an alternative to meaningful parliamentary democracy for the next century.

The system of local government established by Bonaparte in 1800 came ironically close to the kind of royal centralization that public opinion had roundly condemned in 1789. Bonaparte eliminated the local elections that the Revolution had empha-sized. Instead, each department was now admin-istered by a *prefect* appointed by the ruler. The four-hundred-odd subprefects on the district level as well as the forty thousand mayors of France's com-munes were likewise appointed. With minor changes the unquestionably efficient prefectorial system survived in France for 150 years, severely limiting local autonomy and self-government.

Police-state methods finished what constitu-tional change began: the suppression of inde-pendent political activity. From the legislature to the grass roots, France was depoliticized. The government permitted no organized opposition, reduced the number of newspapers drastically, and censored the remaining ones. The free jour-nalism born in 1789 gave way to government press releases and news management. In 1811 only four newspapers remained in Paris, all hew-ing to the official line. Political clubs were pro-hibited, outspoken dissidents deported, and oth-ers placed under police surveillance. All these restrictions silenced liberal intellectuals as well as former political activists.

The Concordat Napoleon's religious policies promoted tranquillity at home and a good image abroad. Before Brumaire the Republic tolerated Catholic worship in theory but severely restricted it in practice. Continued proscription of the re-fractory clergy; insistence on the republican cal-endar, with its ten-day weeks that made Sunday a workday; and a drive to keep religious instruc-tion out of elementary schools curtailed the free and familiar exercise of Catholicism. These poli-cies provoked wide resentment among the mass of citizens whose commitment to Catholicism re-mained intact throughout the Revolution.

Though not a believer himself, Napoleon judged that major concessions to Catholic senti-ment were in order, provided that the Church re-mained under the control of the state. In 1801 he negotiated a Concordat, or agreement, with Pope Pius VII. It stipulated that Catholicism was the "preferred" religion of France but protected reli-gious freedom for non-Catholics. The Church was again free to operate in full public view and to re-store the refractory priests. Primary education would espouse Catholic values and use Catholic texts, as it had before the Revolution, and clerical

Chronology

NAPOLEON'S ASCENDANCY IN FRANCE

Nov. 1799	Coup d'etat of 18 Brumaire
Dec. 1799	Bonaparte becomes First Consul
Feb. 1800	Inauguration of prefectorial system
July 1801	Concordat with the Church
May 1802	Legion of Honor founded
Aug. 1802	Bonaparte becomes Life Consul
March 1804	Promulgation of Civil Code
May 1804	Napoleon becomes emperor
Aug. 1807	Suppression of the Tribunate
March 1808	Organization of the Imperial Nobility

salaries would be paid by the state. Though nom-inated by the ruler, bishops would again be con-secrated by the pope. But as a major concession to the Revolution, the Concordat stipulated that land confiscated from the Church and sold dur-ing the Revolution would be retained by its pur-chasers. On the other hand, the government dropped the ten-day week and restored the Gre-gorian calendar.

The balance of church-state relations tilted firmly in the state's favor, for Napoleon intended to use the clergy as a major prop of his regime. The pulpit and the primary school became in-struments of social control, to be used, as a new catechism stated, "to bind the religious con-science of the people to the august person of the Emperor." As Napoleon put it, the clergy would be his "moral prefects." Devout Catholics came to resent this subordination of the Church. Even-tually Pope Pius renounced the Concordat, to which Napoleon responded by removing the pontiff to France and placing him under house arrest.

Family and Gender Roles under the Napoleonic Civil Code

◆

"Art. 148. The son who has not attained the full age of 25 years, the daughter who has not attained the full age of 21 years, cannot contract marriage without the consent of their father and mother; in case of disagreement, the consent of the father is sufficient.

"Art. 212. Married persons owe to each other fidelity, succor, assistance.

"Art. 213. The husband owes protection to his wife, the wife obedience to her husband.

"Art. 214. The wife is obliged to live with her husband, and to follow him to every place where he may judge it convenient to reside: the husband is obliged to receive her, and to furnish her with everything necessary for the wants of life, according to his means and station.

"Art. 215. The wife cannot plead [in court] in her own name, without the authority of her husband, even though she should be a public trader . . . or separate in property.

"Art. 217. A wife . . . cannot give, alienate, pledge, or acquire by free or chargeable title, without the concurrence of her husband in the act, or his consent in writing.

"Art. 219. If the husband refuses to authorize his wife to pass an act, the wife may cause her husband to be cited directly before the court of first instance . . . which may give or refuse its authority, after the husband shall have been heard, or duly summoned.

"Art. 229. The husband may demand a divorce on the ground of his wife's adultery.

"Art. 230. The wife may demand divorce on the ground of adultery in her husband, when he shall have brought his concubine into their common residence.

"Art. 231. The married parties may reciprocally demand divorce for outrageous conduct, ill-usage, or grievous injuries, exercised by one of them towards the other."

THE ERA OF THE NOTABLES

With civil equality established and feudalism abolished, Napoleon believed that the Revolution was complete. It remained to encourage an orderly hierarchical society to counteract what he regarded as the excessive individualism of revolutionary social policy. Napoleon intended to reassert the authority of the state, the elites, and, in family life, the father.

In the absence of electoral politics, Napoleon used the state's appointive powers to confer status on prominent local individuals, or *notables*, thus associating them with his regime. These local dignitaries were usually chosen from among the largest taxpayers: prosperous landowners, former nobles, businessmen, and professionals. Those who served the regime with distinction were honored by induction into the Legion of Honor, nine-tenths of whose members were military men. "It is with trinkets that mankind is governed," Napoleon once said. Legion of Honor awards and appointments to prestigious but powerless local bodies were precisely such trinkets,

and they endured long after their creator was gone.

Napoleon offered more tangible rewards to the country's leading bankers when he chartered a national bank that enjoyed the credit power derived from official ties to the state. In education, Napoleon created elite secondary schools, or *lycées*, to train future government officials, engineers, and officers. The *lycées* embodied the concept of careers open to talent and became part of a highly centralized French academic system called the *University*, which survived into the twentieth century.

The Civil Code Napoleon's most important legacy was a civil code regulating social relations and property rights. Baptized the Napoleonic Code, it was in some measure a revolutionary law code that progressives throughout Europe embraced. Wherever it was implemented, the Civil Code swept away feudal property relations and gave legal sanction to modern contractual notions of property. The code established the right to choose one's occupation, to receive equal treatment under the law, and to enjoy religious freedom. At the same time, it allowed employers to dominate their workers by prohibiting strikes and trade unions. Nor did the code match property rights with popular rights like the right to subsistence.

Revolutionary legislation had emancipated women and children by establishing their civil rights. Napoleon undid most of this by restoring the father's absolute authority in the family. "A wife owes obedience to her husband," said the code, which proceeded to deprive wives of property and juridical rights established during the 1790s and to curtail the right to divorce while establishing a kind of double standard in the dissolution of a marriage (see "Family and Gender Roles under the Napoleonic Civil Code," p. 737). The code also expanded the husband's options in disposing of his estate, although each child was still guaranteed a portion.

The prefectorial system of local government, the Civil Code, the Concordat, the University, the Legion of Honor, and the local bodies of notables all proved to be durable institutions. They fulfilled Napoleon's desire to create a series of "granite masses" on which to reconstruct French society. His admirers emphasized that these institutions contributed to social stability amid France's chronic political unrest, arguing that they were skillful compromises between revolutionary liberalism and an older belief in hierarchy and central authority. Detractors point out that these institutions were class oriented and excessively patriarchal. Moreover they fostered overcentralized, rigid structures that might have sapped the vitality of French institutions in succeeding generations. Whatever their merits or defects, these institutions took root, unlike Napoleon's attempt to dominate all of Europe.

▼ **Deputies from the Cisalpine Republic of Italy proclaim Napoleon Bonaparte their president in 1802.**
Nicolas André Monslau, "The Council of the Cisalpine Republic Proclaims Napoleon President," 1802. Giraudon/Art Resource.

▲ **Admiral Nelson's heavily armed three-decker ship of the line, which inflicted devastation on the French fleet at Trafalgar.**
Nicholas Pocock, "Nelson's Flagships at Anchor." National Maritime Museum, London.

III. Napoleonic Hegemony in Europe

◄●►

After giving France a new government, Bonaparte's first task was to defeat the second anti-French coalition on the battlefield, especially in northern Italy. The outcome of this campaign against Austria would reinforce or destroy the settlement he had imposed on France after Brumaire. Napoleon's dictatorial tendencies became obvious enough within France, but it was in the arena of international relations that his ambitions lost all semblance of restraint. There he evolved from a general of the Revolution to an imperial conqueror. Napoleon's conquest of Italy, Germany, Spain, and other lands set into motion contradictory responses of collaboration and resistance. French expansion sparked nationalism abroad, but also liberalism and reaction.

MILITARY SUPREMACY AND THE REORGANIZATION OF EUROPE

Bonaparte's strategy in 1800 called for a repeat of the 1797 campaign: He would strike through Italy while the Army of the Rhine pushed eastward against Vienna. Following French victories at Marengo in Lombardy and Hohenlinden in Germany, Austria sued for peace. The Treaty of Lunéville (February 1801) essentially restored France to the position it had held after Bonaparte's triumphs in Italy in 1797.

In Britain a war-weary government now stood alone against France and decided to negotiate. The Treaty of Amiens (March 1802) ended hostilities and reshuffled territorial holdings outside Europe, such as the Cape Colony in South Africa, which passed from the Dutch to the British. But this truce proved precarious since it did not settle the future of French influence in Europe or of commercial relations between the two great powers. Napoleon abided by the letter of the treaty but soon violated its spirit. Britain and Austria alike were dismayed by further expansion of French influence in Italy, Switzerland, and North America. Most important, perhaps, France seemed determined to exclude British trade rather than restore normal commercial relations. Historians agree that the Treaty of Amiens failed to keep the peace because neither side was ready to abandon its century-long struggle for predominance.

The Third Coalition   A third anti-French coalition soon took shape, a replay of its predecessors. France ostensibly fought to preserve the new regime at home and its sister republics abroad. The coalition's objectives included the restoration of the Netherlands and Italy to "independence," the limitation of French influence elsewhere, and if possible, a reduction of France to its prerevolutionary borders. Like most such alliances, the coalition would be dismembered piecemeal.

French hopes of settling the issue directly by invading Britain proved impossible once again. At the Battle of Trafalgar (October 1805), Admiral Nelson's fleet crushed the combined naval forces of France and its ally Spain. Nelson, an innovative tactician who broke rule-book procedures on the high seas just as French generals did on land, died of his wounds in the battle but ensured the security of the British Isles for the remainder of the Napoleonic era.

Napoleon meanwhile had turned against the Austro-Russian forces. Moving 200,000 French soldiers with unprecedented speed across the continent, he took his enemies by surprise and won a dazzling succession of victories. After occupying Vienna he proceeded against the coalition's main army in December. Feigning weakness and retreat at the moment of battle, he drew his nu-merically superior opponents into an exposed position, crushed the center of their lines, and inflicted a decisive defeat. This Battle of Austerlitz was Napoleon's most brilliant tactical achievement, and it forced the Habsburgs to the peace table. The resulting Treaty of Pressburg (December 1805), extremely harsh and humiliating for Austria, imposed a large indemnity and required the Habsburgs to cede their Venetian provinces.

France and Germany   By now the French sphere of influence had increased dramatically to include most of southern Germany, which Napoleon reorganized into the Confederation of the Rhine, a client realm of France (see map 21.2). France had kept Prussia neutral during the war with Austria by skillful diplomacy. Only after Austria made peace did Prussia recognize its error in failing to join with Austria to halt Napoleon. Belatedly, Prussia mobilized its famous but antiquated army; it was rewarded with stinging defeats by France in a number of encounters culminating in the Battle of Jena (October 1806). With the collapse of Prussian military power, the conquerors settled in Berlin and watched the prestige of the Prussian ruling class crumble. Napoleon was now master of northern Germany as well as the south. For a while it appeared that he might obliterate Prussia entirely, but he restored its sovereignty—after amputating part of its territory and imposing a crushing indemnity.

Napoleon was free to reorganize central Europe as he pleased. After formally proclaiming the end of the Holy Roman Empire in 1806, he liquidated numerous small German states and merged them into two new ones: the Kingdom of Westphalia, with brother Jérôme on the throne, and the Grand Duchy of Berg, to be ruled by his brother-in-law Joachim Murat. His ally Saxony became a full-scale kingdom, while a new duchy of Warsaw was carved out of Prussian Poland. This "restoration" of Poland had propaganda value; it made the emperor appear as a champion of Polish aspirations, compared to the rulers of Prussia, Russia, and Austria, who had dismembered Poland in a series of partitions between 1772 and 1795. Moreover, Napoleon could now enlist a Polish army and use Polish territory as a base of operations against his remaining continental foe, Russia.

▲ **Napoleon amidst the carnage on the battlefield of Eylau, the bloodiest engagement to date of the revolutionary-Napoleonic era, where the French and Russians fought each other to a stalemate in 1807.**
C. Meynier, "The Day After the Battle of Eylau, February 9, 1807." Giraudon/Art Resource.

France and Russia In February 1807 Napoleon confronted the colossus of the east in the Battle of Eylau; the resulting carnage was horrifying but inconclusive. When spring came, only a dramatic victory could preserve his conquests in central Europe and vindicate the extraordinary commitments of the past two years. Fortunately for the emperor, the Battle of Friedland in June was a French victory that demoralized Russia's Tsar Alexander I and persuaded him to negotiate.

Meeting at Tilsit, the two rulers buried their differences and agreed in effect to partition Europe into eastern and western spheres of influence. Each would support the other's conquests and mediate in behalf of the other's interests. The Treaty of Tilsit (July 1807) sanctioned new annexations of territory directly into France and the reorganization of other conquered countries. The creation of new satellite kingdoms became the vehicle for Napoleon's domination of Europe. Like the French Republic, the sister republics became kingdoms between 1805 and 1807. And it happened that Napoleon had a large family of brothers ready to wear those new royal crowns.

The distorted shape of Napoleonic Europe is apparent on maps dating from 1808 to 1810 (see map 21.2). His chief satellites included the Kingdom of Holland, with brother Louis on the throne; the Kingdom of Italy, with Napoleon himself as king and his stepson Eugène de Beauharnais as viceroy; the Confederation of the Rhine, including brother Jérôme's Kingdom of Westphalia; the Kingdom of Naples, covering southern Italy, with brother Joseph the ruler until Napoleon transferred him to Spain and installed his brother-in-law Murat; and the Duchy of Warsaw. Belgium, the Rhineland, Tuscany, Piedmont, Genoa, and the Illyrian provinces had been annexed to France.

▲ MAP 21.2 EUROPE AROUND 1810

Switzerland did not become a kingdom, but the Helvetic Republic (as it was now called) received a new constitution dictated by France. In 1810, after yet another war with Austria, a marriage was arranged between the house of Bonaparte and the house of Habsburg. Having divorced Joséphine de Beauharnais, Napoleon married princess Marie Louise, daughter of Francis II, who bore him a male heir the following year.

NAVAL WAR WITH BRITAIN

For a time it seemed that Britain alone stood between Napoleon and his dream of hegemony over Europe. Since Britain was invulnerable to invasion, Napoleon hoped to destroy its influence by means of economic warfare. Unable to blockade British ports directly, he could try to close off the continent: keep Britain from its markets, stop its exports, and thus ruin its trade and credit. Napoleon reasoned that if Britain had nowhere to sell its manufactured goods, no gold would come into the country and bankruptcy would eventually ensue. Meanwhile overproduction would cause unemployment and labor unrest, which would turn the British people against their government and force the latter to make peace with France. At the same time, French advantages in continental markets would increase with the elimination of British competition.

The Continental System Napoleon therefore launched his "Continental System" to prohibit British trade with all French allies. Even neutral ships were banned from European ports if they carried goods coming from the British Isles. Britain responded in 1807 with the Orders in Council, which in effect reversed the blockade: It *required* all neutral ships to stop at British ports to procure trading licenses and pay tariffs. In other words, the British insisted on regulating all trade between neutral states and European ports. Ships that failed to obey would be stopped on the high seas and captured. In an angry response, Napoleon, in turn, threatened to seize any neutral ship that obeyed the Orders in Council by stopping at British ports.

Thus a total naval war between France and Britain enveloped all neutral nations. Indeed, neutral immunity virtually disappeared, since every ship was obliged to violate one system or the other and thus run afoul of naval patrols or privateers. While the British captured only about forty French ships a year after 1807 (for few were left afloat), they seized almost three thousand neutral vessels a year, including many from the United States.

The Continental System did hurt British trade. British gold reserves dwindled, and 1811 saw widespread unemployment and rioting. France was affected, in turn, by Britain's counterblockade, which cut it off from certain raw materials necessary for industrial production. But the satellite states, as economic vassals of France, suffered the most. In Amsterdam, for example, shipping volume declined from 1,350 ships entering the port in 1806 to 310 in 1809, and commercial revenues dropped calamitously. Out of loyalty to the people whom he ruled, Holland's King Louis Bonaparte tolerated smuggling. But this action so infuriated Napoleon that he ousted his brother

▲ **Emperor Napoleon I on his imperial throne in 1806, by the great portrait painter Ingres. Note the dramatic contrast in appearance with the young, intense military hero of the Republic in David's portrait at the beginning of this chapter.**
J. A. D. Ingres, "Napoleon I Enthroned." Giraudon/Art Resource.

from the throne and annexed the Kingdom of Holland directly to France. Smuggling was in fact the weak link in the system, for it created holes in Napoleon's wall of economic sanctions that constantly needed plugging. This problem drove the emperor to ever more drastic actions.

Chronology

NAPOLEON AND EUROPE

June 1800	Battle of Marengo and defeat of the Second Coalition
Feb. 1801	Treaty of Lunéville with Austria
March 1802	Treaty of Amiens with Britain
Sept. 1802	Annexation of Piedmont
1805–1806	Third Coalition forms
Oct. 1805	Battle of Trafalgar and defeat of French fleet
Dec. 1805	Battle of Austerlitz; defeat of Austria
1806	Battle of Jena and humiliation of Prussia
1807	Stalemate with Russia; battles of Eylau and Friedland
July 1807	Treaty of Tilsit with Russia Consolidation of satellite kingdoms
1807	Launching of Continental System against British trade
Feb. 1808	Invasion of Spain
July 1809	Battle of Wagram; Austria defeated again
April 1810	Napoleon weds princess Marie Louise of Austria
Dec. 1810	Annexation of Holland
July 1812	Invasion of Russia
Oct. 1812	Retreat and destruction of Grand Army
Oct. 1813	Battle of Leipzig and formation of Fourth Coalition
March 1814	Battle of France and Napoleon's abdication

THE NAPOLEONIC CONSCRIPTION MACHINE

One key to Napoleon's unrestrained ambitions in Europe was the creation of an efficient administrative state in France and its annexed territories. State penetration of the countryside under Napoleon achieved its most dramatic impact by creating a veritable conscription machine, which continuously replenished the ranks of the imperial army.

The National Convention's mass levy of August 1793 had drafted all able-bodied unmarried men between the ages of eighteen and twenty-five. But this unprecedented mobilization had been meant as a one-time-only emergency measure, a temporary "requisition." There was no implication that subsequent cohorts of young men would face conscription into the army as part of their civic obligations. When the war resumed in 1798, however, the Directory passed a conscription law that made successive "classes" of young men (that is, those born in a particular year) subject to a military draft should the need arise. The Directory immediately implemented this law and called up three classes, but local officials reported massive draft evasion in most of the departments. Many French youths found the prospect of military service repugnant. From this shaky foundation, however, the Napoleonic regime developed a successful conscription system.

The Rules of the Game After much trial and error with the details, timetables, and mechanisms, the system began to operate efficiently within a few years. The government assigned an annual quota of conscripts for each department. Using parish birth registers, the mayor of every community compiled a list of men reaching the age of nineteen that year. These youths were then led by their mayor to the cantonal seat on a specified day for a draft lottery. Panels of doctors at the departmental capitals later verified or rejected claims for medical exemptions. In all, about a third of French youths legally avoided military service because they were physically unfit—too short, lame, or deformed or suffering from poor eyesight, chronic diseases, or other infirmities.

In the draft lottery, youths picked numbers out of a box; marriage could no longer be used as an exemption, for obvious reasons. Those with high numbers were spared (for the time being), while

▲ **The departure of a group of conscripts from the "class" of 1807 in Paris.**
Boilly, "The Departure of Conscripts at St. Denis," 1807. Musée Carnavalet/Photo Bulloz.

those who drew low numbers filled the local in-duction quota. Two means of avoiding service re-mained: The wealthy could purchase a replace-ment, and the poor could flee. True, the regime had a bad conscience about allowing draftees to hire replacements, because the practice made its rhetoric about the duties of citizenship sound hol-low. But to placate wealthy notables and peasants with large holdings (who were sometimes des-perate to keep their sons on the farm), the gov-ernment permitted the hiring of a replacement un-der strict guidelines that made it difficult and expensive but not impossible. The proportion of replacements was somewhere between 5 and 10 percent of all draftees.

Draft Evasion For Napoleon's prefects, con-scription levies were always the top priority among their duties, and draft evasion was the number one problem. Dogged persistence, bu-reaucratic routine, and various forms of coercion gradually overcame this chronic resistance. From time to time, columns of troops swept through ar-eas in which evasion and desertion were most common and arrested culprits by the hundreds. But draft evaders usually hid out in remote places—mountains, forests, marshes—so coer-cion had to be directed against their families as well. Heavy fines assessed against the parents did little good since most were too poor to pay any-thing. A better tactic was to billet troops in the draft evaders' homes; if their families could not afford to feed the troops, then the community's wealthy taxpayers were required to do so. All these actions created pressure on the youths to turn themselves in. By 1811 the regime had bro-ken the habit of draft evasion, and conscription was generally becoming accepted as a disagree-able civic obligation, much like taxes. In fact, just as draft calls were beginning to rise sharply, draft evasion fell dramatically. In 1812 prefects all over France reported that the year's levies were more successful than ever before.

Napoleon had begun by drafting 60,000 French-men annually, but by 1810 the annual quotas had risen steadily to 120,000, and they continued to

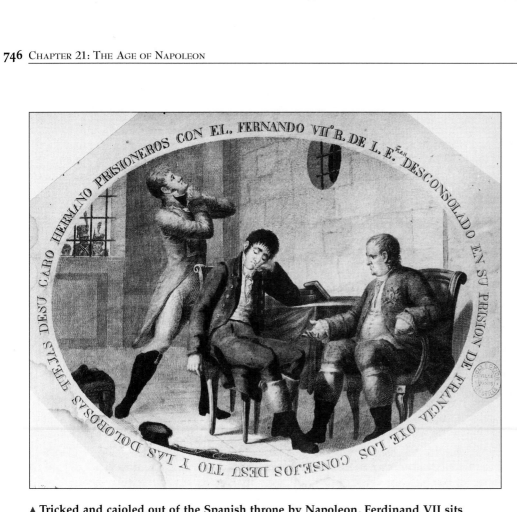

▲ **Tricked and cajoled out of the Spanish throne by Napoleon, Ferdinand VII sits
unhappily as a virtual prisoner in Bayonne, across the French border.**
Musée Carnavalet/Photo Bulloz.

climb. Moreover, in 1810 the emperor ordered the
first of many "supplementary levies," calling up
men from earlier classes who had drawn high lottery numbers. In January 1813, to look ahead,
Napoleon replenished his armies by calling up the
class of 1814 a year early and by making repeated
supplementary calls on earlier classes.

IV. Opposition to Napoleon

In 1808, with every major European power except
Britain vanquished on the battlefield, Napoleon
felt that nothing stood in his way. Since Spain and
Russia seemed unable or unwilling to stop smuggling from Britain, the emperor decided to deal
with each by force of arms, assuming that his design against Britain could then be pursued to its
conclusion. On all counts he was mistaken.
Napoleon's confrontations with Spain and Russia proved that his reach had exceeded his grasp.

THE "SPANISH ULCER"

Spain and France shared a common interest in
weakening British power in Europe and the colonial world. But the alliance they formed after making peace with each other in 1795 brought only
troubles for Spain, including the loss of its
Louisiana Territory in America and (at the Battle
of Trafalgar) most of its naval fleet. The Spanish
royal household, meanwhile, was mired in scandal. Prime Minister Manuel de Godoy, once a
lover of the queen, was a corrupt opportunist and
extremely unpopular with the people. Crown
Prince Ferdinand despised Godoy and Godoy's
protectors, the king and queen, while Ferdinand's
parents actively returned their son's hostility.

Napoleon looked on at this farce with irritation.
At the zenith of his power, he concluded that he
must reorganize Spain himself to bring it solidly
into the Continental System. As a pretext for military intervention, he set in motion a plan to invade Portugal, supposedly to partition it with

Spain. Once the French army was well inside Spain, however, Napoleon intended to impose his own political solution to Spain's instability.

Napoleon brought the squabbling king and prince to France, where he threatened and bribed one and then the other into abdicating. The emperor then gathered a group of handpicked Spanish notables who followed Napoleon's scenario by petitioning him to provide a new sovereign, preferably his brother Joseph. Joseph was duly proclaimed king of Spain. With 100,000 French troops already positioned around Madrid, Joseph prepared to assume his new throne, eager to rule under a liberal constitution and to believe his brother's statement that "all the better Spanish people are on your side." As he took up the crown, however, an unanticipated drama erupted.

Popular Resistance Faced with military occupation, the disappearance of their royal family, and the crowning of a Frenchman, the Spanish people rose in rebellion. It began on May 2, 1808, when an angry crowd in Madrid rioted against French troops, who responded with firing squads and brutal reprisals. This bloody incident, known as the Dos de Mayo and captured in Goya's famous paintings, has remained a source of Spanish national pride, for it touched off a sustained uprising against the French. Local notables created committees, or *juntas*, to organize resistance, mainly by peasants and monks, and to coordinate campaigns by regular Spanish troops. These troops were generally ineffective against the French, but they did produce one early victory: A half-starved French army was cut off and forced to surrender at Bailén in July 1808. This defeat broke the aura of Napoleonic invincibility.

The British saw a great opportunity to attack Napoleon in concert with the rebellious Spanish people. Landing an army in Portugal, the British actually bore the brunt of anti-French military

▼ **The great Spanish artist Francisco Goya memorably captured the brutality of French reprisals against the citizens of Madrid who dared to rebel against the Napoleonic occupation on May 2, 1808.** Erich Lessing/Art Resource.

▲ In a relentlessly bleak series of drawings collectively entitled "The Horrors of War,"
Goya went on to record the savagery and atrocities committed by both sides of the
struggle in Spain.
Francisco de Goya y Lucientes, "The Disasters of War: Populacho." Etching. Harris 148. 1st Edition.
The Norton Simon Foundation.

Spanish Liberals Draft a Constitution, 1812

"The general and extraordinary Cortes of the Spanish nation, duly organized . . . in order duly to discharge the lofty objective of furthering the glory, prosperity and welfare of the Nation as a whole, decrees the following political Constitution to assure the well-being and upright administration of the State.

"Art. 1: The Spanish Nation is the union of all Spaniards from both hemispheres.

"Art. 3: Sovereignty resides primarily in the Nation and because of this the right to establish the fundamental laws belongs to it exclusively.

"Art. 4: The Nation is obligated to preserve and protect with wise and just laws civil liberty, property and the other legitimate rights of all the individuals belonging to it.

"Art. 12: The religion of the Spanish Nation is and always will be the Catholic, Apostolic, Roman and only true faith. The Nation protects it with wise and just laws and prohibits the exercise of any other.

"Art. 14: The Government of the Spanish Nation is an hereditary limited Monarchy.

"Art. 15: The power to make laws resides in the Cortes with the King.

"Art. 16: The power to enforce laws resides in the King.

"Art. 27: The Cortes is the union of all the deputies that represent the Nation, named by the citizens.

"Art. 34: To elect deputies to the Cortes, electoral meetings will be held in the parish, the district, and the province.

"Art. 59: The electoral meetings on the district level will be made up of the electors chosen at the parish level who will convene at the seat of every district in order to name the electors who will then converge on the provincial capital to elect the deputies to the Cortes.

"Art. 338: The Cortes will annually establish or confirm all taxes, be they direct or indirect, general, provincial or municipal. . . .

"Art. 339: Taxes will be apportioned among all Spaniards in proportion to their abilities [to pay], without exception to any privilege."

From James B. Tueller, (trans.), *Political Constitution of the Spanish Monarchy*, proclaimed in Cadiz, March 19, 1812.

---

operations in Spain, in what they called the Peninsular War. In a grueling war of attrition, their forces drove the French out of Portugal, and after five years of fighting and many reversals they pushed the French back across the Pyrénées in November 1813. The British commander, the Duke of Wellington, had grasped the French predicament when he said: "The more ground the French hold down in Spain, the weaker they will be at any given point."

About 30,000 Spanish guerilla fighters helped wear down the French and forced the occupiers to struggle for survival in hostile country. The guerillas drew French forces from the main battlefields, inflicted casualties, denied the French access to food, and punished Spanish collaborators. In short, the Spanish fighters established the model for modern guerilla warfare. Their harassment kept the invaders in a constant state of anxiety, which led the French to adopt harsh measures in reprisal. But these "pacification" tactics only escalated the war's brutality and further enraged the Spanish people.

Together, the juntas, the Spanish regulars, the guerillas, and the British expeditionary force kept a massive French army of up to 300,000 men pinned down in Spain. Napoleon referred to the war as his "Spanish ulcer," an open sore that would not heal. Though he held the rebel fighters in contempt, other Europeans were inspired by their example of armed resistance to France.

The Spanish Liberals The war, however, proved a disaster for Spanish liberals. Torn between loyalty to Joseph, who would have liked to be a liberal ruler, and nationalist rebels, liberals faced a difficult dilemma. Those who collaborated with Joseph hoped to spare the people from a brutal war and to institute reform from above in the tradition of Spanish enlightened absolutism. But they found that Joseph could not rule independently;

Napoleon gave the orders in Spain and relied on his generals to implement them. The liberals who joined the rebellion organized a provisional government by reviving the ancient Spanish parliament, or Cortes, in the southern town of Cádiz. Like the French National Assembly of 1789, the Cortes of Cádiz drafted a liberal constitution in 1812 (see "Spanish Liberals Draft a Constitution, 1812," p. 749), which pleased the British and was therefore tolerated for the time being by the juntas.

In reality, most nationalist rebels despised the liberals. Most rebels were royalists who were fighting for the Catholic Church, the Spanish monarchy, and the old way of life. When in 1814 Wellington finally drove the French out of Spain and former crown prince Ferdinand VII took the throne, the joy of the Cádiz liberals quickly evaporated. As a royalist mob sacked the Cortes building, Ferdinand tore up the constitution of 1812, reinstated absolutism, restored the monasteries and the Inquisition, revived censorship, and arrested the leading liberals. Nationalist reactionaries emerged as the victors of the Spanish rebellion and the Peninsular War.

Independence in Spanish America The Creoles, descendants of Spanish settlers who were born in the New World, also profited from the upheaval in Spain. Spain had been cut off from its vast empire of American colonies in 1805, when the British navy won control of the Atlantic after the Battle of Trafalgar. In 1807 a British force attacked Buenos Aires in Spain's vice-royalty of the Río de la Plata (now Argentina). The Argentines—who raised excellent cattle on the *pampas,* or grassy plains—were eager to trade their beef and hides for British goods, but Spain's rigid mercantilism had always prevented such beneficial commerce. The Argentines welcomed the prospect of free trade, but not the prospect of British conquest. With Spain unable to defend them, the Creoles organized their own militia and drove off the invaders. Gaining confidence from this victory, they pushed aside the Spanish viceroy and his bureaucrats and took power into their own hands, though they still swore allegiance to the Spanish crown. The subsequent upheaval in Spain, however, led the Argentines to declare their independence. After Ferdinand regained the Spanish throne in 1814, he sent an army to reclaim the

colony but the Argentines, under General José de San Martín, drove it off, and Argentina made good on its claim to full independence.

Rebellion spread throughout Spanish America, led above all by Simón Bolívar, revered in the hemisphere as "The Liberator." After Napoleon removed the king of Spain in 1808, the Creoles in Spain's vice-royalty of New Granada (encompassing modern-day Venezuela, Colombia, and Ecuador) elected a congress, which declared independence from Spain. An arduous, protracted war with the Spanish garrisons followed, and by 1816 Spain had regained control of the region. But Bolívar resumed the struggle and gradually wore down the Spanish forces; in one campaign his army marched six hundred miles from the torrid Venezuelan lowlands over the snow-capped Andes Mountains to Colombia. Finally in 1819 the Spanish conceded defeat. Bolívar's dream of one unified, conservative republic of Gran Colombia soon disintegrated under regional pressures into several independent states, but not before Bolívar launched one final military campaign and liberated Peru, Spain's remaining colony in South America (see map 21.3 p. 751).

THE RUSSIAN DEBACLE

Napoleon did not yet realize in 1811 that his entanglement in Spain would drain French military power and encourage resistance in central Europe. On the contrary, never were the emperor's schemes more grandiose. Surveying the crumbling state system of Europe, he imagined that it could be replaced with a vast empire, ruled from Paris and based on the Napoleonic Code. He mistakenly believed that the era of the balance of power among Europe's nations was over and that nationalist sentiments need not constrain his actions.

Russia now loomed as the main obstacle to Napoleon's imperial reorganization and domination of Europe. Russia, a restive ally with ambitions of its own in Eastern Europe, resented the restrictions on its trade under the Continental System. British diplomats, anti-Napoleonic exiles such as Baron Stein of Prussia, and nationalist reactionaries at court all pressured the tsar to resist Napoleon. Russian court liberals, more concerned with domestic reforms, hoped on the contrary that Alexander would maintain peace with France, but

LOUISIANA
French 1800–1803;
sold to U.S. 1803

UNITED STATES
(from 1783)

TEXAS

ATLANTIC OCEAN

New
Orleans

FLORIDA
Spanish 1783–1819;
sold to U.S. 1819

REPUBLIC OF
MEXICO
| 1821 / 1821 |

Gulf of Mexico

Cuba

REPUBLIC
OF HAITI
| 1804 |

*VICEROYALTY
OF NEW SPAIN*

Caribbean Sea

UNITED PROVINCES
OF CENTRAL AMERICA
| 1821 / 1823 |

VENEZUELA
| 1830 |

BRITISH
GUYANA

DUTCH
GUIANA

FRENCH
GUIANA

*VICEROYALTY OF
NEW GRANADA*

REPUBLIC OF
GREATER COLOMBIA
| 1811 / 1830 |

ECUADOR
| 1830 |

EMPIRE OF
BRAZIL
| 1822 |

*VICEROYALTY
OF PERU*

PERU
| 1821 / 1821 |

PACIFIC OCEAN

BOLIVIA
| 1825 |

PARAGUAY
| 1811 |

*VICEROYALTY
OF LA PLATA*

**REMAINING COLONIAL
POSSESSIONS**

Spanish Possessions

Former borders of Spanish viceroyalties

PERU Former names of Spanish viceroyalties

British Possessions

French Possessions

Dutch Possessions

URUGUAY
| 1814 / 1828 |

Buenos Aires

ARGENTINE
CHILE CONFEDERATION
| 1810 / 1818 |
| 1810 |

Date of   Date of
independence separation
from colonial from other
power   states
| 1821 / 1823 |

*Islas Malvinas/
Falkland Islands*
British 1765–1770;
Spanish 1770–1820

▲ **MAP 21.3 SPANISH AMERICA AFTER INDEPENDENCE**

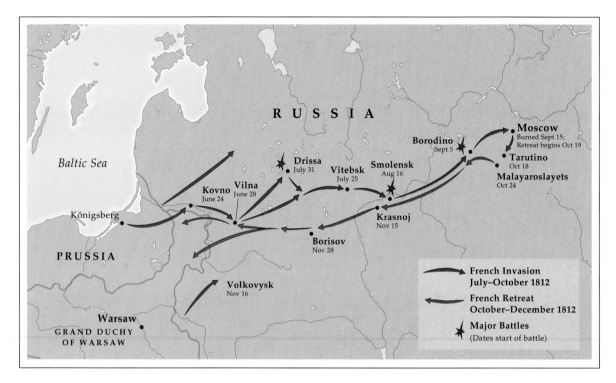

▲ MAP 21.4 THE RUSSIAN CAMPAIGN OF 1812

by 1812 their influence on the tsar had waned. For his part, Napoleon wanted to enforce the Continental System and humble Russia. As he bluntly put it: "Let Alexander defeat the Persians, but don't let him meddle in the affairs of Europe." Once again two major powers faced each other with diminishing interest in maintaining peace.

Napoleon prepared for his most momentous military campaign. His objective was to annihilate Russia's army or, at the least, to conquer Moscow and chase the army to the point of disarray. To this end he marshaled a "Grand Army" of almost 600,000 men (half of them French, the remainder from his satellite states and allies) and moved them steadily by forced marches across central Europe into Russia. The Russians responded by retreating in orderly fashion and avoiding a fight. Many Russian nobles abandoned their estates and burned their crops to the ground, leaving the Grand Army to operate far from its supply bases in territory stripped of food.

At Borodino the Russians finally made a stand and sustained a frightful 45,000 casualties, but the remaining Russian troops managed to withdraw in order (see map 21.4). Napoleon lost 35,000 men in that battle; but far more men and horses were dying from hunger, thirst, fatigue, and disease in the march across Russia's unending, barren territory. The greatly depleted ranks of the Grand Army staggered into Moscow on September 14, 1812, but the Russian army was still intact and far from demoralized.

The Destruction of the Grand Army   In fact, the condition of Moscow demoralized the French. They found the city deserted and bereft of badly needed supplies. The next night Moscow was mysteriously set ablaze, causing such extensive damage as to make it unfit to be the Grand Army's winter quarters. Realistic advisers warned the emperor that his situation was dangerous, while others told him what he wished to hear—that

▲ Just as Goya's drawings captured the unique ferocity of the Spanish campaign, this illustration evokes the particular agonies of climate and logistics in the Russian debacle.
Photo Archives, Nationalbibliotek Austria.

Russian resistance was crumbling. For weeks Napoleon hesitated. Logistically it was imperative that the French begin to retreat immediately, but that would constitute a political defeat. Only on October 19 did Napoleon finally order a retreat, but the order came too late.

The delay forced an utterly unrealistic pace on the bedraggled army as it headed west. Supplies were gone, medical care for the thousands of wounded nonexistent, horses lacking. French officers were poorly prepared for the march, and the soldiers grew insubordinate. Food shortages compelled foraging parties to sweep far from the main body of troops, where these men often fell prey to Russian guerillas. And there was the weather—Russia's bitter cold and deep snow, in which no commander would wish to find himself leading a retreat of several hundred miles, laden with wounded and loot but without food, fuel, horses, or proper clothing. Napoleon's poor planning, the harsh weather, and the operation of Russian guerilla bands made the long retreat a nightmare of suffering for the Grand Army. No more than 100,000 troops survived the ordeal. Worse yet, the Prussian contingent took the occasion to desert Napoleon, opening the possibility of mass defections and the formation of a new anti-Napoleonic coalition.

GERMAN RESISTANCE AND THE LAST COALITION

Napoleon was evidently impervious to the horror around him. On the sleigh ride out of Russia he was already planning how to raise new armies and set things aright. Other European statesmen, however, were ready to capitalize on Napoleon's defeat in Russia and demolish his empire once and for all. Provocative calls for a national uprising in the various German states to throw off the tyrant's yoke reinforced the efforts of diplomats like Prussia's Baron Stein and Austria's Klemens von Metternich to revive the anti-Napoleonic coalition.

Reform from Above in Prussia   In Prussia after the defeat of 1806, the government had introduced reforms intended to improve the quality of the bureaucracy by offering non-nobles more access to high positions and by reducing some of the nobility's privileges. The monarchy hoped thereby to salvage the position of the nobility and the authority of the state. Prussian military reformers adopted new methods of recruitment to build up a trained reserve force that could be rapidly mobilized, along with a corps of reserve officers to take command of these units. Prussia, in other words, hoped to achieve French-style efficiency and military mobilization without resorting to new concepts of citizenship, constitutions, legislatures, or the abolition of seigneurialism. On the level of propaganda and the symbolic gesture, writers in Prussia and other German states called for a popular war of liberation under the slogan "With God for King and Fatherland."

Against this background of Prussian military preparation and growing nationalist sentiment, the diplomats maneuvered and waited. Finally, in March 1813, King Frederick William III of Prussia signed a treaty with Russia to form an offensive coalition against Napoleon. A great struggle for Germany ensued between the Russo-Prussian forces and Napoleon and his allies. Austria continued to claim neutrality and offered to mediate the dispute, but at a meeting in Prague, Napoleon rejected an offer of peace in exchange for restoring all French conquests since 1802.

In August, as Napoleon learned of new defeats in Spain, Habsburg Emperor Francis finally declared war on his son-in-law. Napoleon called up underage and overage conscripts and was able to field one last army, but his major southern German ally, Bavaria, finally changed sides. A great battle raged around Leipzig for three days in October, and when the smoke cleared, Napoleon was in full retreat. Germany believed that the war of liberation had been won. German states were free from Napoleon's domination, but Prussia's rulers were also free from the need to concede further reforms in the political and social order.

The Fall of Napoleon   In the belief that he could rely on his conscription machine, Napoleon had rebuffed offers by the allies to negotiate peace in 1813. In fact, however, he reached the end of the line in November 1813 with a desperate call for 300,000 more men to defend France against the allies. Difficulties were inevitable, wrote one prefect, "when the number of men required exceeds the number available." Another reported: "There is scarcely a family that is not oppressed by conscription." Alongside sizable contingents of Italians, Germans, and other foreigners from the annexed territories and satellite states, nearly 2.5 million Frenchmen had been drafted by Napoleon. At least 1 million of those conscripts never returned.

With Napoleon driven back into France, British troops reinforced the coalition to ensure that it would not disintegrate once central Europe had been liberated. The coalition offered final terms to the emperor: He could retain his throne, but France would be reduced to her "normal frontiers." (The precise meaning of this term was left purposely vague.) Napoleon, still hoping for a dramatic reversal, chose to fight, and with some reluctance the allies invaded France. Napoleon led the remnants of his army skillfully but to no avail. The French had lost confidence in him, conscription had reached its limits, and no popular spirit of resistance to invasion developed as it had in 1792. Paris fell in March 1814. The price of this defeat was unconditional surrender and the emperor's abdication. Napoleon was transported to the island of Elba, between Corsica and Italy, over which he was granted sovereignty. After twenty-two years of exile, the Bourbon dynasty returned to France.

NAPOLEON JUSTIFIES HIMSELF IN 1815

"I have cleansed the Revolution, ennobled the common people, and restored the authority of kings. I have stirred all men to competition, I have rewarded merit wherever I found it, I have pushed back the boundaries of greatness. Is there any point on which I could be attacked and on which a historian could not take up my defense? My despotism? He can prove that dictatorship was absolutely necessary. Will it be said that I restricted freedom? He will be able to prove that license, anarchy, and general disorder were still on our doorstep. Shall I be accused of having loved war too much? He will show that I was always on the defensive. That I wanted to set up a universal monarchy? He will explain that it was merely the fortuitous result of circumstances and that I was led to it step by step by our very enemies. My ambition? Ah, no doubt he will find that I had ambition, a great deal of it—but the grandest and noblest perhaps, that ever was: the ambition of establishing and consecrating at last the kingdom of reason and the full exercise, the complete enjoyment, of all human capabilities!"

From B. Las Cases, ed., *Mémorial de Sainte-Hélène.*

THE NAPOLEONIC LEGEND

For Napoleon, imperial authority—originating with him in France and radiating throughout Europe—represented the principle of rational progress. In his view, the old notion of balance of power among European states merely served as an excuse for the British to pursue their selfish interests. While paying lip service to the notion of Italian, Spanish, and Polish nationhood, Napoleon generally scorned patriotic opposition to his domination as an outmoded, reactionary sentiment—exemplified by the "barbaric" guerillas in Spain fighting for king and religion. Modern-minded Europeans, he believed, would see beyond historic, parochial traditions to the prospect of a new European order. Indeed, Napoleon's credibility with some reformers in Europe was considerable. The Bavarian prime minister, for instance, justified his collaboration with France in 1810 in these words: "The spirit of the new age is one of mobility, destruction, creativity. . . . The wars against France offer the [unfortunate] possibility of bringing back old constitutions, privileges, and property relations."

During his final exile, however, Napoleon came to recognize that nationalism was not necessarily reactionary—as one could plainly see in the nationalistic but liberal Cortes of Cádiz of 1812. Progressive thinking and nationalist aspirations could coexist. From exile Napoleon rewrote his life story to portray his career as a series of defensive wars against selfish adversaries (especially Britain) and as a battle in behalf of the nations of Europe against reactionary dynasties. In this way Napoleon brilliantly (if falsely) put himself on the side of the future.

These memoirs and recollections from exile formed the basis of the Napoleonic legend, as potent a force historically, perhaps, as the reality of the Napoleonic experience. The image they projected emphasized how General Bonaparte had consolidated what was best about the French Revolution while pacifying a bitterly divided nation and saving it from chaos. They cast the imperial experience in a deceptively positive light, glossed over the tyranny and unending military slaughter, and aligned Napoleon with pragmatism, efficiency, and modernity (see "Napoleon Justifies Himself in 1815").

The Napoleonic legend also evoked a sense of grandeur and glory that moved ordinary people in years to come. Napoleon's dynamism and energy became his ultimate inspirational legacy to succeeding generations. In this way the Napoleonic legend fed on the romantic movement in literature and the arts. Many young romantics (including the poet William Wordsworth and the composer Ludwig van Beethoven) saw in the French Revolution a release of creativity and a liberation of the individual spirit. Napoleon's tyranny eventually alienated most such creative people. But the Napoleonic legend, by emphasizing the bold creativity of his career, meshed nicely with the emotional exaltation and sense of individual possibility that the romantics cultivated. Napoleon's retrospective justifications of his reign may not be convincing, but one can only marvel at the irrepressible audacity of the man.

In the confrontations between Napoleon and his European adversaries, France still embodied the specter of revolution. Even if the revolutionary legacy in France amounted by that time to little more than Napoleon's contempt for the inefficiency and outmoded institutions of the old regime, France after Brumaire remained a powerful challenge to the status quo. Napoleon intended to abolish feudalism, institute centralized administrations, and implant the French Civil Code in all of France's satellite states. But by 1808 his extravagant international ambitions relied on increasingly tyrannical and militaristic measures. These in turn provoked a range of responses, including nationalist rebellions. Britain and Russia, then Prussia and Austria, joined forces once more to bring the Napoleonic Empire down, to restore the balance of power in Europe, and to reinstall the Bourbons in France. But the clock could not really be set back from Europe's experience of revolution and Napoleonic transformation. The era of modern political and social conflicts had begun.

Recommended Reading
(See also chapter 20)

Sources

De Caulaincourt, Armand. *With Napoleon in Russia.* 1935. A remarkable account of the diplomacy and warfare of the 1812 debacle by a man at Napoleon's side.

Herold, J. C. (ed.). *The Mind of Napoleon.* 1961.

Thompson, J. M. (ed.). *Napoleon Self-Revealed.* 1934.

*Walter, Jakob. *The Diary of a Napoleonic Foot Soldier.* M. Raeff (ed.). 1991. A vivid and appalling account of the Russian campaign.

Studies

Alexander, Don. *Rod of Iron: French Counterinsurgency Policy in Aragon during the Peninsular War.* 1985. A case study of French responses to Spanish guerilla warfare.

Anderson, Eugene. *Nationalism and the Cultural Crisis in Prussia, 1806–1815.* 1939. The intellectual roots of German resistance to Napoleon.

*Bergeron, Louis. *France under Napoleon.* 1981. A fresh and insightful evaluation of the Napoleonic settlement in France.

*Broers, Michael. *Europe under Napoleon 1799–1815.* 1996. An incisive and up-to-date synthesis on French expansion in Europe.

*Carr, Raymond. *Spain 1808–1975.* 1982. An authoritative general history with fine chapters on this period.

Chandler, David. *Napoleon's Marshals.* 1986. By a leading expert on Napoleonic military history.

Cobb, Richard. *Reactions to the French Revolution.* 1972. On the violent aftermath of the second revolution in the provinces.

*Connelley, Owen. *Blundering to Glory: Napoleon's Military Campaigns.* 1988. An irreverent but incisive account of Napoleon's military leadership.

———. *Napoleon's Satellite Kingdoms.* 1965. A study of the states conquered by France and ruled by the Bonaparte family.

*Ellis, Geoffrey. *Napoleon.* 1997. A concise profile.

———. *Napoleon's Continental Blockade: The Case of Alsace.* 1981. A case study of the period's economic warfare.

Elting, John. *Swords around a Throne: Napoleon's Grande Armee.* 1988. An eminently readable military history.

Forrest, Alan. *Conscripts and Deserters: The Army and French Society during the Revolution and Empire.* 1988. A study of popular resistance to revolutionary and Napoleonic conscription.

Gates, David. *The Spanish Ulcer: A History of the Peninsular War.* 1986. On the Spanish rebellion, the French response, and Wellington's expeditionary force.

*Geyl, Pieter. *Napoleon, For and Against.* 1949. Napoleon and the historians, as reviewed by a Dutch scholar with no illusions.

*Herold, J. Christopher. *The Age of Napoleon.* 1963. A brilliant popular history of the era.

Lefebvre, Georges. *The Thermidorians.* 1964. A detailed narrative of 1794–1795.

*———. *Napoleon.* 2 vols. 1959. A general history of the period by a master historian.

Lucas, C., and G. Lewis (eds.). *Beyond the Terror: Essays in French Regional and Social History, 1794–1815.* 1983. Local studies by students of Richard Cobb.

*Lynch, John. *The Spanish American Revolutions, 1808–1826.* 1973. A comprehensive account of the independence movements in Spanish America and their aftermath.

Lyons, Martyn. *France under the Directory.* 1975. A brief topical survey of the Revolution's later, unheroic phase.

*———. *Napoleon Bonaparte and the Legacy of the French Revolution.* 1994. A good recent textbook.

Marcus, G. J. *A Naval History of England, II: The Age of Nelson.* 1971. The standard history of British naval supremacy.

*Markham, Felix. *Napoleon.* 1966. Perhaps the best biography in English.

Mitchell, Harvey. *The Underground War against Revolutionary France: The Missions of William Wickham 1794–1800.* 1965. On British attempts to subvert the French Republic.

*Palmer, Robert R. *The World of the French Revolution.* 1971. Emphasizes the interplay of French power and revolutionary movements outside of France.

Rosenberg, Hans. *Bureaucracy, Aristocracy, and Autocracy: The Prussian Experience, 1660–1815.* 1958. On reform from above in Prussia that largely preserved the status quo.

Rothenberg, Gunther. *The Art of Warfare in the Age of Napoleon.* 1978. A good analysis of strategy and tactics.

*Sutherland, D. M. G. *France, 1789–1815: Revolution and Counter-revolution.* 1985. A fine general history of France in this period.

Tulard, Jean. *Napoleon: The Myth of the Savior.* 1984. A synthesis by the leading French expert on Napoleon.

Woloch, Isser. *Jacobin Legacy: The Democratic Movement under the Directory.* 1970. On the ideas and practice of democratic activism after the fall of Robespierre.

*Woloch, Isser. *The New Regime: Transformations of the French Civic Order, 1789–1820s.* 1994. A thematic study of new civic institutions and how they fared, from the beginning of the Revolution to the Restoration of the Bourbons.

Woolf, Stuart. *A History of Italy, 1700–1860.* 1979. An authoritative general history, with fine chapters on this period.

*Woronoff, Denis. *The Thermidorian Regime and the Directory.* 1984. A synthesis by a French historian on France between Robespierre and Bonaparte.

*Available in paperback.

▲ **The contrast of new and old: The train from Vienna to Baden frightened the horses in this watercolor done in 1847 by Leander Russ.**
Archiv für Kunst und Geschichte.

FOUNDATIONS OF THE NINETEENTH CENTURY: POLITICS AND SOCIAL CHANGE

fter twenty-five years of war, peace was in itself a dramatic change. The first concern of the powers that had opposed Napoleon was to guarantee that in the future no one state would be able to dominate the continent. They began by redrawing the map, shifting boundaries to create an interlocking patch-work of states that could resist aggression. They accomplished that at the peace conference in Vienna.

The wars against France had been about more, however, than territory or the balance of power. The allies had fought to preserve monarchy, and they sought a peace that would prevent events like the French Revolution anywhere in Europe. The first step was to impose regimes that would be safely conservative. For the most part they restored the dynasties that had been overturned, but these governments were nonetheless new and not merely a continuation of tradition. Establishing them raised classical questions about the body politic—about how power should be organized, what institutions should direct society, and who should participate in deciding policy. The conflicts that followed made the possibility of revolution a fact of life, dreaded by some and hoped for by others, to be reinvoked in each country by the risings, acts of repression, and major reforms of the next thirty years.

New governments, determined to enforce stability while at the same time adapting many of the institutions and techniques that had made Napoleonic rule effective, confronted another far-reaching challenge. Industrialization and economic development brought changes in production that gradually transformed society. These social changes raised new questions about the role of government and made the struggle between conservatives and advocates of change a central theme of nineteenth-century history. The Europe restructured in 1815 to preserve the status quo had in fact entered a new era of passionate, volatile politics and of rapid and pervasive social change.

I. The Politics of Order

In setting the terms of peace, allied leaders expected to secure stability through domestic political arrangements supported by international agreements. Conservative monarchies were to keep order in their own lands, to cooperate in stamping out the threat of revolution anywhere in Europe, and to sustain an intricate balance of power as the guarantee of peace.

THE CONGRESS OF VIENNA

To forge these arrangements, the great international conference known as the Congress of Vienna met in September 1814, an occasion for serious deliberations and elaborate pomp centered on the crowned heads of Austria, Prussia, Russia, and dozens of lesser states. Officials, expert advisers, princesses and countesses, dancers and artists, and the ambitious of every rank flocked to the Austrian capital. Their contrived gaiety and bewigged elegance made the Congress a symbol of aristocratic restoration.

Its business remained the responsibility of the four great powers—Austria, Great Britain, Russia, and Prussia—an inner circle to which France was soon admitted. Prince Klemens von Metternich, who had led the Austrian Empire to this triumph, conducted the affairs of the Congress with such skill that its provisions can be seen as largely his work. Handsome, elegant, and arrogant, Metternich was the epitome of an aristocrat, fluent in all the major European languages, a dandy who dabbled in science and shone in the ballroom. More consistently than any other single figure, he had understood the extent of Napoleon's ambitions and had welded the international alliance that defeated the French emperor. Metternich was named foreign minister of Austria in 1809 and would hold that position for nearly forty years, tying his vision of European order to Austria's interests. Metternich was generally supported by Lord Castlereagh, England's able foreign minister. Russia's Tsar Alexander I, who acted as his own chief diplomat, was more unpredictable. Educated in the ideas of enlightened despotism, Alexander was now more given to mysticism and conservative fear and was attracted to grandiose programs upsetting to the careful calculations of self-interest by which the Congress reached agreement.

▲ **In the tradition of aristocratic portraits, Prince Metternich is conveyed as a polished courtier; the medals, symbolic of his position and power, are also a reminder of the purpose of his policies.** Mansell/Time, Inc..

The Peace Terms The most pressing issue these statesmen faced was the future of France. Most of the allies favored restoring some sort of monarchy, and the Treaty of Paris, signed in May 1814, had recognized as king Louis XVIII, a brother of the executed Bourbon, Louis XVI. The treaty also granted France its expanded frontiers gained by 1792. A settlement covering all the territory affected by the Napoleonic wars would take longer. Warily watching one another, the allies soon included Prince Talleyrand, the French representative, in their deliberations. A former bishop who had served the First Republic and then the Directory, he had helped Napoleon to power and been his foreign minister for eight years. Talleyrand was now the indispensable servant of Louis XVIII, using all his famous shrewdness to regain for France its former influence.

The concerns of these men focused on continental Europe, for only Great Britain among the victors had extensive interests overseas, and British designs on South Africa, Ceylon, and

▲ **The Congress of Vienna is portrayed here as a kind of elegant salon in which the very clothes these statesmen wore mix the styles of the old regime and the new century.**
Archiv für Kunst und Geschichte.

Malta were modest enough to be accepted by the other European states. Europe was considered the sphere of the great powers; each closely weighed the claims of the others, and all especially watched Russia, with her mammoth armies, undefined ambitions, and quixotic tsar.

Conflicting interests kept Austria, Prussia, and Russia from dividing up Poland as they had in the eighteenth century, but neither did they want to risk creating an independent Poland. So Russia received most of Poland to be ruled as a separate kingdom, and Prussia took about half of Saxony—a triumph of old regime diplomacy in which each of the powers got something (see map 22.1). Prussia was also given greatly enlarged territories in the Rhineland, ensuring that formidable Prussian armies would stand along the French border. The former Austrian Netherlands were absorbed into a new, independent Kingdom of the Netherlands, which created another strong buffer against France

and met the British desire that no major power control the Low Countries' important river ports across the channel from England. Austria, in return for ceding the southern Netherlands, acquired Venetia and recovered Lombardy, which greatly strengthened Austrian dominance of northern Italy. The other duchies of northern Italy went to dukes with close Austrian ties (in a touch of chivalry, Marie Louise, Napoleon's now throneless Austrian wife, was given Parma to rule).

The terms agreed on at Vienna constituted the most extensive European peace settlement since the treaty of Westphalia in 1648.[1] Each of the victors had gained territory, and France was surrounded by states capable of resisting any future

---

[1] The Kingdom of Sardinia would have liked Lombardy but got Genoa, the last of the ancient Italian republics to fall. Russia took Finland from Sweden, which in turn got Norway from Denmark.

▲ Map 22.1 Europe, 1815

French aggression. The final act was signed in June 1815 by the five great powers and by Sweden, Spain, and Portugal, a gracious recognition of their past importance.

The Hundred Days The deliberations of the Congress were interrupted in March 1815 by the terrifying news of Napoleon's escape from exile. He had tried to make the best of ruling the island of Elba and had even showed something of his old flair as he designed uniforms, held receptions, and inquired into the local economy. But the island principality was far too small to contain an emperor's ambition. Landing in the south of France, he was joined by units of the French army as he moved toward Paris. Louis XVIII waited for signs of resistance that did not develop, then climbed into his carriage and once again headed for the eastern border. Napoleon became the ruler of France without firing a shot. He then tried to negotiate with the allies, but they declared him an outlaw and quickly assembled their troops. After several minor battles, Napoleon was defeated for the last time at Waterloo on June 18 and surrendered to the British. They dispatched him to the more distant island of St. Helena, in the South Atlantic.

Napoleon's dashing venture lasted only a hundred days, but its effects were felt far longer. The terms of peace were altered, and the possibility of restoring a stable monarchy was called into question. Allied armies had quickly defeated Napoleon, and France was required to pay an indemnity and her boundaries reduced to those of 1789 (which entailed the loss of much of the Saar region to Prussia). The Bourbons again returned to the French throne, haunted by the specter of renewed revolution and permanently embarrassed by the ease with which Napoleon had retaken power. Napoleon had used his Hundred Days to soften the memory of his despotism with a series of liberal measures (he even banned slave traffic in the French colonies) and the promise of a constitution. Even from St. Helena, he continued to propagandize for Bonapartism, redefining it as a system for achieving both national strength and social change. Allied statesmen, with power on their side, paid less attention to popular opinion.

Principles of International Order The restorations of 1815 acknowledged many of the changes of the past twenty-five years. The Bourbons were restored in France but now governed with a constitution. In Germany, the Holy Roman Empire and hundreds of minor German principalities, all abolished by Napoleon, were not restored but were consolidated into thirty-nine states, including Prussia and Austria, and joined in a loose confederation. The diplomats at Vienna were also innovative in their use of experts as advisers on technical matters of history and law. The Congress established the principle that navigation on international riverways should be open to all and set down rules of diplomatic conduct useful to this day. For the next hundred years Europe would be free of European war, due in part to the complicated arrangements negotiated at Vienna.

The Congress was less impressive in the realm of ideas. Recognizing the need to invoke some general principle to justify such far-reaching arrangements, Talleyrand suggested they were only restoring governments made legitimate by tradition and public support; but that justification gave more weight to public opinion than his colleagues could accept. Aiming for something more stirring, Tsar Alexander proposed a Holy Alliance, an agreement that all states would conduct their affairs according to Christian teachings. The principle seemed vague enough; and though some were publicly skeptical, nearly all European governments signed. Three refused: The Ottoman sultan cared too little for Christian teachings, the pope cared too much, and Britain rejected any permanent commitments on the continent. Historians, too, have tended to dismiss the Holy Alliance as a meaningless expression of Alexander's mysticism. Yet there was something modern, and maybe wise, in the tsar's desire to give the new order moral appeal.

Opposition to the Settlement Proponents of change—Europe's liberals, reformers, and nationalists—would later recall the Congress of Vienna as the occasion during which aristocrats danced while foisting reactionary regimes on the people of Europe. Such critics cited not its realistic compromises but the brutal shuffling of territory without regard to the claims of nationality or constitutions. In fact, the new order was not so solid as it seemed. In 1820 and 1821 uprisings occurred in both Italy and Spain, led by young army officers who were influenced by memories of Napoleonic reforms and convinced that individual advancement and efficient government required a constitution. Metternich quickly called for a "concert of Europe" to snuff the flames of revolution by force, but unanimity among the former allies was breaking down. Great Britain disapproved sending foreign troops to put down a constitutional government in Naples and did not attend the conference, which approved Austrian intervention in Naples and called on France to send troops against the revolution in Spain. French forces met little resistance in Spain, and their royal parade was welcomed by conservatives throughout Europe as evidence of the French monarchy's revived

METTERNICH ANALYZES THE THREAT TO TRANQUILLITY

On December 15, 1820, Metternich wrote the Habsburg emperor from the international conference he had called to deal with the threat of revolution. Metternich argued that all monarchs must act together against the common threat, which he blamed on the middle class.

"Europe presents itself to the impartial observer under an aspect at the same time deplorable and peculiar. We find everywhere the people praying for the maintenance of peace and tranquillity, faithful to God and their Princes. . . . The governments, having lost their balance, are frightened, intimidated, and thrown into confusion by the cries of the intermediary class of society, which, placed between the Kings and their subjects, breaks the scepter of the monarch, and usurps the cry of the people—that class so often disowned by the people, and nevertheless too much listened to. . . .

"We see this intermediary class abandon itself with a blind fury and animosity. . . . to all the means which seem proper to assuage its thirst for power, applying itself to the task of persuading Kings that their rights are confined to sitting upon a throne, while those of the people are to govern, and to attack all that centuries have bequeathed as holy and worthy of man's respect—denying, in fact, the value of the past, and declaring themselves the masters of the future.

". . . . The evil is plain; the means used by the faction which causes these disorders are so blamable in principle, so criminal in their application, and expose the faction itself to so many dangers, that. . . . we are convinced that society can no longer be saved without strong and vigorous resolutions on the part of the Governments. . . .

"By this course the monarchs will fulfill the duties imposed upon them by Him who, by entrusting them with power, has charged them to watch the maintenance of justice, and the rights of all, to avoid the paths of error. . . . and to show themselves as they are, fathers invested with the authority belonging by right to the heads of families, to prove that, in days of mourning, they know how to be just, wise, and therefore strong. . . .

"The Governments, in establishing the principle of stability, will in no wise exclude the development of what is good, for stability is not immobility. But it is for those who are burdened with the heavy task of government to augment the well-being of their people! It is for Governments to regulate it according to necessity and to suit the times. It is not by concessions, which the factious strive to force from legitimate power, . . . that wise reforms can be carried out. That all the good possible should be done is our most ardent wish; but . . . even real good should be done only by those who unite to the right of authority the means of enforcing it."

From Mrs. Alexander Napier, (trans.), Prince Richard Metternich (ed.), *Memoirs of Prince Metternich, 1815–1829.* Scribner's Sons Publishers, 1970.

prestige. Subsequent talk of reestablishing European authority in Latin America, however, brought stern warnings from Britain and the proud announcement of the Monroe Doctrine from the United States, declaring the Americas outside the sphere of European power politics. Metternich's concept of a European concert to maintain order was being circumscribed.

The Concert of Europe was hardly invoked at all when the Greeks revolted against Ottoman Turk rule in 1821. Cries for freedom from that home of ancient democracy excited liberals throughout Europe, an early demonstration of the power of nationalist movements that would be repeated throughout the century. Metternich restrained Russia from rushing to war against the Ottomans as it often had in the past, but he could not keep the British and French fleets from intervening in 1827, when the sultan seemed at last about to subdue the Greeks. Russia declared war a few months later. Greece was granted independence in 1829 on terms arranged by the European powers, stipulating that it must have a king but one who was not a member of the ruling family of a major power. With that policy, the leading European states altered the status quo after all. They did so partly in response to public opinion, but they also made sure that the Greek rising would go no further. In the name of Greek freedom, Britain, France, and Russia displayed a willingness to use force, a preoccupation with their own self-interest, and an eagerness to carve up the Ottoman Empire that foreshadowed the practice of imperialism later in the century.

▼ *Eugène Delacroix*
GREECE EXPIRING
The Greek revolution captured the imagination of many Europeans, and Delacroix's *Greece Expiring* **has all the elements of that fascination. Greece is symbolized by an ordinary peasant girl who is also a classical figure of liberty, come alive. The Turk in the background, a colorful and exotic figure of oppression, evokes centuries of conflict. Romanticism, nationalism, and political liberty come together on the stones of Greek culture and the arm of a martyred freedom fighter.**
Giraudon/Art Resource.

Chronology

CHALLENGES TO THE VIENNA SETTLEMENT

May 1814	Treaty of Paris
September 1814 – June 1815	Congress of Vienna
March 1815 – June 1815	Napoleon's 100 days
1817	German students at Wartburg
1820 – 1821	Revolts in Spain and Italy
1821 – 1829	Greek war of independence
1825	Decembrist rising in Russia
1830	Revolution in France, Belgium

THE PILLARS OF THE RESTORATION: RUSSIA, AUSTRIA, PRUSSIA

To maintain social order in the nineteenth century, the state would need to be more effective than before in order to maintain large armies and collect more taxes, support a better-trained bureaucracy, dispense justice more evenly, and provide more services. Because they would thus affect the lives of their subjects more directly, governments would have to be more concerned with popular sentiment. Even the most reactionary rulers accepted some of the changes (and the potential for increased power) brought by revolution, war, and Napoleonic occupation. The organization of the state became an issue even in conservative Russia, Austria, and Prussia, the guardians of the European restoration.

The Russian Empire   By 1820 Tsar Alexander had abandoned his earlier enthusiasm for new ideas. As Metternich's staunchest ally, Alexander imposed harsh censorship, increased restrictions on universities, and made sure that the constitution granted to the newly organized Kingdom of Poland was largely ignored. On Alexander's death in 1825, a group of young army officers, the Decembrists, attempted a coup and called for a constitution in Russia. Like the leaders of the revolts in Naples and Spain a few years earlier, the Decembrists saw a constitution as an essential step toward a more efficient and progressive administration. Their poorly planned and isolated conspiracy was easily defeated, but it would be remembered by conservatives as an ever-present danger and by revolutionaries as part of Russia's radical tradition. Alexander's younger brother, Nicholas I, succeeded him, convinced that only a loyal army and his own decisiveness had prevented revolution. He turned Russia into Europe's strongest pillar of reaction by his example at home and his willingness to use force abroad. He was a diligent administrator who gave his closest attention to the army and the police and who established a more effective bureaucracy by making it more directly responsible to the state and less attached to the nobility.

Nevertheless, petty corruption, the arrogance of local officials, and fear of change continued to undermine the government's capacity to manage a vast land of varied peoples in which communications were poor and few had the means or the will to effect reform. Most thoughtful people, including the state's highest officials, agreed that serfdom had become a hindrance to Russia's development. The commissions ordered to study the matter gathered data and noted that hundreds of peasant uprisings had had to be suppressed by force, but they proposed no solution. Despite fears that education bred discontent, the government built schools; and among the literate minority, discussion of Russia's future became a compelling theme. The government even attempted to establish a kind of official philosophy based on the teachings of the Russian Orthodox Church. Intellectuals who expected Russia to develop along familiar European lines were known as Westernizers. Those who stressed the uniqueness of Russia were called Slavophiles, and they argued that Russia's religion, peasant communes, and traditional culture gave Russia a unique destiny. Despite this urgent questioning about Russia's place in a changing world and despite loquacious exiles, bitter Poles, angry peasants, and its own im-

mobility, the authority of the Russian state remained. Nicholas would watch with pride in 1848 as his empire escaped the revolutions that swept over most of the thrones of Europe.

The Habsburg Empire Habsburg rule over German, Italian, and Eastern European lands relied on a well-organized bureaucracy. Forged by Maria Theresa and Joseph II, that system of government had enabled Austria to survive the Napoleonic wars without dramatic transformation despite repeated defeat. Metternich and others recognized the need for domestic reform, but their projects for better fiscal planning, stronger local government, and recognition of the empire's diverse nationalities came to nothing. Habsburg rule remained locked in stalemate between an increasingly cautious central bureaucracy and a selfish local aristocracy.

Hungary proved particularly troublesome for the Habsburg empire, for the dominant Magyar aristocracy had a strong sense of their historical identity and a good deal of power, although they remained a minority in their own country. Emperor Francis I grudgingly acknowledged many of their claims, and by the 1840s Magyar had replaced German as the official language of administration and schooling in Hungary. More demands followed. The campaign for a more representative parliament and related reforms was led by Lajos Kossuth, who became Hungary's leading statesman, able through newspapers and public meetings to reach much of the nation. This widespread agitation, stimulated by the example of nationalist ferment in Italy, encouraged other groups subject to Habsburg rule to claim national rights of their own. Much of Polish Galicia rose in revolt in 1846; but weakened by the bitter antagonism between Polish peasants and their masters, the uprising was soon suppressed. In Croatia and Bohemia, too, angry peasants and nationalists often had different aims. The various national groups opposed to Habsburg rule, often hostile to each other, were also internally divided by class, religion, and language. Their conflicts helped sustain Habsburg rule. Throughout the empire, however, growing nationalist movements sought to overcome these social divisions, giving broader appeal to criticisms of Habsburg rule that came mainly from merchants and lawyers. At the center, despite much good advice and many promising plans, inaction remained the safest compromise.

Prussia and the German Confederation Germans called the later battles against Napoleon (1813–1814) the Wars of Liberation; and after that common national experience, talk of "Germany" meant more than it had before. The Congress of Vienna acknowledged this awareness with the creation of the German Confederation. A cautious gesture toward national sentiment that preserved the position of the strongest local rulers while tacitly acknowledging the changes that French dominance had brought, a confederation required some coordination among Germany's many states. Any stronger union was prevented by the rivalry of Austria and Prussia, distaste for reform among restoration regimes, and the conflicting ambitions of German princes. The Confederation's diet, more a council of ambassadors from member states than a representative assembly, was permitted to legislate only on certain matters—characteristically, restriction of the press was one of them.

In practice, the German Confederation was important in German politics largely when Metternich wished to make it so. He used it, for example, to suppress agitation led by nationalist and reformist student groups in the universities. In 1817 some of these groups organized a celebration of the tercentenary of Luther's theses with a rally, the Wartburg Festival. Several hundred young people gathered to drink, listen to speeches

▼ German authorities worried greatly that university students would be a center of political agitation, and this print from a series on student life in the 1820s suggests why. Privileged, educated, and idle young men meeting to drink and smoke were all too likely to talk about politics, spread radical ideas, and maybe even hatch plots.
Archiv für Kunst und Geschichte.

Policing Universities—The Carlsbad Decrees

The Carlsbad Decrees, drafted by Metternich, were adopted by the Diet of the German Confederation in 1819 to be applied in all its member states.

"1. There shall be appointed for each university a special representative of the ruler of each state, the said representatives to have appropriate instructions and extended powers, and they shall have their place of residence where the university is located. . . .

"This representative shall enforce strictly the existing laws and disciplinary regulations, he shall observe with care the attitude shown by the university instructors in their public lectures and registered courses; and he shall, without directly interfering in scientific matters or in teaching methods, give a beneficial direction to the teaching, keeping in view the future attitude of the students. Finally, he shall give unceasing attention to everything that may promote morality . . . among the students. . . .

"2. The confederated governments mutually pledge themselves to eliminate from the universities or any other public educational institutions all instructors who shall have obviously proved their unfitness for the important work entrusted to them by openly deviating from their duties, or by going beyond the boundaries of their functions, or by abusing their legitimate influence over young minds, or by presenting harmful ideas hostile to public order or subverting existing governmental instructions. . . .

"Any instructor who has been removed in this manner becomes ineligible for a position in any other public institution of learning in another state of the Confederation.

"3. The laws that for some time have been directed against secret and unauthorized societies in the universities shall be strictly enforced. . . . The special representatives of the government are enjoined to exert great care in watching these organizations.

"The governments mutually agree that all individuals who shall be shown to have maintained their membership in secret or unauthorized associations, or shall have taken membership in such associations, shall not be eligible for any public office.

"4. No student who shall have been expelled from any university by virtue of a decision of the university senate ratified or initiated by the special representative of the government, shall be admitted by any other university. . . .

"As long as this edict remains in force, no publication which appears daily, or as a serial not exceeding twenty sheets of printed matter, shall be printed in any state of the Confederation without the prior knowledge and approval of the state officials. . . ."

Excerpt from Louis L. Snyder (ed.), *Documents of German History* Rutgers University Press, 1958, pp. 158–159.

full of mystical nationalist rhetoric, sing songs, and cheer as a corporal's cane and a Prussian military manual were tossed into a bonfire. Even such symbolic challenges to military authority alarmed governments in both Berlin and Vienna. When a well-known reactionary writer was assassinated, the Confederation was pressed into issuing the Carlsbad Decrees of 1819, which intensified censorship, proscribed dangerous professors and students, outlawed fraternities and political clubs, and required each state to guarantee that its universities would be kept safely conservative (see "Policing Universities—The Carlsbad Decrees").

Despite these fears, there was less agitation within the German Confederation than in most of the rest of Europe. In fact, the cultural life of these largely rural lands thrived in complacent university and market towns that seemed to eschew politics on a larger scale. Meanwhile, Prussian influence increased. Its national educational system was capped by the new but prestigious University of Berlin, its administration and its army seemed models of modern efficiency, and its policies included measures that stimulated economic growth. In 1818 Prussia lowered tariffs, allowing raw materials free entry into both its eastern and western Prussian territories. The results were so impressive that within a decade the Prussian tariff was adopted by many of the smaller states that Prussia nearly surrounded. By 1833 most German governments except Austria had joined Prussia's customs union, the *Zollverein,* which proved a further spur to commerce. One of the most important steps toward German unification under Prussia had been taken without nationalist intent. Prussia was finding ways to win the benefits of liberal institutions without liberal politics.

THE TEST OF RESTORATION: SPAIN, ITALY, AND FRANCE

The durability of the conservative order that the Congress of Vienna sought to impose would depend less on the autocracies in Russia, Austria, and Prussia than on the new regimes imposed in Spain, Italy, and France. There, the effects of revolution and Bonapartism had been woven into the fabric of public life. Intensely divided over questions of government—its form, powers, and policies—conservatives and liberals alike considered politics central to everything else.

Spain and Italy   In Spain the Bourbon king Ferdinand VII regained his throne in 1814 when Napoleon's army was expelled. Strong enough to denounce the constitution he had promised, Ferdinand was too weak to do much more. He benefited from patriotic resentment against French rule, but his government found no solution for its own inefficiency or the nation's poverty. In Spain's American colonies the revolts led by José de San Martín and Simón Bolívar gained strength, and in 1820 the army that was assembled in Spain to reconquer the colonies mutinied instead and marched on Madrid. The king was then forced to grant a constitution after all, and for three years the constitutional regime struggled to cope with Spain's enormous problems, weakened by its own dissension and its uncooperative monarch. The regime's restrictions on religious orders raised powerful opposition from the Church, freedom of the press produced more devastating criticism, and a constitution in Spain was no help in reconquering the rebellious colonies. When a French army once again crossed into Spain in 1823, this time with the blessing of the Concert of Europe and in the name of order, the Spaniards who had fought French invasion so heroically just ten years earlier were strangely acquiescent. The

constitution disappeared again, but the threat of revolution did not.

In Italy, restoration meant the return to power of the aristocracies the French had ousted and reestablishment of the separate Italian states.[2] Yet the years of Napoleonic rule had established institutions (and hopes) that the new regimes could not ignore, and they promised constitutions, enlightened administration, peace, and lower taxes even though their insecure rulers were hardly prepared to take such initiatives. Cautious, moderately repressive, and conveniently corrupt, these regimes provided the sleepy stability Metternich thought appropriate for Italians. Such an atmosphere bred some conspiracy and rumors of far more. Secret groups began to meet across Italy. Known collectively as the *Carbonari* (charcoal burners), they varied in membership and program. Most were middle class although their name suggested a life of rural simplicity. Some talked of tyrannicide, some promised equality and justice, and some sought mild reform; they had in common the excitement of secret meetings, terrifying oaths, and ornate rituals.

By 1820 news of revolution in Spain was enough to prompt revolts in Italy. Young army officers led the demand for a constitution in Naples; but as the Neapolitan army turned to put down a rising in Sicily, an Austrian army was dispatched to Naples to remove the new constitutional regime. A similar revolt erupted in Piedmont, causing the king to abdicate in favor of his son, and Charles Albert, the prince regent, hastily granted a constitution. But when the new monarch arrived, the Austrian army was with him. Piedmont's constitution lasted two weeks. These revolutions, which left Italy's reactionary governments more rigid and Austrian influence more naked, demonstrated the inadequacy of

---

[2] Italy was divided into three monarchies, four duchies, and a republic. The Kingdom of Sardinia (Sardinia and Piedmont), the Papal States, and the Kingdom of the Two Sicilies were monarchies. The Grand Duchy of Tuscany and the duchies of Lucca, Modena, and Parma were all tied to the Habsburgs, who annexed Lombardy and Venetia. The disappearance of the republics of Genoa (part of Piedmont) and Venice left tiny San Marino, safe on its mountain top, the oldest republic in the world.

romantic conspiracies but affirmed an Italian radical and patriotic tradition that would continue to grow.

The Bourbons Restored in France More than anything else, Europe's conservative order was meant to prevent France from again becoming the center of military aggression or revolutionary ideas, and the restoration there was an especially complex compromise. France was permitted a constitution called the Charter, presented as a gift from Louis XVIII and not as a right. It granted the legislature more authority than Napoleon had allowed but left the government largely in the hands of the king. The old estates were wisely forgotten, replaced by a Chamber of Peers with hereditary members and a Chamber of Deputies chosen by an electorate limited to prosperous landowners. Napoleon's centralized administration and effective system of taxation were willingly kept intact.

The regime's supporters, shaken by Napoleon's easy return during the Hundred Days, were determined to crush their enemies. A violent "white terror" broke out in parts of the countryside as those tainted with a revolutionary past were ousted from local office or even killed. Yet Louis XVIII resisted as best he could the more extreme demands of the reactionary ultraroyalists; land confiscated from the Church and from the émigré aristocracy during the Revolution was not returned to them, and most of those who had gained office or wealth since 1789 were allowed quietly to live out their lives. The king and his ministers, moderate and able men, pursued a course of administrative efficiency and political restraint. From 1816 to 1820 they governed well in a relatively peaceful and prosperous country, and Paris became again Europe's most brilliant center of science and the arts.

The Catholic Church, weakened in the intervening years by the loss of property and a decline in the number of new priests, revived remarkably. Missions of preachers toured the countryside calling for a return to the faith, praising the monarchy, and ceremonially planting crosses of repentance for the sins of revolution. The nobles, traditionally rather skeptical in matters of religion, were now more pious; and so, too, for the first time in more than a century, were France's

leading writers. To the surprise of many Catholics, however, the Concordat of 1801 remained in effect, another of Napoleon's institutional arrangements to prove remarkably lasting.

From Opposition to Revolution in France Despite its achievements, the regime remained insecure and uncertain, satisfying neither Catholics nor anticlericals, neither ultraroyalists nor liberals. The assassination of the duke of Berry in 1820 reminded everyone of how fragile the monarchy was. The duke was the son of Louis' younger brother and the last Bourbon likely to produce an heir. The royal line seemed doomed until the widowed duchess gave birth to a son eight months later. Louis XVIII reacted to the assassination by naming more conservative ministers, increasing restrictions on the press, and dismissing some leading professors. The air of reaction grew heavier in 1824 when his brother succeeded to the throne as Charles X. A leader of the ultraroyalists, Charles had himself crowned at Reims in medieval splendor, in a ceremony redolent with symbols of the divine right of kings and the alliance of throne and altar.

The new government gave the Church fuller control of education, declared sacrilege a capital crime, and granted a cash indemnity to those who had lost land in the Revolution. In reality, the law against sacrilege was never enforced, and the indemnity, which helped end one of the most dangerous issues left from the Revolution, was a limited one. France remained freer than most European countries, but Charles' subjects worried about the intentions of an ultraroyalist regime that disliked the compromises on which it rested. Public criticism increased, leading politicians joined the parliamentary opposition, and radical secret societies blossomed. Disturbed by liberal gains in the elections of 1827, Charles X dutifully tried a slightly more moderate ministry, but he could not conceal his distaste for it. By 1829 the king could stand no more. While political disputes grew more inflamed, he appointed a cabinet of ultraroyalists only to have the Chamber of Deputies reject them. He called new elections, but instead of regaining seats the ultraroyalists lost still more. Determined not to show the hesitancy of Louis XVI, Charles X reacted with firmness. In 1830 he and his ministers suddenly issued a set of secretly drafted decrees, the July Ordinances, which dissolved the new Chamber of Deputies even before it met, further restricted suffrage, and muzzled the press. Having shown his fiber, the king went hunting.

A shocked Paris slowly responded. Crowds began to mill about, some barricades went up, and stones were thrown at the house of the prime minister. Newspapers disregarded the ordinances and denounced the violation of the constitution, and the government responded with enough troops to raise tempers but too few to enforce order. Charles began to back down, but people were being killed (nearly seven hundred died in the three days of Paris fighting), some of the soldiers were mingling with the crowds, and liberal leaders were planning for a new regime. Once again, Paris was the scene of a popular uprising, and Charles X, victim of what he most detested, abdicated on August 2. For fifteen years, and for the only time in its history, France had been administered by its aristocracy, which had performed with probity and seriousness. The nation had prospered at home and enjoyed some success in foreign affairs, but the monarchy had been meant above all to provide political stability, which the Bourbon regime, the restoration's most important experiment, had failed to do.

II. The Progress of Industrialization

Political instability was one sign of a larger process of economic and social change. Economic growth stimulated further growth as new inventions, the demand for more capital, factory organization, more efficient transportation, and increased consumption created a cycle of economic expansion. All of society would feel the effects as land ceased to be the primary and surest source of wealth and the poor crowded into cities to seek the wages on which survival depended.

THE TECHNOLOGY TO SUPPORT MACHINES

Industrialization required the efficient use of raw materials, beginning with cheap metals, such as

▲ This official portrait of Charles X by François Gerard, in the up-to-date romantic style, echoes the portraits of Louis XIV and suggests the way a regime that looked to the past wanted to be seen. Chateau de Versailles/Giraudon/Bridgeman.

iron, which could be formed into machines, and cheap fuel such as coal. The increased importance of iron and coal gave England an important advantage, for it was well supplied with deposits of coal that lay conveniently close to its iron ore.

Coal, Iron, and Steam The English had increasingly turned to the use of coal as the once-great forests were cut down, and miners had begun taking coal from deeper veins, often beneath the water table. The need for powerful pumps to remove the water stimulated experiments to harness

▲ The crucial resource of industrialization was coal, and coal mining was one of the earliest industrial activities, employing steam engines to pump water and creating large, polluting enterprises in which hundreds of workers labored as drones, as at this English mine in Northumberland.
Mary Evans Picture Library.

steam. Coal was not useful in smelting iron, however, because its impurities combined with the iron, resulting in an inferior product. For high-quality wrought iron, ironmasters therefore traditionally used charcoal, which was expensive. This problem stimulated experiments by eighteenth-century engineers in smelting with coke prepared from coal to produce pig iron, which could be cast but not worked or machined. As demand for iron and steel increased, the search for new techniques continued, resulting in the 1780s in the puddling process, the first commercially feasible effort to purify iron using coke alone. It was a breakthrough that convinced ironmasters like John Wilkinson that iron would be the building material of a new age. His improved techniques for boring cylinders made it possible to make better cannons and steam engines, and he built the world's first iron bridge over the Severn River in 1779, experimented with iron rails, launched an iron boat, and at his death was buried in an iron coffin.

The development of steam power also had a long history. In the third century Hero of Alexandria had employed a jet of steam to spin a small wheel, and the account of his experiments, translated into English in 1575, suggested one means by which heat could be converted into motion. The first modern steam engines were based on another principle, however. In the seventeenth century several scientists proved that the atmosphere has weight, and Otto von Guericke in Germany used atmospheric pressure to push a piston through a cylinder, overcoming the efforts of twenty men to restrain it. Such sensational experiments encouraged construction of an "atmospheric engine," which required creating a partial vacuum, and before the end of the seventeenth century, atmospheric machines using the condensation of steam to create the needed vacuum were being designed both in England and on the continent.

The Steam Engine   The first commercially successful atmospheric engine was invented in England by Thomas Savery, who described it in a book published in 1702 and significantly entitled *The Miner's Friend.* Used as a pump, Savery's engine was woefully inefficient; but a decade later another Englishman, Thomas Newcomen, returned to the piston and cylinder design, which completely separated engine and pump and proved a third more efficient. Newcomen engines were soon being used not only in Great Britain but in France, Denmark, Austria, and Hungary.

The most fundamental step in the development of steam was the work of James Watt, a young mechanic and instrument maker working at the University of Glasgow. In the 1760s he made important improvements on the Newcomen engine, while still relying on atmospheric pressure pushing against a vacuum. But he also recognized the enormous potential in the direct pressure created when expanding steam pushed against a piston. His work took years, for it required new levels of precision in machining cylinders and pistons, new designs for valves, and new knowledge of lubricants and the properties of steam itself. Patented in 1782, Watt's first practical model was nearly three times more efficient than the Newcomen engine. Once he added a system of gears for converting the

II: THE PROGRESS OF INDUSTRIALIZATION **775**

piston's reciprocating motion to the rotary motion needed to drive most machines, the steam engine had become much more than a pump.

Getting these inventions into use required the business talents of Watt's partner, the Birmingham industrialist Matthew Boulton. He recognized that the demand for cheap power had become more critical with the new inventions in the textile industry (including Arkwright's water frame, Crompton's spinning mule, and Cartwright's power loom). From the 1780s on, the steam engine was being used in factories, and some five hundred were built before 1800. Even these early machines represented a remarkable improvement over traditional sources of power. They produced between six and twenty horsepower,[3] comparable to the largest windmills and water mills, and did so more reliably and wherever they were needed. An economy traditionally starved for sources of power had overcome that obstacle.

THE ECONOMIC EFFECTS OF REVOLUTION AND WAR

Great Britain's lead over continental countries in goods produced, capital invested, and machinery employed had widened steadily from 1789 to 1815. Nonetheless, there had been economic growth on the continent, too, where the exploitation of resources became more systematic, population increased, transportation generally improved, the means of mobilizing capital for investment expanded, and more and more political and business leaders were concerned with speeding industrial growth. In important respects the French Revolution and the Napoleonic era had cleared the way for future industrialization. In France, western Germany, northern Italy, and the Low Countries, land tenure was no longer the most pressing economic and social issue. Less

constrained by custom and legal restrictions, landowners, including peasant proprietors, could more easily shift their production to meet the demands of a national market. The abolition of guilds and old commercial restrictions had eliminated some obstacles to the free movement of workers and the establishment of new enterprises. The Napoleonic Code and French commercial law not only favored free contracts and an open marketplace but also introduced the advantages of uniform and clear commercial regulations. The French government had exported a common and sensible standard of weights and measures, encouraged the establishment of technical schools (the Polytechnic School in Paris long remained the world's best), and honored inventors and inventions of every sort, from improved gunpowder to new techniques for raising sugar beets. Under Napoleon, Europe had benefited from improved highways and bridges and a large zone of free trade; and the Bank of France, as restructured in 1800, had become the European model of a bank of issue providing a reliable currency.

In the short run, however, the years of war had slowed and disrupted Europe's economic growth. Vast resources in material and men were destroyed or wastefully used up. When peace came, governments were burdened with heavy debts, and returning soldiers had to find ways to support themselves in a changed economy. The Continental System, which had initially swung production and trade in France's favor, had collapsed with Napoleon's fall, bringing down many of the enterprises that it had artificially sustained. Both political change and renewed British competition discouraged daring capital investment. During the war, Great Britain had found compensation in American markets for its exclusion from continental ones and had avoided the shock of military invasion; but it, too, suffered a severe slump in the postwar years when the anticipated continental demand for British goods failed to materialize and the transition to a peacetime economy proved difficult to achieve.

PATTERNS OF INDUSTRIALIZATION

By the mid-1820s, however, British trade was reviving, and by 1830 its economy was being transformed. Although no single industry was yet fully mechanized, the pattern of industrialization was

---

[3] The average man working hard can muster about one-tenth horsepower, or about seventy-five watts; the horse itself works continuously at a power output of only one-half horsepower. James Watt first defined the unit of horsepower as 33,000 foot-pounds per minute, but this could be achieved only by the strongest horses and only for short periods. The largest windmills in the eighteenth century could develop probably as much as fifty horsepower, but perhaps two-thirds of this was lost in friction. The best water mills seem to have produced ten horsepower, but most of them rarely surpassed five.

clear. Later, that pattern would be repeated in much of the world, but contemporaries attributed England's leadership to unique advantages. Cotton had become the most important industry, benefiting from a large consumer market as spinning cotton thread and then weaving the cloth were mechanized. Growth in one economic sector stimulated growth in others. Increased textile production, for example, accelerated the use of chemical dyes; greater iron production required more coal. A few factories in one place encouraged the growth of others in the same region, where they could take advantage of the available work force and capital; this concentration of production in turn increased the demand for roads, canals, and later, railways. All this growth required more capital, and on the cycle went. In continuity, range of industries affected, national scope, and rate of increase, Great Britain's industrial growth in the first half of the nineteenth century was the greatest humankind had yet experienced.

Railroads New inventions became whole industries and were integrated into the economy with dazzling speed. The steam engine's application to rail travel is a classic case. The first successful steam railway line was built in England in 1825; a few years later an improved engine impressed spectators by outracing a horse, and in 1830 the first passenger line took its riders the thirty-two miles from Liverpool to Manchester in an hour and a quarter. Just more than a decade later, there were 2,000 miles of such rail lines in Great Britain; by 1851 there were 7,000 (see "Gladstone Argues for Regulating Railroad Fares," p. 777).

Railroads constituted a new industry that stimulated further industrialization. They bought huge quantities of iron and coal. They carried food and raw materials to cities, manufactured products to consumers, and building materials and fertilizers to the countryside. And they made it easier for the men and women who crowded into dirt-stained railway cars to travel in search of work. Similarly, the telegraph, developed by a generation of scientists working in many countries and quickly adopted as an adjunct of railroading, expanded to other uses, becoming a military necessity and a conveyor of news to the general public. The most impressive of the early long telegraph lines was Samuel F. B. Morse's

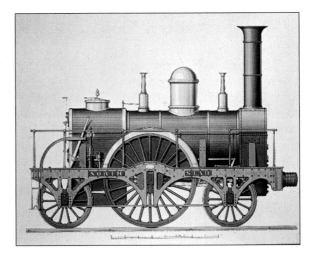

▲ Stephenson's North Star engine of 1837 was meant to be an object of beauty, combining technology and craftsmanship.
Science Museum, London/Bridgeman Art Library.

from Philadelphia to Washington, opened in 1843. Less than a decade later, Britain laid 4,000 miles of telegraph lines, and a cable to the continent was in operation.

Yet the leap from new invention to industrialization was not necessarily direct or predictable. Often dozens of subsidiary inventions or improvements were necessary to make a new machine competitive. Everywhere, but more often on the continent than in Britain, small-scale manufacturing and crafts persisted alongside the new. Machines themselves were usually made of wood and were frequently still driven by wind, waterpower, or horses. But the water-driven mills, charcoal-fired smelters, and hand-powered looms that dotted the countryside would be gradually but relentlessly displaced, as would hundreds of thousands of skilled artisans and rural families working in their homes to make products in the old ways—a transformation that accounted for much of the human suffering occasioned by industrialization.

National Differences In 1815 many regions of the continent, including such traditional commercial centers as Barcelona and Naples, had seemed ready to follow the British example of industrial growth, but by the 1850s the zone of industrialization had narrowed to include only

GLADSTONE ARGUES FOR REGULATING RAILROAD FARES

Sir Robert Peel supported his young colleague, William Gladstone, in trying to push a bill for the regulation of railroads through the English Parliament. Conflicting interests eventually forced Gladstone's plan to be watered down (there was great fear that the government would seek to purchase private railroad companies and considerable opposition to its regulating them very heavily); but Gladstone won his point, set forth in his speech on July 8, 1844, that Parliament should have a voice in setting rates as a matter of social policy.

"Of the forty Clauses of the Bill, twenty-four related to the provisions respecting purchase; those from the twenty-fifth to the twenty-eighth related to third-class passengers. He must say that he felt strongly that the case of the third-class passengers by those trains was becoming a national question of great importance, and though averse to any general interference by Government with the management of these Companies, he did think it was wise to make a provision while it could be done without any breach of public faith, whereby those persons—being, as they were frequently, the least able to bear exposure to the cold, and obliged to remove frequently in search of bread, from one part of the country to the other—might be able to transfer themselves at the charge of 1*d.* a mile, without such exposure to the severity of the weather as amounted in many cases to severe personal suffering. It was on that ground they had introduced Clauses which certainly, so far as they went, were of the nature of interference. There were other Clauses regarding the public service, access of the public to the station and yards, conduct of inspectors, the prosecution of Railway Companies who exceeded the powers for which they were incorporated, contracts with Government, loan notes, and other matters so trivial that he need not mention them. . . .

" . . . With railways the Legislature were dealing with a new system producing new results, and likely to produce unforeseen effects. Was it not wise, then, to make provision for the future? Was it wise to trust themselves to all changes which the next ten or fifteen years might produce with regard to public communication by railway, without a thought for providing for the difficulties that might arise. Was it wise to place themselves in a position in which, whatever might be the exigency, they would be debarred from any interference."

From *Hansard's Parliamentary Debates:* Third Series, Volume LXXVI, 1844.

northeastern France, Belgium and the Netherlands, western Germany, and northern Italy. Industrial change in this zone was uneven but more extensive than outside it. Countries poorly endowed in coal and iron, such as Italy, faced formidable obstacles. Although Saxony in eastern Germany was an early industrial center, most of Germany remained an area of quiet villages in which commerce relied on peddlers and trade fairs, even though by midcentury the German states were crisscrossed by the continent's largest railway network. Except for pockets of industrial development, Eastern Europe remained a world of agricultural estates. The centuries-old Atlantic triangular trade declined in importance as did the European ports that had depended on commerce in sugar and raw materials, now overshadowed by the export of manufactured goods and the entrepreneurial activity of merchants on both sides of the ocean.

Belgium, which had prospered from its former connections with Holland, built on its tradition of technological skill, its geographical advantages as a trade center accessible by water, and its excellent supplies of coal to become the continent's first industrialized nation. Belgium extracted more coal than did France or Germany and was the first country to complete a railway network. The French railway system, on the other hand, was not finished until after Germany's, for it was slowed by political conflict despite early and ambitious plans. France's canals, considered good in 1815,

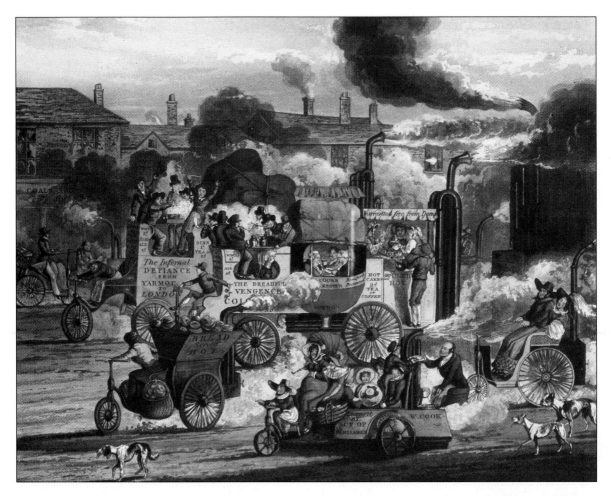

▲ **By 1830 it was possible to conceive of life transformed by technology as in this imagined view of what London's important White Chapel road might soon become, with traffic jams and smog but on an unpaved road with room for dogs.**
National Railway Museum, York/Bridgeman Art Library.

had trebled by 1848; and its production of iron, coal, and textiles increased severalfold in the same period. This growth would have been impressive a generation earlier, but Britain's expansion in each of these sectors was several times greater. In iron production, for example, the two countries were about equal in 1800, but by 1850 Britain's output was six or seven times greater. Britain outstripped France still more in textiles and coal, producing by midcentury half the world total of these items.

Everywhere, increased production led to more commerce and closer international ties as capital, techniques, workers, and managers moved from Britain across the channel and spread from Belgium and France into the rest of Europe. Finance became so internationally linked that the Bank of France granted an emergency loan to the Bank of England in 1825, only a decade after Waterloo; and the domestic banking policies of the United States, in response to a financial panic in 1837, led to a wave of crises in the financial centers of Europe.

State Politics Although many writers argued that the new prosperity followed from natural economic laws that worked best unimpeded by government, by midcentury the state was centrally involved in the process of economic growth. Railroads required franchises and the power of eminent domain before a spike was pounded. Inevitably, routes, rates, and even the gauge of the

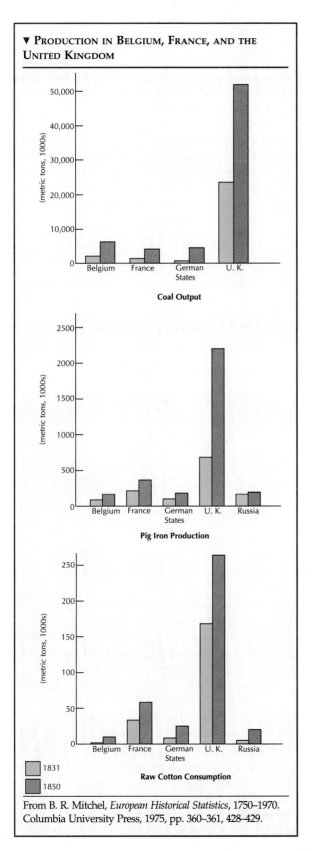

▼ Production in Belgium, France, and the United Kingdom

Coal Output

Pig Iron Production

Raw Cotton Consumption

☐ 1831
☐ 1850

From B. R. Mitchel, *European Historical Statistics, 1750–1970.* Columbia University Press, 1975, pp. 360–361, 428–429.

track became political matters to be settled by parliaments or special commissions. In Belgium and in most of Germany, railroads were owned as well as planned by the state.

Tariffs, the dominant issue in British politics in the 1840s, became a critical question in every country. In 1846, after a wrenching public campaign, Britain abolished the tariff on grain, known as the Corn Laws. In doing so the nation expressed confidence in its position as the world's greatest center of manufacture and sided with those who favored trade and a lower price for bread rather than with the landowners who benefited from higher grain prices. Equally important to economic development was the role of government in banking and currency. Just before the middle of the century, Parliament granted the Bank of England a monopoly on issuing money and required companies to register with the government and publish their annual budget as a guide to investors. Similar steps were taken across Europe. Before industries could effectively tap private wealth, investors needed assurance that they risked only the money they invested, without being liable (as in a partnership) for all a firm's debts. That assurance required new legislation establishing limited liability and encouraging the formation of corporations, and every major country passed such measures.

The Role of Government The growth of cities and the benefits of new technology created additional social demands involving government. By the 1840s most cities had a public omnibus, some sidewalks, and gas lighting in certain areas. Such services, usually provided by private companies, had to be subsidized, regulated, and given legal protection by the government. As the cost and importance of these services increased, so did the state's participation in them, often extending to full ownership. The growing role of government was exemplified by the postal service, which most states had provided since the seventeenth and eighteenth centuries. These postal systems, which were with few exceptions graft-ridden and unreliable, proved inadequate for an industrial era. In Britain demands for improvement led a little-known inventor and radical to propose a solution that captured the thinking of the new age. He called for standard envelopes and payment in advance by means of an adhesive stamp. That, he said, using current arguments, would not only eliminate graft and reduce costs but the service would pay for itself because lower rates would increase volume. His reforms, denounced as dangerous and impractical, passed nevertheless in 1840; and within twenty years the volume of mail in Britain increased sixfold. By then, money orders, savings accounts, and the telegraph had been added to postal services. In France mail delivery was extended to rural areas, and by the 1850s every major government was adopting the new system, including the postage stamp, which quickly became the object of a fashionable middle-class hobby.

Effective government, in short, was now expected to further economic development—by subsidizing ports, transportation, and new inventions; by registering patents and sponsoring education; by encouraging investment and enforcing contracts; and by maintaining order and preventing strikes. In the 1840s the leaders of Britain, France, and Belgium busily did these things—in Great Britain the number of government employees increased about fourfold in the first half of the century—and the desire in other countries to have governments that would similarly foster economic development was an important element in the revolutions of 1848 and the nationalist movements of the period that followed.

The Crystal Palace The British celebrated their position as the masters of industrialization in 1851 with the first international industrial exhi-

▼ **A glass cathedral enclosing trees, statues, and fountains, the Crystal Palace organized national exhibits as a kind of encyclopedia of world industry, with subcategories for different products, as in the Indian exhibit at the left.**
Art Resource, NY, Guildhall Library, London/Bridgeman, Radio Times/Hulton Picture Library.

was the wealthiest nation in history,[4] and over the next twenty years, it would continue to increase its lead in goods produced.

III. The Social Effects

Economic growth on such a scale was accompanied by far-reaching social change. Even in its early stages, industrialization impinged on all of society, from the state to the family, affecting governmental functions, the nature of work, women's roles, and childhood. Child labor, tyrannical foremen, teeming slums, and unemployment brought new social problems and required new social policies as the growing prosperity and security of the middle class contrasted all the more sharply with the destitution of the urban poor.

THE DIVISION OF LABOR

The Factory The factory quickly became the symbol of the age. Well before industrialization there had been workplaces in which hundreds of people labored under one roof, and conversely even in industrialized societies, most wage earners did not work in factories. But the factory symbolized a different kind of power—the power of steam and of technology, the power of capital to assemble machinery and laborers, the power of competition to drive down prices and wages, the power of markets to absorb ever more production and determine what would be produced. Above all, the factory symbolized the capacity of this whole system to change the landscape, to erect or transform cities, and to reshape the lives of masses of men, women, and children.

The factory model was most clearly triumphant in the production of textiles. Spinning and weaving had always been domestic tasks; even in Europe's most important textile centers, where merchants collected the output from hundreds of looms, the actual work had been done primarily in the home, where it might involve all the family. The most successful weavers often employed other workers, so

▲ British products dominated the machinery section of the Crystal Palace Exhibition. Here men and women marveled at Joseph Whitworth's lathe for forming railway wheels, a machine for making machines.
Guildhall Library, London/Bridgeman Art Library.

bition. Prominent people from the aristocracy, business, and government joined in the planning, and a specially designed pavilion was built in London, a sort of giant greenhouse called the Crystal Palace, which proved to be an architectural milestone. Many governments feared that Britain risked revolution by attracting huge mobs to London, but the admiring crowds proved well behaved.

The exhibition provided a significant comparison of the relative economic development of the participating countries. Russia displayed primarily raw materials; Austria showed mainly luxury handicrafts. So did the German *Zollverein* and the Italian states, whose appearance as single economic units foretold the advantages of national unification. Although unable to fill all the space it had demanded, the United States impressed viewers with collections of fossils, cheap manufactured products for use in the home, mountains of dentifrice and soap, and a series of new inventions, including Colt revolvers, a sewing machine, McCormick's reaper, and a vacuum coffin. French machines, which ranged from a much-admired device for folding envelopes to a submarine, were generally considered the most elegant. But British machines surpassed everyone's in quantity, size, and variety. It is, explained London's *Morning Chronicle*, "to our wonderful industrial discipline—our consummately arranged organization of toil, and our habit of division of labour—that we owe all the triumph." By 1850 Great Britain

---

[4] Although all estimates for this period are uncertain, it seems likely that by 1860 the per capita wealth of the French was about two-thirds and of the Germans about two-fifths that of the British.

▲ **This Nasmyth steam hammer looms above the men who endure heat and noise to feed it— in every way the symbol of a new era.**
Science Museum, London.

that the average domestic establishment contained about a half-dozen weavers. Pay and working conditions varied with the region, the season, and the ability of middlemen to control the prices of the thread they supplied and the cloth they purchased and resold. Textile factories, on the other hand, required an investment in buildings, machinery, and raw materials far beyond the reach of most weavers; and production per worker increased more than a thousandfold with the factory's efficient organization and power-driven machinery. By the 1830s cotton factories in Manchester, larger than most, averaged nearly three hundred employees.

These factories would slowly drive the older forms of textile production out of business, although the flexibility of domestic production (and the weavers' hatred of factories) long kept the older ways alive in some regions and for special products. Those who came to work in a factory might be former weavers, but they were likely to be less skilled laborers (often migrants) driven by poverty. Most were women and children, hired to tend power looms, splice thread, or sweep the floor. Children were paid less than women and women less than men, who did the heaviest work and served as carpenters and mechanics. At first, children usually worked with their parents, even

in the factories; but increased specialization meant that, like their mothers and fathers, children came to be employed and supervised without regard to family ties.

Factory Life The workday usually began at 5:30 or 6:00 in the morning and lasted for twelve hours of work plus whatever time was allotted for meals and for recesses (when belts were replaced and machinery fixed). The workroom, hot in summer and cold in winter, was usually kept moist so the taut thread would break less readily. Employers, concerned about keeping the expensive machinery running, found their workers too often lethargic and sullen, prone to drunkenness and indifference. To maintain the discipline that efficient production demanded, foremen used whips, curses, and most of all, fines (fines for lateness, for slacking off, for flawed work, for talking, and sometimes even for singing or whistling).

The best employers, like the middle-class reformers and the inspectors subsequently appointed as the result of factory legislation, were shocked by these conditions, and by the workers themselves, in whom they discovered foul language, filthiness, poor health, ignorance, and promiscuity. Factory owners could see no solution beyond more discipline, and nearly all employers opposed such measures as the law finally passed in England in 1847 that limited the workday to ten hours. Even that legislation was primarily an embarrassed response to the evils of child labor, which had been bitterly criticized by reformers and intellectuals, as in this excerpt from Elizabeth Barrett Browning's poem *The Cry of the Children* published in 1843:

And well may the children weep before you!
    They are weary ere they run.
They have never seen the sunshine, 'nor the glory,
    Which is brighter than the sun.
They know the grief of man, without his wisdom.
    They sink in man's despair, without its calm;
Are slaves, without the liberty in Christendom,
    Are martyrs, by the pang without the palm,—
Are worn, as if with age, yet unretrievingly
    The harvest of its memories cannot reap,—
Are orphans of the earthly love and heavenly,
    Let them weep! Let them weep!

▲ Under the foreman's close supervision, women kept the textile looms running.

Many workers, especially those with established skills—hatters, masons, tanners, typesetters, bakers, and eventually, steam-engine makers—took the lead in forming labor organizations and agitating for political redress. Although skilled laborers tended to look down on factory workers, the latter were, in income at least, better off than about half of all laborers; and their lot improved a bit as legislation hesitantly restricted hours and set some standards of hygiene and safety.

Differentiation The increased division of labor was not limited to the allocation of work within factories, and sociologists use the term *differentiation* to describe the spread of specialization among groups and institutions that was a characteristic of the nineteenth century. Just as factories separated work from family life, so money exchange and legal contracts differentiated economic from personal or social relationships. Business affairs and governmental functions became more specialized, matters determined by calculation or regulation rather than status or social connection. Maintaining the peace, collecting taxes, inspecting factories and schools, and administering welfare measures fell to separate agencies. In addi-

tion, social tasks (such as the registration of births and deaths and provisions for education and charity) that had once been performed more informally and largely through the churches, were now increasingly absorbed by the state—another reason for the importance of politics in this period. Just as each trade and each locality followed its own course of social change, so each nation differed in the pace and manner of institutional differentiation. Britain, more than continental states, left many public matters to local government and private groups; in France the role of the national government increased; and the German states tended to combine centralizing bureaucracies with considerable local autonomy. Whatever the pattern, the growth of differentiation brought increased professionalization and exposed tensions between government and established interests, between national policy and local custom.

THE FAMILY

To a great many nineteenth-century observers, social change threatened to undermine the family, and moralists of every sort warned that the very institution most central to civilization was in danger. Recent research has suggested a different view. The heightened concern for the family was a response to real stress, but it was also an expression of a growing belief in the importance of the family, which would prove to be an extraordinarily adaptable institution.

Traditional Roles Family life in Europe had always been related to social status. For the aristocracy, family encompassed a wide network of relatives, privilege, and power. Women played a critical but subordinate role as carriers of the dowries that joined estates, as managers of large domestic staffs, and as centers of the social circles in which aristocrats met. Among peasants, the family unit might include grandparents or, where plots were large enough, even in-laws, cousins, and nephews. Particularly in the Mediterranean regions, such extended families often shared housing in the village but worked in different nearby fields. When they could, however, a young couple generally set up a household of their own. In regions where peasants owned land, they had difficulty keeping it intact while giving something to all their children. Law and custom might require equal division of inheritance (as in France), primogeniture (inheritance by the eldest son, as in England), or other more complicated arrangements. But everywhere bitter disputes were frequent, for the elderly feared dispossession and the children feared that they would not get their share in time.

The family was the basic economic unit, pooling income from various sources and dividing labor in customary ways. Women usually handled household chores and the smaller animals, the men were responsible for the heavier work, and everyone worked together in critical periods of planting and harvest. Often the women had more access than the men to additional sources of income—piecework from a nearby mill or domestic service for the well-to-do—and they played a central role in marketing. Men, on the other hand, were more likely to travel considerable distances, especially in difficult times, in order to pick up a bit of work on roads or docks or at some great landlord's harvest. As population increased, the children were more often pushed out to seek employment in the nearest mills and towns.

▲ The bourgeois family at breakfast: perfect domestic harmony, father looks up from the morning newspaper to enjoy the scene of an angelic child and adoring wife, a servant tends to them in front of the Chinese screen that sets off the eating space. Tallandier.

The Impact of Industrialization For artisans, too, the family was often the unit of production, although the division of tasks by sex was usually more explicit, and even small workshops had long tended to exclude women, at least from the better-paid tasks. Working-class women and children were accustomed to long hours of labor. The strain on the family in the industrial age came rather from the lack of housing, the conditions of work, and the need for cash, which was compounded by the risk of unemployment. Not only did women and children have to supplement the father's income, but they were less and less likely to work side by side; if taught a trade, children were less likely to learn it from their parents. Sometimes the father, with his preindustrial skills, remained unemployed and did housework while his wife and children earned wages, which the socialist Friedrich Engels believed was another source of "the righteous indignation of the workers at being virtually turned into eunuchs."

Adolescents in factory towns, hardened at an early age, were probably more likely to leave home when their pay allowed, and urban conditions made it more difficult for the family to support the aged and the sick. Such factors did weaken family ties, as did—at least in the eyes of the upper classes—the common practice for working men and women to live together without the trouble or expense of formal marriage rites. Yet among workers, too, the family survived, and the home remained a special place expected to provide protection for small children, a haven for wage earners, and temporary shelter for relatives come to seek a job.

Women's Roles The fact that women worked for pay may also have slowly lessened their domestic subordination, even if it did not lead directly to the new and superior stage of family life that Karl Marx thought it might. In the lower-middle class, especially in France, women were as important as and frequently more visible than men in operating small shops. The life of the middle-class woman, however, contrasted greatly with that of her poorer sisters, and the role allotted to wife and mother became one of the most apparent and important indicators of social status. Women continued to be the organizers, patrons, critics, and ornaments of many of Europe's most cultivated circles; but the middle class isolated women from the harsh competition of business and politics. As the contemporary French historian Jules Michelet complained, "By a singular set of circumstances—social, economic, religious—man lives separated from woman." In Victorian England gentlemen met in their clubs or withdrew from the ladies after dinner for their cigars and weighty talk.

Except for the well-to-do who had domestic (female) servants, wives of every class—no matter what their other burdens—were expected to prepare and serve the food, wash and mend clothes, and clean the home. Victorian discourse often made the ideal of femininity appear to be an idle and pallid creature, encased in corset or bustle, whose tendency to faint was a sign of delicacy. In reality women's roles were far more significant and varied, but the image may well have reflected values widely shared. Allowing a wife to be idle even if her husband worked hard was a kind of conspicuous consumption, a partial imitation of aristocratic elegance. There were signs, too, of an unconscious effort to sustain a sort of counterculture. If men must be competitive, hard, and practical, women should be tender, innocent, and gracious—the weak but pure upholders of morality and aesthetic sensibility. The middle-class woman with no estate to manage and few servants to direct was almost literally placed on a pedestal. Neither her needlework nor her piano playing was viewed as serious, but her role in maintaining the protective calm of the home and as exemplar of the moral virtues was.

Moral Seriousness Middle-class concern with the family also emphasized the special moral role of women within the home, conceived as a private citadel largely closed to the outside world. The liberal dream of combining individualism and social order found its model in the family, where the patriarchal father, devoted mother, and carefully trained children were meant to live in disciplined harmony. Childhood itself lasted longer in the middle class, for manners, education, and character required elaborate preparation. The mother was the core of this home; and books, newspapers, magazines, and sermons enthusiastically described the talents her role required. Motherhood was treated as an honored occupation, fondly depicted in novels and in the new women's magazines founded, like the Parisian *Journal des Femmes* of 1832, to make women "skilled in their duties as companions and mothers."

Clearly, these attitudes were related to the famous prudery of the age and the distrust of sexual passion. In 1818 Thomas Bowdler produced his *Family Shakespeare,* a "bowdlerized" version "in which . . . those words and phrases are omitted which cannot with propriety be read in a family," a strange sensitivity after two hundred years of admiration for Shakespeare's dramas. And "the anti-English pollution of the waltz . . . the most degenerating that the last or present century can see"

Reports on the Housing Crisis in France and Germany

The housing crisis was not limited to cities with a lot of new industry, as these two descriptions, expressing the shock of middle-class reformers, show. The first is from André Guépin, Nantes au XIXe siécle (Nantes, 1835); the second, giving Dr. Bluemner's impression of Breslau, is from Alexander Schneer, Über die Zuständer der arbeitenden Klassen in Breslau (Berlin, 1845).

"If you want to know how he [the poorer worker] lives, go—for example—to the Rue des Fumiers which is almost entirely inhabited by this class of worker. Pass through one of the drain-like openings, below street-level, that lead to these filthy dwellings, but remember to stoop as you enter. One must have gone down into these alleys where the atmosphere is as damp and cold as a cellar; one must have known what it is like to feel one's foot slip on the polluted ground and to fear a stumble into the filth: to realise the painful impression that one receives on entering the homes of these unfortunate workers. Below street-level on each side of the passage there is a large gloomy cold room. Foul water oozes out of the walls. Air reaches the room through a sort of semi-circular window which is two feet high at its greatest elevation. Go in—if the fetid smell that assails you does not make you recoil. Take care, for the floor is uneven, unpaved and untiled—or if there are tiles, they are covered with so much dirt that they cannot be seen. And then you will see two or three rickety beds fitted to one side because the cords that bind them to the worm-eaten legs have themselves decayed. Look at the contents of the bed—a mattress; a tattered blanket of rags (seldom washed since there is only one); sheets sometimes; and a pillow sometimes. No wardrobes are needed in these homes. Often a weaver's loom and a spinning wheel complete the furniture. There is no fire in the winter. No sunlight penetrates [by day], while at night a tallow candle is lit. Here men work for fourteen hours [a day]."

"*Question:* What is the condition of the living quarters of the class of factory workers, day labourers and journeymen?

Reply of the City Poor Doctor, Dr. Bluemner: It is in the highest degree miserable. Many rooms are more like pigsties than quarters for human beings. The apartments in the city are, if possible, even worse than those in the suburbs. The former are, of course, always in the yard, if places in which you can hardly turn round can be called apartments. The so-called staircase is generally completely in the dark. It is also so decrepit that the whole building shakes with every firm footstep; the rooms themselves are small and so low that it is hardly possible to stand upright, the floor is on a slope, since usually part of the house has to be supported by struts. The windows close badly, the stoves are so bad that they hardly give any heat but plenty of smoke in the room. Water runs down the doors and walls. The ground-floor dwellings are usually half underground."

From Sidney Pollard and Colin Holmes (eds.), *Documents of European Economic History*, Vol. 1. St. Martin's Press, 1968, pp. 494–495, 497–498.

was denounced in *The Ladies' Pocket Book of Etiquette* of 1840. The middle classes sought to maintain an orderly world through convention. At a time when prostitution and drunkenness were believed to have reached new heights, prudery was more than repression; it was an effort to bend society to the self-discipline on which morality, a thriving commerce, the advancement of knowledge, and personal fulfillment were thought to rest.

THE STANDARD OF LIVING

Historians agree more about the general pattern of social change in the first half of the nineteenth century than about its effects on the standard of living, particularly of the working class. For this period, England is the critical case; scholars agree that between 1790 and 1840 national wealth about doubled but that the upper classes were the principal beneficiaries. Did workers gain, too? Certainly they were poor, but poverty, even of the bleakest sort, was not new (and the growing protest against such destitution was in itself one of the important changes of the period). The poorest peasants of Sicily who lived in caves or those of Sweden or Ireland who lived in holes dug into the ground may have been victims of the social system; they were hardly victims of industrialization.

Living Conditions   What *was* new was the terrible crowding in industrial areas and the workers' helpless dependence on their employers. The conditions in which workers lived made poverty more miserable, more obvious to all, and more threatening to the general welfare. The crowding was partly the result of increased population, but it followed directly from the rapid growth of factory towns. There, hastily built housing may often have been drier and cleaner than peasant hovels that had served for centuries, but squeezing whole families into a single room and cramming hundreds and thousands of people into slums with little light, with a single source of insalubrious water, and with no means for disposing of sewage created problems so different in scale as to be different in kind (see "Reports on the Housing Crisis in France and Germany," p. 786). Industrialization also added the special hazards of lead and phosphorous poisoning; and the assault on the lungs of coal mining, cotton spinning, and machine grinding combined with poor nutrition to make tuberculosis ubiquitous. Everywhere in Europe members of the working class were recognizably thinner, shorter, and paler than other people.

The work available had always changed with the seasons, and laborers in many regions and trades were accustomed to migrating to follow harvests and other temporary opportunities for work. Industrialization, however, often brought a demoralizing dependence. Most new factories employed between 150 and 300 men, women, and children whose well-being was largely tied to a single employer. A high proportion of these people were new to the area in which they lived, starkly dependent on cash to pay their rent, to purchase rough cotton for clothes, to provide the bread that was the staple of their diet, and to buy some candles and coal. For millions, employment was never steady; for millions of others, unem-

ployment was the norm. It was common for a third of the adult males of a town to be without work, especially in the winter, and pauperism was acknowledged to be the social disease of the century, a condition that included some 10 percent of the population in Britain and only slightly less in France. Workers, of course, suffered most in the periodic economic depressions that baffled even the most optimistic observers. The depression of 1846 was nearly universal, and that of 1857 extended from North America to Eastern Europe. Layoffs in the Lancashire cotton industry ran so high in the 1860s as a result of the American Civil War that at one time more than 250,000 workers, better than half the total, lived by what they could get on relief. The recipes for watery soup handed out by the charitable agencies of every city define the thinness of survival.[5]

Purchasing Power   Although most workers everywhere suffered from the changing conditions of employment, workers in some trades and places were distinctly better off; and overall, real wages—measured, that is, in terms of what they could buy—may have begun to increase somewhat even before the general rise in wages in the mid-1840s and notably again in the 1850s, though these gains meant less in new factory towns, where workers could be forced to buy shoddy goods at high prices in company stores. Alcoholism was so extensive that in many a factory town paydays were staggered in order to reduce the dangerous number of drunks, a sign of alienation that may also have reflected an increase in available money. Technology brought benefits as well. The spread of the use of soap and cotton underwear was an enormous boon to health, and brick construction and iron pipes had improved

---

[5] The French chef of the Reform Club of London was much admired for his "good and nourishing" recipe: 1/4 lb. leg of beef, 2 oz. of drippings, 2 onions and other vegetables, 1/2 lb. flour, 1/2 lb. barley, 3 oz. salt, 1/2 oz. brown sugar—and 2 gallons of water! It was by no means the cheapest soup. Cited in Cecil Woodham-Smith, *The Great Hunger*, 1964, p. 173.

▲ Hopelessness dominates J. Leonard's painting of the poor coming to the charitable doctor in an endless stream.
Musée des Beaux-Arts, Valenciennes/Bridgeman Art Library.

housing even for many of the relatively poor by midcentury. Luxuries such as sugar, tea, and meat were becoming available to the lower-middle class and to the more prosperous artisans.

The vigorous debate among historians over whether industrialization raised or lowered workers' standard of living in the first half of the century has become in large measure a judgment about the effects of capitalism. But historians generally agree that whatever improvements occurred reached the masses slowly and often could not compensate for the added burdens of industrial employment or the growing chasm between the destitute and the regularly employed. In industrial Europe the urban poor remained a subject of baffled concern. The more fortunate workers and the

middle classes were unquestionably more prosperous than they had been in the recent past, which made the contrast with the poverty of those beneath them even more striking. A luxury restaurant in Paris (by 1830 Paris had more than 3,000 restaurants of every type in contrast to only 50 or so before the Revolution) might charge twenty-five or thirty times an average worker's daily wage for a single meal; even modest restaurants charged twice a worker's daily wage—to a clientele that ate three or four times a day, in contrast to the two meals of many workers. From the top to the bottom of society, the gradations in status and wealth were subtle, but the differences between the comfortable minority and the poor majority were palpable in every aspect of daily life.

The Industrial Revolution and the Standard of Living

Debates among historians about the impact of the industrial revolution in England on the standard of living of workers is likewise a debate about capitalism and social policy, but its evolution is also a result of increased historical knowledge and new methods. These excerpts show the diverse emphases and shifting conclusions but not the careful reasoning and the extraordinary range of the research that makes this literature still worth reading.

From John L. and Barbara Hammond, The Rise of Modern Industry, *M. S. G. Haskell House, 1925.**

"The apologies for child labour were precisely the same as the apologies for the slave trade. Cobbett put it in 1833 that the opponents of the Ten Hours Bill had discovered that England's manufacturing supremacy depended on 30,000 little girls. This was no travesty of their argument. The champions of the slave trade pointed to the £70,000,000 invested in the sugar plantations, to the dependence of our commerce on the slave trade. . . . The argument for child labour followed the same line. . . . Sir James Graham thought that the Ten Hours Bill would ruin the cotton industry and with it the trade of the country. . . . Our population, which had grown rapidly in the Industrial Revolution was no longer able to feed itself; the food it bought was paid for by its manufactures: those manufactures depended on capital: capital depended on profits: profits depended on the labour of the boys and girls who enabled the manufacturer to work his mills long enough at a time to repay the cost of the plant and to compete with foreign rivals. This was the circle in which the nation found its conscience mangled.

" . . . Thus England asked for profits and received profits. Everything turned to profit. The towns had their profitable dirt, their profitable smoke, their profitable slums, their profitable disorder, their profitable ignorance, their profitable despair. The curse of Midas was on this society: on its corporate life, on its common mind, on the decisive and impatient step it had taken from the peasant: to the industrial age. For the new town was not a home where man could find beauty, happiness, leisure, learning, religion, the influences that civilize outlook and habit, but a bare and desolate place, without colour, air or laughter, where man, woman and child worked, ate and slept. This was to be the lot of the mass of mankind: this the sullen rhythm of their lives. The new factories and the new furnaces were like the Pyramids, telling of man's enslavement, rather than of his power, casting their long shadow over the society that took such pride in them."

From Thomas S. Ashton, "The Standard of Life of the Workers in England, 1790–1830," Journal of Economic History, *Vol. 9, 1949.**

"Let me confess at the start that I am of those who believe that, all in all, conditions of labour were becoming better, at least after 1820, and that the spread of the factory played a not inconsiderable part in the improvement. . . . One of the merits of the factory system was that it offered, and required, regularity of employment and hence stability of consumption. During the period 1790–1830 factory production increased rapidly. A greater proportion of the people came to benefit from both as producers and as consumers. The fall in the price of textiles reduced the price of clothing. Government contracts for uniforms and army boots called into being new industries, and after the war the products of these found a market among the better-paid artisans. Boots began to take the place of clogs and hats replaced shawls, at least for wear on Sundays. Miscellaneous commodities, ranging from clocks to pocket handkerchiefs, began to enter into the scheme of expenditure, and after 1820 such things as tea and coffee and sugar fell in price substantially. The growth of trade-unions, friendly societies, savings banks, popular newspapers and pamphlets, schools, and nonconformist chapels—all give evidence of the existence of a large class raised well above the level of mere subsistence."

From Eric J. Hobsbawm, "The British Standard of Living, 1790–1850," Economic History Review *1957.**

"We may consider three types of evidence in favour of the pessimistic view: those bearing on (a) mortality and health, (b) unemployment and (c) consumption. . . . We must not forget that mortality rates did not improve drastically until very much later—say, until the 1870s or 1880s—and may therefore be less relevant to the movement of living standards than is sometimes supposed. . . . The rise in mortality rates in the period 1811–41 is clearly of *some* weight for the pessimistic case, all the more as modern work . . . tend[s] to link such rates much more directly to the amount of income and food consumption than to other social conditions.

" . . . It is too often forgotten that something like "technological" unemployment was not confined to those workers who were actually replaced by new machines. It could affect almost all pre-industrial industries and trades . . . Doubtless the general expansion of the early industrial period (say 1780–1811) tended to diminish unemployment except during crises: doubtless the decades of difficulty and adjustment after the wars tended to make the problem more acute. From the later 1840s, the working classes began to adjust themselves to life under a new set of economic rules . . . but it is highly probable that the period 1811–42 saw abnormal problems and abnormal unemployment. . . . These notes on unemployment are sufficient to throw doubt upon the less critical statements of the optimistic view, but not to establish any alternative view. . . . Per capita consumption can hardly have risen. The discussion of food consumption thus throws considerable doubt on the optimistic view."

From Ronald M. Hartwell, "The Rising Standard of Living in England, 1800–1850," Economic History Review *1961.**

"People lived longer because they were better nourished and sheltered, and cleaner, and thus were less vulnerable to infections and other diseases (like consumption [tuberculosis]) that were particularly susceptible to improved living standards. Factory conditions also improved. . . . But increasing life expectation and increasing consumption are no measures of ultimate well-being, and to say that the standard of living for most workers was rising, is *not* to say that it was high, *nor* that there was no dire poverty, and cyclical fluctuations and technological unemployment of a most distressing character.

" . . . Thus much misunderstanding has arisen because of assumptions—mainly misconceptions—about England before the Industrial Revolution; assumptions, for example, that rural life was naturally better than town life, that working for oneself was better and more secure than working for an employer, that child and female labour was something new, that the domestic system . . . was preferable to the factory system, that slums and food adulteration were peculiar products of industrialization, and so on. . . . The new attitude to social problems that emerged with the industrial revolution was that ills should be identified, examined, analysed, publicised and remedied, either by voluntary or legislative action. Thus evils that had long existed—child labour, for example—and had long been accepted as inevitable, were regarded as new ills to be remedied rather than as old ills to be endured. It was during the industrial revolution, moreover, and largely because of the economic opportunities it afforded to the working class women, that there was the beginning of the most important and most beneficial of all the social revolutions of the last two centuries, the emancipation of women."

From Theodore S. Hamerow, The Birth of a New Europe, *State and Society in the Nineteenth Century.* University of North Carolina Press, 1983, pp. 140–141.

"The debate goes on and on because the evidence is ambiguous, lending itself to a variety of interpretations. Yet taken as a whole, it does point to a few tentative conclusions. The first generation or two of workers under the industrial revolution experienced no major change in its standard of living as a result of the economic transformation of which it was a part. There were some members of the labor force, especially those in the textile trades, who undoubtedly suffered a decline, as skilled handicraftsmen found themselves unable to compete with machinery. On the other hand there were others, in metallurgy or engine building, for example, who improved their position as a result of the rationalization of production. For most of them, however, the coming of the industrial revolution made little difference with regard to income, workday, diet, or housing.

"This was especially true of those employed in agriculture, who still made up the great bulk of the labor force Yet even those engaged in manufacture experienced only minor changes in their accustomed level of subsistence. The goods and services generated by early industrialization remained largely inaccessible to them. But the new hardships imposed on the working population by the rationalization of production were less the result of a long-term decline in income than of psychological disorientation.

Millions of people who had grown up amid the certainties and traditions of the village or small town were suddenly thrown into an alien environment of factories, shops, tenements, and slums, where the values of rural society soon disintegrated before the hard realities of the urban experience. The outcome was a profound demoralization, which primarily reflected not a change in the standard of living but a change in the way of life.

"Such generalizations about the initial effect of the industrial revolution may be open to challenge, but there can be little doubt about what happened subsequently. Within fifty years the standard of living of the lower classes began to rise. The evidence on this point is incontrovertible."

*From Philip A. M. Taylor (ed.), *The Industrial Revolution in Britain: Triumph or Disaster?* D. C. Heath, 1970.

In 1815 the reorganization of Europe following the Napoleonic wars had concentrated on politics as the key to social order. The conservative political solutions that the victors favored continued to be challenged, however. Many of the effects of the French Revolution could not be undone, and compromises that allowed limited freedoms led to demands for more. Competing visions of political order could not be eliminated, while the very meaning of social order was being transformed by the painful process of industrialization. For the rest of the century, Europeans would struggle in their daily lives and in their thinking to understand accelerating social change and the problems that accompanied it. Arguments about change—about its extent and its causes, about its benefits and its evils, about how it could be contained or controlled, and about whether the most fruitful responses were fundamentally moral, economic, or social—would stimulate debates and conflicts in the streets, the press, and parliaments. They would lead to new political parties, important philosophies, and the development of the social sciences, all of which in turn added to the momentum for political and social change.

Recommended Reading

Sources

Memoirs of Prince Metternich. 5 vols. Published in the United States in the 1890s, this edition was reissued in 1970. The published memoirs and correspondence of diplomats are a wonderful source, and larger libraries will have editions of *The Memoirs and Correspondence of Viscount Castlereagh* (12 vols.) and the *Memoirs of the Prince of Talleyrand* (5 vols.). All of these books give a lively picture of the Congress of Vienna.

For the subsequent years, *France and the European Alliance, 1816–1821: The Private Correspondence between Metternich and Talleyrand,* 1948, is particularly useful.

Wilson, Charles, and Geoffrey Parker. *An Introduction to the Sources of European Economic History, 1500–1800.* 1977.

Studies

*Briggs, Asa. *The Making of Modern England, 1784–1867.* 1967. A wide-ranging and readable survey of English society and politics.

*Carr, Raymond. *Spain, 1808–1975.* 1982. The most balanced and comprehensive account in any language.

*Cipolla, Carlo M. (ed.). *The Industrial Revolution, 1700–1914.* 1973. The essays collected here give a good sense of the range of factors and interpretations important for understanding industrialization.

Davies, Norman. *God's Playground: A History of Poland.* Vol. 2: *From 1789 to the Present.* 1981. Effectively studies the development of a nation without a national government.

*Frader, Laura L., and Sonya O. Rose. *Gender and Class in Modern Europe.* 1996. A collection of essays exploring the relationship between social change and conceptions of gender and class in several countries from 1800 to after World War I.

*Gash, Norman. *Aristocracy and People: Britain, 1815–1865.* 1979. An incisive and balanced account of how British politics adapted to social and economic change.

*Gideon, Siegfried. *Mechanization Takes Command.* 1948. This provocative analysis of the social and aesthetic implications of the machine age has become a classic.

Goodman, J., and K. Honeyman. *Gainful Pursuits: The Making of Industrial Europe, 1600–1914.* 1988. Attentive to the variety of interests that made industrialization a continuing process.

Hamerow, Theodore S. *The Birth of a New Europe: State and Society in the Nineteenth Century.* 1983. A systematic, informative consideration of the major social changes of the nineteenth century, noting their connection to industrialization and the role of the state.

*Henderson, W. O. *The Industrialization of Europe: 1780–1914.* 1969. A general study contrasting developments in England and on the continent.

*Hobsbawm, E. J. *The Age of Revolution, Europe 1789 to 1848.* 1970. A sparkling, influential Marxist assessment of the period.

Kissinger, Henry A. *A World Restored: Metternich, Castlereagh, and the Problems of Peace, 1812–22.* 1957. The author's subsequent fame adds to the interest of this account, which is very sympathetic to Metternich.

Kossman, Ernst H. *The Low Countries, 1780–1940.* 1978. Valuable and balanced treatment of a region that was an important participant in all the trends of modern European history.

*Landes, David S. *The Unbound Prometheus: Technological Change and Development in Western Europe from 1750 to the Present Day.* 1969. Emphasizes the role of technology.

*Macartney, C. A. *The Habsburg Empire, 1790–1918.* 1968. Detailed and authoritative.

Magraw, Roger. *France, 1815–1914: The Bourgeois Century.* 1986. A clear general account attentive to social change.

Nibberdey, Thomas. *Germany from Napoleon to Bismarck, 1800–1866.* 1996. An invaluable modern synthesis.

*Nicolson, Harold. *The Congress of Vienna. A Study in Allied Unity: 1812–1822.* 1970. A lively account of the process of peacemaking by a British official who was at the Paris peace conference one hundred years later.

O'Brien, Patrick, and Caglar Keyder. *Economic Growth in Britain and France, 1780–1914.* 1978. A thorough examination of statistical methods and data for the period, focusing in particular on wages and productivity.

*Pollard, Sidney. *Peaceful Conquest. The Industrialization of Europe 1760–1970.* 1981. A provocative new study that focuses on the importance of geographical regions and not political units.

Price, Roger. *An Economic History of Modern France, 1730–1914.* 1981. Underlines the importance of modes of communication and transportation in the development of the marketplace.

*Rich, Norman. *Great Power Diplomacy, 1814–1914.* 1992. A classic kind of diplomatic history, in which the century is seen in terms of international relations; includes a very useful bibliography.

Seton-Watson, Hugh. *The Russian Empire, 1801–1917.* 1967. A solid, largely political survey.

*Smith, Bonnie G. *Changing Lives: Women in European History Since 1700.* 1989. Discussion of the major trends affecting all classes; excellent bibliographies.

*Tilly, Louise, and Joan Scott. *Women, Work and Family.* 1978. Discusses the impact of industrialization on women and on the family economy.

*Trebilcock, Clive. *The Industrialization of the Continental Powers, 1780–1914.* 1981. A synthesis that uses modern research to emphasize the political implications of industrialization.

*Wandycz, Piotr S. *The Lands of Partitioned Poland, 1795–1918.* 1974. A standard, balanced account.

*Available in paperback.

▲ **Delacroix's painting presents the revolution of 1830 in France as the heroic rising of the people, poor and middle class together, being led by liberty into a new era.**
Louvre, Paris, France/Peter Willi/Bridgeman Art Library, London/New York.

LEARNING TO LIVE WITH CHANGE

*n the first half of the nineteenth century European intellectuals and artists responded to the experiences of war, revolution, and industrialization with new ideas and new forms of creative expression. Change—in society, the arts, and politics—had become a central concern. In philosophy and in the arts, romanticism—like the ideologies of conservatism, liberalism, and socialism—dealt directly with change and its results. Intellectuals had reason to be concerned, for the very structure of society was being transformed. Social relations based on custom were giving way to ones controlled by impersonal rules of law and economics. Populations were growing larger, people were becoming more mobile, and more and more of them lived in cities, where lifestyles were different. Industrialization subjected millions to hardships for which neither individual charity nor government had adequate answers. These changes, experienced more intensely in cities than in the countryside and more in Western than in southern or Eastern Europe, were coming to be understood as the result of a historical process likely to affect all of Western Civilization and to raise explosive questions about how society should respond.

I. Ideas of Change

Political ideas, social theories, and new movements in the arts were all closely interconnected in the early nineteenth century. New movements altered the way pictures were painted, poetry was written, statistics were collected, society was analyzed, biology was studied, and history was understood. Several elements served to connect all this creative diversity and increase its impact. The professors, writers, scientists, and artists whose works were most influential increasingly saw themselves as having a special place in society because of their talents and knowledge. Primarily male and largely from the middle class, they depended less on patronage than on their connections to established institutions such as academies, universities, publishing houses, magazines, and newspapers. Through exhibitions, public lectures, and publications, they sought to reach others like themselves and then a broader audience. Their need to explain modern society, like their effort to comprehend the French Revolution, produced competing interpretations that were in fact debates about the nature of society and the sources of historical change.

ROMANTICISM

Romanticism, a movement in philosophy and the arts, cannot be captured in any simple definition. Associated with the great burst of creativity in

▼ A convert to Catholicism and a leading student of Gothic architecture, Augustus Pugin was one of the architects of the Houses of Parliament. These illustrations, part of a book on *Contrasts* comparing Catholic and Protestant society, sum up the romantic and conservative critique of modern society for replacing church spires with smokestacks, cottages and artisanship with massive tenements and factories, and charities with prisons. (The new prison in the foreground is Jeremy Bentham's Panopticon, designed so that a single guard can see down all the cellblocks.)
New York Public Library.

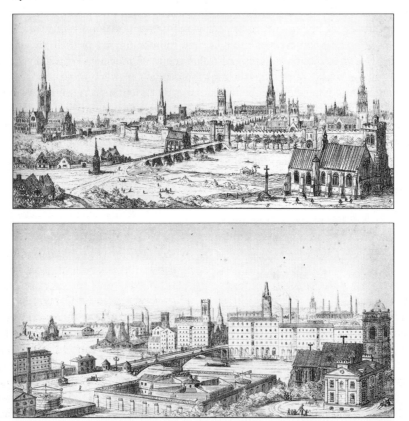

Germany in the latter part of the eighteenth century and with the ideas of Jean-Jacques Rousseau (see chapter 19), romanticism was also a set of attitudes and aesthetic preferences. Strongest initially in Germany and England, it spread across the continent and to North America, an international trend that paradoxically emphasized local difference and that varied in each country. Romanticism is difficult to pin down because it took so many forms and, although challenged and largely superseded by the middle of the nineteenth century, it continued to influence taste and creativity into the twentieth century.

Certain themes emerged as characteristic: an emphasis on feeling, emotion, and direct experience more than on universal principles and abstract logic; a preoccupation with erotic love, often unrequited, and mortality; fascination with nature understood as an unconquerable power, raw and unpredictable; a search for the organic relatedness of all life that went beyond the cold analysis of cause and effect; a concern for spirituality, deep and mysterious, that tended to dismiss thinkers of the Enlightenment as shallow; interest in the momentary, the accidental, and the uniquely colorful in human affairs; and an admiration for imagination and originality that hailed the individual genius who was capable of experiences and feelings more profound than those of ordinary mortals. These preferences were revealed in matters of fashion as well as content. English gardens became the vogue. Carefully arranged to look natural, with great trees and hidden copses along a rolling terrain dappled with flowers of varied colors and heights, gardens in the English style replaced, or were added to, the geometrical plots and cropped hedges of the classical garden. Romantic artists and writers favored flamboyant dress that distinguished them from aristocrats or bourgeois and presented themselves as pensive and passionate.

Romantic Philosophy and Literature Romantic modes of thought flourished in conjunction with the revival of religion, the increased interest in history, and rising nationalism, all of which are discussed in the next chapter; but their core was philosophical. Romantic thinkers wrote about metaphysics, aesthetics, the philosophy of nature, and in Germany and Scandinavia, even a romantic philosophy of science. While envisioned in terms of grand systems (F. W. J. Schelling's works were widely read in Germany despite their almost mystic complexity), romantic philosophies were often expressed piecemeal in poetry, aphorisms, meditations on death, and autobiographical accounts of youthful yearning and the quest for truth. In Germany Friedrich Schlegel and in England Samuel Taylor Coleridge (heavily influenced by German philosophy) were among the most influential romantic thinkers, through intense personal friendships with other intellectuals as well as their published work. Both wrote poetry, drama, and essays on philosophy and theology. Friedrich's brother, August Wilhelm Schlegel, was a major critic and theoretician. Coleridge's *Rime of the Ancient Mariner,* one of the great long poems in English, is a tale of guilt, redemption, and the supernatural. Full of evocative nautical lore, the poem tells of a seaman cursed to wear a dead albatross around his neck, a result of his violence against nature, and who is in the end released from that weight as he feels God's love. With William Wordsworth, his closest friend, Coleridge campaigned for a new kind of poetry, direct and emotive. Wordsworth's poems contrasted the beauty of nature with urban corruption, the clear-eyed and innocent responsiveness of youth with the jaded sadness of age. Like William Blake before him, he denounced the materialism of his age. Blake, whose drawings and poems were filled with religious mystery, also believed that poets had a special wisdom that society should heed; and many other romantics could have joined in Blake's cry:

> Hear the voice of the Bard,
> Who present, past, and future, sees
> The Holy Word
> That walk'd among the ancient trees.

The anguish, depression, and despair experienced in their personal lives became for romantic poets a sign of their own sensitivity and a summons to a higher vision of the meaning of life.

In France, where romanticism developed somewhat later, Madame Anne-Louise de Staël's essays on the German thinkers stimulated a whole generation of philosophers, historians, and novelists, ranging from the young Victor Hugo, whose plays and novels (*The Hunchback of Notre Dame* is the best known) made him the towering figure of French letters through most of the century, to the

Wordsworth on the Role of the Poet

Wordsworth was one of England's most popular poets, and the success of his Lyrical Ballads *may have encouraged him to write a preface to the second edition, explaining what he was up to. He points out that his poems differ from classical poetry with its greater formality and lofty themes, and he justifies his use of ordinary speech. In making his case, he touches on many of the themes characteristic of the romantic movement.*

"The principle object of these Poems was to choose incidents and situations from common life, and to relate or describe them, throughout, as far as was possible in a selection of language really used by men, and, at the same time, to throw over them a certain colouring of imagination, whereby ordinary things could be presented to the mind in an unusual aspect. . . . Humble and rustic life was generally chosen because, in that condition, the essential passions of the heart find a better soil in which they can attain their maturity, are less under restraint, and speak a plainer and more emphatic language; because in that condition of life our elementary feelings co-exist in a state of greater simplicity, and, consequently, may be more accurately contemplated and more forcibly communicated; because the manners of rural life germinate from those elementary feelings . . . ; and, lastly, because in that condition the passions of men are incorporated with the beautiful and permanent forms of nature. . . .

" . . . For all good poetry is the spontaneous overflow of powerful feelings: and though this be true, Poems to which any value can be attached were never produced on any variety of subjects but by a man who, being possessed of more than usual organic sensibility, had also thought long and deeply. . . .

"The Man of science seeks truth as a remote and unknown benefactor; he cherishes and loves it in his solitude; the Poet, singing a song in which all human beings join with him, rejoices in the presence of truth as our visible friend and hourly companion. Poetry is the breath and finer spirit of all knowledge; it is the impassioned expression which is the countenance of all Science. Emphatically may it be said of the Poet, as Shakespeare hath said of man, 'that he looks before and after.' He is the rock of defence for human nature; an upholder and preserver, carrying everywhere with him relationship and love . . . ; the Poet binds together by passion and knowledge the vast empire of human society, as it is spread over the whole earth, and over all time."

From William Wordsworth, "Preface to the Second Edition of *Lyrical Ballads*" in *William Wordsworth: Selected Poems and Prefaces* edited by Jack Stillinger, Houghton-Mifflin Co., 1965.

---

swashbuckling stories of Alexander Dumas' *Three Musketeers*. Novelists and dramatists in Italy and Russia, as well as in England, France, and Germany, often set their tales in the distant past and tended to favor vivid description and singular settings appropriate to occurrences beyond rational understanding. Turning from the Enlightenment and its veneration for the Renaissance, they preferred the rougher, sprawling picture of human experience in seventeenth-century writers like Shakespeare and Cervantes (stimulating an important revival of interest in their work) and felt a kinship with the Middle Ages as an age of faith and spontaneity that produced such achievements as Dante's poetry and Gothic architecture.

The Wider Influence of Romanticism The fairy tales of Hans Christian Andersen combined the romantic delight in folk culture and affection for childhood. Throughout the Western world there was a new taste for tales of ghostly spirits (Edgar Allen Poe was one of the first American writers to achieve international recognition) and paintings of storms and ruins that evoked unseen powers, as in the landscapes of William Constable and J. M. W. Turner in England and Caspar David Friedrich in Germany (note the Turner painting on p. 799).

Literary and artistic works thus burst beyond classical forms. Romantic painters like Théodore Géricault in France emphasized vibrant color and swirling lines without the sharp outlines and balanced composition so important to their predecessors. Like Eugène Delacroix (note his paintings on pp. 767 and 794), they were drawn to exotic scenes from the past and from North Africa and the Middle East. Romantic values came together with particular power in music, admired for its ability to communicate an ineffable understanding deeper than words. The response to the works of Beethoven had brought great seriousness to music. Critics wrote of his symphonies and string quartets in terms of their philosophic profundity, and audiences listened in reverent silence, finding in that shared experience something akin to religion. Subsequent romantic composers appealed even more directly to the heart, emphasizing melody and using freer harmonies. When words and music were combined, as in the song cycles of Franz Schubert and Robert Schumann, or in grand opera (often hailed as the highest of the arts), it was the music that mattered most.

Both conservatives and radicals drew upon the romantic movement, for it was both a call for change and a response to it, attentive to politics as well as to philosophy and the arts. Conservatives found in romantic values powerful arguments for rejecting the French Revolution and considered it the necessary result of Enlightenment rationalism and the universalism that ignored the local variety and tradition conservatives treasured. Stability, they argued, was possible only in a society organically connected, held together as it had been in the Middle Ages by respect for custom and religion. They contrasted their vision of an organic society with the competition and selfish individualism of modern capitalism. Radicals, however, used romantic themes to argue that a new era required the shattering of old institutional constraints, much as creativity in the arts fostered the breaking of established art forms. Romantic thinkers tended to see folk culture and language as natural expressions of the nation. For conservatives these values validated rural life and custom; for radicals the promise of this culture would be realized when the people spontaneously arose to achieve new freedoms. In Germany and England many romantics had, like Wordsworth, initially welcomed the French Revolution only to turn away from it in disgust. Victor Hugo, on the other hand, turned from con-

▲ The evocation of nature and time, favorite romantic themes, made the ruins of Tintern Abbey the subject of a poem by Wordsworth and of this watercolor by J. M. W. Turner.
Victoria and Albert Museum, London/Art Resource.

servatism to become a lifelong advocate of radical change. A younger generation of English poets, led by Lord Byron, Percy Bysshe Shelley, and John Keats, were persistent critics of church and state drawn to the promise of revolution. In short, romanticism in its aspirations and its tumultuousness expressed the preoccupation with change that marked the age.

SOCIAL THOUGHT

Conservatism Conservatism grew from opposition to the French Revolution to become what today would be called an ideology—a coherent view of human nature, social organization, political power, and the sources of change that generally justified the status quo. Not that conservatives always agreed. But in arguing for social order, they tended to emphasize the limitations of human understanding, the wisdom of established customs, the value of hierarchy, and the social importance of religion. From those concerns, conservatives mounted a powerful critique not just of radical programs but of modern society itself as perilously inclined toward antisocial individualism, materialism, and immorality. More than a matter of temperament or interest, conservatism would remain a vigorous part of European intellectual life and political discourse throughout the nineteenth century.

From the late eighteenth century on, the powerful English prose of Edmund Burke (see discussion on p. 703) provided what was perhaps the most influential formulation of the conservative position. Society, he argued, exists through continuity. By granting special privileges to certain groups, it fulfills social needs in a way that sustains order, achieving a delicate arrangement in which rank is related to social function and in which differences of status, having evolved through time, are acceptable to all. This "natural" historical order, Burke argued, was far wiser than the "artificial" plans of radicals, no matter how well intentioned. The Burkean view thus allowed for gradual change, at least in theory; in practice, such arguments could be used against any plan for general reform. This tendency was strengthened by a distrust of reason that rejected the ideas of the Enlightenment as dangerously abstract. No social schemes or written constitutions could reconstitute society, because it was a great interconnecting web, and slogans about rights or equality merely concealed selfish interests and encouraged false hopes.

Conservatives found in history the record of how painfully civilization had developed and how fragile it remained, and many saw evidence not only of human error but of divine will in events since the French Revolution. Christianity was the source of Europe's strength, and Christian fear a necessary restraint on humanity's selfish and prideful nature. Without it, society dissolved into revolution and anarchy. Political battles were part of a far larger millennial conflict.

Such views gave conservative thought both militancy and depth. Europeans were used to re-

ceiving radical ideas from France, and two of the most pungent exponents of conservatism were men who wrote in French, Joseph de Maistre and Louis de Bonald. Society's first task, they argued, is self-preservation. Only authority can check the selfish wills of individuals, and authority requires undivided sovereignty, social hierarchy, close links between church and state, and the vigilant suppression of dangerous ideas. These writers thus connected religion to politics and tied the Church to aristocracy and monarchy. Revolution, de Maistre explained, is divine retribution for false ideas (see "De Maistre's Opposition to Reform," p. 801). This sort of conservatism, very different from Burke's, contained little that was humane or tolerant. With its praise of hangmen and censors, it spoke only to those who already shared its fears. Terrified of weakening the dikes that held back revolution, it left little room for compromise, divided while calling for unity, and relied on power while speaking of the social good. Nevertheless, as a way of understanding change, mobilizing opposition to it, and criticizing modern life, conservatism would be a profoundly influential element in modern thought.

Political Liberalism Liberalism, like conservatism, was not so much a compact doctrine as a set of attitudes; but whereas conservatism emphasized tradition and hierarchy, liberalism was associated with ideas of social progress, belief in economic development, and values associated with the middle class. Confident that their ideas would triumph, liberals generally welcomed change and looked forward to the future.

Liberal political thought was rooted in the writings of John Locke and of the philosophes; and liberals in the nineteenth century believed that their programs would benefit individuals and society as a whole. A leading French liberal, Benjamin Constant, put the case succinctly: "The liberty of the individual is the object of all human association; on it rest public and private morality; on it are based the calculations of industry and commerce, and without it there is neither peace, dignity, nor happiness for men." By this creed, freedom would lead to morality, prosperity, and progress. The freedom that liberals sought was primarily political and legal, and they generally favored a constitution and representative institutions, freedom of the press and of assembly, an ex-

DE MAISTRE'S OPPOSITION TO REFORM

Over the course of the past twenty years, most European governments had adopted constitutions when Joseph de Maistre, writing from exile in Russia, set forth his objections to them in his Essay on the Generative Principle of Political Constitutions. *First published in Russia in 1810 and in Paris in 1814, the essay was reprinted many times.*

"Every thing brings us back to the general rule— *man cannot create a constitution; and no legitimate constitution can be written.* The collection of fundamental laws, which must essentially constitute a civil or religious society, never has been written, and never will be, *a priori.* It is only when society finds itself already constituted, without being able to say how, that it is possible to make known, or explain, in writing, certain special articles; but in almost every case these declarations or explanations are the effect of very great evils, and always cost the people more than they are worth.

" . . . Not only does it not belong to man to create institutions, but it does not appear that his power, *unassisted,* extends even to change for the better institutions already established. . . . *Nothing* [says the philosopher, Origen] . . . *can be changed for the better among men, without God.* All men have a conscious-

ness of this truth, without being in a state to explain it to themselves. Hence that instinctive aversion, in every good mind, to innovations. The word *reform,* in itself, and previous to all examinations, will be always suspected by wisdom, and the experience of every age justifies this sort of instinct.

" . . . To apply these maxims to a particular case . . . the great question of parliamentary reform, which has agitated minds in England so powerfully, and for so long a time, I still find myself constrained to believe, that this idea is pernicious, and that if the English yield themselves too readily to it, they will have occasion to repent."

From Scholars' Facsimiles & Reprints (New York: Delmar, 1977), reprinting of the edition of Joseph de Maistre, *Essay on the Generative Principle of Political Constitutions* (Boston: Little and Brown, 1847).

▶ **Known for his biting satire, Honoré Daumier began the 1830s expecting liberty to bring social and political progress that would light up the sky like fireworks.**
Collection Viollet.

tension of the jury system, separation of church and state, public education, and administrative reform. Most liberals were not democrats—political wisdom, they thought, required the advantages of education and leisure and the restraint that came with owning property—but nearly all believed that giving ideas a free hearing and propertied voters a free voice would result in policies beneficial to all.

Economic Liberalism Although liberal politics and liberal economic theory were closely related, they were nevertheless separable. The advocates of one were not always committed to the other. Still, England's example of economic growth as well as political liberty made it the model of nineteenth-century liberalism. Adam Smith's argument that government intervention in the free play of the market restricted economic forces, which if left to themselves would increase productivity and prosperity, became liberal dogma. As systematically expounded by Englishman David Ricardo in his *Principles of Political Economy and Taxation* (1817), liberal theory became the keystone of modern economics. Ricardo, a financier who became wealthy during the Napoleonic wars and then retired from business, became an important public figure; but his great influence lay in his precise, flat prose that presented economics as a science.

The wealth of the community, Ricardo declared, comes from land, capital, and labor; and these three "classes" are compensated by rent, profit, and wages. A product's value results from the labor required to make it: This was the labor theory of value, which socialists would later use for very different purposes. For Ricardo, this theory led to principles of property similar to those of Locke and to an emphasis on labor saving as the source of profit, which had been foreshadowed by Adam Smith. The value of land or of work was determined not by individual decisions but by economic laws. The poorest land in cultivation simply sustains those who work it; but the most fertile land produces more for the same labor, and that increment constitutes profit, paid to the landlord as rent. As population pressures bring more (and poorer) land into cultivation, rents rise because the difference between the best and worst land increases. Similarly, wages subtract from profit, but the rate of pay is set by an "iron law of wages" (Ricardo's phrase is characteristic). It decrees that when labor is plentiful, the workers tend to be paid at the subsistence level. Short-term fluctuations in prices are the natural regulator within this system, pushing people to activities for which demand is high. Ricardan economics thus extended the sphere of inexorable economic laws to social relations.

For Ricardo, both land and labor are commodities, their value quite unaffected by any sentimental talk about the virtues of rural life or artisanship, and society is a congeries of competing interests. Legislation cannot raise wages or prevent the marketplace from working in its natural way; but if people acknowledge economic laws and act in their own best interest, a natural harmony and progress follow.

Ricardo called his subject *political economy*, and a powerful reform movement developed from it. Landed interests, liberals argued, had misused political power for their own benefit while harming the rest of society. Throughout Europe liberal economic theory thus added important weight to demands that special privilege be eliminated (as the French Revolution had done), that governments be responsive to their citizens (who best know their own interests), and above all that the state not try to regulate production and trade. As economic growth became more impressive, it was natural for liberals to add that politicians should adopt some of the openness, efficiency, and energy of the men of action who were transforming the economy.

Utilitarianism   The call for political and social reform could also lead to renewed emphasis on the role of the state, as it did in the utilitarianism of another Englishman, Jeremy Bentham. Like the philosophes, Bentham believed he could rationally deduce practical programs from universal principles, and he was ready to write a constitution for Russia or codify the laws of Latin American republics. Bentham began his reform campaign by criticizing the legal system, and he remained all his life an opponent of the precedent-bound courts of England. Some of his most important writings before 1789 appeared first in French (the revolutionaries gave him French citizenship).

In contrast to most philosophes, he rejected the doctrine of natural rights as a meaningless abstraction. In his system utility replaced natural rights as the basis of public policy, and utility was measured by determining the greatest good for the greatest number. In the Enlightenment tradition, he combined plans of detailed reform with a theory of psychology. The good is that which avoids pain and gives pleasure—a calculation all people make for themselves anyway and that better education would enable them to make more wisely.[1] Thus just as self-interest built great industry, so it could create a just and happy society. In contrast to Burke's emphasis on tradition and many liber-

---

[1] Bentham called this the "felicific calculus," but his verbal pomposity was famous: After-dinner walks were "postprandial perambulations."

als' preference for limited government, Bentham gave the state a central role. It should assign penalties for undesirable actions and awards for desirable ones, distributing pain and pleasure to induce socially beneficial behavior.

Bentham's followers, sober intellectuals who called themselves *philosophic radicals,* did not necessarily adopt all his doctrines, but they applied his principles in every sphere. By his death in 1832, they were among the most important reformers of Parliament, law, prisons, education, and welfare. A special group within a larger liberal movement, they shared and contributed to the tendency of liberals everywhere to press for humane reforms on grounds of common sense and natural harmony.

John Stuart Mill Liberals appraised society primarily in terms of freedom for individual choice and opportunities for individual growth, an emphasis that gave some ethical dignity to the pain of industrialization and lent promise to the process of social change. They believed their principles were universally valid; yet, to the perpetual surprise of its adherents, liberalism proved a creed of limited appeal, forever subject to attack and internal division. Enthusiasm for limited constitutional reform produced disagreements over how limited it should be. In practice reconciling liberty with order or equal rights with private property proved contentious and led to attacks on liberalism and divisions among liberals themselves. Some theorists reduced liberalism to little more than the narrow justification of individual success. Others expanded it until the demand for social justice overshadowed its founding principles of competition and individualism. In each country the temper of liberalism was different, shaped by a national history liberals never wholly dominated.

Its very malleability, however, enabled liberalism to endure as a doctrine and a political force; and its broader meaning is best exemplified in John Stuart Mill, the most important liberal spokesman of the nineteenth century. Mill's father was a leading Benthamite, and he raised his son in the strictest utilitarianism; but the younger Mill gradually came with searching candor to modify received doctrine. Mill was extraordinarily learned—a philosopher, economist, and publicist—and he wrote some of the most influential

▲ This photograph of John Stuart Mill shows a sensitive intellectual who is also distinctly middle class; compare the Ingres portrait on p. 816.
The Granger Collection.

classics of modern thought. Fearful of the intolerance and oppression of which any social class or political majority was capable, he made freedom of thought a first principle. He advocated universal suffrage as a necessary check on the elite and proportional representation as a means of protecting minorities. Influenced by Auguste Comte, the French social theorist who was one of the founders of sociology, Mill acknowledged the critical role of institutions in social organization, and he admitted that the institutions, even liberal ones, suited to one stage of historical development might not be appropriate for another.

To counterbalance the influence of the established elites, Mill favored a more open administration, organized interest groups, and workers' cooperatives. Moved by the problems of the industrial poor, he tried to distinguish between production (to which liberal economics could still apply) and distribution (in which the state might intervene in behalf of justice), and he came to see that collective action by the workers could enhance freedom rather than restrict it. He sought a

MILL OPPOSES THE SUBJECTION OF WOMEN

◆

John Stuart Mill published his essay The Subjection of Women *in 1869. His arguments were based on familiar ideas about individualism and modern progress, but their extension to women's rights and in such absolute terms went much further than most contemporary discussion.*

"The object of this Essay is to explain, as clearly as I am able, the grounds of an opinion which I have held from the very earliest period when I had formed any opinions at all on social or political matters, and which, instead of being weakened or modified, has been constantly growing stronger by the progress of reflection and the experience of life: That the principle which regulates the existing social relations between the two sexes—the legal subordination of one sex to the other—is wrong in itself, and now one of the chief hindrances to human improvement; and that it ought to be replaced by a principle of perfect equality, admitting no power or privilege on the one side, nor disability on the other.

" . . . The masters of all other slaves rely, for maintaining obedience, on fear; either fear of themselves, or religious fears. The masters of women wanted more than simple obedience, and they turned the whole force of education to effect their purpose. All women are brought up from the very earliest years in the belief that their ideal of character is the very opposite to that of men; not self-will, and government by self-control, but submission, and yielding to the control of others. All the moralities tell them that it is the duty of women, and all the current sentimentalities that it is their nature, to live for others; to make complete abnegation of themselves, and to have no life but in their affections.

" . . . So far as the whole course of human improvement up to this time, the whole stream of modern tendencies, warrants any inference on the subject, it is, that this relic of the past is discordant with the future, and must necessarily disappear.

"For what is the peculiar character of the modern world—the difference which chiefly distinguishes modern institutions, modern social ideas, modern life itself, from those of times long past? It is, that human beings are no longer born to their place in life, and chained down by an inexorable bond to the place they are born to, but are free to employ their faculties, and such favourable chances as offer, to achieve the lot which may appear to them most desirable.

"If this general principle of social and economical sciences is . . . true, we ought to act as if we believed it, and not to ordain that to be born a girl instead of a boy, any more than to be born black instead of white, or a commoner instead of a nobleman, shall decide the person's position through all life. . . .

"At present, in the more improved countries, the disabilities of women are the only case, save one, in which laws and institutions take persons at their birth, and ordain that they shall never in all their lives be allowed to compete for certain things. The one exception is that of royalty.

" . . . The social subordination of women thus stands out an isolated fact in modern social institutions; a solitary breach of what has become their fundamental law; a single relic of an old world of thought and practice exploded in everything else, but retained in the one thing of most universal interest."

From John Stuart Mill, "The Subjection of Women," *Three Essays* (Oxford: Oxford University Press, 1975).

place for aesthetic values within the colder utilitarian doctrine he inherited, and in later years Mill courageously advocated causes, such as the emancipation of women and the confiscation of excess profit, that seemed fearfully radical to most contemporaries (see "Mill Opposes the Subjection of Women"). His liberalism, thus modified and extended, remained firm; and his essay, *On Liberty,* published in 1859, stands as one of the important works of European political theory, a careful but heartfelt, balanced but unyielding declaration that society can have no higher interest than the freedom of each of its members.

THE EARLY SOCIALISTS

Socialist thought offered a radical alternative to conservative and liberal ideologies, varied as each of those were. Among scores of socialist schemes, those of Saint-Simon, Fourier, and Owen were notable for the attention they won among intellectuals and political leaders. All three men had lived through the French Revolution and had personal experience of burgeoning capitalism in the early stages of industrialization, and each of them founded a movement that disseminated telling criticisms of capitalism. Competition, they argued, is wasteful and cruel, induces hard-hearted indifference to suffering, misuses wealth, and leads to frequent economic crises. They offered instead scores of suggestions for organizing production differently and creating a harmonious, orderly, and truly free society.

Saint-Simon As a young French officer, Claude Henri de Rouvroy, Comte de Saint-Simon, fought alongside George Washington at Yorktown. During the French Revolution he abandoned his title, made and lost a fortune speculating in land, and then devoted himself to the difficult career of a seer. Injustice, social divisions, and inefficiency could be overcome, he believed, in a society directed by experts standing above the conflict: scientists, men of affairs (*industriels*), and artists. These specialists, chosen for their ability, would design plans to increase productivity and prosperity for the benefit of all. The integrated, organic quality of Greek city-states and of the Middle Ages could be recaptured in the industrial age with scientists and managers (who would have the authority once granted priests and soldiers) leading humanity to self-fulfillment and love.

Saint-Simon's theories won a significant following especially among the bright engineers at France's École Polytechnique, and an extraordinary number of France's leading engineers and entrepreneurs in the next generation fondly recalled the Saint-Simonian enthusiasms of their youth. In their penchant for planning, in their grand economic projects and in their schemes for social reform, they carried elements of his teaching into the world of affairs and respectable politics. There were important Saint-Simonian movements in every country, and later socialists would long sustain his respect for industrialization and the power of planning.

Fourier François Marie Charles Fourier had been a traveling salesman before dedicating himself, at the same time as Saint-Simon, to a theory that he firmly believed would rank among the greatest discoveries ever made. His cantankerous yet shrewd writings on contemporary society were so copious that his manuscripts have still not all been printed, despite the devotion of generations of admirers. Largely self-taught, he committed to paper his fantasies of the strange beasts and incredible inventions that would abound in the future. His central concept, however, was an ideal community, the phalanstery (from "phalanx"). Once even one was created, the happiness and well-being of its members would inspire the establishment of others until all of society was converted.

A phalanstery should contain some sixteen hundred men, women, and children, representatives of all the types of personality identified in Fourier's elaborate psychology. He listed a dozen passions that move human beings and proposed to organize the phalanstery in such a way that individuals would accomplish the tasks society required simply by doing what they wanted. Each member would perform a variety of tasks, engaging in no one task for too long; pleasure and work would flow together. Largely self-sufficient, a phalanstery would produce some goods for export and pay its members according to the capital, labor, and talent that each contributed. Although no phalanstery was ever established exactly as Fourier planned (he even offered designs for the architecture), communities were founded on Fourierist principles; from the United States to Romania and if few of them survived for long, the vision did of a society in which cooperation replaced compulsion and joy transformed drudgery.

Robert Owen Robert Owen was one of the success stories of industrial capitalism: A self-made man, he rose from selling cloth to be the manager and part owner of a large textile mill in New Lanark, Scotland. Owen ran the mill in a way that transformed the whole town, and by the end of the Napoleonic wars, distinguished visitors were traveling from all over Europe to see the miracle he had wrought in New Lanark. The workday was shortened from seventeen to ten hours. New housing eventually allowed an employee's family several rooms; inspection committees maintained cleanliness; gardens were planted and sewers installed. In nursery schools with airy, pleasant rooms, children were given exercise, encouraged

▲ **A saintly father figure, Fourier instructs his disciplines from a hill overlooking an idyllic setting and an imagined phalanstery, Fourier's orderly community for four hundred families.**
Archiv für Kunst und Geschichte.

to sing and dance, taught without corporal punishment, and trained in the useful arts. Most promising of all, the subjects of this paternalistic kingdom developed a pride in their community, productivity rose, and profits increased.

Owen had, he felt, disproved Ricardo's dismal economic laws; and he set about establishing ideal communities elsewhere. Like Fourier's, they would be placed in a rural setting and would supply most of their own needs. Members would take meals and enjoy entertainment in common, and children would be raised communally. The young would be educated to the age of eight and then engage in productive labor until they were twenty-six; after five years in distributive or managerial jobs, adults would assume the tasks of government, cultivating the sciences and the arts in their increasing leisure time. The controlled environment would assure good character among community members, and the division of tasks would provide them with varied and interesting lives. Standardized production would offer more goods at lower cost (the snobbery that made luxuries attractive would disappear), and higher wages would increase sales (see "Owen Tells Congress about the Science of Socialism," p. 807).

Even after losing most of his wealth when the community of New Harmony, which he founded in Indiana, failed, Owen remained the single most important figure in the labor movement and in the workers' cooperatives that he helped spread across England in the 1830s and 1840s. But by the

Owen Tells Congress about the Science of Socialism

◈

Robert Owen made a number of trips to the United States in connection with the Owenite community on the Wabash River at New Harmony, Indiana. His international fame was such that on one of these trips he was invited to give two addresses to the U.S. Congress. In the first he called on Congress to adopt his principles; and in the second—delivered on March 7, 1825—he set out in some detail his plan for a community of up to 5,000 people on 1,000 or 2,000 acres, with a square of large buildings at the center (each 1,000 feet long). These buildings would house the "school, academy, and university" as well as washrooms, kitchens, dining halls, dormitories for children over the age of two, and apartments. Owen described the arrangements for central heating and cooling, gardens, manufacturing, and farms, and discussed how the community would be governed by an elected committee. But before entering into such specific matters, he presented the general principles of his program:

"Then it should be ever remembered, that the first principle of the science is derived from the knowledge of the facts, *that external circumstances may be so formed as to have an overwhelming and irresistible influence over every infant that comes into existence, either for good or evil . . . and thus, at pleasure, make any portion, or the whole, of the human race, poor, ignorant, vicious, and wretched; or affluent, intelligent, virtuous, and happy.*

"And thus, also, form man to understand and to practice pure and genuine religion, which never did nor ever will consist in unmeaning phrases, forms, and ceremonies; but in the daily, undeviating practice . . . of charity, benevolence, and kindness . . . [this] is the *universal religion* of human nature.

" . . . Having then discovered, as I believe I have, the science of the influence of circumstances, and a rational, and therefore, a pure and genuine religion, the next important consideration is, to ascertain in what manner the new science and the new religion can be applied to produce the promised practical results. I have been frequently urged to apply these principles to the present state of society, and not attempt to disturb it, but endeavor to make them unite harmoniously together. . . . The inventor of the Steam Engine might as well have been required to unite his new machinery with the inefficient and clumsy horse engine. . . . The fact is . . . the system which I propose now for the formation and government of society, is founded on principles, not only altogether different, but directly opposed to the system of society which has hitherto been taught and practised at all times, in all nations.

" . . . My conviction is, that, from necessity and inclination, the individual or old system of society would break up, and soon terminate; from necessity, because the new societies would undersell all individual producers, both of agricultural productions, and manufactured commodities. And from inclination, because it is scarcely to be supposed that anyone would continue to live under the miserable, anxious, individual system of opposition and counteraction, when they could with ease form themselves into, or become members of, one of these associations of union, intelligence, and kind feeling."

From Oakley C. Johnson (ed.), *Robert Owen in the United States.* Humanities Press, 1970.

---

time of his death, in 1858, Owen, who had converted to spiritualism, was largely ignored by the world he had sought to remake.

The Socialist Critique Although much in these socialist movements was easily ridiculed, the values they stressed echoed those of growing workers' movements everywhere. These early socialists sought to combine an older sense of community with the possibilities of a new era. They imagined a society enriched by new inventions and new means of production, in which new forms of social organization would foster cooperation and love. Their indictment of capitalism, their insights into the nature of productivity and exchange, and their attention to social planning and education had an impact far beyond their relatively small circles of believers. The dream of fraternity and of work that was fulfilling echoed through later socialist and anarchist movements; yet nearly everyone ultimately rejected their ideas as impractical and too radical. Bucolic isolation and artisanal production became increasingly unrealistic in the face of industrialization, and these theories were incredibly vague about problems of politics and power.

The nature of their radicalism, however, deserves a closer look. The criticisms of liberal society mounted by Saint-Simon, Fourier, and Owen were not so different overall from the conservative attack. With some restrictions (Saint-Simon, for example, insisted on the abolition of inheritance), they even allowed private property, and none of them was thoroughly democratic. What most shocked contemporaries were their views on the status of women, sexual mores, and Christianity. All rejected the place allotted women in bourgeois society, and Owen not only specified that women should share in governing but believed that their emancipation required lessening their family responsibilities. All wrote of sensual pleasure as good and of its repression as a characteristic European error. The Saint-Simonians publicly advocated free love, and Fourier carefully provided that neither young nor old should be deprived of the pleasures of the flesh. Owen was only slightly less outspoken in his contempt for Christian marriage. At the same time, all three stressed religion as the source of community feeling, brotherhood, and ethics. Their efforts to replace what they had eliminated therefore led to imitations of Christian ritual and foggy mysticism that provided an easy target for their opponents. By the end of the nineteenth century, these thinkers would be remembered as "utopian socialists"; for by then, socialist thought would center on the more hard-headed and systematic theories of Karl Marx (see chapter 26).

II. The Structure of Society
◆◈◆

SOCIAL CLASSES

Theories of change intermixed with everyday experience to form nineteenth-century perceptions of society. In the old regime, discussion of the "orders" or "ranks" in society had referred to an imaginary social pyramid rising from the lowliest peasant to the ruler. In this idealized picture, each person had an assigned place in that pyramid and social relations were governed by elaborate networks of reciprocal responsibilities. By the beginning of the nineteenth century, increased reference to the "middle" or "middling classes" conveyed a different conception of society. In this view, society consisted of broad strata, called classes, and social relations were matters of free contract between individuals, undetermined by rank or custom. A person's class reflected the status of his or her or her husband's occupation as well as something of the values held, the style of life led, and later, the political and social interests likely to be favored. Descriptive of an expanding, fluid, unequal, national society, the concept of class gained urgency with the sharpening contrast between the middle class and the urban poor.

The Aristocracy   The class most easily identified was the aristocracy. Recognized since the Middle Ages as a special group, it included all nobles (whose rank gave them a number of formal privileges) and their immediate relatives, whether they held noble titles or not; members of the upper gentry, who were large landholders and lived like nobles; and (in the ancient commercial cities of the Netherlands, northern Germany, and northern Italy) the established and wealthy patrician families, who dominated the cities though they might not bear titles.

The aristocracy had been a principal target of the French Revolution, and its privileges and influence were further threatened in the nineteenth century by new industrial wealth (which overshadowed the fortunes of large landholders), wider participation in politics, the growth of the state, and cultural change. The aristocracy's relative decline was so clear, in fact, that its continued importance is easily overlooked.

In most countries aristocrats continued to control most of the wealth, were closely allied to an established church, and dominated the upper levels of administration and the military. By training and tone the most international of social classes, aristocrats would remain the preeminent diplomats even in governments dominated by the middle class. Aristocrats also stimulated some of the most influential critiques of nineteenth-century society, denouncing the middle class for selfishness and materialism, proclaiming urban life morally inferior to rural, and lamenting the loss of gentlemanly honor. The efforts of the aristocracy to defend its position, the means used, and the success achieved provide an important measure of social and political development in each country.

National Differences in Aristocracies   In much of Europe, especially the south and east, the aristocracy held on to local power and tremendous wealth, a social pattern exemplified by the Kingdom of Naples and by Russia. In both states the nobility, constituting only about 1 percent of the population, in effect ruled over most of the peasant masses. Three-fifths of the people in southern Italy lived on baronial estates, and after the defeat of Napoleon the aristocracy there worked with king and church to reestablish its authority. In Russia a fraction of the nobility held one-third of the land, and most of the rest of the land, although owned by the state, was administered by nobles. Tyrants on their estates and dominant over local administration, Russia's aristocracy was a pillar of tsarist rule.

In countries in which the nobles made up a higher proportion of the population, the pattern was somewhat different. In Poland, Hungary, and Spain, many of the nobility were extremely poor, and they tended to alternate between desperate allegiance to an empty title and sympathy for radical change, thus becoming another important source of political instability. In some countries, however, aristocrats sought to strengthen their influence through representative government and decentralization, thereby cooperating with political and economic reformers. The confident Magyars took this position in Hungary, and so, even more open-mindedly, did the aristocrats of northern Italy, Belgium, and Great Britain. They were thus prominent during the revolutions of 1848 in Hungary and northern Italy and in the subsequent nationalist movements in those countries. The Belgian aristocracy cooperated with liberals in the revolution of 1830 and afterward, accepting an endless string of concessions and reforms. In England, above all, the aristocracy proved willing to accept liberal programs in exchange for keeping their political prominence. Of the 100

men who served as cabinet ministers in Britain between the reform bills of 1832 and 1867, 64 were sons of nobles; and perhaps four-fifths of the members of Parliament were landholders or their representatives, closely tied to the aristocracy. On the other hand, younger sons and lesser aristocrats in England were more closely associated with the upper-middle class, which lessened the sharpness of social division.

In Prussia, the most influential aristocrats were the Junkers of east Prussia, owners of large estates, some of which included sizable villages. The Junkers maintained their traditional position even when the state became the instrument of dramatic and rapid change. Considered crude and ignorant by most of the aristocracies of Europe—which set great store by polished manners, elegant taste, and excellent French—the Junkers had a proud tradition of service to the state and loyalty to their king. In local government, in the bureaucracy, in the army, and at the court, their manners and their values—from rectitude to fondness for dueling, from arrogance to loyalty—set the tone of Prussian public life.

France is thus the European exception, for there the old aristocracy was reduced to a minor role in national politics after the revolution of 1830. Its members retained major influence in the Church, army, and foreign service, but those institutions were also on the defensive. Yet even in France, aristocrats maintained a strong voice in local affairs and were a major influence on manners and the arts. Everywhere, however, aristocrats were in danger of being isolated from important sources of political and economic power. Lineage was once of such importance that tracing family lines had been a matter of state; now, pride of family was becoming a private matter.

Peasants   The overwhelming majority of all Europeans were peasants, a social class as firmly tied to the land and to tradition as the aristocracy. They also felt the effects of change as agriculture became more commercial, its production increasingly intended for market rather than for mere subsistence or local consumption. Profits increased with the cultivation of one or two cash crops and with the use of improved fertilizers and machinery, but these changes were easier for those farmers with more capital and bigger holdings than most peasants enjoyed. Because larger farms were more likely to be profitable, landed nobles, bourgeois investors, and richer peasants sought to expand and consolidate their holdings, a trend encouraged by legislation in much of northern Europe.

An important change in peasant life occurred with the emancipation of peasants from obligations to the lord denounced as "feudal," obligations that typically might have required the peasant to give the lord a number of days of labor or to use the lord's grain mill at rates the lord set. The French Revolution abolished such requirements, a policy carried to much of Western Europe by Napoleon, decreed in Prussia as part of the reforms of 1806, and spread to most of Eastern Europe with the revolutions of 1848. These changes encouraged peasant producers to enter the commercial market; but they also deprived peasants of such traditional protections against hard times as the use of a common pasture, the right to glean what was left after the first harvest, and the practice of foraging for firewood in forests owned by others. Similarly, the decline of the putting-out system and of local industries took away critical income, especially during the winter months. Gradually and with considerable local variation, peasants were becoming more dependent on the little piece of land to which they had some legal claim or on the wages that could be earned from labor. Although additional land was put under cultivation to meet rising demand, especially in the West, it was usually of poor quality and divided into small plots, and thus it did not greatly improve the peasant economy. As governments became more efficient, they reached more deeply into peasant society for taxes and conscripts, while population growth and competition from more distant markets added other pressures.

Peasant Activism Peasants, however, were not just passive victims of outside forces. They tenaciously maintained old loyalties to their region, their priests, and their habitual ways; and they were the despair of reformers, who were often defeated by peasant suspicion of outsiders, ignorance, and opposition to change. But peasants also used elaborate ties of family and patronage to build effective social networks, and they were frequently shrewd judges of their interests, cooperating with measures that promised immediate benefits while resisting all others with the skepticism of experience.

Their hunger for land, resentment of taxes and military service, and sense of grievance against those above them could also become a major political force. Peasant involvement made a crucial difference in the early days of the French Revolu-

◄ **This idealized picture of prosperous peasants and bustling farmyard is a German lithograph of 1850.**
Archiv für Kunst und Geschichte.

tion, in the Spanish resistance to Napoleon, in the wars of German liberation, and in the strength of nationalism in Germany and Italy. Rulers were kept on edge by eruptions of peasant violence in southern England in the 1820s; Ireland in the 1830s and 1840s; Wales, Silesia, and Galicia in the 1840s; and on a smaller scale in most other countries. The outbreaks of 1848 would topple the system of feudal service in the Austrian Empire and eastern Prussia, though rural indifference to constitutional claims and to workers' demands undermined the urban revolutions there.

The peasantry was deeply divided between those who owned land and those who were forced to sell their labor. Some of the former, especially in the West, grew relatively prosperous and joined the influential notables of their region. More of them survived on small plots by being as little dependent on cash as possible, vulnerable to the slightest change in weather or market, and by supplementing their income by whatever odd jobs family members could find. In most of Europe peasants received only a part of the crops they raised, with the rest going to their landlords. Such arrangements could provide significant security, but they also tended to be inflexible, discouraging adaptation to changes in prices, markets, and technology. Rural laborers were the poorest and most insecure of all, the tinder of violence and the recruits for factory work.

Peasants and Social Change A central problem for nineteenth-century European society was how to integrate the agricultural economy and the masses dependent on it into the developing commercial and industrial economy. By the 1850s the process had gone farthest in France and Great Britain but by opposite means. In Britain the peasantry was largely eliminated as the continuing enclosures of great estates reduced the rural poor to laborers, shifting from place to place and hiring out for the season or by the day. The concentration of landholding in Great Britain was one of the highest in Europe: Some 500 aristocratic families controlled half the land; and some 1,300 others, most of the rest. In France, on the other hand, peasants owned approximately one-third of the arable land and were gradually gaining more. They made the most of their situation by favoring crops that required intense cultivation, such

as grapes and sugar beets, and by maintaining small-scale craft industries.

Patterns elsewhere lay between these two extremes. Small landholding persisted in western Germany, northern Italy, Switzerland, the Netherlands, Belgium, and Scandinavia alongside a trend toward the consolidation of larger farms that reduced millions to becoming day laborers. In Germany emancipation from personal obligations to the lord usually required peasants to pay for their freedom with part (often the best part) of the land they had previously cultivated. New historical research has also established that the situation of peasants varied greatly with local conditions—the quality of the soil, the favored crop, government policy, and legal custom.

The clear distinction remained, however, between these western and central regions and Eastern Europe, where peasants were more directly subject to the power of the lord, most of all under Russian serfdom. In the West, developments that increased agricultural productivity often made the life of peasants more precarious. In the East, the landowners' authority over their peasants included claims to their unpaid labor, which in Russia ranged from a month or so of work each year to several days a week. The disadvantages of such a system were many, and the eventual emancipation of Russian serfs in the 1860s proved necessary for economic growth and minimal military and administrative efficiency. As urbanization and industrialization advanced, many writers waxed nostalgic for the bucolic purity and sturdy independence of peasant life, but the social and economic problems of the peasantry were, in fact, some of the gravest and most intractable of European society.

Workers Industrial workers attracted far more attention than did the peasantry; yet even in Britain industrial workers were a minority among paid laborers (there were more domestic servants than factory hands). Industrial workers, however, were taken to be indicative of the new age because of the environment in which they lived and worked and because of their absolute dependence on wages set by employers, who could fire them at will and who determined the tasks performed as well as the conditions of work and the length of the workday. To many, such workers seemed a

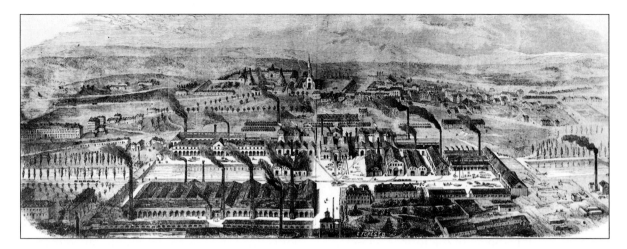

▲ **Le Creusot was a carefully planned and controlled company town that provided housing for the workers in its foundries.**
Collection Viollet.

social threat, and in the 1830s and 1840s, serious French analysts wrote of the "dangerous classes" crowding into Paris.

Most factory workers earned too little to sustain a family even when work was steady, and the employment of women and children became as necessary to their survival as it was advantageous to employers, who appreciated their greater dexterity and the lower wages they would accept. The largest factories were cotton mills, in which commonly half the laborers were women and a quarter, children. In coal mines, women and children, who were hired to push carts and work in the narrower shafts, made up a smaller proportion of the workforce. A class of men, women, and children was thereby formed of people dependent on cash for their subsistence and subject to the rigid discipline of their employers. Awakened before dawn by the factory bell, they tramped to work, where the pace of production was relentless and the dangers from machinery and irate foremen were great. Any lapse of attention during a workday of fourteen hours or more, even stopping to help a neighbor, brought a fine and a harsh reprimand. Children were frequently beaten, just as men had been beaten before fines proved more effective, and workers were spurred by the hated system of payment for tasks completed.

Industrial workers were thus set apart by the conditions of their labor, the slums in which they lived, and special restrictions such as the *livret*, or passport, that all French workers were required to present when applying for a job and on which previous employers recorded comments on the worker's conduct and performance. Life was still more precarious for the millions without regular employment, who simply did such tasks as they could find, hauling or digging for a few pence. Understandably, the powerful worried about the social volcano on which they lived, and the sensitive feared the effect of the immorality and degradation that accompanied industrial life.

Artisans and Skilled Workers The most independent workers were the artisans, who had been stripped of their tight guilds and formal apprenticeships by the French Revolution, by a series of laws passed in Britain in the years before the 1830s, and by a similar process in Germany that was completed by the revolutions of 1848. Nevertheless, artisans continued to ply their crafts in a hierarchy of masters, journeymen, and apprentices, working in small shops in which conditions varied as much according to the temper of the master as to the pressures of the market. Skilled workers, from carpenters and shoemakers to mechanics, moved in a less organized labor market but were distinctly better paid than the masses of the unskilled. Although they were vulnerable to competition from machines and new products and, above all, to unemployment during the frequent economic slumps, in general these skilled workers were among the beneficiaries of industrialization. Their real wages tended slowly to increase, and they could expect to earn enough to support their families in one or two bare rooms on a simple diet.

In contrast, uneducated and exhausted industrial workers, often strangers to one another, for the most part lacked the means necessary for effective concerted action to improve their lot. Their frequent outbursts of resentment and intermittent strikes usually ended in some bloodshed and sullen defeat. Sometimes riots, demonstrations, and strikes became local revolutions, spreading across the north of England in 1811 and 1812, breaking out in Lyons in 1831 and 1834, Bristol in 1831, Lancashire in 1841, and Silesia in 1844. Significantly, most of these outbursts were led by artisans, who felt most keenly the threat of economic change and held clearer visions of their rights and dignity. Although the authorities usually blamed such disturbances on the sinister plots of a few agitators, they were for the most part expressions of resentment and of a growing sense of a common interest.

Early Labor Movements Trade unions were banned everywhere except in England after 1824, and even there the laws against conspiracy restricted their activity; but various local organizations had developed since the eighteenth century to take the place of the declining or outlawed guilds. By midcentury more than 1.5 million British workers may have belonged to such groups, called friendly societies in England, which tended to form around a few of the more skilled workers and to meet in secret, often of necessity but also as a sign of brotherhood and trust. Although their members were fond of elaborate

▼ An etching of Dean Mills in 1851 shows cotton spinning as contemporaries liked to think of it: women working together with nimble industriousness under the watchful but gentle eye of a sturdy foreman, all in the iron grandeur of an immaculate, orderly, huge new factory.
Mansell/Time, Inc.

rituals and terrifying oaths, these societies served specific purposes that were tellingly modest, such as providing burial costs for members or assistance in times of illness. There were also movements that aimed to increase the workers' control over their lives. Consumers' cooperatives were numerous by the 1830s in England, as were artisans' production cooperatives, often established with church support, in France and Italy. Such programs sometimes became associated with radical politics, a specter likely to rouse crushing opposition even from liberal governments. For the most part, however, these expressions of workers' insistence on their rights and dignity remained small in scale and local in influence.

The hundreds of strikes that occurred throughout Western Europe in the first half of the century suggested what unions might accomplish; but without funds, organizational experience, or effective means of communication, these labor movements usually petered out after a few years or sometimes a few months. Not even the Workingman's Association for Benefiting Politically, Socially, and Morally the Useful Classes, launched with some fanfare in England in 1836, managed to survive for long or bring off the general strike its more radical members dreamed of. Yet these organizations did influence Parliament to favor factory legislation. The meetings, torchlight parades, and special workers' newspapers and tracts all contributed to the growing sense of belonging to a distinctive class. So, above all, did the repression by police and courts that usually followed. By midcentury millions of workers in Britain, somewhat fewer perhaps in France, and smaller numbers elsewhere shared heroes and rituals, believed they faced a common enemy, and adopted organization as the prime means of defending themselves in a hostile world. In Britain the national trades unions of skilled workers formed in the 1830s and 1840s (with only some 100,000 members then) steadily increased their size and influence, reaching more than a million members a generation later.

The vast majority of the working class, however, remained essentially defenseless, possessing meager skills, dependent on unstable employment, and living in the isolation of poverty. Ideas of *fraternité* and *égalité,* of the rights of freeborn English people, and of simple patriotism, often expressed in Biblical prose, communicated a com-

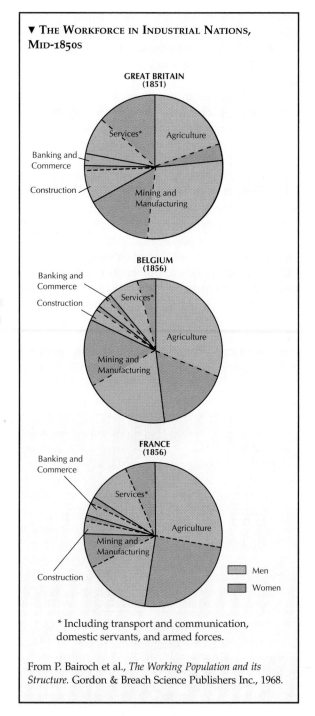

▼ **The Workforce in Industrial Nations, Mid-1850s**

GREAT BRITAIN
(1851)

Services*
Agriculture
Banking and Commerce
Construction
Mining and Manufacturing

BELGIUM
(1856)

Banking and Commerce
Construction
Services*
Agriculture
Mining and Manufacturing

FRANCE
(1856)

Banking and Commerce
Services*
Agriculture
Mining and Manufacturing
Construction

☐ Men
▨ Women

* Including transport and communication, domestic servants, and armed forces.

From P. Bairoch et al., *The Working Population and its Structure.* Gordon & Breach Science Publishers Inc., 1968.

mon sense of hope and outrage to the millions of men and women who attended rallies, met in dingy cafés, and read the working-class press (or listened as it was read to them). Newspapers and pamphlets intended for workers were numerous in England after 1815, less widespread in France in the 1830s and 1840s, and present everywhere in 1848. The common themes were people's natural rights, pride of work, and the claims of social justice.

The Middle Classes Of all the social classes, the most confident and assertive was the middle class. At the top stood the great bankers, who in London and Paris were often closely connected to the liberal aristocracy and whose political influence after 1830 was considerable. Just below them in status, the great industrialists and the wealthiest merchants were more separate from and a little contemptuous of the traditional elites. The bottom of the middle class consisted of office clerks, schoolteachers, and small shopkeepers, often distinguishable from artisans only by their pretensions. This *petite bourgeoisie* constituted most of the middle class numerically, but the class was epitomized by those neither at the top nor bottom but in between: most merchants, managers, and upper bureaucrats and nearly all lawyers, doctors, engineers, and professors. The view that such disparate groups made up a social class resulted as much from ideas shared as from common interests. Opposed to aristocratic privilege, they saw themselves as the beneficiaries of social changes that allowed talented people to gain security and influence.

They were primarily an urban class and intimately connected with the commerce and politics of city life. In Paris they constituted nearly all of that part of the population (between one-fourth and one-fifth) that was prosperous enough to pay some taxes, have at least one maid, and leave an estate sufficient to cover the costs of private burial.[2] In other cities their proportion was probably somewhat smaller. Among nations, they were most numerous in Great Britain, a sizable fraction in France and Belgium, and a smaller minority elsewhere. The middle class was the only social class that it was possible to fall out of, and people established their membership in it by economic self-sufficiency, literacy, and respectability. Their manner, their dress, and their homes were thus symbols of their status and were meant to express values of probity, hard work, fortitude,

prudence, and self-reliance. No matter how favored by birth or fortune, they tended to think of themselves as self-made.

Middle Class Values While industrial centers were notoriously drab, the middle-class home became more ornate, packed with furnishings that boasted of elaborate craftsmanship. Women's fashions similarly featured ornamental frills, and shops translated Parisian elegance into forms available to more modest purses. Masculine garb, by contrast, grew plainer, a point of some pride in a practical age; and clerk and banker tended to dress alike. Those who forged great industries out of daring, foresight, and luck; those who invented or built; and those who taught or tended shop or wrote for newspapers came to share a certain pride in one another's achievements as proof that personal drive and social benefit were in harmony and as a harbinger of progress yet to come.

▼ **Fashion magazines like** *La Mode Illustré* **kept middle-class women informed of the latest styles and elegant touches to which they might aspire.** Photo Bulloz.

---

[2] Perhaps the most detailed study yet made of the middle class in this period is Adeline Daumard's *La Bourgeoisie parisienne de 1815 . . . 1848* (1963).

More than any other, the middle class was associated with an ideology; and the triumph of the middle class in this period—so heralded then and by historians since—related as much to constitutionalism and legal equality, individual rights, and economic opportunity as it did to any explicit transfer of power. The conquests of the middle class were measured not just by its rise in importance but also by a more general adoption of values associated with it. Even being in the middle, between the extremes of luxury and power and of poverty and ignorance, was seen as an advantage, a kind of inherent moderation. Most of Europe's writers, scientists, doctors, lawyers, and businesspeople would have felt no need to blush on finding themselves called by a London paper in 1807 "those persons . . . always counted the most valuable, because the least corrupted, members of society," or on hearing John Stuart Mill speak a generation later of "the class which is universally described as the most wise and the most virtuous

▼ **Dominique Ingres portrayed the entrepreneur Louis Bertrand as the very epitome of the self-reliant, aggressive man of the industrial middle class.**
Giraudon/Art Resource.

part of the community, the middle rank." Society was understood in terms of social class at a time when the hallmarks of the era—flourishing commerce, science, and technology; great works of art and institutions of culture; triumphant movements of liberalism and nationalism—were seen as achievements of the middle class.

THE CHANGING POPULATION

While Europeans grappled with political, economic, and social changes, they also faced the fact that there were more and more people—more people to feed, more seeking work, and more living in cities.

Demographic Growth The effects of population growth were particularly visible in areas in which industrialization was under way, and historians used to think that industrialization had stimulated a rising birthrate with new opportunities for employment, particularly of children. But demographic research has challenged that view, and current explanations emphasize a decline in disease-carrying germs, an increase in the food supply, a lowering of the age at which people married, and, after 1870, some improvement in public sanitation.

Admittedly spotty data suggest that the world experienced a decline in some common diseases beginning in the eighteenth century. Microbes have cycles (like those of locusts but less regular), and remissions had undoubtedly occurred many times before. Now, however, better supplies of food allowed the larger number of babies surviving the perilous years of infancy to reach adulthood and form families of their own.

The food supply rose because of better transportation, more effective agricultural techniques, and the potato. Agricultural associations, usually led by enlightened aristocrats, campaigned for more scientific farming; and the humble potato, not common on the continent before 1750, was a staple of the peasant's diet in most of Europe by 1830.[3] Potatoes are easy to cultivate in a small space and can yield more calories per acre than

---

[3] William L. Langer made an effective case for the potato's importance in "Europe's Initial Population Explosion" *American Historical Review*, 1963, pp. 1–17.

any other crop. While infant mortality remained enormously high by modern standards, even a slight decline in death rates could make a great difference in the total number of people, so close to subsistence did most Europeans live.

Population and Society   The reasons for the trend toward earlier marriage are less clear, but peasants freed from servile obligations apparently tended to marry and form new households at a younger age. Early marriage was facilitated by the spread of cottage industry, which preceded the new factories and enabled families to add to their income by spinning or weaving at home. The increased number of people in a single generation—only a slight rise in a single decade or province—multiplied in the next generation and led to an enormous increase in the aggregate. As population grew, the proportion who were young and in the childbearing years grew still faster, which increased the ratio of births to the total population. The net result was that the 180 to 190 million Europeans of 1800 had become 266 million by 1850 and 295 million by 1870.

The effects of a larger population were far-reaching. More people consumed more food, which necessitated more intensive cultivation and the use of land previously left fallow. An increasing population also meant an expanding market for goods other than food, an element of growth that would have stronger impact later in the century. More people meant a larger potential workforce readier to leave the countryside for industrial jobs; and this mobility became a social change of immeasurable importance, for it reduced the isolation of country folk and stimulated a pattern of migration to the Americas that would become a flood. Young people constituted a greater proportion of the population, which may have made for increased restiveness and a larger pool of potential radical leaders.[4] There was also a distinc-

tion in birthrates by social class, which demographers call *differential fertility*. On the whole, the higher a man stood on the social scale, the fewer the children in his family, which led some to interpret the lower classes' fertility as a lack of foresight and moral restraint and to worry that they would eventually overwhelm society.

The most influential analysis of population was Thomas R. Malthus' *An Essay on the Principle of Population as It Affects the Future Improvement of Society*, first published in 1798 and reissued in many revisions. Observing the Britain of his time, Malthus argued that human population, unless checked by death (through war, famine, or pestilence) or deliberate sexual continence, increases faster than the supply of food. A clergyman, he advocated continence; but he remained pessimistic that human beings were capable of such restraint. An economist as well, Malthus presented demography as a science closely attached to liberal economic theory, with the convenient corollary that the misery of the poor resulted from their own improvidence.

Urbanization   At the turn of the century, greater London reached 1 million in population. No European city since imperial Rome had ever approached this size. Paris, with about half that number, would reach 1 million a generation later. The third largest European city in 1800, Naples, had some 350,000 inhabitants; and in all Europe there were then only twenty-two cities with populations of more than 100,000. By midcentury there were forty-seven. Great Britain was the leader, with six cities over the 100,000 mark; London's population had surpassed 2.5 million by 1856, Liverpool had grown from 80,000 to almost 400,000, and Manchester and Glasgow each had more than 300,000 people. By the 1850s, half of Britain's population lived in towns or cities, making it the most urbanized society since the classical era.

On the continent most old cities increased by at least 50 percent in the first half of the century, and many a town became a city. The major capitals burgeoned. Paris reached a population of nearly 1.5 million by 1850; Berlin almost trebled, to 500,000; and a similar growth rate pushed Brussels to 250,000. St. Petersburg, Vienna, and

---

[4] In 1789 perhaps 40 percent of France's population was between twenty and forty years old and another 36 percent under twenty, the highest proportion of the young that France has ever known. The nationalist organization Young Italy limited membership to those under forty, and probably most of the leaders of the revolutions of 1848 would have met that standard. The relation of youth to revolution is interestingly discussed in Herbert Moller, "Youth as a Force in the Modern World," *Comparative Studies in Society and History*, April 1968.

Budapest all had populations between 400,000 and 500,000.

By the 1860s the English countryside was actually losing people, as were some sections of France. The tide of urbanization was overwhelming, and nearly all the subsequent increase in European population would end up in cities swelling with immigrants, as rural folk moved to nearby villages, villagers to towns, and town dwellers to cities. Clearly, the tide of urbanization was strongest where industry was great, but the growth of ports and national capitals demonstrated the importance of great commercial, financial, and political centers as well.

Urban Problems Society had neither the experience nor the means to cope very well with such an expansion. Urban conditions for all but the reasonably prosperous were unspeakable. Narrow alleys were littered with garbage and ordure that gave off an overpowering stench. The water supply in Paris, better than in most large cities, offered access to safe water only at fountains that dotted the city (the affluent paid carriers by the bucket), and in London the private companies that provided water allowed it to flow only a few hours a day. In most cities the water supply came from dangerously polluted rivers. Sewage was an even more serious problem. A third of Manchester's houses used privies in the 1830s, and a decade later the ratio of inside toilets to population was 1 to 212. In London cesspools menaced health only slightly less than still more public means of disposal.

The most dramatic inadequacy, however, was in housing. A third of Liverpool's citizens lived crowded into dark, cold cellars, and conditions in Lille were similar. In every city the poor of both sexes crowded into filthy, stuffy, unheated rooms; and over the cities, especially manufacturing and mining towns, chemical smog and coal smoke darkened the sky. It is hardly surprising that crime was rampant, that often more than a third of the births were illegitimate, and that the number of prostitutes soared (reaching perhaps 80,000 in London, where 9,000 were officially registered; 3,600 were registered in Paris).

Maintaining public order became a new kind of problem. Governments had used the police primarily as secret agents whose job was to ferret out real or potential enemies. But the protection of lives and property in great cities, the effective handling of crowds, and the enforcement of local ordinances required something other than spies or the military. London's police force was established by Sir Robert Peel in 1829,[5] and the Paris Municipal Guard was created under Guizot a few years later.

For all their misery, cities continued to grow; and through the century the worst conditions were slowly alleviated by housing codes, public sewers, and reliable water supplies. These improvements were made possible in part by industrialization, which gradually provided iron pipes, water closets, gas lighting, better heating, and sounder buildings. Urban life developed a style of its own, increasingly distinct from life in the countryside. Towns clustered around factories and railway stations, and cities teeming with the poor and indigent were also the thriving centers of communication, commerce, politics, and culture.

SOCIAL WELFARE

Social questions were debated in hundreds of speeches and pamphlets and in newspaper articles that worried about public health and morals, class division, and pauperism. These discussions were filled with the appalling facts uncovered through parliamentary and private inquiries in Britain and scholarly investigations in France. Using the rational techniques that seemed to work brilliantly when applied to issues of profits and politics, these humanitarian attempts to improve the lot of the lower class had discouragingly modest results, although individual employers, especially in Britain and Alsace, improved conditions somewhat by building special housing for their workers, drab barracks that nonetheless seemed marvels of cleanliness and decency.

Charity Middle-class radicals supported efforts like those of the Society for the Diffusion of Useful Knowledge, founded in 1826 to carry enlightenment to the lower classes. They contributed to and gave lectures at night schools for the work-

---

[5] The role played by Sir Robert Peel led to the nickname "Bobbies," by which the police are still called.

▲ In this famous engraving of London by Gustave Doré, the rhythmic sameness and cramped efficiency of new housing suggest a machine for living appropriate to the age of the railroad.
New York Public Library.

ingman, many of which were run by the Mechanics' Institutes (of which there were more than 700 in Great Britain by 1850) and by the Polytechnic Association of France (which had more than 100,000 participants on the eve of the revolution of 1848). Thousands of middle-class people personally carried the lamp of truth to the poor in the form of Bibles, pious essays, moral stories, and informative descriptions of how machines worked. Ambitious members of the lower-middle class were, however, more likely than workers to take advantage of these opportunities.

For the truly poverty-stricken, charities were established at an astounding rate; more than 450 relief organizations were listed in London alone

in 1853, and whole encyclopedias cataloging these undertakings were published in France. A revival of Christian zeal provided powerful impetus to such groups in Britain, and on the continent new Catholic religious orders, most with specific social missions, were founded by the hundreds. They sponsored lectures, organized wholesome recreation to compete with the temptations of the tavern, set up trade apprenticeships, provided expectant mothers with a clean sheet and a pamphlet on child care, opened savings banks that accepted even the tiniest deposit, campaigned for hygiene and temperance, gave away soup and bread, supported homes for abandoned children and fallen women, and ran nurseries, schools, and

▲ **The visitation of the poor by charitable members of the middle class was expected to bring a good example as well as food and clothes.**
Jean-Loup Charmet.

hostels. These good works were preeminently the province of women. Catholic nuns and Protestant matrons in the middle class were expected to uplift the poor by example as well as charity. The Society of St. Vincent de Paul believed that pious men could have a similar effect. Organized in Paris in 1835, it soon spread to all of Catholic Europe, requiring thousands of educated and well-to-do men to visit the poor regularly so that they might teach thrift and give hope by their very presence. Although these heroic efforts were important for some lucky individuals and were a significant means of informing the comfortable about the plight of the poor, they were never adequate to the social challenge. Most of Europe's urban masses remained largely untouched by charity or religion.

Public Health In matters of public health, standards of housing, working conditions, and education, governments were forced to take a more active role. By modern standards the official measures were timid and hesitant, and the motives behind them were as mixed as they were in factory legislation, which was favored not only by humanitarians but by landed interests happy to restrict industrialists. Vaccination, enforced by pro-

gressive governments, made smallpox less threatening; but beyond that, advances in medicine contributed little to public health. The great work of immunization would come later in the century. The most important medical gain of the 1840s was probably the use of anesthesia in surgery, dentistry, and childbirth.

Serious epidemics broke out in every decade. Typhus, carried by lice, was a constant threat, accounting for one death in nine in Ireland between 1816 and 1819, and infected water spread typhoid fever in city after city. A cholera epidemic, which apparently began along the Ganges River in 1826, spread through East Asia, reaching Moscow and St. Petersburg by 1830; 100,000 people died of cholera in Russia in two years. From Russia it spread south and west, to Egypt and North Africa, to Poland, Austria, and into Germany, where it was reported in Hamburg in 1831. Despite efforts to put ports in quarantine (a move opposed by shipping interests), the disease reached northern England and then France in that same year and continued slowly to the south, taking a ninth of Palermo's population in the period from 1836 to 1837.

Reaction to the cholera epidemic in Britain, France, and Germany revealed much about social change. An official day of fasting, prayer, and humiliation in England and warnings of the archbishop of Paris that the cholera was divine retribution expressed the strength of traditional faith and revealed widespread distrust of an era of materialism and its claims to progress.

But governments were expected to act. Torn between two inaccurate theories of how the disease spread,[6] governments mobilized inspectors to enforce such sanitary regulations as existed (not infrequently the inspectors faced riots by a populace fearful of medical body snatchers eager to dissect corpses). In Paris and Lille tenements were whitewashed by the tens of thousands, foods inspected, streets and sewers cleaned by official order; similar steps were taken in the German states and in Britain, where the demonstrated inadequacy of local government prompted establishment of a national Public Health Commission

---

[6] The cholera bacillus was finally identified by Robert Koch in 1883.

with extraordinary powers over towns and individuals. Carefully collected statistics led to a new understanding of how disease spread and of the importance of social factors for public health. Over the years, doctors and inspectors reported with troubled consciences on the terrible conditions they had found among lower-class neighbors whose quarters they had never visited before. Another cholera epidemic followed in the 1840s and lesser ones thereafter, but the shock and uncertainty of what to do was never again so great. Gradually, hospitals, too, came under more direct state supervision as the cost and complexity of medical treatment increased. By midcentury housing and sanitary codes regulated most of urban construction throughout the West, and inspectors were empowered to enforce these rules.

The Irish Famine   Liberalism showed its other face in England's handling of the terrible potato famine in Ireland. As the potato blight struck late in 1845, disaster for a population so dependent on a single crop was not hard to predict. By winter hundreds of thousands of families sold what little they had to survive, were forced off the land, and began to suffer the diseases that accompany famine. Hope rested on a good harvest the following year. In spring and summer the potato plants emerged promisingly; but when desperate peasants dug them up, there was only stinking rot. In 1846 the blight was nearly total; and in that year and the next millions died, about a quarter of the population—the exact number will never be known. Roads were lined with bodies, huts abandoned. For several years some of England's ablest officials struggled with bureaucratic earnestness to collect information, organize relief, and maintain order in a corpse-strewn land; yet they were so inhibited by respect for the rules of liberal economics and the rights of property that their efforts had limited effect. In England, even those public figures most concerned to provide help to the Irish tended to view the famine as a natural disaster rather than a failure of policy; and many blamed Irish laziness for the country's dependence on potatoes, an easy crop to grow.

Ireland did produce grain, but that brought a better price in Britain. The landowners, mainly English and absentee, followed market principles and continued to export most of their wheat to England even as famine spread. Most Irish farmers rented the tiny plots they worked and paid for them principally by selling the pig or two they could raise on the same potatoes that provided their subsistence. When that crop failed and they had no money for rent, landlords usually forced them off the land. The relief law that denied aid to anyone who farmed more than a quarter acre of land had a similar effect, forcing tenants to abandon farming so their families might have food. The Irish famine, which made migration to the United States a part of Irish life and stimulated increased hatred of English rule, also fostered debate about what the responsibilities of a liberal government should be.

Government Regulation   In the 1830s and 1840s governments also began reluctantly to regulate child labor, banning employment of those under nine years old in textile mills in Britain and factories in Prussia, under eight in factories in France, and under ten in mines in Britain. By the end of the 1840s, similar measures had been adopted in Bavaria, Baden, Piedmont, and Russia. Generally, the laws variously held the workday to eight or nine hours for children under twelve or thirteen years old and to twelve hours for those under sixteen or eighteen. Britain and France included additional requirements that the very young be provided with a couple of hours of schooling each day. To be effective, such regulations required teams of inspectors, provided for only in Britain, where earnest disciples of Jeremy Bentham applied the laws diligently. This expansion of government authority had been vigorously opposed by industrialists and many liberals; but mounting evidence of the harmful effects of industrial work made the need apparent, and the ability to gather such evidence became one of government's most important functions.

The most bitterly controversial welfare measure of the period was Britain's Poor Law of 1834. The old system of relief required each county to supplement local wages up to a level of subsistence determined by the price of bread. The system, expensive and inadequate to changing needs, was attacked by liberal economists, who charged that it cost too much and discouraged workers from migrating to new jobs. An extensive campaign for reform led to the Poor Law of 1834, based on the Benthamite notion that unemployment had to be made unattractive. Those receiving relief were required to live in workhouses, where discipline was harsh, conditions were kept suitably mean, and the sexes were separated. The new law was resented as a cruel act of class conflict, and it proved unenforceable in much of the nation, though recent studies suggest that it was somewhat less harsh in either practice or intent than its critics charged. On the continent welfare measures kept more traditional forms while gradually shifting the responsibility for directing them from local and religious auspices to the state.

Education   Public education also became a matter of national policy. Prussia had declared local schooling compulsory in 1716, and efforts to enforce and regulate that requirement culminated in 1807 with the creation of a bureau of education. In the following decades the government, with the cooperation of the Lutheran clergy, established an efficient system of universal primary instruction with facilities to train the teachers now needed and to guarantee that the subject matter taught would remain rudimentary and politically safe. The network of secondary schools was also enlarged but kept quite separate, generally not admitting graduates of the ordinary primary schools. Most of the German states had similar arrangements, establishing nearly universal elementary education. In France the French Revolution had provided the framework for a national system of public schools meant as a substitute for the extensive but more informal and largely religious schools of the old regime. Slowly that vision of a national system of public schools took effect. By 1833 every commune was required to support a public school, and schooling steadily expanded while the quality of teachers improved and the power of inspectors over tightfisted local authorities increased. By the revolution of 1848, three-fourths of France's school-age children were receiving some formal instruction. In Britain conflict between the Church of England and other Protestant churches prevented creation of a state-controlled system of elementary schools, a lack welcomed by those conservatives who opposed educating the masses. Nevertheless, Parliament voted in 1833 to underwrite the construction of private schools, and subsidies for education gradually increased in amount and scope each year

thereafter. From Spain to Russia, elementary schools were favored by every government and passionately demanded by liberals. The public schools of Europe, inadequate and impoverished, offered little chance of social advancement to those forced to attend them, but few doubted that they could be a major instrument for improving society as well as a force for social peace.

III. The Spread of Liberal Government

Such social programs were part of the great age of liberalism that began in 1830, made England its model, and spread to the continent with revolution in France and the revolt that created Belgium. With the establishment of these liberal governments, the representative monarchies of the West stood in sharp contrast to the autocratic governments of central and Eastern Europe.

GREAT BRITAIN

Britain's withdrawal in the 1820s from Metternich's Concert of Europe represented more than insular habit. The world's leading example of liberalism, Britain was coming to favor liberal programs in other countries, too. But the triumph of liberalism at home had not come without serious conflict.

Pressure for Change   The turmoil of the postwar years was heightened by the economic crisis that resulted from demobilization and the collapse of wartime markets, and popular meetings echoed with cries of class resentment. The issues were both social and political. The government's economic policies—removal of the wartime income tax and a higher tariff on grains, which made bread more expensive—favored the rich. To change policies required reform of the political system; and the agitation for that reform, which swept the country, was heated and sometimes violent.

The government had responded with repression. Habeas corpus was suspended for the first time in English history in 1817. A mass meeting for reform at St. Peter's Field, Manchester, in 1819 so terrified the local magistrates that they called out troops. In the ensuing charge, hundreds of demonstrators, including women and children, were wounded, and several were killed. With bitter mockery people called it the Peterloo Massacre. Parliament responded by passing the Six Acts of 1819, which restricted public meetings, facilitated the prosecution of radicals, and imposed a stamp tax intended to cripple the radical press. In 1820 the discovery of a clumsy plot to blow up the cabinet at dinner added to the atmosphere of political danger. Support for the established order continued to ebb, and the scandal of George IV's personal life earned public contempt. Old restrictions on Protestant dissenters and Roman Catholics (they could not hold public office, for example) now brought rising criticism of the special privileges accorded the Church of England.

Even an unreformed Parliament could be sensitive to public opinion, however, and it began to support temperate compromises on some critical issues. Under the leadership of George Canning, the government gave a voice to people like William Huskisson, a businessman well known for his belief in the new economics. It reduced some tariffs and repealed the Combination Acts that had banned unions, although an amendment effectively outlawing strikes was soon added. As the minister in charge of the Home Office, Sir Robert Peel ceased the prosecution of newspapers and the use of political spies, halved the list of capital crimes, and by creating a police force put domestic order in the hands of civil authority. The Tories, who opposed such measures, looked to the conservative duke of Wellington, the prestigious victor over Napoleon at Waterloo, to resist further change; yet as prime minister even he saw the need to push through Parliament a measure he himself disliked, allowing Catholics and religious dissenters to vote and to hold public office. All of these issues—religious freedom, the legitimacy of labor unions, tariffs, restrictions on the press—led to agitation that from London to Ireland increasingly focused on the need to reform Parliament itself. Elections in 1830, required by the death of King George IV and the accession of William IV, only raised the political temperature. In the countryside, laborers set haystacks afire by night; by day, stern magistrates ordered laborers accused of seditious activity transported to Australia.

The Reform Bill of 1832   As public turmoil rose (and British leaders watched with concern the rev-

olution of 1830 in France), a new cabinet presented a bill to reform the electoral system. The measure was approved in the House only after a new election and was then rejected in the Lords until the king reluctantly threatened to create enough new peers to get it through. Each defeat made the public mood uglier, and the king's intervention came amid demonstrations, the burning of the town hall and the bishop's palace in Bristol, and much dark talk about the French example.

The bill itself offered a good deal less than the more outspoken radicals had wanted, but it marked a fundamental change in Britain's electoral system. Suffrage was increased, allowing some 800,000 well-to-do men to vote, based on the property they owned or the rents they paid.[7] More important than the increased suffrage was the elimination of local variation in favor of a uniform national standard which, as many Tories warned, could easily be broadened in the future. Before the Reform Bill was passed, many boroughs that sent representatives to Parliament were barely villages (the most notorious, Old Sarum, was uninhabited), and the bustling cities of Birmingham and Manchester had had no representatives at all. Perhaps a third of the members of Parliament owed their seats to the influence of some lord. Now representation was at least crudely related to population, and the voices of commerce and manufacturing were both more numerous and louder.

Although restricted suffrage and social tradition (and the open voting) guaranteed the continued dominance of the upper classes, Parliament was ready after 1832 to turn to other reforms. Slavery was abolished in Britain's colonies in 1833, a victory for Protestant reformers and humanitarian radicals. The Factory Act, limiting the hours children worked,[8] soon followed, as did the Poor Law

---

[7] This electorate was considerably broader than that established in either France or Belgium in 1830, though Belgium, the only country to give elected representatives a salary, had in many respects Europe's most liberal constitution. About 1 Frenchman in 160 could vote in 1830; 1 Briton in 32, after the Reform Bill of 1832. About 1 Belgian in 95 could vote by 1840; and 1 in 20, by 1848. Universal male suffrage permits approximately one-fifth of the total population to go to the polls.

[8] The work week was limited to 48 hours for children between the ages of six and thirteen, and to 69 hours for those between ages fourteen and eighteen.

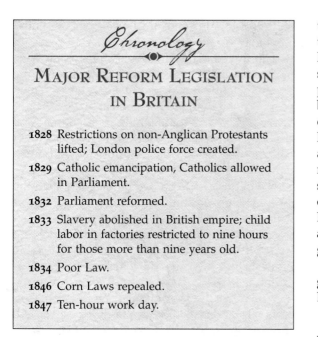

MAJOR REFORM LEGISLATION IN BRITAIN

1828 Restrictions on non-Anglican Protestants lifted; London police force created.

1829 Catholic emancipation, Catholics allowed in Parliament.

1832 Parliament reformed.

1833 Slavery abolished in British empire; child labor in factories restricted to nine hours for those more than nine years old.

1834 Poor Law.

1846 Corn Laws repealed.

1847 Ten-hour work day.

of 1834. A law granting all resident taxpayers the right to vote in municipal elections challenged aristocratic influence even more directly than the Reform Bill of 1832. When young Victoria ascended the throne in 1837, representative government was stronger than ever. Her reign of more than six decades would rival that of Queen Elizabeth I as a period of British glory and power, but she would remain subordinate (often against her wishes) to an increasingly flexible political system.

Chartism and the Corn Laws Two great popular movements helped define the limits of that political system. Chartism was a huge, amorphous workers' movement, the central aim of which was political democracy, spelled out in what was called the People's Charter.[9] With articulate leaders and a working-class base, Chartists propagandized widely; held huge demonstrations in 1839, 1840, and 1848; and were accused of causing riots that ended with scores of deaths. Al-

though treated by the state as dangerous revolutionaries, their principal tactic was to present Parliament with petitions containing thousands of signatures (see "The Great Charter," p. 826). These petitions were summarily rejected, however, and by 1842 the movement was weakening. It failed, despite its size, to find a program that could for long mobilize the masses struggling for survival; and it failed, despite its emphasis on political rather than more threatening economic goals, to stir the consciences of those in power. Angry or desperate workers could riot here or there, but in England they were too isolated from one another and from other classes to gain even their political goals.

The other great popular movement, against the grain tariff, was victorious. The Anti-Corn Law League grew out of urban resentment over the

▼ **The British House of Commons sat in a new building of gothic splendor that made parliamentary liberty seem ancient and the two-party system inevitable.**
Houses of Parliament, Westminster, London/Bridgeman Art Library.

---

[9] The six points of the People's Charter were universal male suffrage, a written ballot, abolition of property qualifications for members of Parliament, payment of the members, constituencies of equal population, and annual elections. All but the last of these points were adopted by 1918.

▲ Mass meetings had been one of the Chartists' most effective devices, and this one held on Kensington Common in London, April 10, 1848, was one of the most publicized. With revolution on the continent and famine in Ireland, radical hopes were as high as conservative fears. The 20,000 who attended this meeting had passed armed soldiers, poliecmen, and special constables. The expectation of violence explains the small number of women and children in this photograph. What might have been the beginning of a revolution in England was instead the Chartists' last national demonstration.
Royal Archives, Windsor Castle.

high cost of bread resulting from grain tariffs—the Corn Laws—that benefited the landowning classes. From Manchester the movement spread throughout the country, becoming a kind of crusade, an attack on the privileges of aristocracy in the name of the "productive orders" of society, the middle and working classes. The league's propaganda used the new techniques of popular politics: parades and rallies, songs and speeches, pamphlets and cartoons. Its slogans were printed on trinkets for children, ribbons for women, drinking cups for men. Two manufacturers, Richard Cobden and John Bright, proved effective spokesmen who became influential figures in public life, spreading the gospel of free trade across the land. To the upper classes, such activity seemed in terrible taste; and conservatives argued that the nation's greatness was rooted in its landed estates.

In the face of this sort of coalition of the middle and working classes, however, British politics was more responsive. Twice Sir Robert Peel's government lowered duties on a wide range of items, including grain, but the league demanded more. Finally, in 1845, Peel announced his support for outright repeal of the Corn Laws. The threat of famine in Ireland had decided the issue for him. Almost simultaneously, the Whig leader, Lord John Russell, affirmed his conversion to the principles of free trade. Yet neither man was eager to carry the fight through the houses of Parliament. Ultimately, Peel undertook the task, and in 1846 he shepherded the measure through both the Commons and the Lords. The grain tariff was reduced to almost nothing, and nearly all duties were abolished or greatly lowered. As in 1832, the political system had bent when demands for reform gained widespread support among the

The Great Charter

The Chartist movement reached its peak in 1842 with the presentation to the House of Commons of the Great Charter. There were more than 3 million signatures on this petition calling for universal male suffrage, annual parliaments, lower taxes, and greater attention to the needs of the poor.

TO THE HONOURABLE THE COMMONS OF GREAT BRITAIN AND IRELAND, IN PARLIAMENT ASSEMBLED.

"The petition of the undersigned people of the United Kingdom,

"Sheweth—That Government originated from, was designed to protect the freedom and promote the happiness of, and ought to be responsible to, the whole people.

"That the only authority on which any body of men can make laws, and govern society, is delegation from the people.

"That as Government was designed for the benefit and protection of, and must be obeyed and supported by all, therefore all should be equally represented.

"That any form of Government which fails to effect the purposes for which it was designed, and does not fully and completely represent the whole people, who are compelled to pay taxes to its support, and obey the laws resolved upon by it, is unconstitutional, tyrannical, and ought to be amended or resisted.

"That your honourable House, as at present constituted, has not been elected by, and acts irresponsibly of, the people; and hitherto has only represented parties, and benefited the few, regardless of the miseries, grievances, and petitions of the many. Your honourable House has enacted laws contrary to the expressed wishes of the people, and by unconstitutional means enforced obedience to them, thereby creating an unbearable depotism on the one hand, and degrading slavery on the other. . . .

"That the existing state of representation is not only extremely limited and unjust, but unequally divided, and gives preponderating influence to the landed, and monied interests, to the utter ruin of the small-trading and labouring classes.

"That bribery, intimidation, corruption, perjury, and riot, prevail at all parliamentary elections, to an extent best understood by the Members of your honourable House.

"That your petitioners complain that they are enormously taxed to pay the interest of what is termed the national debt, a debt amounting at present to £800,000,000, being only a portion of the enormous amount expended in cruel and expensive wars for the suppression of all liberty, by men not authorised by the people, and who, consequently, had no right to tax posterity for the outrages committed by them upon mankind. . . .

"That your petitioners would direct the attention of your honourable House to the great disparity existing between the wages of the producing millions, and the salaries of those whose comparative usefulness ought to be questioned, where riches and luxury prevail amongst the rulers, and poverty and starvation amongst the ruled.

"That your petitioners, with all due respect and loyalty, would compare the daily income of the Sovereign Majesty, with that of thousands of the working men of this nation; and whilst your petitioners have learned that her Majesty receives daily for her private use the sum of £164 17s. 10d., they have also ascertained that many thousands of the families of the labourers are only in the receipt of 3 3/4d. per head per day. . . .

"That your petitioners believe all men have a right to worship God as may appear best to their consciences, and that no legislative enactments should interfere between man and his Creator.

"That your petitioners maintain that it is the inherent, indubitable, and constitutional right, founded upon the ancient practice of the realm of England, and supported by well approved statutes, of every male inhabitant of the United Kingdom, he being of age and of sound mind, non-convict of crime, and not confined under any judicial process, to exercise the elective franchise in the choice of Members to serve in the Commons House of Parliament."

middle class, but Peel's courage split his party and ended his ministry. He was jeered by angry Tories as a young backbencher, Benjamin Disraeli, rose to decry Peel's treachery to the aristocracy. The growing weight of public opinion and the liberal creed had triumphed; the sphere of political debate had expanded to include vexing social issues.

THE REVOLUTIONS OF 1830

Uprisings across Europe Reform in Britain had benefited from the warning of events on the continent. In France, Charles X's abdication led to a provisional government. Organized largely in newspaper offices, it had a faintly republican coloration but soon settled for a liberal monarchy. Most of France was ready to accept that compromise when the Marquis de Lafayette, still a republican and a popular hero, stepped out on the balcony of the Hôtel de Ville to present Louis Philippe as the candidate for the throne. The revolution, brief and largely limited to Paris, was a revolution nevertheless, and any uprising in France was a European event. Minor revolts stimulated by the French example occurred in central Italy, Spain, Portugal, and some of the German principalities, and revolution broke out in Poland. But Austria once again extinguished revolt in Italy, and the Russian army crushed Poland's rebels.

Belgium In the southern Netherlands, Catholics and liberals took the occasion to rise against Dutch rule. This revolt was a direct challenge to the provisions of the Congress of Vienna. Britain opposed any intervention by the great powers, however, once convinced that France had no territorial designs on the Netherlands; and Britain led in arranging international guarantees for the independence of the southern Netherlands, which became Belgium. The British and French then pressured the Dutch to acquiesce.

The Belgian monarchy established in 1830 was one of the triumphs of liberal constitutionalism; and the new state, which owed its existence both to French restraint and British protection, took as its king Leopold I, who had lived long in England (he was an uncle of Queen Victoria) and who soon married the daughter of Louis Philippe. The constitution went further than France's in guaranteeing civil rights and the primacy of the Chamber of Deputies; and politics continued to revolve around a coalition—rare in Europe—of Catholics and liberals, aristocrats and members of the upper-middle class.

Rapidly becoming the most industrialized nation on the continent, Belgium was prosperous; and if its lower classes were more miserable and a greater proportion of them illiterate than in France, that very fact permitted the social isolation of its leaders. Self-confident and satisfied with the new order of things, they built on the administrative traditions left from earlier Austrian and French rule as well as that of the Dutch and proved themselves remarkably adept at planning railroads, reforming taxes and schools, and making timely political concessions.

Switzerland Liberal institutions spread to Switzerland, too, as part of the international trend spurred by the revolutions of 1830. Beginning in 1828, some cantons adopted such liberal measures as representative government and freedom of the press, and ten cantons formed a league in 1832 to agitate for religious freedom and for a stronger, secular central government within the Swiss confederation. These policies were resisted by seven largely Catholic cantons, which were dominated by their aristocracies and soon formed an alliance, the Sonderbund. By 1847 the two leagues were at war. The Sonderbund looked for support from conservative and Catholic states, but none came (the papacy, Austria, and Piedmont had their hands full with revolts in Italy), and the liberal sympathies of Britain and France once again proved decisive. With the Sonderbund's defeat, Switzerland became a federal state with a new constitution, influenced by the example of the United States, that provided for universal male suffrage.

France's July Monarchy The symbols of revolution and moderation were neatly combined in France's new monarchy under the House of Orléans, the liberal branch of the royal line headed by Louis Philippe (his father had voted with the Jacobins for the death of Louis XVI). Louis

▲ Jeanron's depiction of a Parisian barricade in 1830 (later used to illustrate Louis Blanc's socialist history of the period) presents a more realistic scene of the fighting than Delacroix's more famous version but a very similar heroic vision of workers and middle class together (see p. 794).
Collection Viollet.

Philippe's posters proclaimed him citizen-king, and the Revolution's tricolor replaced the Bourbon flag. Known as the July Monarchy, the new regime began with a constitution presented as a contract the king swore to keep, not as a gift he granted. Similar to the one it replaced, the contact offered stronger guarantees of political freedom, lowered property requirements for voters (nearly doubling their number to some 170,000, safely restricted to men of means), and replaced the hereditary upper house with lifetime peers. Because most of the old aristocracy resigned their offices, never to return to public life, there was an important change in government personnel. Those who replaced the aristocracy, professional people and bearers of newer (often Napoleonic) titles, differed from their predecessors more in outlook than in social origin. In his appeal to the people of Paris, Louis Philippe sounded more radical than he was, and the new government hastened to assure Europe's other monarchs that this French revolution would send no militants to sponsor or support revolution elsewhere.

The overriding political question of the 1830s in France was the July Monarchy itself, which was attacked from left and right. Louis Philippe presented himself as a good bourgeois, while the regime's opponents on both sides sought broader support. With strong Catholic support, legitimists (those in favor of the Bourbons) campaigned in the countryside and the newspapers. A mass held in Paris on the anniversary of the death of Charles X's son and heir, who had been assassinated in 1820, became a demonstration that in turn prompted an anticlerical crowd to sack and loot the archbishop's palace and a nearby church. In 1832 the duchess of Berry, whose infant son was now the legitimist claimant to the throne, tried to stage an uprising. Republicans were active, too, often in secret groups that had provocative names like the Society of the Rights of Man. When the silk workers of Lyons went on strike, it was viewed as a republican revolt and was suppressed with the bitterness of class hatred by the bourgeois National Guard. That political climate encouraged another contender, the Bonapartist heir, Louis Napoleon, to attempt to stir an uprising in 1836 and again in 1840.

Limited Liberalism in France   Yet all these attempts failed; and the July Monarchy presented itself as a center of stability and patriotism, even laying claim to the cult of Napoleon I by bringing the emperor's body back from St. Helena and placing it with nationalist pomp in the marble crypt of the Invalides. The government built on the administrative system that had been developed under the Revolution and Napoleon to promote public education, new if limited social services, and industrialization. With time (and restrictions on the press) opposition quieted, and many of the middle-class notables of France rallied to a government of cautious moderation that talked of progress.

A regime largely isolated from workers, peasants, and the old aristocracy had found in nationalism its most effective means of reaching a larger public. Yet it remained divided between those who wanted further reform and wider suffrage and those, like the king himself, who believed the proper balance between liberty and order had been achieved. The former were led by Adolphe Thiers; the latter, by François Guizot. Both were journalists and historians of great talent; but their skillful verbal duels, often models of parliamentarism, failed to mobilize opinion in France as agitation over the Corn Laws had done in England. From 1840 to 1848 the government was dominated by Guizot. A Protestant in a Catholic country, an intellectual in politics, a man who held broad principles rigidly, Guizot had in excess failings common to many liberals of the nineteenth century. He spoke of liberty, progress, and law in eloquent terms that made his cautious practices seem hyp-

ocritical. In 1848 the whole regime fell as easily as incumbents losing an election.

The two freest and most prosperous of Europe's great nations had developed similarly since 1830. In both, liberal governments led by able men sought through reasonable compromise, the rule of law, and parliamentary politics to unify their nations and to make "progress" compatible with stability. Discontent and workers' misery, though frightening, were understood in the councils of government primarily as a threat to order. In England reform had to be wrung from a powerful aristocracy that was, in the end, secure enough to cede under pressure. In France the aristocracy counted for little after 1830; but the government, fearful of the more radical hopes for democracy and social justice that it excluded, remained uncertain of its popular support.

Spain   The victories of French and British liberalism seemed part of a general trend. In Spain the monarchy itself wooed liberals. When King Ferdinand VII died in 1833, he had carefully arranged for his three-year-old daughter, Isabella, to succeed him. But the king's brother, Don Carlos, denounced the arrangement as illegal[10] and began an uprising that lasted until 1839. The Carlists, who favored autocracy and the traditional claims of Spanish Catholicism, found their greatest support in rural areas and regions of the north that were resentful of rule from Madrid. Despite eventual defeat, Don Carlos won a place in Spanish legend as a dashing and chivalric hero, protector of old Spanish virtues; and Carlism would remain a conservative rallying cry in every subsequent Spanish revolution.

To win liberal support, the regency ruling in Isabella's name granted a constitution in 1834. Cautiously modeled on the French constitution of 1814, with narrow suffrage and protection of royal power, it established representative institutions as

---

[10] Don Carlos cited the Salic law, dating from Merovingian times, which prohibited women from acceding to royal thrones. Generally followed on the continent, the law meant that in 1837 England's Queen Victoria could not also assume rule over Hanover as her father had. In Spain Ferdinand VII had abolished the Salic law in 1830 by what was known as a pragmatic sanction.

a lasting feature of Spanish politics. Even so modest a step placed Spain in the liberal camp, and Isabella's government relied on extensive support from Britain and France against threats from abroad, an alliance joined by Portugal after similar concessions there. Internal war brought generals into politics and conflict between two camps: the moderates (who supported the constitution of 1834 and admired Guizot's France) and the anti-clerical progressives (who demanded a democratic constitution and the election of local officials). Only after a couple of military coups did moderates establish a regime in the 1840s strong enough to hold power for a decade. Everywhere, the changes and the aspirations that brought constitutions, limited suffrage, and circumscribed freedoms were based on a delicate balance that proved difficult to maintain.

Clusters of ideas about the nature of historical change, about how to prevent revolutions or achieve them, and about the kind of future that industrialization might lead to had become the ideologies that have divided Western social thought ever since. In the arts and philosophy, romanticism pointed nostalgically to the past but also toward the new, hailing individual genius yet yearning for community. Conservatives sustained standards critical of the new age; liberals gained strength from their confidence in the future; and socialists envisioned an alternative to capitalist industrialization. From 1815 on, a variety of political experiments, each claiming to be permanent, had been tried in Europe. The problem for conservative regimes was to increase their political effectiveness while preserving as much of the old social order as possible. Although liberal regimes experienced the benefits of uniform justice, legal equality, individual rights, and broader political participation, they faced the question of how far such principles could be taken without creating instability. In fact all available ideas, institutions, and policies were challenged by the social changes that accompanied industrialization, factory labor, demographic growth, and urbanization. There was an explosive mixture in these intellectual, social, and political trends; and they came together in the revolutions that swept across Europe in 1848 and in the increased emphasis on the importance of the state, especially a national state that could demand the loyalty of its citizens.

Recommended Reading

◆

Sources

Engels, Friedrich. *The Condition of the Working Class in England.* Written in 1844 and available in many modern editions, this influential work by Karl Marx's friend and coauthor paints a dark picture of the working-class slum and conveys the moral outrage radicals felt.

Ure, Andrew. *The Philosophy of Manufactures.* 1835. An early and classic justification of liberal economics, emphasizing its promised benefits for all.

Novels are important sources for understanding nineteenth-century society. Elizabeth Gaskell (*Mary Barton* and *North and South*) and Charles Dickens (*Hard Times* and *Oliver Twist*) provided contemporaries with an influential picture of social conditions in England; Honoré de Balzac's *Père Goriot* set the tone for criticisms of the selfishness of the middle class.

Studies

Berdahl, Robert M. *The Politics of the Prussian Nobility: The Development of a Conservative Ideology.* 1988. Shows how political interests and social structure led to the formation of a conservatism that dominated much of German history.

*Briggs, Asa. *Victorian Cities.* 1970. Colorful studies of the urban politics and social life of individual cities.

Brock, Michael. *The Great Reform Act.* 1974. Analyzes the significance of the Reform Bill of 1832 through a close examination of the political and social forces that brought it about.

*Chevalier, Louis. *Laboring Classes and Dangerous Classes in Paris during the First Half of the Nineteenth Century.* Frank Jellinek (tr.). 1981. This detailed study of the Parisian poor also says much about French society in general during the early years of industrialization.

Church, Clive H. *Europe in 1830: Revolution and Political Change.* 1983. A study that emphasizes the significance of the revolutions of 1830 by noting their transnational connections and impact.

Coffin, Judith G. *The Politics of Women's Work: The Paris Garment Trades, 1750-1915.* 1996. The quintessential women's work was in the garment industry, and this study reveals the long evolution of women in the labor movement and of ideas about gender, issues that concerned all of society.

*Davidoff, Leonore, and Catherine Hall. *Family Fortunes: Men and Women of the English Middle Class, 1780–1850.* 1985. A wonderfully rich and concrete picture of the aspirations and concerns of middle-class life.

Dennis, Richard. *English Industrial Cities of the Nineteenth Century.* 1984. A comprehensive study of the special nature and problems of this new kind of city.

De Ruggiero, Guido. *The History of European Liberalism.* R. G. Collingswood (tr.). 1977. A classic comparison of the different concepts of liberalism that were dominant in each of the major European nations.

Franklin, S. H. *The European Peasantry: The Final Phase.* 1969. Taken together, these essays on different countries reveal not only the striking differences in peasants' lives but the importance of the peasantry for understanding the general history of European nations.

*Hamerow, Theodore S. *Restoration, Revolution, and Reaction: Economics and Politics in Germany, 1815–1871.* 1958. A complex analysis of the relationship of social classes and the state to economic change in this revolutionary period.

Harrison, J. F. C. *The Early Victorians, 1832–1851.* 1971. A lively account of the personalities and issues that marked the beginning of a new era.

*Heilbroner, Robert L. *The Worldly Philosophers.* 1972. A good introduction to the ideas of the economic liberals.

Himmelfarb, Gertrude. *On Liberty and Liberalism: The Case of John Stuart Mill.* 1974. Penetrating and controversial analysis of the still-controversial philosopher of liberalism.

Holmes, Stephen. *Benjamin Constant and the Making of Modern Liberalism.* 1984. The biographical focus offers a valuable insight into the evolution of liberalism on the continent.

Johnson, Douglas. *Guizot: Aspects of French History.* 1963. Insightful essays focusing on the dominant figure of the July Monarchy and revealing the tensions between aspirations for a liberal society and conservative fear for order.

Katznelson, Ira, and Artistide R. Zolberg (eds.). *Working-Class Formation: Nineteenth-Century Patterns in Western Europe and the United States.* 1986.

Significant interpretative essays by some leading scholars that take a fresh look at how working-class awareness was formed and at the values and attitudes associated with it.

*Lichtheim, George. *A Short History of Socialism.* 1975. Well-constructed treatment of the evolution of socialist ideas in their historical context.

*Lindemann, Albert S. *A History of European Socialism.* 1984. Establishes the line of continuity from the early socialists through labor movements and the eventual dominance of Marxism.

*Lukács, Georg. *The Historical Novel.* Hannah and Stanley Mitchell (trs.). 1962. Insightful and learned study of the social significance of the nineteenth-century novel by one of Europe's leading Marxist scholars.

*Manuel, Frank. *The Prophets of Paris.* 1965. An excellent discussion of French utopian thinkers.

Perkin, Harold. *The Origins of Modern English Society, 1780–1860.* 1969. Provides a clear picture of the diverse sectors of English society and how they adapted to the changes of the period.

Porter, Roy, and Mikul Teich (eds.). *Romanticism in National Context.* 1988. Particularly useful for the student because this volume of interpretive essays includes many on smaller European nations.

Price, Roger. *A Social History of Nineteenth-Century France.* 1987. A clear synthesis of recent research that provides an excellent introduction.

*Riasanovsky, Nicholas V. *The Emergence of Romanticism.* 1992. An excellent introduction to the origins of European Romanticism.

*Rudé, George. *The Crowd in History, 1730–1884.* 1964. Argues that there was a fundamental change in the social composition and demands of crowds, and therefore of their significance, after industrialization.

Segalen, Martine. *Love and Power in the Peasant Family: Rural France in the Nineteenth Century.* J. C. Whitehouse and Sarah Mathews (trs.). 1983. Shows the active role of peasant society in the process of social change.

*Sewell, William H., Jr. *Work and Revolution in France. The Language of Labor from the Old Regime to 1848.*

1980. An important study that shows the radical potential and continuing strength of a preindustrial working-class culture in the industrial area.

*Shanin, Teodor (ed.). *Peasants and Peasant Society.* 1987. Essays treating the varied aspects of peasant society, reflecting important recent scholarship; especially useful on Eastern Europe.

Snell, K. D. M. *Annals of the Laboring Poor: Social Change and Agrarian England, 1660–1900.* 1985. A pioneering look at the position of the rural underclass in Britain and the transformation of their world in the nineteenth century.

*Stromberg, Roland N. *European Intellectual History since 1789.* 1975. A graceful and thorough presentation of the major trends.

*Thompson, Dorothy. *The Chartists: Popular Politics in the Industrial Revolution.* 1984. A lively and sympathetic account that relates working-class action to the larger social context.

*Thompson, Edward P. *The Making of the English Working Class.* 1964. A remarkable work of sympathetic insight and exhaustive research that continues to influence studies of the working class in all societies.

Valenze, Deborah. *The First Industrial Woman.* 1995. Establishes the connection between new modes of production, ideas of gender, and women's economic roles.

Walker, Mack. *German Home Towns: Community, State, and General Estate, 1648–1871.* 1971. Sensitive and original treatment of the response of small-town life to political and social change, showing the historical significance of the ambivalence felt toward the state, liberalism, and nationalism.

*Weiss, John. *Conservatism in Europe, 1770–1945: Traditionalism, Reaction, and Counter-Revolution.* 1977. Provides a valuable survey of the rich variety and social insight in conservative thought and of the political importance of conservative movements.

---

*Available in paperback.

▲ **Victory and the birth of a new Germany: The Halls of Versailles ring as Prussian officers hail the proclamation of Prussia's King Wilhelm as German Kaiser.**
Bismarck Museum/Bildarchiv Preussischer Kulturbesitz, Berlin.

NATIONAL STATES AND NATIONAL CULTURES

*I*n the spring of 1848 revolution swept across Europe from France to Hungary, and within a few weeks the revolutionaries appeared victorious. These revolts had in common the pressures of economic distress and their emphasis on political freedoms. Their spontaneity in capital after capital demonstrated the widespread belief that liberty and representative institutions could make all the difference. Their internal divisions and eventual defeat taught other lessons. Radical social programs raised as much opposition as support. Nationalist appeals could be as powerful as calls for liberty, and stability required a strong state. Over the next thirty years, Italy and Germany each formed a single state as much of Europe adopted a model, exemplified by Britain and France, that expected the modern national state to shape public life through parliamentary legislation and an efficient bureaucracy, watch closely over the economy, establish universal schooling, foster measures for public health, and support the institutions of high culture.

I. The Revolutions of 1848

Two years of poor harvests and industrial recession in most of Europe preceded the outbreak of revolution, but economic crisis alone does not make a revolution. In Ireland more than a million people died from starvation during the famine years from 1846 to 1849; yet that tragedy did little more to shake British rule than the Chartist movement. In Switzerland, Belgium, and the Netherlands major liberalization occurred without a serious revolt. Revolutions occurred where governments were distrusted and where the fear and resentment fed by rising food prices and unemployment found focus in specific political demands.

THE OPENING PHASE

France   In France Guizot's government refused to widen the suffrage. The parliamentary opposition then launched a protest movement that staged large banquets across the country. When a nervous government, aware of its unpopularity, banned the banquet scheduled for Paris in late February 1848, some members of the Chamber of Deputies announced they would attend anyway. Crowds gathered in the streets, and workers who could never have afforded banquet tickets started to build barricades. The rituals of revolution had begun. Louis Philippe, ever sensitive to middle-class opinion, held a review of his citizen militia, the National Guard. When they sullenly refused to cheer him, Louis Philippe knew his days were numbered. He abdicated in favor of his grandson and left for England, much as Charles X had done just eighteen years before. This time, too, the effort to preserve a dynasty was ignored, and a provisional government of men chosen by two rival newspapers appeared at the Hôtel de Ville and declared France a republic. The Paris crowds cheered, and political clubs organized. The new cabinet—led by Alphonse de Lamartine, a handsome and much-admired romantic poet—was dominated by moderates who at first cooperated with more radical members (including a socialist, Louis Blanc). They agreed that the republic should adopt universal male suffrage, a degree of democracy allowed in no other large nation, and that the citizen's right to work was a principle of govern-ment, establishing a commission to hold public hearings on problems of labor. Noting that each French revolution "owed it to the world to establish yet one more philosophic truth," the republic abolished the death penalty.

At the same time, the new regime was careful to demonstrate its restraint. It rejected intervention in behalf of revolutions in other countries, rejected proposals for adopting a red flag as the symbol of socialism and kept the familiar tricolor but with a red cockade, and levied new taxes to balance the budget. Relations with the Catholic Church were the best in a generation, and April elections for a constituent assembly took place in good order. Nearly 85 percent of the eligible electorate voted, giving moderate republicans an overwhelming majority. The Second Republic seemed solidly established.

Revolution Spreads   As news of the events in France sped across Europe, a conservative nightmare became a reality. Nearly every capital had citizens who found exciting promise in words like "constitution," "rights," "liberty," and "free press." In Hungary the Diet cheered the Magyar leader, Louis Kossuth, as he called on March 3 for representative government; and in the same week demonstrations with similar demands erupted in the cities of the Rhineland, soon giving way to revolution there and then in Vienna (March 12), Berlin (March 15), Milan (March 18), and Venice (March 22). Each of these revolutions followed a similar pattern. The news from France would attract excited crowds; groups of men—especially journalists, lawyers, and students—would meet in cafés to discuss rumors and newspaper reports. Governments that did not quickly grant constitutions (as they had tended to do in Italy) would call out troops to maintain order; and with a kind of inevitability, some incident would occur—a shot fired by a soldier insulted once too often or by someone in the crowd with an unfamiliar gun.

Then barricades would rise in the style that came from Paris, constructed of paving stones, a passing coach ceremoniously overturned, nearby trees, and furniture. Barricades became the people's voice, threatening but vague, as workers and professional people, men, women, and children labored together. When blood was shed, the crowd had its martyrs. In Paris corpses were car-

▲ **Lamartine persuades the crowd to reject the red flag and let the new French republic keep the tricolor.**
Musée du Petit Palais, Paris/Giraudon/Bridgeman Art Library.

ried around on a cart as a spur to revolutionary determination; in Berlin the king, supporting his fainting queen, acceded to the crowd's demands and paid his respects, bareheaded, to the subjects his troops had killed. When new concessions were won, the atmosphere would grow festive. New flags would fly, often a tricolor, an echo of the French Revolution but with colors symbolizing national union. In the almost universal dedication to politics, newspapers and pamphlets appeared in floods (100 new newspapers in Vienna, nearly 500 in Paris). Radicals would seek ever after to recapture the unanimity and joy of those early days of revolution. Others, and not just conservatives, would never forget fearsome mobs, fanatical faces, and ugly threats.

Central Europe In the Austrian Empire, the Hungarian Diet had by mid-March established a free press and a national guard, abolished feudal obligations (with compensation to the lords), and required nobles to pay taxes. Everyone noticed the parallel to 1789. Reluctantly Vienna agreed that Hungary could levy its own taxes and direct its own army. The Hungarian example encouraged students in Vienna to demand representative government for Austria as well, and crowds soon clashed with the troops and formed specific demands. In rapid order Metternich resigned, censorship was abolished, a constitution was promised, and firearms were passed out to the students. When students rejected the proposal that all men except factory workers and servants be allowed to vote, universal male suffrage was conceded. Hungarian autonomy then brought similar demands from Czechs in Bohemia, Croatians in Croatia, and Romanians in Transylvania (these last two domains under Hungarian rule). The old Austrian Empire had all but collapsed.

When Frederick William IV of Prussia learned the incredible news of an uprising in Vienna and the fall of Metternich, he granted the concessions on which he had stalled for months, relaxing censorship and calling a meeting of the Landtag. Fighting broke out anyway, and Frederick William then agreed to remove his hated troops from Berlin, used the evocative word *Germany* in proclamations to "my dear Berliners," and wore the German national colors: black, gold, and red. A constituent assembly was elected in May by universal

Chronology
THE OPENING PHASE,
1848

France	German States		Italian States
	Habsburg Empire	*Prussia*	
Feb. 22 Barricades in Paris	**Mar. 3** Hungarian demands	**Mar. 15** Berlin rising	**Jan. 12** Palermo revolt
Feb. 23 Louis Philippe abdicates, Republic proclaimed	**Mar. 12** Student risings in Vienna	**Mar. 18 – 21** Prussian king calls Landtag	**Feb. 10** King in Naples grants constitution
Apr. 23 French elections	**Mar. 13** Metternich resigns	**May 18** Frankfurt national assembly meets	**Feb. 17** Constitution granted in Tuscany
	Mar. 15 – 31 Liberal legislation; Hungarian autonomy	**May 22** Prussian constituent assembly meets	**Mar. 4** Constitution granted in Piedmont
	Apr. 8 Czechs promised a constituent assembly		**Mar. 14** Pope grants constitution
	Apr. 25 Emperor proclaims constitution for Austria		**Mar. 18 – 22** Milan revolt: Five Glorious Days
	May 15 Vienna: Demonstrators demand democracy		**Mar. 22** Venice declares republic
	May 17 Emperor flees		**May 30** Italian troops defeat Austrians

▼ **In one of the early triumphs of the 1848 revolutions, the citizens of Milan forced the Austrian Army to leave the city. Everyone now knew how to build barricades, and the whole family helped, using whatever was available.**
Milan, Museo del Risorgimento. Photo, G. Costa/Index.

but indirect male suffrage, and when it met in Berlin, where a civic guard now kept order, revolution seemed to have triumphed in Prussia, too. Events in the rest of Germany confirmed that victory. In May, 830 delegates elected by universal male suffrage convened at Frankfurt to write a constitution for all of Germany. They were mostly from the smaller states of the more liberal west, and more than half of them were lawyers and professors. But there were also businessmen, members of the liberal gentry, and even nobles, suddenly awkward in such society. The great majority favored a monarchical German state with an almost democratic constitution as the brilliant, difficult, and noisy assembly set about to write a constitution for a united Germany.

The arrangements contrived in 1815 at the Congress of Vienna were under siege in Italy as well, where in the 1820s and 1830s the kingdoms of Piedmont in the north and Naples (including Sicily) in the south had barely weathered earlier revolts, which had also threatened the smaller duchies in between. A well-organized rising in Palermo against rule from Naples was actually the first of the revolutions in 1848; but it was news of the revolution in Paris that made it possible to demand constitutions in Naples, Tuscany, and Piedmont. Even the Papal States got a constitution, though it awkwardly preserved a veto for the pope and the College of Cardinals. Lombardy and Venetia had been ruled as part of the Habsburg Empire since 1815, but shortly after the revolution in Vienna, a revolt broke out in Milan against the Austrian forces there. The Austrians were forced to retreat, and the "Five Glorious Days of Milan" were added to the heroic legends of March. Then Venice rose up to reestablish the Venetian republic of old, and the possibility that the Italian peninsula might be freed from foreign rule stimulated a nationalist fervor that forced Piedmont to join the war against Austria.

THE FATAL DISSENSIONS

Social Class Everywhere, however, the new freedom exposed divisions among those who had fought for it. In France these divisions were primarily social—between Paris and the countryside, between the middle class and the workers. Finding conditions little improved under a republic, workers agitated for a social program and pinned their hopes on the national workshops that had been established as an echo of ideas popularized by the socialist Louis Blanc. Imagined as cooperatives in which workers would work for themselves and share the profits, the workshops that the Republic established were in practice little more than a program of temporary relief. Unemployed men from Paris and the countryside nevertheless enrolled by the tens of thousands. To moderate republicans the workshops represented a dangerous principle and outrageous waste. The government ordered them disbanded in June. To workers the workshops represented an explicit promise and the beginning of a new era. They responded by building barricades in the working-class sections of Paris. For three days the poor fought with the ferocity of hopelessness before the Republic's troops under General Cavaignac systematically crushed the threat to order.

More than a thousand people died; thousands more would be sent to prison or into exile. The June Days remained the very symbol of class conflict for socialists, and radicals never quite recaptured their faith that democracy alone would lead to social justice. Given almost dictatorial powers, Cavaignac took steps to restrict the press, suppress radical societies, and discipline workers. Yet Cavaignac remained a convinced republican; and the assembly continued to write a constitution that maintained universal suffrage and provided for a president directly elected by popular vote. But after June there was something a little hollow about the Second Republic.

National Ambitions In Germany and Austria, also, revolution uncovered latent conflicts between workers and the middle class and among artisans, peasants, and nobles; but the outcome was determined more by competing nationalism

▼ A silent street in Paris, its rubble, bodies, and blood—the emblems of revolution defeated in this painting by Ernest Meissonier.
Giraudon/Art Resource.

Chronology

FATAL DISSENSIONS,

1848

France

June 23 – 26 June Days insurrection

Nov. 4 Constitution

German States

Habsburg Empire

June 12 Prague bombarded; Pan-Slav congress dissolved; military dictatorship

June 22 Assembly in Vienna adopts constitution, peasants emancipated

Sept. 17 Austria army from Croatia invades Hungary

Oct. 31 Vienna bombarded, occupied

Prussia

June – Sept. Frankfurt assembly supports Prussia against Danes in Schleswig-Holstein

Italy

July 24 Austrians defeat Italian army

Nov. 25 Pope flees Rome

▼ **An engraving of the violence in Frankfurt in September 1848 contrasts the fighting styles of troops and people.**
The Granger Collection.

and the fact that kings still had their armies. The Frankfurt parliament had little sympathy for uprisings by other nationalities against German rule. Instead of protesting the repression of revolution, it congratulated the Austrian field marshal who bombarded Prague, where Czechs had staged a Pan-Slav conference, on his German victory; and it applauded the Austrian forces that regrouped in northern Italy and fought their way back into Milan. It called on the Prussian army to put down a Polish uprising in Posen and to fight against Denmark in Schleswig and Holstein. In September when riots broke out in Frankfurt itself, the assembly invited Austrian and Prussian troops to restore order. Conflicts among multiple nationalities were also strengthening the Habsburgs at home, where the emperor mobilized Croatians, who had been demanding autonomy from Hungary much as Hungary had from Austria.

The armies that soon moved on Frankfurt and Vienna confronted a rising that, like the June Days in Paris, revealed an even greater popular fury and more radical demands than the risings of February and March. Politics turned more radical in Rome, too, where the pope had proved not to be an Italian nationalist; economic conditions worsened, and a government that had promised much accomplished little. When his prime minister was assassinated, Pius IX slipped across the border into the Kingdom of Naples, allowing a representative assembly to give the eternal city its ancient title of Roman Republic. Venice and France were also republics, and assemblies were still busy drafting constitutions in Vienna, Berlin, and Frankfurt, but there could be no doubt that conservative forces were gaining ground.

THE FINAL PHASE

New Leaders In December, France elected a president, and the candidates who had been prominent in the new republic finished far behind Louis Napoleon Bonaparte, who won 70 percent of the votes. The ambitious nephew of Emperor Napoleon, he had campaigned as a republican. He had written more about social questions and workers' needs than any other candidate; and he was supported by the Catholic Church and the monarchists, for want of anyone else, as a man of

order. Above all, he had his name.[1] Austria, too, found a strong new leader in Prince Felix von Schwarzenberg, who filled the place Metternich left vacant; and in December he persuaded the emperor to abdicate in favor of his eighteen-year-old nephew, Francis Joseph I, who could promise a fresh start. In Prussia the king felt confident enough to dissolve the Landtag and promulgate a constitution of his own, one very similar to Piedmont's and Belgium's. Ten months of turmoil had led back to the arrangements of February.

Military Force One by one, the remaining revolutionary regimes were subdued. The Frankfurt Assembly, having completed its constitution for a unified Germany, in March 1849 elected the Prussian king as German emperor, only to have him reject a crown from the "gutter," declaring that the ones he recognized came by grace of God. The Frankfurt constitution—with its touching list of old abuses to be abolished, its universal male suffrage and promises of civil rights and education—would never be tested (see "The Frankfurt Constitution," p. 843). New revolutions broke out in the Rhineland, Saxony, and Bavaria, but all were quashed in June and July with the aid of Prussian troops. The Habsburgs' multinational armies bombarded the revolutionaries of Vienna into submission and soon turned on Hungary, where a republic had been declared because Schwarzenberg refused to permit Hungary to have a constitution. The Hungarians battled for months against the armies of Austria and against Croatians, several groups of Slavs, and Romanians until Russia intervened in June to seal the fate of the Hungarian republic.

In Italy, too, military force was decisive. Austria defeated Piedmont one more time, leaving it nothing to show for its support of Italian independence except an enormous debt, an unpopular government, a new ruler, a cautious constitution, and the red, white, and green flag of Italian

---

[1] On trial for his attempted coup in 1840, Louis Napoleon had concluded his defense with these words: "I represent before you a principle, a cause, and a defeat: the principle is sovereignty of the people; the cause, that of the Empire; the defeat, Waterloo. The principle you have recognized; the cause you have served; the defeat you want to avenge."

Chronology

THE FINAL PHASE,
1848 – 1849

France	German States		Italy
	Habsburg Empire	*Prussia*	
Dec. 20 Louis Napoleon elected president	**Dec. 2.** Francis Joseph, emperor	**Dec. 5** Prussian assembly dissolved	**Feb. 9** Roman Republic established
	Jan. 5 Budapest occupied	**Mar. 27** Frankfurt constitution completed; rejected by Prussia on Apr. 21	**Mar. 23** Decisive defeat of Piedmont by Austria
	Mar. 4 Austrian Reichstag dissolved, its constitution replaced		**Apr. 24** French army lands in Papal States
	Apr. 13 Hungary declares a republic		**June 30** Rome falls to French
	June 17 Russia invades Hungary		**Aug. 28** Venice surrenders
	Aug. 13 Hungary capitulates		

---

nationalism. Ten years later the constitution and the flag would seem quite a lot; for the time being, Austrian power once again dominated the Italian peninsula. There was soon a further foreign presence in the center of Italy, for Louis Napoleon sent French armies to restore the pope and defeat the Roman Republic, which fought with heroic tenacity for three months before being overrun. The Kingdom of Naples did not reconquer Sicily until May 1849 and only after a bombardment of the city of Messina that made Ferdinand II known throughout Europe as King Bomba. The last of the revolutionary regimes to fall was the Venetian republic, defeated in August 1849 more by starvation and cholera than by the Austrian artillery that accomplished the unprecedented feat of lobbing shells three miles from the mainland into the island city.

The Results A famous liberal historian has called 1848 "the turning-point at which modern history failed to turn,"[2] and his epigram captures

the sense of destiny thwarted that still colors the liberal view of 1848. Current historical analysis of the failures of 1848 generally makes five broad points. First, liberal constitutions, new economic policies, and increased civil rights failed to pull strong and lasting support from artisans, peasants, and workers, whose more immediate needs were neither met nor understood. Second, the revolutions of February and March were made primarily by the middle classes, strengthened by popular discontent; but when radicals sought more than representative government and legal equality, the middle classes worried about order and private property. Isolated from the masses, they were too weak to retain power except in France; and there order came only after repression of the urban poor and erosion of constitutional lib-

---

[2] George Macaulay Trevelyan, *British History in the Nineteenth Century and After*, 1937, p. 292.

The Frankfurt Constitution

◆◇◆

The Frankfurt Parliament completed its work on a constitution for Germany in 1849. It was a long and detailed document, carefully proscribing the repressive acts that had been most common in the preceding years. Its proud assertions of German freedom remain significantly vague, however, about the enforcement of its provisions and what the boundaries of the German nation will be.

THE FUNDAMENTAL RIGHTS OF THE GERMAN PEOPLE

"Article 1

¶ 131. The German people consists of the citizens of the states, which make up the Reich.

¶ 132. Every German has the right of German Reich's citizenship. He can exercise this right in every German land. Reich's franchise legislation shall provide for the right of the individual to vote for members of the national assembly.

¶ 133. Every German has the right to live or reside in any part of the Reich's territory, to acquire and dispose of property of all kinds, to pursue his livelihood, and to win the right of communal citizenship.

The terms of living and residence shall be established by a law of settlement; trade regulations shall be established by regulations affecting trade and industry; both to be set by the Reich's administration for all of Germany.

¶ 134. No German state is permitted to make a distinction between its citizens and other Germans in civil, criminal, and litigation rights which relegates the latter to the position of foreigners.

¶ 135. Capital punishment for civil offenses shall not take place, and, in those cases where condemnation has already been made, shall not be carried out, in order not to infringe upon the hereby acquired civil law.

¶ 136. Freedom of emigration shall not be limited by any state; emigration levies shall not be established.

All matters of emigration remain under the protection and care of the Reich.

"Article 2

¶ 137. There are no class differences before the law. The rank of nobility is abolished.

All special class privileges are abolished.

All Germans are equal before the law.

All titles, insofar as they are not bound with an office, are abolished and never again shall be introduced.

No citizen shall accept a decoration from a foreign state.

Public office shall be open to all men on the basis of ability.

All citizens are subject equally to military service; there shall be no draft substitutions.

"Article 3

¶ 141. The confiscation of letters and papers, except at an arrest or house search, can take place with a legally executed warrant, which must be served on the arrested person at once or within the next twenty-four hours.

¶ 142. The secrecy of letters is inviolable.

Necessary exceptions in cases of criminal investigation and in the event of war shall be established by legislation.

"Article 4

¶ 143. Every German shall have the right freely to express his opinion through speech, writing, publication, and illustration.

The freedom of the press shall be suspended under no circumstances through preventive measures, namely, censorship, concessions, security orders, imposts, limitation of publication or bookselling, postal bans, or other restraints."

From Louis L. Snyder (ed.), *The Documents of German History,* Rutgers University Press, 1958.

---

erties. Third, the leaders of the revolutions, inexperienced in practical politics, often mistook parliaments for power and left intact the established authorities that would soon turn on them. Fourth, nationalism divided revolutionaries and prevented the cooperation that was essential for durable success. Fifth, no major nation was ready to intervene in behalf of change. Britain was sympathetic, France encouraging, and the United States (its consulates centers of republicanism) enthusiastic; but none of that sympathy matched the military assistance Russia gave the Austrian emperor or the formidable armies of Austria and Prussia.

The events of 1848 had significant effects nonetheless. Revolution so widespread measured the failures of restoration, displayed again the power of political ideas, and uncovered the effects of a generation of social change. Many of the gains won in that year endured: The peasants of eastern Prussia and the Austrian Empire were emancipated in 1848 and remained free of servile obligations; Piedmont and Prussia kept their new, limited constitutions. The monarchs triumphant in 1849 punished revolutionaries with execution, flogging, prison, and exile, but they also learned that they must pay more attention to winning some popular support. Liberals would never again depend so optimistically on the spontaneous power of the people, and advocates of social reform would be more skeptical of political liberalism. International power clearly constrained domestic policy, but political leaders of every hue now also recognized the potential force of nationalism.

II. The Politics of Nationalism

Why nationalism assumed such importance in the nineteenth century and has retained it to the present day remains one of the important questions of modern history. As an ideology, it presents itself as a natural, age-old sentiment arising spontaneously; yet nationalism is essentially a modern phenomenon and often seems to require generations of propaganda. Associated with liberalism in the first part of the nineteenth century, nationalism came to be embraced and used by both the left and the right.

THE ELEMENTS OF NATIONALISM

Nationalism's deepest roots lie in a shared sense of regional and cultural identity, especially as those roots are expressed in custom, language, and religion. This shared culture had been greatly affected, even shaped, by the development of the state, whose power and importance had increased since the state building of the seventeenth century. But it was the experience of the French Revolution that established nationalism as a political force capable of mobilizing popular enthusiasm, of reforming society, of creating seemingly irresistible political movements, and thus of greatly adding to the power of the state.

Liberation and Modernization   Napoleon I had appealed to national feeling in much of Europe, most notably Poland and Italy. The fight against Napoleon was called a national war of liberation in Germany, and the Allies had evoked national feeling somewhat more timidly to recruit opposition to the French in Spain and (less successfully) Italy. The association of liberation and nationalism had been particularly marked in the New World, where the American Revolution had fostered a fervent nationalism and where, as a result of their revolt against Spanish rule, elite groups had carved Central and South America into new states and claimed a national identity for each of them.

Nationalism was also a movement for self-conscious modernization, embraced by people who believed that their societies might equal the industrial wealth of England and acquire political systems as responsive and efficient as those of Britain and France. In the course of the nineteenth century, increased communication, literacy, and mobility further stimulated the sense of belonging to a larger but definable community. Nationalism was thus a response to social and economic change, one that promised to bring middle classes and masses together in support of common goals. Nationalists, like conservatives and socialists, stressed the values of community; like liberals, they tended to believe that change could bring progress.

National Identity   As an intellectual movement, nationalism was an international phenomenon, everywhere emphasizing the importance of culture; yet it was informed by cultural romanticism, with its rejection of the universalism of the Enlightenment. Thus German intellectuals such as Johann Gottfried von Herder and Johann Gottlieb Fichte were characteristic in urging their countrymen to put aside values imported from France in favor of a uniquely German culture.

The exploration of ethnic origins took many forms. A group of German scholars made philology a science, and by the 1830s and 1840s an extraordinary revival of national languages had occurred across Europe. Gaelic was hailed as the national tongue of Ireland; in Finland the first public lecture in Finnish marked a break from the dominant Swedish culture; intellectuals in Bohemia began abandoning their customary German to write in Czech. More remarkable still was the number of languages consciously contrived out of local dialects and invented vocabularies. Norwegian became distinct from Danish, Serbian from other Slavic languages, and Slovak from Czech—all literary languages by the 1840s, each the work of a handful of scholars whose task of establishing a national language was made easier by widespread illiteracy.

This fascination with folk culture and a national past was reinforced by an emphasis on history as popular genre but also a special, scholarly form of knowledge that revealed each nation's historic mission. Germans wrote of a special sense of freedom embodied in Germanic tribes, expanded in the Reformation, and now extended to the state. French historians wrote eloquently of France's call to carry reason and liberty across Europe, and Italian writers proclaimed that Italy was destined to lead Europe once again as it had as the home of Roman civilization and the center of Christianity. The poet Adam Mickiewicz, lecturing in Paris, inspired Polish nationalists with his descriptions of how Poland's history paralleled the life of Christ and had yet to achieve Resurrection. Francis Palacky pioneered in stressing the role of the Czechs as leaders of the Slavs. Such visions were repeated in poetry and drama, which now blossomed in the native tongue and justified resistance to alien rule. This cultural nationalism, which circulated among intellectuals, students, professional people, and journalists, served as a weapon of middle-class self-assertion, whereby people who felt cramped by their society's social hierarchy, unsympathetic bureaucracy, or stagnant economy could win broader support for their own dreams of progress.

Political Goals   In places subject to foreign rule, the political goal of nationalist movements was independence. Everywhere, economic issues were central. Campaigns for agricultural improvement, promoted by the liberal aristocracy, became nationalist programs in Hungary and Italy. In Germany Friedrich List, a leading liberal economist, argued that the American example proved the need for tariffs to protect fledgling industries and made his analysis into a nationalist battle cry. Only a united Germany with a national tariff, he insisted, could create an internal area of free trade sufficient to develop the industry and vigorous middle class necessary for competitive strength and independence. Everywhere nationalist groups generally demanded public education, more political freedom, and efficient government. Strengthened by its promises of economic growth and its respect for native traditions, nationalism generated political movements of broad appeal, capable of mobilizing popular enthusiasm. Daniel O'Connell's inflammatory speeches won thousands to his Young Ireland organization and its demands for the end of union with Great Britain; by the 1830s he commanded the largest movement of political protest Europe had yet seen.

A NEW REGIME: THE SECOND EMPIRE IN FRANCE

Elections in France had left the Second Republic ruled by a president, Louis Napoleon, who would eventually subvert it, and a Chamber of Deputies in which a majority were monarchists who had not wanted a republic at all.

From Republic to Empire   Often at odds with the deputies, Napoleon continued to play to public opinion; and when, in the third year of his four-year term, the Chamber rejected a constitutional amendment that would have allowed him a second term, he struck. His coup d'état came on the eve of December 2, 1851—the anniversary of the first Napoleon's coronation as emperor in 1804 and of his victory at Austerlitz in 1805. Potential opponents, including 200 deputies, were quickly taken into custody; troops occupied the streets and overran hastily built barricades. At the same time, Napoleon restored universal manhood suffrage, which the conservative Chamber had restricted.[3] Resistance was serious in many parts of

---

[3] They did so by using a residence requirement that excluded "unstable" workers, that is, those who had recently moved.

France—hundreds were killed and more than 20,000 people arrested—but brief. Three weeks later Napoleon's actions were ratified by more than 90 percent of the voters in a national plebiscite. Exactly one year after this first coup, Napoleon had the Second Republic transformed into the Second Empire and became Emperor Napoleon III, a change even more overwhelmingly supported in another plebiscite. Citizens could do no more than vote yes or no, to accept changes already effected or risk whatever might follow from a negative vote.

The Second Empire claimed a democratic mandate but held authoritarian power. It was supported by most businessmen and the Catholic Church, accepted by most monarchists, local notables, and peasants. It sponsored programs for social welfare as well as economic growth and promised both peace and national glory. Napoleon III was influenced by Saint-Simonian socialism, attracted by liberal nationalism, and obsessed by belief in his own destiny—Napoleon the Little to his opponents, the Emperor to most of the French.

The economy boomed in the 1850s; and the French government fostered economic growth more systematically than any other government in Europe, using tax incentives to stimulate investment, making it easier to form companies with limited liability, and adding its own special investment funds (of which the Crédit Mobilier for industry was the most famous). Among its many programs of public works, the rebuilding of Paris was one of the most elaborate. A pioneering venture in city planning, the project typified the imperial style. Plans were reviewed by Napoleon III himself, who favored ostentatious structures of equal height, and directed by his extraordinarily able prefect Georges Haussmann. New parks were created and slums cleared, often with painful dislocation for their residents; wide

▼ **Haussmann's rebuilding of Paris began with the demolition of buildings that had stood for centuries.**
Lauros-Giraudon/Art Resource.

boulevards, planned for their striking vistas and as an aid to traffic, incidentally made it hard to build barricades. Facades often received more attention than the buildings behind them, but the buildings were now served by a vast new sewer and water system. Such massive projects stimulated land speculation and profiteering; yet the result was a city healthier and more convenient, envied and imitated throughout the world. The court of Napoleon and Empress Eugénie was brilliant, and French prestige in the arts and sciences (enhanced by the fame of Louis Pasteur's discoveries in biology) was never higher. The emperor presented himself as the patron of educational and social reform and, in the Napoleonic tradition, rewarded talent with honors and promotions, and he took credit for heightened prestige— more credit, in fact, than was his due.

The Liberal Empire   By the 1860s, however, the empire's fortunes were changing, its policies at home and abroad subject to rising criticism. The coalition of interests that had supported Napoleon was breaking up. Foreign ventures intended to extend French influence and satisfy national pride had their political costs. Support of Italian unification antagonized French Catholics, and the attempt to gain imperial glory by intervention in Mexico ended in disaster. Steps toward free trade, including a major tariff agreement with Great Britain in 1860, appealed to liberal economists but upset many producers. At the same time, workers wanted more from the government than public works projects and support for mutual-aid societies. Restrictions of political freedom were increasingly resented, and opponents' criticisms became more intense.

Napoleon's response was a gradual liberalization that in 1860 enlarged the role of the legislature and by 1868 included freedom of the press and of assembly; a full-fledged parliamentary system was in place two years later. The government also encouraged workers' organizations and acknowledged the right to strike. Like the establishment of public secondary schools, which the Church opposed, these new measures alienated some old supporters without, however, mollifying an opposition that gained in each election. Republicans held nearly half the lower house in 1869, and a republican was prime minister the fol-

▲ The ladies and gentlemen of the court and diplomatic corps assembled in 1860 to watch Napoleon III take the imperial prince in a rowboat. The family scene with the emperor as father reflected the popular appeal that a modern ruler needed, especially if elected by plebiscite.
Harlinque-Viollet.

lowing year, which turned out to be the Second Empire's last.

NATIONALISM AND INTERNATIONAL RELATIONS

The Politics of Patriotism   The conflicts of 1848 and 1849 had suggested the political potential of nationalism, a lesson that Prussia, Austria, Britain, Piedmont, and France would all seek to apply. In 1849 Prussia still hoped to lead a confederation of North German states, finding the nationalist dreams of the Frankfurt assembly more attractive once the assembly itself had no voice. Austria promoted a competing solution. Eager to reassert Habsburg influence in Germany after revolution in Hungary had been quelled, Schwarzenberg shrewdly reconvoked the diet of the old German Confederation, putting the German states in the dangerous position of having to choose between Austrian and Prussian leadership. With the clear support of Russia, Austria then threatened Prussia with war; before so grave a challenge, Prussia backed down, abandoning its scheme for a German union. Habsburg hegemony over Germany seemed assured.

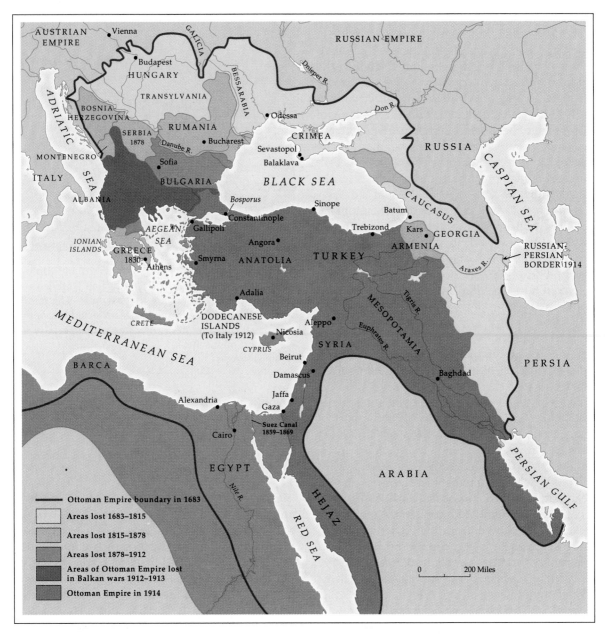

▲ MAP 24.1 THE DECLINE OF THE OTTOMAN EMPIRE, 1683-1914

The British foreign secretary also exploited the nationalist appeal of an assertive policy. Henry John Temple, Viscount Palmerston, was a flamboyant aristocrat, frequently at odds with his cabinet colleagues, often indifferent to procedural niceties, but shrewdly alert to public opinion. Thus he made the claims against the Greek government of one Don Pacifico into an issue of British national honor. An Athenian mob had burned Pacifico's house because he was a Portuguese Jew; but he had been born in Gibraltar and held British citizenship. Palmerston vigorously supported Pacifico's demands for compensation from the Greek government, sending notes, threats, and finally the British fleet to Greece until an indemnity was paid. Palmerston defended

▲ The Crimean War generated considerable enthusiasm in Britain and France, with the help of colorful accounts from the front. This dramatic illustration from a British paper shows Florence Nightingale rushing to aid wounded soldiers, a service that made her and professional nurses famous.
The Granger Collection.

his stand in the House of Commons. Dramatically, he recalled the pride of ancient Romans, who could say *"Civis Romanus sum"* ("I am a Roman citizen") and know themselves secure throughout their empire. A British subject, Palmerston declared, "in whatever land he may be, shall feel confident that the watchful eye and strong arm of England will protect him against injustice and wrong." To the public at least, Palmerston was vindicated.

The Crimean War The restless search for international prestige led France and Great Britain to war against Russia in 1854 over competing claims by Roman Catholic and Greek Orthodox monks to be the guardians of Jerusalem's holy places. France, citing traditions going back to the time of the crusades and the policies of Cardinal Richelieu several centuries later, supported the Latin monks. France pressed the Ottoman sultan, whose

empire included Jerusalem, to grant them specific privileges. Russia, as defender of the Orthodox faith, demanded a protectorate over Orthodox churches within the Ottoman Empire and showed its determination by occupying Wallachia and Moldavia, Danubian lands under Ottoman suzerainty. This Russian expansion, part of a long-term pattern, worried the English, who saw a threat to their own empire in any extension of Russian influence in the direction of Persia or Afghanistan. Britain encouraged the sultan to resist Russia's demands.

Negotiations repeatedly broke down; Britain and France sent their fleets into the Aegean Sea, and in October 1853 the sultan exuberantly declared war on Russia. Russian forces destroyed an Ottoman fleet, however, and Britain and France decided to fight Russia to preserve the balance of power in the Middle East. That announcement in March 1854 was greeted with patriotic enthusiasm

MAZZINI'S NATIONALISM

"On the Duties of Man" is one of Giuseppe Mazzini's most famous essays. It was first written in 1844 for Italian workers living in England, and the excerpts here are from the fifth chapter, which was added for a new edition in 1858. Despite the events of the intervening years, Mazzini's romantic faith had changed little. The essay's title was meant to contrast with the French Revolution's Declaration of the Rights of Man, which Mazzini criticized for encouraging selfishness and materialism.

"Your first duties—first as regards importance—are, as I have already told you, towards Humanity . . . . If you do not embrace the whole human family in your affection, . . . if, wheresoever a fellow-creature suffers, or the dignity of human nature is violated by falsehood or tyranny—you are not ready, if able, to aid the unhappy, and do not feel called upon to combat, if able, for the redemption of the betrayed or oppressed—you violate your law of life, you comprehend not that Religion which will be the guide and blessing of the future.

"But what can each of you, singly, *do* for the moral improvement and progress of Humanity? . . . The watchword of the faith of the future is *Association*, and . . . [the] means was provided for you by God when he gave you a country; when, even as a wise overseer of labour distributes the various branches of employment according to the different capacities of the workmen, he divided Humanity into distinct groups or nuclei upon the face of the earth, thus creating the germ of Nationalities. Evil governments have disfigured the divine design. Nevertheless you may still trace it, distinctly marked out—at least as far as Europe is concerned—by the course of the great rivers, the direction of the higher mountains, and other geographical conditions. They have disfigured it by their conquests, their greed, and their jealousy even of the righteous power of others. . . .

"These governments did not, and do not, recognize any country save their own families or dynasty, the egotism of caste. But the Divine design will infallibly be realized. Natural divisions, and the spontaneous, innate tendencies of the peoples, will take the place of the arbitrary divisions sanctioned by evil governments. The map of Europe will be redrawn. The countries of the Peoples, defined by the vote of free men, will arise upon the ruins of the countries of kings and privileged castes. . . .

"O my brothers, love your Country! Our country is our Home, the house that God has given us, placing therein a numerous family that loves us, and whom we love. . . . Our country is our common workshop, whence the products of our activity are sent forth for the benefit of the whole world. . . . In labouring for our own country on the right principle, we labour for Humanity."

From Giuseppe Mazzini, *On the Duties of Man*, Greenwood Publishing Group.

in London and Paris. Six months after war was declared, not having found a more convenient battlefield, British and French forces landed in the Crimea. The war was conducted with remarkable incompetence on both sides. Russia was unable to mobilize or effectively deploy the large armies that made it so feared, and Britain's supply system proved inadequate for hostilities at such a distance. In 1855 the allies welcomed the aid of little Piedmont and, a full year after invading the Crimea, finally took Sevastopol. Russia sued for peace and agreed to accept terms to be defined at a European congress in Paris.

Congress of Paris The Congress signified an important shift in the European balance. It met in Paris rather than Vienna and was preoccupied with issues of nationalism. In 1856 Russia counted for less than it had in 1815, and the conservative alliance of Austria, Prussia, and Russia that had dominated the continent for a generation had broken up over competing ambitions in the Balkans and Germany. The Congress required Russia to cede some territory at the mouth of the Danube River, to surrender its claims to any protectorate over Christians in the Ottoman Empire, and to accept a ban on warships in the Black Sea. Only this last point really rankled. The more troublesome issues all had to do with national claims. Britain and France did not want to give the Danubian principalities to either Russia or Austria. The issue was postponed because the obvious resolution—unit-

▲ In his portraits and in his personal life Mazzini seemed as much a romantic poet as a revolutionary agitator.
The Granger Collection.

ing the two territories and allowing them autonomy, a procedure that began a few years later—would create the basis for a Romanian national state, and Austria was learning to fear nationalism as a threat to the Habsburg empire. Such fears prevented Napoleon III from putting the question of Polish independence on the agenda as he wanted to; but the Congress did discuss the rising discontent in Italy, the only concession Piedmont won for having helped the victors in the Crimea. Even that was enough to produce patriotic outbursts in Italy and to frighten Austria.

Almost 500,000 soldiers died in the Crimean War, the highest toll of any European conflict from the Napoleonic wars to World War I. Two-thirds of the casualties were Russian, and two-thirds of all losses resulted from sickness and bad care. Yet the outbreak of war produced a surge of enthusiasm no government could ignore. The public diplomacy that led to the war, the parades of magnificently uniformed soldiers, and the heroic stories reported by an aggressive journalism underscored its political importance. Under Western pressure, the Ottoman Empire began to adopt the modernizing institutions of the West; and Russia, sobered by defeat, launched an era of fundamental reform unequaled since the days of Peter the Great. In Italy and Germany the way was opening for still more drastic changes.

A NEW NATION: THE UNIFICATION OF ITALY

Giuseppe Mazzini Across the Italian peninsula, all the revolutions of 1848 had declared an independent nation to be one of their primary goals; and in doing so they employed the ideas of Giuseppe Mazzini, one of Europe's most important revolutionaries (see "Mazzini's Nationalism," p. 850). For fifteen years, Mazzini had lived in exile, mainly in London, organizing conspiracies and writing passionate propaganda in pamphlets and thousands of letters. His nationalist movement, Young Italy, had stimulated similar efforts in Ireland, Switzerland, and Hungary. Until 1848, the conspiracies he fostered had resulted in tragic failures; yet like the clandestine committees, secret meetings, and smuggled newspapers that surrounded them, these plots, though unsuccessful, had disseminated the belief that once corrupt regimes were toppled, the people would rise in common cause. Revolutionary and democratic, Mazzini was also a moralist who criticized the French Revolution for stressing rights over moral duty and who rejected socialism as materialistic. In nationalism he saw the expression of natural communities, the basis for popular democracy and international brotherhood.

Italy renewed would lead the way. A man of letters steeped in romanticism, Mazzini nonetheless wrote tellingly about the specific grievances of peasants, artists, professionals, and intellectuals. His influence was especially strong in northern Italy, where in the 1830s and 1840s young lawyers, liberal landowners, and some members of the aristocracy began to find national implications in nearly everything they did. Annual congresses of Italian scientists became quiet demonstrations of patriotic aspirations; disputes over where railroad lines should be built became means of expressing discontent with Austrian rule. Literary journals and societies for agricultural improvement took up the nationalist theme.

For Mazzinians, 1848 was the great chance (Mazzini himself was one of the leaders of the

Roman Republic), and the defeats that followed were an even greater blow to Mazzinianism than to Italian nationalism. As Austria regained dominance of the peninsula, Mazzini had returned to exile and Italian nationalists began to look elsewhere for leadership. The papacy, restored by French arms, was no longer sympathetic to Italian unity; Austria ruled Lombardy and Venetia repressively, and all the other Italian regimes except Piedmont were Austrian dependencies.

The Role of Piedmont Although a small state, Piedmont held some promise for patriots. It had fought Austria, and its young king, Victor Emmanuel II, though no liberal, ruled with a parliament. The kingdom had a tradition of military strength and bureaucratic rectitude. More recently, its government had encouraged commerce and industry, and its efforts to win trade away from Austria through commercial treaties excited Italians elsewhere. These policies acquired firmer purpose in 1852, when Count Camillo Cavour became prime minister. Cavour was a gentleman-farmer who had traveled in France and England. He believed in economic and scientific progress, representative government with limited suffrage, the rule of law, and religious tolerance. Nationalism he understood primarily as an avenue to modernization, and he found in free trade, sound finances, and railroads a power that could remake Piedmont.

Cavour pursued his liberal goals with tactical brilliance, skillfully using newspapers and parliamentary debate to mold public opinion. He created a centrist parliamentary coalition with which he dominated both king and parliament from 1852 until his death in 1861. In that brief time he established himself as one of the outstanding statesmen of the century. Piedmont's internal strength was Cavour's first concern, but he also sought to make his state the center of Italy's resurgence, the Risorgimento.[4] He welcomed exiles from other parts of the peninsula, encouraged the nationalist press, and sought every opportunity for symbolic gestures of patriotism. He was aided in this goal by the Italian National Society, one of whose founders was the president of the Venetian republic in 1848. The National

Society propagandized for Italian unity under Piedmont's king and established secret committees in most of the cities of Italy. Its members were predominantly liberal aristocrats, local lawyers, and professors; and in calling for Italian unity, the society combined Mazzinian rhetoric with hardheaded insistence on the need for international alliances and military force. Economic liberalism largely replaced more generous and vaguer social theories.

War against Austria Most of all, Cavour depended on astute foreign policy. He had pushed for Piedmont's participation in the Crimean War and was rewarded with the discussion of the Italian question at the Congress of Paris. Using his state's enhanced international position, he argued that Italy repressed would remain a danger to European order. He appealed for liberal sympathy throughout Western Europe, and he courted Napoleon III. At last, in July 1858, Cavour and Napoleon III met secretly. It was easy to argue that war was inevitable, given Austria's resentment of Piedmont's growing prominence. If France would support Piedmont against Austria, Cavour promised to accept a complicated set of arrangements designed to benefit France and limit Piedmont's expansion. The plan, too delicately balanced to be practical, sought cautious ends through cynical daring.

Austria, watching young Lombards and Venetians escape conscription by streaming to Piedmont as volunteers, determined to end the nationalist threat once and for all. It sent Piedmont an ultimatum so strong that Cavour needed only to reply with cautious dignity in order to have his war. On April 29, 1859, Austria invaded Piedmont, and France went to the rescue of a small state attacked by her giant neighbor. The rapid movement of large French armies was impressive, but thereafter the war was fought with little tactical brilliance on either side. The Austrians suffered a serious defeat in June, but a larger battle three weeks later was as indecisive as it was bloody. As the Austrians retreated to the fortresses controlling the Lombard plain, Napoleon suddenly lost his taste for war and unilaterally assented to a truce. The emperors of France and Austria agreed that Piedmont should have Lombardy but not Venetia and that the other Italian states should remain as before.

Formation of the Italian Kingdom Those other Italian states, however, had not survived the ex-

---

[4] *Risorgimento*, now the historian's label for the whole period of Italian unification, was a term meaning "resurgence," often used by nationalists and made the title of a liberal newspaper that Cavour helped to found and edit.

citement of a national war. Gentle revolutions accompanied the march of Piedmontese troops throughout northern Italy. When local patriots gathered in the streets, the dukes of Modena, Parma, and Tuscany simply fled, to be replaced by provisional governments led by members of the National Society. These governments quickly adopted Piedmontese laws and held elections to representative assemblies. The terms of the truce arranged by France and Austria could not be carried out; and after a few months, the provisional governments held plebiscites—a device Napoleon could hardly reject—on the question of annexation to Piedmont. Italians trooped to the polls with bands playing and flags waving, peasants behind their lords and workers with their guilds. The result was as one-sided as in the plebiscites in France. Piedmont's King Victor Emmanuel ruled from the Alps to Rimini on the Adriatic. The province of Savoy and the city of Nice were turned over to France.

Moderate liberals had united half of Italy. Sputtering revolts in Sicily gave more democratic nationalists a chance to lead a different sort of Risorgimento. Former Mazzinians, eager to promote a Sicilian uprising, gathered guns in Genoa and planned an expedition that Cavour dared neither support nor oppose. Its leader would be Giuseppe Garibaldi, Italy's most popular hero. Exiled for his Mazzinian activity in the 1830s, Garibaldi had spent ten years fighting for democratic causes in South America, returning to Italy in time to take part in the wars of 1848. He had directed the heroic defense of the Roman Republic in 1849 and led the most effective corps of volunteers in 1859. In his greatest exploit of all, he set sail for Sicily one night in May 1860, with a thousand men, mainly middle-class youths from Lombardy, Venetia, and the Romagna.

Garibaldi Goes South No event in the nineteenth century so captured the popular imagination as that daring venture. The Expedition of the Thousand was like some ancient epic come to life in an industrial age: Untrained men, wearing the red shirts Garibaldi had adopted in South America, fought with bravery and discipline, enthusiastically supported in the Sicilian countryside. Garibaldi's tactics confused and defeated the Neapolitan generals, despite their far larger and better-equipped forces. In two weeks the Red Shirts occupied Palermo and within two months almost all of Sicily. Volunteers flocked from all over Italy to join Garibaldi, and money was raised in his behalf in all the towns of northern Italy and from New York to Stockholm.

The epic continued when, against all odds, Garibaldi sailed across the strait and landed on the Italian mainland. He declared his goal to be Rome itself and not just Naples. That worried Cavour, who considered Garibaldi irresponsible and believed that an attack on Rome might lead Austria and France to intervene on behalf of the pope. So Cavour encouraged uprisings in the Papal States and then sent Piedmontese troops to preserve order. Carefully skirting the area around Rome, they moved south to meet Garibaldi. On September 18, between lines of suspicious men, Giuseppe Garibaldi and Victor Emmanuel rode out to shake hands and unite Italy. Garibaldi added to his legend by thus giving way in the interests of union, and the Piedmontese took over. Plebiscites confirmed the union, and in March 1861 the Kingdom of Italy was proclaimed.

United Italy The Kingdom of Italy included almost all of Italy except for Rome and Venetia. Catholics throughout the world opposed the

▼ The handshake of Victor Emmanuel and Garibaldi, which sealed the unification of Italy as their armies met in 1860, became a favorite subject for illustrations of the Risorgimento. This engraving is English.
Culver.

▲ MAP 24.2 THE UNIFICATION OF ITALY

annexation of Rome, which Napoleon III was pledged to protect; and Austrian troops were massed in Venetia. Italy acquired Venetia in 1866 as a by-product of the war between Austria and Prussia. Austria offered it in return for neutrality; Prussia promised that Italy should have it if allied to a victorious Prussia. Italy kept a prior pledge to Prussia and went to war. It fought poorly but got Venetia anyway following Prussia's rapid victory. Rome was annexed when French troops withdrew during the Franco-Prussian War of 1870; the new nation finally had its ancient capital.

More lasting problems remained. To many Italians, especially in the south, unification felt like a foreign occupation, and Italy's leaders were appalled at the poverty and corruption they could not overcome. Pius IX forbade Catholics to take part in national elections and rejected the indemnity and guarantees of protection the government offered. United Italy was poor and overwhelmingly agricultural. It had no coal or iron, and three-quarters of the population was illiterate. With liberal conviction the Italian government assumed the debts of all the former governments and struggled to balance the annual budget. Despite taxes that were among the highest in Europe, Italy continued to lag in schools, railways, and roads. The sale of Church lands failed to benefit peasants as much as hoped, and the lower Piedmontese tariffs brought instant distress to hundreds of small producers. For millions of artisans and peasants, few tangible benefits followed from replacing reactionary dukes with a liberal national state.

▼ **A demonstration in Florence's historic piazza della Signoria in 1866 for the annexation of Venetia to the new Kingdom of Italy.**
Scala/Art Resource.

A NEW NATION: THE UNIFICATION OF GERMANY

German cultural identity had grown throughout the first half of the nineteenth century, from the battles against Napoleon to the statements of the Frankfurt Parliament. It was strengthened by achievements in philosophy, science, literature, and music that were seen as German accomplishments no matter what German kingdom, principality, or free city they occurred in. What the political expression of that identity should be was far from resolved, however. The German Confederation was ineffectual; none of the schemes for unification in 1848 had been adopted, and Austria had blocked Prussian plans for leadership in 1850. Yet it was Prussia that created modern Germany.

The Dominance of Prussia Several factors account for Prussia's eventual dominance. One was economic. The *Zollverein*, the tariff union Prussia led, continued to prosper with industrialization in the Rhineland and Prussia, and by 1853 every German state except Austria had joined it. Another factor was Austria's multiple and multinational preoccupations, and its vulnerability was highlighted by the campaign for the unification of Italy. Most important of all was the dynamism of Prussia itself. It was the largest German state, with a powerful army and an efficient administration, and Prussian politics began a new era in 1858 with the rule of William I.[5]

After a long period of reaction in which the press and public discussion were severely repressed, politics had become more open and livelier. Liberal nationalists, particularly in the Rhineland, campaigned for a more representative government; William sought to strengthen the army, and a constitutional crisis resulted. The Prussian constitution of 1850 allowed universal male suffrage but avoided democracy by dividing voters into three classes according to the taxes they paid. Each of the three classes elected an equal number of representatives, ensuring that those chosen by the two wealthier classes would be a majority. In addition,

the king could veto any legislation and appoint the ministers of his choice.

Although designed to ensure conservative dominance, the three-class system had the unexpected effect of magnifying the voice of new industrial wealth, and the majority of the Landtag was now prepared to challenge the monarch. The military budget became their battleground. With William's support, General Albrecht von Roon, minister of war, and Helmuth von Moltke, his chief of staff, proposed to double the army and add to its equipment. Although the proposal was defeated, the government went ahead with its plan. Liberals, who distrusted Prussian militarism and an army dominated by the Junkers, insisted the government must be responsible to the legislature; and the opposition gained in the elections of 1862. Convinced that royal authority was at stake, William called on God and conscience, threatened abdication, and named Otto von Bismarck his chief minister.

Bismarck's Leadership Bismarck was a member of the Junker class, better educated than many. His pride of caste and reactionary views were resented by liberals, and most conservatives considered him to be as erratic and dangerous as Napoleon III. An experienced diplomat familiar with Europe's major capitals, he stood out by reason of his cosmopolitan outlook as much as his enormous self-confidence. For thirty years officials and legislators would have to live with his stinging sarcasm, bruising contempt, and brilliance. Bismarck surprised conservatives with his appeal to nationalism, shrewdly used power wherever he found it, and made success in foreign policy his justification. He lectured the deputies: If Germans looked to Prussia, it was because of its powerful army, not because of any liberal institutions; and he added, in the most famous statement he ever uttered, that "the great questions of the day will not be settled by speeches and majority decisions—that was the mistake of 1848 and 1849—but by blood and iron."

Bismarck dissolved the parliament and used heavy government pressure in the subsequent elections but with little effect. So Bismarck ignored parliament whenever he could and encouraged divisions within the legislature when-

---

[5] William I became regent in 1858—when his brother, Frederick William, was judged insane—and king on his brother's death in 1861.

ever possible. He closed opposition newspapers and manipulated the rest. Promotions in the civil service and judiciary went to those unquestionably loyal; and, once confident of his position, Bismarck spent funds and collected taxes without parliamentary authorization.

In return he offered a remarkable string of foreign triumphs. While blocking Austria's efforts to lead the German Confederation, he courted Russian friendship. When in 1863 Russia repressed a Polish uprising with such severity that Austria, France, and Britain joined in protest, Prussia supported the tsar. Bismarck used conflict over Schleswig and Holstein to assert leadership in German affairs. German nationalists were outraged at attempts by the king of Denmark to annex Schleswig and to extend his authority over Holstein, but Prussia overshadowed the German Diet by persuading Austria to join in war against Denmark in January 1864. Bismarck then foiled international negotiations until the Danes were defeated. Schleswig was placed under Prussian administration and Holstein, surrounded by Prussian troops, under Austrian control, in an awkward arrangement sure to breed contention between Austria and Prussia.

The Austro-Prussian War, 1866   Friction with the Habsburg Empire increased almost daily, and Bismarck prepared for war while ensuring Austria's diplomatic isolation. He dangled visions of territory along the Rhine before Napoleon III, won Italy's support by promising it Venetia, and gained Russia's assurance of neutrality. Both Austria and Prussia were already mobilizing when Prussian troops found an excuse to march into Holstein in June 1866. Initially, Austria had the support of most of the German Confederation, but Hanover surrendered to Prussia within two weeks. Three Prussian armies swept into Bohemia, and at the

▼ **Crowds cheer as Prussian troops parade through the Brandenburg Gate in Berlin in 1866, celebrating Prussia's victory over Austria and the formation of the North German Confederation.**
Archiv für Kunst und Geschichte.

Battle of Sadowa, Austria suffered overwhelming defeat. The Austro-Prussian War lasted just seven weeks. Experts had predicted a long fight, but Prussia, well equipped and ready, applied the lessons of the American Civil War, using railroads and telegraph to move with a speed for which Austria was unprepared.

Many Prussian conservatives had been shocked at Bismarck's disrespectful and belligerent treatment of Austria, but now they were eager to take advantage of Austria's defeat and looked forward to significant territorial gains. Instead, Bismarck insisted on leniency, against the wishes of his king and generals. Austria surrendered no territory, but Prussia's gains elsewhere changed the face of Europe. It annexed several states that had sided with Austria,[6] established a confederation of North German states under Prussian leadership, and got the South German states to accept a military alliance with Prussia.

The North German Confederation The North German Confederation was a Bismarckian structure that seemed to protect local interests and to point toward democracy yet ensured the dominance of Prussia. It left member states free to regulate their local affairs but joined them through a common army under Prussian officers and a bicameral federal parliament. The upper house, the Bundesrat, was composed of forty-three delegates sent in varying numbers from the separate states; Prussia's seventeen gave it more than the one-third necessary for a veto. The lower house, the Reichstag, was elected by universal male suffrage; but the king of Prussia appointed the chancellor, who was responsible to no one else.

After Prussia's victories, the Prussian Parliament retroactively legalized the taxes and expenditures Bismarck had imposed. No German nationalist believed Bismarck's federation to be a satisfactory or permanent solution. Germany's unification, like Italy's, would be achieved in stages and through war and diplomacy. North Germany, Protestant and more industrial than the south, offered a sound foundation for the kind of Germany Bismarck envisioned, as different from the largely

agricultural and Catholic south as northern Italy was from Naples. With their own cultural traditions and ancient dynasties, Germany's southern states still looked to Vienna as their traditional center, admired Paris, and remained suspicious of Berlin.

The Franco-Prussian War More than elections and trade were necessary if Germany was to be quickly united, and war with France filled the need. Historians once hotly disputed who was to blame for that war and whether it was "necessary." New research and changing perspectives have lessened the controversy. The war was wanted by Bismarck but first declared by France, the result more of nationalism on both sides than of long-range calculation. It was provoked by competition over influence in Spain. Queen Isabella II had been forced to abdicate in 1868, and the provisional government there, seeking a replacement, picked a Hohenzollern prince. He declined, under heavy French pressure; but a shaky French government, eager to curry popular favor at home, continued to press its case. In a famous interview at the western German spa of Ems, where William I was taking the baths, the French ambassador demanded a public guarantee that the Hohenzollern candidacy would not be put forward again. The king refused and telegraphed a report to Bismarck, who edited the Ems dispatch to make French demands seem more imperious and the king's refusal more abrupt, then released it to the press. Bismarck, Roon, and Moltke correctly assumed that war would follow. The French government responded to the patriotic fury it had helped ignite and declared war on Prussia in July 1870.

France hoped for support from Italy and Austria but had failed to establish formal agreements, and these states remained neutral. The French army, more formidable than Austria's had been, possessed modern equipment in some respects superior to that of the Germans, but the Germans were better prepared and far more decisively led. In rapid movements German armies pushed through Alsace and encircled the French army at Metz. After heavy losses on both sides, another French force, attempting to relieve Metz, was defeated at Sedan in September. There Napoleon III surrendered and was taken prisoner. Major fight-

---

[6] They were Hanover, Nassau, Electoral Hesse, and Frankfurt.

▲ **MAP 24.3 THE UNIFICATION OF GERMANY**

ing was over, but French resistance continued. Paris, quickly surrounded by German troops, held out under a long siege, and a provisional French government kept an army in the field. An armistice came only at the end of January 1871, when Paris capitulated.

The brief war had profound effects. A German national state was created. In France the Second Empire fell to be succeeded by the Third Repub-

lic after bitter internal conflict. France was required to pay an indemnity of 5 billion francs and to cede Alsace and Lorraine, harsh terms that established enmity between France and Germany as a central fact of European affairs.

The German Reich   The decision to annex Alsace-Lorraine was primarily a military one, intended to provide Germany with strong fortifications in case of future conflict with France. But it was also a response to the demands of German nationalists, whose support Bismarck still needed, for there were many Germans who did not welcome unification under Prussia. Well before the final French surrender, Bismarck began difficult negotiations with each of the South German states. They had joined in fighting France with a mixture of enthusiasm and fear, but it took threats, concessions, and secret funds to arrive at terms for a permanent union of North Germany. William I was then crowned German kaiser (emperor) in the Hall of Mirrors of the French palace of Versailles on January 18, 1871, the anniversary of the founding of the Prussian monarchy.

With modifications, the constitution of the North German Confederation was extended to all the new nation. Many domestic matters were reserved to the twenty-five states that made up the Reich. There was no doubt, however, that the great new nation would be dominated by Prussia. The Second Reich[7] was from its inception a powerful nation. Germany in 1871 was already more populous than France, and its rate of demographic growth was the fastest Europe had ever known. Germany's industrial production increased at an astounding rate. Because it had developed later than Great Britain and France, its industrial equipment was more modern, and the French indemnity added to the available capital. The German government made heavy investments in railroads and spurred industrialization with tax benefits, tariffs, and policies encouraging the formation of large combines, the famous German cartels. German universities led all others in the application of scientific methods to every discipline.

Such rapid growth fed tensions between powerful conservative circles, a growing but insecure middle class, and workers increasingly aware of their distinct interests. Nowhere were materialistic and urban values more intensely attacked than in industrial Germany. Bismarck, worried about internal threats to the new nation, chose to demonstrate the supremacy of the state by moving against two potential opponents: first the Catholic Church and then the socialist party.

---

[7] The old Holy Roman Empire was patriotically honored as having been the first Reich.

Internal Conflict Rather grandiosely named the Kulturkampf ("Struggle for Civilization"), the conflict with the Catholic Church centered on the state's right to approve appointments, restrict religious orders, and supervise seminaries. Many of these measures were common in much of Europe, but there was a harshness in the new state's execution of them and in the rhetoric surrounding them. Intended to assure the "Germanization" of Alsace and the Polish parts of Prussia (both largely Catholic), the measures accentuated regional and ideological differences. Yet the Kulturkampf was not a success. It made martyrs of many a priest and nun, and Catholics rallied to their Church as a majority of bishops went into exile. The Catholic Center party steadily gained votes, and when the more flexible Leo XIII became pope in 1878, Bismarck sought an understanding with the Vatican. That battle of civilization subsided as Bismarck turned his sights on another growing movement.

Socialism did not offend Bismarck either in its criticism of laissez-faire economics or in its call for the state to be socially active, and he had gotten on well with the leading German socialist of the 1860s, Ferdinand Lassalle. But as socialists sought a mass following and in 1875 established the Social Democratic party, their attacks on autocracy, the military, and nationalism seemed dangerous. Using as justification two attempts in 1878 to assassinate the kaiser (neither by a socialist), Bismarck demanded laws repressing socialism. The Reichstag refused, and the election of 1878 in which conservatives and the Center party made some gains was fought largely on that issue. Most socialist publications were banned and socialist meetings prohibited unless supervised by the police. The Social Democrats were, in effect, forced underground, although they were free to speak in the Reichstag, and their party gained support with every election.

The campaigns against Catholics and socialists were abandoned by the 1880s as no longer needed or effective, but they were part of a larger political realignment. The conservatives and Catholics who had resisted the new Germany came to accept it, while liberals, torn between Bismarck's accomplishments and their old principles, grew weaker. A more durable coalition was formed around the tariff of 1879. Its higher duties, a re-

BISMARCK'S SOCIAL PROGRAM

◆

Between 1883 and 1887 the German parliament passed three laws that created a new model for the role of the state in social legislation. Bismarck introduced the first of these (providing for sickness insurance) in April 1881 in a speech to the parliament that reflects the power of his personality as well a the clarity of his reasoning and of his prejudices.

"For the past fifty years we have been talking about the social question. Since the Socialist Law was passed, I have been repeatedly reminded, in high quarters as well as low, of the promise I then gave that something positive should be done to remove the causes of Socialism. . . . I do not believe that our sons, or even our grandsons, will be able finally to solve the question. Indeed, no political questions can ever be mathematically settled, as books are balanced in business; they crop up, have their time, and give way to other questions propounded by history. Organic development wills that it shall be so. I consider it my duty to take up these questions without party feeling or excitement, because I know not who is to do so, if not the imperial government.

"Deputy Richter has pointed out the responsibility of the state for what it is now doing. Well, Gentlemen, I feel that the state should also be responsible for what it leaves undone. I am not of the opinion that *laissez faire, laissez aller,* 'pure Manchester policy,' 'everybody takes care of himself,' 'the weakest must go the wall,' 'to him who hath shall be given, from him who hath not shall be taken even that which he hath,' can be practiced in a monarchically, patriarchically governed state. . . .

"An appropriate title for our enterprise would be 'practical Christianity,' but we do not want to feed poor people with figures of speech, but with something solid. Death costs nothing; but unless you will put your hands in your pockets and into the state Exchequer, you will not do much good. To saddle our industry with the whole affair—well, I don't know that it could bear the burden."

From Louis L. Snyder (ed.), *The Documents of German History.* New Brunswick Rutgers University Press, 1958.

sponse to the economic problems caused by rapid growth and by a European agricultural depression, protected manufactured and agricultural goods, drawing together the most powerful interest groups in German society. Supported by Junker landlords, industrialists, the army and navy, and nationalists, the new tariff gave the conservative state and its powerful leaders their political base. In the 1880s Bismarck also established a system of national insurance to aid workers in times of illness and unemployment and to help provide for pensions upon retirement. Paid for by contributions from employers and workers, these measures became an influential model of modern social policy (see "Bismarck's Social Program" above).

RESHAPING THE OLDER EMPIRES

In a Europe of industrial growth and national states, war more than ever stood as the ultimate test of the state's efficiency. The wars that made Italy and Germany were understood to require drastic political changes in the nations that lost—Russia in 1856, Austria in 1859 and 1866, and France in 1870.

The Russian Empire   Of the 74 million people in Russia, some 47 million were serfs. Their emancipation began in 1861 by the tsar's decree. Intellectuals had argued against serfdom for generations, and peasants spoke through frequent uprisings. Serfdom was constricting economic development, and any major political reforms required its abolition. Defeat in the Crimean War added urgency; and Tsar Alexander II, who had assumed the throne in 1855, announced his commitment to modernization. Quietly he pressed the nobles to lead the way; but while secret committees drafted proposals for ending serfdom, most nobles dragged their feet.

Emancipation was thus imposed by edict, a daring step cautiously framed. More than 22 million serfs gained legal rights and were promised

▲ In this 1861 photograph a Russian official is reading to peasants on a Moscow estate the "Regulations Concerning the Peasantry," the decree that abolished serfdom.
Novosti/Sovfoto.

title to the land they worked or its equivalent. If they accepted one-quarter of that, they would owe no payments; otherwise they contracted a long-term debt to the state, which compensated the lord. In practice, the lord usually kept the best land for himself and often got an inflated price for the land he lost. Former serfs on the whole found themselves with less land than they needed to support families and make their payments. Although they were required to fulfill other obligations to their former masters for only two more years, they often remained dependent on those nobles for pasture and water rights and for the wage labor that had become a necessity. A few years later the government liberated the nearly 25 million state peasants, who worked on government–owned estates, granting them somewhat more favorable terms. Russia's peasants nevertheless remained a caste distinguishable in

dress, speech, and customs, with special laws and punishments, including flogging, applicable only to them.

The law of 1861 also gave the *mir*, or village commune, new importance. It elected its own officials, and they assigned plots of land, decided what would be planted, and assessed the taxes owed the state. The former serfs could not leave the commune or sell their land without permission. The *mir*, which came to be considered a characteristic Slavic institution, thus sustained traditional ways and served as the agent of the state at the same time that it provided peasants a voice in communal decisions. Other reforms followed. In 1864 district councils (*zemstvos*, elected through a three-class system like Prussia's) were made responsible for local primary schools, roads, and welfare. These steps were part of a process that—along with increased schooling, relaxed censorship, and reduced military service[8]—made Russia more like other European nations. Each reform, however, uncovered more that needed to be done, and leaders remained fearful. Concessions in Poland were followed by revolution in 1863. It was harshly quelled, and Poland's separate status ended. Repression increased in Russia, too, as censorship and police surveillance tightened. While pan-Slavists stressed Russia's special destiny and disdained liberal parliamentarianism as alien, an isolated intelligentsia was drawn to more radical ideas, and conspirators plotted more drastic remedies. Yet when a bomb killed Alexander II in 1881, his son smoothly succeeded him as Alexander III; tsarist Russia could survive an assassination.

The Austro-Hungarian Empire Following the revolutions of 1848, the Habsburg monarchy under the young Franz Joseph I had sought to create a modern, unitary state. For the first time in its history, the empire was subjected to uniform laws and taxes. But military defeats in Italy and then at the hands of Prussia plus mounting debts

---

[8] The old military system, which required selected serfs to serve twenty-five years, was changed in 1874 to one of universal service, with generous exemptions and only six years of active duty. Those who completed primary school were liable for only four years of duty; those who finished secondary school, for two years; and those with university education, for just six months.

proved that more changes were needed. In 1860 Franz Joseph announced a new federal constitution, giving considerable authority to regional diets. Intended to reduce resentment against high-handed government, it was a failure from the start, opposed by liberals and bureaucrats alike while provoking dangerous arguments among the empire's diverse nationalities. So the emperor reversed himself the next year and established a bicameral parliament for the entire empire. Having stirred visions of local self-government and autonomous nationalities, he now wanted to subordinate local governments to rule from Vienna and to a parliament in which a lower house elected by a four-class system ensured the dominance of the German-speaking middle class.

Hungary in particular objected, led by the liberal nationalist Ferencz Deák, who had campaigned for Hungary's Constitution of 1848. Neither side was strong enough to have its way, and the war with Prussia finally brought a compromise. In 1867 Hungary became an autonomous state, joined to Austria only through the emperor, Franz Joseph, who became king of Hungary, and through common policies for defense and diplomacy. The emperor had kept his authority in foreign policy, which was what he cared about most, by conceding to one nationality what he denied to others. Within Hungary itself, domestic politics centered on conflict between the dominant Magyars and the non-Magyar majority and between the diverging interests of Austrian industry and Hungary's great landholders.

Within Austria's imperial parliament, the emperor turned for support first to the German liberals, who offended him by their anticlericalism, and then to the Czechs and Poles, who disturbed him with their nationalist demands. More fundamental reform proved difficult; and although ministers were now responsible to parliament, policy rested more on a conservative bureaucracy dominated by Germans. An awkward compromise, the Dual Monarchy gave power to wealthy landlords and merchants; and it rested on the dominance of Magyars (over Romanians, Croatians, and Serbs) and of Germans in cooperation with Czechs and Poles (over Slovenes, Slovaks, and Ruthenians). It lasted for fifty years as one of Europe's great powers, an empire of diversified peoples and cultures, threatened by nationalism,

changing even while resisting change, with more freedom in practice than in principle, and sustained at its center by the graceful civilization of Vienna.

III. Nineteenth-Century Culture

Europe's cultural life was as dynamic as its economy and politics. In the nineteenth century the arts were understood to be national and urban rather than centered in courts, salons, or villages (*provincial* had become a pejorative term); and they were remarkable for quantity as well as quality. There were more writers, artists, musicians, and scholars than ever before; and they reached larger audiences through expanding cultural institutions and markets.

THE ORGANIZATION OF CULTURE

Before the nineteenth century, most paintings and musical compositions were commissioned for a particular place or occasion. Now music moved from palaces, churches, and private salons to public concert halls; artists sold their paintings to any purchaser and, by midcentury, in galleries created for that purpose; and writers found themselves engaged in commercial activity. Theaters ranged from the new music halls to the great stages and opera houses built (usually by the state) to rank with parliament buildings as monuments of national or civic pride. Most major cities supported choirs, bands, and symphony orchestras, which grew larger and technically more proficient. Conservatories and museums became national public institutions, maintaining official taste and considerably increasing Europe's stock of highly trained artists, musicians, and scholars. Some of the greatest of these institutions—the British Museum in London, the Bibliothèque Nationale in Paris, the Hermitage in St. Petersburg, the Alte Pinakothek in Munich—opened to the public in the 1840s. Whether in palaces once private or in imposing new structures, cultural institutions were treated as civic and national monuments. Lending libraries, charging a few pence per volume, were common even in smaller cities. In Paris the Louvre became the model art museum that provided access to everyone and expressed the era's understanding of culture by displaying works of art by country of origin and in chronological order. This was an urban, bourgeois culture that sought to make the city itself a cultural statement.

Cultural life—associated with the state, tied to a market economy, and promulgating shared values and taste—helped to create national identity and to establish social status. The intended public was, for the most part, the same public that was active in politics, the professions, and business—or rather, such people and their wives. They bought tickets for concerts just as they frequented restaurants with famous chefs, enjoying in both cases pleasures once part of private society and now open to all who had the inclination and money. Participation in this exciting culture also set boundaries of decorum that distinguished the middle class from those below them and defined the distinctive roles thought appropriate to men and women. High culture was expected to sustain those values, although individual artists and intellectuals often criticized that fact and attacked a system that left one's artistic fate dependent either on administrators or what would sell to the public. The tension between creative expression and market, which sometimes stimulated creativity in itself, became a much lamented hallmark of modernity.

Reaching a Wider Public This public culture encompassed an expanded range of activities. For those who sought self-improvement, there were public lectures on the sober implications of political economy or the wonders of steam power or newer marvels like photography, which was being enthusiastically applied to the needs of science and exploration, widely used for portraits, and recognized as the newest of the arts.[9] No cultural institution was more important than the press, and the newspaper became a major instrument of culture and politics. By 1830 there were more than two thousand European newspapers, and liberals everywhere fought the censorship, special taxes, and police measures with which governments sought to constrain so awesome a

social force. *The Times* of London had a circulation of 5,000 in 1815 and of 50,000 by midcentury; two of the most popular French papers, the *Presse* and *Siècle*, reached a circulation of 70,000.

As newspapers came to rely more on advertising than on subscriptions for their revenue, they increased in size, they published articles on a wider range of topics (including items on fashion and domestic concerns aimed at women), and they attracted readers by serializing novels by writers as famous as Honoré de Balzac, the elder Alexandre Dumas, and Charles Dickens. Technology aided these changes. Press services such as the Agence Havas and Reuters quickly adopted the telegraph; and the *London Illustrated News*, which created the picture magazine in 1842, was immediately copied in every large country. Satirical magazines (*Punch* was founded in London in 1840, a few years after the *Caricature* and *Chiarivari* in Paris) made the cartoon a powerful political weapon, raised to art by Honoré Daumier's biting pictures of fat bankers and complacent bourgeois.

The Cultural Professions Professionalization affected the arts as well as other occupations. The violinist Niccolò Paganini, who transformed violin technique, commanded huge fees and enormous crowds wherever he played; the soprano Jenny Lind, "the Swedish Nightingale," was the rage of Europe as was Franz Liszt, piano virtuoso and composer. Many a young man announced that he was a painter and proudly starved, in Paris if possible, out of loyalty to his career (there were 354 registered artists in Paris in 1789, 2,159 in 1838). A few, among them England's great landscape painter J. M. W. Turner, became wealthy.

The most popular writers—Balzac, Sir Walter Scott, Victor Hugo, Dickens—were able to live by their pen alone, among the most honored figures of their age. There were also many women novelists. Expected to write light romances, they generally were not taken very seriously; and to escape that prejudice a number of women writers adopted masculine pen names. Still, the rising prestige of the professional writer enabled some extraordinary women, like George Eliot (Mary Evans Cross) and Elizabeth Gaskell in England and George Sand in France, to be recognized as influential thinkers. For a middle-class public

---

[9] Daguerre announced his photographic process to the French Academy in 1839, which persuaded the government to purchase his rights and give the new technique to the world, unencumbered by royalties.

faced with so much new work to choose from, critics became important; like professors, they were professional intellectuals who guided taste much as the popular books on etiquette and gastronomy taught manners to people of new means and prepared the bourgeois palate for haute cuisine.

THE CONTENT OF CULTURE

Varied Forms   The most admired artistic works were valued for a moral seriousness and formality that distinguished them from popular culture. In painting, great historical scenes were the most admired, ranked considerably above genre painting or portraits. Music was increasingly treated as a kind of spiritual essay, to be heard reverentially in concerts suitable to its distinctive forms—symphony, concerto, quartet, and sonata—all considered to have a social and intellectual importance. The novel's great popularity was related to the social panorama it presented. Balzac attempted in his novels to encompass all the "human comedy" (the phrase contrasted with Dante's divine concerns), showing the wealthy, the ambitious, and the poor in their roles as husbands, wives, soldiers, bankers, politicians, and writers. Novelists used social types to analyze society and challenge the public conscience, and no reformer was more influential than Dickens. Scott's swashbuckling stories of romance and chivalry in an earlier age probed the connection between personal character and social tension in a way that influenced writers throughout Europe. Theater and opera featured historical settings; and Hugo, Alexander Pushkin, and Alessandro Manzoni promulgated patriotism by connecting high ideals to the national past, painting in words (much as the most admired paintings put on canvas) monumental interpretations of historical events. The novel's most common theme, the conflict between personal feeling (especially romantic love) and social convention, explored critical contemporary issues of individualism and social change.

Conceptions of culture were also strongly gendered. Women were held to have qualities—including a natural sense of beauty and openness to emotion—that made them especially responsive to art. Women were thought to be the principal readers of novels, and novels presented women's lives in ways that underscored the in-equities of their social subordination and ultimately enlarged the perception of women's abilities (as in Gustave Flaubert's *Madame Bovary* and Thomas Hardy's *Tess of the d'Urbervilles*). Women were especially associated with the intimate side of middle-class culture, the popularity of poetry, lithographs, watercolor paintings, and piano music[10]—all to be savored in the parlor with the woman of the house at the center.

Changing Styles   In culture as in philosophy there was also a strong desire for synthesis, for ideas and forms that would tie everything together. In the arts this urge gave lyric opera special resonance. Opera was first of all theater, combining popular appeal with aristocratic elegance, and performances were important civic events. Elaborate plots, often in historical settings, and flowery poetic texts were closely followed along with the varied, tuneful, and complex music, the whole further enriched by ballet, colorful sets, and special effects. The two leading operatic composers of the period were Giuseppe Verdi and his exact contemporary Richard Wagner. Verdi was an Italian national hero, whose compelling and often patriotic music explored human emotion and character in diverse contexts, often historical ones explicitly about politics. Wagner carried the search for an artistic synthesis still further. He wrote his own texts and increasingly used Germanic myths with nationalist intent. In his operas recurrent musical themes were identified with major ideas and characters to create a whole in which voices, instruments, words, and visual experience moved inseparably to a powerful climax.

By the 1840s rapidly changing and competing artistic styles had become a characteristic of modern culture, a response to social change and new audiences but also an expression of the creative artist's sense of self. Some artists adapted romanticism's emphasis on individual genius to claim that the merit of a piece of art was independent of any social or moral purpose and to adopt, therefore, the cry of art for art's sake. For others, the goal of the artist should be to capture the essence of "modernity," extracting "from fashion whatever

---

[10] Industrial techniques had made the piano, with its iron frame, economical enough to be a common sight in middle-class homes.

▲ Courbet, a leader in the shift toward social realism in painting, presents the artist in his studio in touch with all classes of men and women. Many of those portrayed here were well-known artists and radicals.
Scala/Art Resource.

element it may contain of poetry within history," in the words of Charles Baudelaire.[11] By midcentury, realism was becoming the dominant style, as writers and painters reemphasized close observation in a socially concerned effort to portray ordinary people, sometimes with shocking directness, as in Flaubert's acid account of a young middle-class wife's aimless existence in a small French town or Gustave Courbert's paintings of rural workers and villages. Innovation was often taken for a sign of genius, and the belief that artists must be in an avant-garde, ahead of their duller public, became a cliché. Often disturbing to their audiences, the arts were never more honored

nor artists more critical of their own society than in the nineteenth century.

Religion Religion was regarded with comparable ambivalence. In some respects the nineteenth century was a very religious age, for thoughtful people cared greatly about religion. Protestant and Catholic missions campaigned with an intensity not seen since the seventeenth century, and the pious became more militant and turned to social action, preaching temperance, teaching reading, and establishing charities. This focus on the problems of modern life was connected, however, to the fear that religion was losing its social importance. Some intellectuals became bitter anticlericals, seeing in the church the barrier to progress. More typically, especially in England, stern morality and propriety were substituted for theology. Theological works nevertheless accounted for a high proportion of the titles publishers produced. Friedrich

---

[11] From his essay on the painter Constantin Guys in Charles Baudelaire, *The Painter of Modern Life and Other Essays*, Jonathan Mayne (tr. and ed.), 1965, p. 12.

Schleiermacher's writings were as influential in German philosophy as in Protestant theology, and it made headlines when the Abbé Lamennais, once a powerful spokesman of Catholic renewal, broke with the Church in the 1830s because it would not accept the connection he made between Christianity and democracy. The impact of historical research on religion created a sensation across Europe when the Protestant David Strauss published his *Life of Jesus* in 1835, for it cast erudite doubt on the accuracy of the Gospel, frightening many with the apparent need to choose between scholarship and Christ. In Denmark the writings of Søren Kierkegaard starkly explored ethical dilemmas in a passionate search for faith; and his intense, semi-autobiographical essays that interweave biblical stories and personal symbols have continued to fascinate twentieth-century thinkers.

The Sense of History Nineteenth-century intellectual life emphasized historical thinking. A romantic respect for the past, the nationalists' desire to rest their claims on the historical record, explanations of revolution, economic theory, and a modern need to understand change reinforced an interest in history. Its systematic study became an admired profession. In England, France, and Germany, national projects were launched for publishing historical documents and for training scholars to interpret them. Some historians were as widely read as novelists, among them Jules Michelet, for whom French history was a dramatic story of the people's fight for freedom, and Thomas B. Macaulay, for whom the history of England was a record of progressive change through moderation and compromise. In each country certain events and themes—in England, the Glorious Revolution of 1688; in France, the Revolution; in Germany, the rise of Prussia—were favored as part of an intense search for national roots, heroes, and patterns of development significant for the present. Many a political leader first gained fame as a historian.

This preoccupation with history received its most powerful philosophic expression in the writings of Georg Wilhelm Friedrich Hegel, a German Rhinelander who watched with fascination the unfolding of the French Revolution and the spread of Napoleon's influence. Thoroughly trained in philosophy and Lutheran theology, Hegel set out to establish a philosophy as comprehensive as that of Thomas Aquinas or Aristotle. He was determined to reconcile contradictions between science and faith, Christianity and the state, the ideal and the real, the eternal and the temporal. The key, he believed, lay in the meaning of history and the nature of the historical process.

According to Hegel, that process is dialectical. Society in any era constitutes a thesis, an implicit statement about life and values expressed through social structures and actions. That thesis, however, is never adequate to every need, and its incompleteness generates contrary views, institutions, and practices—the antithesis. Thus every society gives rise to conflict between thesis and antithesis until from that dialectic a new synthesis is molded. This synthesis becomes in turn another thesis that generates a new antithesis. History thus moves by this dialectic in a steady unfolding of what Hegel called the World Spirit, and it always moves toward greater human freedom and self-awareness. In the ancient East, Hegel said, only one man was free; in Greece and Rome, some were free; in the Germanic Christian kingdoms after the Reformation, all were free. Since the French Revolution, people have consciously acted on history, knowing what they want and fulfilling the World Spirit at the same time. Thus cosmic order and human reason ultimately work together; history has a religious meaning.

Hegel's important philosophy was—as he would have said it had to be—an important expression of his age. Like most nineteenth-century thinkers, he was determined to find eternal meaning in historical change and was convinced that his own nation was the highest articulation of that meaning. After Hegel, philosophy and literary criticism both tended to become increasingly historical, and historians sought more systematically for relationships among all aspects of a culture. Within a generation of his death in 1831, just after another wave of the revolutions he abhorred, some of his followers claimed to find humanity's highest ethical expression in the Prussian state at war, while others—led by Karl Marx, the most famous of the Hegelians—predicted the state's withering away. By then it was a European habit to approach any question of society, culture, or politics in terms of historical change.

In 1848 a wave of revolutions, the most spontaneous and widespread Europe had ever known, brought new governments to power. Defeated before they could complete their democratic and egalitarian programs, these revolutionary regimes left important legacies not only in measures passed but lessons learned. In the future, radicals would not rely on middle-class support and political reform, liberals would be more willing to sacrifice democracy for social order. In these circumstances the most effective governments of the 1850s were those that adopted parts of the revolutionaries' programs and some of their techniques for reaching a broader public while keeping the forces of order on their side. Thus the Second Empire of Napoleon III was the principal guarantor of that social order and economic growth important to the propertied classes. Piedmont and Prussia, as the focus of nationalist movements, won significant followings and triumphed dramatically in the creation of national states in Italy and Germany. From England to Prussia, astute political leaders found ways to undertake new social responsibilities, facilitate industrialization, and mobilize popular support without giving way to full democracy or radical programs. Closely associated with the nation, cultural institutions flourished, supporting a diverse and dynamic culture that was one of the great achievements of the age. While it lasted, the social cohesion that sustained change and stability, wealth and culture would give European nations unprecedented power in the world.

Recommended Reading
◄●►

Sources

Marx, Karl. *The Class Struggles in France, 1848–1850* and *The Eighteenth Brumaire of Louis Napoleon.* Early and brilliant applications of Marx's ideas to contemporary political events, these essays on the revolution of 1848 in France and on Napoleon's coup d'état also show Marx's power as a polemicist.

Treitschke, Heinrick. *History of Germany in the Nineteenth Century.* Written shortly after German unification, this vast work exemplifies the importance of history as nationalist propaganda.

Trollope, Frances Milton. *Travels and Travellers.* 2 vols. 1846. A novelist well known for travel essays, Mrs. Trollope's chatty descriptions contain insightful comments on European society and the position of women on the eve of revolution.

Studies

*Agulhon, Maurice. *The Republican Experiment, 1848–1852.* Janel Lloyd (tr.). 1983. An authoritative study of politics and society during the Second French Republic, sensitive to popular attitudes and concerns.

*Alter, Peter. *Nationalism.* 1989. A valuable introduction to the history of European nationalism organized around a very interesting classification of the different kinds of nationalism.

*Anderson, Benedict. *Imagined Communities: Reflections on the Origin and Spread of Nationalism.* 1983. An important and provocative analysis of modern nationalism around the world, stressing its origins in European culture and capitalism.

*Barzun, Jacques. *Classic, Romantic, and Modern.* 1961. A famous and provocative defense of romanticism by a cultural historian.

*Beales, Derek. *The Risorgimento and the Unification of Italy.* 1982. Concise, skeptical introduction to the history of Italian unification.

Branca, Patricia. *Women in Europe since 1750.* 1978. A helpful survey, emphasizing England and addressing many of the important issues of modern social history.

*Chadwick, Owen. *The Secularization of the European Mind.* 1975. Perceptive, careful introduction to changing patterns of thought affecting attitudes toward religion.

*Gellner, Ernest. *Nations and Nationalism.* 1983. An effort to build a theory by analyzing the relation of industrialization to nationalism.

*Greenfield, Liah. *Nationalism: Five Roads to Modernity.* 1992. An ambitious comparison of nationalism and state making in England, France, Russia, Germany, and the United States.

Greenfield, Kent R. *Economics and Liberalism in the Risorgimento: A Study of Nationalism in Lombardy, 1814–1848*. 1978. A classic study of the connection between economic change and nationalism.

*Hamerow, Theodore S. *The Social and Economic Foundations of German Unification, 1858–1871*. 2 vols. 1969 and 1972. The politics and ideas of unification placed in the context of a developing economy.

Hemmings, F. W. J. *Culture and Society in France, 1789–1848*. 1987. *Culture and Society in France, 1848–1898*. 1971. A literary scholar's provocative and comprehensive analysis of the relationship between cultural styles and social context.

*Howard, Michael. *The Franco-Prussian War*. 1969. Exemplary study of how war reflects (and tests) an entire society.

*Jelavich, Barbara. *History of the Balkans*. 2 vols. 1983. An impressively thorough survey of both society and politics, from the eighteenth century to the present.

*Mack Smith, Denis. *Cavour*. 1985. An expert and well-written assessment of the personalities and policies that created an Italian nation.

*McLeod, Hugh. *Religion and the People of Western Europe, 1789–1970*. 1981. A well-conceived interpretive survey of the impact of social change on religious practice.

*Mosse, George L. *The Nationalization of the Masses: Political Symbolism and Mass Movements in Germany from the Napoleonic Wars through the Third Reich*. 1975. One of the most recent and complete efforts to find the roots of Nazism in popular nationalism.

Olsen, Donald J. *The City as a Work of Art: London, Paris, Vienna*. 1986. Combines an analysis of how ordinary people really lived with an appreciation of the aesthetics of the modern city and the economic and political realities behind it.

Pflanze, Otto. *Bismarck and the Development of Germany: The Period of Unification, 1815–1871*. 1963. A balanced assessment that places each of Bismarck's actions in its larger context.

*Pinkney, David. *Napoleon III and the Rebuilding of Paris*. 1958. Studies the political background to one of the most extensive, influential, and successful examples of urban policy.

*Plessis, Alain. *The Rise and Fall of the Second Empire, 1852–1871*. Jonathan Mandelbaum (tr.). 1985. A balanced assessment of this important political experiment, making good use of current scholarship.

*Poovey, Mary. *Making a Social Body: British Cultural Formation, 1830–1864*. This study of how the public was conceived in literature and politics exposes the ways in which public institutions helped construct categories of gender and class.

*Read, Donald. *England 1868–1914. The Age of Urban Democracy*. 1979. Political change presented in terms of economic and social conditions.

Reardon, B. M. G. *Religion in the Age of Romanticism: Studies in Early Nineteenth-Century Thought*. 1985. An excellent introduction to the formation of one of the most important intellectual traditions of the century.

Riasanovsky, Nicholas V. *Nicholas I and Official Nationality in Russia*. 1959. An important study of how a conservative regime sought to use nationalism to strengthen the state.

Rich, Norman. *Why the Crimean War? A Cautionary Tale*. 1985. A concise synthesis and engaging interpretation of the political and diplomatic problems involving the major powers.

Salvemini, Gaetano. *Mazzini*. 1957. Still the best introduction to Mazzini's thought and its relationship to his revolutionary activities.

Saville, John. *1848: The British State and the Chartist Movement*. 1987. A careful study of why Chartism failed to win its aims at the moment revolution succeeded elsewhere.

*Sperber, Jonathan. *The European Revolutions, 1848–1851*. 1994. A fresh synthesis that pays attention to popular attitudes and symbolic actions as well as political and social conflict.

*Stearns, Peter N. *1848: The Revolutionary Tide in Europe*. 1974. Assesses conflicting interpretations in bringing together accounts of these diverse revolutions.

Szporluk, Roman. *Communism and Nationalism: Karl Marx versus Friedrich List*. 1988. By drawing attention to the ideas of List, one of the most influential figures of his day, this study suggests that in central and Eastern Europe nationalism and Marxism were, from the first, competing programs for modernization and economic development.

Wandycz, Piotyr S. *The Lands of Partitioned Poland, 1795–1918*. 1974. An excellent overview of the history of divided Poland.

*Williams, Roger L. *The French Revolution of 1870–1871*. 1969. An introduction to the long-standing controversies about the Paris Commune.

*Zeldin, T. *France: 1848–1945*. 2 vols. 1973–1977. Reissued in five paperback volumes, 1979–1981. Lively essays on an unusual array of topics that add up to an important look at French society and culture.

---

*Available in paperback.

▲ The Reverend John Williams was an English missionary who had extraordinary success converting native populations on the islands of the South Seas. He wrote codes of law for them and taught them European construction techniques before moving on to win more converts elsewhere. This painting depicts his arrival in November 1839 on an island in the New Hebrides, where on the following day the natives killed him.
Maidstone Museum and Art Galley, Kent/Bridgeman Art Library.

European Power: Wealth, Knowledge, and Imperialism

Economic development in the second half of the nineteenth century was more extensive than ever before, moving beyond the regions that had been centers of industrialization in the past. More extraordinary still, economic growth now came to be expected and was understood to be a self-sustaining process. New technologies, large-scale industry, better communication, and greater capital investment made unprecedented productivity possible, and these gains were in turn a triumph of social organization and of the capacity to generate new knowledge. The connection of economic growth to social change, political institutions, and scientific discoveries had never been so apparent, and there was thus a demand for social theories that could explain how all these diverse developments were interrelated, how they came about, and where they were leading.

This expansive civilization with its ever-increasing trade, investment, population, migration, missionary activity, and cultural curiosity spread European influence to all parts of the globe. Influence hardened into imperialism as commercial contacts were institutionalized and Europe's competitive states embraced imperialism as an essential assertion of national power. Ironically, this dominance over non-European peoples was thus stimulated by tensions within European society, not only between nations but within industrial capitalism and domestic politics. The extension of European power around the world would raise the possibility that the conflicts on which it fed might explode beyond society's capacity to contain them.

I. The Economics of Growth

The dynamism of Europe's economy in the second half of the nineteenth century was unprecedented. As economic growth accelerated, it reached into sectors previously little affected and spread beyond Europe's industrial heartlands into most of the continent. While Europe's population grew more rapidly than ever before, the value of manufacturing went up three times as fast. For the first time in history, economic growth became an expectation, and most of society would experience some of its benefits. Factories, especially those that produced steel and chemicals, coupled large-scale production with new technologies, like those connected to electricity. The impact of these developments was so great that historians often speak of this as the second industrial revolution. Distribution and marketing operated on a larger scale, too, and department stores used new techniques of merchandising to entice a wider public to higher levels of consumption.

THE SECOND INDUSTRIAL REVOLUTION

Industrial growth in this period was closely tied to new technology. By 1890 Europe was producing even more steel than iron. The Bessemer converter developed in the 1860s permitted far higher temperatures in smelter furnaces, and subsequent discoveries made it profitable to use lower-grade ores. British, German, and French maritime shipping, which doubled between 1870 and 1914, depended on faster and larger steamships. New chemical processes and synthetics led to improved products ranging from dyes, textiles, and paints to fertilizers and explosives. A whole new industry developed to produce and supply electricity, and with the invention of the incandescent lamp, the demand increased for large generating stations to distribute power over a wide area. By 1900 the manufacture of generators, cables, and motors, an important new industry in itself, allowed greater and cheaper production in scores of other fields.

Equally striking was the speed with which the new technology was adapted to commercial uses. The telephone, invented in 1876, became a business necessity and an established private convenience within a few decades. Thomas Edi-

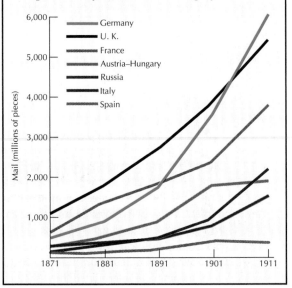

▼ MAIL (MILLIONS OF PIECES)

The volume of mail has been used by some scholars as an indicator of modernization, reflecting increased literacy, internal communication, and commercial activity. In these terms, then, the relative position of the several nations on this chart is suggestive of more than gross population, as are the points at which Germany surpasses first France and then the United Kingdom or at which Russia surpasses Italy and Austria-Hungary.

son's incandescent lightbulb was developed in the 1870s; central power stations for public lighting were built in New York and London in 1882 and in Berlin a few years later. The steam turbine, shown in the 1880s to be more efficient than the reciprocating engine, was soon widely employed in ships and factories, fueled by oil as well as coal.

Home sewing machines spread rapidly, first in the United States and then across Europe, the most important of many new labor-saving devices that allowed women to increase their contribution to the home economy even when they also worked outside the home. The bicycle granted new mobility and independence to women as well as men. Inventions were now expected to change people's lives, and products created directly for the consumer market responded to the growing purchasing power of the masses. The automobile in the 1890s, the airplane in the 1900s, and the ra-

▲ The Bessemer process of removing impurities from molten iron, which revolutionized the industry, was based on English and American patents; but the Krupp steelworks installed these massive converters in 1862 and continued to lead in steel production in both size and efficiency when this photograph was taken in 1880.
Ullstein Bilderdienst.

dio a decade later were all greeted with enthusiasm even before their commercial possibilities were established.

Germany's Economic Growth The German economy expanded spectacularly following unification. Already rich in natural resources, Germany acquired more raw materials as well as factories with the annexation of Alsace-Lorraine. Its system of railroads provided excellent communications; the famous educational system produced ample numbers of the administrators and engineers the commercial sector now required. The government, which had played an active role in every facet of industrialization, continued to cooperate with business interests. Military needs stimulated basic industry, and a growing population provided an eager domestic market.

German factories, being newer than those of Britain or France, employed the latest and most efficient equipment, obtaining the necessary capital through a modern banking structure. By 1900 those plants were far bigger than anyone else's, and firms engaged in the various stages of production often combined in huge cartels that dominated an entire sector of industry, from raw material to finished product, as Germany became preeminent in new fields such as chemicals and electricity (see "Making the Deals That Created a Cartel," p. 874). German salespeople appeared all over the world with catalogs in local languages and products suited to local conditions, selling

MAKING THE DEALS THAT CREATED A CARTEL

◆

Cartels, strongest in Germany, existed in other countries, too. Here the general manager of an iron rolling mill that made rails describes how in 1878 a cartel of rail producers came to be formed in Austria.

"In 1878 there were in Austria-Hungary nine rail rolling mills with an annual capacity of about 120,000 tons. A large part of these mills had been set up in the years 1869–73, that is to say in a period in which railway building flourished in Austria-Hungary as never before. . . . The picture changed in the course of 1873. The lines that had been started were being finished, but no new ones were being built. . . .

"I was then the general manager of one of these rail rolling mills. . . . If our works did not get an annual minimum quantity of orders of 10,000 tons, it would be faced with the impossibility of employing its work force. We should have had to close and face bankruptcy. . . . My task was therefore a simple one; to get orders at all costs.

"In 1878 . . . on the day when contracts were awarded [by the Kaiser Franz-Joseph Railway], the manager . . . told me: 'Yours was the lowest; but since two other works are also prepared to come down to our price, I shall divide the order into three parts. . . .' I tired to make representations; in vain, the decision stood. After I had left the office of the managing director, I met the managers of the other two works which had come down to my price. Because of the years of bitter competition, our personal relations had also suffered, but this time we shook hands, and the rail cartel, the first cartel in Austria, the model for other later cartels, also in Germany, was born. At the moment when it became clear that no works could succeed in getting sufficient orders to stay fully employed, each reached the conviction that there was nothing left but at last to attempt to get higher prices. The course of the tendering negotiations with the Franz-Joseph Railway had shown the way. We reached agreement to distribute the total demand according to certain ratios among all the works, and sought then to get the highest prices possible in the light of foreign competition, and the rates of freight and of customs duty."

From Karl Wittgensteing, "Kartelle in Österreich" in Gustav Schmoller (ed.), *Über wirtschaftliche, Kartelle in Deutschland und im Auslande,* Leipzig, 1894, as quoted in Carroll and Embree, *Readings in European History since 1814,* 1930.

with a drive and optimism British merchants resented as bad manners.

Older Industrial Economies The older industrial economies of Great Britain, Belgium, and France continued to grow but more slowly. By 1900 France's industrial production, despite the loss of important textile and iron centers in Alsace, had reached the level of Great Britain's a generation earlier, when Britain had led the world. French iron production more than doubled in the first twenty-five years of the Third Republic, and new processes made the nation's ore output second only to that of the United States. In value of production per capita, a figure that suggests something of a nation's standard of living, France remained ahead of Germany, though behind England.

By the turn of the century, Great Britain, whose industrial superiority had seemed a fact of nature, was clearly being surpassed in some of the critical indexes of production by both Germany and the United States. Although the British economy did continue to grow, the fear that it was falling behind became a serious issue in English public life; and economic historians remain fascinated by the question of why an economy once so dynamic was sluggish. Several factors stand out. British plants and equipment were old, and owners hesitated to undertake the cost of modernizing or replacing them. Well-established firms often made it hard for new companies to get a start. Without technical secondary schools like those of Germany and France, English schooling remained weak in technical subjects and provided less opportunity for social mobility than on the continent. Indeed, social attitudes, always difficult to analyze precisely, may explain more than strictly economic factors. British industrialists, slow to appreciate

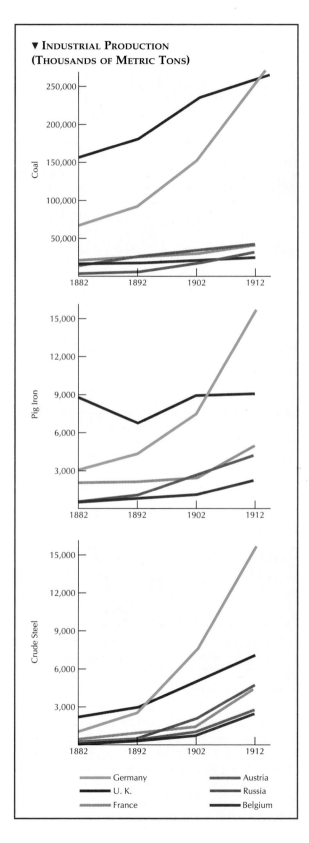

▼ **Industrial Production**
(Thousands of Metric Tons)

Coal

Pig Iron

Crude Steel

Germany — Austria
U. K. — Russia
France — Belgium

the value of specialists and resistant to new ways, became less venturesome and perhaps a little complacent. Even so, London remained the financial capital of the world.

The Spread of Industrialization That world was increasingly industrialized. The industrial potential of the United States was apparent by the time of the Civil War, although few expected subsequent growth to be so dramatic as it was by the turn of the century. Rich in natural resources, America had a continent in which to expand, millions of immigrants eager to supply needed labor, schooling that sustained technological inventiveness, an openness and mobility that encouraged enterprise, and a democracy that pioneered in creating a consumer society.

But other nations were industrializing, too: Italy and Japan, which had very limited natural resources; and Russia and Sweden, which had appeared rural, poor, and backward compared to industrialized Western Europe. Assumptions that related industrial progress to European values, Protestantism, or Anglo-Saxon institutions were belied by the changes in the nature of industrialization itself. It no longer depended so directly on the possession of critical resources like coal and iron ore but could be accomplished with foreign investment and imported technology. Newly industrializing countries, reluctant to leave their fate to market forces and the interests of foreigners, expected government and investment banks to favor and protect new industries.

Agriculture Although greater prosperity and growing populations increased the demand for food, the percentage of the population that made its living in agriculture continued to decline, down to only 8 percent in Britain, 22 percent in Belgium, and 35 percent in Germany toward the end of the century. In France, which maintained a more balanced economy (as did the Netherlands and Sweden), 43 percent of the population lived off the land. But everywhere the wider use of machinery and chemical fertilizers increased the capital investment required for farming, and improved transportation intensified international competition. These factors encouraged much greater specialization. The most famous example is Denmark, where agriculture began to center on

▼ ECONOMICALLY ACTIVE POPULATION, CA. 1900

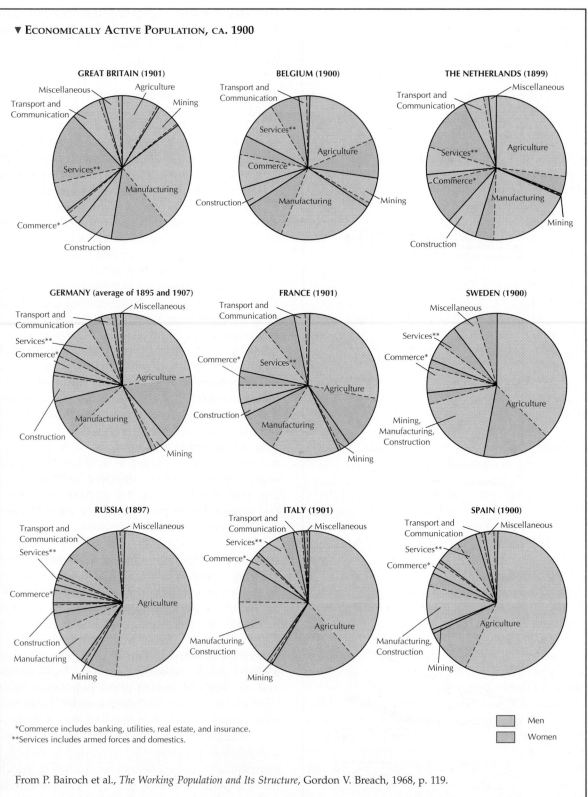

*Commerce includes banking, utilities, real estate, and insurance.
**Services includes armed forces and domestics.

From P. Bairoch et al., *The Working Population and Its Structure*, Gordon V. Breach, 1968, p. 119.

a highly capitalized and profitable dairy industry. But in France, too, wheat and sheep production declined in favor of wine grapes and sugar beets, which farmers could raise more profitably.

Global connections were increasingly important. Civil war in the United States, which cut off Europe's supply of cotton from the southern states, caused unemployment in England's mills and created a boom for Egyptian cotton. After 1865, cheaper grain from the Americas and Eastern Europe, especially Russia, poured into Europe on larger ships to be distributed on improved railroads, pushing prices down at a time when farmers needed cash for the improvements required to make farming profitable. Britain now imported almost all its grain, and Germany, a great deal. More young men abandoned the countryside, and landed interests pressed their governments for help in the face of recurrent agricultural crises. The most common response was protective tariffs, which were raised in France, Germany, Austria, Russia, Italy, and Spain. Initially applied primarily to agriculture, the new tariffs were soon extended to manufactured goods as well, reversing the trend toward liberal policies from the 1830s to the 1870s that had favored free trade.

The Long Depression   But the trade barriers did not stop the general decline in prices. Strangely, the second industrial revolution occurred in one of the longest and most severe periods of deflation in European history. From the 1870s to 1896, prices, interest rates, and profits fell, with far-reaching effects. This dynamism in which one part of the economy soared while another declined was socially disruptive. Handicraft industries, which had survived side by side with mechanized manufacturing throughout Europe, were forced out of business. So were numerous smaller and less efficient industrial firms. The great boom in railroad building ended, and governments had to save socially or politically important lines deserted by bankrupt companies.

As competition sharpened, many industrialists welcomed the support governments could give through tariffs, state spending, and colonial policies. Economic demands became a central theme of politics as more and more of economic life centered on great factories owned by large corporations (and closely tied to banks and government) that employed hundreds or even thousands of workers who, in turn, increasingly organized into industrial labor unions.

THE DEMOGRAPHIC TRANSITION

Europe's population continued to grow during the second industrial revolution and did so at an increasing rate. The 295 million Europeans in 1870 had become nearly 450 million by 1914, but the age distribution or demographic profile had changed completely.

Declining Rates of Mortality and Fertility   The population had increased despite the fact that in most of Europe birthrates had begun to decline, and it did so because mortality rates were falling still more steeply. This pattern of a declining birthrate accompanied by a more rapidly falling mortality rate, which is called the *demographic transition,* continues in our own time and has become one of the marks of modernity that spread from Europe to the rest of the world.

Death rates initially declined because of lower infant mortality rates, a result of improved sanitation, better diet, and the virtual elimination of diseases such as cholera and typhus. By the turn of the century, improvements in medical care lowered mortality rates among adults as well. Thus the population grew despite the declining birthrate.

Lower mortality rates reflected the benefits of industrial prosperity, but the declining birthrates marked a subtler change.[1] The number of children in a family was becoming more a matter of choice, aided by the spread of contraception; and where bourgeois values took root and child labor declined, workers followed the upper classes in the trend toward later marriage, fewer births, and smaller families.

The Social Impact   Although the issues are complicated and the statistics uncertain, the estimates of crude birthrates in about 1910 suggest the social significance of this changing pattern: Birthrates were highest in Romania, Bulgaria, Portugal,

---

[1] *Birthrate* is used here as the more familiar term, but *fertility rate*—the ratio of the number of children born to the number of women of childbearing age—is the more precise term preferred by demographers.

Hungary, Italy, and Spain; they were lowest in Switzerland, Belgium, and France. Parents who were confident their children would live, who wanted them to inherit property and receive some education, chose to have fewer of them. Before 1850 population growth had been higher in Western than in central and Eastern Europe. That pattern was now reversed, and the enormous increases in populations to their east gave the French added reason to fear Germany's larger and younger population and the Germans cause to worry in turn about the Russian giant. Another outcome of population growth was a new mobility as the growing numbers of people in the countryside moved to towns and from towns to cities. Mainly the young and the poor, they were responding to new ambitions as well as perennial misery. In doing so, they added to the sense of restless change within Europe. In most cities a majority of residents had been born elsewhere.

These economic, demographic, and social changes reached into the peasant hut and the urban slum. Meat and white bread became regular, although not daily, parts of the diet for most people in the industrialized countries. Commerce offered cheap products at fixed prices, and jobs in sales and distribution provided new opportunities to rise into the lower-middle class for both men and women. Although domestic service remained the primary occupation for young girls, those with some education could increasingly consider teaching, nursing, or clerical work. For most workers, however, there was little prospect of social mobility; but there were gains in wages and stable employment as the result of an improved economy and the pressure from growing working-class movements. Women still constituted about one-third of the workforce and remained concentrated in poorly paying jobs. Those with full-time jobs tended to be young, between the ages of fifteen and twenty-five, but most working-class women continued to supplement the family income with work as laundresses and seamstresses or as the makers of artificial flowers or matchboxes, usually with the aid of their small children. Male industrial workers, as they became better paid, were pleased to see their wives give up factory jobs, and unions argued for a "family wage" to make that possible. Ordinary people thus shared, more than they had in the past, in Europe's increased prosperity and dynamism.

II. The Knowledge of Nature and Society

Knowledge was expanding, too. Scientific discoveries underlay technological innovation far more directly than in the first industrial revolution, and science itself was becoming ever more organized into distinctive specialties pursued by professional researchers (the term *scientist* was first used in the 1830s). The educated public could understand the new scientific theories, and scientific ideas were an important part of the general discourse about religion, progress, and ethics. Establishing the laws of nature rekindled hope that laws of social development might similarly be discovered and beneficially applied; and the new inventions, discoveries, and theories that were hailed as evidence of modern advancement justified increased devotion to research.

THE CONQUESTS OF SCIENCE

The clearest intellectual triumphs were in the natural sciences. Understood as contributions to general philosophy, new findings in the sciences were expected to affect learning in all spheres of study but also to have practical effects on the economy and ordinary life.

Physics *Thermodynamics*, the study of the relationship between heat and mechanical energy, became the core of nineteenth-century physics. Building on theorems stated by Nicolas Sadi Carnot early in the century, the study of thermodynamics developed in many directions at once, addressing both fundamental properties of matter and the practical problems of steam engines. By midcentury laws predicting the behavior of gases came to be applied to the field of mechanics as well. The combined work of scientists in many countries culminated in the mathematical formulation of the two fundamental laws of thermodynamics. One states the principle of the conservation of energy: Energy can be transformed into heat or work but neither created nor destroyed, and heat or work can be transformed into energy. The other law declares that any closed physical system tends toward equilibrium, a system in which heat becomes uniformly distributed

▲ **Michael Faraday at work in his laboratory at the Royal Institution.**
Courtesy of the Director of the Royal Institution, London.

and which therefore cannot be used to produce work.[2] In practical terms, this second law means that heat can be made to do work only when connected through an engine to some cooler body. Philosophically, the law invited troubled speculation about the universe as a giant machine in which the level of energy must inexorably decline.

The study of magnetism advanced in a similar way from the work of Michael Faraday. He had shown in the 1830s and 1840s that lines of mag-

netic force are analogous to gravity and that electricity can induce magnetism (in reverse, the principle of the dynamo). In 1873 James Clerk Maxwell published equations that described the behavior of electricity, magnetism, and light in terms of a single, universal system. Thus gravity, magnetism, electricity, and light were all related. By the end of the century, physics had established mathematical laws of theoretical beauty and practical power extending from the universe to the atom, which was then conceived of as a miniature solar system. Thermodynamics led to the development of more efficient sources of power. The investigations of electricity led to the telegraph by midcentury and

---

[2] The measure of the energy unavailable for work is called *entropy,* a term coined by the physicist Rudolf Clausius in 1865.

to electric lights and motors for hundreds of uses a generation later.

Chemistry and Biology The fundamental generalizations of chemistry are contained in the periodic law and periodic table published by Dmitri Mendeleev in 1869. The distinction between compounds and elements had been clearly established for only half a century, and the difference between molecules and atoms came to be generally accepted only in 1860. Yet Mendeleev's table established a marvelous symmetry, so precise that the elements could all be charted by atomic weight, with similar elements occurring at regular intervals. This regularity even allowed for the prediction of unknown elements that would, when discovered, fill the gaps in the table. By the 1880s inorganic and organic chemistry were becoming two separate fields.

The recognition of germs and the realization that they were not spontaneously generated had immediate practical results, for in the 1860s the discoveries of Louis Pasteur in France led to the techniques for destroying germs called *pasteurization*, which were of crucial importance to the wine, dairy, and silk industries. As a result of his work in immunology, Pasteur also developed a preventive vaccine against rabies. In England Joseph Lister discovered that germs could be killed by carbolic acid, and the application of that knowledge made surgery a reasonable remedy rather than a desperate gamble. A decade later Robert Koch in Germany showed that different diseases were caused by distinct microbes, discovered the microorganism responsible for tuberculosis, and opened the way to new techniques in bacteriology and in the battle against communicable diseases. Advances such as these not only improved agriculture and medicine but also stimulated the drive to make sanitation and public health into systematic sciences.

Such achievements resulted from the efforts of hundreds of scientists freely exchanging ideas across national boundaries and working with precise methods and the logic of mathematics. Experiments admired in the 1820s seemed crude by the 1870s, and science became the province of carefully trained professionals rather than inspired amateurs. Research demanded even more systematic organization and larger and more expensive laboratories. The success of science stimulated a general expansion of secondary and higher education, and most of the academic disciplines that constitute the modern university achieved their separate identity in the late nineteenth century, establishing professional organizations and scholarly journals that created communities of specialists and fostered communication within them. Tangible evidence in the form of practical benefits as well as intellectual pride sustained the optimistic view that science progressed at an unprecedented pace for the benefit of all humankind.

SOCIAL SCIENCE AND IDEAS OF PROGRESS

Auguste Comte The philosophy of Auguste Comte (1798–1857), enormously influential from midcentury on, was characteristic of much nineteenth-century thought. Clearly rooted in the ideas of the Enlightenment, his philosophy gave greater attention to the process of historical change. Like Hegel a few years earlier, Comte sought to erect a comprehensive philosophical system that would encompass all human knowledge. Like Hegel, Comte believed that his own era had opened the final stage of historical development. Comte was especially impressed, as were most contemporary intellectuals, by the social role of religion, the conquests of natural science, and the possibilities of human progress. For many years private secretary to Saint-Simon (see p. 805), Comte retained a confidence characteristic of the early socialists that society would soon be reorganized on rational principles.

He systematically elaborated his philosophy, which he called *positivism*, in ten volumes published between 1830 and 1845; and these, with his other writings, established positivism as an international movement even before his death in 1857.[3] The key to civilization, he argued, is humanity's understanding of the world, which has developed through three historical stages. In the first, the theological stage, humankind interpreted everything

---

[3] Later, the term *positivism* came to refer not so much to Comte's specific theories as to a method he advocated: the construction of logical theories based on facts established through empirical research.

in terms of gods who lived in nature. In the second, or metaphysical stage, people learned through Christianity to think in more abstract terms. In the third, or positive stage now dawning, human understanding was becoming scientific through objective and precise observation followed by generalization in the form of scientific laws. Every science, he argued, has already passed through the first two stages and into the third—astronomy first, then physics, chemistry, and biology. Now a new science, *sociology* (Comte coined the term), must crown the progression.

While thus honoring the role of established religion, Comte announced its demise, substituting a "religion of humanity" of his own invention. Some devoted followers accepted his complex scheme whole; and many more would find inspiration in Comte's conviction that progress and social order could be made compatible with the proper organization of society. More generally, Comte's ideas contributed greatly to the widespread acceptance of the view that civilization progresses with increased knowledge discovered through the scientific method and that the great need now was for the scientific study of society and of humankind itself. This creed inspired and shaped much of the rapid development of the social sciences—economics, political science, anthropology, sociology, and psychology—later in the century.

Karl Marx   No theory about society and history has proved more influential than the work of Karl Marx. Marx was born in 1818 into a middle-class Rhineland Jewish family that had prospered with the lifting of civil disabilities that accompanied the revolutionary armies from France. He was an able student and received an excellent education at the leading German universities. Too radical to be permitted an academic career, he turned to journalism and became editor of a famous liberal newspaper, the *Rheinische Zeitung*. But his attacks on censorship and his views on economics led the Prussian government to demand his removal, and in 1843 Marx left for Paris. There he met other exiles and leading French radicals, men to whom he would later give the dismissive and enduring label of "utopian" socialists, and there he established a friendship with Friedrich Engels that would become a lifetime's collaboration.

▲ **Something of the power of his personality shows through in this photograph of Karl Marx, bourgeois and scholar (with reading glass).**
The Granger Collection.

Trained in German philosophy, abreast of contemporary economics, and in touch with the currents of radical thought, Marx began in Paris the systematic development of his own ideas. He outlined his theory of history in a powerful, apocalyptic tone in the *Communist Manifesto*, written jointly with Engels, which was published just before the revolutions of 1848. Little noticed at first, it proved to be one of the greatest pieces of propaganda of all time, a specific program and a general call to action combined with a philosophy of history. Marx devoted the rest of his life—from 1849 to 1883, which he spent in poverty-stricken exile in London—to the painstaking elaboration of his ideas in essays, letters, and the comprehensive treatise *Das Kapital,* the first volume of which was published in 1867. Engels, who shared Marx's exile in Britain, edited the second and third volumes, which appeared in 1885 and 1894.

Marx's Theory of History Marx wrote with verve on contemporary affairs—his essays on the revolutions of 1848 and Louis Napoleon's coup d'état are classics—but fundamentally he wanted, like so many thinkers of his time, to build a comprehensive philosophical system. Later in the century his followers would compare him with Darwin as the "discoverer" of the "law" of history: dialectical materialism. The dialectic came from Hegel, who had said that history evolved through the struggle between thesis and antithesis leading to a synthesis that formed the next stage of history. Marx kept the idea of a dialectic but rejected Hegel's idealism—the view that the dialectic works through ideas that constitute the spirit of the age—and insisted instead that any society rests fundamentally on the organization of its economy, on its mode of production.

Political systems, Marx said, grow from these material underpinnings, and in each system, the dominant social class expresses the needs, values, and interests associated with a particular mode of production. The agricultural economy of the Middle Ages required the feudal system with its particular social values and laws, upheld by the landowning aristocracy. That system produced its antithesis in the middle class. But the industrial society of capitalism, dominated by the middle class, was now producing a new antithesis embodied in the rising working class. Class conflict is the mechanism of historical progress, and the triumph of the proletariat will bring a new synthesis, a classless society.

By its own inevitable laws, history would thus lead to a new era, one similar to the future envisioned by other socialists. In the classless society, people would no longer be forced into the inequality that capitalist production required. At present, the primary purpose of the state was to protect property and enforce inequality, but in the new era the state would wither away, unneeded. Revolutions, in this analysis, mark the arrival to power of a new class. They are, however, more than mere transfers of power. A new class brings changes in law, religion, and customs, which it

then maintains in its own interest. The middle class, in Marxist terms, had represented a great, progressive force. But capitalism, despite all the ideologies and social institutions designed to shore it up, will fail through its own internal contradictions.

Marx's Analysis of Capitalism Marx's detailed analysis of capitalism took much from the classical economists (at a time when they were beginning to be outmoded). The value of a product, he insisted somewhat obscurely, comes from the value of all the labor required to produce it, all the labor necessary to transform raw materials into manufactured goods. The capitalist makes a profit by keeping part of the value added by all this labor done by others, that is, by exploiting the working class. But capitalists must compete with each other, and to do so, they are forced to lower prices, which in turn reduces profits. This reduction in profits has two effects. First, the capitalist must exploit labor more harshly, cutting wages to the minimum required for subsistence. Second, the smaller producers will fail, which will lead to larger concentrations of capital and force more and more members of the middle class into the proletariat, the class of people who have nothing but their labor to sell. Thus a shrinking capitalist class suffering from declining profits will face a growing proletariat. Capitalism therefore lays the basis for socialism by depriving all but a few of property. The contradictions will be resolved when the whole system fails.

Many of Marx's specific predictions now seem wrong. Although some of the rich have grown richer, the poor are not poorer as Marx predicted. Marx simply did not see much that is central to the modern economy—ever-expanding technology, the spread of ownership through public sale of stocks, and mass consumption. He did not anticipate the social effects of literacy, popular democracy, and mass communication. Marxist psychology is inadequate, with little acknowledgment of the loyalties and the irrationality so important in human personality. He sought to combine in one system Hegel's most difficult ideas, the economic theories of liberalism, the "scientific" method of positivism, and the moral vision of socialism—a combination awkward at best. Such critical terms as *class* and *state* remained ambiguous, and the concept of class struggle, applied elastically to a single event and to centuries of history, lost its analytic force. The goal of history, according to Karl Marx, is the classless society; yet he sketched that condition only vaguely and left unanswered fundamental questions about it and about the means of obtaining it.

The Appeal of Marxism Despite such weaknesses, and the theory's every flaw has been widely broadcast, Marxism has deeply affected all modern thought, shaped the policies of all sorts of governments, and provided a core for some of the most powerful political movements of the last hundred years. Such impact requires explanation, and perhaps four points can capture something of the answer.

First, Marxism not only sees society as a whole and explains historical change but demands systematic and detailed analyses of the interrelationship of social values, institutions, politics, and economic conditions. It also suggests methods for conducting such analyses. These qualities and the impressive body of important Marxist studies that have resulted account for its continuing importance in all the social sciences.

Second, Marxism accepts and indeed hails industrialization as inevitable and beneficial even while accepting most criticism of industrial society. Many reformers dreamed of green gardens and simpler days; but Marx believed that the machine can free human beings from brute labor and that it can, through greater productivity, provide well-being for all. Industrialization could be made to provide solutions to the very problems it created. Thus Marxism has had special appeal for societies eager to modernize.

Third, the theory is rich in moral judgments without having to defend any ethical system. Although social values are considered relative, and those of his opponents are denounced as hypocritical, Marx's own rage at injustice rings out in a compelling call to generous sentiments that rejects sentimentality.

Finally, Marxism not only claims the prestige of science but offers the security of determinism. Knowing where destiny leads, Marxists can accept the uneven flow of change, confident that any defeats are temporary. Opponents are to be recognized and fought less for what they say or do than for what they represent—for their "objective" role in the structure of capitalism. Their con-

cessions do not alter their destiny, and the Marxist is free to adopt whatever tactics will further the inevitable movement of history toward the victory of the proletariat. Just as Marx believed that small (quantitative) changes may lead to sudden qualitative ones, so Marxists can favor short-term reforms as well as revolution. The variety inherent in Marx's system has been a source of bitter division as well as strength among socialists, but it helped keep Marxism more vigorous and coherent than any other of the grand theories spawned in the nineteenth century.

Charles Darwin A more concrete and more shocking theory of human progress emerged from Charles Darwin's *On the Origin of Species*, a milestone in the history of science published in 1859.[4] With sober caution, Darwin had worked much as Comte said a scientist should. Born into a well-known family of clergy and doctors with ties to many of England's leading intellectuals, Darwin had difficulty in finding a suitable career. But his respect for facts led him to collect evidence about natural history from every available source—his own observations from travel in the South Seas, the work of others, the lore of farmers. He first formulated his concept of natural selection in 1838, but not until Alfred R. Wallace independently developed a very similar theory could Darwin be persuaded to publish his findings.

Although Darwin's presentation was the more fully and carefully developed, the parallel theories of the two men suggest how much both owed to ideas already current. Biologists had shown in impressive detail the close relationship between biological forms and their functions in supporting life. Geologists had begun to analyze the earth in terms of the effect of natural forces over a long period of time, without recourse to sudden cataclysms or divine intervention. Classical economists, especially Malthus, had stressed the importance to social development of the cruel conflict for food, which Darwin made the essential key to natural selection.

---

[4] The full title of Darwin's work suggests its broad and provocative implications: *On the Origin of Species by Natural Selection, or the Preservation of Favoured Races in the Struggle for Life.* The first edition sold out on the day of publication.

▲ **With self-conscious art, the photographer of an elderly Charles Darwin suggested some timeless mystery.**
New York Public Library.

Darwinian Evolution Darwin established that the variety of species is potentially infinite—rejecting the classical and Christian ideas of immutable forms in nature—and argued that there is an almost constant modification of species, each tested in the universal struggle for existence. He not only presented detailed evidence for evolution but described its mechanism: Only those well adapted to their environment survived to reproduce, as their progeny would. Over millions of years, through the process of natural selection, more complex or "higher" forms of life emerged, each form proliferating as its environment permitted and as competition for food and survival dictated.

This scientific theory, expressed with caution and supported by massive evidence, almost instantly became the center of controversies that raged throughout Europe for a generation. Evolution, mutable species, survival determined by brute conflict rather than divine will—each of these theories challenged established assumptions in science and theology. Nor did Darwin hide his belief that the same laws apply to the development of human beings and beasts. This seemed to many a scandalous disregard of divine providence and Christian teaching. Nowadays, most theologians and scientists generally agree that there is no necessary conflict between the concept of evolving species and Christian doctrine, but such tolerance required a differentiation between the study of natural laws and religious tradition that few in the nineteenth century were willing to make.

Social Darwinism People eager to apply science to society quickly extended Darwin's principles to more current concerns, a tendency that came to be called *Social Darwinism.* Few of the claims of Social Darwinism were logically necessary extensions of Darwin's views; but reference to his grand theories added universal meaning, scientific prestige, and a new vocabulary to contemporary debate. Social Darwinists tended to ignore the unimaginably long time span in which Darwinian theory operated and to extend the formal concept of species by loose analogy to groups, classes, nations, or civilizations. An invitingly tough-minded way to reason, Social Darwinism was used to argue for opposing policies. Thomas Huxley, the greatest intellectual propagandist for Darwin's theories, battled clergy who rejected human evolution as contrary to the Bible, but his conception of Social Darwinism held it to be consonant with the teachings of Indian philosophy, Buddhism, ancient Greece, and Christianity (see "Huxley's Social Darwinism," p. 885).

Some writers in Great Britain and the United States used the vocabulary of Social Darwinism to argue that better education and social welfare constitute a higher stage of evolution and that an environment thus improved would produce a superior species. But Darwinism was more commonly used to justify competition in the marketplace or between nations, as the mechanism of evolution in which the fittest triumph. At its most extreme, Social Darwinism presented the law of the jungle as realistic, scientific, and beneficial.

Huxley's Social Darwinism
◆

"Evolution and Ethics," a much reprinted lecture that T. H. Huxley gave at Oxford in 1893, was perhaps the most famous statement of what can be called the gentle interpretation of the social implication of Darwin's theories.

"Man, the animal, in fact, has worked his way to the headship of the sentient world, and has become the superb animal which he is, in virtue of his success in the struggle for existence. The conditions having been of a certain order, man's organization has adjusted itself to them better than that of his competitors in the cosmic strife. In the case of mankind, the self-assertion, the unscrupulous seizing upon all that can be grasped, the tenacious holding of all that can be kept, which constitute the essence of the struggle for existence, have answered. For his successful progress, throughout the savage state, man has been largely indebted to those qualities which he shares with the ape and the tiger; his exceptional physical organization; his cunning, his sociability, his curiosity, and his imitativeness; his ruthless and ferocious destructiveness when his anger is roused by opposition.

"But, in proportion as men have passed from anarchy to social organization, and in proportion as civilization has grown in worth, these deeply ingrained serviceable qualities have become defects. . . . In fact, civilized man brands all these ape and tiger promptings with the name of sins, he punishes many of the acts which flow from them as crimes; and, in extreme cases, he does his best to put an end to the survival of the fittest of former days by axe and rope.

" . . . The history of civilization details the steps by which men have succeeded in building up an artificial world within the cosmos. Fragile reed as he may be, man, as Pascal says, is a thinking reed: there lies within him a fund of energy operating intelligently and so far akin to that which pervades the universe, that it is competent to influence and modify the cosmic process.

" . . . Moreover, the cosmic nature born with us and, to a large extent, necessary for our maintenance, is the outcome of millions of years of severe training, and it would be folly to imagine that a few centuries will suffice to subdue its masterfulness to purely ethical ends. Ethical nature may count upon having to reckon with a tenacious and powerful enemy as long as the world lasts. But, on the other hand, I see no limit to the extent to which intelligence and will, guided by sound principles of investigation, and organized in common effort, may modify the conditions of existence, for a period longer than that now covered by history. And much may be done to change the nature of man himself."

From Thomas H. Huxley, *Evolution and Ethics and Other Essays* (New York: D. Appleton and Company, 1916).

Usually not so unmodulated, the assumptions of Social Darwinism nevertheless infiltrated many aspects of late nineteenth-century social thought. Ideas of genetic determinism employing (often fallacious) theories of genetics were widespread; and these ideas cropped up in loose talk about national characteristics and theories that ranked races as superior or inferior, in the codification of traditional views about gender in which male dominance was said to be based on innate differences between men and women, in elaborate systems for identifying criminal types by physiology, in a science of eugenics that looked for ways to discourage the unfit from breeding, and in the emergence of inherited characteristics as a literary theme in novels and drama.

Herbert Spencer   One of the grandest statements of the laws of progress was the *Synthetic Philosophy* of Herbert Spencer, published in a series of studies that first appeared in the 1850s and continued to 1896. Spencer's ideas were closely tied to those of Comte and Darwin, and his contemporaries (especially in Great Britain and the United States) ranked him among the major philosophers of all time. Spencer's central principle, which made progress "not an accident, but a necessity," was the evolution of all things from simplicity to complexity, from homogeneity to diversity. With heavy erudition, he traced this process in physics and biology, sociology and psychology, economics and ethics. Such comprehensiveness was part of his appeal, and he applied his theses to physical matter, to human understanding, and to social institutions. He was admired for his claim to be hardheaded and practical; but while he refused to worry about the metaphysical abstractions of traditional philosophy, he maintained the assumptions of a narrow and rigid liberalism.

Spencer argued that the marketplace is the true test of the fittest, and that it must be uninhibited by state intervention even in behalf of welfare or public education. When he died in 1903, much of his work was already outmoded. Strict laissez-faire had been abandoned even by most liberals, his sort of rationalism had come under heavy attack, and the disciplines of the social sciences had moved toward subtler theories. His confidence that universal laws of development enshrined the values of middle-class English Protestants would soon seem quaint.

The Study of Other Societies Interest in other societies had long been a significant current in European thought, shaped by centuries of conflict with Islam and still engaged even in the nineteenth century with Greek and Roman thought. Curiosity about other ways of life had increased in the age of exploration, stimulated by the reports of missionaries and the experience of trade, conquest, and rule. Subsequently, Enlightenment thinkers had observed other societies as a way to study the effects of diverse environments, customs, and political forms. Admiration for the Chinese or Persians was a way of criticizing European societies while searching for universal patterns in human behavior. This effort to establish a science of society continued in the nineteenth century. An important part of liberal economic theory and utilitarianism, the effort expanded with the experience of industrial change, to be furthered by ideas of historical evolution and increased contact with other lands.

Much as Darwinian ideas were influenced by economic theory and discoveries in geology, so anthropology, which now became a distinctive field of study, bore the imprint of the new work in sociology and history and of increased contact with the Americas and Asia. Many of the great scholars of ancient law and of linguistics developed their methods through the study of Indian civilization. And many of the leading advocates of reform in England formed their views from the experience of governing in India.

Confident of their own place on the evolutionary scale, Europeans tended to see other societies as recapitulating their own historic past, a view that encouraged both affectionate interest and disdain for cultures stuck in a distant past. At the same time, Europeans learned from non-European

▼ *James McNeill Whistler*
THE PRINCESS FROM THE LAND OF PORCELAIN.
Increased familiarity with Chinese and Japanese art strongly influenced Western artists interested in new styles, including the impressionists or their friend, James McNeill Whistler, who painted this portrait of *The Princess from the Land of Porcelain* **in 1864.**
James McNeill Whistler (American, 1834–1903). "Rose and Silver: The Princess from the Land of Porcelain," 1863–1864. Oil Color on canvas: 199.9 × 116.1 cm. Courtesy of the Freer Gallery of Art, Smithsonian Institution, Washington, D.C. 03.91.

civilizations, most obviously in the social sciences but in many other fields as well. Asian and later African art influenced the arts in Europe, and European medical practice adopted herbs and drugs used elsewhere. On the whole, however, these growing global connections strengthened the sense that Europe's was a distinctive civilization and the one that led the world.

III. The European Presence Around the Globe

From the French Revolution to the last third of the nineteenth century, European influence on other continents was not primarily a matter of conquest but came rather from cultural, economic, and political connections. The energy of Europe and its example nevertheless spilled across the world in multiple ways: economic exploitation, humanitarian opposition to slavery, the harsh treatment of Native Americans and denunciations of that treatment, Christian missions, political advice, trade, and military conflict. Whatever the intent or the mixture of motives, the result was disruptive; for the European presence brought new ideas, manners, technologies, and interests accompanied by irrepressible power.

THE APPARENT DECLINE OF COLONIAL EMPIRES

Most liberals truly believed that the age of empire, which they associated with an outmoded mercantilism, had passed.

Latin America Latin American history seemed to prove the point. In the twenty years from 1804 to 1824, France lost control of Haiti, Portugal of Brazil, and Spain of all the rest of Latin America save Cuba and Puerto Rico. Deeply affected by the examples of the French and American revolutions, the independence movements of Latin America were in turn models of the kind of nationalism and state making that would soon sweep Europe. Although subsequent conflicts among the new states of Latin America created plenty of opportunities for British and French involvement, empire was not at issue.

Garibaldi had been hailed as the hero of two worlds when he returned to Italy from Latin America in 1848, because it was believed he fought on both continents for the same principles of freedom and national independence. Creoles, the descendants of Europeans who now ruled Latin America, maintained and strengthened their cultural ties to Spain and France. They followed the latest continental trends in music and literature, fashion and science; shared an intellectual life close to Europe's (positivism was especially strong in Latin America); adapted constitutions modeled on that of the United States; and purchased the goods brought by English merchants. Independence from European rule had not eliminated Europe's cultural influence or profitable trade.

The Middle East In the Middle East, too, Europe's liberal governments tended to favor local efforts to throw off foreign domination as the power of the Ottoman Empire declined. Britain and France had ensured the independence of Greece. When Mohammed Ali, the Ottoman governor in Egypt, set out on an independent course that led Egypt to war with Turkey (1832–1833, 1839, and 1841) and to his conquest of the Sudan, he formed an alliance with France. Determined to create a more modern and efficient regime, Mohammed Ali also adopted institutions like those of the Napoleonic state, established French as the language of administration in Egypt, and opened the country to other European influences. As early as 1833, Saint-Simonian engineers arrived with plans for building a Suez canal, a project that would eventually lead to European dominance in Egypt.

EUROPE'S INCREASING INFLUENCE

The greater European presence brought with it the competition among European states. The desire of Britain and France to restrict Russia's claims against the Ottoman Empire had led to the Crimean War (see p. 848), and the war's effect was to increase European influence in the region. Russian pressure on Afghanistan and Persia brought British counterpressure. The pattern was significant. To resist one European state, local leaders turned to another European state for help, but that help would come with demands for

▲ After elaborate ceremonies, the opening of the Suez Canal in 1869 was marked by a parade of ships, including new steamships and a sailboat with the lateen sail characteristic of the Mediterranean. Both the empress Eugénie of France and the emperor Franz-Josepf of Austria attended the ceremonies for which the khedive of Egypt commissioned Verdi to write an opera, *Aida*, first performed two years later.
Mary Evans Picture Library.

special concessions and offers of military alliances which would result in the sending of European military and political advisers. The process that began with efforts to strengthen local autonomy led to formal arrangements legitimating the presence of European officials and interests.

Explorers Exploration was no longer expected to reveal previously unknown civilizations, but it continued in the name of science and could have practical importance (the continued search for a northwest passage across northern Canada incidentally benefited whaling). Most expeditions made no claims to conquest and were not investigating lands their governments possessed, as Lewis and Clark had done when Jefferson sent them to explore the newly purchased Louisiana Territory. But Europeans freely charted the seas in more detail than ever before, while European geologists, botanists, and cartographers scrambled over the mountains and along the rivers and trails of the world without claims of sovereignty. Their tables, lists, maps, and descriptions of local peoples nevertheless constituted a kind of dominion of the world, a poten-

tial for the exercise of power benignly assembled in the name of science in the libraries and learned societies of European capitals.

Missionaries Humane and pious intentions similarly tended to result in an extension of European influence. Campaigns against the slave trade led to British intervention in parts of East Africa and to the French creation of Libreville in the Congo in 1847 as a haven for freed slaves. Liberia, where the first colonists of American blacks arrived in 1822, became an independent state in the same year. David Livingston made his way across central Africa in the 1850s, opposing the slave trade while stimulating interest in that vast continent among traders and statesmen.

Catholic and Protestant missionaries competed for influence in Madagascar, and the British and French governments were soon involved in a parallel competition for influence there. Seeking support against local enemies, the emperor of Ethiopia turned to the English. The interaction of European interest and internal developments was preparing the way for more radical changes in Africa. Christian missionaries were important in Asia, too, where they had been active for centuries; but traders and European governments now began to show more consistent concern to protect their economic and political interests.

Military Intervention The English reformers who objected to slavery also opposed the opium trade between India and China, long a source of profit for English merchants. Yet Chinese efforts to restrict that trade resulted in a conflict with Britain that ended with China's cession of Hong Kong (1841) and grant of special rights to foreigners. The disruptive impact of a European presence, including missionaries, was further demonstrated in the Taiping Rebellion (1850–1864). Social discontent and the resentment of foreigners mixed together in a Chinese-led millenarian movement that incorporated elements of Christian belief and soon fostered revolts that threatened the Chinese empire.

When the rebels attacked Europeans, their governments put new pressure on China; and the Chinese government, battling for survival, was forced to grant further concessions to Britain, the United States, France, and Russia, guaranteeing them extraterritorial rights, trading privileges, and the protection of their missionaries. In 1860 British and French forces occupied Peking and burned the summer palace in retaliation for the seizure of their envoys, and Russia took Vladivostock—that loss was recognized by China's Department of Foreign Affairs, a ministry not needed before.

Elsewhere, too, conflicts that began as local issues often resulted in the further exercise of European political power. The persecution of Christians in Cochin China brought French and Spanish forces to the scene. They occupied Saigon in 1858, the beginning of an intrusion that in twenty years saw the eastern provinces of Cochin China transformed into French Indochina. The mistreatment of American castaways in Japan prompted the arrival of an American fleet with demands that went beyond that issue to include trading rights. The treaty signed with the United States in 1854 was quickly followed by similar ones between the major European nations and Japan, ending that nation's centuries-old policy of isolation.

The process that led to greater European domination did not require conscious imperial designs, and the privileges that Europeans demanded usually did not include outright control. An inherent dynamic, however, led to European domination. The growing European presence, upsetting to local institutions and customs, disrupted established society. When these disruptions undermined stability and threatened some European national or legal claim, European governments responded with a show of force and increased demands. Resistance to this pressure brought more European force and a more permanent European presence.

Direct Rule Important examples of direct imperial rule could also be found, and in those cases, too, resistance led to expanded and tighter European control. A revolt in Java against the Dutch (1825–1830) resulted in their firmer control over the entire Dutch East Indies. Just before its fall in 1830, France's Bourbon monarchy had invaded Algeria to reestablish order there. Significantly, succeeding French governments found themselves extending the efforts of their predecessors until all of Algeria had been conquered. Officials responded to guerrilla attacks or a lack of cooperation on the part of local leaders by expanding

the area under military control, then by placing administration ever more firmly in French hands. Algeria was made part of metropolitan France after 1848.

Similarly, Britain's well-established interest in India assumed a greater place in the government's policy. Protecting access to India stirred British interest in Afghanistan and led to wars in Burma and the opening of Siam to European trade in 1855. Within India itself, the East India Company, under charter from the British government, had long exercised authority through local princes. But empire building was already under way during the governor-generalship of Lord William Bentinck (1828–1835). Maintaining order led to border skirmishes that ceased only with British forces in command of a larger territory. Campaigns against the bands of *thags* (the source of the English word *thugs*) resulted in more intrusive British policing.

When reformers in London denounced corruption within the East India Company and demanded more humanitarian measures, the result was an extension of British involvement in Indian affairs. The custom of *sati* (in which a widow placed herself on her husband's funeral pyre) was banned, trade opened to merchants not connected to the company, and the production of tea and coffee encouraged. The country's first railroad was built in 1853, and a school system was established the following year. Administrative reforms made officials more responsible and intrusive, and Thomas Macaulay, historian and reformer, was commissioned to design a law code for India that extended British influence deeper into Indian society.

This British activity, which often ran counter to traditional practices and religious beliefs, provoked resistance and then the shock of rebellion in 1857. It began with a revolt among the native troops whom the British employed in northern India and spread to popular risings eventually put down but only after terrible atrocities on both sides. In Britain, public opinion was outraged at the ungrateful Indians but also at the brutality of English officials. The upshot was more reforms of British administration, further annexations of Indian territories to guarantee more acceptable politics, and the promotion of the governor-general to viceroy. The British crown had established direct sovereignty over India.

Law and Money These worldwide arrangements and interventions stemmed from more than the superiority of European arms and technology. Europe simply assumed (and then insisted) that European laws and standards of conduct applied to their relations with authorities outside Europe. Similar assumptions about the universal validity of European mores accompanied the thousands of resolute missionaries and avid traders who poured across the globe. In the Middle East, Africa, and Asia local rulers recognized that self-protection and their own ambitions required that they try to deal with those traders, seek alliances with these powerful foreign nations, and adopt some of their techniques and institutions. Such policies required money, which Europeans were ready to lend. As debts mounted, payments often fell into arrears, which became a justification for more forceful European intervention.

Efforts at modernization in Egypt, which resulted in the completion of a railway from Alexandria to Cairo and the concession to Ferdinand de Lesseps of the rights to construct the Suez Canal, also included Egypt's first foreign loan in 1854. A serious burden by 1863, the debt grew to be thirty times larger in the following decade. The Bey of Tunis was so badly in debt by 1869 that he accepted international (meaning European) control of Tunisian finances that would lead to French conquest a decade later. Mexico's suspension of debt payments in 1861 led to a joint intervention by Britain, Spain, and France, which was followed by Louis Napoleon's disastrous efforts to establish a lasting influence there by arranging the appointment of Archduke Maximilian of Austria as emperor of Mexico. Maximilian's regime was soon toppled, and he was executed in 1867.

In general, however, Europeans were injected into the affairs of other continents not so much as the result of official plans as by the effects of burgeoning commerce and capital, the advantages of European technology and firearms, and the ambitions of individual diplomats, military officers, and merchants who found themselves in foreign lands.

Migration Ordinary people also carried European languages and cultures around the world in the greatest voluntary movement of peoples in human history. This wave of migration continued a century-old trend but on an unprecedented

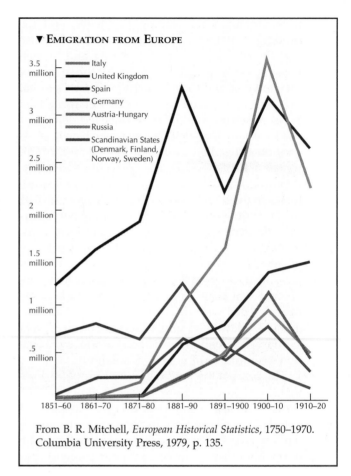

▼ EMIGRATION FROM EUROPE

Italy
United Kingdom
Spain
Germany
Austria-Hungary
Russia
Scandinavian States (Denmark, Finland, Norway, Sweden)

From B. R. Mitchell, *European Historical Statistics*, 1750–1970. Columbia University Press, 1979, p. 135.

scale, facilitated by more rapidly increasing populations, an established pattern of migration from rural areas to cities, and larger boats with cheaper fares. Unemployment in Europe, opportunities in the New World, and visions of a better life pushed Europe's poor to crowd into the steerage of ship after ship.

Between 1875 and 1914 some 26 million Europeans emigrated overseas, more than half of them to the United States, with Latin America the next most common destination. Smaller numbers sought their fortunes in Asia and Africa. More people left the United Kingdom than any other country, going to Australia, Canada, and South Africa as well as to the United States. Before 1890 the United Kingdom, the Scandinavian countries, and Germany sent migrants in highest proportion to their domestic population. After 1890 the leaders were the United Kingdom, Italy, Spain, and Portugal. Overall, the

▲ *C. J. Staniland*
The Emigrant Ship.
Staniland's painting shows English men (mainly young) and some women crowding on board ship to start a new life overseas. By this time, toward the end of the century when emigration from Europe was at its height, the ships were larger and the voyage shorter and less dangerous than it had been a generation earlier.
Bradford Art Galleries and Museum/Bridgeman Art Library.

greatest exodus in proportion to population came from Ireland. But every nation except France (Europe's major receiver of immigrants) contributed significant numbers to the movement. Perhaps a third of those who left their homeland to go overseas eventually returned, and they, too, added to the experiences and human networks that connected Europe to the world.

Most of these migrants were from rural areas, often members of peasant families who hoped to add to their family holdings with the money they could earn abroad. Some, like Scandinavians in the northern plains of the United States or Italians in California and parts of South America, were fortunate enough to find new land in climates similar to those they had left, where they could successfully employ farming techniques they already knew. When they could, migrants with special skills continued in the trades they knew. En-

glish and Polish miners were drawn to the coal fields of Pennsylvania and the mines of northern Michigan; Italian masons looked for work in the construction industry that flourished in expanding cities.

Cities offered the most opportunities, and cities are where most European migrants went, taking whatever jobs they could find when they could not make a living in the trades they knew as tailors or leather workers or seamstresses. Their large numbers produced concentrations of ethnic groups that sustained much of their old culture and thereby enriched the culture of the places in which they settled with their cuisine, music, tastes, and habits: Eastern European Jews (escaping pogroms as well as poverty) in London and Paris as well as New York; Irish, Italians, and Eastern Europeans in cities across North America; Italians and Spaniards in South America.

IV. Modern Imperialism

THE MEANINGS OF IMPERIALISM

Empire and, to a lesser extent, *imperialism* are terms that have been used throughout Western history, but the meanings have changed. For most of European history, ancient Rome stood as the model of empire, and that usage continued well into the last third of the nineteenth century. Spain's empire and the British Empire were often compared to Rome; and Rome's grandeur was consciously evoked by the tsars of Russia, the Habsburg monarchs, and both Napoleons when they called themselves *emperors*.

Late Nineteenth-Century Usage This emphasis had shifted by the 1870s. By then when contemporaries spoke of imperialism (and they spoke and wrote about it a great deal), they generally meant a European state's intervention in and continuing domination over non-European territory. The altered meaning reflected a striking new reality. In the single generation preceding World War I, European states suddenly spread their political dominion over vast territories. Most of the newly acquired lands had few European settlers (the primary means of exploiting local wealth in the past), and most of the new lands lay in tropical zones that Europeans had heretofore found unappealing and unhealthy. Dramatic evidence of Europe's dynamism, imperialism was justified as progress—carrying higher civilization and Christianity to backward lands—that was also in the national interest. Imperialism became a central concern of international relations and a reason to abandon free trade, and it injected a more competitive nationalism into political campaigns and infected public discourse throughout the West with ideas of superiority based on race, class, and gender.

Capitalism and Culture Since World War II, *imperialism* often refers to economic and cultural domination with or without direct political control. Such imperialism is seen as a complex system fundamentally related to the development and expansion of capitalism, with Europe (mainly Western Europe and by the end of the nineteenth century the United States as well) its core and with the poor and distant lands of Africa, the Americas, and Asia its periphery. Studies of imperialism thus often focus on the unequal relations between core and periphery and trace the development of those relations with the spread of a world market, from the trade in luxuries and slaves during the seventeenth century to the multinational corporations of today.

Understood in this sense, modern European imperialism has existed over four centuries but clearly increased enormously in the nineteenth century, especially from the 1860s on. Trade expanded both in value and in geographical range. Wherever commerce took them, Europeans built docks and warehouses, established companies, and made new investments. Whether directed by business managers in Europe, by European settlers, or by non-European merchants in the periphery, these commercial enterprises adopted European techniques of management, accounting, and technology. Businesses expanded by attracting European capital, and much of the profit generated returned to European banks and investors.

These enterprises tied to foreign markets in turn transformed local economies through their purchases of local goods and services and their labor policies. This process expanded with improved communication. Steamships required better ports, more reliable and expensive provisions, and larger cargoes. Telegraph lines connected India to Europe in 1865, and a cable ran from Vladivostok to Shanghai, Hong Kong, and Singapore by 1871. By the 1880s rail lines operated on every continent;

▼ Bourdeax had been a major Atlantic port for centuries, but in the 1860s Éduoard Manet could still portray the harbor as a colorful clutter of fishing boats and vessels for coastal shipping.
Buhrle Foundation, Zurich/Bridgeman Art Library.

▲ **By the end of the century shipping was associated with power and empire as in this painting by Frederick Scarborough, which shows lighters ready to tend to the needs of the great steamships in the harbor of London, the world's greatest port.**
Rowles Fine Art, Powis/Bridgeman Art Library.

and more were being built, all requiring European equipment, engineers, and investment. By the turn of the century the automobile began to generate a demand not only for highways and bridges but also for a steady flow of petroleum, the basis for new international corporations.

Merchants and migrants, missionaries and officials, scientists and reporters carried European languages and law and customs around the world, deeply affecting local cultures. In the second half of the nineteenth century, universities on the European model were established from Constantinople to India; and students from China, Japan, India, and the Middle East became familiar figures in European and American centers of learning. These developments, which affected ordinary social life, challenged the position of traditional elites and contributed to that larger process—by which Western interests used power and prestige to increase their wealth while disrupting and transforming non-Western societies—that the term *imperialism* evokes today.

EXPLANATIONS OF IMPERIALISM

The phenomenon of nineteenth-century imperialism demands explanation, and by the turn of the century, its opponents in particular had an explanation for the pervasive imperial fever.

J. A. Hobson In 1902 J. A. Hobson, a British economist, published *Imperialism: A Study,* a critical tract that has been heavily attacked by subsequent scholars yet remains the starting point of modern analysis (see "The Interpretation of Imperialism," p. 894). Writing during the Boer War (discussed later in this chapter), Hobson was eager to show that imperialism offered little real benefit to restless Europeans or to commerce. Emigrants, he noted, preferred to go to the Americas, and Britain's trade with the European continent and the Americas was far greater and growing faster than its trade with its colonies.

Hobson found the economic explanation of imperialism to lie in the influence of speculators and financiers, a small number of people who controlled great wealth and looked for quick profits by investing outside Europe. Through their social and political connections such people got their governments to protect their investments in undeveloped lands and made calculated use of the missionaries, soldiers, and patriotic dreamers who glorified empire. Imperialism thus stemmed from the manipulation of public opinion in the interest of certain capitalists.

The Interpretation of Imperialism

Debate on the interpretation of imperialism has not ceased since the publication of J. A. Hobson's Imperialism: A Study *in 1902. The work went through many editions and remains worth reading today. Hobson was a highly respected British economist and social scientist, and his study is filled with statistics and careful argument. His conclusions capture some of the essence, and polemic tone, of the case he made.*

"If Imperialism may no longer be regarded as a blind inevitable destiny, is it certain that imperial expansion as a deliberately chosen line of public policy can be stopped?

"We have seen that it is motivated, not by the interests of the nation as a whole, but by those of certain classes, who impose the policy upon the nation for their own advantage. . . . The essentially illicit nature of this use of the public resources of the nation to safeguard and improve private investments should be clearly recognized.

" . . . Analysis of Imperialism, with its natural supports, militarism, oligarchy, bureaucracy, protection, concentration of capital and violent trade fluctuations, has marked it out as the supreme danger of modern national States. The power of the imperialist forces within the nation to use the national resources for their private gain, by operating the instrument of the States, can only be overthrown by the establishment of a genuine democracy."

Joseph A. Schumpeter, who was born in Austria, achieved international fame with the publication of The Theory of Economic Development *in 1912, when he was 29 years old. The famous essay title "The Sociology of Imperialism," written a few years later, was an extension of his interest in economic growth under capitalism and was in part a rebuttal of economic explanations of imperialism, particularly those of Hobson and of Marxists from Lenin on. Imperialism, Schumpeter argued, was not a natural outgrowth of capitalism but rather a leftover from the precapitalist era centered in the policies of the aristocracy.*

"Here we find that we have penetrated to the historical as well as the sociological sources of modern imperialism. It does not *coincide* with nationalism and militarism, though it *fuses* with them by supporting them as it is supported by them. It too is—not only historically, but also sociologically—a heritage of the autocratic state, of its structural elements, organizational forms, interest alignments, and human attitudes, the outcome of precapitalist forces which the autocratic state has reorganized, in part by the methods of early capitalism. It would never have evolved by the 'inner logic' of capitalism itself. This is true even of mere export monopolism. It too has its sources in absolutist policy and the action habits of an essentially precapitalist environment. . . . But export monopolism, to go a step further, is not yet imperialism. And even if it had been able to arise without protective tariffs, it would never have developed into imperialism in the hands of an unwarlike bourgeoisie. If this did happen, it was only because the heritage included the war machine, together with its socio-psychological aura and aggressive bent, but because a class oriented toward war maintained itself in a ruling position. This class clung to its domestic interest in war, and the promilitary interests among the bourgeoisie were able to ally themselves with it. This alliance kept alive war instincts and ideas of overlordship, male supremacy, and triumphant glory—ideas that would have otherwise long since died. It led to social conditions that, while they ultimately stem from the conditions of production, cannot be explained from capitalist production methods alone. And it often impresses its mark on present-day politics, threatening Europe with the constant danger of war.

"This diagnosis also bears the prognosis of imperialism. The precapitalist elements in our social life may still have great vitality; special circumstances in national life may revive them from time to time; but in the end the climate of the modern world must destroy them."

Wolfgang Mommsen, a distinguished member of a family of famous historians, for years served as director of the German Historical Institute in London and a professor of history at the University of Düsseldorf. His Theories of Imperialism *began as a series of lectures given at the University of Amsterdam in 1970, and it reflects the complexity and ambiguities of current interpretations.*

"Despite the changes in our attitude towards the imperialist age now that the classic type of formal imperialism has become a thing of the past, a remarkable degree of continuity can be seen in both bourgeois and Marxist studies of the subject. The broad lines of a possible interpretation of imperialism were already laid down by such classic theorists as Hobson, Hilferding, Schumpeter and Lenin; later writers have endeavored, on the basis of these studies, to produce more differentiated models taking into account recent research and developments in the world situation. An important new light is cast by recent British research, which on the one hand has developed the idea of 'informal imperialism' and thus widened the scope of the enquiry in general, and on the other has drawn attention to the independent role of the 'periphery,' especially the indigenous ruling classes, which have often had much to do with the character, timing and direction of imperial expansion.

"It must be said that the older theories of imperialism have lost much of their usefulness because they are too Eurocentric and also tend to reduce the whole phenomenon to a single cause. A modern theory which gives due weight to the periphery, while recognizing that its so-called crises were themselves the result of informal European penetration, is better able to comprehend the phenomenon of third-world underdevelopment without necessarily subscribing to the tautologies of neo-Marxist theory. The 'objectivist' argument that imperialist processes were generally stimulated by the marginal groups in European society, in conjunction with 'men on the spot,' gives sufficient reason to review the 'endogenous type of theory' according to which imperialism is a necessary outcome of the policies or economic structures of the industrial states. Finally, it seems as though the long discredited political theories of imperialism are to some extent enjoying a 'comeback,' chiefly in combination with sociological and socioeconomic explanations. The 'official mind' is certainly not nowadays conceived as brashly imperialist, as was formerly the case. The picture is rather one of statesmen who were powerless to control the self-propelled course of imperial expansion, which began with more or less informal methods and then called for the use of formal power in one case after another, often against the wishes of the politicians concerned.

"Classic economic theories of imperialism, whether Marxist or bourgeois, have lost much of their attraction. . . . In the present state of research into the subject it appears to us that a new form of theory is required which would not simply repeat the traditional formulae. . . . On the other hand, a new theory should not, as is frequent in the Western world, content itself with regarding imperialism as a thing of the past: it must take account of the after-effects of imperialism in the world as we know it, not least the disturbing fact that the gap between rich and poor nations is growing steadily wider. Many may even develop nostalgia for the days of formal colonial rule, when the European powers were, at least in principle, responsible for developments at the periphery, whereas today they are formally relieved of the burden. But the question remains of how far these developments are rooted in the era of formal imperialism, and whether the forms of economic, cultural and political dependence which have survived the end of colonialism are not partly to blame for the 'development of underdevelopment' in many parts of the third world. Any modern theory of imperialism must face the question of how far the international capitalist system contains latent or manifest imperialist tendencies, or even whether it *is* manifestly imperialist."

From J. A. Hobson, *Imperialism: A Study* (London: George Allen & Unwin, Ltd., 1961; sixth impression of the third revised edition of 1938, first published in 1902), excerpts from pp. 356, 358, 360; From Heinz Norden (trans.), *Two Essays by Joseph Schumpeter: Social Classes, Imperialism,* Meridian Books, 1951, pp. 97–98; From Wolfgang J. Mommsen, P. S. Fall (trans.), *Theories of Imperialism,* Weidenfald & Nicolson Ltd., London, 1980.

V. I. Lenin Hobson's analysis inspired the still more influential theory of V. I. Lenin. The leader of Russia's Marxist revolutionaries, Lenin provided a Marxist interpretation of a subject on which Marx had written little. In *Imperialism: The Last Stage of Capitalism* (1916), Lenin agreed with Hobson that the stimulus behind empire building was basically economic and that the essence of colonialism was exploitation. Lenin argued, however, that imperialist ventures grew not just from the policies of a few but from the very dynamics of capitalism itself.

Competition lowered profits and resulted in monopolies, forcing surplus capital to seek investments overseas. The alternative, to enlarge the domestic market by raising wages, would be uncompetitive and thus further reduce profit. Imperialism was therefore the last "stage" of capitalism, the product of its internal contradictions. Looking back on the outbreak of World War I, Lenin would add that imperial rivalries involved whole nations and led to wars that further hastened the end of capitalism. For many, *imperialist* became an epithet for a system considered decadent as well as immoral.

Current Views   Although influenced by these interpretations, most historians have remained uncomfortable with them. The emphasis on capitalism contributes little to an understanding of the actual process of imperial conquest, in which capitalists were often reluctant participants. It does not explain why imperialists called for political control beyond treaty rights or for the swift spread of European power into areas that offered small financial return. In fact, even British investment and trade remained much greater with other independent nations than with its own colonies. Nor do economic arguments tell us much about the role of the popular press, explorers, earnest missionaries, and ambitious soldiers in pressing hesitant politicians to imperial conquest.

Many other factors are needed to help explain the sudden increase in the pace and importance of European imperialism in the late nineteenth century, although all analysts today would agree that economic interests, at least in the long run, played a major part. Even early in the century the European economy had been closely tied to imports of raw materials such as cotton and timber and of commodities like tea and sugar. Policies that guaranteed those supplies were sure to win broad domestic support. A general increase in trade and the growing demand for rubber, oil, and rare metals stimulated interest in access to critical or profitable resources.

Military commanders tended to favor imperial policies not only because they brought increased budgets but also because telegraph posts and coal-ing stations which enabled navies to remain far from home acquired strategic as well as commercial importance. Nineteenth-century technology facilitated imperialism, providing the portable power of European arms and making communication with distant places easier. Dynamite lessened the difficulty of building roads, and modern medicine reduced the dangers of the tropics. Competition between nations made colonies seem more important, and competition in international commerce taught businesses to seek special protection for their colonial ventures from their home governments. The experience of rapid economic growth made it easier to believe that new lands offered the chance to make a fortune.

IMPERIALISM'S DOMESTIC CONNECTIONS

Beyond such rational calculations, imperialism flourished because of the values that Europeans held and because of the institutions of their own society.

Religion and Class   Religious missions increased enormously throughout Europe. Many of the hundreds of new religious orders and missionary societies initially created in response to the social problems of industrialization also sent increasing numbers overseas to convert the heathen. For churches often at odds with the culture of their day and in conflict with the state, imperialism offered a dramatic outlet and a welcome reassurance of their importance in modern life. British, Swiss, and German missionaries were competing for souls on the Nigerian coast well before the area had been targeted by any foreign office.

Imperial activities had particular importance for members of the aristocracy, especially in Britain and France. The younger sons of aristocratic families in Britain had a long tradition of government and military service, and now their best chances for the experience of governing and of military command were in the empire. In France, where the Republic turned anticlerical after 1875, Catholic and monarchist nobles who were largely excluded from public positions at home could find them in the colonies. Aristocrats, after all, expected to feel distant from the people they ruled, and the language of subordination was applicable to both European and colonial societies.

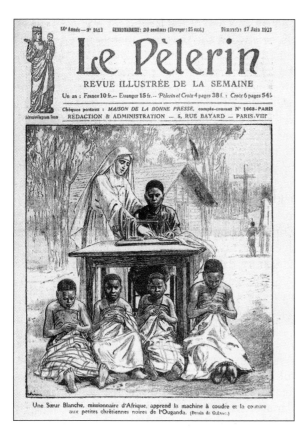

Le Pèlerin
REVUE ILLUSTRÉE DE LA SEMAINE

Une Sœur Blanche, missionnaire d'Afrique, apprend la machine à coudre et la couture aux petites chrétiennes noires de l'Ouganda. (Dessin de Guénac.)

▲ **This illustrated French Catholic weekly presented the popular European view of imperial influence: a saintly (and beautiful) member of the White Sisters teaches a well-behaved group of newly converted Ugandan girls to use a sewing machine. Faith, order, civilization, and technology went together. At home, too, Catholic orders emphasized the importance of teaching poor girls a useful trade.**
Mary Evans Picture Library.

Descriptions of ignorant, lazy, uncooperative natives were much like those used by the upper classes to complain about workers and peasants at home. While conservatives were often tempted to use empire to argue for the necessity of inequality, labor leaders and radicals were equally quick to note the parallels, to compare the treatment of strikers and radicals to the brutality of imperial armies, and to protest that the poor workers and peasants (in Wales, Scotland, southern Italy, or eastern Germany) were treated like colonial subjects.

State Policy   Even the campaigns for reform at home proved remarkably relevant to imperial rule. Governments were increasingly engaged in collecting statistics, providing for public health, building schools, and establishing welfare programs, and they found it natural to undertake similar measures in their colonies. Officials with colonial experience proved particularly useful back home. Organizing hospitals in the tropics taught doctors and nurses about health care in the slums; and the courts, police, and prisons being built across Europe and in the United States (which had pioneered in creating them to rehabilitate criminals) were equally useful for maintaining order in the colonies.

Even the work colonies and model farms sponsored by religious communities and utopian socialists had coercive imperial imitations. Britain's best-known organization in the campaign for public education was called the British and Foreign Schools Society. Indeed the arguments for such measures, from schooling to railroads, were similar at home and abroad. Overcoming isolation and ignorance in the colonies was much like making good citizens in the nation. In both cases governments saw themselves combating local dialects, provincial outlooks, corruption, and lack of civic spirit.

Public Opinion   The propaganda for empire, which appealed effectively to nationalism, contained other ideological messages as well. Descriptions of encounters with native peoples were rich in images of Europeans mistaken for gods, of a superiority in knowledge and technology that made dominance inevitable and usually beneficial; and they were often written in gendered language that equated European qualities with masculine virtues (rationality, decisiveness, dominance) and those of other societies with feminine ones (intuitive sensitivity, passivity, subordination). Mass-circulation newspapers gloried in imperialism, writing of adventure and wealth and of Christianity and progress in the virile language of force.

To the people of the late nineteenth century, exploration and conquest were high and noble adventure. Geographical societies became prominent in every European country, proudly acclaiming yet another association of new knowledge with increased power. Press reports made popular heroes of daring men like Henry M. Stanley, who followed the rivers of South Africa and penetrated the interior of the Congo, and Pierre de Brazza, who traveled up the Congo River, overcoming hardship and danger after dismantling a steamship so it could be carried around the rapids.

The Appeal of Imperialism Exploration seemed, in itself, an expression of progress, the brave adventurer the personification of individual initiative. If the explorer also gained wealth, that completed the parable. The missionaries who risked their lives to build a chapel in the jungle and convert the heathen made for appealing stories of humane concern and heroic sacrifice, while social Darwinists could hardheadedly note the inevitable conflict of race with race and the resultant spread of civilization, by which they meant, of course, their own.

In countries in which class tensions were high and domestic conflict serious, colonial expansion offered all citizens a share in national glory and gain. Rudyard Kipling's poems of imperial derring-do in exotic lands hail the simple cockney soldier; whatever his lot at home, he was a ruler abroad. Thus in politics, imperialism, like nationalism, cut across social divisions. It was an important part, especially in Great Britain and Germany, of the political resurgence of the right, allowing conservative groups strong in the army, the Church, and the aristocracy to ally themselves with commercial interests in a program of popular appeal. Employment as well as glory was promised as the fruit of a policy of strength.

Significantly, imperialism never achieved comparable political effect in France, the nation with the second largest of the European empires, though this empire, too, was built principally by soldiers and priests. French nationalism retained ideas associated with the Revolution that often conflicted with those of imperialism; patriots were preoccupied with avenging the loss of Alsace and Lorraine to Germany, and the right fumbled its effort at mass appeal in the Dreyfus affair (discussed in the next chapter). Still, in France, too, imperial triumphs were welcomed when they came. Everywhere empire offered the appeal of individual daring and direct action in a society becoming more bureaucratized, gave openings to groups often disparaged at home, and illustrated popular ideologies with concrete tales of risk, gain, glory, and conquest.

Imperialism in Britain Imperialism became an increasingly important issue in Britain's domestic politics and one of the important points of difference between the parties. Liberals had generally joined the call for the reform of British rule in India following the great uprisings of 1857, and that precedent made it easier in 1867 to pass the important act that gave Canada the self-governing autonomy of dominion status. The Liberal commitment to imperial reform included criticism of many of the techniques of imperial expansion, including the use of ambiguous treaties and the hasty reliance on force. William Gladstone, the leader of the Liberals, won the election of 1880 after campaigning against the immoral and unChristian imperialist policies of the Conservatives. Yet it was the Liberals who occupied Egypt just more than a year later, for Gladstone could not withstand the public outcry once incidents occurred that were deemed a threat to British interests and a challenge to British honor.

The Conservatives, led by Benjamin Disraeli, embraced empire in principle as well as practice. When the debt-ridden Khedive of Egypt (who ruled as a monarch although still nominally under the Ottomans) had to sell a large bloc of Suez Canal shares, Disraeli had snatched the chance to get them for Britain and thus gain a voice in Egyptian affairs (that would counterbalance French influence). As prime minister, he had Queen Victoria declared Empress of India in 1876, a flamboyant title that caught the popular imagination, and imperialism proved politically popular even as it began to draw the British into armed conflicts around the world.

The Boer War The most costly of these conflicts—in blood, money, and prestige—was the Boer War (1899–1902) in South Africa. Ultimately a conflict between the Dutch-speaking white farmers, called *Boers,* and the British government, its origins were far more complex. The Boers, who had lived in South Africa for centuries, resented Britain's organization of the Cape Colony and in the Great Trek of 1835–1837 had literally moved away, across the Orange River, where they established two (frankly racist) republics and were almost constantly at war with neighboring African peoples.

From the Cape Colony, British forces, too, were often at war, most significantly with the powerful Zulus. The situation became more explosive in the 1870s and 1880s with the discovery of diamonds and gold in the Boer republics. The rush was on. Prospectors poured in, mining companies amassed enormous wealth, railroads were hurried to completion, and African blacks were forced to work for meager wages or be driven away. Ambitious Englishmen on the scene urged the expansion of the territory under British rule, and the most notable among them was Cecil Rhodes, who had gained a near monopoly of the world's diamond production before he was thirty. He became prime minister of the Cape Colony and used his position to scheme and propagandize for a South African federation dominated by the British.

By 1890, the Boer republics were swarming with British citizens and surrounded by British colonies. Conflicts between the two groups grew more heated, and in 1899 the Boers declared war. British forces rapidly occupied the major cities of the Boer republics, but it took two years to subdue the Boers'

skillful guerrilla resistance. The rest of Europe watched that slow progress with surprise and then shock as farmhouses were destroyed and homeless Boers herded together in guarded areas called concentration camps. In Great Britain, however, the Boer War produced patriotic fervor. British victory allowed the establishment a few years later, in 1910, of the Union of South Africa, a partial fulfillment of Rhodes's ambitions.

PATTERNS OF IMPERIALISM

Despite the general popularity of imperialist ideas, few wholehearted imperialists held high political office even in Great Britain.

The Process of Empire Building The history of colonial conquest in this period was less one of long-range schemes than of a series of decisions

▼ **This engraving of 1897 typically shows Cecil Rhodes as popular hero. Leaving the Cape Town railway station, his carriage is drawn by a private army (called the Matabili boys after the Zulu warriors) through a crowd meant to depict the romance and color of empire.**
The Granger Collection.

that appear almost accidental when viewed singly. Frequently, individual explorers, traders, or officers—acting independently of their home governments—established claims in a given region through treaties with native leaders whose agreement was won by fear, the lure of profit, the promise of investment, or the hope of help against some nearby enemy. Once so involved, European interests proved difficult to dislodge.

When enforcing contracts and maintaining order, Europeans on the scene often exceeded their instructions and then sought the backing of their governments after the fact. Anxious not to appear weak in the eyes of voters or of other powers, the governments acquiesced in initiatives that had not been authorized. Those steps in turn led to further efforts to maintain order and institutional regularity; trading concessions and protectorates became colonies. This pattern of expansion required little premeditation. Applying their own laws and practices to other cultures, Europeans were surprised when natives failed to honor Western rules, and they responded with increased force.

Even those Europeans attracted by non-Western cultures or devoted to helping local populations in the name of Western religion and medicine undermined their host societies—introducing alien ideas, institutions, and technology and overwhelming them by sheer wealth and power. There is, in fact, a whole other history of imperialism now being written from the perspective of the indigenous peoples that shows how native political, economic, and religious organization was disrupted by the arrival of outsiders. To the confident people of empire, such unstable conditions left no alternative but further European control.

The Conquest of Africa   European involvement in Africa had produced only limited territorial claims prior to 1875 (see map 25.1)—despite the growing pressures of traders, missionaries, and officers, despite the vigorous exploration of the Congo sponsored by King Leopold II of Belgium, and despite conflicts like those between the British and the Boers. Twenty years later, seven European states had partitioned almost the entire continent.

The Suez Canal was completed in 1869, and after 1875 France and Britain were the largest shareholders. Determined to protect their investments, two countries established joint control over Egyptian finances. A nationalist revolt in 1882 by

the Egyptian army against both the khedive and foreign influence threatened this arrangement. The British government decided to mount a show of strength (the French Parlement refused to allow France to take part), and the Royal Navy bombarded Alexandria to teach Egyptians that contracts must be met.

In the resulting chaos, the British attempted to restore order. That quickly led to their occupying Egypt, which remained a British protectorate until after World War II. (Later, British troops would join Egyptian forces in bloody fighting in the Sudan, which added the Anglo-Egyptian Sudan to the British Empire.) In Tunisia a similar pattern of increased foreign investments followed by a financial crisis and intricate diplomatic maneuverings brought about French occupation in 1881. Both events accelerated the European competition for African Empire.

Competition South of the Sahara   In sub-Saharan Africa, European nations found themselves drawn piecemeal into scores of treaties that prescribed arrangements for societies they little understood and defined boundaries in areas whose geography was barely known. Africa had become a site of competition among European states; and European governments, although reluctant to accept responsibility for all that their ambitious citizens did, were afraid to disown any local advantage.

The International Association for the Exploration and Civilization of Central Africa, founded in Brussels in 1876, quickly became a private operation of Leopold II. The association paid less attention to its lofty aims of furthering science and ending slavery than to the vast territorial claims it might make by sponsoring Stanley's explorations. From their outposts along the west coasts, the French, English, Spaniards, and Portuguese responded with a hurried push inward into what are now Senegal and Nigeria.

As the European states were drawn into the scramble for Africa, they sought through diplomacy to lessen the clear danger that clashes there would lead to war in Europe. At Berlin in 1885 the powers established rules for one another. The most important was that coastal settlement by a European nation would give it claim to the hinterlands beyond. Straight lines drawn from haphazard coastal conquests cut across little-known

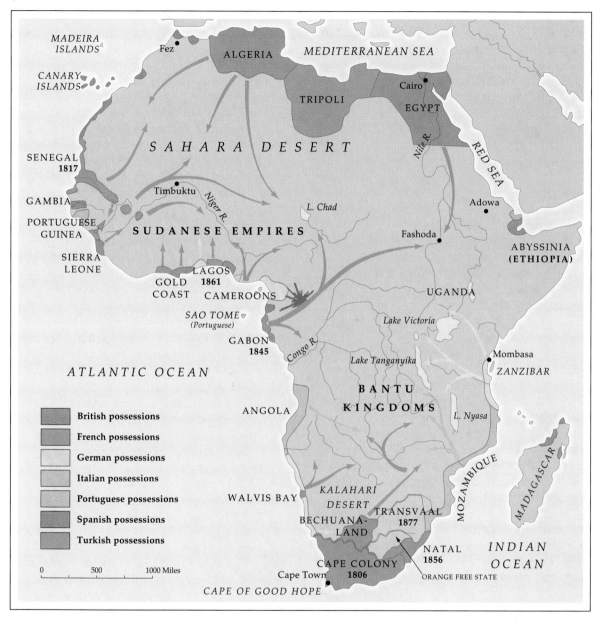

▲ MAP 25.1 AFRICA, ca. 1885

indigenous cultures, but they restrained the anarchy of European ambition. Germany and Italy could safely occupy the remaining bits of Africa not already held by a European state. The powers also agreed at Berlin to prohibit slavery; and five years later they banned liquor and limited arms in the zone between the Sahara and the Cape Colony. Humanitarian considerations had not been wholly forgotten, and by the turn of the century, the ruthless exploitation of the Belgian Congo was considered an international scandal.

The Fashoda Crisis French gains in West Africa were the most extensive of all, and in 1898 a group of soldiers who had pushed two-thirds of the way across the continent at its widest point arrived at Fashoda, on the Nile, a few days before British forces that were moving into the Sudan. Both

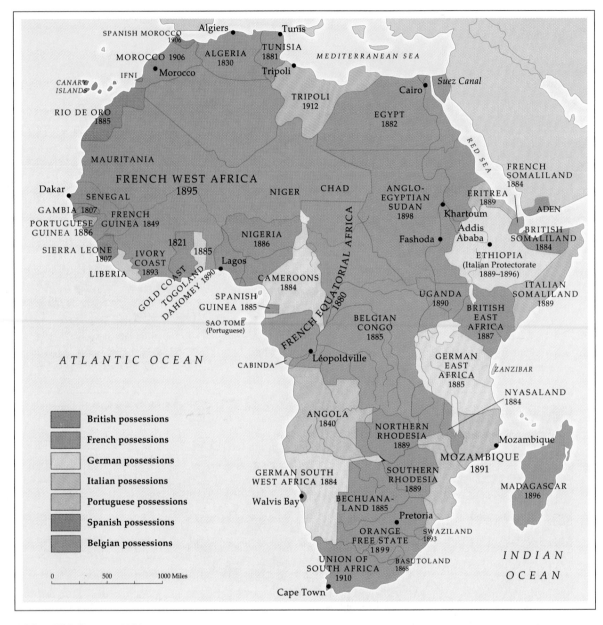

▲ Map 25.2 Africa, 1914

nations considered the encounter of their troops at Fashoda a matter of national honor, and imperialists plotted on maps how dominance over Africa was at stake. The French imagined holdings stretching from west to east across the continent, controlling the headwaters of the Nile. The British talked in terms of territory and maybe even a railway from the Cape of Good Hope to Cairo, a north-south axis through the continent.

Thus for weeks Great Britain and France were on the brink of war over the obscure outpost at Fashoda, sought by neither nation's general staff. The confrontation ended when the French, facing serious political divisions at home, chose to give way.

Those officials who bravely planted their flags and wrote out treaties for chieftains to sign did not doubt that theirs was a beneficial achievement to

▲ A latecomer to African Empire, Germany shared the general sense that Europeans were bringing civilization to a primitive world, the results of which were lampooned in this German cartoon on the effects of Teutonic order in Africa.

The Granger Collection.

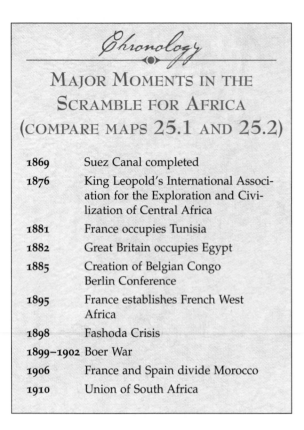

Chronology

MAJOR MOMENTS IN THE SCRAMBLE FOR AFRICA
(COMPARE MAPS 25.1 AND 25.2)

1869	Suez Canal completed
1876	King Leopold's International Association for the Exploration and Civilization of Central Africa
1881	France occupies Tunisia
1882	Great Britain occupies Egypt
1885	Creation of Belgian Congo Berlin Conference
1895	France establishes French West Africa
1898	Fashoda Crisis
1899–1902	Boer War
1906	France and Spain divide Morocco
1910	Union of South Africa

be measured by mission hospitals and schools, by new roads and political order, as well as by their profit. By 1912 only Liberia and Ethiopia were formally free of European domination. The social, cultural, religious, and political life of Africans was everywhere submerged under an imposed European order based on raw power and used for prestige and profit, whatever its other intentions.

India   India remained the jewel of the British Empire, the envy of all imperial powers. As Britain's trading partner, India stood on a par with France (only the United States ranked higher in British commerce). India's wealth and the prestige of its culture made it the very symbol of empire. Many of the leading figures of British political life made their reputations in the India service, and their techniques of administration through local lords and British courts were often proclaimed as models of enlightened rule. Yet the growth of trade and industry did not prevent devastating famines in the 1890s, and concessions to local government only stimulated increasingly organized and nationwide demands for a native voice in political life.

Southeast Asia   East of India and south of China, only Siam (Thailand) preserved its independence of European control through its willingness to modernize—that is, to adopt European forms of political and economic organization—and through the countervailing pressures of the three European powers in neighboring realms, who, in effect, constrained one another. The Dutch were established on Java, Sumatra, and Borneo as a result of treaties with the British, who after the Napoleonic wars restored much of the territory previously in the hands of the Dutch East India Company. Revolts against Dutch rule (in 1825, 1849, and 1888) resulted each time in its strengthening and further consolidation. The British annexed upper Burma in 1886 and part of Malaya in 1896 and on a northern strip of Borneo (called Sarawak) benefited from the reign of an English rajah, who in 1841 acquired lands subsequently held by his descendants until 1946.

French influence in Cambodia and Cochin China steadily increased during the 1860s despite the indifference of the governments in Paris. Whenever Christians were attacked or a trader murdered, the local commander pressed native rulers for further political concessions without waiting for instructions from home. Even the modest goal of providing their enclave with a secure frontier—a European conception that ignored social realities—usually led to war and the extension of French power into another ancient realm. France in this way eventually found itself at war with China in 1883; and though the parliament voted down the government of Premier Jules Ferry, France's leading imperialist, the war nevertheless resulted in an enlarged French protectorate, which was reorganized in 1887 as French Indochina. By the 1890s France had begun the kind of full-scale program to build roads and schools and headquarters that marked a well-run colony.

China   The weakness of China and the strengthening of Japan were the central realities of Asian history in the second half of the nineteenth century. Both proud nations had sought to keep intruding Europeans at a distance, and both failed, but with contrasting results. Western missionaries and traders were especially disruptive in the huge Chinese Empire, its administrative system threatened by inefficiency and by provincial warlords. Thus French gains in Indochina, the exten-

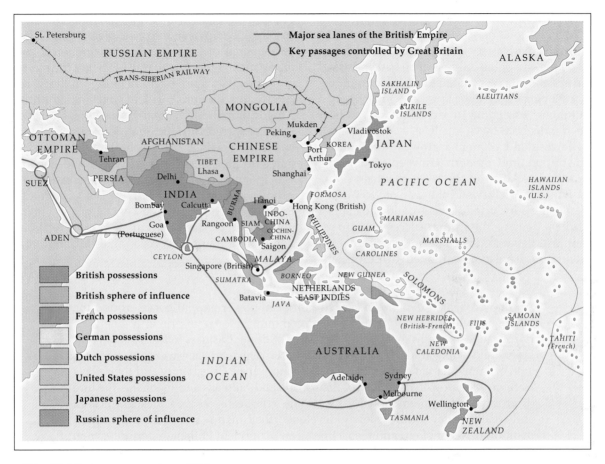

▲ Map 25.3 Imperialism in Asia, 1900

sion of Russian interests in Manchuria, the arrival of more and more missionaries, and China's further trading concessions were all part of a continuing process. Again and again, a local riot, a missionary murdered, or a contract broken would provoke military intervention from the great powers and demands for new privileges.

European governments competed in this systematic exploitation of new opportunities. In 1898 China's inland waters were opened to foreign shipping (mainly British), and the Germans laid claim to Kiaochow Bay, as Germany and Japan entered the lists of those with claims on China. Chinese efforts to raise revenues, reform administration, and stimulate railroads required, in turn, further loans from and concessions to Western nations. The Boxer Rebellion (1900–1901)—a complicated response by local militias outraged at foreigners and at the weakness of their own government—brought another round of violence.

Scores of Western missionaries, agents, and some diplomats were killed, prompting heavy military intervention, especially by Russia and Germany. When order was restored, China agreed to a large indemnity. Ironically, the only defense against European imperialism even in a great and ancient nation like China appeared to be a Westernization that deepened European influence. Such pressure accelerated changes that resulted in the revolution of 1911, led by Sun Yat-sen, and the establishment of the Chinese Republic.

Japan Once Japan—which for centuries had preserved its isolation—had been pressured into permitting trade with the West and protecting foreigners, the country experienced the familiar pattern of misunderstandings, broken agreements, antiforeign feeling, and renewed Western demands. But domestic political transformation came quickly in Japan. A new generation of leaders joined with the emperor, after a brief civil war, in carrying out the Meiji Restoration (1868). An essentially feudal system that had lasted seven centuries was ended, and by the end of the century Japan had embarked on a systematic policy of adapting Western industry, technology, education, laws, and governmental institutions, including a constitutional system (much influenced by Germany's).

The resultant economic growth, efficient administration, and modern army enabled Japan, like the imperialists of the West, to attack China and win easy victories in the war of 1894–1895. Japan's gains included Formosa and the control of Korea, demonstrating that successful imperialism, like the ambitions and power from which it stemmed, need not be limited to Europeans.

The United States also now acquired an overseas empire. It had played the principle part in the initial opening of Japan to foreign commerce, and the Spanish-American war of 1898 had the marks of imperialism: an overwhelming military response to a dubious incident (the sinking of the American battleship, *Maine*), sensational journalism that stirred patriotic outrage, exciting tales of heroism, one-sided battles, and a quick, decisive outcome. The United States, which had gone to war in support of a Cuban revolt against Spanish rule, acquired from Spain the island of Puerto Rico in the Caribbean and control of the Philippines. The Western system of power relations dominated Southeast Asia and encircled the globe.

An unprecedented dynamism carried European power and influence around the world. Initially, the flow of culture and communication was primarily one-way: European technology, dress, etiquette, ways of doing business, wage payment, religion, and political ideas spread everywhere. Wherever they went, whether for gain or humanitarian concern, Europeans taught their Christianity and their ways of controlling power, the utility of their roads and railways and medicine, the lure of profit through international trade. While Europeans enjoyed prestige, power, and wealth, other cultures slowly developed their own ways of using European institutions, technology, and ideas. Europeans, confident of their superiority, were slower to borrow from non-Western cultures; but gradually, from foreign foods to Eastern and African art to Oriental religions and philosophy, European civilization would in turn be influenced by the cultures it had been so quick to overpower.

In fact, late nineteenth-century imperialism was not the simple triumph its advocates made it seem. Imperialist ventures were costly and faced resistance that would continue, however sporadically, through the first half of the twentieth century, until a weakened Europe was forced to retreat. And much of the dynamism of imperialism was a response to conflicts at home—between nations, social classes, interests, and ideologies—that threatened to explode.

Recommended Reading

Sources

Darwin, Charles. A number of volumes provide good selections from Darwin's writings, which demonstrate his gifts for observation and his reflectiveness. Some eight volumes of his *Correspondence* have appeared in the new edition edited by F. Burckhardt and Sydney Smith, which began in 1985. These letters show him to have been a well-connected and self-aware intellectual.

Lugard, Frederick J. D. *The Rise of Our East Africa Empire.* 2 vols. 1893. This colorful account provides a superb example of the mixture of qualities in a dynamic English imperialist: curious and arrogant, well-intentioned and domineering.

Studies

*Avineri, Shlomo. *The Social and Political Thought of Karl Marx.* 1971. There are dozens of excellent introductions to Marx's thought; this one stands out for the clarity and freshness of its treatment.

*Barzun, Jacques. *Darwin, Marx, and Wagner.* 1958. This famous essay finds a good deal to connect three of the most famous thinkers of midcentury.

Bowler, P. *Evolution: The History of an Idea.* 1989. Combining recent work in the history of science with more general intellectual history, this book traces the various conceptions of evolution in different fields.

Burrow, J. W. *Evolution and Society: A Study in Victorian Social Thought.* 1968. A distinguished essay on the origins of anthropology and the scientific study of society in Britain.

Cameron, Rondo. *France and the Economic Development of Europe, 1800–1914.* 1961. Demonstrates the importance of capital and engineers for the economic growth of Europe and the important role played by France in the development of central and Eastern Europe.

Clark, Ronald W. *The Survival of Charles Darwin.* 1984. A detailed biography that also discusses the impact of Darwin's work.

*Fieldhouse, D. K. *The Colonial Empires: A Comparative Study from the Eighteenth Century,* 1982. A valuable introduction to this complicated subject that combines older and newer approaches in looking at imperialism around the world.

Headrick, Daniel R. *The Tools of Empire: Technology and European Imperialism in the Nineteenth Century.* 1981. The author discusses an array of fascinating examples in arguing convincingly for the importance of technology in European domination.

*Himmelfarb, Gertrude. *Darwin and the Darwinian Revolution.* 1968. Relates Darwinian ideas to the intellectual currents of the age, not just in geology and other sciences but in liberal thought as well.

Hobsbawm, Eric. *The Age of Empire, 1875–1914.* 1987. An interesting interpretive essay emphasizing England that argues for the importance of imperialism in domestic life.

Kennedy, Paul. *The Rise of the Anglo-German Antagonism, 1860–1914.* 1980. This massive study of international relations includes economic and political factors as well as imperialism in accounting for the rising tension between the two nations.

Kiernan, V. G. *European Empires from Conquest to Collapse, 1815–1960.* 1981. A good survey of European imperial activity around the globe.

Kindelberger, Charles. *Economic Growth in France and Britain, 1851–1950.* 1964. Comparing the two economies reveals a good deal about the role of the state and social structure in the economic history of each.

*McLellan, David. *Karl Marx. His Life and Thought.* 1977. Considers the more youthful writings as well as *Das Kapital,* bringing out their essential unity.

Milward, Alan S., and S. B. Saul. *The Development of the Economies of Continental Europe, 1850–1914.* 1977. Excellent study of the second great wave of industrialization, which shows the significant difference between this later continental experience and the earlier English one.

*Mommsen, Wolfgang J. *Theories of Imperialism.* P. S. Falla (tr.). 1977. A careful assessment of the dominant approaches that argues the need for a new theory without producing it.

*Owen, Roger, and Bob Sutcliffe (eds.). *Studies in the Theory of Imperialism.* 1972. Telling essays evaluate current and older theories, while case studies treat particular historical examples; a heterogeneous collection, both Marxist and non-Marxist.

Reddy, William M. *Money and Liberty in Modern Europe: A Critique of Historical Understanding.* 1987. A critical look at the social impact of the expansion of capitalism in England, France, and Germany, probing the nature of the inequality that resulted.

*Robinson, Ronald, John Gallegher, and Alice Denny. *Africa and the Victorians: The Climax of Imperialism.* 1961. An influential study that has affected all subsequent writing through its emphasis on the importance of the domestic history of the societies subjected to imperialist pressure and its argument for the continuity in European imperialism.

Rotberg, Robert I. *Africa and Its Explorers: Motives, Methods, and Impact.* 1970. A lively account that incorporates modern scholarship on European imperialism.

———. *The Founder: Cecil Rhodes and the Pursuit of Power.* 1988. A biography that uses psychology and the astounding events of Rhodes's life to explain the dynamic of imperialism in Africa.

Simmel, Bernard. *The Liberal Ideal and the Demons of Empire.* 1993. A penetrating study of the contradictory relations of liberalism to empire by a leading expert on the ideas behind British imperialism.

*Thornton, A. P. *The Imperial Idea and Its Enemies: A Study in British Power.* 1959. A well-written account of the appeal of imperialism in Britain and of the movement against it.

Wiener, Martin. *English Culture and the Decline of the Industrial Spirit, 1850–1980.* 1981. Argues that English society and culture never really held the values or accepted the social practices necessary to sustain economic growth.

*Available in paperback.

▲ This early and famous painting by Claude Monet, which partakes of the Impressionists' delight in scenes of outdoor leisure and in seascapes, also conveys the calm satisfaction of middle-class life against a background of the commerce plying the English Channel that made such a lifestyle possible.

Claude Monet, "Garden at Sainte-Adresse" Oil on Canvas. 38 5/8 × 51 1/8". The Metropolitan Museum of Art. Purchased with special contributions and purchase funds given or bequeathed by friends of the Museum 1967. (67.241)

Chapter 26

THE AGE OF PROGRESS

*I*n the last decades of the nineteenth century, European society seemed to have entered a new era of progress, marked by expanding production and trade, a rising standard of living, greater leisure, and new opportunities for education and employment. More people than ever lived in the growing cities, and millions shared in the diversion of a popular commercial culture. The creative arts had never been more inventive or varied, but that made for significant conflicts as the most innovative artists rejected traditional styles and formal rules as "academic." Art thus helped by example to make a burning issue of the question of where this civilization was headed. That issue was also a central topic of major movements of social thought.

Nor was conflict merely intellectual, for late nineteenth-century public life was dominated by large-scale institutions—business corporations, government agencies, political parties, labor unions, national associations, newspapers, and churches. In the long run such institutions may have encouraged accommodation and compromise, but more immediately they amplified tensions among workers and employers, interest groups and advocates of conflicting ideologies. These differences, openly and even aggressively expressed wherever there was some form of representative government, seemed to threaten social order. While many, perhaps most, thoughtful intellectuals heralded this age as one of increasing knowledge, prosperity, and justice, others mounted a fierce attack on this modern civilization. And each European nation struggled in its domestic politics to work out a way to contain and temper these conflicts.

I. The Belle Epoque

With a touch of nostalgia, the thirty years or so before 1914 has come to be called the *Belle Epoque,* a phrase evocative of the Paris of the 1890s, the city of lights where the Eiffel Tower was new, the grand boulevards were crowded with cafés, and great department stores propagandized for consumerism. It was the era in which millions of Europeans came to share an urban life of public ceremonies, strolls through parks, relaxation and light entertainment. Regular leisure for the masses was part of an essentially new way of life that offered something for every taste and pocketbook.

POPULAR CULTURE

Men and women had carried their culture with them as they moved to cities, and the dialects, songs, and stories of rural regions continued to be heard in specific sections of the major cities. Nevertheless, traditional festivals and games, once tied to the local region, gradually become less important than other amusements.

The Business of Entertainment Folk songs about work, the life of the soldier or sailor, and young love continued to be sung but more often now by paid singers in pubs or cafés or beer halls that featured singing and dancing. Music halls combined adaptations of opera, theater, and symphony with forms borrowed from the circus and vaudeville. The entertainments available in outdoor gardens (there were more than two hundred such places in London alone) and less-expensive theaters also used elements of folk and high culture.

More people could now afford to pay for entertainment, and it was an important business whose clientele included families from the lower-middle and working classes (see "G. B. Shaw Explains the Appeal of Popular Theater," p. 911). Performances designed to appeal to different social classes—revues, operettas (those by Gilbert and Sullivan are the best known), melodramas, and comedy routines (especially popular at the beach resorts now opening up to families from the lower-middle and working classes)—reached an ever larger part of the population. Then silent motion pictures won a still larger audience by the turn of the century.

▲ Department stores, like this one in Paris—a combination of theater and commercial display—were the seductive symbols of consumerism and prosperity.
Tallandier.

Professional Sport Something similar happened with sport. Its roughest forms (free-for-alls and animal baiting) had been banned and were replaced by more regulated activities (the Marquis of Queensberry rules for boxing, for instance, date from 1867). Many traditional games faded away, leaving a trace in ball games like cricket, soccer, and rugby. By midcentury, these ball games had become the sports of elite English secondary schools and had earned increasing notice in the press. Then teams formed in cities (the industrial cities of Birmingham and Liverpool each had more than two hundred cricket teams by the 1890s) with players from the working classes, and the best of these teams began to be paid. Leagues were formed, and their matches became important communal events.

G. B. SHAW EXPLAINS THE APPEAL OF
POPULAR THEATER
◆◆◆

The famous playwright George Bernard Shaw was even better know as a drama critic. In this review published in the April 9, 1898, issue of The Saturday Review, *a prestigious general magazine, he contrasts the high culture of the theaters in London's West End, where internationally admired artists such as Sarah Bernhardt performed, with the more vaudeville-like popular theater.*

"The Britannia Theatre is in Hoxton, not far from Shoreditch Church, a neighbourhood in which the *Saturday Review* is comparatively little read. The manager, a lady, is the most famous of all London managers. . . . Over 4000 people pay nightly at her doors; and the spectacle of these thousands, serried in the vast pit and empyrean gallery, is so fascinating that the stranger who first beholds it can hardly turn away to look at the stage. Forty years ago Mrs. Sara Lane built this theatre; and she has managed it ever since. It may be no such great matter to handle a single playhouse . . . ; but Mrs. Lane is said to own the whole ward in which her theatre stands. Madam Sarah Bernhardt's diamonds fill a jewel-box: Mrs. Lane's are reputed to fill sacks.

" . . . The enthusiasm of the pit last night, with no stalls to cut it off from the performers, was frantic. There was a great throwing of flowers and confectionery on the stage; and it would happen occasionally that an artist would overlook one of these tributes, and walk off, leaving it unnoticed on the boards. Then a shriek of tearing anxiety would arise, as if the performer were wandering blindfold into a furnace or over a precipice. Every factory girl in the house would lacerate the air with a mad scream of 'Pick it up, Topsy!' 'Pick it up, Voylit!' followed by a gasp of relief, several thousand strong, when Miss Topsy Sinden or Miss Violet Durkin would return and annex the offering. I was agreeably astonished by Miss Topsy Sinden's dancing. Thitherto it had been my miserable fate to see her come on, late in the second act of some unspeakably dreary inanity at the West End. . . . At the Brittania Miss Sinden really danced, acted, and turned out quite a charming person. I was not surprised; for the atmosphere was altogether more bracing than at the other end of the town. These poor playgoers, to whom the expenditure of half a guinea for a front seat at a theater is as outrageously and extravagantly impossible as the purchase of a deer forest in Mars is to a millionaire, have at least one excellent quality in the theatre. They are jealous *for* the dignity of the artist, not derisively covetous of his (or her) degradation. . . . Altogether, I seriously recommend those of my readers who find a pantomime once a year good for them, to go next year to the Britannia, and leave the West End to its boredoms and all the otherdoms that make it so expensively dreary."

From George Bernard Shaw, "The Drama in Hoxton," in *The Saturday Review,* April 9, 1899, reprinted in George Rowell (ed.), *Victorian Dramatic Criticism* (London: Methuen & Co., 1971).

By the 1880s, professional soccer teams were attracting huge, noisy, paying Sunday crowds; and the game spread across Europe. Most of the European professional teams that are famous today were (like the older American baseball teams) founded around the turn of the century. Their games became an important part of civic life, and teams depended on their ability to appeal to workers as well as to members of the middle class, while the upper-middle classes took to individual games like golf and tennis, which had recently adopted new sets of rules.

Britain's elite schools had emphasized athletics, believing they inculcated the "manly virtues" of perseverance, sacrifice for the team, and playing by the rules. Sport, it was said, trained leaders (especially the sort of leaders empire required) and fostered religion, a "muscular Christianity" that was embraced by schools in the United States, Canada, and Australia. But sports soon demonstrated the capacity to promote communal identity on a much broader civic and national scale. Competition could invoke both individualism and nationalism, as it did in the modern Olympic games, established in 1896 through the efforts of Baron Pierre de Coubertin of France.

Leisure Increased leisure was made possible by "the English week" (Sundays and half of Saturdays off) and laws restricting working hours that were adopted in most of Europe. For all the talk of manliness, the changing position of women was also fundamental to the new use of leisure. As women's opportunities to attend the theater or café concerts increased, impressarios catered to their tastes. Strolls in public parks, picnics, and boating provided occasions for young couples to be unchaperoned. So did women's participation in sports, which raised heated debates about women's physical capacity as well as the propriety of their wearing more revealing athletic garb in public. Despite all the warnings and doubts, women increasingly took part in such activities;

and the bicycle had a further revolutionary effect, stimulating changes in fashion and offering unprecedented freedom.

Limited hours of work (and long tram rides home) left employees with time to read newspapers, and the papers quickly discovered ways to increase their circulation. Appealing to a broader public, several newspapers now approached daily sales of a million copies. The most popular of them publicized professional sport and fostered a less literary style of writing, abandoning the tone of sober reflection on public affairs characteristic of older papers. Instead, the new kind of newspaper gave more space to sensational accounts of crime and disasters (and imperial adventures) and sought out colorful human interest features.

Like the millions of popular novels (now more specialized into romances, adventure stories especially for children, and penny thrillers), such

▼ The street life and vaudeville of Paris provided an international model, and all Europe's great cities delighted in an urban life that provided attractions for every class.
Christie's, London/Bridgeman Art Library.

writing candidly sought a wide audience rather than a learned one. For the first time in Western history, in the wealthier nations at least, a majority of the adult population could read and write. By the 1880s governments almost everywhere, recognizing the importance of literacy to politics and industry, had made education universal and compulsory and had reduced or eliminated school fees.

In 1850 Prussia was the only major nation in which a majority of the adult population could read and write; by 1900 more than 90 percent of the adult population of Germany, France, and Great Britain was literate, and the proportion elsewhere was climbing rapidly. Mass schooling was usually limited to a few years of the most elementary subjects, and aside from special supplementary instructions in workers' classes, night schools, and special vocational institutes, few of the poor had any opportunity for further training. In fact, the amount and kind of education received was one of the clearest distinctions between the middle class and those below it. Nevertheless, the schooling available to everybody would be steadily extended and access to secondary school, technical school, and university gradually increased.

"THE WOMAN QUESTION"

From the 1860s on, women everywhere had begun to organize in behalf of their own, distinctive interests. While they pressed for further change, the existence of these organizations also reflected important changes already taking place in the workplace, in social attitudes, and in the educational opportunities available to women.

Women's Movements   Often divided over goals and tactics, these movements tended to fall into three types. The first and largest were led by middle-class women and often reflected their experience in charitable work and education. Usually cautious in outlook, they could effectively demonstrate the contradictions between a social reality that subjected millions of women to desperate poverty and sometimes brutal conditions and a cultural ideal of female purity and motherhood. The meeting of the International Congress of the Rights of Women on the occasion of the Paris exposition of 1878 brought together representatives from twelve countries, including the United States. Women's issues were becoming a regular part of the public agenda.

By the 1880s and 1890s, this growing awareness led to a second, politically more radical type of movement, less intent upon protecting women and more explicitly concerned with equal rights. Particularly in Germany, England, and France, these movements realized that their demands required fundamental social change, and they often looked toward the traditional left for support. But they met a mixed response. Working men, who were the strength of Britain's Labour party and the continental socialist parties, feared competition from women, who were traditionally paid less. And many feminist leaders worried that to seek special laws regulating women's work would tend to preserve paternalistic attitudes and close off new opportunities.

A third response centered in the growing women's trade union movement, which was concerned primarily with the immediate problems of pay and working conditions. Employers' resistance, low pay, the nature of the jobs most working women were permitted, and a lack of sympathy from men's unions made it difficult to establish strong women's unions. When a British trade union leader declared it men's "duty as men and husbands . . . to bring about a condition of things where wives should be in their proper sphere at home," he spoke for most of his sex of every class (and quite possibly for a majority of women).

Working Women   The fact remained that in the late nineteenth century most women in industrial nations worked for wages from their early teens until they married and increasingly afterward, once their children were no longer infants, as an often essential contribution to family income. The increase in the number of women workers was especially noticeable in countries in which industrialization was more recent, such as Germany, Italy, and the Scandinavian countries. The proportion of women who worked for pay was highest in France—about 40 percent. (The proportion of married women who worked was twice as high there as in England.)

Jobs remained tightly tied to gender. More women in England and Germany were employed

▲ New developments like the small electric motor created new jobs for women as in this German metal-working plant.
Bettmann.

as domestic servants than in any other field. The next most common employment for a woman was as a laundress, seamstress, chambermaid, or waitress. Only about one-fifth of working women were employed in factories, where they were usu-

▼ Middle-class women were the leaders in feminist movements, and efforts to organize women workers concentrated on industrial work; but far more women earned money in menial drudgery, like these women in a French laundry.
Göteborg Konstmuseum/Edimedia.

ally assigned tasks associated with domestic skills. In the textile industries the proportion of women workers steadily rose to become the majority everywhere. Paid less than men in any case (from one-half to two-thirds as much for comparable work), women were less numerous in the burgeoning industries of the second industrial revolution than in more stagnant ones in which pay was lower; and far more women than men did piecework, fabricating buttons or cardboard boxes in shops or at home. The garrets of every city were filled with women living in tiny rooms where they worked late into the night making hats, artificial flowers, and lace; and a measure establishing a minimum rate for piecework in England was an unusual protection, even in 1910. Many women found jobs in the growing service sector—washing, ironing, and mending clothes—the classic employment for the young woman newly arrived in the city.

New Opportunities But there were some significant changes in women's employment, and these changes were helpful to the women's movement generally. With the spread of elementary schooling, women slowly took over as bookkeepers, office clerks, and secretaries, occupations in which prestige, opportunities for advancement, and pay declined as they came to be women's work. Some professions also opened to women, especially nursing (primarily provided by nuns in Catholic countries) and teaching in elementary school. By the end of the century three-quarters of the elementary school teachers in England were women, as were more than half the teachers in Sweden and France and one-fifth of those in Germany.

The expanding field of social work began to pay women, often the sort of middle-class women whose earlier charitable work had pioneered in creating the field. Small shops and, more slowly, the great department stores also hired women as clerks, preferably women from the lower-middle class who were trained to speak and dress in the ways considered proper by a bourgeois clientele. A few of the famous stores provided dormitories for their women employees, although the city life of single women who supported themselves and lived alone continued to worry moralists and titillate readers of the sensational press.

Public Policy These developments, along with the women's movements and the formidable resistance to them, made "the woman question" a persistent topic of debate in newspapers, from pulpits, and in learned essays. The very awkwardness of the phrase suggested some embarrassment and confusion. Feminists found themselves combating customary attitudes present throughout society as well as the prejudices of doctors who cited women's physical weakness and psychological instability and of social Darwinists who declared that civilization required women to concentrate on their biological function. Nevertheless, dominant attitudes did begin to change.

Women's colleges were established at Oxford and Cambridge in the 1870s; and in Italy, where universities had never been closed to women, Marie Montessori's lectures at the end of the century on "the new woman" were widely hailed. Outstanding achievements by individual women (and their number was growing) in science, medicine, education, literature, art, economics, and social reform challenged stereotypes; and it was far less unusual now for women to attend school beyond the elementary grades, to take part in demonstrations, and even to speak at public meetings.

As women lived longer and bore fewer children, legal and cultural constraints that assumed their lives would be circumscribed by marriage and motherhood became harder to defend. By 1910, most European nations had passed laws protecting women workers and increasing women's rights to dispose of property (France in 1884 and 1910 granted wives control of the money they earned, independent of their husbands); to share in decisions affecting their children; and to take part in civic life (the ban forbidding women to attend public political meetings in Germany was lifted in 1908). Wherever suffrage was universal for men, demands that women be allowed to vote were becoming louder.

THE ARTS

The creative arts continued to flourish, benefiting from high prestige and ever larger and more sophisticated audiences. Yet the forms and styles employed grew so diverse that the arts hardly seemed to speak for a single civilization. One rea-

▲ This advertisement in a German magazine was typical in selling not just an inexpensive means of transport but the joys of youth, style, and a new freedom for women.
May Evans Picture Library.

son for the change (and the one most welcomed) was the trend toward national styles. The use of folk elements and distinct traditions gave an instantly recognizable national identity to English or Russian novels and French, German, or Russian music. Another reason for the variety of artistic styles was the tendency of artists to act as social critics, thereby bringing into the realm of aesthetics the issues of politics and values that troubled society. Thus the tension between the individual and society, between the artist's personal perceptions and the unstable conventions of a world undergoing rapid change, remained a central theme of nineteenth-century art.

Divergent Schools These concerns and then the reaction against them in favor of a "purer" art led to a bewildering variety of competing movements.

"Naturalism," the "Pre-Raphaelites," "Impressionism," the "Decadents," "Symbolism"—such self-conscious labels for new artistic movements were frequently proclaimed with angry manifestos against previous art and present culture.

Naturalists claimed that the artist, like a scientist, should present life in objective detail after careful research. This aim was particularly suited to the novel; and Emile Zola, with his precise descriptions of industrial and Parisian life, was a master of the school. Determinism, the view that behavior was determined by social circumstance or blood inheritance, was a favorite theme in this Darwinian age. It proved especially effective on the stage, where the protagonist's destiny inexorably unfolded before the new audience gradually won over to realistic drama in the plays of Henrik Ibsen of Norway, August Strindberg of Sweden, and Anton Chekov of Russia.

The realistic painters of midcentury had turned to scenes from ordinary life yet tended, like England's Pre-Raphaelites (who took their name from the pious and simpler art of the early Renaissance), to believe that much of a painting's importance lay in the message it conveyed and therefore in its subject matter. For them art was still to be uplifting.

Toward a More Subjective Art A new generation of painters broke with this tradition to concentrate

▼ *Auguste Renoir*
Le Moulin de la Galette
Renoir's festive scene of the outdoor Sunday dance at *Le Moulin de la Galette*, an outdoor café in Paris that catered to the working class and the lower-middle class as well as to artists, is characteristic of the Impressionists' interest in urban life.
Erich Lessing/Art Resource.

on capturing the effects of light and color, making the artist's brilliance in analyzing and recreating such effects in itself a purpose of painting. In 1867 some of these artists were denied exhibition space by the academic judges of the annual Paris Salon; and they exhibited instead at a Salon des Refusés, proudly contesting the validity of official taste. These are the painters we remember, for they included some of the leaders of Impressionism, whose golden age was the 1870s and 1880s, among them Auguste Renoir and Claude Monet. They and the post-Impressionist Paul Cézanne were recognized in their own lifetimes as ranking among the great artists of Western history, and today their works remain the most reproduced and widely enjoyed of Western art. Yet painters only slightly younger, like Paul Gauguin and Vincent van Gogh, quickly turned to still newer, more challenging, and more personal styles.

Poetry, like painting, became an increasingly private expression, often obscure, indifferent to conventional morality, and constructed according to complex aesthetic doctrines. The fashionable fascination with death, languid despair, and perfumed aestheticism was called *Decadent* by its critics, a label the artists willingly accepted until that term gave way to *Symbolism*. A movement of French poets that spread throughout Europe, Symbolism interpreted the things one sees and describes as signs of a deeper and more spiritual reality. Art, like life itself, was to be complexly understood on several levels of meaning at once, and individual style became a personal conquest, a private bridge between the artist's identity and external society.

Art and Society   Architecture, the most immediately social of all the arts, was the least innovative. Perhaps the tension between individual and society that was so fruitful in literature was stultifying to so public and functional an art. Even when they achieved real beauty, the great buildings of the nineteenth century were eclectically dressed in the styles of other periods. Churches evoked the spiritual coherence of the High Middle Ages; banks and public buildings expressed in stone the civic virtues of Greece and Rome. Even apartment houses usually imitated some earlier epoch, as if to make new wealth feel more

▲ *Vincent van Gogh*
Much influenced by the impressionists, Vincent van Gogh was one of the important artists to move away from their emphasis on cohesion and control in favor of vigorous strokes that made a dazzling, and often fervently mystical, personal statement. By 1890, when he painted this picture of a village church, impressionism was being superseded.
Erich Lessing/Art Resource.

secure. Only at the very end of the century were the structural and aesthetic possibilities hidden in railroad sheds, bridges, and exhibit halls developed into a new architectural style that included the skyscraper. Even as that was happening, the international style known as art nouveau turned its back on the practical and efficient industrial world of the turn of the century and delighted in applying ornamental arabesques to everything from wrought iron to poster lettering and printed cloth.

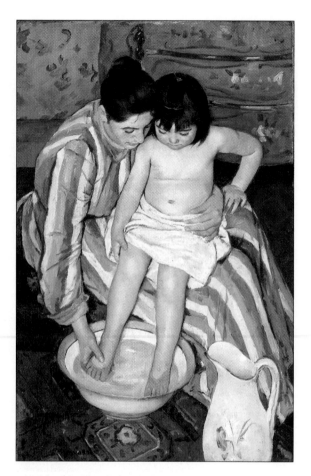

▲ *Mary Cassatt*
THE BATH

**The American, Mary Cassatt, was the first woman
painter to achieve recognition as a member of the
impressionists. The unusual composition, which
emphasizes the relationship between mother and
daughter, is characteristic of the experimentation
found in many impressionist works (with composition, the effects of thick paint on the surface, and
strong patches of color) that pointed in directions
that would be explored by the next generation of
painters.**

Mary Cassatt, American, 1844–1926. "The Bath" 1891–92.
Oil on canvas. 39 1/2 × 26". Art Institute of Chicago. Robert
A. Waller Fund, 1910, 2. Photograph © 1998, The Art Insti-
tute of Chicago. All Rights Reserved.

In the decade preceding World War I far more
radical changes (changes that would shape the art
of the twentieth century and will therefore be discussed in chapter 28) further separated the artist
from the broad public. That separation, like the
quality of popular entertainment and mass journalism, seemed to some commentators an ominous new threat to Western culture. For most contemporaries, however, European culture at the
end of the century was characterized primarily by
an extraordinary commitment to education and to
the dissemination of knowledge, encouraging evidence (along with political liberty and industrial
prosperity) of progress.

▼ *Georges de Feure*
PORCELAIN VASE

**With playful elegance, art nouveau was even more
influential in the design of household objects than
in architecture. Graceful curvilinear suggestions of
natural objects were echoed in the shape of vases,
gates, and furniture in porcelain, metal, and wood.
Georges de Feure, who made this vase, had a whole
room of porcelain on display at the Paris Exposition
of 1900.**

Georges de Feure, porcelain vase. c. 1900. 12 1/2" height.
The Metropolitan Museum of Art, Purchase, Edward C.
Moore, Jr. Gift, 1926. (22.228.9). Photograph by Schecter Lee.

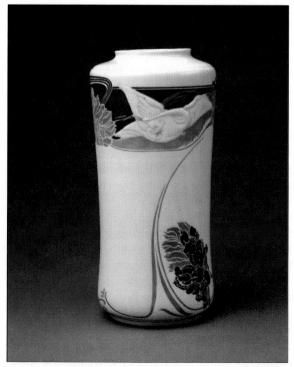

▲ *Edvard Munch*
Dance of Life
**In Norway Edvard Munch's use of Symbolism
pointed the way to German Expressionism, using
color and line to convey the anxiety underlying ordinary life as in this bitter comment on the tragedy
of the *Dance of Life*.**
Nasjonalgalleriet, Oslo/Bridgeman Art Library.

II. Attacks on Liberal Civilization

This dynamic, prosperous Europe with its constitutional liberties could be seen as fulfilling much
of liberalism's promise; yet liberalism came under
a heavy critique as many intellectuals joined with
artists in expressing contempt for middle-class society, as radicals sought the end of the capitalist
system, and as conservatives and Christians
mounted new attacks on liberal values. These attacks had their intellectual foundations in well-
developed systems of thought, but they had their
greatest impact in organized movements that
clamored for public attention and fought for political power.

WORKING CLASS MOVEMENTS

Although Marx had done most of his work in the
library of the British Museum, he and Engels intended to lead an effective social movement.

The First International   When in 1864 a group of
English labor leaders called a small international
conference in London, Marx readily agreed to attend as a representative of German workers. The
International Working Men's Association, usually
called the First International, was founded at that
meeting, and Marx dominated it from the start.
He did his best to replace traditional radical
rhetoric about truth and justice with the hard language of Marxism. During the eight years of the
First International, he gradually succeeded in ex-
pelling those who disagreed with him.

The French members were generally followers
of Louis-Auguste Blanqui and Pierre Joseph
Proudhon, socialists for whom Marx had little use.
He dismissed the Blanquists, with their fondness
for violence and dreams of conspiracy, as romantic revolutionaries; and his earliest socialist writing had criticized Proudhon's plans for workers'
cooperatives and his sympathy for anarchy. Marx
also antagonized the English members of the International who did not accept his emphasis on
revolution or his claim that the Paris Commune
of 1871 (discussed later in this chapter) was "the
glorious harbinger of a new society."

Bakunin   Marx's most important conflict, however, was with Mikhail Bakunin. A Russian anarchist, Bakunin had established himself in 1848 as
one of Europe's more flamboyant revolutionaries
(see "Bakunin on Why He Opposes the State,"
p. 920). Later sentenced to exile in Siberia, he escaped in 1861 and eventually joined the International in 1867. Bakunin respected Marx and understood his materialist philosophy, while Marx
seems to have felt some of the fascination of
Bakunin's personality. But Bakunin supported nationalism and praised the revolutionary spirit of
countries like Italy and Spain, whereas Marx insisted that the revolutionary cause was international and most certain to triumph where industrialization was farthest advanced. The Russian's
delight in conspiracies and plots seemed childish
to the German expatriate; and Bakunin, who distrusted any state, found a dangerous authoritar-
ianism in Marx and Marxism.

The 1872 meeting, at which Bakunin was expelled, was the First International's last, for Marx
and Engels then let the association die. Its membership had never been large or even clearly defined. Yet it played a part in building a workers'
movement by disseminating Marxism, by teaching others to view each strike or demonstration as

BAKUNIN ON WHY HE OPPOSES THE STATE

◆

A professional revolutionary, Mikhail Bakunin took part in the Polish revolution of 1863 and spent most of the next six years in Italy organizing workers there. In 1870 he took part in an uprising in Lyons aimed at creating a regime like that of the Paris Commune, which he greatly admired. In the spring of 1871 he was in Geneva, where he published three lectures "To the Swiss Members of the International," part of which is given here. Always eager to present his interpretation of European history and his arguments for anarchism, he was an important figure in the International Working-ingmens Association until his conflicts with Marx led to his expulsion in 1872.

"This ruination and general oppression of the working masses, and partly of the bourgeois class, had for its pretext and as its acknowledged goal the grandeur, power, and magnificence of the monarchical, nobiliary, bureaucratic, and military State, a State which had usurped the place of the Church and proclaimed itself a divine institution. Accordingly, there was a State morality entirely different from, or rather wholly opposed to, the private morality of men. Private morality has an everlasting basis that is more or less recognized, understood, accepted, and achieved in every human society, insofar as it is not vitiated by religious dogmas. This basis is nothing but human respect, respect for human dignity and for the right and freedom of every human individual. To respect [these principles] is a virtue; to violate them, on the contrary, is a crime. State morality is wholly opposed to this human morality. The State presents itself to its subjects as the supreme goal. Virtue consists of serving its power and grandeur, by all means possible and impossible, even contrary to all human laws and to the good of humanity. Since everything which contributes to the power and growth of the State is good, everything contrary to them is bad, be it even the noblest and most virtuous action from the human point of view.

" . . . The contradiction lies in the very idea of the State. Because the worldwide State has never been realized, every State is a limited entity comprising a limited territory and a somewhat restricted number of subjects.

" . . . This is why we are passionate opponents both of the State and of every State. For so long as there exist States, there will be no humanity; and so long as there exist States, war and its horrible crimes and inevitable consequences, the destruction and general misery of the peoples, will never cease.

"So long as there are States, the masses of the people will be *de facto* slaves even in the most democratic republics, for they will work not with a view to their own happiness and wealth, but for the power and wealth of the State. And what is the State? People claim that it is the expression and the realization of the common good, universal rights and freedom. Well, whoever so claims is as good a liar as someone who claims that God Almighty is everyone's protector. Ever since the fantasy of a Divine Being took shape in men's imagination, God—all gods, and among them above all the God of the Christians—has always taken the part of the strong and the rich against the ignorant and impoverished masses. Through His priests, He has blessed the most revolting privileges, the basest oppressions and exploitations.

"The State is likewise nothing but the guarantor of all exploitation, to the profit of a small number of prosperous and privileged persons and to the loss of the popular masses. In order to assure the welfare, prosperity, and privileges of some, it uses everyone's collective strength and collective labor, to the detriment of everyone's human rights. In such a set-up the minority plays the role of the hammer and the majority that of the anvil."

From Robert M. Cutler (trans. and ed.), *Mikhail Bakunin: From Out of the Dustbin: Bakunin's Basic Writings, 1869–1871*, Ardis Publishers, 1985.

part of a larger conflict, by stressing the international ties of workers in a period of nationalism, and by exemplifying the advantages of militant discipline. In these ways and in its intolerance of doctrinal error and its intense polemics, the First International helped set the tone of the growing socialist movement.

Socialist Parties and Trade Unions Between 1875 and World War I, socialist parties became an important part of political life in nearly every European country. Except in Great Britain, most socialist parties were at least formally Marxist. As they began to win elections, socialists disagreed over whether to follow a more moderate policy aimed at electoral success or to adhere rigidly to the teachings of Marx. The most common compromise combined moderate policies with flaming rhetoric, and the Second International, formed in 1889 with representatives from parties and unions in every country, sought to maintain doctrinal rigor and socialist unity. The Marxist critique of liberalism and capitalism was spread through books, newspapers, and magazines; in parliamentary debate; and in every election.

Labor organizations outside Germany were not often consistently Marxist, but trade unions everywhere were class conscious, frequently tempted by anarchism, and suspicious of politics. Their membership soared, with millions of workers paying dues in the industrialized countries, and the strike became the common expression of social protest. Skilled artisans, threatened by new modes of production yet strengthened by their own traditions of cooperation, often continued to be the leaders in militant action; but it was the successful organization of workers in larger factories that led to a great wave of strikes, larger, better organized, and more orderly than any that had come before.

Anarchism Most people did not distinguish very clearly among the various radical movements, and newspapers were quick to associate socialists and labor leaders with the anarchist "propaganda of the deed," violent acts that made headlines. In the 1880s and 1890s, bombs were thrown into parades, cafés, and theaters in cities all over Europe. Acting on their own, individual anarchists assassinated the president of France in 1893, the prime minister of Spain in 1897, the empress of Austria in 1898, the king of Italy in 1900, and the president of the United States in 1901. Such incidents were followed by the arrest of known radicals, spectacular trials, and denunciations of leftists.

But bomb throwers and assassins were only a tiny part of the broad anarchist movement. Anarchism's intellectual tradition was continuous from the time of the French Revolution. Its most famous figure after Bakunin was Prince Peter Kropotkin,

an exiled Russian aristocrat. Kropotkin was a theorist whose gentleness and compassion made him a kind of spiritual leader, but his prescriptions for what he called anarcho-communism did not unify the movement. Some anarchists stressed individualism, some pacifism, and some the abolition of private property. All rejected imposed authority and denounced the state as a repressive machine serving the interests of wealth.

They won their largest following among the poor who felt crushed by industrialization: immigrants to the United States, peasants in southern Spain, artisans and some industrial workers in Italy and France. Anarchism was an influential element in the opposition to bureaucratic centralization and to militarism; and it appealed to artists and writers who shared the anarchists' contempt for bourgeois values, while it contributed heroes and martyrs to the growing mystique of the radical left.

Socialism, anarchism, and trade unions all fostered feelings of brotherhood and addressed the sense of justice and common interest that had developed within working-class life. Expressed in songs and speeches at meetings, demonstrations, and strikes, these shared values had developed over generations to be reinforced now by militant organizations but also by changes that made the conditions of labor in different industries more similar and by housing patterns that created working-class districts. One of the functions of radical movements, then, was to sustain this solidarity by linking the immediate issues of the workplace to broad principles and to national politics. The result was a powerful challenge to the established system. Nevertheless, the left was far from united. Different interests often divided skilled from unskilled workers, those in established trades from those employed in new industries, male from female workers, and labor unions from political parties.

THE CHRISTIAN CRITIQUE

Many Protestants, especially in Great Britain and the United States, felt a natural affinity with liberalism; yet attacks on liberalism came from the pulpits of every Christian denomination. Some Protestants were drawn to a Christian socialism, and even conservative Protestant ministers excoriated the tendency to mistake selfishness for individualism, toleration for moral indifference, and materialism for progress. As official churches closely connected to the state and to governing elites, the Lutheran churches of Germany and Scandinavia, the Church of England, and the Russian Orthodox Church generally supported nationalism and the established social system. Even so, churches often found themselves opposing the growing claims of the state, especially in education and welfare; and both Protestants and Catholics engaged in social work were likely to denounce the injustices of capitalist society as forcefully as socialists did.

Roman Catholic Opposition Since the French Revolution, the Roman Catholic Church had found itself at odds with many modern trends, and it was particularly hostile to liberalism. In 1864 Pope Pius IX issued an encyclical, *Quanta Cura*, accompanied by a syllabus of "the principal errors of our time." Taken from earlier statements by the pope, its eighty items were written in the unbending tones of theological dispute. The syllabus was a list of false propositions, for example, that "it is no longer expedient that the Catholic religion should be held as the only religion of the State, to the exclusion of all other forms of worship."

Catholics more politic than the pope were quick to point out that declaring such statements not to be general truths is not the same as advocating religious intolerance, but such subtleties were easily lost. The syllabus denounced total faith in human reason, the exclusive authority of the state, and attacks on traditional rights of the Church; but its most noted proposition was the last, which declared it false to think that "the Roman Pontiff can, and ought to, reconcile himself, and come to terms with progress, liberalism and modern civilization."

The Vatican Council of 1869–1870, the first council of the Church in three hundred years, confirmed the impression of intransigence. It was a splendid demonstration of the Church's continued power, and prelates came from around the world to proclaim the dogma of papal infallibility. It declared that the pope, when speaking *ex cathedra* (that is, formally from the chair of Peter and on matters of faith and morals), is incapable of error. This belief had long been a tradition, and its elevation to dogma confirmed the trend toward

increased centralization within the Church and affirmed the solidarity of Catholics in the face of new social and political dangers. Even as the council met, the outbreak of the Franco-Prussian war allowed Italy to take the city of Rome from the pope and make it the Italian capital. But throughout Europe political leaders wondered if Catholics who now followed an infallible pope could be reliable citizens of a secular state.

Church and State The expanding role of government, especially in matters of education and welfare, made conflicts between church and state a major theme of European life. Theories of evolution, positivism, and biblical criticism put defenders of traditional beliefs on the defensive and made them seem opponents of science. Politicians, on the other hand, worried about the influence that the clergy might exercise in elections, especially in rural areas, among national minorities, and among men who had never voted before.

In the United Kingdom, the Church of England had steadily been stripped of its special privileges in moves opposed at every step by the clergy, by most peers, and by many conservatives. And religious differences continued to inflame the Irish question. As chancellor of the new German state, Bismarck launched and then abandoned attacks on the Catholic Church as his government relied more and more on the Catholic Center party. In Russia the Orthodox Church became, in effect, a department of state, used to strengthen the dominance of Russians in the multinational empire; while the Austrian government, in contrast, broke its close ties (and its concordat) with the Roman Catholic Church in an effort to lessen nationalist opposition to rule from Vienna. The conflict between church and state was most open and bitter, however, in Spain, Italy, and France, where it was the central political division of the 1880s and 1890s.

Generally, these conflicts subsided somewhat after the turn of the century. Relatively secure states, having established the breadth of their authority, tended to become more tolerant; and anticlericalism came to seem outmoded as governments faced the rising challenge from the left. The churches, too, became more flexible, in the style of Pope Leo XIII (r. 1878–1903), who established an understanding with Bismarck and encouraged French Catholics to accept the Third Republic.

Social Action At the same time, Christianity displayed renewed vigor. There was a general revival of biblical and theological studies among Protestants and Catholics, marked in the Roman Catholic Church by emphasis on the theology of St. Thomas Aquinas, whose arguments for the compatibility of faith and reason brought greater clarity and confidence to Catholic positions. Christian political and social movements learned to mobilize enormous support and became more active in social work (the Protestant Salvation Army was founded in 1865). This engagement in charity, religious missions at home and overseas, education, labor unions, and hundreds of special projects not only strengthened Christian social influence but gave concreteness to the outspoken denunciations by religious leaders of immoral and unjust conditions.

In his social encyclicals, especially *Rerum Novarum,* issued in 1891, Leo XIII added a powerful voice to the rising cry for social reform. He restated Catholic belief in private property, the sanctity of the family, and the social role of religion, but he went beyond these well-known views to speak to modern industrial conditions. The Catholic Church, he wrote, recognizes the right of workers to their own organizations and to "reasonable and frugal comfort"; but the state, he warned, should not favor any single class, and society must not consider human beings as merely a means to profit.

Strongest in rural areas and with more support among women than men, Christian churches knew a lot about those who had not necessarily benefited from modern social change. The churches now made more effort to reach workers and the middle class, urban groups whose special needs had often been overlooked in the past, and they spoke more readily for those discontented groups that tended not to rely on close ties to the state. By 1910 Christianity was more respectable among intellectuals, more active in society, and more prominent in politics than it had been since the early nineteenth century. Whether of the political left or right, Protestants and Catholics found in Christian teaching a whole arsenal of complaints against liberalism and industrial capitalism.

BEYOND REASON

Until World War I European political thought remained predominantly liberal, but some of its optimism was fading. Liberals themselves worried more about problems of community and social justice, and others questioned the power of human reason and argued for leadership by a small elite.

Georges Sorel and Henri Bergson The Frenchman Georges Sorel shared the growing suspicion that public opinion owed more to prejudice than to reason. Like many intellectuals, he felt contempt for middle-class society, but he argued that its overthrow would not come in the way predicted by Marx. His most important book, *Reflections on Violence* (1908), postulated rather that historic changes like the rise of Christianity and the French Revolution come about when people are inspired by some great myth beyond the test of reason. As a myth for his times, he proposed the general strike, a possibility then much discussed by European unions. Sorel thus contributed to the widespread syndicalist movement, which called on workers' organizations, or *syndicats,* to bring down bourgeois society. And he rejected bourgeois rationalism in favor of violence as an expression of the will that could create powerful political movements. Like many contemporary writers in Italy and Germany, he found the energy for change in humanity's irrationality.[1]

Sorel's countryman, Henri Bergson, the most eloquent and revered philosopher of his day, expounded gentler, more abstract theories; yet he, too, pictured much that is best in human understanding as arising not from reason but intuitively from subjective and unconscious feelings. Bergson was close to contemporary movements in the arts, psychology, and religion; and he believed society needed the new spirit of energy and common endeavor that could be achieved through spontaneity. That concern to translate feeling into action led away from liberalism's emphasis on the importance of law and formal procedures.

---

[1]Vilfredo Pareto and Sorel, both trained as engineers, are usually grouped together with Robert Michels as leading theorists of the new political "realism."

Friedrich Nietzsche The revolutionary challenge that such ideas contained was clearest in the works of Friedrich Nietzsche. He, too, emphasized human will in a philosophy that lashed contemporary civilization on every page. His disdain for ideas of equality and democracy was balanced by his hatred of nationalism and militarism; he rejected his society not only for what it was but also for what it meant to be. The only hope for the future was the work of a few, the supermen who would drop the inhibitions of bourgeois society and the "slave morality" of Christianity. Nietzsche's tone had the violence of a man trying to bring everything crashing down, but he was no mere nihilist. He was a brilliant analyst of culture and of language, who wrote his passionate aphorisms as a man in terror for himself and his world. A deeply original thinker who would prove vastly influential for twentieth-century thought, he was a child of his times in his concern for civilization, in his emphasis on history, and above all, in his anger.

Antisemitism Like Nietzsche's philosophy, antisemitism, which he detested, was part of the rising current of opposition to liberal society. Antisemitism in the 1890s was more than a continuation of centuries-old prejudices, and it was remarkably widespread. Venomous assertions of Jewish avarice and lack of patriotism were used to discredit the entire republic in France and the opponents of imperial policy in Great Britain. Sixteen deputies from antisemitic parties won seats in the German Reichstag in 1893, and Germany's prestigious Conservative party added antisemitism to its program (see "The Argument of Antisemitism," p. 925). The lord mayor of Vienna from 1895 to 1910 found antisemitism invaluable in his electoral victories, and antisemitism was an official policy of the Russian government from the terrible pogroms of 1881 on.

There is no simple explanation for a phenomenon seemingly so contrary to the major trends of the century, but scholars note that Jews were often perceived as a symbol of liberal, capitalist society. They had received their civil rights at the hands of Napoleon and in liberal revolutions, lived primarily in urban environments, and found their opportunities for advancement in the expanding professions and businesses of the nineteenth century. They were prominent leaders in many of the most venturesome enterprises, important scientific discoveries, and striking social theories. Nationalism, especially in Germany, had come to stress folk culture and race; by attacking Jews, conservatives could make the liberal, capitalist world itself seem alien to national traditions. Crude adaptations of Darwinism gave racial theories a pseudoscientific panache,[2] and indeed quack science generally flourished, for credulity was encouraged by the fact that much of academic science, especially physics, was no longer comprehensible to the layperson. Theories of conspiracy gave concrete and simple explanations for the baffling pace of social change, offering the hope that by circumscribing specific groups—such as the Jews—society could resist change itself.

The Revival of the Right Neither irrationalism nor antisemitism belongs inherently to a single political persuasion, but both were used primarily by the political right in the decades preceding World War I. Rightist movements revived notably in these years, building among those social groups that felt most harmed by the changes of the century: aristocrats, rural people, members of the lower-middle class whose status was threatened, and many Christians. Often incongruously, they defended established constitutions—the House of Lords in Britain, the concordat with the Roman Catholic Church in France, three-class voting and government independent of the Reichstag in Germany, limited suffrage and an intrusive monarchy in Italy, the authority of the tsar in Russia.

They added to this conservatism contemporary concerns about the shallowness of middle-class culture and the evils of unchecked capitalism. A reinvigorated right tried, frequently with success, to use patriotism and national strength as their battle cry, learning to make the effective mass appeal that had often eluded it in the past. They declared socialism the menace of the hour and the

---

[2]An important example is Houston Stewart Chamberlain's *The Foundation of the Nineteenth Century,* published in Germany in 1899. A Germanophile Englishman, son-in-law and intense admirer of Richard Wagner, who had become more antisemitic, Chamberlain traced all that was best in European civilization to its "Aryan" elements. The work was widely admired until the collapse of the Nazi regime.

The Argument of Antisemitism

◀●▶

Antisemitism became more organized and more vocal in most European countries in the 1880s. Despite important variations of tone and tactic in each nation, certain myths and themes were common to most of these movements. In 1883 a German publication calling itself The Journal for the Universal Rally for Combatting Jewdom (Zeitschrift für die Allgemeine Vereinigung zur Bekämpfung des Judentums) *repeated many of these themes. The article was presented in the form of a petition to Chancellor Bismarck, calling for a ban on Jews holding important offices and a restriction on their immigration.*

"Wherever Christian and Jew enter into social relations, we see the Jew as master and the native-born Christian population in a servile position. The Jew takes only a vanishingly small part in the hard work of the great mass of our people; in field and workshop, in mines and on scaffolding, in swamps and canals—everywhere it is only the calloused hand of the Christian that is active. But it is above all the Jew who harvests the fruits of this labor. By far the greatest portion of capital produced by national labor is concentrated in Jewish hands. Jewish real estate keeps pace with the growth of mobile capital. Not only the proudest palaces of our cities belong to the Jewish masters (whose fathers or grandfathers crossed the borders of our fatherland as peddlers and hawkers), but the rural estate—this highly significant and conserving basis of our state structure—is falling into Jewish hands with ever greater frequency.

"Truly, in view of these conditions and because of the massive penetration of the Semitic element into all positions affording power and influence, the following question seems justified on an ethical as well as national standpoint: *what future is left our fatherland if the Semitic element is allowed to make a conquest of our home ground for another generation as it has been allowed to do in the last two decades?* If the concept of 'fatherland' is not to be stripped of its ideal content, if the idea that it was our fathers who tore this land from the wilderness and fertilized it with their blood in a thousand battles is not to be lost, if the inward connection between German custom and morality and the Christian outlook and tradition is to be maintained, then an alien tribe may never, ever rise to rule on German soil. This tribe, to whom our humane legislation extended the rights of hospitality and the rights of the native, stands further from us in thought and feeling than any other people in the entire Aryan world.

"The danger to our national way of life must naturally mount not only when the Jews succeed in not only encroaching upon the national and religious consciousness of our people by means of the *press*, but also when they succeed in obtaining state offices, the bearers of which are obliged to guard over the idealistic goods of our nation. We think above all of the professions of *teacher* and *judge*. Both were inaccessible to Jews until very recently, and both must again be closed if the concept of authority, the feeling for legality and fatherland, are not to become confused and doubted by the nation. Even now the Germanic ideals of honor, loyalty, and genuine piety begin to be displaced to make room for a cosmopolitan pseudoideal."

From Richard S. Levy (trans. and ed.), *Antisemitism in the Modern World*, D.C. Heath and Co., 1991.

natural consequence of liberal error, while Marxists denounced both liberals and conservatives as defenders of reactionary capitalism.

Thus critics from the right and the left gained by addressing the discontents that liberalism tended to ignore and by criticizing the modern changes that most people still labeled progress. So many simultaneous assaults created grave political crises in many states. How those assaults were dealt with in each country reshaped the political system that would guide it through the challenges ahead. Despite ominous signs of division and disaffection and major policy failures, despite giant strikes and an arms race, most observers believed that the international trend by 1910 was for governments to accept more responsibility for social justice, politics to become more democratic, and society to grow more tolerant. Overall, Europeans had never been so free to move about as they wished and say what they liked.

III. Domestic Politics

◆

Most governments had come to recognize the importance of winning popular support and had discovered new ways of doing so. In many respects political systems were more similar at the end of the nineteenth century than they had been since before the French Revolution, and everywhere they faced some of the same issues. Yet each nation evolved its own distinctive response and its own way of balancing the pressures for continuity and change, the interests of business and agriculture, the values of old aristocracies and new elites, the claims of workers and factory owners, the demands of democracy and differences of wealth and status.

COMMON PROBLEMS

There were certain issues that every political system had to deal with. One was who should participate in political life. The trend was to increase suffrage until every adult male had the right to vote, and extending that right to women had become a divisive issue in many countries by the turn of the century. Each political system also found its own ways of constraining democracy, through royal prerogatives, a conservative second chamber, or limits on what legislatures could do.

The state—the center at which political parties, economic interests, and ideologies competed—had become the focus of patriotism, a sponsor of culture, an agent of economic growth, and a source of public welfare. But its precise role in these matters was often hotly contested, especially its responsibility for social welfare (including education, housing, and public health) and its economic policies as they affected banks, commerce, and labor unions. Powerful groups such as the church, the military, or the aristocracy sought to enlist the state on their side; and sometimes these competing interests could be balanced (as in tariffs that protected both industry and agriculture) or resolved through compromise (as in reforms that preserved social distinctions but expanded access to public schooling and to positions in the civil service). Often these conflicts reinforced older ideological divisions that threatened to undermine the political system itself.

Large-Scale Organizations As governments took on increased responsibilities for public health, social welfare, transportation, the post, and the telegraph, the civil service expanded. Government agencies carried out their duties by means of bureaucratic procedures within formal hierarchies. Businesses tended to become bigger and more bureaucratic, with a few large companies dominating whole national industries from steel and shipping to retail sales. Smaller firms thus tended to organize in associations that could represent their interests in dealings with government and with other interest groups.

Workers, too, were increasingly organized in national trade unions that negotiated for particular industries, and companies also often grouped together (especially in Germany and Britain) to increase their political influence and economic weight. In every industrial country from the 1880s on, there were great strikes in which the two well-organized sides battled while competing for political protection and public support. Political parties also tended to adopt some form of national organization and a permanent staff, especially where universal male suffrage made such efforts worthwhile. And the German Social Democratic party, with its Marxist program, national organization, and thousands of local centers for recreation and instruction, was the most impressive example of all.

Professional associations set standards, lobbied governments, and conferred prestige on the physicians, lawyers, engineers, and teachers that belonged to them. Like political parties, associations offered a means whereby scattered groups and new interests could make their presence felt in public life. This institutionalization of society was in many respects a source of stability, providing rapidly expanding activities with norms, internal discipline, and a means for negotiating conflicts. But the very size of these organizations amplified their disagreements and encouraged intransigence as a means for keeping followers in line, deepening social divisions.

Not surprisingly, nearly every country struggled with the very definition of national community and whether some groups—ethnic minorities, foreigners, Catholics, Jews, anarchists, or socialists—should be excluded as alien or of uncertain loyalty. Identifying such groups, which evoked extreme patriotism and aroused passionate fears, could become extremely disruptive; and the way each society responded to this challenge became an important measure of its political system. Peaceful resolutions were possible: When Norway voted for separation from Sweden in 1905, the decision was accepted on both sides, and the two nations lived thereafter in harmony, among the most democratic in the world. In this period comparative politics became a formal academic subject, in part because the similarities among European political systems made their differences more revealing.

FRANCE: THE THIRD REPUBLIC

In France political conflict revolved around the form of government following the fall of the Second Empire.

Monarchy or Republic Shortly after Louis Napoleon surrendered in the Franco-Prussian War of 1870, Parisian crowds cheered the proclamation of a republic; and new leaders sought to mobilize the nation as an earlier republic had done in 1792. German forces quickly surrounded Paris, but Léon Gambetta, the most dynamic of the republicans, made a daring escape, flying off in a balloon to set up headquarters and organize resistance outside the capital. French forces, strengthened by newly recruited peasants, even made some gains until, overmatched, they were pushed back in December.

Paris remained under German siege. Refusing to surrender, its citizens held out for four months. They cut down the trees of the boulevards for fuel, slaughtered pets, and emptied the zoo as a starving city continued to resist during a winter as severe as any on record. But heroism and patriotic fervor could not defeat a modern army, and at the end of January Paris capitulated. German troops marched into a denuded and quiet city.

France's newly elected assembly met at Versailles and quickly accepted peace on German terms. The assembly, divided between monarchists (elected as proponents of peace) and republicans, could not agree, however, on the form of government. It compromised by naming Adolphe Thiers, a moderate politician who had been prominent in the July Monarchy thirty years earlier, as chief of the "Executive Power," thereby postponing the issue of whether France was to have a king or a president.

The Paris Commune Thiers knew that his government must establish control of Paris, which had been cut off from the rest of France. As a first step, he decided to disarm the city's National Guard. When troops from Versailles tried to remove some cannons, however, they were confronted by an angry crowd. Shots were fired; and by day's end, two generals lay dead. Faced with insurrection, Thiers withdrew his army, determined first to isolate the revolution and then to crush it. The municipal council of Paris, in another echo of the French Revolution of 1789, declared the city a self-governing commune and prepared to fight. While German armies idly watched, the French engaged in civil war.

Many of the well-to-do had left Paris during the armistice, but the poor and the radical remained. Hardened by months of siege, their

▼ Onlookers reacted with fury when the Versailles government sent troops into Paris to seize artillery left in the city after the siege. Shouts and stones led to shots and bloodshed, then someone recognized Generals Lecomte and Clément-Thomas. They were lined up and shot, while citizens watched (and someone took a photograph).
Collection Viollet.

resentments mounted as the government at Versailles stopped payments to the National Guard, the only income for many Parisians, and suddenly ended the moratorium on the payment of personal debts (including rents) that had been in effect while Paris was under siege. The Paris Commune included moderate and radical republicans, some followers of Pierre Joseph Proudhon and Louis-Auguste Blanqui, militant socialists in the tradition of Saint-Simon and Fourier, and a few members of the Marxist First International. Its program, favoring democracy and federalism, was not very specific on other matters; and it had little time to experiment.

Civil War The conservative assembly in Versailles sent its armies to assault the Paris Commune, and the mutual hatred in this civil war was exacerbated by the recent anguish of siege and defeat as well as by the long-standing differences, ideological and social, between rural France and the capital. The two camps fought for competing visions of what the nation should become, and they fought with rising fury. On both sides hostages were taken and prisoners shot (the communards executed the archbishop of Paris), and it took almost two months of bloodshed before government troops broke into the city in May.

Even then the fighting continued, barricade by barricade, into the working-class quarters, where the group commanded by Louise Michel was among the last to fall. The most famous of hundreds of militant *citoyennes* she would later tell her captors, "I belong entirely to the Social Revolution." Solid citizens shuddered at revolutionary excess (and especially at the part played by women), but on the whole, the victors were more brutal. Tens of thousands of Parisians died in the streets, and summary courts-martial ordered execution, imprisonment, or deportation for tens of thousands more.

Throughout Europe, the commune raised the specter of revolution. From the first, Marxists hailed it as a proletarian rising, the dawning of a new era, though Marx was indignant with the communard's lack of revolutionary daring and their respect for property and legality. Former communards became the heroes of socialist gatherings for the next generation, and to this day the cemetery where many of them were executed remains a shrine honored by socialists and com-

munists.[3] Historians have been at great pains to show how little socialism, still less Marxism, there was in the Paris Commune (it respectfully left the Bank of Paris intact); yet myth has its historical importance, too. This indisputably was class conflict, and the rage on both sides was more significant than mere differences of program. After 1871 a proletarian revolution became a credible possibility to radical and conservative alike, and working-class movements across Europe pointed to the martyrs of the Commune as evidence of the selfish cruelty of bourgeois rule.

The Founding of the Third Republic Remarkably, a stable republic gradually emerged from this unpromising beginning. The administrative structure of the French state remained, stronger than any political group, and Thiers used it effectively. The loan needed to pay the indemnity to Germany was soon oversubscribed. As elections produced victories for moderate republicans, monarchists feared that their chance was slipping away. They ousted Thiers, put a monarchist in his place, and looked for a chance to restore the monarchy. They never found it.

The monarchists themselves were divided between the conservative supporters of the grandson of Charles X and those who favored the grandson of Louis Philippe. The two factions differed on issues of democracy, social policy, relations with the Church, and even symbolism (the more conservative claimant refused to accept the tricolor, the flag of French patriotism, because it was the flag of revolution). Meanwhile moderate republicans continued to gain in popularity, and in 1875 the assembly passed a law declaring that "the president of the republic" should be elected by the two legislative houses. The Third Republic was thus quietly established, without ringing phrases, as the government that, as Thiers put it, divided Frenchmen least.

There was a Chamber of Deputies, elected by direct universal male suffrage, and a Senate, indirectly elected by local officials. In elections the following year, republicans captured two-thirds of the seats in the Chamber and almost half those in the Senate. The presidency, which had been so

---

[3] A century later a Russian sputnik proudly carried to the moon not only a Soviet flag but a red flag from the Commune of 1871.

strong under Thiers, was still in monarchist hands; but its authority continued to decline. That established a further precedent: The Republic would have a weak executive. Made acceptable by having crushed the Commune and by having a conservative Senate, this republic was a regime of compromise; and it would last longer than any French regime since 1789.

Successive republican governments guaranteed political freedom and deferred to the middle class while France's public institutions preserved the remarkable administrative continuity that had characterized them since 1800. Economic growth, less dramatic than in Great Britain or Germany, was also less disruptive. France had found its own balance between the demands for order and the need for change.

Conflicts and Crises For twenty years, from 1879 to 1899, the leading politicians were moderate republicans who found in lack of daring the best guarantee of stability and in anticlericalism their most popular plank. Strong defenders of free speech and individualism, they recognized unions but initiated few projects of public works or social welfare. They made elementary education in state schools compulsory and established restrictions on the Catholic Church that were intended to weaken its political influence, policies that carried the parliamentary conflicts between left and right into the villages of France.

In 1889 General Georges Boulanger gained the popularity that the republic's more cautious leaders lacked through speeches expressing concern for workers and patriotic denunciation of Germany. There was even danger that Boulanger would attempt a coup d'état; and even after that danger had passed, scandals threatened the republic's stability. Companies planning a canal through Panama went bankrupt, and investigations uncovered political graft. There followed a stormy campaign against republican politicians, liberal newspapers, and Jewish financiers. Only when the regime seemed close to toppling did its defenders pull together.

The Dreyfus Affair The Third Republic's great trial came with the Dreyfus case. In 1894 a court-martial convicted Captain Alfred Dreyfus, a Jew and a member of the General Staff, of providing the German military attaché with secret French

> ## Chronology
> ## CRITICAL MOMENTS IN THE THIRD REPUBLIC
>
> | | |
> |---|---|
> | **1871** | Paris Commune. |
> | **1875** | Republic formally established. |
> | **1889** | Boulanger crisis. |
> | **1894–1906** | Dreyfus affair. |
> | **1905** | Separation of church and state. |

documents. Although the sensational press shouted Jewish treachery, the issue only became the center of public attention three years afterward, when evidence appeared implicating another officer as the guilty party.

The army's principal officers, refusing to reopen the case, spoke darkly of honor and state secrets, and the right-wing press hailed their patriotism. The controversy escalated with charges and countercharges in parliament and the press, a series of sensational trials, and huge public demonstrations. The nation was divided. The majority of Catholics, monarchists, and conservatives joined in patriotic indignation against Jews and socialists who were allegedly conspiring to sell out France and weaken a loyal army. The left—intellectuals, socialists, and republicans—came to view Dreyfus as the innocent victim of a plot against republican institutions.

Figures like the novelist Emile Zola, who was twice convicted of libel for his efforts, led in demanding a new trial. The military courts, however, were reluctant to admit past mistakes. A court-martial in 1898 instead acquitted the man who forged the principal evidence against Dreyfus and a year later it convicted Dreyfus a second time but "with extenuating circumstances," a confusing ruling that led to a presidential pardon. The defenders of Dreyfus won the battle for public opinion, though barely,[4] and that victory set the

---

[4]A few Dreyfusards continued collecting evidence and finally won acquittal in a civil trial in 1906. Dreyfus was then decorated and promoted to the rank of major.

▲ Every stage of the Dreyfus affair was the occasion for public demonstrations. *Le Petit Journal*, which had the largest circulation of any Paris newspaper, printed this scene of a crowd of magistrates and ordinary citizens hailing the news in February 1898 that Zola has been convicted of libel.
Edimedia.

tone of subsequent French politics, cementing traditions of republican unity on the left and greatly reducing the political influence of the Church and monarchists. Years of polemics and confrontation, however, left deep scars.

A Stable Republic From 1900 until World War I, government was in the hands of firm republicans who, despite their cautious position on social issues, called themselves the Radical party. They set about purging the army of the most outspoken opponents of the republic, and they launched new attacks on the Church that subsided only with the passage of a law separating church and state in 1905. Yet they administered with restraint. Solicitous of the "little man," of small businesses and

peasant farmers, they solidified support for the republic. Indeed, part of the Third Republic's achievement was its ability to draw radical politicians to moderate policies. A socialist even entered the cabinet in the aftermath of the Dreyfus affair (thereby earning the condemnation of the Second International for cooperating in a bourgeois state). The prime minister from 1906 to 1909 was Georges Clemenceau, a man once considered a militant leftist, who now shrewdly combined policies of reform and conciliation. The trade union movement doubled its membership, but frequent strikes never culminated in the revolutionary general strike so much talked about. On the eve of world war, France, prosperous and stable, appeared to have surmounted its most dangerous divisions.

GERMANY: THE REICH

Bismarck had given Germany a constitution that established representative institutions but left power in the hands of a conservative monarchy, and throughout its history the Reich would be haunted by the question of whether this awkward system could hold together or must veer sharply toward autocracy or democracy. Until 1890 Bismarck dominated German public life with an authority few modern figures have equaled. Scornful of criticism, he won many enemies but remained untouchable until William II ascended the throne in 1888. Twenty-nine years old, bright but ill-prepared, William was infatuated with all things military, anxious to make himself loved, and eager to rule. He disagreed with parts of Bismarck's foreign policy and opposed the antisocialist laws, but theirs was primarily a conflict of wills. In 1890 the emperor, impatient with Bismarck's paternal arrogance, forced his resignation.

The Army and the Conservative Leagues Bismarck's policies had allowed for great concentrations of political and economic power in a rapidly expanding society, one in which court, army, bureaucracy, and business were treated as semiautonomous interests. Holding the system together while balancing the demands of parliament and public opinion was the growing challenge Bismarck's successors faced. They sometimes tried to match his dazzling foreign policy, and they followed him in attending to the army. Bismarck had won a sizable electoral victory in 1887 on the issue of enlarging the army over the parliament's objections, and military appropriations were a source of intense conflicts between right and left again in 1893, 1898, and 1911–1913; each time the army grew larger, the government's statements became more nationalist, and society seemed more divided.

Germany's conservatives had also learned from Bismarck the value of appealing to the public, and they did so through the strident propaganda of political leagues—the Landlords', Peasants', Pan-German, Colonial, and Naval Leagues—organized in the 1890s. Well-financed by Prussian Junkers and some industrialists, these leagues campaigned for high tariffs, overseas empire, and the military, with attacks on socialists, Jews, and foreign enemies. As pressure groups, they won significant victories, including the naval bill of 1898, which proposed to create a fleet that could compete with Britain's. In addition to building railroads, roads, and schools, the government extended the comprehensive social welfare programs begun under Bismarck, and William II was hailed as "the Labor Emperor" for supporting social security, labor arbitration, the regulation of workers' hours, and provisions for their safety.

The Social Democrats   But Bismarck's hope that such measures would weaken socialism was not realized. The well-organized Social Democrats continued to gain in the 1890s, and they became the largest party in the Reichstag in 1912 (and the strongest socialist party in Europe) despite the distortions of the electoral system. Socialists also dominated Germany's vigorous labor unions, which had 2.5 million members by 1912, and the Social Democratic party sustained an influential subculture that had its own newspapers, libraries, and recreation centers.

In theory, at least, the Social Democrats remained firm revolutionaries, formally rejecting the revisionism of Eduard Bernstein, who in his book *Evolutionary Socialism* (1897), argued for less emphasis on economic determinism or revolution and a greater focus instead on improving working conditions and strengthening democracy. The subject of international debate, Bernstein's criticism of Marx and his alternative

▲ **At a mine entrance in the Ruhr in 1912, striking German mine workers read an official proclamation warning that the police are authorized to shoot.** Ullstein Bilderdienst.

theory implied a less militant socialism willing to cooperate with other democratic parties, and it was an important moment in the history of socialism when Germany's powerful Social Democrats chose instead to make a rigorous Marxism their official policy.

An angry rigidity had developed in Germany's politics. The last peacetime chancellor (and the first of bourgeois origin), Theobald von Bethmann-Hollweg took office in 1909. A cautious bureaucrat who presided over a government rife with cabals, he tried to placate parliament and hold in check a royal court in which people spoke openly of using the army against radicals. Bethmann-Hollweg's mild programs for political reform came to nothing. The continent's most powerful nation remained dominated by Prussia, where voting continued to be by the three-class system, and Germany's chancellor remained responsible to the crown and not to the Reichstag.

ITALY

Italy's liberal monarchy was committed to modernizing the nation while balancing the budget and steadily sponsoring modest reforms, but the political system in which only the well-to-do could vote and in which the government kept its parliamentary majority by means of political favors made it hard to win broad popular support.

The Crisis of the 1890s　As a hero of Italian unification and former radical, Francesco Crispi, prime minister in the late 1880s and 1890s, tried to change that. His policies—which included anticlericalism, a trade war with France, and imperial adventure—proved divisive instead. To end a protest movement among Sicilian peasants, Crispi resorted to martial law; and in 1894, he launched an invasion of Ethiopia to establish an Italian protectorate there. Two years later, he had to resign when 25,000 Italian troops were nearly wiped out at Aduwa by well-prepared Ethiopian forces four times their number.[5]

Domestic unrest increased both in the poverty-stricken agrarian south and in the rapidly industrializing north, where anarchist bombs, socialist demonstrations, and waves of strikes culminated in riots that reached revolutionary scale in Milan in 1898. The government restored order but at the cost of bloodshed, the suppression of scores of newspapers, and a ban on hundreds of socialist, republican, and Catholic organizations. Many conservatives argued for still firmer measures; yet the Chamber of Deputies, although frightened, refused further restriction of civil liberties, a stand supported in the elections of 1900. In Italy, as in France at the same time, the political campaign of a revitalized right was defeated by parliament and public opinion.

Limited Liberalism　The political system acquired a broader base of support under Giovanni Giolitti, prime minister from 1903 to 1914. He acknowledged the right to strike, nationalized railroads and life insurance, sponsored public health measures, and in 1911 supported universal male suffrage. Giolitti also encouraged Catholics to enter the national politics they had boycotted since 1870, and he, too, acquiesced in an imperial venture. Italy went to war against the Ottoman sultan in 1912, took Rhodes and the other major Dodecanese Islands, and landed at the port city of Tripoli in Libya, all of which the sultan ceded. The

▲ **Social tension in an era of prosperity: The excitement and uncertainty of a riot contrasts with the stable warmth of an elegant café.**
Umberto Boccioni, "Riot in the Galleria, 1910," oil on canvas, Pinacoteca di Brera, gift of Emilio and Maria Jesi, Scala/Art Resource, NY.

year of war inspired an enthusiasm that Italian governments had rarely enjoyed. Although the economic problems of the south remained grave and the discontent of more and more militant workers went largely unappeased, the Italian economy, less developed than that of the great industrial powers, experienced the fastest growth rate in Europe during the decade ending in 1914. In the elections of 1913, the first under the broadened suffrage, Giolitti's compromises would prove an easy target for critics from the left and the right, and they were the notable winners. Still, Italy appeared firmly set on a liberal, democratic course.

RUSSIA

In Russia the pressures for political change were held in check for a generation by official policies

---

[5]Subsequent governments held on to Eritrea as an Italian colony.

that centered on a program of "Russification," meant to create a united nation. But defeat in war and the first stages of industrialization produced a revolution.

Reaction   Alexander III had become tsar in 1881 on his father's assassination, an event that he believed to be the result of too much talk about further reform following the abolition of serfdom. He sought instead to achieve stability by using the Orthodox Church and the police to extend an official reactionary ideology through public life, and he gave nobles an increased role in regional councils, the *zemstvos*, and in rural administration. Local governors were authorized to use martial law, to restrict or ban the religions and languages of non-Russian peoples, and to persecute Jews.[6] These policies were continued with equal conviction but less energy by Tsar Nicholas II, who ascended the throne in 1894. As unrest increased in cities and in the countryside, many in the government searched for other ways of achieving the solidarity that repression had failed to create.

The Russo-Japanese War   War, and the patriotism it evokes, was thus welcomed in 1904, when Japan suddenly attacked the Russians at Port Arthur. Russia had leased Port Arthur from China in 1898 as part of its expansion into East Asia and Manchuria. For years these moves had troubled the Japanese, and Russia had neither kept its promises to withdraw nor acknowledged Japan's proposals for establishing mutually acceptable spheres of influence. The war was a disaster for Russia. Surprise attack was followed by defeats in Manchuria, the fall of Port Arthur, and then the annihilation of a large Russian fleet that sailed around the world only to be sunk in Japanese waters. In the peace treaty, signed at Portsmouth, New Hampshire— the United States, like Japan, wished to demonstrate its status as a world power—Russia ceded most of its recent gains, including Port Arthur and the southern half of Sakhalin Island, and recognized Japanese interest in Korea.

The Revolution of 1905   So dramatic a defeat increased pressure for major reforms just as the Crimean War had done fifty years before, but this time the pressure came from deep within Russian society. Peasant agitation had been on the rise since a terrible famine in 1891. Secret organizations were growing among the non-Russian nationalities, and workers drawn to St. Petersburg and Moscow by industrialization had begun to form unions. The Social Revolutionaries, a party combining the traditions of populism and terrorism, grew more active; and the Marxist Social Democrats, hitherto composed of rather disparate groups, now organized in exile and strengthened their ties within Russia.

In this atmosphere liberal members of the *zemstvos* held a national congress in 1904, though forbidden to by the government, and insisted on civil liberties. Then in January 1905 striking workers in St. Petersburg marched on the Winter Palace to petition the tsar for a national constitution and the recognition of labor unions. The workers carried icons and sang "God save the tsar"; but when they had assembled, the army opened fire, killing scores and wounding hundreds more.

"Bloody Sunday" led to agitation so widespread that in March the tsar promised to call an assembly of notables and announced immediate reforms: religious toleration, reduced restrictions on Jews and non-Russian nationals, and cancellation of part of the payments peasants owed for their land. Agitation for a constitution only grew stronger, expressed through urban strikes, peasant riots, and mutinies in both the army and navy. In August the tsar conceded more, declaring he would consult a national assembly, the Imperial Duma. Many close to the throne were shocked by so radical a step. A public wanting something more concrete responded with a wave of strikes.

A Russian Constitution   For the last ten days of October, Russia's economic life came to a halt, the most effective general strike Europe had ever seen. It won from the tsar the October Manifesto, which granted a constitution. Crowds danced in the streets, but proponents of change were divided. Those willing to work with this constitution, which guaranteed freedom of speech and assembly but was vague on much else, became known as Octobrists. Liberals who insisted on a

---

[6]One of history's famous forgeries, the *Protocols of the Elders of Zion,* was published (and written) by the Russian police in 1903. The protocols purported to be the secret minutes of a Jewish congress that revealed a conspiracy to control the world.

▲ On Bloody Sunday in January 1905 protesters, led by a priest and carrying a petition to the tsar, marched to the Winter Palace where they were fired on by Russian soldiers. That bloodshed, following rising demands for a representative assembly, marked the beginning of the Revolution of 1905; thousands of people died that day. Sovfoto.

constituent assembly and broader guarantees formed the Constitutional Democratic party, called Cadets for short. Further to the left, socialists and revolutionaries rejected compromise, and the St. Petersburg Soviet, a committee of trade union leaders and socialists, called another general strike. It was only partially successful, and an emboldened government arrested the leaders of the Soviet in December and bloodily defeated the Moscow workers who revolted in protest.

The Fundamental Laws announced in May 1906 defined the limitations of the tsar's concessions. He would keep the power of veto, the right to name his ministers, and full command of the executive, the judiciary, and the armed forces; the national legislature would have an upper house in addition to the Duma, with half its members appointed by the tsar. Elections under this new system, however, brought the Cadets a large majority, which demanded representative government. Nicholas then disbanded the legislature and

held new elections, but they produced an even more radical assembly; and it, too, was disbanded. Only a new electoral law favoring the propertied classes ensured conservative majorities in subsequent legislatures.

The Revolution of 1905 had nevertheless brought important changes. Russia now had parliamentary institutions and organized parties, the power of the aristocracy had been greatly reduced, and the nation was clearly set on a modern course. The prime minister from 1906 to 1911, Peter Stolypin, reformed education and administration and strove to stimulate the economy by turning away from the *mir* system of communal lands in favor of the full private ownership of land, and he created land banks and a program of social insurance. With the aid of foreign capital, the pace of industrialization rapidly increased. While discontent among workers and poorer peasants remained serious and radical movements were sternly repressed, the Cadets were finding it possible to work with the new system. Liberals throughout Europe rejoiced that the giant of the East had at last begun to follow the path of Western progress.

AUSTRIA-HUNGARY

The political problems of Austria-Hungary were revealed not so much in crises as in stalemate. Creation of an autonomous regime in Hungary led to conflicts with the rest of the empire, and these political and nationalist issues were exacerbated by the divergent economic interests of the Empire's industrializing and agrarian regions. The conservative instincts of the imperial court, the aristocracy, and the bureaucracy stymied further reforms.

Shifting Stalemates   These groups, the pillars of the empire, settled on a cautious prime minister, Count Eduard von Taafe, who held office from 1879 to 1893. Taafe's parliamentary supporters included Czechs and Poles. But they wanted concessions that Taafe's other supporters would not accept so that inaction was the safest course. Social change brought further disagreements. The spread of education, for instance, heightened conflict over what language should be used in schools. In response to workers' agitation, Taafe proposed welfare measures but repressed socialists, antagonizing both left and right. After his fall, governments came to rely more on decree powers and support from the crown than on parliament. After universal manhood suffrage was introduced without conviction in 1907, the Christian Socialists and the Social Democrats became the two largest parties; but neither was acceptable to the leaders of the empire. Kept from imperial office, they competed in the city of Vienna, where the Christian Socialists gained sway by combining social programs with demagogic antisemitism.

Within Hungary Magyar notables maintained their dominance over other nationalities by requiring that the Magyar language be used in government and schools, by tightly controlling the electoral system, and by subverting the bureaucracy through corruption. Their policies protecting large landowners and seeking greater independence from the imperial government weakened

the empire. In 1903, when they demanded greater autonomy for their own army, they touched one issue about which Emperor Francis Joseph I cared too much to yield. He suspended the Hungarian constitution, ruled without parliament, and frightened the Magyars into submission by threatening to subject them, a minority in their own country, to universal male suffrage. Magyars and the empire needed each other; and Magyar politics, admired in the 1840s as a model of liberal nationalism, had turned by 1906 into the defensive strategy of a threatened aristocracy. For mutual survival the leaders of Austria and Hungary avoided dangerous changes and relied on imperial foreign policy to strengthen from the outside a political system in danger at home.

SPAIN

Spain developed a remarkable tradition of parliamentarism in which governments were careful to keep the support of the army, the Church, big business, and regional interests. By emphasizing the economy, a liberal coalition held power from 1854 to 1863, years in which Spain experienced on a smaller scale the waves of speculation, railroad building, economic growth, and ostentation associated with the Second Empire in France.

Revolution and Restoration   This growth brought new demands that old alliances, palace intrigue, and electoral manipulation could not check. Rising discontent led in 1868 to the flight of the unpopular Queen Isabella II and to revolution. The leaders of the revolution were political moderates who quickly agreed on a constitutional monarchy with universal manhood suffrage, trial by jury, and freedom of religion and the press. It proved easier to adopt a new constitution, however, than to find a new king. Candidate after candidate declined to become entangled in Spanish politics and the sort of international complications that precipitated the Franco-Prussian War. The Italian prince who finally did accept the throne gave it up after three years in the face of rising opposition from left and right. The subsequent republic lasted only two years before the military installed Isabella's son on the throne as Alfonso XII.

He began his reign in 1875 with a new constitution closer to the one in effect at midcentury than to the more democratic ones that had succeeded it. In a parliamentary system based on limited suffrage, the Conservative and Liberal parties alternated in power with little change in policy, a system that by keeping the state weak masked the bitter divisions between regionalists and centralists, Catholics and anticlericals, the poor and the propertied. As in Russia and Austria, however, industrialization exacerbated these tensions. Unable to establish a consistent program for the colonies, the government met unrest in Cuba with alternating policies of repression and laxity. Cuban resistance became guerrilla war, and in 1898 the United States entered the conflict with an imperialist enthusiasm of its own. Spain was forced to withdraw from Cuba and to cede Puerto Rico, Guam, and the Philippine Islands to the United States.

Those losses led to a great deal of soul searching. A group of Spanish intellectuals known as the generation of 1898 brought new vitality to Spanish public life, but neither the caution of conservatives nor the mild reforms of liberals could stem the increasing dissension in which the Church denounced the liberals while growing anarchist and socialist movements attacked the whole establishment. In 1909 these conflicts burst forth in a week of violence in Barcelona during which churches were burned and looted and private citizens were murdered. Yet the authorities soon restored order. Spain's unadmired moderate regime remained less divisive than the alternatives.

GREAT BRITAIN

From Russia to Spain, European nations had adopted parliamentary systems; and until the end of the century, Britain provided the model of how such a system was supposed to work. Legislation addressed the most pressing social issues, however cautiously; and parliament gradually reduced legal inequalities, opening the civil service to those who passed competitive examinations, removing legal disabilities on Jews, and eliminating special taxes on behalf of the Church of England. At the same time order was maintained through respect for law, toleration, and social deference. There were serious domestic tensions, but they were attenuated by a thriving two-party system.

The Liberal and Conservative Parties   The creation of modern political parties led by two brilliant leaders facilitated Britain's adaptation to change. William Gladstone was instrumental in transforming the Whigs into the Liberal party, and Benjamin Disraeli led in making the Tories into the modern Conservative party. Gladstone was a skilled parliamentary tactician sympathetic to liberal reformers and even radicals, for whom political liberalism was a moral cause. Somewhat hesitantly, he made increased suffrage, which had been talked about for a generation, a central plank; but his complicated bill was defeated in Parliament.

Instead, Disraeli persuaded his startled party to support a simpler, more generous reform, which passed in 1867. It doubled the electorate by extending the right to vote to all men who paid property taxes directly or indirectly through rent (about one adult male in three). Equally important, imperial policies and major programs of reform now became part of the systematic competition for popular favor. The parliamentary clashes of Gladstone and Disraeli became a dramatic part of British public life.

Political Reforms   The enlarged electorate gave the Liberals a great victory; and for six years Gladstone's first ministry fundamentally altered the relations between government and society. State aid to elementary schools, both religious and secular, brought Britain closer to universal education. The Liberals also reformed the army (even the purchase of commissions was abolished, despite great resistance from the House of Lords) and disestablished the Anglican Church of Ireland (so that an overwhelmingly Catholic population no longer paid taxes to support a Protestant church). Recognizing the festering poverty and discontent in Ireland, new laws restricted the abuses of absentee landlords and provided peasants some protection against eviction.

The Conservatives, returned to power in the elections of 1874, were more willing than the Liberals to expand the authority of the state. A public health act established a national code for housing and urban sanitation; and new measures allowed striking workers to picket, making unions more effective. These social concerns, often called Tory democracy, which offered a British parallel to the policies of Bismarck and Napoleon III, became the cornerstone of the revived Conservative party.

Gladstone in turn adopted the principle of universal male suffrage, which became law in 1885. Men with an independent place of residence could now vote, and it says much about the life of the poor that this one requirement—which excluded domestic servants, sons living with parents, and those with no permanent address—was enough to exclude roughly one-third of all adult males. Gladstone's perpetual compromises, however, were losing their appeal; and imperial issues were his undoing. His renewed efforts in behalf of Irish peasants failed to satisfy Irish nationalists who wanted an independent parliament of their own; and when Gladstone acquiesced to Irish home rule in 1886, his party split. A group of Liberals led by Joseph Chamberlain allied with the Conservatives. A radical in social matters, Chamberlain had adopted the popular cause of imperialism, which would help the Conservatives stay in office for sixteen of the nineteen years between 1886 and 1905.

Rising Social Tensions While projecting British power around the world, Conservative governments remained active at home. In 1888 and again in 1894 they restructured local government, a traditional source of the aristocracy's political power, making country councils elective and thus more democratic. They extended the reforms of the civil service, and in an act of 1902 established a national education system that for the first time included secondary schooling. Yet these important changes did not address the needs of the working class, whose rising dissatisfaction was marked by the dramatic strikes of London match girls in 1888 and dock workers the next year. The strikes, which won public sympathy, were part of a "new unionism" that included unskilled workers in a more militant labor movement. Social conflict became public in Britain as never before.

In 1900 a combination of union representatives and some prominent intellectuals formed the Labour party on a platform of democratic socialism. Both the Labour and Liberal parties campaigned for social programs that the Conservatives resisted, hoping that the popular appeal of empire would keep them in power. Instead,

▲ **London's dock workers had gained national sympathy with their orderly demonstrations in the great strike of 1899 and had won some of their demands, but the agitation and unrest continued. Here, during a subsequent strike, police guard a convoy of food trucks making their way to city markets.** Bettmann.

in 1906 the Liberals won the most one-sided electoral victory since 1832. They immediately established systems of workers' compensation, old-age pensions, and urban planning. These measures—and the expanding arms race—required new revenues, and in 1909 David Lloyd George, the Chancellor of the Exchequer, proposed a "people's budget." A skilled orator who delighted in the rhetoric of class conflict, he promised to place the costs of social welfare squarely on the rich.

Constitutional Crisis An aroused House of Lords rejected his budget, an unprecedented act that forced a constitutional crisis and new elections. The king's threat to appoint hundreds of additional peers finally forced the upper house to accept not only the hated budget but also a major change in the constitution. New legislation established that the Lords could no longer veto money bills or any measure that passed the Commons in three successive sessions.

Emmeline Pankhurst on Women's Rights
◆

Emmeline Pankhurst founded the Women's Social and Political Union in 1903. As the militant leader of the British suffragettes, she won headlines and eventually significant support for her cause with her disruptive tactics and powerful speeches. Her fame was international by the time she went on a speaking tour in Canada in 1912, where on January 14 she gave a long speech from which this passage is taken. Delighting her audience with stories of the resistance she had met, she focused on the right to vote but made clear that her vision of women's roles was much broader.

"There has been a great deal of talk lately of new legislation for those who are about to enter into marriage. Women should have a say as one of the contracting parties. There are the questions of divorce and of the training of children. Who knows better of these matters than do women? There are also the trades and professions which are at the present time open to women. It is only right that we should have some say in the legislation concerning us. We have heard much of the English divorce law. It is a disgrace to any civilized country. The only redeeming feature of the matter is that the bulk of men are better than the law allows. But there is the minority, and the law should be severe for them. They are as bad as the law allows them to be. If woman only had weight in politics this would be rectified soon. She will serve to call more attention to such questions of national welfare. If we are to have any divorce law at all, and that is a much-debated question, it should be a law that is equal both for man and woman. Unless women get the vote we have no guarantee that it will be so.

" . . . Men are responsible if they allow the present condition of things to continue. Women have the power to work out their own salvation. But as it is, if a woman is ruined, if a child is injured, man is responsible for it all. It is a responsibility I would not care to have, and, as things are, I would not be a man for all the world. If women fail as men have failed, then they will bear the burden with them. But since men cannot protect and shield us, let us share the duty with them, let us use our power so that woman may be a participant, not to tyrannize over man but to take a share in the responsibilities of ruling, without which there is no real representative government. What we really are interested in in this fight is the uplifting of the sex and better conditions of humanity than men can secure. In the legal home there is but the man. What we want is the combined intelligence of man and woman working for the salvation of the children of the race. This will make for the world a better time than ever before in its history. It will raise mankind to heights of which now it has little conception. We must only make this last fight for human freedom that as the class distinction disappeared so that sex distinction may pass, and then you will get better things than men can by themselves secure."

From Emmeline Pankhurst, "The Last Fight for Human Freedom," speech given in Canada in 1912, in Brian MacArthur, *Twentieth-Century Speeches* (New York: Viking, 1992).

The peers' intemperate outburst, which cost them so much, was part of a general rise in social tension. From 1910 to 1914 strikes increased in frequency, size, and violence; a general strike became a real and much-talked-of threat. Women campaigning for the right to vote interrupted public meetings, invaded Parliament itself, smashed windows, and planted bombs. Arrested, they went on hunger strikes until baffled statesmen ordered their release. Such behavior from ladies was shocking in itself; but as the movement gained strength, recruiting women (and some men) from every social class, its outraged attack on smug male assumptions reinforced the rising challenge to a whole social order (see "Emmeline Pankhurst on Women's Rights").

Nor was the threat of violence limited to the left. In 1914 the Commons for the third time passed a bill granting Irish home rule, which made it immune to a veto in the House of Lords. The Protestants of northern Ireland, with support from many in England, openly threatened civil war. Squads began drilling, and the British officer corps seemed ready to mutiny rather than fight to impose home rule on Protestant loyalists.

The outbreak of world war generated the national unity that neither imperialism nor social reform had been able to achieve. But if the death of Queen Victoria in 1901 had symbolized the end of an age of British expansion, the ascent of George V to the throne (r. 1910–1936) marked the opening of new and terrible conflicts. Edward VII's brief reign (r. 1901–1910) would soon be remembered a little sadly as the Edwardian era, a happy time of relaxed confidence in prosperity, progress, and peace.

In the period from 1870 to 1914 every European nation had faced major political crises; yet as political systems worked to balance class conflict and clashing interests, the trend toward greater democracy and large-scale organization seemed irresistible. For good or ill, there had been few major upheavals, save in backward Russia, and no European war, facts that contemporaries often cited as proof of progress. In most countries there was greater freedom of expression, more political participation, more leisure, increased literacy and education, and better health care than in the past. In general, productivity and prosperity, already at levels never achieved before, continued to rise. Science and technology promised still greater wonders. Even in retrospect, the level of creativity in the arts and scholarship and the growth of knowledge and professional standards in every field remain impressive.

Yet the civilization that achieved all these changes was bitterly denounced not only for its manifest injustices, which by contrast with its achievements seemed all the more blatant, but more fundamentally for its lack of coherent values, for its materialism, for the ugliness of industrial society, and for the privileged position of a middle class portrayed as self-serving and philistine. Perhaps European society was evolving toward solutions of these deficiencies, as many believed. Or maybe the positive trends were less significant than the effects of imperialism, domestic social conflict, and the arms race. In 1914 the very compromises that had held society together and kept the peace exploded—not in revolution, but in total war.

Recommended Reading

Sources

*Hélias, Pierre-Jackez. *The Horse of Pride: Life in a Breton Village.* June Guicharnaud (tr.). 1980. A compelling memoir of a preindustrial society about to be transformed at the turn of the century.

MacDougall, H. A. (ed.). *Lord Acton on Papal Power.* 1973. A leading figure in Britain's intellectual life and a thoughtful historian, Lord Acton was a committed Catholic who was also an outspoken opponent of the doctrine of papal infallibility proclaimed at the Vatican Council in 1871. This collection of his public writings and private correspondence with important contemporaries provides a touching glimpse of Acton's anguish as well as the widespread attention these issues received.

Snyder, Louis L. *The Dreyfus Case: A Documentary History* 1973. These well-edited documents convey the passions that this famous affair evoked and the broad implications that all sides saw in it.

Weintraub, Stanley. *The Yellow Book: Quintessence of the Nineties.* 1964. The stories and articles in this collection are all taken from the most daring literary quarterly of the day; nearly every piece is an exercise in the rejection of Victorian proprieties, and in that respect characteristic of the new movements in the arts.

Studies

Berghahn, Voker R. *Germany, 1871–1914: Economy, Society, Culture, and Politics.* 1993. A thematic survey unusual in its breadth, particularly attentive to public culture and social structure.

Berlanstein, Lenard R. *The Working People of Paris, 1871–1914.* 1984. Looks at the important changes in the lives of wage earners, in the nature of work, and in the workplace, as well as their impact on working-class movements.

Boxer, Marilyn, and Jean Quataert. *Socialist Women: Socialist Feminism in the Nineteenth and Twentieth Century.* 1978. Looking at the important figures, the book explores the tortured ambivalence among socialists toward feminism in all the major countries.

Canning, Kathleen. *Languages of Labor and Gender: Female Factory Work in Germany, 1850–1914.* 1996. Connects social changes in the nature of work to changes in women's lives and to the shifting discourse on gender.

*Craig, Gordon. *Germany: 1866–1945.* 1978. A well-written and capable analysis that stresses the failure of liberalism to overcome preindustrial forces as a key to public life.

*Dangerfield, George. *The Strange Death of Liberal England.* 1935. A skillfully and argumentatively written description of a society in crisis that has influenced subsequent interpretations of the period.

*Derfler, Leslie. *Socialism since Marx: A Century of the European Left.* 1973. Thoughtful discussion of the movements that stemmed from Marx, showing their variety, creativity, and contradictions.

*Evans, Richard J. *The Feminist Movement in Germany, 1894–1933.* 1976. Establishes the importance of these movements and their connection to German politics and parties more generally.

*———. *The Feminists: Women's Emancipation in Europe, America, and Australia.* 1979. The similarities and differences in feminist campaigns reveal a good deal about the dominant ideologies, social structure, and politics of their respective societies.

*Gay, Peter. *The Education of the Senses.* 1984. A sensitive treatment of sexuality during the Victorian Age and the first part of a major study of the values of the bourgeoisie, written from a Freudian perspective.

Gillis, John R. *Youth and History: Tradition and Change in European Age Relations, 1770 to the Present.* 1981. An original study of youth transformed by social change that highlights the late nineteenth century as a pivotal period.

*Gullickson, Gay L. *Unruly Women of Paris: Images of the Commune.* 1997. A richly illustrated study of the hysterical press accounts of the role of women in the Commune.

*Hughes, H. Stuart. *Consciousness and Society: The Reorientation of European Social Thought, 1890–1930.* 1958. A gracefully written and indispensable analysis of the currents of modern thought in this time of transition from midcentury certitudes.

Johnson, Douglas. *France and the Dreyfus Affair.* 1966. A standard account of the affair that explains its extraordinary impact.

*Joll, James. *The Anarchists.* 1964. Provides a particularly clear discussion of the ideas and motives of very disparate groups, all claiming to be anarchist.

*———. *The Second International, 1889–1914.* 1966. A general history of the socialist movement in this period, with striking portraits of the major figures.

Kern, Stephen. *The Culture of Time and Space 1880–1918.* 1983. An imaginative study of ideas and experiences related to technological and cultural change reflected in art, literature, politics, and social life.

Lidtke, Vernon. *The Alternative Culture: Socialist Labor in Imperial Germany.* 1985. A significant analysis of how German socialists created Europe's most organized working-class subculture.

*Löwith, Karl. *From Hegel to Nietzsche: The Revolution in Nineteenth-Century Thought.* 1964. A sober essay on the pessimistic and irrationalist transformations in modern thought and the powerful insights that resulted.

Lyons, Francis S. *Ireland since the Famine.* 1971. A broad social history of a society in crisis.

*Mayeur, Jean-Marie, and Madeleine Rebérioux. *The Third Republic from Its Origins to the Great War, 1871–1914.* J. R. Foster (tr.). 1984. A balanced synthesis of recent scholarship on the establishment of a stable republic amidst social conflict.

Miller, Michael. *The Bon Marché: Bourgeois Culture and the Development of the Department Store.* 1981. A fascinating study that explores the department store as a significant cultural institution.

Moses, Claire. *French Feminism in the Nineteenth Century.* 1984. Reveals the vigor of a feminist movement quite different from its British and German counterparts.

*Mosse, George L. *The Crisis of German Ideology.* 1964. Looks for the currents of Nazi ideology in the views of nation and race embodied in the popular ideas and movements of the late nineteenth century.

Pugh, Martin. *The Tories and the People, 1880–1935.* 1985. A study of the basis for and limitations of the Conservatives' mass appeal.

*Pulzer, Peter G. *The Rise of Political Anti-Semitism in Germany and Austria.* 1964. A clear and balanced survey of a difficult topic that shows the remarkable scope of antisemitism.

Ralston, David B. *The Army of the Republic, 1871–1914.* 1967. Treats a question of central importance to the establishment of democracy: the problem of the military in France both before and after the Dreyfus affair.

Rearick, Charles. *Pleasures of the Belle Époque.* 1985. Captures the cultural and social vitality of the period, emphasizing popular culture and the uses of leisure.

*Robertson, Priscilla. *An Experience of Women: Pattern and Change in Nineteenth-Century Europe.* 1982. A social and intellectual history of middle- and upper-class women in Western Europe, useful for the breadth of its coverage.

*Romero, Patricia W. *E. Sylvia Pankhurst: Portrait of a Radical.* 1987. This biography of Britain's feminist leader gives a good sense of the development of the movement overall.

*Schorske, Carl E. *Fin-de-Siècle Vienna: Politics and Culture.* 1980. Unusually sensitive and imaginative assessment of one of the important moments in European cultural history.

Seton-Watson, Christopher. *Italy from Liberalism to Fascism.* 1967. A thorough general, political account of Italy in its first period of rapid industrialization.

*Shattuck, Roger. *The Banquet Years.* 1968. A brilliant study of the role of artists in late-nineteenth-century Paris, showing the connections among social attitudes, institutions, and the birth of modernism in the arts.

Sheehan, James J. *German Liberalism in the Nineteenth Century.* 1978. An important assessment of a much disputed and critical issue, the place of liberalism in German intellectual and political life.

Stone, Norman. *Europe Transformed, 1878–1919.* 1984. An insightful and fresh new survey of the period, outlining the weaknesses of the liberals.

Tannenbaum, Edward R. *1900: The Generation before the Great War.* 1976. Interesting essays on the major facets of society.

*Wagar, Warren W. *Good Tidings: The Belief in Progress from Darwin to Marcuse.* 1972. A wide-ranging account of the period's principal yet beleaguered concepts.

*Weber, Eugen. *Peasants into Frenchmen: The Modernization of Rural France, 1880–1914.* 1976. A provocative treatment stressing the resistance of rural France to the pressures for change and the lateness of their arrival.

Wehler, Hans-Ulrich. *The German Empire 1871–1918.* Kim Traynor (tr.). 1985. A comprehensive structural analysis that synthesizes the most recent empirical research.

*Wohl, Robert. *The Generation of 1914.* 1979. Theories of generations in conflict are related to the intellectual and political discontent preceding World War I in this important book.

*Available in paperback.

▲ A British surgeon and painter, Henry Tonks, was sent to the front in 1917 to paint this scene of a dressing station at the Somme, where officers classify the wounded while the artillery barrages go on.
Imperial War Museum.

WORLD WAR AND DEMOCRACY

n 1914 Germany, Russia, Austria-Hungary, France, and Great Britain suddenly found themselves at war—a war different from any that had gone before, a war that permanently altered society and politics, and a war that even in retrospect stands as the dividing point between two eras. Interpreting its origins is thus crucial to any understanding of modern history and is still the subject of controversy. Historians have given few subjects the close study devoted to the system of alliances and the diplomatic moves that led to World War I, and we have a clear understanding of the events that culminated in catastrophe.

The larger question is whether these fatal steps were themselves a result of nineteenth-century developments—economic expansion, imperialism, social divisions, ideological conflicts, and representative government—that favored an arms race and strident nationalism. Once it came, the war strained every resource of the belligerents and mobilized civilian life as never before. As it ended, the victors were shaken, their societies and politics different. The losing states crumbled, opening the way to still more dramatic political changes. The complicated peace settlement, which changed the map of Europe and tried to make democracy universal, was meant above all to ensure that there would not be another world war.

I. The Coming of World War

International relations held center stage in the period from 1870 to World War I for a variety of reasons. The balance of power established at the Congress of Vienna in 1815 had been overturned by the unification of Italy and Germany and by Prussia's defeat of Austria in 1866 and France in 1870. The heightened sense of insecurity that followed led to an intricate web of alliances requiring constant attention. At the same time, imperialism, economic competition, and an escalating arms race multiplied the arenas in which national interests might clash. In addition, every threat, insult, or setback was magnified in daily journalism and domestic politics, for nationalism sold newspapers and made political careers. Foreign ministries worked to keep these conflicting pressures under control through diplomacy conducted by gentlemen, largely in secret and according to elaborate rules.

DIPLOMATIC ALLIANCES

Bismarck's diplomatic skill had been essential to the creation of the Second Reich, and for the next twenty years he continued using that skill to make the new German nation secure from any foreign

▼ **Bismarck dominated the Congress of Berlin in 1878 much as he dominates this portrait, which shows him being congratulated by the Russian delegate, with Count Andrassy of Austria-Hungary on the left.**
Staatliche Museum, Berlin/Archiv für Kunst und Geschichte.

threat. The treaties he fostered plus those created as a counterweight, which seemed to increase security in the short run, ultimately stimulated a dangerous arms race.

The Berlin Conference of 1878 The immediate issue at the Berlin Conference of 1878 was the expansion of Russian influence in the Balkans beyond what the other European powers would allow. With few German interests directly involved, Bismarck presented himself as an "honest broker" and masterfully orchestrated agreements in which everyone got something. Russia's military gains in 1876 had forced the sultan to cede territory across the Caucasus Mountains to Russia, allow an enlarged Montenegro and Serbia, and grant full independence to a large and autonomous Bulgaria, which everyone believed would be a Russian puppet. The aim of the Congress was to restrain Russian ambitions while finding a response to Balkan nationalism and Ottoman weakness that avoided war.

The settlement granted autonomy to a greatly reduced Bulgaria (thus lessening Russia's gains) and recognized the independence of Serbia, Romania, and Montenegro (acknowledging rising nationalism).[1] Austria-Hungary, nervous about the presence of new Balkan states, was authorized in compensation to occupy Bosnia and Herzegovina, which nevertheless remained formally under Ottoman rule. In addition Britain's occupation of Cyprus was confirmed, and Tunis was in effect promised to France. The Berlin Conference achieved a balance among competing nations by extending European dominion at the expense of a weakening Ottoman Empire—a pattern characteristic of imperialism.

The Bismarckian System Bismarck subsequently persuaded Austria-Hungary, worried by Russia's ambitions and grateful for Germany's support at the Conference, to a mutual defense pact with Germany. It became the foundation of German foreign policy. The secret pact promised

---

[1] The tsar's nephew was elected to the Bulgarian throne. Rumelia, the southern part of Bulgaria, remained under Turkish rule as a separate province. The provinces of Wallachia and Moldavia had been joined in 1862 to form Romania and received their own prince two years later. A Hohenzollern, he became King Carol in 1881.

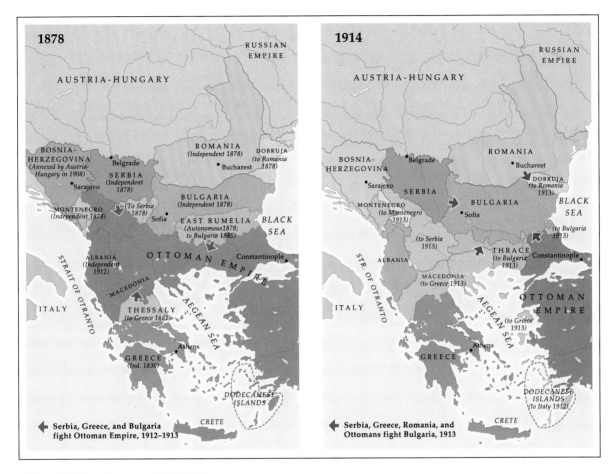

▲ Map 27.1 The Balkans, 1878–1914

that either nation would come to the defense of the other if either should be attacked by Russia. The Conference had also demonstrated Russia's diplomatic isolation, and so in 1881 Bismarck audaciously persuaded Russia to join Germany and Austria-Hungary in promising to remain neutral in the event of war between any of them and a fourth power. To these understandings, Bismarck added a third—the Triple Alliance of Italy, Germany, and Austria-Hungary—a renewable five-year pact first signed in 1882. Bismarck took advantage of Italy's resentment at France's occupation of Tunis in 1881 to achieve a major goal of his own, the diplomatic isolation of France, for Bismarck continued to fear France's resentment over the loss of Alsace-Lorraine (see "The Terms of the Triple Alliance," p. 946).

Formally, these treaties were defensive, although the secrecy surrounding them fostered a sense of insecurity. They gave Germany an international influence rare in peacetime, but holding them together took great skill. Italy and Russia had more reasons for conflict with Austria-Hungary than with anyone else, and it was hard to keep them tied to Germany. Russia and Austria-Hungary let their alliance lapse in 1887 because of their disagreements in the Balkans, and Bismarck could only partially repair the damage by signing a separate Reinsurance Treaty with Russia in which the two nations promised to remain neutral toward each other if one of them was at war. In order to persuade Italy to renew the Triple Alliance in 1887, Bismarck had to recognize Italian ambitions in the Balkans, Africa, and elsewhere.

The Shifting Balance Afer Bismarck's dismissal in 1890, German diplomacy was erratic and often

THE TERMS OF THE TRIPLE ALLIANCE

These articles are from the treaty of 1912 in which Austria-Hungary, Germany, and Italy renewed the Triple Alliance for the fifth time since 1882. This version essentially continued earlier ones, except for articles VI through XI, not printed here, which dealt rather vaguely with the Balkans, Ottoman territories, Egypt, and North Africa. With respect to those regions, the signatories reassured each other that they preferred to maintain the status quo but promised mutual understanding and even support if Austria-Hungary or Italy found it necessary temporarily to occupy territory in the Balkans or if Italy had to take measures against French expansion in North Africa. The promises of support to Italy indicated the higher price now required to keep Italy in the Alliance.

"ARTICLE I. The High Contracting Parties mutually promise peace and friendship, and will enter into no alliance or engagement directed against any one of their States.

"They engage to proceed to an exchange of ideas on political and economic questions of a general nature which may arise, and they further promise one another mutual support within the limits of their own interests.

"ARTICLE II. In case Italy, without direct provocation on her part, should be attacked by France for any reason whatsoever, the two other Contracting Parties shall be bound to lend help and assistance with all their forces to the Party attacked.

"This same obligation shall devolve upon Italy in case of any aggression without direct provocation by France against Germany.

"ARTICLE III. If one, or two, of the High Contracting Parties, without direct provocation on their part, should chance to be attacked and to be engaged in a war with two or more Great Powers nonsignatory to the present Treaty, the *casus foederis* will arise simultaneously for all the High Contracting Parties.

"ARTICLE IV. In case a Great Power nonsignatory to the present Treaty should threaten the security of the states of one of the High Contracting Parties, and the threatened Party should find itself forced on that account to make war against it, the two others bind themselves to observe towards their Ally a benevolent neutrality. Each of them reserves to itself, in this case, the right to take part in the war, if it should see fit, to make common cause with its Ally.

"ARTICLE V. If the peace of one of the High Contracting Parties should chance to be threatened under the circumstances foreseen by the preceding Articles, the High Contracting Parties shall take counsel together in ample time as to the military measures to be taken with a view to eventual cooperation.

"They engage, henceforth, in all cases of common participation in a war, to conclude neither armistice, nor peace, nor treaty, except by common agreement among themselves.

"ARTICLE XII. The High Contracting Parties mutually promise secrecy as to the contents of the present Treaty."

From Sidney Bradshaw Fay, *The Origins of the World War,* Macmillan, 1930.

---

abrasive. His successors understood the importance of Germany's alliances, but it was easy from Berlin to overlook a new factor that could draw other nations together: common fear of Germany. When Germany's new leaders let the Reinsurance treaty with Russia expire (partly from concern that it contradicted the Triple Alliance), France pressed Russia for an understanding, which by 1894 had become a full alliance. France and Russia promised that each would support the other if either was attacked by Germany or by another member of the Triple Alliance aided by Germany. Such an accord between the Russian autocracy and the French republic had seemed politically impossible, despite Russia's having already turned to France for loans and arms purchases. Now the tsar greeted French delegates while a band played the "Marseillaise," previously outlawed in Russia as a song of revolution.

In response, German diplomats sought to reassert Germany's importance in world affairs while renewing their efforts to reach some understanding with Great Britain. Those aims conflicted. In 1896, for example, William II sent a telegram congratulating the president of the South African Republic on the Boers' defeat of a small private army organized by Englishmen. The gesture, intended to show the British how much they needed German friendship, was instead resented. The kaiser's talk of the "yellow peril" during a period of turmoil in China, when he instructed his soldiers to behave like the barbaric Huns of old, did nothing to enhance his reputation for stability. Neither did the talk of a "natural" alliance between the Teutonic and Anglo-Saxon races when at the same time Germany was exploring a continental coalition against Great Britain. The specific issue in contention was the expanding German navy, and some negotiated limit seemed possible until the Germans demanded a formal alliance first. The British concluded that the German fleet was aimed at them.

Anglo-French Understanding The colonial competition between Great Britain and France, which had seemed to risk war, was in the meantime giving way to mutually defined spheres of influence. Following the confrontation at Fashoda in 1898, the French set about turning humiliation into good relations. They accepted British domination in Egypt in return for Britain's recognition of French interests in North Africa, particularly Morocco. Further understandings followed, culminating in the Anglo-French Entente Cordiale of 1904 in which France and Great Britain eliminated the major issues of imperial conflict between them from Siam to Newfoundland and from the Niger River to North Africa. Formally a mere understanding, the Entente implied much more, as the exchange of public visits between Edward VII and the president of France was meant to demonstrate.

Rising Tensions Germany's diplomatic position remained strong, and German leaders reasoned that an assertive foreign policy would demonstrate that strength. But the tenor of international relations was changing. As armaments increased and treaties proliferated, each power became more obsessed with its own security, and public opinion grew more sensitive to questions of national honor. Within seven years, three diplomatic crises—each of which initially seemed a German

victory—in fact drew Germany's opponents closer together.

The first of these crises arose over Morocco. France, its designs there well known, had carefully won acquiescence from the other powers except for Germany; and the German chancellor, Bernhard von Bülow, demanded an international conference to settle Morocco's future. He expected the conference to expose France's isolation; and in fact the architect of French policy, the foreign minister Théophile Delcassé, was forced from office before the conference met at Algeciras in 1906. The agreement reached there confirmed that Morocco had a special international status, but it also recognized the primacy of French interests. The crisis was a disaster for German diplomacy. Only Austria-Hungary loyally voted with its ally. Italy, Russia, Great Britain, and the United States (now a regular participant in such international agreements) supported France; and Germany's threatening tactics led French and British officials to begin talks about their mutual military interests.

Testing Alliances The second crisis arose over the Balkans. Austria was concerned that Serbia, led by a new king and a radical nationalist government, had become a dangerous antagonist and was fearful that Turkey's influence in the Balkans would grow following the revolution in 1908 by the Young Turks, who determined to modernize their nation. Austria-Hungary decided to annex Bosnia and Herzegovina.

That move, which threatened Serbia, outraged Russian Slavophiles. Nationalists who believed that Russia should defend the interests of Slavs everywhere demanded an international conference. Britain and France agreed. Germany, though angered by the suddenness of the annexation, supported Austria-Hungary. Diplomatic crises were becoming tests of alliances (and significantly, Italy expressed resentment at not being consulted by Austria-Hungary rather than loyalty to the Triple Alliance). There had been earlier signs that Italy might drift away when in 1902 France recognized Italian ambitions in Libya. The two nations then pledged neutrality if either was attacked by a third power (i.e., Germany). Although the Triple Alliance was renewed in the same year, Italy now sat on the fence between the Franco-Russian and the Austro-German alliances.

German Blunders The third major crisis once again involved Morocco, which France now wanted to annex. It had consulted all the European powers, and talks with Germany seemed to be going well when suddenly in 1911 the Germans sent the gunboat *Panther* to the Moroccan port of Agadir (a show of power and a classic imperialist gesture) and then asked for all of the French Congo as the price for accepting France's annexation of Morocco. Both the demands and the method seemed excessive, and in Great Britain David Lloyd George publicly denounced them. Once again, eventual compromise (France would cede parts of its Congo lands and bits of its other African territories adjacent to German colonies) counted for less than the rising tension and growing international distrust of the Germans.

The dangers of a European arms race, especially the naval competition between Britain and Germany, were thus very apparent; and two great conferences on disarmament and compulsory arbitration were held at The Hague in 1899 and again in 1907. No power was willing to sacrifice any of its strength, but Germany's delegates bluntly rejected any limitation on their sovereign right to make war. And at that moment Kaiser William complained to the British press that England should be grateful for German neutrality in the Boer War. British officials and journalists replied in public recriminations that were part of an important shift in policy.

The Triple Entente In 1902 Britain ended its long tradition of refusing peacetime alliances by signing a treaty with Japan. That was followed in 1907 by an accord among France, Russia, and Japan that defined their areas of interest and promised to preserve the integrity of China. That agreement opened the way for a more important understanding between Great Britain and Russia. Surprisingly those old imperial antagonists were able to resolve their points of contention from the Black Sea to Persia, Afghanistan, and Tibet. Thus the Triple Entente was formed, an informal coalition of France, Russia, and Britain that now balanced the Triple Alliance. Its implications became clear when Britain decided in 1912 to withdraw its battleships from the Mediterranean, leaving the French navy to defend its interests there while the British fleet concentrated on the German threat in the North Sea.

The Balkan Threat The Triple Alliance and the Triple Entente glared menacingly at each other, and for each of them turmoil in the Balkans was a test of strength. The ferment there of nationalism, modernization, militarism, and shaky parliamentarism echoed European-wide trends but was complicated by centuries of oppression, by disputed boundaries (most of recent invention), and by social, ethnic, and religious rivalries. The competition between Russia and Austria-Hungary quickly became enmeshed in these conflicts, and so did the Balkan ambitions of Germany (with railway and economic interests in the peninsula) and of Italy.

The first Balkan War was triggered by Italy's defeat of Turkey in 1912, when Italy gained Libya and important Mediterranean islands. In the fall of that year Bulgaria, Serbia, and Greece declared war on Turkey. In a few months they drove the Ottomans from all their remaining European holdings except Constantinople. After a partial truce and months of border skirmishes, the great powers hammered out the terms of peace at the end of May 1913.

One month later Serbia and Greece, quickly joined by Romania and Turkey, again went to war, this time against Bulgaria, the big winner in the previous war. This conflict ended in a few weeks, but local anger and international concern did not. The great powers pressured the belligerents to accept peace, but their primary attention was directed toward each other.

The Assassination of an Austrian Archduke In this atmosphere of growing distrust Austria-Hungary threatened Serbia with the use of force if it did not abandon some of its nationalist claims, while groups of Serbian nationalists agitated in behalf of their fellow Slavs living under Austrian rule in Bosnia and Herzegovina. Against this background Archduke Francis Ferdinand, the heir to the Austrian and Hungarian thrones, chose to parade in Sarajevo, the capital of Bosnia, on June 28, 1914. If the archduke wished to display Habsburg authority, others were eager to demonstrate their opposition. As the archduke's car moved down the street, a bomb just missed him. Then other conspirators lost their courage and failed to fire as his car passed by. At that point his driver made a wrong turn, started to back up, and yet

▲ **The assassination of Archduke Francis Ferdinand and his wife in Sarajevo, painted as a dramatic moment when a single act affected the course of history.** Bettmann.

another young Bosnian revolutionary fired point-blank, killing both the archduke and his wife.

The leaders of Austria-Hungary, convinced that the Serbian government was involved, believed that a strong response was imperative. They dispatched a special emissary to Berlin, where he was promised Germany's full support, and on July 23 they sent an ultimatum to Serbia. Meant to be unacceptable, it gave Serbia forty-eight hours in which to apologize, ban all anti-Austrian propaganda, and accept Austria-Hungary's participation in investigations of the plot against Francis Ferdinand.

Serbia replied with great tact, accepting all terms except those that diminished its sovereignty and offering to submit even these to arbitration. Great Britain proposed an international conference, to which France and Russia reluctantly agreed, and Germany hinted that Serbia and Austria-Hungary alone should settle the matter. Another crisis seemed about to pass when, on July 28, Austria-Hungary declared war on Serbia.

Stumbling into War   The system of alliances, increasing armament, bluster, and compromise had become a trap. Austria-Hungary was in fact not yet ready to fight. Germany and Great Britain still hoped the Austrians would limit themselves to occupying Belgrade and then agree to an international conference. But Russia could not be seen to abandon its role as protector of the Slavs nor let Austria-Hungary unilaterally extend its sway in the Balkans.

On July 29 Russia ordered partial mobilization, making clear that its move was aimed at Austria-Hungary only. The following day, however, the Russians discovered they lacked the organization for a partial call-up and so announced a general mobilization instead. On July 31 Germany proclaimed a state of readiness, sent Russia an ultimatum demanding demobilization within twelve hours, and requested France to declare what it would do in case of a Russo-German war.

France answered that it would act in its own interests and then mobilized but held its troops ten kilometers (about six miles) from the German frontier to prevent any incidents. The Germans, who had planned next to demand that France guarantee its neutrality by surrendering its border fortresses, were unsatisfied. On August 1 Germany mobilized and declared war on Russia. Convinced this step meant war on the Western front as well, Germany also invaded Luxemburg and sent an ultimatum to the Belgians demanding the unobstructed passage of German troops. On August 3 Germany declared war on France and invaded Belgium. The following day Great Britain declared war on Germany. Within forty-eight hours each nation had 2 million soldiers under orders. World War I had begun.

The Origins of World War   The question of what caused the Great War—or, more simply, who was to blame—would become an important issue in European affairs. Four years later the victors in that war blamed Germany so insistently that they would write its guilt into the peace treaty. Most

▲ **By 1912 this Krupp factory at Essen was devoted to the arms race that was consuming an increasing proportion of Europe's energy and wealth.**
Archiv für Kunst und Geschichte.

historians have considered that assessment to be one-sided. German scholars rejected it with special force, which explains the furor some forty years later (after another world war) that greeted the research of the German historian Fritz Fischer. He found evidence that Germany's leaders had, in fact, looked forward to war and nurtured almost boundless ambitions for military dominance. But the question remains without a final answer, for the causes adduced depend very much on how long-range a view one takes.

The immediate cause, the assassination of the archduke, almost did not happen. The tensions that made it so significant had deeper roots, however: in Balkan struggles for independence, in Austria-Hungary's declining power, and in each nation's fears for its safety. Human judgment was also involved, and individual leaders and governments can be blamed for Austria-Hungary's untoward haste in attacking Serbia, Germany's irresponsible support of Austria-Hungary, Russia's

clumsy and confused diplomacy, and France's eagerness to prove loyalty to the Russians. British leaders were at fault as well. Not wanting to admit that they were already attached to one side, they failed to warn the Germans that an attack on France meant war with Britain.

The Limits of Diplomacy Such an analysis, however, may make statesmen seem to have been more autonomous and therefore more to blame than they were. The system of alliances that was intended to achieve security had been hardened by habit, military imperatives, and domestic politics. The fear that cemented these commitments was related to Britain's conviction that empire required supremacy at sea; France's eagerness to revenge the defeat of 1870 and regain Alsace-Lorraine; Russia's 150 years of territorial expansion; Italy's need to show itself a great power; Austria's dependence, since Metternich, on foreign policy to sustain a shaky regime; and Germany's fear of encirclement and use of prestige abroad to reduce conflict at home.

The arms race itself contributed to the outbreak of war. In 1889 Great Britain had adopted the principle that its navy must equal in size the two next-largest fleets combined, and in 1906 it had launched the *Dreadnought*, the first battleship armed entirely with big guns. By 1914 Britain had 29 ships of this class afloat and 13 under construction. The German navy had 18, with 9 being built. The standing armies of France and Germany doubled between 1870 and 1914, and all able-bodied men had some military responsibilities from the age of twenty to their late fifties.

Strategy was a factor, too. Germany's victory over France in 1870 had been understood to prove the superiority of the Prussian system of universal conscription, large reserves, and detailed military planning. Furthermore, it was believed that technology gave an attacker overwhelming advantages. It took immense organization and many days to locate millions of reservists, get them to their proper units, equip them, and then effectively deploy them.

Mobilization, which in the eyes of some diplomats was a cumbersome but effective show of seriousness, was considered by military men in each country to be an essential act of self-defense. By 1914 it had become tantamount to war. Even slight disadvantages in numbers, weapons, speed, or tactics might prove fatal. Thus each increase in personnel and weapons was quickly matched, often with enormous effort; France, for example, had only 60 percent of Germany's potential manpower and yet equaled its rival through more burdensome conscription. The arms race, justified by the fear that it was meant to allay, fed on itself.

Public Opinion   Such expenditures of money and resources had to be justified to parliaments. Ultimately, these enormous forces, like foreign policy, rested on domestic politics. In every country

▼ Summer hats in the air, an August crowd in London's Trafalgar Square cheers the declaration of war on Austria, as it had a week earlier the announcement of war with Germany. Similar scenes occurred throughout that week of 1914 in France and Germany.
Bettmann.

▲ **In Berlin during August 1914, German volunteers march down the street hailing their good fortune; they will soon fight for their country.**
Ullstein.

flag-waving could win votes and nationalism seemed a way to overcome domestic divisions. Special interest groups associated with the military and imperialism and political groups fearful of socialist gains joined in dramatizing issues of national honor as a way to appeal to the masses. This pattern was especially strong in Germany, where economic growth and social change threatened the political system that preserved the dominance of Prussia and of the Junker class.

Few Europeans really wanted war; yet everywhere there was popular joy at its outbreak. After decades of economic, demographic, and imperial competition, after decades of threats and fears, armed conflict was almost a relief; and it generated a sense of unity and common purpose that was a welcome contrast with ordinary public life. In immediate terms, world war could have been avoided; in a larger sense, it was a product of the very structures it nearly annihilated.

II. The Course of the War

For decades European military staffs had prepared detailed plans for the situation they now faced. The French intended to drive into Alsace and Lorraine in coordinated dashes that reflected their almost mystic belief in the spirit of a patriotic offensive. German strategy began from the desire to avoid fighting on two fronts simultane-

ously: A detailed plan adopted years earlier called for assigning minimal forces to hold the Russians in the East and to slow the expected French attack in Alsace while Germany's main armies wheeled through Belgium and on to Paris. The German aim was to knock France out of the war before Russia could bring its massive armies into play and before British aid could make a difference. That strategy, which envisioned the German army as a coiled spring to be released the moment war began, required the invasion of neutral Belgium, further labeled Germany as the aggressor, and determined Britain's entry into the war.

THE SURPRISES OF THE FIRST TWO YEARS

In 1914 the belligerents all assumed the war could not last long. It was thought that modern economies, intricately connected by trade, would be unable to sustain a long conflict and that modern

▼ **MAP 27.2 WORLD WAR I, THE WESTERN FRONT**

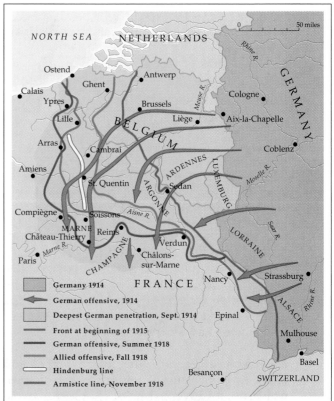

▲ **Newly mobilized French recruits pose in front of the flower-decked train that will carry them off to military duty.**
Tallandier.

weapons would make for brief wars of rapid movement (as in 1870). But in a few months it began to be clear that the war being fought was not the one planned, though commanders were slow to admit it. Increased firepower gave defensive forces unexpected strength. Cavalry was ineffectual, for rifles could now hit horses from great distances; infantry, loaded down with equipment, could not go far very rapidly; and the common soldier proved able to absorb more punishment than anyone had thought possible.

The German Offensive After making some slight gains, the French offensive in Alsace was stopped, with heavy losses on both sides. The Germans were

more nearly successful. The French command had underestimated by half the forces they would face at the outbreak of war, and in the first weeks the Germans drove to within thirty miles of Paris. But the German army was as battered as the defenders, its casualties as high, and its lines of communication and supply dangerously stretched.

These factors, added to unanticipated Belgian resistance, infuriated and worried German commanders; for their elaborate plans, first drawn up by Count Alfred von Schlieffen in 1891 and regularly modified thereafter relied on a different outcome. The Schlieffen plan was based on a series of assumptions: that there was no decisive strategic objective on the Eastern front (which proved true), that Russia would be slow to mobilize (less true than expected), and that modest German forces would therefore be sufficient to hold the Russians off while Germany gained an overwhelming advantage on the Western front by throwing two-thirds of its forces against the French (French forces, however, had grown larger and stronger in the decade before the war broke out).

The plan called for the German armies wheeling through northern France to capture Paris and knock France out of the war. For so great and quick a victory, the general staff was willing to violate Belgian and Dutch neutrality and leave the Eastern front largely to Austrian forces for which they had little respect. Despite initial successes, a number of things went slightly wrong. When a small British force arrived sooner than expected and Russian armies made unanticipated advances, the indecisive German chief of staff, Helmuth von Moltke (nephew of the field marshal who had led Germany to victory in 1866 and 1870), modified the Schlieffen plan. He ordered troops intended for the Western front to the East and sent extra forces to Alsace in hope of a breakthrough there. The German army cut east of Paris instead of running beyond it as planned. After each bloody encounter, the enemy retreated but

was not routed, and German officers were surprised they took so few prisoners.

Allied Offensives On the other side, the French commander in chief, Joseph Joffre, remained imperturbably confident of the ultimate success of a great French drive. In September the French launched a counteroffensive along the Marne River that saved Paris and hurled the Germans back to the natural defenses of the Aisne River. There, despite repeated Allied attacks, the Germans held. In the next few months the armies tried to outflank each other but succeeded only in extending the front northward to the sea. With changes of only a few miles, the battle lines that were established at the end of 1914 would remain those of the Western front for the next four years. France had not been knocked out of the war, but Germany held the important industrial and agricultural area of northeastern France, a tenth of its territory, and nearly all of Belgium.

On the Eastern front, Russian armies scored important gains in early August, taking eastern Galicia from Austria-Hungary and beginning an invasion of eastern Prussia in the north. Moltke talked in panic of a general retreat until the battle of Tannenberg late in August. There generals Paul von Hindenburg and Erich Ludendorff, who soon became Germany's greatest war heroes, surrounded and destroyed a Russian army and then pushed on almost to Warsaw before being stopped.

In the south, Austria-Hungary halted the Russian advance with German aid and took Belgrade despite the strong resistance of the Serbian army. By the end of 1914, Germany and Austria-Hungary had made impressive gains at every hand, and the entry of the Ottoman Empire on their side threatened Britain and France through the eastern Mediterranean all the way to Suez.

The War of Attrition On the Western front especially, the great armies found themselves bogged down in a terrifying kind of siege warfare. Artillery became increasingly important, and shells were fired at rates unimaginable a few months before, devastating the pockmarked land and making any movement difficult. Dug into trenches and clinging to pillboxes, neither side could be uprooted. Military units worked out complex systems of communication by laying ca-

▲ **The ruins of Verdun stood like a broken tombstone after the siege that bled both armies.**
AP/Wide World.

bles, building bridges, and maintaining roads and railways. For the first time, poison gas was used, but the German troops could not follow up the momentary gains their new weapon permitted (and the British were no more successful when they experimented with gas some months later).

Again and again, the Allied armies attempted to mount a great offensive, only to be stopped when German reinforcements arrived and with gains of only a few miles and hundreds of thousands of men lost. Battles were now numbered— the Second Battle of Ypres (April–May 1915), the Second Battle of Artois (May–June), the Second Battle of Champagne (September–November), the Third Battle of Artois (September–October)— and after a year's bloodshed, the Western front remained essentially the same.

Italy Joins the Allies Nothing broke the stalemate, neither desperate new offensives nor Italy's

entry into the war. Italy had announced its neutrality when war broke out, declaring the attack on Serbia an offensive action that did not meet the terms of the Triple Alliance. Both sides then negotiated with Italy; Britain and France could offer much more. In April 1915 Italy signed a secret agreement, the Treaty of London, and committed itself to the Allies, as the opponents of Germany and Austria-Hungary had come to call themselves. In return Italy was promised considerable territory along its border with Austria-Hungary, important Dalmatian islands, and expansion of its colonial holdings. Italy declared war in May and soon advanced to a line along the Isonzo River. Eleven battles would be fought along that line in the next two years.

Costly Offensives Early in 1916 the Germans launched another all-out offensive to knock France out of the war. They stormed the fortifica-

▲ MAP 27.3 TERRITORIAL GAINS, 1914–1919

tions at Verdun. Their aim, knowing the French would be determined to hold, was more to bleed the enemy than to take territory. For days shells poured down, and then the Germans attacked in overwhelming numbers. From February to July 1916 the fighting continued at full pitch. German forces captured two outlying forts, but the French managed a brief counterattack. Verdun held; and though the French losses, more than 300,000 men, weakened the subsequent Allied offensive, Germany casualties were only slightly less.

The Allied attack in the Battle of the Somme, from July to November, brought still heavier casualties and a maximum advance of seven miles.

The doctrine of the offensive, like general morale, was sinking in mud and gore. If tactics could not guarantee victory, then attrition, systematically exhausting men and resources, was the alternative.

There was more movement on the Eastern front but no decisive result. The Central Powers (Germany, Austria-Hungary, and the countries on their side) launched an offensive through Galicia in May 1915, drove forward a hundred miles, and followed that with a general offensive in July. By late September—while their new ally, Bulgaria, pushed into Serbia—the Central Powers were massed on a line from Riga in the north to the easternmost part of Hungary. Russia lost Poland and Lithuania.

▲ **Massive German forces cross the Schara river, the opening of the drive into Galicia in May 1915 that would carry the Central Powers into Russia.**
Archiv für Kunst und Geschichte.

The following year, however, in one of the few really well-conducted Russian campaigns, General Alexis Brusilov regained a large part of those losses. The effort cost Russia a million men and used up the capacity to do more. Although the Russian offensive brought Romania into the war on the Allied side, Austria-Hungary took Bucharest at the end of the year.

The Naval War   Naval strength, so significant to the arms race, proved more important in terms of supply lines than combat. The single large-scale attack by sea, the dramatic landing of Allied forces on the Gallipoli peninsula in April 1915, was a failure. The Allies were grateful to withdraw in December without having either opened the Dardanelles as a pipeline to Russia or forced the Ottomans out of the war.

Britain's naval blockade of Germany was more effective. As the blockade began to hurt, Germany countered in 1915 by announcing a submarine blockade of Britain; but the angry reaction of neutrals, led by the United States, forced them to abandon the tactic. The sinking of passenger ships—most sensationally the *Lusitania,* killing more than a thousand civilians—gave way in 1916 to attacks on armed merchant ships and then, in the face of American warnings, to the renunciation of "unlimited" submarine warfare.

Chronology

THE WESTERN FRONT, *1915 – 1916*

1915

Feb. 16–Mar. 30	Battle of Champagne, French attacks.
Apr. 22–May 25	Second Battle of Ypres, Germans gain, using gas, halt.
May 9–June 18	Second Battle of Artois, French short advance.
Sept. 22–Oct. 15	Second Battle of Champagne and Third Battle of Artois, broad Allied attack, limited gains.

1916

Feb. 21–July 11	Battle of Verdun, nearly 350,000 casualties on each side.
Aug. 29	Hindenburg and Ludendorff replace von Falkenhayn.
July 1–Nov. 18	Battle of the Somme, British lose about 400,000 men; French, 200,000; Germans nearly 500,000.
Dec. 12	Nivelle replaces Joffre as commander of French armies.

The one great naval battle of the war, at Jutland in May 1916, was indecisive. British and German fleets lost the same number of ships, though three British battle cruisers were sunk and only one German capital ship. The British retained a two-to-one naval superiority, however; and after Jutland the feared German fleet stayed in its harbors.

ADJUSTMENT TO TOTAL WAR

By every measure, this was war on an unprecedented scale, and adjustment to its demands strained the very fabric of society. The first response was national unity. The German parliament unanimously voted the funds for war, the public convinced that theirs was a just and defensive war. The French hailed their "sacred union," and a leading socialist joined the cabinet.

In Great Britain the Liberal government soon gave way to a coalition that included Conservatives, and in Russia the government seemed almost popular.

Domestic Mobilization There was also immediate dislocation. At first, factories closed and unemployment rose despite conscription; a labor shortage followed as war production became crucial. Everywhere agricultural output dropped, contributing to the food shortages of subsequent years. Prices rose rapidly and consumer hoarding further strained faltering systems of distribution. Just as the rules of warfare were bent or shattered by unlimited submarine warfare, poison gas, and a blockade that included consumer goods, so governments expanded their powers to move workers, censor the press, control railroads and shipping, and direct the economy. Unprepared for the ever greater amounts of ammunition and supplies required by the war, governments quickly learned to use paper money, rationing, and central planning.

In Great Britain the government requisitioned supplies and forced industry to new efficiency. Despite voluntary enlistments that raised the largest army in British history, it had to adopt conscription in 1916, a step Winston Churchill would call "the greatest revolution in our system since the institution of feudalism under William the Conqueror." Rebellion in Ireland that Easter was quickly put down; yet it was a serious diversion for British troops and a disturbing reminder of how cruelly war tested every weakness in the social structure.

Germany, deprived of critical raw materials, developed the most fully controlled economy of any of the combatants, under the brilliant direction of Walther Rathenau. Private firms were organized into sectors of production so that the most important could be favored, inefficient firms closed, and national planning enforced. The chemical industry created rubber substitutes, culled aluminum from local clays, manufactured fertilizers from nitrates in the air, and made textiles from wood pulp. Substitutes, which made ersatz an international word, included chestnut flour and clover meal used in the "war bread" that, like meatless days and conscription, soon made civilians feel the burden of all-out war.

In the first weeks of the fighting, France lost half of its iron ore and coal fields and more than half its heavy industry; yet as commissions established quotas and allocated supplies, production steadily increased. Although Joffre exercised virtually dictatorial powers and censorship was severe, the tradition of political dispute was in large part preserved. In France, as in Great Britain, civilian authority had begun to reassert itself by 1915.

Great Britain, France, and Germany adjusted effectively to the new challenge of fielding vast armies while increasing industrial production and maintaining intricate logistical networks. The Austro-Hungarian and Russian empires could not match these feats. Their industries were less well developed; supplies and trained personnel were often lacking. Equally important, neither government knew how nor dared try to squeeze from the economy the quantities of food, ammunition, and clothing that war required. Russian armies increasingly showed the effects of fighting ill-fed and ill-shod, with inadequate weapons and ammunition, and without good communication. (Orders to Russian troops were broadcast uncoded, and the German ability to intercept them contributed to Ludendorff's reputation as a great tactician.) In adversity, Austria-Hungary could not rely on the continued loyalty of subject peoples, and soldiers were carefully dispatched to zones far from their native lands so as not to be fighting against people who spoke their own language.

Social Effects By the winter of 1916–1917, the strains were visible to all. Everywhere on the bloodied continent, Europeans were thinner and more shabbily dressed, overworked, and grieved by the endless losses of husbands, sons, and homes. Poor crops and overloaded transportation systems further reduced the diet; this winter was Germany's "turnip winter," when the best organized of the domestic war economies could barely keep its people healthy. Society itself was subtly altered from the first month, when Belgian refugees poured into France, until years after the war. The strains of war were changing society. As the queue became a kind of public rite and rationing a way of life, distinctions of social class blurred. Each government awkwardly tried to restrict the consumption of alcohol and worried about rising rates of illegitimacy.

Women on the Home Front The role of women in the workplace took on added meaning. Women were essential in sustaining what was now called "the home front" while the men fought on the battle front, and even most feminists became active supporters of their nation's war effort. Though war propaganda reinforced traditional gender roles by emphasizing the enemy's brutality toward women and the maternal care that nurses provided the wounded, governments were soon eager for women to go to work. British women were asked in 1915 to take any jobs they could, and by 1917 the government denied contracts to employers unwilling to hire women (see "Meet the 'Khaki Girls,'" p. 960). Women went to work in the new munitions factories and other war-related industries that previously had employed only men. In every country, women left home and domestic service to work in industry, transportation, and business. The French government forbade hiring men for jobs that women could do; and the Krupp works, which had no women employees in 1914, counted 12,000 by 1917. In Great Britain, the number of women workers soared to 5 million by 1918. In the munitions industries especially, the number of women workers rose steadily to become one-third or more of the total. Women also ran farms, became firefighters and bus conductors, and worked in offices. On the front, they served as nurses.

Women's contributions outside the home were publicly acknowledged, and for some women wartime activities had brought increased independence. Women became more likely to live on their own and go out in public alone. Inevitably, questions arose about unequal pay and whether men might be permanently displaced, the debate over the proper role of women, which the suffrage movement had stimulated before the war, intensified.

Although general labor agitation remained below prewar levels, signs of growing discontent among workers had to be taken seriously. Trade unions were treated with new respect, and officials began to talk of the benefits to be granted after the war to those making such heavy sacrifices now. Even the kaiser spoke of ending the three-class voting system in Prussia and hinted at a government that would be responsible to parliament, while the House of Commons, in a notable reversal, declared its support in principle for women's suffrage. Meanwhile, month upon month of bloodshed in muddy, disease-filled trenches took a psychological as well as physical toll. Morale was sinking.

New Generals Having gained the initiative on the Eastern front, the Central Powers in December 1916 indicated their willingness to discuss a settlement; but the Allies' terms were wholly unacceptable. The war would continue, and the belligerents looked to new leaders. In France Joffre's intolerance of civilian leaders brought his downfall in December 1916; and he was replaced by the tactful and dashing General Robert Georges Nivelle, who planned a massive new offensive. This one, he promised, would break through German defenses.

In Germany two heroes of the Eastern front had been promoted. Hindenburg received overall command and with Ludendorff took charge of campaigns in the West in the fall of 1916. To destroy the shipping on which Britain depended, Germany returned to unlimited submarine warfare in January 1917. Aware that such a step might bring the United States into the war, the Germans calculated that Britain would have to sue for peace before American power could make a difference.

Political Changes The political changes were more revealing. Lloyd George, made minister of war in June 1916, became prime minister in December. Eloquent and energetic, once a radical orator who had terrified the upper classes, he now seemed the kind of popular and decisive leader who could galvanize the British war effort. After French morale hit a dangerous low, that country made the fiery Clemenceau premier again in November 1917.

Change came to Russia too—through revolution. In March 1917 the tsar was forced to abdicate, and a new provisional government proclaimed sweeping democratic reforms while promising to continue the war. Both sides knew that Russia was now more vulnerable than ever but that its immense resources had yet to be effectively tapped. For the Allies these changes in Russia gave the war itself new meaning. Now democracies, led by politicians with ties to the left, were fighting together against authoritarian

MEET THE "KHAKI GIRLS"

The two women who wrote this brief article, published in June 1917 in The Englishwoman, *a lady's magazine, present it as an upbeat account of the dedication of women workers, but it is also a document about class distinctions.*

"We got out of the tram and walked up the short, muddy path, past the sentry, who with fixed bayonet guards the entrance to A_3, the 'shop' in which we work. It was twenty minutes past two—ten minutes before the hour for the shift to begin—so there were plenty of our fellow-workers passing through the door. Among the three hundred girls employed on this shift there are not more than four of five lady-workers, so the crowd was made up of 'khaki girls', the colloquial name given to the industrial hands, originating from the fact that when women were admitted last July to the munition shops they wore khaki overalls, which since have been replaced for economical reasons by those made of black material.

"We had grown accustomed to the sight of the endless procession of girls pouring into the factory . . . all of the same type, rather wild, yet in their quieter moods giving an impression of sullen defiance, ready to answer you back if you should happen to tread on their very tender corns. So long, though, as you keep off those corns, and do not let these wayward creatures feel you are intruding nor provide yourself with anything which they have not, even though it be merely a newspaper to sit upon in preference to a dusty board, they will show their good nature to you—and they have plenty. Then there is their good humour and their gay spirits. No matter how strenuous the work, nor how wearing the hardships, they will always give out from this wonderful gaiety of spirits, and keep the ball rolling with their sense of humour—obvious and childlike—running as it does mostly to nicknaming, pelting the mechanics with orange peel, or skipping with a rope of steel shavings cut from the shell on the lathe.

"Every one of them carries a brown or green despatch-case. Most of them are flashily dressed: a cherry-coloured coat, a black-and-white check skirt, a satin blouse trimmed with swansdown, a hat, small in shape but too large to fit, so it drops over one eye, and down-trodden boots, is typical of what they wear. Some of them are exceedingly pretty; they are all heavily powdered, and in some cases rouged. Their hair is dressed with great care, and even if it does fall about their eyes it is not untidiness, but an effect purposely arranged by the aid of the small mirror—often a beautiful thing to look upon, either encrusted with shells or mounted on scarlet plush—carried in that despatch-case which is the essential part of a khaki girl's equipment, since it contains the food with which she is obliged to provide herself.

"We stood in the doorway a moment looking at the sun shining down upon the river. 'Do you think the Zeppelins will come tonight?' one of us said to the other. 'It will be a good night for them.' 'There's no moon.' 'Nor wind—and they were at Paris last night.'

"Then we went to our work, and the absorption of screwing plugs into shells, turning them on the lathe, taking them out and gauging them, working to exceed the standard number, swallowed up every other thought."

From Brenda Girvin and Monica Coxens, "Meet the 'Khaki Girls'" *The Englishwoman,* 1917.

governments. A war that involved the people more fully than any before it took on an ideological meaning. The Allies' sense of democratic purpose was strengthened in April when the United States—resentful that Germany was sinking its ships and making overtures to Mexico that included promises of the return of former Mexican lands now part of the United States—declared war on Germany.

THE GREAT TRIALS OF 1917–1918

In the fighting itself, neither new leaders nor shared ideals seemed to make much difference (see "Wilfred Owen Describes Trench Warfare," p. 962).

Fighting in the West On the Western front, Nivelle launched his great offensive in April and May 1917 despite multiple handicaps. The Germans

▲ In March 1917 women demonstrated in Petrograd, demanding that the rations of soldiers' families be increased.
VA/Sovfoto.

had strengthened their defenses; disagreements arose between the British and French commands; and some French troops, dispirited by two years of endless death on the same desolate terrain, mutinied, refusing to fight. The Second Battle of the Aisne and the Third Battle of Champagne took a toll as great as their predecessors and made even slighter gains. Nivelle was replaced by General Henri Philippe Pétain, the hero of Verdun, who began a concerted effort to raise morale, but it would be months before France dared another offensive.

The British went ahead with plans for an attack in the north, spurred by the desperate need to knock out at least some of the submarine bases from which German U-boats were sinking such enormous tonnages that the Admiralty openly wondered how many months Great Britain could last. The noise of battle could be heard in England, and hundreds of thousands of men fell, but the British fared no better in the Third Battle of Ypres (July–November) than the French had in their spring offensive. British morale, too, was shaken; yet stalemate continued. Germany's submarine warfare had come close to its goal, but Allied losses dropped to a tolerable level in mid-

1917 with the development of the convoy in which fleets of armed ships accompanied merchant vessels across the ocean. With America's entry into the war, the tonnage those convoys delivered grew still greater.

▼ Desolation surrounded weary Allied soldiers as they made their way across the mud on the battlefield at Ypres.
Imperial War Museum.

Wilfred Owen Describes Trench Warfare

Wilfred Owen's moving poems about World War I were published after he was killed in action in 1918, and they continue to be widely read. His first tour of duty had ended when he was sent home suffering from "shell shock." Some months later, he was back in France; and on January 4, 1917, he wrote his mother that "on all the officers' faces there is a harassed look that I have never seen before," adding, "I censored hundreds of letters yesterday, and the hope of peace was in every one of them." He was back in the fighting a few days later, when he wrote her this letter.

Tuesday, 16 January 1917
[2nd Manchester Regt, B.E.F.]
"My own sweet Mother,

" . . . I can see no excuse for deceiving you about these last 4 days. I have suffered seventh hell.

"I have not been at the front.

"I have been in front of it.

"I held an advanced post, that is, a 'dug-out' in the middle of No Man's Land.

"We had a march of 3 miles over shelled road then nearly 3 along a flooded trench. After that we came to where the trenches had been blown flat out and had to go over the top. It was of course dark, too dark, and the ground was not mud, not sloppy mud; but an octopus of sucking clay, 3, 4, and 5 feet deep, relieved only by craters full of water. Men have been known to drown in them. Many stuck in the mud & only got on by leaving their waders, equipment, and in some cases their clothes.

"High explosives were dropping all around us, and machine-guns spluttered every few minutes. But it was so dark that even the German flares did not reveal us.

"Three quarters dead, I mean each of us ¾ dead, we reached the dug-out, and relieved the wretches therein. I then had to go forth and find another dug-out for a still more advanced post where I left 18 bombers. I was responsible for other posts on the left but there was a junior officer in charge.

"My dug-out held 25 men tight packed. Water filled it to a depth of 1 or 2 feet, leaving say 4 feet of air.

"One entrance had been blown in & blocked.

"So far, the other remained.

"The Germans knew we were staying there and decided we shouldn't.

"Those fifty hours were the agony of my happy life.

"Every ten minutes on Sunday afternoon seemed an hour.

"I nearly broke down and let myself drown in the water that was now slowly rising over my knees.

"Towards 6 o'clock, when, I suppose, you would be going to church, the shelling grew less intense and less accurate: so that I was mercifully helped to do my duty and crawl, wade, climb and flounder over No Man's Land to visit my other post. It took me half an hour to move about 150 yards.

"I was chiefly annoyed by our own machine-guns from behind. The seeng-seeng-seeng of the bullets reminded me of Mary's canary. On the whole I can support the canary better.

"In the Platoon on my left the sentries over the dug-out were blown to nothing. One of these poor fellows was my first servant whom I rejected. If I had kept him he would have lived, for servants don't do Sentry Duty."

From Harold Owen and John Bell, (eds.), *Wilfred Owen: The Collected Letters*, Oxford University Press, 1967.

Allied Defeats: Russia and Italy Elsewhere the picture was different. On the Eastern front, Russian advances in July soon turned into almost constant retreat, and in November the communists gained control of the government. They invited all nations to join in peace without annexations or indemnities, then entered into independent negotiations with the Central Powers. The most populous of the Allies had been defeated.

Able now to engage more troops on the Italian front, Germany and Austro-Hungary launched a concentrated attack there in October, scoring an overwhelming victory at the Battle of Caporetto. Italy's armies collapsed as tens of thousands died, surrendered, or deserted. But the Italians regrouped along the Piave River; Britain and France rushed in reinforcements, and the Austro-German onslaught was slowed and then stopped.

Chronology
THE WESTERN FRONT,
1917 – 1918

1917

April 6 — United States declares war on Germany.

Apr. 9–20 — Battle of Arras; Second Battle of the Aisne; Third Battle of Champagne; major Allied assaults bring minimal gains.

May 15 — Pétain replaces Nivelle as mutinies break out in French army.

July 31–Nov. 10 — Third Battle of Ypres; British assault costs 400,000 casualties.

1918

Mar. 21–Apr. 5 — Great German offensive, major gains, finally checked.

Mar. 26 — Foch named commander of all Allied armies in France.

May 27–June 6 — Third Battle of the Aisne, major German attack, initial gains, then slowed; first major engagement of American troops.

July 15–Aug. 7 — Second Battle of the Marne, German attack and Allied counterattack, Germans forced back over Marne.

Sept. 26–Oct. 15 — Battle of Argonne; Fourth Battle of Ypres; slow Allied advance.

Nov. 11 — Armistice.

The Last Year Although the Russians stopped fighting in February 1918, the Central Powers did not. Their eastward march ended only with the Treaty of Brest Litovsk, signed in March. Russia surrendered Russian Poland, the Baltic provinces, the Ukraine, and Transcaucasia. Germany had acquired invaluable wheat and oil and a respite on one front when it needed them most. But merely patrolling such immense gains required great numbers of badly needed troops, and the incredibly harsh terms of the treaty stiffened resistance elsewhere. Both Lloyd George and President Wilson now stated formal war aims that expressed their confidence in victory and put revolutionary emphasis on the right to self-government.

On the Western front, the Germans, their reserves of personnel and resources nearing exhaustion, opened a great offensive. Attacking sector after sector from March through June, they made the greatest advances seen there in four years. It was a triumph of careful strategy, improved tactics, heavy artillery, and gas. To correct the weakness of divided command, the Allies named General Ferdinand Foch supreme commander of all their forces; and they retained their reserves while the Germans exhausted theirs. Enemy guns once more bombarded Paris before the Allied counteroffensive began in July. Slowly, then faster, the Germans were driven back over the familiar and devastated landscape. By the end of August, German armies had retreated to the Hindenburg line. The Allies continued their push in battles of the Argonne and Ypres in September and October, gaining inexorably even if less rapidly than hoped or expected.

The Collapse of the Central Powers On other fronts the Central Powers collapsed dramatically. In the Middle East Turkish and German troops were defeated by British and Arab forces led by T. E. Lawrence, whose exploits became part of the romantic lore in which this war was poorer than most. In October the sultan was deposed, and a new government sued for peace. Combined Serbian, French, British, and Greek forces under French leadership drove up the Balkan Peninsula. Bulgaria surrendered at the end of September, and the Allies moved toward Romania.

Czech, Yugoslav, Romanian, and Polish movements for independence, encouraged by the Allies, gained strength throughout 1918. The Austro-Hungarian Empire was disintegrating. Austria-Hungary attacked once more on the Italian front but withdrew after heavy losses. Its armies, defeated at Vittorio Veneto at the end of October, began simply to dissolve as the various nationalities left for home and revolution. Czechoslovakia and the kingdom later called Yugoslavia both declared their independence. In November Austria-Hungary surrendered unconditionally to the Italians.

At the end of September, Ludendorff had demanded that Germany seek an armistice, but that required political changes as well. Twice in 1917 Kaiser William II had promised to make his cabinet subject to a majority in the Reichstag; and in October 1918, he appointed Prince Max of Baden as chancellor to begin this transformation from above. Ludendorff resigned his command at the end of October, and Germany asked for peace on the terms of President Wilson's Fourteen Points. But Wilson now insisted on the evacuation of occupied territories and a democratic German government with which to negotiate.

The German Republic Accepts an Armistice While German leaders hesitated, they faced the threat of revolution at home. A liberal believer in parliamentary government, Prince Max represented a compromise that might have worked earlier but now could not in the face of uprisings in the name of peace, democracy, and socialism. Germany threatened to break apart. Prince Max pleaded with William to abdicate and, when revolt spread to Berlin, simply announced that the kaiser had done so. William II abdicated on November 9 after a mutiny in the German fleet and revolution in Munich. The government was handed over to Friedrich Ebert, the leader of the Social Democrats; a German Republic was proclaimed and an armistice commission sent to meet with Foch. The commission agreed to terms on November 11. By then Allied troops were approaching German borders in the West and had crossed the Danube in the East, taken Trieste on the Adriatic, and sailed through the Dardanelles. In the meantime, revolution was sweeping across central Europe.

THE EFFECTS OF WORLD WAR I

The war itself had some of the effects of revolution. Even among the Allies, it had forced such changes that no one could be sure what postwar society would be like.

The New State of Affairs To the east of Germany, new regimes and sometimes whole new nations replaced the defeated states. In Germany itself, radical groups staged a number of local revolts, creating an air of instability sustained by *Frei-*

korps ("free corps"), mercenary squads made up of former soldiers available to any movement that could pay them for street fighting and marauding. Throughout central Europe political conflict adopted the techniques of force. The victorious governments, having shown the capacity to mobilize society for war, would now be held more responsible than in the past for society's peacetime needs, as evidenced in a spate of postwar legislation on housing, education, and pensions. Clemenceau, Lloyd George, and Wilson, the spokesmen of victory, had all been vigorous reformers; but now they watched with apprehension the revival of the radical left.

Life in wartime had affected social classes differently. Even where there was no open revolution, the aristocracy and other traditional elites had been weakened by the general democratization of political life and by the decline in purchasing power that resulted from inflation, reduction in the value of land, and increased taxes (especially in England). A middle class confident in 1914 found itself exposed and vulnerable after the war, its savings threatened, its possibilities limited, its values challenged. Those on salary or fixed income suffered more from inflation than those on workers' wages; middle-class life became less lavish, and there were fewer servants (some 400,000 English women left domestic service in the course of the war). Workers, particularly the skilled, were on the whole relatively well off. Although rates of pay usually lagged behind inflation, the years of full employment and more jobs for women had increased family income; and trade unions used their greater influence to maintain shorter hours and higher pay. Peasants, though declining in number, were also often better off, helped by the demand for food and by inflation, which made it easier to pay off their debts.

Social Mores Even ordinary manners and dress were different. Gentlemen, forced to use public transportation, had abandoned their top hats; women's clothes grew simpler and their skirts shorter. Women of the working class took to wearing cosmetics and high-heeled shoes and smoking and drinking in public, as did their middle-class sisters. Such changes in customs, even more than the increase in violent crime and juvenile delinquency, shocked moralists who associated them with casual encounters between the sexes, increased illegitimacy, and the popularity of dance halls.

Public appearance thus added to the economic and political disruptions of wartime in suggesting a new openness and uncertainty, a more fluid society in which old standards could not be recaptured. Millions of refugees constituted more tangible displacement, and millions of other Europeans (especially peasants and women) were not eager to return to their old way of life. Of course most people more or less did, and by the 1920s prewar constraints of class and gender were largely back in place, despite some relaxation.

The psychological impact of war, harder to demonstrate than the social changes, may have been just as important. Throughout society, there was a tendency following the war to expect instability. Intellectuals suffered what one historian has called "minds scorched by war"; and among the populace, a cynical distrust of leaders and institutions seems to have spread after years of wartime promises. There was a cleavage, too, between those who had fought and those who stayed home, those whose lives were transformed and those who had more nearly maintained business as usual. Bitterness about these inequalities of sacrifice surfaced in public denunciations of war profiteers and in a more inflammatory political rhetoric. At the same time, with a kind of selective nostalgia, many regretted the loss of that sense of common purpose and national unity that war had brought, and some even yearned again for the thrill of combat.

Economic Effects   Military needs had stimulated the rapid development of certain technologies. When World War I began, the cavalry was a major element of every army, pack horses and horse-drawn wagons the principal form of transport from rail lines to the front. By war's end, the practical importance of automobiles and airplanes, radio, and the chemical industry had become clear to all. In many factories the effort to speed up industrial production altered the nature of work as tasks were reorganized in ways thought to be

▼ It would take years to recover from the damage to roads and bridges and private housing in Belgium and northeastern France. The French village of Craonne, where Napoleon once won a battle and which was the scene of fighting in 1917 and 1918, looked like this in 1919.
Roger-Viollet.

more rational and efficient but that workers found increasingly impersonal and demanding.

Although some sectors of the economy gained from their wartime importance, the overall losses were dramatic. World trade had been disrupted and Europe's place in it transformed. In 1914 Europe was the world's greatest lender of money; in 1918 its nations were debtors. The physical destruction of property, aside from the billions lost in war matériel, was greatest in Belgium and France. In France alone, thousands of bridges and factories as well as a million buildings were destroyed. Total European production in the 1920s would fall below the level of 1913.

The Dead and Wounded   The effects of the war required enormous adjustments from individuals, institutions, and society as a whole. So did the war's simplest accomplishment: the killing of 10 to 13 million people, perhaps one-third of them civilians. Moreover, for every soldier who died, two or three were wounded; millions were maimed for life. The casualty figures tell much about the history of the first third of the twentieth century. Among the armed forces, casualties ran about 50 percent for the major combatants except France, which suffered higher losses. Able to mobilize some 7 percent of its population, Russia could only estimate fatalities. Germany mobilized some 16 percent and France, 19 percent. In each country whole classes from the elite schools were virtually wiped out. For France, with its older population and low birthrate, the war was a demographic catastrophe in which a large part of an entire generation disappeared on the Western front. And throughout Europe, the one-armed, the one-legged, and the blind would live on, supported by pensions and performing menial tasks, in silent testimony to the cost of total war.

With all these losses before them, the leaders of exhausted nations sat down to make a lasting peace. The gigantic effort that victory required had increasingly been fueled by the vision of a better world in which governments would use their enhanced powers to ensure greater justice and fuller democracy. With Wilson as its moralistic voice, democracy—meaning popular participation in public life and opportunity for all—seemed a guarantee of peace. And democracy, Wilson urged, would put an end to the old secret diplomacy that

▼ MILITARY FATALITIES IN WORLD WAR I (MAJOR POWERS)	
Germany	1,900,000
Russia	1,700,000
France	1,400,000
Austria-Hungary	1,200,000
British Empire	900,000
Ottoman Empire	700,000
Italy	600,000
United States	100,000

juggled spheres of influence and national interests without regard for public opinion.

III. The Peace

From the Rhine to Russia so many governments were new and so many boundaries undecided that, by default as well as victory, the Allies seemed free to construct the new Europe of peaceful democracies their wartime statements had foreshadowed. Instead, the diplomats assembled at the Peace Conference in Paris found their task complicated by the very extent of victory and beset by more interests than they could satisfy. So great an opportunity and so grand an undertaking fed the extremes, first of hope, then of disillusionment. Meanwhile, away from Paris, more direct means were being used to shape the postwar world.

THE REVOLUTIONARY SITUATION

The revolution in Russia was the most important of the revolutions that resulted from World War I, but there were many others. Among the defeated nations, only Bulgaria's government survived. From Asia Minor to Ireland, nationalist movements sought to capture power.

Eastern Europe   The peoples suddenly released from Habsburg and Russian rule fought to define the boundaries of their new nations. In the Baltic lands, Lithuanian, Estonian, and Latvian republics marked their independence by war with Russia. Lithuania was also at odds with the new republic of Poland; and Poland faced conflict on all its other borders—against Russians, Ukranians, Czechs, and Germans. The creation of Czechoslovakia and the new kingdom of Yugoslavia led to renewed warfare as Hungary attacked Czechoslovakia, while in the Balkans Romania attacked both Hungary and Yugoslavia, just the kind of hostility that had preceded World War I.

Russia's communists had good reason then to hope that revolution would sweep from East to West, and Marxists throughout Europe looked to the miraculous events in Russia as the beginning of the socialist future they had so long imagined. In March 1919 delegates from a score of countries met in Moscow to establish the Third International. Communists were active in the Baltic states, and in 1919 Lenin's friend Béla Kun led a communist government in Hungary until Romanian armies ended his brief reign. There was also communist agitation in Vienna, where the provisional government of truncated Austria, all that was left of the Habsburg Empire, looked forward to union with the new German republic.

Marxists, however, had long set their eyes on highly industrialized Germany, finding revolutionary promise in its class tensions and strong socialist movement. Germany's defeat and a shaky new German republic appeared the fulfillment of old portents. In January 1919 a communist revolt broke out in Berlin, and in the following spring another uprising managed for a few weeks to make Bavaria a Soviet republic. Both were quickly defeated by remnants of the German army. Russia remained the center of the communist world.

THE PEACE TREATIES

President Wilson's Fourteen Points had won acceptance as a basis for defining a new European order. The points dealt mainly with territorial adjustments but idealistically proclaimed the self-determination of peoples to be a matter of policy. Wilson's call for free trade and open seas had long been part of the liberal canon. His attention to the dangers of colonial warfare, the need for disarmament, and the benefits of open diplomacy was more radical but echoed the common belief that such policies would have averted world war. Wilson's final point, and the one closest to his heart, called for a League of Nations to guarantee the safety of all. The American president's talk of "impartial justice," a "peace that will be perma-

nent," and covenants that will be "sacredly observed" caught the imagination of the world.

The Paris Conference At the Paris Peace Conference, which opened in January 1919, all parties agreed not to repeat the mistakes of the Congress of Vienna a century earlier. No defeated nations would take part in the early discussions; no German Talleyrand would divide the Allies. The atmosphere was one of sober business, organized around commissions of expert advisers. Thirty nations had joined the Allies, at least formally,[2] but the major decisions would be taken by the five big powers: France, the United Kingdom, Italy, Japan, and the United States.

In practice, since most questions did not directly concern Japan, primary authority resided in four men: Clemenceau, Lloyd George, Premier Vittorio Orlando, and Wilson. Disagreements among the Big Four soon became the center around which the negotiations turned. All were elected leaders, sensitive to public opinion, faced with grave domestic problems, and worried by the turmoil in central and Eastern Europe. Experienced politicians, they knew they had to hurry.

The Treaty with Germany To settle by May the complicated terms for peace with Germany was a remarkable achievement. Haste itself probably made the treaty more severe than it might otherwise have been. Commissions, assuming their proposals would be subject to later bargaining, tended to begin with maximum terms, but these were often simply written into the treaty itself.

The territorial provisions were not extremely harsh. Germany lost territory and colonies but remained a great state. Except for Alsace-Lorraine, however, the new boundaries were a source of continuing difficulties. France did not get the left bank of the Rhine as it had wanted. Instead, the Allies were to occupy the Rhineland for fifteen years; and the coal-producing regions along the Saar River, while remaining under German sovereignty, would be supervised by France until a later plebiscite by universal suffrage determined the final disposition. Plebiscites would also decide

---

[2] The newly created nations of Yugoslavia, Czechoslovakia, and Poland were treated as Allies; the new republics of Austria, Hungary, and Germany as the defeated Central Powers.

whether Germany surrendered part of Schleswig to Denmark and part of upper Silesia to Poland.

The Polish provinces of eastern Prussia, where Germans formed about 40 percent of the population, were immediately ceded to Poland. That created the controversial Polish corridor to the sea, which awkwardly separated eastern Prussia from the rest of Germany. Although a majority of the population within the corridor was Polish, its outlet was the German port city of Danzig, restored to its ancient status as a free city. Poland would always feel insecure with an arrangement the Germans never accepted.

Germany was to have no large artillery, submarines, or military air force, and no more than 100,000 men under arms—requirements that would have been less controversial if they had led to the general disarmament the treaty implied. The lists of matériel Germany had to deliver to the Allies were more punitive: horses and railway carriages, quantities of coal, most of its present ships, and some new vessels to be specially built. The required reparations were more burdensome still.

Reparations   Despite fine talk of not requiring an indemnity, the Allies declared that Germany should pay for civilian damages. The claims of Belgium, a neutral attacked without warning, were easily justified; and Clemenceau could argue that the most destructive fighting had occurred in Belgium and France. But Lloyd George had campaigned on a platform of making Ger-

▼ When Woodrow Wilson paraded through the streets, Parisians cheered the representative of a new democratic era as well as an ally in victory.
The Granger Collection.

▲ MAP 27.4 TERRITORIAL SETTLEMENTS, 1919–1926

many pay. He insisted, over American objections, on including Allied military pensions as civilian costs. Pandora's box was opened. Germany was made liable for sums unspecified and without foreseeable end and was forced to accept "responsibility" for losses from a war "imposed . . . by the aggression of Germany and her allies." The "war guilt clause" became a subject of controversy

▲ **The Treaty of Versailles was signed by elected political leaders in the Hall of Mirrors at Versailles and presented as a great public event, in self-conscious contrast to the Congress of Vienna a century earlier.**
National Portrait Gallery, Smithsonian Institution, Washington/Art Resource.

in every country and a source of bitter resentment, official and private, in every part of Germany.

In German eyes, the treaty was an intolerable *Diktat*; German delegates had no chance to discuss until it was already drafted, when only minor objections were accepted. Faced with these terms, the German government resigned, and the parliament at first rejected the treaty's stipulation of German guilt. But when the Allies held firm, parliament angrily acquiesced. The treaty was signed on June 28, 1919, the fifth anniversary of the assassination at Sarajevo, in the Hall of Mirrors at Versailles, where Bismarck and Kaiser Wilhelm I had announced the German Empire forty-eight years before. The symbolism was complete.

Italian Aims For the Big Four, Italy's expectations were especially difficult, and Italian insis-

tence on them particularly irksome. The Treaty of London of 1915 had promised Italy much of the Slavic-speaking lands of the Dalmation coast, and the Italian delegates expected to get them. Wilson was determined to prevent further violations of the principle of nationality beyond allowing Italy, for strategic reasons, to have the Tyrol south of the Brenner Pass through the Alps, although that former Austrian land was German-speaking.

Using a press interview, Wilson in effect spoke directly to the Italian people, asking them to reject the position taken by their representatives at the conference. The Italian delegation withdrew in protest, to a great outpouring of nationalist feeling at home. Eventually, Italy was given the Istrian Peninsula and some islands but not Dalmatia. For years to come, resentment over the promises not kept at Paris would be a disruptive issue in Italian domestic politics.

The Other Treaties With the signing of the Treaty of Versailles, the Big Four dispersed, leaving the details of the remaining settlements to their foreign offices. The treaty with Austria in September was closely modeled on the treaty with Germany; but reparations and demilitarization, including naval restrictions, hardly seemed appropriate for the shaky little landlocked Austrian republic. Boundaries for the other new states were settled on the basis of nationality in some cases and strategic needs in others.

Treaties with Bulgaria in November and with Hungary in June 1920 gave Bohemia to Czechoslovakia on historical grounds, while Hungarian claims to a larger historical kingdom were largely ignored. Hungary lost almost three-quarters of its former lands. Although Bulgaria surrendered relatively little territory, resentment over its borders was also great. Every state of Eastern Europe could cite some injustice it had suffered, usually with exaggerated statistics and with tales, too often true, of inhumane treatment. Railways, economic ties, "natural" boundaries, historical claims, and nationality simply did not coincide. It would fall to the new League of Nations to make these arrangements work.

Much remained to negotiate. The fate of many territories was determined later, sometimes by plebiscite. The promise of just treatment for minorities, an expression of the Allies' decent intent, would confront the sensitivity of new states about protecting their sovereignty. Many of the arrangements were just not workable. The reparations required from Austria-Hungary, for example, were divided among the new states carved out of the former Habsburg Empire, which left some of them paying reparations to others, a perpetual source of dissension.

The Middle East   The final treaty, with Turkey, was not signed until August 1920, and much of it never went into effect. The Allies' aims had been contradictory all along, and the postwar situation spawned indigenous movements in the former Ottoman Empire as complex and uncontrollable as those in Eastern Europe. The Russian and Habsburg empires no longer competed for influence there, and the Soviet government's release of earlier secret Allied plans for partitioning the Ottoman Empire reinforced suspicions that Britain and France were more commited to an old imperialism than to any new arrangements.

A nationalist revolt in Turkey had brought the reforming Mustafa Kemal to power, and he succeeded in ensuring Turkey's territorial integrity. Arabia's independence was also recognized, although internal conflict there created further opportunities for European influence. The pressing need to create political order on the eastern shores of the Mediterranean was met by a solution defined as temporary. France was to have a supervisory authority in Syria; and a vaguely defined area—carved from Palestine, Trans-Jordan, and Iraq—would be subject to British authority. Aside from recognizing the presence of Britain and France in the Middle East, the treaty settled little, and lasting boundaries would be determined only through the conflicts and diplomacy of the next few years.

British intentions in separating Palestine from Trans-Jordan were especially confusing. Anti-imperialist sentiment was especially strong in the Middle East, where it was often connected to Islam. During the war, the European powers had competed with each other in showing sympathy for the region's nationalist movements; and the Allies had encouraged Arab nationalism. In 1917 the British foreign secretary, Arthur Balfour, had also promised that a "national home" for Jews would be created in Palestine. In accord with the propaganda and humanitarian concern of that difficult year, the Balfour Declaration also guaranteed the rights of Muslims. In short, British intentions for Palestine remained uncertain, and their subsequent statements provided little clarification.

Colonial Mandates   In their effort to codify French and British interests, these arrangements did lead to an important innovation. Colonial territories were declared "mandates" of the League of Nations and assigned to classes. The parts of the Ottoman Empire newly placed under British or French rule were Class A mandates, states considered on the verge of self-government. Most of the reassigned African territories (primarily former German colonies) were Class B mandates, ones in which European rules were to guarantee freedom of religion, prohibit trade in liquor and arms, refrain from subjecting natives to military training, and encourage commerce. Class C mandates were primarily Pacific islands, to be ruled essentially as colonies.

In every case, the mandate power had to submit annual reports to the League of Nations for review. Like much else in the treaties, the system of mandates can be seen both as an expression of conscience toward the rest of the world and as a device for absorbing former German colonies while legitimating continued European dominance.

Europe's Diminished Position   Taken together, all these arrangements confirmed Europe's importance in world affairs and the dominance of Britain and France among the European powers. Yet these provisions also reflected changes in Europe's position. The French and British could take pride in the contributions of wealth and people they had received from their empires, but imperialism was weakened by the war. Its assumptions and ideals were under challenge around the world, and the very system of mandates was a response to widespread criticism of European rule. The independence of former colonies was now recognized as an official and desirable goal. China and Siam (Thailand) had been able during the war to eliminate many of the treaties that had granted special rights to European states, and powerful movements in India, South Africa, Madagascar, and Egypt were demanding self-government.

Economically, while Europe had been enormously weakened, its suppliers (including countries with a single valuable crop, like Chile or Cuba) had prospered. The two that benefitted most were Japan and the United States. Japan sold munitions and weapons to the belligerents, especially Russia, and quickly replaced German traders throughout East Asia. American production reached new heights in sector after sector (steel production doubled); and by war's end the United States had a huge new merchant fleet. The United States, increasingly willing to intervene in South America, economically, politically, and militarily, now dominated that continent while its financiers directed the flow of world capital.

In the conflict everyone called "The Great War," the battles that mattered most had all taken place in Europe, but it had been a world war in the sense that its effects were felt around a globe that was getting smaller. The improved communications that carried supplies more rapidly across the seas (the Panama Canal opened in 1914) and on railroads from Japan to Russia and across Africa (the railroad from the Cape of Good Hope to Cairo was completed in 1918) also opened the possibility of communications and trade independent of Europe.

Disillusionment Not since 1848 had liberal conceptions so thoroughly dominated European politics. There was much to hope for in the call for self-determination and plebiscites, the League of Nations, the system of colonial mandates, and the establishment of representative regimes throughout central Europe. By 1920, however, the limitations of what had been accomplished at Paris were all too apparent. Many of the agreements reached there reflected a cold assertion of national interest and a realistic appraisal of power, but the Allies had propagandized standards of high principle and injected ideology into international affairs.

Living in a time of revolutionary changes that they largely welcomed, the leaders who forged the peace were not revolutionaries. They never managed to find a place for Russia at the conference. They took little account of the social and economic complexities of Eastern Europe. Believers in democracy, they were baffled by the turmoil it created. They stimulated nationalist movements but recognized the dangers of nationalism. Slogans that sounded radical in November 1918 gave

way to frightened insistence on order a few months later. None of the leaders of democracy yet fully understood how much had changed.

Disillusionment came quickly. In March 1920 the Senate of the United States rejected the treaties for the final time. Having claimed moral leadership, America would in the end not enter the League of Nations. In the process, it added France to the list of aggrieved states, for France had abandoned demands that Germany be weakened further in return for a joint guarantee against German aggression from the United States and Great Britain, which it did not get. China refused to sign the treaties because of terms that gave Japan, in addition to other gains, extensive rights in China. Japan was offended by the conference's rejection of a formal declaration that all races are equal.

The reparations were denounced in a brilliant and influential pamphlet in which the English economist John Maynard Keynes castigated the Carthaginian peace the victors had exacted.[3] He argued that the Allies owed one another more money than Germany could pay and that reparations would merely slow Europe's economic recovery. His analysis helped undermine confidence in the terms of peace, but his prescriptions—cancellation of international war debts and recognition that the international economic system was essentially artificial—were as utopian in their way as any of Woodrow Wilson's points. Keynes's criticisms, like those that for decades would ring from party platforms in every country, tended to exaggerate how much of the postwar world could be shaped by worried statesmen quarreling in Paris.

IV. Postwar Democracy

From Finland to the Balkans, most of the states of Eastern Europe were new, and most of them had democratic constitutions. The disappearance of the Russian, Austrian, and Ottoman empires opened the way for systematic modernization us-

---

[3] John Maynard Keynes, *The Economic Consequences of the Peace*, 1920; and the famous rebuttal, Etienne Mantoux, *The Carthaginian Peace: Or the Economic Consequences of Mr. Keynes*, 1946. The reference is to the harsh peace terms that Roman senators demanded upon the defeat of Carthage in the Third Punic War, 149–146 B.C.

ing the administrative institutions and practices they left behind. There were hopeful signs. Schools, for example, were built by the thousands and functioned fairly effectively despite issues of language and nationality. But stability was threatened by economic, social, and ethnic conflict.

THE NEW GOVERNMENTS

Economic Issues New tariff barriers interrupted trade that had flowed more freely within the former empires, compounding the dislocations of war and the burden of reparations. Extensive help from the new League of Nations proved essential as growing populations, widespread illiteracy, and lack of capital plagued economic development. Only Austria and Czechoslovakia had advanced industries that could compete in European markets; elsewhere, land remained the central economic issue.

Independence brought the eviction of "foreign" landlords, the breakup of large estates in the Baltic countries, and land reform in Bulgaria, Romania, and Czechoslovakia. These measures, less effective than expected, fostered accusations in each region of special treatment for favored nationalities. In Poland and still more in Hungary (where 40 percent of the peasants were landless and 90 percent held less than 3 hectares, or 7.4 acres), the great estate owners of the aristocracy succeeded in protecting their interests.

Ethnic Conflict The resulting resentments favored peasant parties, soon dominant in Eastern Europe, which tended to combine agrarian radicalism with distrust of urban values, of modernizing changes, and of parliaments. Social conflicts were reinforced by ethnic and religious differences. The German minorities in Poland, Czechoslovakia, Hungary, and Bulgaria were generally among the resented well-to-do. Town-country antagonisms often put the rural Slovaks at odds with the Czechs of industrialized western Czechoslovakia. Antisemitism was especially virulent in Poland and Romania, where it was partly an expression of rural hostility toward village money lenders and urban values. In Yugoslavia the claims of Greek Orthodox Serbians to be the "national" people angered the Roman Catholic Croatians and Slovenes. Macedonians—their home-

land divided among Yugoslavia, Greece, and Bulgaria—agitated in all three countries and produced chaotic insurrection in Bulgaria from 1923 to 1925.

Such circumstances encouraged military intervention in politics, as in the new Greek republic and in the authoritarian rule in Hungary of Admiral Miklós Horthy, regent for an empty throne, who abolished the secret ballot in rural areas. But most of the governments of Eastern Europe worked more or less within their constitutions; and Czechoslovakia, under President Tomás Masaryk and Foreign Minister Eduard Benes, became a model of the order, freedom, and prosperity that democracy was supposed to bring.

The Weimar Republic The German provisional government had been established just in time to sign the armistice. Its officials referred proudly to the German "revolution" and promulgated decrees promising democracy, freedom of speech, a return to the eight-hour workday, and improvements in social security. Frightened of a communist revolution, the government quickly reached an accommodation with the army, which was already encouraging the legend that it had not lost the war but had been stabbed in the back by politicians and radicals at home. General Wilhelm Groener, who replaced Ludendorff as Hindenburg's principal

▼ Friedrich Ebert took the oath of office as provisional president of Germany in February 1919; note the absence of men in uniform.
Keystone/Ullstein.

aide, promised to assist the government provided it would not meddle in the army's affairs.

President Ebert accepted those terms; and when an uprising of left-wing Marxists, the Spartacists, gained control of most of Berlin in January 1919, the army crushed the revolt and shot its leaders. Lenin's best hope for a communist revolution in Germany died with them. One of those murdered was Rosa Luxemburg, who had drafted the Spartacist platform calling for a proletarian revolution. An effective leader and impressive intellectual, she had urged the Spartacists to avoid useless violence and had recognized that most workers remained loyal to Ebert's social democratic government. But she would not abandon her party when hotter heads chose armed conflict. Her death was a lasting blow to the radical left, and the government's reliance on the army a blow to Germany's new democracy.

Committed democrats nevertheless, Germany's new leaders held elections in January 1919 for a constituent assembly. It met in Weimar, with nearly three-quarters of the delegates intent on installing a republic. They wrote a thoroughly democratic constitution that joined proportional representation to universal suffrage. The president, directly elected for a seven-year term, would nominate the chancellor, or prime minister, who would have to be approved by the Reichstag. The Reichsrat, the upper house, would still represent the single states but with reduced powers. In the new Germany, government would be responsible to parliament, minorities would be fairly represented, the aristocracy would hold no political privilege, and civil rights and private property would be guaranteed. With women voting, the Social Democrats in power, and a broad spectrum of parties, German politics was launched on a new course.

German Inflation   The gravest problem of these years was inflation. Early in 1923 French and Belgian forces occupied the Ruhr district following Germany's failure to make the coal deliveries required as reparations. The local populace responded with passive resistance, a kind of general strike that made the occupation fruitless. The resulting dislocation and scarcity drastically accelerated the already serious inflation. The German government, which from 1920 on found it

▲ **By November 1923 German children could play with their nation's worthless paper money.**
Archiv für Kunst und Geschichte.

easier to print more money than to raise taxes, continued that practice in 1923 as its expenses rose (it provided payments to the striking workers of the Ruhr) and its revenues declined.

The German mark, valued at 4 to 1 U.S. dollar in 1914 and 9 to 1 in 1919, was exchanged at 500 to 1 by 1922. Its subsequent fall was cataclysmic. One dollar was worth 18,000 marks in January 1923; 350,000 marks in July; nearly 5,000,000 in August; and inflation accelerated after that. New money was run off the presses at top speed, and old notes with additional zeros printed on them were rushed to the banks before they, too, became valueless. Prices changed within hours, always upward. By November a newspaper could sell for nearly 100 billion marks (see "German Inflation," p. 975).

By the end of the year a restructuring was begun. The government imposed stringent new fi-

GERMAN INFLATION
◆

The German statistical office published this description of the effects of inflation in 1923. Obviously concerned that foreigners did not understand how bad the effects of inflation were, the account also expresses the rising insecurity of the middle class.

"The greater part of the population has been forced down far below their old standard of living, even with regard to the most important necessities of life.

"Consequently the foreigner, for example, who has visited Germany since the war, would do well to ask himself whether, in the overcrowded first-class railway carriages, he has found many Germans, or whether in the best seats at the theatre Germans are in the majority. He would do well to inquire whether in fashionable places of entertainment the German or the foreign public predominates, and if he does see Germans present spending their money for light entertainment, let him consider whether these are the majority of the German people. He must not forget either that many people today are influenced by the psychological fact that saving is no longer of any use: 100 marks today will perhaps be only 50 marks tomorrow. He who before the war, for example, had saved 5,500 marks could purchase for that amount furniture for a middle-class flat of three rooms as well as clothing, for a married couple with two children. In the middle of February 1923 (with an average dollar rate of 27,819 for February) the same person, for the same articles, would have had to spend 26.3 million marks in paper money. The man who did not spend the 5,500 marks, but preferred to save it together with the interest thereon might have over 7,000 marks today,

with which, however, he cannot even buy a shirt! Who would care to 'save' under such conditions? Does the stranger realize, moreover, that such violent changes in the valuation of German money have meant for many thousands of German savers the annihilation of their savings? Does the stranger see the formerly well-to-do men and women of the middle class who today with a heavy heart carry their old family jewellery to the dealer, in order to prolong their physical existence a little longer? He who before the war could spend the interest on 1 million marks was a rich man, even up to 1919 he could still live upon it with reasonable comfort; today he is poor, for with his 50,000 marks interest he can today barely provide his own person with the necessities of life for a week! Does the stranger see the women and girls from the higher circles, even up to the highest, who are compelled to take up some occupation or who help to eke out the family income by working in their homes for a miserable wage? Does the stranger see the 1½ millions of war cripples, who are struggling desperately to earn their living, because the pensions that the State can afford to pay them are utterly inadequate?"

From Sidney Pollard and Colin Holmes (eds.), *Documents of European Economic History*, Vol. 3: *The End of Old Europe, 1914–1939*, St. Martin's Press, 1972.

nancial measures, aided by foreign loans, a moratorium on reparations, and subsequently a new schedule of payments. Some fortunes had been made during the inflation, especially by speculators and financiers; many large industries and property owners had fared quite well. Small businesses were more often hurt, as were nearly all wage earners. Savings held in cash had been wiped out, but a slow recovery began.

Domestic Conflict   At the height of the Ruhr crisis, a little-known man named Adolf Hitler led a nationalist *putsch*, or coup, in Munich. Notable for

Ludendorff's participation, it was quickly defeated, and the plotters' punishment was ludicrously light. Ludendorff was acquitted, and Hitler was given a five-year sentence in comfortable prison quarters, where he composed *Mein Kampf* ("My Struggle") during the thirteen months he actually served. Such attacks on the new government were becoming less frequent, however. Its moderate policies and general prosperity brought relief from the assassinations and revolts of the earlier years, and it was reasonable to believe in 1924 that Germany was on the road to stability.

But the divisions in German society were sharpening, and there was no significant group with primary loyalty to the existing regime. The leading statesman was Gustav Stresemann, who sat in every cabinet, usually as foreign minister, from 1923 to his death in 1929. A nationalist of the center-right, he acquiesced in the army's violations of the disarmament clauses; but the right denounced him for his conciliatory tone toward former enemies and for bringing Germany into the League of Nations. German workers felt little was being done for them. The middle class could not forgive the inflation. The political extremes were growing at the expense of the center. When President Ebert died in 1925, a rightist coalition elected General von Hindenburg as his successor, defeating the candidate supported by both the Center and the Social Democratic parties; significantly, the 2 million votes given the Communist nominee would have made the difference.

THE ESTABLISHED DEMOCRACIES

Except for Italy, where Fascism came to power, democracy at first fared rather well in the postwar years. Belgium, despite the ruins left by the war and conflicts over language and religion, recaptured its place among Europe's most prosperous and freest countries. Although the Netherlands faced nationalist unrest in its colonies, especially the East Indies, such problems hardly threatened democratic institutions at home. The Scandinavian countries, while often at odds among themselves, sustained effective democracies.

Social Changes European society had not been radically reformed, although in every country the most militant Marxists felt strengthened by the presence of the Soviet Union as an international homeland for the proletariat. But the founding of Communist parties and allegiance to the Soviet Union split and weakened the left in domestic affairs. Economic recovery, though slower than expected, brought a general prosperity by the mid-1920s that contributed to the electoral victories of moderate and conservative parties. Constitutional democracy was the European norm, and many were convinced that even the Soviet Union and Italy would in time return to that standard.

Generally, the central government now spent a higher proportion of national wealth; and although most of that went to the military, to interest on the national debt, and to pensions (all costs left from the war), some of it was used to lay the basis for broader measures of social security for all. Politically, both business interests and labor unions exercised a more direct influence, supporting efforts to achieve economic stability. Yet despite periods of prosperity and a genuine boom in certain industries, the 1920s did not provide the steady growth of the prewar decade. Economic uncertainty, increased by inflation and unemployment, tended, like the disillusionment over reparations or the specter of Bolshevism, to favor caution.

Changes in Women's Lives Women's suffrage, once hotly debated, had been adopted in the Scandinavian countries (Finland, 1906; Norway, 1907; Denmark, 1917; Sweden, 1919) and in Great Britain (right after the war, as promised) and was part of the new constitutions of Austria and Germany. The effects on public life were less dramatic than either advocates or opponents had predicted. Politics was not transformed and the family not harmed, but there was significance in the spreading sense that for women to vote was a natural extension of democracy.

The most fundamental social changes of the period were usually not the result of deliberate policy. Employment in services such as sales and office work increased more rapidly than in industry, and the number of domestic servants declined. These changes affected unmarried women especially. In most countries more women were gainfully employed than before the war (at those jobs thought suitable for women) despite a sharp decline from the wartime peak and despite the strong tendency for women to leave work upon marriage. Everywhere women received more years of schooling than before, and the number of (middle class and still primarily male) youths enrolled in universities increased sharply. A rising standard of living and the automobile, especially in France and Britain, began to alter middle-class life.

France Life in France quickly returned to prewar patterns. The nation had become par excellence the land of the middle class, the artisan, and the peasant proprietor fiercely attached to a tiny plot of land. Though the expected cornucopia of reparations never materialized, ordinary people accomplished miracles of reconstruction, carefully making their new buildings look as much as possible like those destroyed. The Chamber of Deputies elected in 1919 at the height of patriotic pride in victory was the most conservative since the founding of the Third Republic; and politics, too, focused on restoration.

Depreciation of the franc, for a century one of the world's stablest currencies, became the focus of President Raymond Poincaré's conservative program. Inadequate taxation during the war (it took great political courage to raise taxes in France) lay at the root of the problem, and budgetary contraction was the preferred solution. The rigid focus on a stable franc and military security reflected the psychological as well as the economic and demographic costs of war.

In the subsequent prosperity, competent leaders presided over governments content with policies that permitted domestic stagnation and encouraged inflexibility in foreign affairs. Poincaré's concern for national honor and a stable currency appealed to a cautious middle class much as the complicated maneuvers of Aristide Briand, the leading figure of the 1930s, did to parliamentarians, but neither encouraged their followers to face more difficult long-term issues of working conditions, social inequality, cultural change, or international peace.

The United Kingdom In the United Kingdom, also, the elections of 1919—the first in which women (those over thirty years old) were allowed to vote—produced an overwhelming victory for leaders who promised to extract enough from Germany to make winning the war worthwhile. Lloyd George remained prime minister, but his government was essentially conservative. The breakup of the wartime coalition exposed the Liberal party's decline; and in 1924 new elections brought the Labour party briefly to power. Except for recognizing the Soviet Union, Labour did little to recall its leftist origins. For most of that decade, Britain was led with dull caution by the Conservatives and Stanley Baldwin, who inherited problems of unemployment, Irish nationalism, and a changing empire.

A crisis in the coal industry led to a ten-day general strike in 1926 that became a lightening rod for social division. Frightened by the bitter class conflict, many of the well-to-do volunteered in maintaining essential services, thus helping to break the strike. That response and the antilabor legislation which followed did much to deepen the resentments of British workers and heighten the angry rhetoric of public life.

Irish Independence The Irish question was equally explosive. The promise of home rule had been suspended during the war, and the Easter Rebellion of 1916 had been firmly suppressed. In 1919, however, the most militant Irish nationalists, led by the Sinn Fein (meaning "We Ourselves") party, refused to take their seats in the House of Commons and met instead at Dublin in a parliament of their own, the Dail Eireann. There, they declared Ireland an independent nation.

To this defiance the London government responded slowly and ineptly, finally choosing to suppress the Sinn Fein party and with it Irish independence. The government then sent reinforcements to the Royal Irish Constabulary in numbers sufficient to spread the fighting without ending it, troops that soon became the most hated symbol of British repression. Violent civilian resisters called themselves the Irish Republican Army; and against civilian terrorists, the British could look only foolish or brutal. By the 1920s the two sides were fighting a bloody war.

With pressure mounting at home and abroad for some settlement, the British government in 1920 passed an Ireland act, creating two Irish parliaments, one in the predominantly Catholic areas of the south and west, and the other in the predominantly Protestant counties of the northeast. Sinn Fein warred against this division of the island during almost two more years of fighting. Nevertheless, in December 1922 the Irish parliament sitting in Dublin in the Catholic south proclaimed, with British acquiescence, the existence of the Irish Free State, which included all Ireland except the six northern counties of Ulster. As Northern Ireland, these counties maintained the traditional union with Great Britain, an uneasy peace that preserved the basis for further tension and conflict that has continued through two more generations.

▲ Demonstrations and parades were banned in Dublin and Belfast, where an armored car stands ready to put down any trouble; violence had become an expected part of political struggle in Ireland.
UPI/Bettmann.

The British Commonwealth Only in imperial affairs did flexible compromise still seem to work. Canadian complaints led the Imperial Conference of 1926 to a significant new definition of all dominions as "autonomous communities . . . equal in status . . . united by a common allegiance to the crown and freely associated as members of the British Commonwealth of Nations." Autonomous in all domestic and foreign affairs, dominions accepted ties to the British crown as the expression of their common traditions and loyalties. Given legal sanction by the Statute of Westminster in 1931, this conception of empire proved a skillful adaptation to new conditions crowned by the stability, prosperity, and loyalty of dominions such as Canada, New Zealand, and Australia.

INTERNATIONAL RELATIONS

From 1924 to 1930 the conduct of international relations reflected some of the idealism of the Paris Peace Conference. The League of Nations, formally established in 1920, successfully resolved a number of disputes, despite the absence of the United States, Britain's greater concern for its empire, and France's tendency to use the League for its own security. The league's special commissions helped restructure the disjointed economies of new states, aided refugees, and set international standards for public health and working conditions. In the late 1920s, at least, the decisions of the Permanent Court of International Justice were treated with great respect as steps toward the rule of law.

Debt Payments Crises over debt payments were dealt with directly by the major powers. As Germany fell behind in its payments, the Allies took the position that they, in turn, could not pay their war debts to the United States. Some compromise was essential, and in 1924 the nations involved accepted the proposals of an international commission of financial experts, headed by the American banker Charles G. Dawes. The Dawes Plan fixed Germany's reparations payments on a regular scale, established an orderly mode of collection, and provided loans to Germany equal to 80 percent of the reparations payment German owed in the first year of the plan.

The Dawes Plan did not admit any connection between Allied debts to the United States and German reparations to the European victors, but it did end the worst of the chaos. For the next six years, Germany, fed by loans largely from the United States, made its reparations payments on schedule. The issue seemed forever resolved with the adoption of the Young Plan in 1929, which finally set a limit to Germany's obligations (fifty-nine years), reduced annual payments, and ended foreign occupation of the Rhineland. Under the leadership of American bankers, the interests of international capital had come to shape policy in the name of economic necessity.

The Locarno Era International efforts to outlaw war foundered on definitions of aggression, but they led to a series of treaties in 1925 known as the Locarno Pact. In the major agreement—entered into by Germany, Belgium, France, Great Britain, and Italy—all parties accepted Germany's western frontier as defined by the Versailles Treaty and promised to arbitrate their disagreements. In addition, France pursued a more traditional diplomacy, signing a mutual-defense alliance with Poland and Czechoslovakia. A continental war caused by German aggression now seemed impossible.

The optimism of the Locarno era was capped by the Kellogg-Briand pact of 1928. The French had suggested that the American entry into World War I be commemorated by a friendship pact, and the Americans proposed to include others as well. More than a score of nations signed the pact, which contained no troubling provisions for enforcement while it renounced war "as an instrument of national policy."

Disarmament   From 1921 on, some League commission was always studying the problem of disarmament. Given the enormous cost of capital ships (Britain no longer aspired to maintain a fleet twice the size of any other), naval disarmament seemed especially promising. At the Washington Conference of 1921–1922, called by President Warren G. Harding, the United States, Great Britain, Japan, France, and Italy agreed after some difficulty to fix their relative strength in capital ships at current levels,[4] not to expand their naval bases, and even to scrap some of their larger vessels. About smaller ships there was less agreement, but the Washington Conference produced tangible results. Never again did discussions of naval disarmament prove so fruitful. At Geneva in 1927 and London in 1930, Italy (citing the special needs of its geography) and France (arguing that all forms of disarmament should be discussed together) refused to accept a treaty. By 1935 Japan would reject even the Washington accord.

Attempts to limit land and air arms were even less successful. League commissions could not agree on which were offensive weapons, on whether a professional army was comparable to a reserve force, and on whether limitations should be expressed in terms of budgets, weapons, or personnel. German and Russian proposals that their own military weakness be made a standard for other nations, one they could achieve by disarming, only aroused suspicion. After much preparation, these League commissions called a conference on general disarmament in 1932. By then, the dream of arms restrictions was more re-

mote than ever. Discussions continued at length, but before agreements were reached, Hitler had come to power in Germany, and a new arms race ensued.

The Beginning of a New Era   To contemporaries, and for historians since, World War I was the beginning of a new era. The war itself was understood to have resulted from a dangerous system of alliances, secret diplomacy, and the arms race. Creation of the League of Nations, agreements like the Locarno treaties, and conferences on disarmament were unusual examples of an extensive effort to learn from history and to correct the errors of the past. Postwar international relations differed in other respects, too; for the nations of Europe, weakened economically and militarily, were now deeply in debt, their hold on empire weakening.

Postwar politics, too, confronted new problems and new opportunities. Multiple new states with contested boundaries, in which nationalism was often the strongest communal bond, wrestled with the unfamiliar complications of democracy. In those countries and in the established democracies the relationship between politics and the general public had changed. Old elites were less trusted, the techniques of mass mobilization now more familiar and available to every party, and groups once treated as peripheral (such as workers, farmers, women, and veterans) were now more assertive. Disillusionment with politics was deep after years of propaganda; yet more was expected of government following its wartime accomplishments, and the range of issues politicians engaged grew wider. Revolutionary new political movements threatened to change the rules of politics altogether.

Economic conditions were different, too. The war and the terms of peace left enormous problems of physical destruction, burdens of debt, broken trade patterns. The flood of former soldiers seeking jobs while war industries shrank (an immediate effect of demobilization) led into more long-term changes involving new technologies and mass markets. The composition of social classes and the relations between them altered, too.

In these circumstances the radical ideas and shocking cultural movements of the 1890s had

---

[4] The current level was defined as parity between the United States and Great Britain at 525,000 tons apiece in capital ships; 315,000 tons for Japan; and 175,000 tons each for France and Italy.

new relevance. Nearly all Europeans had personal experience of lives disrupted—families broken up, women adding new roles to demanding old ones, jobs gained and suddenly lost, savings wiped out, property destroyed, invading armies, civil war, or sickness and death. All these changes at once, from the international to the personal, marked a new era.

The nations of Europe had stumbled into the most destructive war in their history, forcing them to harness the political systems, organizational skills, and technology that had made them powerful. The war had probed every social weakness; eliminated the German, Austro-Hungarian, and Russian empires; and left the victors only marginally better off than the losers. In the course of the war and as part of its justification, the winning alliance had promulgated universal values of democracy; and though these values were tainted in the practical decisions of the peace, they were to some extent embraced across the continent. Gradually, stability and prosperity did return to much of Europe. If broader hopes for social justice and international cooperation lost their luster, the institutions that expressed them remained in place. Only the next round of challenges would reveal whether those institutions could provide a sufficient basis for domestic and international peace.

Recommended Reading

Sources

Chapman, Guy. *A Passionate Prodigality.* 1966. No war stimulated a richer literature, and this searing account of the personal experiences of an English soldier, first published in 1933, is among the best of these works.

*Nicholson, Harold G. *Peacemaking, 1919.* 1965. The retrospective analysis of an experienced diplomat who was a disillusioned participant at the Versailles Conference.

*Remarque, Erich Maria. *All Quiet on the Western Front.* First published in Germany in 1928, this novel with its realistic (and antinationalist) depiction of the war became the subject of great controversy there, and its moving rejection of modern warfare made it a best seller throughout Europe and in the United States.

Studies

Becker, Jean-Jacques. *The Great War and the French People.* 1985. Shows the multiple ways in which the war was a turning point in French life.

Cannadine, David. *The Decline and Fall of the British Aristocracy.* 1990. Traces the extraordinary erosion of the position of a dominant class from the Lloyd George budget of 1906 through World War I and the changes that have followed.

Carsten, F. L. *Revolution in Central Europe, 1918–1919.* 1972. An important treatment of these significant outbreaks following the war.

Downs, Laura L. *Manufacturing Inequality.* 1995. A study of class relations and social attitudes in the organization of women's work in British and French factories.

Falls, Cyril B. *The Great War.* 1961. A skillful account of the war by a noted military historian.

Feldman, Gerald D. *Army, Industry, and Labor in Germany, 1914–1918.* 1966. A fundamental analysis of the war's effects on institutions and power in Germany.

*Ferro, Marc. *The Great War, 1914–1918.* 1973. This stimulating, outspoken essay emphasizes the economic and social impact of the war.

*Fischer, Fritz. *Germany's Aims in the First World War.* 1967. The reassessment that became a center of controversy among Germany historians.

Fridenson, Patrick (ed.). *The French Home Front, 1914–1918.* Bruce Little (tr.). 1992. A valuable collection of essays by social historians on the effects of wartime on the lives of industrial workers.

*Fussell, Paul. *The Great War and Modern Memory.* 1975. A lively study of the cultural impact of the war denouncing modern warfare in all its aspects.

*Herrmann, David G. *The Arming of Europe and the Making of the First World War.* 1997. Uses new archival evidence to show the importance of military considerations in the diplomacy that led to world war.

*Joll, James. *The Origins of the First World War.* 1984. Draws upon the vast literature dealing with a question that was once extremely controversial to establish a balanced perspective.

Kennedy, Paul (ed.). *The War Plans of the Great Powers, 1880–1914.* 1979. Places the arms race in the context of imperialist and political pressures that underlay the planning process leading up to the war.

Kocka, Jürgen. *Facing Total War: German Society 1914–1918.* Barbara Weinberger (tr.). 1984. A leading social historian's assessment of the domestic impact of the war on Germany.

Marwick, Arthur. *War and Social Change in the Twentieth Century: A Comparative Study of Britain, France, Germany, Russia and the United States.* 1975. Develops the case for the revolutionary effects of World Wars I and II on the domestic economy of modern society.

*Mayer, Arno J. *Politics and Diplomacy of Peacemaking: Containment and Counterrevolution at Versailles, 1918–1919.* 1967. Argues that fear of Bolshevism shaped the terms of peace more than publicized principles did.

Miller, S. (ed.). *Military Strategy and the Origins of the First World War.* 1985. These essays assess the role of the military in the decisions that led to war.

Williams, John. *The Home Fronts: Britain, France, and Germany, 1914–1918.* 1972. Pulls together a variety of evidence of the war's domestic impact.

Williamson, S. R., Jr. *The Politics of Grand Strategy: Britain and France Prepare for War, 1904–1914.* 1969.

Winter, J. M., and R. M. Wall. *The Upheaval of War: Family, Work, and Welfare in Europe, 1914–1918.* 1988. An insightful assessment of the effects of the war on domestic society.

Winter, Jay. *Sites of Memory, Sites of Mourning: The Great War in European Cultural History.* 1996. A powerful study of the impact of the war on European culture.

Winter, Jay, and Jean-Louis Robert. *Capital Cities at War: Paris, London, Berlin, 1914–1919.* 1997. An important new study of the social history of the war.

---

*Available in paperback.

▲ This idealized image of Lenin addressing the people conveys the power of Lenin's oratory skills and the sense that his leadership began a new era. The portrait of impassioned workers, soldiers and sailors, men and women—all inspired by their leader—and the careful placement of Stalin just behind Lenin reveal the painting as the subsequent official view of the Soviet government. One of the marks of the new era in Europe was, in fact, the effective propaganda of single-party states.
Itar-TASS/Sovfoto.

THE GREAT TWENTIETH-CENTURY CRISIS

The 1920s and 1930s opened an era of intense hope and great fear, of prosperity and consumerism followed by economic depression, of old and newly established liberal governments across Europe that were immediately challenged by conflict at home and the dynamism of two new revolutionary regimes, and of seering arguments about where all these changes would lead. A flourishing popular culture, flippant and commercial, undermined nineteenth-century standards of propriety (and the confidence that went with them). Europe's most interesting artists and intellectuals seemed unconvinced by the prosperity of the 1920s, and provocative theories, in both the physical and social sciences, invited skepticism about absolute truths and traditional values.

While most European nations embraced representative government, communists consolidated their hold on Russia and fascists seized power in Italy. Relatively isolated at first, these new regimes soon stimulated further divisions in other countries as new movements on the right sprung up in imitation of the nationalist tone and military style of Italian Fascism and socialist parties split between democratic reformers and more revolutionary communist parties with close ties to Russia. These movements could recruit support from among many discontented groups: workers who had expected stronger unions to bring them greater benefits, peasants who found it hard to make a living even where reforms had provided them with small but often inefficient holdings, ethnic groups resentful of sudden minority status as a result of the boundary changes in Eastern Europe, nationalists angry that their new states had not gained more territory, and all those who disliked the culture and society of their era. Then economic depression dramatized the weaknesses of democracy and the limitations of liberalism. Nearly everywhere, communists gained support among many workers and intellectuals, fascists among many defenders of order. Political conflicts, domestic and international, presented themselves as the summation of all these crises at once.

I. The Distinctive Culture of the Twentieth Century

The exciting intellectual and cultural movements of the 1920s built on those of the prewar period, for many of the works that marked new directions in science, philosophy, and the arts had appeared in the decades just before and after the turn of the century. Even then the new trends were disquieting to those who were aware of them. After the war, they gained momentum to became dominant in many fields. Psychology, literature, and art explored the irrational and surreal. The sciences uncovered complexities in nature that made uncertainty a theoretical principle, and theories of society adopted a tough-minded "realism" that spoke of power and interest more than values. Norms of behavior that had been considered the essence of civilization just a generation earlier were now called into question.

FREUDIAN PSYCHOLOGY

No one disturbed accepted views more deeply than Sigmund Freud, a Viennese physician whose clinical studies had taken him gradually from an interest in neurology to the study of psychiatry. Freud followed the method—close and detailed observation—of medical science, and his writings were as careful in their logic as in their literary elegance. Freud had done his most important work before 1914, and in many ways he was old-fashioned. For the most part, he accepted as socially necessary the norms of respectable behavior promulgated by the nineteenth-century middle class. He was deeply influenced by ideas of evolution, and his metaphors and assumptions betray the liberal economist's appreciation of self-discipline and calculated self-interest. His attention to the phenomenon of hysteria and his use of hypnosis built on the work of others to create a startling view of the human mind, which he insisted could be universally applied.

The Unconscious In treating neurotics, Freud found that they often experienced relief of their symptoms by recalling forgotten events under hypnosis. He concluded that the recollection itself was crucial, not for its accuracy but as an expression of the psychic reality with which the patient had been unconsciously struggling. Within the unconscious, conflicting urges contended in what Freud labeled the *id*. Here universal basic desires (similar to instincts) seek satisfaction, and Freud found the most troublesome and psychologically significant desires to be sexual. The *ego* tries to channel and control these desires, directed to do so by the *superego*, which (rather like the conscience in more traditional conceptions) imposes a socially conditioned sense of what is acceptable behavior. Thus mental life is marked by perpetual tension between the id and the superego.

This conflict, uncomfortably mediated by the ego, is unconscious; for one of the mind's responses is to repress from consciousness the id's desires. Most people remain unaware of their own deepest motivations. Repression, however, causes an enormous mental strain that often finds an outlet in neurotic behavior. As the patient comes to face and understand what is being repressed, neurosis is relieved.

Psychoanalysis From this conception of the human psyche, Freud developed an elaborate, subtle, and shocking theory that ascribed sexual lusts to every person at every age. The idea of infant sexuality was especially offensive to contemporaries, but so was the notion of the Oedipus or Electra complex, through which the boy's angry competition with his father (or the daughter's with her mother) could produce a child's unconscious guilt-ridden wish for the death of one parent in order to possess the other. Few in Freud's time could tolerate this ascription of base desires to decent people. Freudian theory proclaimed that such decent people were merely the most repressed. Similarly, religion provided satisfaction for infantile and obsessive needs. Even the greatest human achievements in art and science were the result of sublimation, by which Freud meant the diversion of the id's primitive demands to other, higher purposes.

Psychoanalysis, the name Freud gave his body of theory and his therapeutic technique, calls on the analyst not to pass judgments but rather to help the patient discover aspects of self that proper society held to be quite simply unmentionable. By implication, these ideas and therapeutic techniques called for a shift in aesthetic and

▲ Although Freud believed his theories had universal, scientific validity, his consultation room in Vienna unmistakably reflected the cultivated taste of a central European of the upper-middle class in the late nineteenth century, from its tiled stove and afghans to its pictures and ancient sculptures. Edmund Engelman.

intellectual standards. Freud considered whatever seemed real to the psyche to be important; dreams and slips of the tongue were serious expressions of psychic conflict. Hypnosis and free association (in which patients are encouraged to let their thoughts ramble) were valued as modes of expression in which hidden connections emerged without the intervention of narrative or logic. Freud pioneered ways of comprehending life and literature on several levels at once and provided the model for doing so.

Wider Implications In the 1920s the broad implications of Freud's discoveries gained wider public recognition despite continued hostility. If repression leads to neuroses, one extrapolation went, then greater sexual freedom and, above all, greater candor will produce healthier people. This inference remains perhaps the most widespread popular notion drawn from Freudian teaching,

though it was not a view he held. Related to this view is the belief that guilt is evil, a kind of Christian perversion of human nature. Freudian insights encouraged literary and personal introspection and supported the view that childhood is the most important phase of life. Although his theories stimulated new visions of a freer and happier life, Freud's dark conclusion was that "the price of progress in civilization is paid in forfeiting happiness." Civilization, then, is based on the repression of primitive and still very powerful drives, which may burst forth at any moment. Freud, who feared the explosion he foresaw, died in 1939, driven into exile by the antisemitism of the Nazis.

Freudians strove to maintain these doctrines whole as science and therapy, treating deviations as heresies; but there would be many deviations. The best known came from the Swiss psychologist Carl G. Jung, who soon broke from Freud and developed his theory of the collective unconscious, the common psychic inheritance of whole peoples which they most commonly expressed in the symbols and rituals of religion. Jung's somewhat looser and more mystical perspectives have fascinated religious thinkers, attracted theorists of nation and race, and influenced philosophers and artists. More generally, the concepts and vocabulary of psychoanalysis penetrated much of Western culture, apparent in art and literature, journalism and advertising.

THE HUMANITIES

Art and Literature   Some artists in the postwar period—the Surrealists, with their dreamlike canvases, are an example—applied Freudian ideas directly, and in his manifesto of Surrealism (1924), the writer André Breton proclaimed that art must liberate the subconscious. Quite independent of Freud, explorations of human irrationality fairly exploded in prose and poetry. The novels of Marcel Proust, Franz Kafka, and James Joyce most clearly mark the change in style and content.

Marcel Proust died in 1922, soon to be hailed as one of the great stylists of the French language. His long novel, *Remembrance of Things Past*, built an introverted and delicately detailed picture of upper-class Parisian life into a monumental and sensitive study of one man's quiet suffering, which became a model of interior monologue, of the novel in which the subject is not action seen from the outside but feelings observed from within.

Franz Kafka, who wrote in German though born in Prague, died in 1924, leaving instructions for his manuscripts to be burned. They were not, and they came to be accepted as quintessentially modern, with their realistic and reasonable descriptions of fantasies that convey the torture of anxiety. In *The Trial* the narrator tells of his arrest, conviction, and execution on charges he can never discover, an exploration of the psychology of guilt that foreshadows the totalitarian state.

James Joyce's international fame came with the publication of his novel *Ulysses* (1922), the presentation on a mythic scale of a single day in the life of a modest Dubliner, written in an exuberant, endlessly inventive game of words in which puns, cliché, parody, and poetry swirl in a dizzying stream of consciousness.

Virginia Woolf, who used related devices in her novels, was less widely read at the time but her work would become very influential a generation later. A political activist and feminist who was prominent in England's intellectual circles, her book *A Room of One's Own* (1929), subtly explored the value of a female perspective and the ways in which women were discouraged from intellectual independence. Not all of the most important writers turned away from the objective tone and chronological clarity of traditional narrative. But even those who made use of more familiar techniques—like Thomas Mann in Germany, André Gide in France, and D. H. Lawrence in England—tended to explore topics and attitudes offensive to convention.

The Other Arts   In all the arts, shock became one of the points of creative expression. Dada, a movement that originated during World War I, put on displays, part theater and part art exhibition, of noisy nonsense and absurd juxtapositions that were intended to infuriate the Parisian bourgeoisie. Italian Futurists, poets and playwrights as well as artists, promised to build a new art for a technological age—"The world has been enriched by a new beauty: the beauty of speed"—and in their manifesto of 1909 had issued a call to "burn the libraries . . . demolish the venerated cities" (see "The Futurist Manifesto," p. 987 and the painting by Boccioni, p. 932). The Fauves in France and the Expressionists in Germany and Scandinavia gloried in their reputation for wild and often brutal candor in the style and content of their paintings as well as in their conduct.

Works of art became more difficult to comprehend. Cubist and Expressionist painters, like composers using the twelve-tone scale and dissonance, deliberately eschewed the merely decorative or pleasant and seemed eager to incorporate violence and amorality. Even when more sober traditions prevailed—as in the carefully constructed, cerebral poetry of William Butler Yeats and of the younger Ezra Pound and T. S. Eliot—foreboding and obscurity intertwined. Today the richness and profundity of the greatest of these works are readily apparent; but to contemporaries, they were more threatening than attractive, dangerously widening the chasm between "serious" art and the popular culture most intellectuals disdained.

The Futurist Manifesto
◀◉▶

The Futurist movement was announced in typically provocative language in the "Manifesto of Futurism," written by Filippo Marinetti and published in the Paris newspaper Le Figaro *in 1909.*

MANIFESTO OF FURTURISM

"1. We intend to sing the love of danger, the habit of energy and fearlessness.

"2. Courage, audacity, and revolt will be essential elements of our poetry.

"3. Up to now literature has exalted a pensive immobility, ecstasy, and sleep. We intend to exalt aggressive action, a feverish insomnia, the racer's stride, the mortal leap, the punch and the slap.

"4. We say that the world's magnificence has been enriched by a new beauty; the beauty of speed. A racing car whose hood is adorned with great pipes, like serpents of explosive breath—a roaring car that seems to ride on grapeshot—is more beautiful than the *Victory of Samothrace*.

"5. We want to hymn the man at the wheel, who hurls the lance of his spirit across the Earth, along the circle of its orbit.

"6. The poet must spend himself with ardor, splendor, and generosity, to swell the enthusiastic fervor of the primordial elements.

"7. Except in struggle, there is no more beauty. No work without an aggressive character can be a masterpiece. Poetry must be conceived as a violent attack on unknown forces, to reduce and prostrate them before man.

"8. We stand on the last promontory of the centuries! . . . Why should we look back, when what we want is to break down the mysterious doors of the Impossible? Time and Space died yesterday. We already live in the absolute, because we have created eternal, omnipresent speed.

"9. We will glorify war—the world's only hygiene—militarism, patriotism, the destructive gesture of freedom-bringers, beautiful ideas worth dying for, and scorn for woman.

"10. We will destroy the museums, libraries, academies of every kind, will fight moralism, feminism, every opportunistic or utilitarian cowardice.

"11. We will sing of great crowds excited by work, by pleasure, and by riot; we will sing of the multicolored, polyphonic tides of revolution in the modern capitals; we will sing of the vibrant mighty fervor of arsenals and shipyards blazing with violent electric moons; greedy railway stations that devour smoke-plumed serpents; factories hung on clouds by the crooked lines of their smoke; bridges that stride the rivers like giant gymnasts, flashing in the sun with a glitter of knives; adventurous steamers that sniff the horizon; deep-chested locomotives whose wheels paw the tracks like the hooves of enormous steel horses bridled by tubing; and the sleek flight planes whose propellers chatter in the wind like banners and seem to cheer like an enthusiastic crowd."

Excerpt from "The Founding and Manifesto of Guturism" by F. T. Marinetti in R. W. Flint and Arthur A. Coppotelli (eds. and trans.), *Marinetti Selected Writings*, Farrar, Straus and Giroux, 1971.

Philosophy The philosophical work most widely read in the 1920s was Oswald Spengler's *Decline of the West*, which had appeared in 1918. Spengler treated whole civilizations as biological organisms, each with a life cycle of its own, and presented his study of Western culture as an achievement of German philosophy. But his fame rested on the dire prediction of his title: World War I had begun the final act of Western civilization (see "Spengler's View of History," p. 989). José Ortega y Gasset's *The Revolt of the Masses*, published in 1930, was hardly more optimistic. The masses, he warned, were destined to use their rising power to destroy civilization's highest achievements. Scores of other writers joined in scorn for modern culture as vapid and directionless.

The most striking innovation in philosophy, however, came from another tradition entirely and was monumentally set forth in *Principia Mathematica* (1910) by Bertrand Russell and Alfred North Whitehead. It became the cornerstone of analytic philosophy, which holds that philosophers should concern themselves only with what is precise and empirically demonstrable. On the continent a group known as the Vienna Circle developed a related system, logical positivism; and the work of Ludwig Wittgenstein, especially his

▲ **Like many German Expressionists, Otto Dix challenged the public with a series of paintings that simultaneously lampooned and celebrated the decadence of life in Berlin in the Weimar era.**
Archiv für Kunst und Geschichte.

Tractatus Logico-Philosophicus (1921), influenced both schools of thought.

Wittgenstein attempted in a series of numbered propositions "to set a limit to thought." By insisting on such rigor and seeking through symbolic logic to attain the precision of mathematical reasoning, analytic philosophers tended to exclude most of the general questions of ordinary life. The issues theologians and moral philosophers had argued about for centuries were too imprecise to merit debate. Like the earlier positivists, analytic philosophers consciously emulated the natural sciences, but their stress on the lean language of mathematics led away from positivist confidence in knowledge. The philosopher's task was to analyze every statement, stripping away those connotations and values, however appealing, that do not convey precise meaning. "My propositions," Wittgenstein concluded in the *Tractatus*, "serve as elucidations in the following way: anyone who understands me eventually recognizes them as nonsensical." Philosophy, too, generated doubt and turned to its own specialized challenges.

Spengler's View of History

◆

Oswald Spengler was an obscure German teacher before the publication of The Decline of the West *in 1918. A philosophy of history in two substantial volumes, it presents an original and systematic analysis of world history. The erudition is remarkable, and Spengler elaborately categorized the societies of Asia and Europe while discussing all sorts of topics, beginning with the meaning of numbers and ideas of destiny. They study's central device, however, is to analyze the arts as the symbolic expression of entire civilizations. The passage quoted here is from the last two paragraphs in the book. The final chapter—which follows chapters on the state, politics, and money—entitled "The Form-World of Economic Life (B): The Machine." Although conceived and largely written before the outbreak of World War I, the work was inevitably read as a commentary on the postwar world and prediction of the future.*

"The *private* powers of the economy want free paths for their acquisition of great resources. No legislation must stand in their way. They want to make the laws themselves, in their interests, and to that end they make use of the tool they have made for themselves, democracy, the subsidized party. Law needs, in order to resist this onslaught, a high tradition and an ambition of strong families that finds its satisfaction not in the heaping-up of riches, but in the tasks of true rulership, above and beyond all money-advantage. *A power can be overthrown only by another power,* not by a principle, and no power that can confront money is left but this one. Money is overthrown and abolished only by blood. *Life* is alpha and omega, the cosmic onflow in microcosmic form. It is *the* fact of facts within the world-as-history. Before the irresistible rhythm of the generation-sequence, everything built up by the waking-consciousness in its intellectual world vanishes at the last. Ever in History it is life and life only—race-quality, the triumph of the will-to-power—and not the victory of truths, discoveries, or money that signifies. *World-history is the world court,* and it has ever decided in favour of the stronger, fuller, and more self-assured life—decreed to it, namely, the right to exist, regardless of whether its right would hold before a tribunal of waking-consciousness. Always it has sacrificed truth and justice to might and race, and passed doom of death upon men and peoples in whom truth was more than deeds, and jus-

tice than power. And so the drama of a high Culture—that wondrous world of deities, arts, thoughts, battles, cities—closes with the return of the pristine facts of the blood eternal that is one and the same as the ever-circling cosmic flow. The bright imaginative Waking-Being submerges itself into the silent service of Being, as the Chinese and Roman empires tell us. Time triumphs over Space, and it is Time whose inexorable movement embeds the ephemeral incident of the Culture, on this planet, in the incident of Man—a form wherein the incident life flows on for a time, while behind it all the streaming horizons of geological and stellar histories pile up in the light-world of our eyes.

"For us, however, whom a Destiny has placed in this Culture and at this moment of its development—the moment when money is celebrating its last victories, and the Cæsarism that is to succeed approaches with quiet, firm step—our direction, willed and obligatory at once, is set for us within narrow limits, and on any other terms life is not worth the living. We have not the freedom to reach to this or to that, but the freedom to do the necessary or to do nothing. And a task that historic necessity has set *will* be accomplished with the individual or against him.

"*Ducunt Fata volentem, nolentem trabunt.*"

From Oswald Spengler, Charles Frances Atkinson (trans.), *The Decline of the West,* Alfred A. Knopf, 1970).

THE SCIENCES

Science had also, since the turn of the century, moved beyond the layperson's comprehension. Even when the achievements of science were apparent to everyone, they often rested on theoretical advances that overturned established certain-

ties. And the fields in which scientists worked became ever more highly specialized.

The Nature of Matter One line of scientific investigation stemmed from an experiment by two Americans, Albert A. Michelson and Edward W. Morley, in 1887. By demonstrating that the speed

▲ **Einstein's face remains one of the best known icons of the twentieth century, a symbol of humanity, universal genius, and Jewish exile.**
Karsh, Ottawa/Woodfin Camp & Associates.

of light leaving earth was the same whether the light traveled in the direction of the earth's movement or against it, they challenged the established theory that the universe was filled with a motionless substance called "ether," which was thought necessary because waves could not function in empty space. The implications were fundamental, and exploring them led Albert Einstein to his theory of relativity, which he set forth in two brief papers published in 1905 and 1915. They were of the highest philosophical as well as scientific interest: Space and time are not absolute, he said, but must be measured in relation to the observer and on the most fundamental levels are aspects of a single continuum.

As Einstein developed his theory of relativity, physicists were also achieving a new understanding of matter. Wilhelm Roentgen's discovery of x-rays in 1895 had given the first important insight into the world of subatomic particles. Within two years the English physicist J. J. Thomson showed the existence of the electron, the subatomic particle that carries a negative electrical charge. The atom was not the basic unit of matter. By the turn of the century Pierre and Marie Curie, among others, had found radium and other materials to be radioactive; that is, they emitted both subatomic particles and a form of electromagnetic radiation. Soon, largely through the work of the English physicist Ernest Rutherford, radioactivity was identified with the breakdown of heavy and unstable atoms. These discoveries made it possible to link the structure of atoms with Dmitri Mendeleev's periodic table of elements. Elements with similar chemical properties were also similar in their atomic structures. A simpler and clear understanding of matter seemed in the offing.

Quantum Physics But continuing research soon revealed phenomena that Newtonian physics could not explain. In 1902 the German physicist Max Planck challenged Newtonian assumptions by announcing that energy in the subatomic world was released or absorbed not in a continuous stream but in discrete, measurable, and apparently irreducible units, which Planck called quanta. Energy, in effect, possessed many of the properties of matter.

This finding implied that matter and energy might be interchangeable, and Einstein incorporated the insight into his theory of relativity in the famous equation $E=mc^2$. Energy (E) is equivalent to mass (m) times the square of the speed of light, a constant (c), which means that at least in theory, small quantities of matter could be turned into enormous amounts of energy. In this respect Newtonian physics was wrong; matter could be transformed after all. In 1919 Rutherford produced changes in the structure of the nitrogen atom by bombarding it with subatomic particles, and other atomic changes were soon produced in the laboratory.

By the mid-1920s, however, physicists had to face troubling anomalies. Planck's quantum theory, though verified in numerous experiments, considered particles to behave in probabilistic rather than absolutely regular patterns—a concept Einstein himself could never wholly accept. Furthermore, electromagnetic radiation, including visible light, seemed to behave like a flow of particles in some circumstances and as a wave (a regular disturbance of particles in which the particles themselves do not advance) in others. Nor, the German physicist Werner Heisenberg argued, was it possible at the same time to determine a particle's position and its momentum, for at the subatomic level measurement interfered with the variables measured—a disturbing effect that Heisenberg appropriately named "the uncertainty principle." Conceptions of matter had been transformed in just a few years. Inside atoms there was mostly empty space and particles that did not behave with absolute regularity; and in both the subatomic world and the stellar universe, the position and purpose of the observer fundamentally affected what was observed.

Uncertainty Principle The new theories proved powerful tools, but physicists who chose to philosophize about such matters now spoke in humbler and more tentative tones. Physics became one of the most prestigious, highly organized, and expensive of human activities, recognized rather than understood by the public through its applications: x-ray technology, the electron microscope, and eventually the controlled fission of atomic energy. Newtonian principles, physicists insisted, still obtained in most cases, as solid and predictable as ever. But there was a loss. The Western world had long looked to the sciences for confirmation of its philosophy and even its theology. In the twentieth century no popularizer would build a general outlook on society from the latest scientific discoveries as Voltaire had once done from the ideas of Newton.

The Biological and Social Sciences Although the new work in other fields of science was less revolutionary, it often had immediate impact. Knowledge of the mechanisms of heredity furthered scientific breeding of animals and the creation of plant hybrids that would greatly increase the productivity of agriculture. The isolation of viruses, first achieved in the 1890s, gave medicine a new armory and led the way to invaluable drugs, most notably penicillin, discovered in England by Sir Alexander Fleming and Sir Howard Florey in 1928.

The understanding of society was deeply affected by two giants of modern sociology, the Frenchman Emile Durkheim and the German Max Weber, whose work is central to modern social science. Durkheim's use of statistical tools and Weber's use of the "ideal type" to analyze how societies function remain influential, as does their concern with the customs and beliefs that hold society together. Both, for example, emphasized the importance of religion, although they were concerned not with its metaphysical truth but with its contribution to the development of the state and of capitalism. Both stressed the threat to society when group norms broke down, and both saw a danger of that breakdown in modern trends. Through this emphasis on the function of communal values rather than their validity and on the role of myth and ritual in all societies including our own, anthropology, sociology, and history have tended to share psychology's insistent relativism.

PUBLIC CULTURE

To the public at large, developments in science and the arts were associated with the prosperity and brash excitement of the twenties. Science meant the spread of automobiles, radios, and airplanes; new trends were known through colorful stylish advertising, risqué literature, and vibrant theater. The surprising crisp architecture and applied design of Walter Gropius' Bauhaus school in Germany, with its emphasis on relating form to function, began to win a following, and there was curiosity about the still more daring endeavors in France of Le Corbusier to envision a wholly modern city as a machine for living.

Cinema The distortions of time and perspective through flashbacks and close-ups were less disturbing when conveyed in motion pictures than through words or on canvas. On the silent screen, even the frothiest romance or adventure story could contain subliminal themes of social or national concern, reflecting the experiences of World War I through themes of abandonment in France and of betrayal in Germany.[1] Motion pictures became more popular and more profitable than any

---

[1] Paul Monaco develops this interpretation in *Cinema & Society: France and Germany during the Twenties*, 1976.

▲ **A school of handcrafts, art, and architecture, the Bauhaus defined a modernist aesthetic; and buildings like this one designed by Walter Gropius in 1925 pioneered the functional, international style that would dominate the most admired architecture of the next fifty years. Part of the explosive creativity of the Weimar years, the school broke up with the advent of Hitler when many of its members left Germany, most for the United States.**
Erik Bohr/Archiv für Kunst und Geschichte.

form of entertainment had ever been. Movie theaters were built on the most elegant streets of Paris, London, and Berlin, gaudily combining the exoticism of a world's fair with reassuring luxury. Egyptian and Greek motifs, marble columns, fountains, mirrors, and statues reinforced the fantasies on the screen. The Gaumont Palace built in Paris in 1919 became an international model, with its 5,000 plush seats and an orchestra pit for eighty musicians. Berlin's 300 cinemas included the Sportspalast, redone for motion pictures in 1920, which boasted of being the largest movie theater in the world. By the mid-1920s, Britain, France, Germany, and Italy each counted their movie theaters in the thousands.

Crowds of people from every stratum attended the same movies; and women came, even without male escorts. Influenced by the movies, middle-class and working-class families in the 1920s were more likely to be talking about the same things, and women especially could more easily imagine a different and better life. Reviews and movie magazines helped to provide the publicity essential to success in a business that relied on stars and vast distribution networks. American companies did all this very effectively, filling screens around the world. The United States made more films than any other country. Japan was second and Germany third, with Europe's largest film company.

The rapid transition to talking pictures between 1929 and 1930 underscored national differences, and every country had some ministry empowered to restrain the presentation on the screen of sex and violence. In 1919 an English Watch committee condemned a film of the Johnson-Jeffries fight, fearing it could "demoralize and brutalize the minds of young persons." Sunday showings were an issue for years. Politics was present, too. Many countries restricted or banned German films in the 1920s; France, generally the most tolerant, in effect proscribed films made in the Soviet Union where, with Lenin's encouragement, the director Sergei Eisenstein brilliantly showed how well suited the medium was to depicting official views of the revolutionary power of the masses.

Consumerism While moralists worried about the cynicism of mass entertainment and the amoral excess of nightlife in cabarets and theaters, millions joined a kind of dizzying celebration. Middle-class families bought their first car; millions from every class, their first radio. Sophistication was a kind of shibboleth, used to justify lipstick, short skirts, alcohol, and one brash fad after another but also to underscore the cosmopolitanism that valued American jazz, openly learned from African art, and welcomed the new. For perhaps the only time, Berlin rivaled Paris as a European artistic center, more famous as the home of acid satire in art and theater than for its thriving cultural institutions of a more traditional sort. Modernism turned its back on gentility.

II. The New Revolutions

In Russia and in Italy the aftermath of war was revolution. Both nations had begun rapid industrialization in the 1890s, and both were sorely tested in the world war that followed. Revolution in Russia began while the war was still going on and continued for several years before its outcome was certain. Revolution in Italy occurred quickly a few years after the war. Each resulted in new kinds of political regimes, and only gradually did it begin to be clear that Russian communism and Italian fascism might change the face of Europe.

REVOLUTION IN RUSSIA

When world war broke out in 1914, Russia's parliament (the Duma) and local councils (or *zemstvos*) had helped coordinate the war effort. But when the Cadet party maintained its insistence on further liberal reforms, the Duma was suspended. Resentful that political aims should be pursued in wartime—they still did not see that a more rep-

resentative government could strengthen the war effort—the tsar and his officials grew increasingly isolated from the country. More skilled as a military strategist than as a head of state, Tsar Nicholas II grandly departed to command his army, leaving Tsarina Alexandra and those closest to her to oppose any program for reform. Her chief confidant was Grigori Rasputin, an ignorant and corrupt mystic whose influence symbolized the decadence of this regime.

▼ Gaudy movie palaces like this Parisian theater, one of the first, became prominent monuments in every city, offering the masses an exotic luxury previously associated with the great opera houses. Tallandier.

The February Revolution Throughout 1916 signs of Russia's failures accumulated. Production and transportation were undependable, war refugees filled the roads, inflation soared, and food shortages became critical. All this came on top of years of rising anger among peasants eager for land and workers determined to change their lot. Without realizing the depth of this social strife, officials were well aware of how serious the situation was. Even in the highest circles, there was talk of deposing the tsar. In November in the reconvened Duma, Pavel Milyukov, a noted historian and the leader of the liberal Cadets, courageously delivered a bitter attack on the government. In December a group of nobles murdered Rasputin. Strikes spread; and in March 1917, when strikers filled the streets of Petrograd,[2] their economic demands quickly broadened to include political issues. The army could not be relied on to oppose them. Once again, much as in 1905, the Soviet of Workers' and Soldiers' Deputies became the voice of revolution, and they joined with a Duma committee in seeking a provisional government. They prepared to resist any tsarist force that might be sent against them. None came. The military situation was desperate, the government in disarray, and the tsar unpopular. With nowhere to turn, Nicholas II abdicated, and the February Revolution[3] was hailed with joy and relief throughout the country.

The provisional government's central figure was Milyukov; its only socialist was Aleksandr Kerensky, a member of the Social Revolutionary party and vice-chairman of the Petrograd soviet. The new government quickly established broad civil liberties, an amnesty for political prisoners, and the end of religious persecution. It also proposed granting a constitution to Finland, which Russia ruled, and independence to Russian Poland. Declaring its support for an eight-hour workday and for the abolition of class privileges, it left most other social issues to a constituent assembly, which it promised to call soon.

In fact, the parties of revolution sharply disagreed on these issues. The Cadets, who dominated the provisional government, came to accept the idea of a republic, political democracy, and distribution of land with compensation to former owners. To their left, the Social Revolutionary party and the Menshevik wing of the Social Democratic party, which was especially strong in the soviets forming across the nation, demanded more drastic reforms. These parties were divided, too, however. Some of their members were willing to postpone these further reforms until after the war, which, like the Cadets, they still meant to win. The more radical of them stressed an early end to the war, without yet advocating an immediate armistice. For the time being, the soviets, watching from the outside and ever ready to criticize, allowed the provisional government its chance. To the left of all these factions stood a small group known as the Bolsheviks.

The Bolsheviks In 1898 Russian Marxists had secretly formed the Social Democratic party, which functioned mainly in the conspiratorial world of exile. At the party's second congress, held in Brussels and London in 1903, it had split into two groups, called the Bolsheviks (majority) and Mensheviks (minority); in fact, the Bolsheviks rarely had a majority, but these nicknames stuck. Their differences were theoretical, organizational, and personal. The theoretical issues, which engaged Marxists everywhere, were fought with the special intensity of revolutionaries far from home and power. On the whole, the Mensheviks placed greater emphasis on popular support and parliamentary institutions, which implied cooperation with other parties. The Bolsheviks stressed instead the need for a disciplined revolutionary party to instruct and lead the masses, which might otherwise be likely to settle for immediate gains rather than the European revolution that would bring about socialism. Led by Georgi Plekhanov and V. I. Lenin, the Bolsheviks denounced as enemies all who did not join them. Only later would these party battles waged in foreign cities prove significant for Russian history.

The ideas of socialism that spread in Russia after 1905 were not so much those of the Bolsheviks

---

[2] St. Petersburg was a German name, and in 1914 Nicholas had changed it to the Russian *Petrograd*. The capital until 1918, the city would become Leningrad in 1924 and St. Petersburg again in 1991.

[3] These events occurred on March 8–12 according to the Gregorian calendar used throughout the West. Russia, however, had never abandoned the older Julian calendar (which continues to be the calendar of the Orthodox Church). The revolutions of March 8–12 and November 7, 1917, according to the Gregorian system were dated thirteen days earlier according to the Julian, and they continue to be called the February and October revolutions.

as those of the Mensheviks and the Social Revolutionaries, who were less consistently Marxist and were closer to the peasants. Although Plekhanov tried on his own to heal the breach in the Social Democratic party, Lenin's conception of iron discipline allowed little room for compromise; and Plekhanov, too, was soon consigned to the Mensheviks.

Lenin's Tactics   Removed from events in Russia, Lenin continued from Switzerland to organize selected followers, denounce the heresies of others, and develop his theoretical view of the special role a militant party should play in a country that, like Russia, was just achieving modern capitalism. The party could achieve its aims, he argued, only by recognizing the revolutionary potential in the peasants' hunger for land (most Marxists considered the peasantry a socially backward class and land ownership opposed to socialism). Thus the Bolsheviks, although they lacked a large following in Russia, had a theory of how to make a revolution.

Lenin considered World War I a civil war among capitalists, and in a sense that theoretical stand gave Lenin his chance, for it suggested to the Germans that his presence in Russia as an agitator might be useful in undermining the Russian war effort. In April 1917 the Germans arranged to send Lenin by sealed train through Germany and Scandinavia to Russia. Lenin, however, had something grander than mere agitation in mind; and once again it began from a practical solution to a doctrinal problem.

Marxists were ambivalent in their attitude toward the February Revolution, which they welcomed as progressive but tended to disdain as a bourgeois revolution and not a victory of the proletariat. Lenin offered another interpretation: Revolution in Russia was part of a larger revolution about to sweep all of Europe. Socialists had no interest in the capitalist war, which Russia's provisional government continued to support, but Bolsheviks could seize the chance to push the revolution beyond its bourgeois phase to a "second stage" in which the soviets would be the true representatives of the proletariat. That in turn dictated the tactics the Bolsheviks should follow: They must gain the leadership of the soviets, and then Russia could join in the international revolution that was imminent. Historians have em-

phasized Lenin's tactical flexibility, but in April his views seemed impossibly dogmatic even to radicals. It was the force of his personality, his political skill, and his oratory that kept him leader of the Bolsheviks.

Summer Crisis   While the soviets were building a national organization that claimed authority over railroads, telegraph lines, and troops, the provisional government was falling apart. Its members disagreed over war policy and land reform; its police and officials were abandoning their posts. Workers continued to strike, and nationalist movements erupted in Latvia, Georgia, and the Ukraine. Army morale was sinking when in March the Petrograd soviet issued its famous Order Number I: Officers would be chosen by their men and the army run by elected committees. The order was adopted in most military units, and a good part of the army simply melted away. In the face of a losing war effort, disruptive nationalism, and class conflict, a radical change in political leadership was imperative. Milyukov resigned, four more socialists joined the cabinet, and Kerensky, an energetic leader and effective orator, became the cabinet's leading figure.

The Kerensky government was quickly attacked from left and right. The Bolsheviks criticized Kerensky at the first all-Russian Congress of Soviets in June but gained support from just more than 100 of the 800 plus delegates. In July they attempted a coup in Petrograd. That was decisively defeated, and many of the coup leaders were arrested. Lenin fled to Finland.

Kerensky, still focused on the war, believed he could achieve a more effective and stable government with just one successful military offensive. Although prepared as carefully as possible, the offensive failed. His call for a national congress of all interests, intended to show that the soviets were isolated, revealed instead how deeply divided the nation was over war aims and social policy. Cities were torn by strikes and demonstrations as the situation at the front grew more perilous. In the countryside, manor houses were burned and landlords murdered as peasants rioted for land.

Convinced that a strong military hand was what the nation needed, the army's commander in chief, General Lavr Kornilov, led an attack on Petrograd in September. Kerensky asked the

Soviets (and thus the Bolsheviks as well) to defend the government. Most of Kornilov's men had refused to follow his orders, and the threat passed quickly. But in the meantime Bolshevik leaders had been released from prison, and Bolshevist propaganda was gaining ground with simple slogans promising peace, land, and bread—issues at the heart of daily life and ones for which the provisional government had no clear solutions.

The Bolsheviks won control of the soviets in Moscow and Petrograd, electing Leon Trotsky chairman of the latter. Trotsky, who had worked with Lenin in exile, had until recently stood somewhat aloof from party conflicts. Now firmly in Lenin's camp, he proceeded to organize the armed forces in Petrograd. With the Social Revolutionaries supporting peasant expropriation of land, the provisional government was left politically alone in a city it could not control trying to rule a nation in chaos and still at war.

The October Revolution   To the dismay of many in his party, Lenin boldly decided to seize power. When the second all-Russian Congress of Soviets met on November 7, he would confront it with a new government. Kerensky began countermeasures a few days before that date, but it was too late. On November 6, Red Guards (squads of armed workers), sailors, and soldiers captured the Winter Palace and strategic points throughout the city. A simultaneous movement in Moscow won control of the city in a week. Lenin announced to the Congress that the Bolsheviks held power and sent out a young officer to take command of the armies. At each stop along his route, the troops enthusiastically cheered his announcement of the Bolshevik coup. Their commanders could only acquiesce. Kerensky, who had escaped from the capital, tried to muster support; but the one group of Cossacks who moved on Petrograd was soundly defeated. The world's first Communist government had taken office (see "Two Accounts of Revolution in Russia," p. 997).

"All power to the Soviets!" had been one of the Bolsheviks' most effective slogans, and the Congress readily approved the one-party cabinet

▼ **The armed civilians in the foreground are Red Guards, demonstrating their might and protecting the Bolshevik leaders addressing a large crowd of workers.**
Sovfoto.

TWO ACCOUNTS OF REVOLUTION IN RUSSIA

◆◆◆

The culmination of the Russian Revolution came on November 7, 1917, when the Communists captured the Winter Palace, which was then the seat of the Kerensky government. Eyewitnesses saw the event very differently. The first account is by Pitirim Sorokin, a young member of the Social Revolutionary party, who would soon go into exile and have a distinguished career as a professor of sociology at Harvard. In his memoir, Leaves from a Russian Diary, *he recalled that day. The second description is from* Ten Days That Shook the World, *the famous book by John Reed, an American journalist who admired the Bolsheviks.*

"Lying ill all day on my bed, I listened to the steady booming of the cannon and the spatter of machine-guns and crack of rifles. Over the telephone I learned that the Bolsheviki had brought up from Kronstadt the warship *Aurora* and had opened fire on the Winter Palace, demanding the surrender of members of the Provisional Government, still barricaded there. At seven in the evening I went to the Municipal Duma. With many matters before us, the immediate horror that faced us was this situation at the Winter Palace. There was a regiment of women and the military cadets were bravely resisting an overwhelming force of Bolshevist troops, and over the telephone Minister Konovalov was appealing for aid. Poor women, poor lads, their situation was desperate, for we knew that the wild sailors, after taking the Palace, would probably tear them to pieces. What could we do? After breathless council it was decided that all of us, the Soviets, Municipalities, Committees of Socialist Parties, members of the Council of the Republic, should go in procession to the Winter Palace and do our utmost to rescue the Ministers, the women soldiers, and the cadets. Even as we prepared to go, over the telephone came the despairing shout: 'The gates of the Palace have been forced. The massacre has begun. . . . Hurry! The mob has reached the first floor. All is over. Goodbye. . . . They break in. They are. . . . 'The last word . . . from the Winter Palace was a broken cry. . . .

"Carried along by the eager wave of men we were swept into the right-hand entrance, opening into a great bare vaulted room, the cellar of the east wind, from which issued a maze of corridors and staircases. A number of huge packing cases stood about, and upon these the Red Guards and soldiers fell furiously, battering them open with the butts of their rifles, and pulling out carpets, curtains, linen, porcelain plates, glassware. . . . One man went strutting around with a bronze clock perched on his shoulder; another found a plume of ostrich feathers, which he stuck in his hat. The looting was just beginning when somebody cried, 'Comrades! Don't touch anything! Don't take anything! This is the property of the People!' Immediately twenty voices were crying, 'Stop! Put everything back! Don't take anything! Property of the People!' Many hands dragged the spoilers down. Damask and tapestry were snatched from the arms of those who had them; two men took away the bronze clock. Roughly and hastily the things were crammed back in their cases, and self-appointed sentinels stood guard. It was all utterly spontaneous. Through corridors and up staircases the cry could be heard growing fainter and fainter in the distance, 'Revolutionary discipline! Property of the People'"

From Pitrim Alexandrovitch Sorokin, *Leaves from a Russian Diary.* E. P. Dutton, 1920. Expanded edition Beacon Press, 1950.

Lenin presented it. The rudiments of a new form of government emerged: The Congress of Soviets replaced parliament and elected a Central Executive committee to advise the Council of People's Commissars, or cabinet. From the very first, Bolshevik rule did not depend on any elected body. Elections for the promised constituent assembly, held at the end of November, would be the last open competition among parties for more than seventy years. The Bolsheviks won a quarter of the seats, other socialist parties more than 60 percent, conservatives and liberals the rest. As the assembly met on its second day, the military guards told it to adjourn.

Lenin provided a basis for such ruthlessness in his pamphlet "The State and Revolution," written in Finland in the summer of 1917. It used the Marxist conception that the state is the coercive organ of the ruling class to argue that, once the Bolsheviks held power, the proletariat would be that ruling class. The dictatorship of the proletariat, Lenin reasoned, was the only way to lead backward Russia through the transition to that higher historical stage that Marxists envisioned in which a state would no longer be necessary. The nationalization of land and factories would achieve socialism. Communism would follow once everyone learned to work for the good of society and once production met the needs of all. Until then, the single party, the "vanguard of the proletariat," would be model and guide. That party, as Lenin envisioned it, would sustain its enthusiasm through open discussion in which differences would be reconciled and criticisms would keep officials on their toes. By this combination of theory, attention to such immediate issues as bread and land, and ruthless but flexible tactics, Lenin placed himself beside Marx as a founder of modern communism.

TOWARD A COMMUNIST SOCIETY

Millions of workers, soldiers, and peasants had joined in pulling down the old system, and the Bolshevik leaders were determined to snatch their historical moment. The day after taking the Winter Palace, the new government decreed that land, livestock, and farm equipment belonged to the state but could be "temporarily" held by peasant committees, thereby legitimizing the rural revolution that was taking place anyway.

Initial Policies   No peasant was to work for hire, and committees of the poor would supervise the allocation of land and produce. Workers' committees would share in factory management, and everyone would be paid according to the work done (the state's new leaders assigned themselves laborers' salaries). All social titles and military ranks were abolished. "People's tribunals" and workers' militias replaced tsarist courts and police. Church and state were separated; the equality of the sexes was decreed and followed by regulations allowing divorce by mutual consent, measures that enhanced the reputation of Russian communism in Western Europe. Even the alphabet was reformed and the Gregorian calendar adopted.

In the next few months, railroads, banks, and shipping concerns were nationalized; foreign trade

---

Chronology
THE CONFLICTS THAT RESULTED IN COMMUNIST VICTORY

March 1917	February Revolution
November 1917	October Revolution
March 1918	Peace of Brest Litovsk
1918 – 1920	Civil war
1920 – 1921	War with Poland
1921	Kronstadt mutiny
1922	Japanese troops leave Russian territory

---

became a state monopoly, and Russia's debts were repudiated. The various nationalities of Russia were declared equal and granted the right of secession; and Finland took advantage of that decree to separate from Russia in December 1917, while the Bolsheviks struggled to prevent the Ukraine and the ethnic groups of the Baltic regions from following suit.

Revolutionary measures also made way for a reign of terror. A new secret police, the Cheka, differed from tsarist police in determination more than method. The citizens who sat on the new committees and tribunals often combined revolutionary enthusiasm with personal vengeance, and tens of thousands lost their property, their rights, and their lives for "mistaken" alliances, "false" ideas, or "suspect" gestures. Such practices, which helped the regime solidify support, also threatened to undermine the regular procedures of government.

Ending the War with Germay   The most pressing issue was to find a way out of the war. The Bolsheviks had asked all nations to accept peace without annexations. When rebuffed, they shocked the world by publishing secret Allied agreements that revealed the cynicism of their territorial ambitions. Then in February 1918 a delegation headed by Trotsky, having failed to arrange terms of peace with Germany, proposed a policy of no peace, no war: Russia would just stop fighting. The Germans advanced to within 100 miles of Petrograd, and in March the Russians accepted the Treaty of Brest Litovsk. Russia surrendered more than 1 million square miles of territory to Germany, including a third of its arable land, a third of its factories, and three-quarters of its deposits of iron and coal. It granted the independence of Finland, Georgia, and the Ukraine; left to Germany the disposition of Russian Poland, Lithuania, Latvia, and Estonia; and ceded parts of Transcaucasia to the Ottoman Empire. The communists paid this high price for peace, confident that revolution in Germany would soon nullify the kaiser's gains.

The peace treaty, like the course of the revolution itself, exposed the discontent among non-Russian nationalities, and in July a new constitution tried to meet that problem by declaring Russia a federation—the Russian Soviet Federated Socialist Republic (R.S.F.S.R.). Great Russia, extending through Siberia, was the largest member. Ostensibly, political power rested with the local soviets, organized by occupation and elected by the votes of all men and women except for members of the clergy, former high officials, and those classified as bourgeois "nontoilers." These soviets elected delegates to the congress of soviets of their canton, the smallest administrative unit, and each of these congresses in turn sent delegates to a congress at the next administrative level. The system, which continued by steps up to the all-Russia Congress, allowed considerable control from the top. The constitution did not mention the Russian Communist party, as it was now named, although it was the real center of political authority. Its Central Committee elected the smaller Politburo, which shared ruling power with the governing Council of People's Commissars. Lenin was the dominant figure in both.

Civil War The Bolsheviks were still surrounded by enemies. In March Allied troops in small numbers had landed in Murmansk, Archangel, and Vladivostok to prevent the supplies shipped to Russia from falling into German hands, but those detachments might also be used to support a change of regime (a move some Allied officials favored). In addition, the Soviet government had re-luctantly permitted a Czech brigade of some 30,000 men to go by rail from the Eastern front to Vladivostok in order to sail around the world to the Western front and fight against the Germans. On the long train journey, the Czechs clashed with some Hungarian prisoners of war; the fighting spread, and the Czechs, aided by Russian anti-Bolsheviks, captured one train station after another. Allied leaders decided to seize this opportunity and ordered the Czechs to move back along the railway toward the center of Russia, in effect creating new bases for anti-Soviet military action. At the same time, a number of tsarist generals, among them the army's former commander-in-chief, Kornilov, were preparing to lead a small but excellent army of Cossacks against the Bolsheviks. It was the beginning of a civil war that would last for two terrible years.

While Trotsky undertook to organize the new regime's army, opponents formed fighting units in many regions. Anti-Bolsheviks of every stripe, including the Social Revolutionaries, organized in hundreds of villages and towns. Across Russia, food riots, battles over land, skirmishes between workers and bourgeois, and ethnic hatred added to the violence. With the economy near collapse, the Bolsheviks adopted "War Communism," a program to extract from a country in chaos just enough men and supplies to fight a civil war through propaganda, requisitioning, police repression, and terror. With the firm leadership of Lenin, the military talent of Trotsky, and above all the mistakes of their enemies, they would eventually win.

By mid-1919 the major remaining threat came from armies under the command of former tsarist officers. One army pushed from the Urals toward Moscow but was stopped before it got there. Another took Kiev in August and reached within 300 miles of Moscow by October, while a third stood only 30 miles from Petrograd. These armies were weakened, however, by their conflicting ambitions; and they did little to win popular support. The areas under their control experienced a terror less efficient but at least as brutal as that conducted by the revolutionaries. With each defeat, more of the anticommunist soldiers melted away until hardly more than marauding bands were left. By the end of 1919, they were in general retreat. Their most important group withdrew to the

▲ **Uncomfortable with the pomp of conventional armies, the Bolsheviks were nevertheless proud of the forces that had won the civil war. Here Trotsky reviews the Moscow Brigade of the Red Army.**
Ria-Novosti/Sovfoto.

Crimea early in 1920 and stubbornly fought on before finally heeding Allied advice and evacuating the remaining men in November 1920.

The Last of the Fighting The Communists had to fight against Poland as well. As provided by the Versailles treaty, an Allied commission had determined the Russo-Polish border, placing it along a line that assigned to Poland most areas in which Poles were a clear majority. Poland wanted more and insisted on its boundary of 1772, well to the east, citing cultural and historical arguments. Rejecting Russian offers of compromise, Poland sent an army into the Ukraine in March 1920. Within a month it took Kiev, but the Ukranian nationalists who had fought the Russians were unwilling to fight for the Poles. In August the Red army, by now a relatively efficient military machine,

launched an assault that soon threatened Warsaw. An effective Polish counterattack led in 1921 to a compromise settlement after all, one by which Poland gained considerable non-Polish territory in the Ukraine and White Russia. Once Russia's western border was settled, it was possible to agree on a boundary with Turkey as well. It ignored local independence movements, and assigned Armenia and Georgia to the Soviet federation, Kars and Ardahan to Turkey. Fighting continued in Asia until 1922 when Japan withdrew from eastern Siberia. By then, the Soviet Union was firmly in Communist hands.

Continuing Turmoil Under War Communism, regimentation and bloodshed were the means of survival, and by using them, the Communist party had become increasingly powerful; yet most of the countryside was still subject to the whims of local party officials and roving bands of armed men. Cities were partially empty, a million Russians had gone into exile, tens of millions more had died, manufacturing produced less in 1920 than in 1913, foreign trade had almost ceased, and poor harvests raised the specter of famine. Requisitions spurred resistance, and black markets flourished. Thus the mutiny of sailors at the Kronstadt naval base in March 1921 was an ominous sign.[4] These sailors were the sort of men who had made the October Revolution possible; and though their revolt was soon quelled and their demands for political liberty rejected, Lenin recognized the need for change.

The New Economic Policy   Lenin announced the New Economic Policy (NEP), a major turning point in the development of Communist Russia. To many, the NEP seemed a departure from Marxism, but Lenin saw Russia's problems as the result not of flaws in Marxist theory but of having stormed the "citadel of capitalism" too fast. Russia suffered from old habits hard to uproot and from a lack of technical experts and managers that a modern economy required. With noteworthy pragmatism, Lenin proposed a moderate course that earlier the Bolsheviks would have opposed.

Under the NEP, peasants were no longer subject to requisitions but rather to a tax in kind. Businesses employing fewer than twenty workers could be run as private enterprises, and nationalized industries could be leased to foreigners as a way of training Russians in efficient methods. Fiscal reforms guaranteed a stable currency, helping Russia's external trade to emerge from the pattern of barter into which it had fallen. Recovery was slow. Millions died in the famine of 1920–1921 despite the extensive aid of the American Relief Administration, and not for another six years would production reach prewar levels.

---

[4] Denounced as part of an international counterrevolutionary conspiracy, the members of the Kronstadt base who were captured after the mutiny was crushed were subject to executions and deportations, and for seventy years the event was cited in Soviet histories as an example of the kinds of forces arrayed against the revolution. In 1994 Boris Yeltsin announced the rehabilitation of these rebels, and the event was used as evidence that the brutality of Communist rule had begun with Lenin's ruthlessness.

Communist Rule   Abandoning the hope of creating Communism all at once, the NEP was nevertheless the reaffirmation of Communist determination. Every social institution was recruited to help create a stable new society. Cooperatives and trade unions, newspapers and public meetings taught efficiency and pride in class and nation, as did the school system, which was improved and extended. Its curriculum stressed official doctrines; workers' children were favored for admission to selective schools, and teachers were urged to abandon old-fashioned rote learning. Women were encouraged to work outside the home and were provided a whole series of programs aimed at their special needs as mothers. The problems of ruling over multiple nationalities had eased somewhat with the cession of so much territory in the Treaty of Brest Litovsk, and three-quarters of the remaining population could be called Russian. Officially non-Russian nationalities were given more recognition than ever before, as the Communist government reassembled much of the Russian empire, and the Orthodox Church, while kept under tight supervision, was permitted to function.

In practice, the Communist party, which remained a restricted elite, was the most important instrument of rule. Organized in a hierarchy that paralleled the bureaucracy, it reached into every aspect of public life—factories, hundreds of new centers for adult education, and youth associations—propagandizing and encouraging, pressuring and explaining. In 1922 cultural activities were placed directly under the Ministry of Education, and the Western artistic movements recently welcomed were discouraged in favor of books and art that met the current definition of communist aesthetics: realistic in style, popular in appeal, and useful to the new order. Issues of practical policy were thrashed out within the government and the party, but to be on the losing side could be politically and sometimes personally fatal. Although the Communist government would never abandon the fear of foreign attack established during the civil war, it gave signs of seeking normal diplomatic relations; and by 1924, the year of Lenin's death, every major power except the United States had recognized the new regime. Still an object of fear to liberals and conservatives, the new Communist state became a source of inspiration and hope for the far left throughout

ITALIAN FASCISM

Postwar Europe witnessed another experiment in a new form of government in Italy, economically the least developed of the major Western powers. Italy and Russia had begun extensive industrialization at about the same time in the late nineteenth century, and there were many parallels between the two countries, despite Italy's more urban society, greater freedom, stronger constitutional tradition, and more responsive governments. With the end of the war, Italy was racked by inflation, unemployment, and talk of revolution. In many places peasants simply confiscated the land they had long been promised; and when in 1920 industrialists met a series of strikes with lockouts, workers answered by occupying factories, and many in the upper classes feared a communist revolution. Social conflicts that the state had largely ignored for twenty years now challenged the established system. The peace treaty, too, was disillusioning. Although granted considerable territory, Italy got less than expected, and its treatment by the other Allies was often humiliating. Disposition of the Dalmatian port of Fiume was still being argued in 1919 when a private expedition led by Gabriele d'Annunzio dramatically captured it for Italy. The nation's most famous living poet, d'Annunzio ruled Fiume for more than a year at the head of an "army" of the unemployed, whose nationalist frenzy and vulgar slogans were for many a welcome contrast to the wordy frustration of diplomacy. Eventually, the Italian government evicted him, but he had shown the effectiveness of direct action in a nationalist cause.

The Victory of Fascism The Fascist movement was born amid these crises. The term *fascio*, meaning "bundle," comes from an ancient Roman symbol of authority—a bundle of sticks, individually weak but strong in unity. Echoes of imperial Rome were part of the Fascist mystique. The movement centered around Benito Mussolini, whose polemical skills won him promotion to the editorship of the Socialist party newspaper until he was expelled in 1915 for favoring Italy's entry into the war. Mussolini, who established another paper, became one of Italy's noisiest nationalists, using the rhetoric of the left to denounce liberalism and parliamentary indecision and the slogans of nationalism to castigate Marxists. Fascism grew from this diverse heritage. Both a movement and a party, it employed propaganda, symbols, and activism in new ways, making party militants in their black shirts seem a civilian army.

At first the Fascists had little electoral success, but the changes in Italian politics offered them multiple opportunities. The elections of 1921 were the first in Italy with universal male suffrage, and two newer, well-organized mass parties overshadowed the traditional leaders and groups. The Catholic Popular party demanded major reforms, but much of its real strength came from rural and conservative groups. The Socialists, for all their increased strength, were weakened by the split with their left wing, which formed a Communist party, inspired by the Bolsheviks' success in Russia.

The Fascists, who had won no seats in 1919, gained thirty-five in the new Chamber; and the aging Giolitti, who had been a dominating prime minister in the prewar era, tried to patch together a personal coalition that included the Fascists in a "national bloc" of candidates. Instead of being domesticated to parliamentary ways as Giolitti expected, they used the electoral campaign to demonstrate their style. Fascist squads in black shirts planted bombs, beat up opponents, and disrupted meetings, enjoying violence and intimidation while denouncing Marxists as a threat to order.

The Weakness of Opposition When left-wing unions called a general strike in 1922, raising fears of revolution, Mussolini's Black Shirts grew more threatening and started taking over town councils by force. While politicians struggled to find a parliamentary majority, the Fascists staged a march on Rome in October. Motley squads of party militants moved on the capital in a grand gesture of revolt while Mussolini cautiously waited in Milan. Belatedly, parliamentary leaders called for martial law, but King Victor Emmanuel III refused. Mussolini dashed to Rome, where the king invited him to form a cabinet; the largely symbolic revolt had been enough to capture power. Claiming the office both as a matter of perfect legality and by right of conquest, Mussolini at age thirty-nine became prime minister of a coalition government. In the elections of 1924, Fascists won a massive victory. Intimidation and fraud contributed to this success, but most Italians were willing to give the new party a chance.

In the following year, it became clearer what a Fascist regime would mean. Giacomo Matteotti, a Socialist who bravely stood before the entire Chamber to enumerate Fascist crimes, was subsequently murdered in gangland style. As public condemnation mounted, Mussolini's government seemed about to topple, but the opponents of Fascism were no more able to unite now than when they had been stronger. The Fascists gradually isolated first the Socialist and then the Popular party, which was weakened by the Vatican's distaste for its program of social reform. By 1925 all the opponents of Fascism had been expelled from the legislature, and newspapers either printed what they were told or risked suppression. The Fascist period had begun.

To many in and out of Italy, it seemed merely that the nation at last had a strong, antisocialist leader. Some distinguished Italians were associated with the regime in various ways, men such as the poet Gabriele d'Annunzio, the sociologist Vilfredo Pareto, the composer Giacomo Puccini, the playwright Luigi Pirandello, and some of the avant-garde Futurist artists. Even moderates found it hard to believe that a party whose program contained so many contradictions—Fascists praised revolution and promised a strong state, defended property and called for social change, advocated order and used violence—could be dangerous for long.

Fascist Rule Mussolini moved slowly to institutionalize his power. A series of special laws passed by 1926 declared the Duce (leader) of Fascism the head of state with the right to set the Chamber's agenda and to govern by decree. For twenty years, nearly all the laws of Italy would be issued in that way. Opposition parties were outlawed, scores of potential opponents arrested, and the civil service and judiciary purged of any-

▼ **Mussolini and his bodyguard of Black-Shirted party members in paramilitary uniforms give the Fascist salute. The propaganda and rituals developed by Italian Fascists would be imitated across Europe.** AP/Wide World.

one thought too independent. Italy's newspapers were filled with pictures of Mussolini overawing visitors, captivating vast throngs, leaping hurdles on horseback, flying airplanes, harvesting grains. No story was too silly: The Duce recited the cantos of Dante from memory, he worked all night (the light in his office was carefully left on), he inspired philosophers and instructed economists, American razor blades were inadequate to the toughness of his beard, and his speed in race cars frightened experts. Slogans such as "the Duce is always right" and "Believe, Obey, Fight" soon covered walls throughout Italy. The victory of an Italian athlete or the birth of a child to a prolific mother became an occasion for hailing the new order as Mussolini's propaganda pumped pride and confidence into a troubled nation.

Despite considerable skepticism, the good news and sense of energy were welcome. Mussolini's sensitivity to the masses brought to Italian government a popular touch that it had lacked. By 1931 when the government demanded that all professors sign a loyalty oath, only eleven refused. With most people frightened into silence and organized resistance shattered, the regime had little to fear from some secret Communist groups and an underground centered in France.

The authoritarian single party, completely subordinate to the Duce, reached into every city and town with its own militia, secret police, and tribunals. Recruited in its early years mainly from among the unemployed and alienated, the Fascist party soon won hundreds of thousands of new members eager for the advantages it offered, until by the 1930s the party decided to accept members more selectively in an effort to achieve internal discipline. There were associations for Fascist teachers, workers, and university students. In youth organizations for every age group over four years old, the next generation wore black shirts, marched, and recited official slogans. Citizens were to replace the handshake with the extended right arm of the Fascist salute,[5] and regulations es-

▲ These ten-year-old boys were not, official propaganda declared, just playing at being soldiers but were ready with half-size rifles and lunch kits to defend their country. Millions of Italian children were enrolled in five organizations: one for boys and girls 6 and 7 years old, two separate ones for boys and girls from the ages of 8 to 13, and two more for those from 14 to 17. For the four years after that, they could belong to the Young Fascists.
UPI/Bettmann.

tablished the Fascist names to give one's children and the form of address to use with one's friends.

Fascist doctrine, never wholly consistent, denounced the principles of the French Revolution and of majority rule but hailed "the people." The much-advertised principle of authority was reduced to simple obedience to the Duce. Authority itself was deemed purer when arbitrary. There was said to be a Fascist style in art and philosophy, sport and war. A candid irrationalism suspi-

---

[5] The salute was a stylized form of the greeting used in ancient Rome and portrayed in the statue of Marcus Aurelius that since the Renaissance had stood on the Capitoline Hill in Rome, where Michelangelo designed a piazza to frame it. The salute quickly became an international symbol.

Fascist Doctrine

The most carefully constructed single statement of Fascist doctrine was the article "Fascism: Doctrine and Institutions," written in 1932 for the Enciclopedia Italiana, *one of the most impressive intellectual works accomplished under the Fascist regime. Although the article was officially listed as by Mussolini himself, most of it was written by Giovanni Gentile, a noted philosopher who was an early supporter of Fascism.*

"It [Fascism] is opposed to classical liberalism which arose as a reaction to absolutism and exhausted its historical function when the State became the expression of the conscience and will of the people. Liberalism denied the State in the name of the individual; Fascism reasserts the rights of the State as expressing the real essence of the individual. . . . The Fascist conception of the State is all-embracing; outside of it no human or spiritual values can exist, much less have value. Thus understood, Fascism is totalitarian, and the Fascist State—a synthesis and a unit inclusive of all values—interprets, develops, and potentiates the whole life of a people.

" . . . First of all, as regards the future development of mankind—and quite apart from present political considerations—Fascism does not, generally speaking, believe in the possibility or utility of perpetual peace. It therefore discards pacifism as a cloak for cowardly supine renunciation in contradistinction to self-sacrifice. War alone keys up all human energies to their maximum tension and sets the seal of nobility on those peoples who have the courage to face it. . . .

"Fascism denies the materialistic conception of happiness. . . . This means that Fascism denies the equation: well-being = happiness, which sees in men mere animals, content when they can feed and fatten, thus reducing them to a vegetative existence pure and simple.

"After socialism, Fascism trains its guns on the whole block of democratic ideologies, and rejects both their premises and their practical applications and implements. Fascism denies that numbers, as such, can be the determining factor in human society; it denies the right of numbers to govern by means of periodic consultations; it asserts the irremediable and fertile and beneficent inequality of men who cannot be leveled by any such mechanical and extrinsic device as universal suffrage.

" . . . The State, as conceived and realized by Fascism, is a spiritual and ethical entity for securing the political, juridical, and economic organization of the nation, an organization which in its origin and growth is a manifestation of the spirit. The State guarantees the internal and external safety of the country, but it also safeguards and transmits the spirit of the people, elaborated down the ages in its language, its customs, its faith. The State is not only the present, it is also the past and above all the future. Transcending the individual's brief spell of life, the State stands for the immanent conscience of the nation."

From S. William Halperin (ed.), *Mussolini and Italian Fascism,* Van Nostrand, 1964.

---

cious of intellectuals and traditional culture stressed the virtues of intuitive "thinking with the blood" and joy in war. As the antithesis of the decadent materialism of the democracies, Italy would influence the world and reclaim the heritage of imperial Rome (see "Fascist Doctrine").

The Corporate State The most discussed element of Fascism, the corporate state, was partly a

facade, partly an institutional expression of ideology. The intent was to organize each sector of production into a huge confederation, or corporation. Each corporation encompassed a syndicate of employers and one of workers, each headed by party members appointed by the government. Corporations were to establish industrywide policies and wage scales, and by 1926 the system was sufficiently in place to outlaw strikes, lockouts, and independent unions. In 1934 the number of corporations was set at twenty-two.[6] The Duce, as president of each corporation, appointed its council of delegates, which then also sat in the National Council of Corporations. These institutions, which never attained real autonomy, were further undercut by the strength of established interests and by Mussolini's habit of legislating by decree. They were presented, however, as the Fascist alternative to liberal forms of representation, replacing conflict with coordination.

The new order in its twenty years did not remake Italy, which never became as orderly, efficient, or docile as Fascists wished. A quiet and safely intellectual opposition was tolerated, exemplified by the relative freedom allowed the world-famous philosopher, Benedetto Croce. The twentieth century would witness greater tyranny and worse brutality; but freedom in Italy was crushed, the jails filled, hundreds of prominent figures exiled to dreary southern towns or desolate islands.

Domestic Policies Fascist economic policy sought *autarchy*, a self-sufficient national economy, and emphasized industrialization and technology. Initial distrust of big business soon attenuated, but the government remained active in economic affairs and often favored nationalization. For reasons of prestige, the value of the lira was set to equal the French franc, which hurt Italian exports and required restrictions that led to a painful devaluation. In the interest of self-sufficiency, the government launched its famous battle of grain in 1926, which succeeded (with enormous hoopla) in doubling grain production at great cost in efficiency.

Output per capita declined in the Fascist era. Generally, the industrial giants in steel, automobiles, rubber, and chemicals found it easy to deal with (and often to manipulate) Fascist bureau-

cracy. At the same time, the Institute for Industrial Reconstruction (IRI) established in 1933 provided subsidies to weak industries and often ended up owning them, a significant extension of government ownership. By 1940 real wages were down in both industry and agriculture.

Efforts to keep peasants on the land and to increase the birthrate at most merely slowed the contrary trends. But the regime did score some notable achievements, which it vigorously advertised. It suppressed the activities in Sicily of criminal groups called mafia, drained the malaria-infested marshes near Rome, built new railroads, and launched some superhighways. Enormous building projects contributed to employment. Workers benefited from the creation of centers with recreation halls, meeting rooms, and libraries in most towns and programs for vacations at seaside or mountain resorts. Family bonuses gave the poor an increased sense of security, and educational reforms put more people in school for longer periods.

The Lateran Agreements Fascism's most publicized accomplishment was its accommodation with the Vatican. Although Mussolini and most of his early followers were thoroughly anticlerical, the Fascist government adopted many measures the Church would welcome, putting crucifixes in classrooms and raising the budget for clerical salaries and church repairs. The Lateran treaties of 1929 ended sixty years of conflict between Italy and the Church. They recognized the tiny area of Vatican City as an independent state, and related agreements established religious teaching in public schools, guaranteed that marriage laws would conform to Catholic doctrine, promised to restrict Protestant activities, and set the indemnity to be paid the Church for its losses during Italian unification. A dispute that had seared the consciences of millions of Italians was at last resolved. Abroad, the agreement suggested that Fascism had won special favor from the papacy, an impression little dimmed by an encyclical of 1931 that warned against the worship of the state or by subsequent conflicts between Fascists and Church officials. Although these conflicts were bitter, Catholics were on the whole more generous toward Mussolini's regime than they had been toward its liberal predecessors.

---

[6] A corporation covered an entire sphere of production, from raw materials to manufacture and distribution, and the corporations were divided into three groups: 1) grains, fruits and vegetables, wines, edible oils, beets and sugar, livestock, forestry and lumber, and textiles; 2) metals, chemicals, clothing, paper and printing, construction, utilities, mining, and glass and pottery; 3) insurance and banking, fine arts and liberal professions, sea and air transportation, land transportation, public entertainment, and public lodging.

Within the country, potential opponents were baffled by Mussolini's apparent successes and, surrounded by propaganda, felt isolated and uncertain of what to believe. Indeed, most Italians probably shared some pride in their nation's heightened prestige. Outside Italy, important groups in all European and many South American nations sang the praises of Fascism's "bold experiment" that ended petty squabbling, ran the trains on time, kept order, and eliminated the threat of communism.

▼ **The techniques of modern art combined with evocations of ancient Rome in Fascist posters like this one for an exhibition in 1933 on the eleventh anniversary of the Fascist revolution.**
Studio Pizzi/Index.

III. The Retreat from Democracy

Within less than a decade after the Paris Peace Conference, democracy was in retreat across Europe. By 1929 authoritarian regimes had violated or eliminated the liberal constitutions of Hungary, Spain, Albania, Portugal, Lithuania, Poland, and Yugoslavia as well as Italy. By 1936 political liberty had also been suppressed in Romania, Austria, Bulgaria, Estonia, Latvia, and Greece as well as Germany. Most of these countries were among the poorest in Europe, but their political difficulties illustrate the broader trend. Divided over issues of social reform, nationality, and religion— differences amplified by new and angry socialist and peasant parties—they suffered increased disruption with each economic crisis and foreign threat.

AUTHORITARIAN REGIMES

Authoritarian leaders often flirted with fascism on the Italian model, only to find it dangerously uncontrollable. They sought through decisiveness and force to achieve stability in societies riven by social conflict and where religious and ethnic loyalties could be readily fanned into anger and hatred by ambitious politicians.

Eastern Europe Hungary was among the first to turn to authoritarian rule. Behind a constitutional facade, the Magyar aristocracy relied on a rigged electoral system to maintain its political dominance, protect its privileges, and stifle land reform. Under Admiral Horthy, who became head of state in 1920, the regime made sure that any threats of democracy were kept in check. Hungary was drawn to Italy both as another opponent of the peace treaties and as a model of order. In the 1930s fascist trappings increased, and successive governments became more antisemitic; yet Hungary never became a full-fledged modern dictatorship, and the government dissolved the most threatening fascist parties in 1939.

Romania's liberal government began to give way even before Carol II was called to the throne in 1930. King Carol admired Mussolini and secretly subsidized the Iron Guard, a fascist organization whose political violence and antisemitism imitated the worst of fascism in other countries.

▲ **The men of Romania's fascist Iron Guard movement marched in green shirts, its women's corps in green skirts.**
UPI/Bettmann.

The government stripped most Jews of land and citizenship, tightened censorship, and imposed martial law, but the disruptions that followed and pressure from Britain and France brought a shift in policy. By 1938 the king led the way in suppressing fascist activities.

In Yugoslavia, King Alexander I assumed dictatorial powers in 1929 in an effort to tame the divisive forces of Croatian, Slovenian, and Serbian nationalism. But as these conflicts continued, he tried a restricted parliamentarianism. The regent, who directed affairs after Alexander's death in 1934, pursued a similar course, drawn at first to the example of Germany and Italy, and then de-

ciding by 1939 that Yugoslavia's international position and internal stability would best be served by a federal and democratic system.

In Bulgaria a military coup ended parliament, parties, and free speech in 1934, and the regime moved closer to fascism as it sought both urban and rural support. But by 1936 the king was restricting the military, banning some fascist groups, and talking of constitutions.

Fear of Germany and the need for French support was one reason these regimes turned away from fascism, but there was another. Authoritarians, attracted to fascism because of its ability to mobilize a mass following in the name of order, were soon threatened by this very ability to rouse support, by the ambitions of fascist leaders, and by the backlash against fascist tactics.

The Republics of Poland, Greece, and Austria
Although republican regimes were more necessarily in touch with public opinion, they faced similar conflicts over land reform and labor. Their political systems, too, were subject to the mutual fears of left and right and to international pressures. Poland especially suffered from having powerful neighbors, and Poles disagreed on whether their national interest lay with Germany, Russia, or France. Socialists and Catholics, conservative landowners and radical peasants, looked in different directions for outside support as they battled each other, and the resulting instability brought Marshal Jozef Pilsudski to the fore. A former socialist, he took power in 1926 in a military revolt; and Poland continued to be ruled by men from the military after he resigned in 1930, once his supporters had gained a majority in parliament. Unable to quell the noisy conflicts of fascists and socialists and without a popular base, they persisted in trying to strengthen a nation badly hurt by the worldwide economic depression of the 1930s.

The Greek republic, founded in 1924, lasted little more than a decade. As liberals gradually lost ground and monarchists gained, republicans attempted a coup but failed to prevent a plebescite in 1935, which the monarchists manipulated and which led to King George II's return to the throne. When liberals made gains in the 1936 elections, General Joannes Metaxas proclaimed himself dictator and clung to power in fascist style by balancing severe censorship and the abolition of political parties with extensive social welfare, public works, and armament.

In Austria the republic was undermined by the sharp division between a Catholic German countryside and a cosmopolitan imperial Vienna that no longer had an empire to administer. The Socialists, out of power since 1926, had little strength beyond the city, while the Christian Socialists—whose nineteenth-century programs of welfare, nationalism, and antisemitism had influenced the young Hitler—moved steadily toward fascism. In the 1920s both parties had established paramilitary organizations, and their violent clashes became a regular part of Austrian politics. Chancellor Engelbert Dollfuss drew Austria closer to Fascist Italy and ruled by decree, suspending parliament, outlawing communists, and by 1934, banning all parties ex-

cept his own Fatherland Front. The Socialists responded with a general strike, and the government replied by bombarding Karl Marx Hof, the public housing that Viennese socialists had been so proud of, an act that symbolized the end of Austrian democracy. A new constitution, elaborately corporative and claiming inspiration from papal encyclicals, was announced in 1934 but never really put into operation. Events in Germany, where Hitler and the Nazis had come to power, now overshadowed everything else in Austrian politics. In July a group of Austria's Nazis assassinated the Austrian chancellor. Although the Anschluss, or union with Germany, that they thought would follow did not come immediately, Austria's authoritarian government, having repressed the left, had little basis from which to resist growing Nazi pressure.

▼ Police in Vienna prepare to confront socialists in 1927. The socialists were protesting the release of men believed to have murdered a socialist. In the ensuing riots, the palace of justice was burned and a hundred people were killed, part of the cycle of violence shaking the Austrian republic.
UPI/Corbis-Bettmann.

Spain With its overstaffed army, discontented workers, militant anarchists, and socialists, Spain was already a strife-torn nation in 1921 when its army in Spanish Morocco was routed by Berber tribesmen. The resulting turmoil at home temporarily ended in 1923 when General Miguel Primo de Rivera issued a *pronunciamento* in time-honored style and assumed office as de facto dictator. Without a clear program, he used the themes of modern antiliberalism and Mussolinian techniques, dividing the left with extensive welfare programs and establishing a political party of his own. Experiments with corporatism followed, but by 1926 intellectuals, business people, the Church, and the army were restive. As economic depression hit and the government faltered, King Alfonso lost his taste for Primo de Rivera's attempt at a fascist constitution, and the dictator went into exile. The king, who now presented himself as the protector of liberty, tried another military government, which experimented in turn with both martial law and the promise of constitutionalism, but all the old problems remained. When republicans and socialists triumphed in the municipal elections of 1931, Alfonso also chose exile.

The second Spanish republic briefly held its divergent supporters together with progressive labor legislation and welfare programs ill-adapted to Spain's economy. It granted autonomy to Catalonia but left unresolved other regional conflicts and the critical problem of effective land reform. Its policies separating church and state and secularizing education infuriated half of Spain without satisfying the anticlericals. Neither a conservative government nor a leftist coalition could keep opposition from growing more radical, both on the far left and on the right, where a movement called the Falange (in direct imitation of Italian Fascism), founded by José Antonio Primo de Rivera, the dictator's son, grew stronger. Systematic street violence was commonplace by 1936, when a group of army generals announced their revolt. The Spanish civil war that followed would set the stage for World War II.

International Fascism Whether they won power or not, Europe's fascist movements had much in common. Generally influenced by Italian Fascism, they looked and sounded similar. They liked uniforms, starting with a shirt of one color. Cheap to buy and easy to adopt, it made a group of supporters (however few or poor) look like a movement, a historical force. They used paramilitary organization that promised decisive action to remake society through discipline and force. They created drama in the streets—noise, marches, colorful demonstrations, symbolic acts, and real violence—that undermined conventional standards of public behavior while advertising fascism as something new and powerful. They borrowed heavily from working-class movements and used all the devices of democratic politics, while seeming to stand outside the corrupting process of compromise and responsibility. Populist tactics were thus attached to the promise of order.

Fascists nostalgically evoked the enthusiastic patriotism of World War I to offer simple solutions to real problems. The disruption and inequity of capitalism, class conflict, a faltering economy, and aimless governments were the fault of enemies—liberal politicians, Marxist revolutionaries, Jews, and foreigners. Those enemies, although ridiculed and denounced in fascist propaganda, were credited with hidden powers that only the force of fascism could overcome. Fascism promised to create a united, orderly, prosperous community.

There was more to these movements than their simple myths, camaraderie, and sinister attraction to violence. Fascists addressed real fears. They spoke to a rural society that felt threatened by urbanization, to small-business people threatened by the competition of large corporations and to all business people threatened by workers' demands and government intervention, to a middle class threatened by socialism, to the privileged threatened by democracy, to the unemployed threatened by continuing economic depression, to the religious threatened by a secular society. Everywhere, they played on fear of a communist revolution.

The Appeal of Fascism Fascists could do all this by borrowing freely from ideas current throughout Europe. They used socialist criticisms of liberalism and capitalism, conservative values of hierarchy and order, and intellectual denunciations of modern culture. They amplified a widespread contempt for parliamentary ineffectiveness, used doctrines of race made familiar by war and imperialism, and laid claim to the nationalism that every government liked to invoke. At the same time, as admirers of technology and organization, fascists promised to create more modern societies. And they laid claim to corporatism, which Mussolini's Italy advertised as the wave of the future.

Corporatist thought had a long history and in its current form emphasized the organization of society and parliament according to occupational groups instead of interests or parties. Such structures, it was argued, would preserve natural hierarchies while avoiding the divisiveness of class conflict or conventional politics. The idea of an integrated society sharing a common purpose gained attractiveness in the years of economic depression and prestige with Pope Pius XI's encyclical *Quadragesimo Anno* ("In the Fortieth Year") issued in 1931 on the fortieth anniversary of Leo XIII's *Rerum Novarum*. The new encyclical went further in rejecting the injustices of capitalism and the solutions of Marxism, and it called instead for a harmony based on religion and cooperation through corporative organization. Many anxious people found in that papal pronouncement a sympathy for fascism that seemed to justify overlooking its deeply antireligious qualities.

The appeal of fascism was not limited to poor nations. Its ambiguities made it applicable everywhere. In Britain, Sir Oswald Mosley, once considered a likely Labour prime minister, founded the British Union of Fascists. In Belgium, fascism benefited from the antagonism between Catholics and anticlericals and between French-speaking Walloons and Dutch-speaking Flemings, who were increasingly sympathetic to fascism and to the Nazis. In the Netherlands a National Socialist movement rose to prominence in the 1930s, and there were a number of fascist and protofascist movements in France, including *Action Française*, which had become prominent in the furor of the Dreyfus case. Led by Charles Maurras, its denunciations of the bourgeois republic were echoed by fascist parties everywhere; but *Action Française* lacked the mass appeal of full-fledged fascism and was overshadowed in the 1930s by other movements of uniformed young militants eager to take to the streets.

THE GREAT DEPRESSION

Above all, fascist and Marxist movements benefited from a worldwide economic depression that undermined social and political stability and seemed to many the death knell of capitalism.

The Stock Market Crash   On October 24, 1929, the price of stocks on the New York Exchange began to plummet. Suspecting that speculation had pushed stock prices too high, nervous investors sold their shares. Day after day tens of millions of dollars in paper assets disappeared. Such panics were not new, and they had spread from New York to Europe in the previous century. Now, however, the United States was the world's wealthiest nation and greatest creditor, and this panic settled into full-scale depression as banks failed, businesses cut back, consumption declined, factories closed, and unemployment rose. Its banks and exchanges shaken, the European economy suffered further from the decline in world trade and the withdrawal of American investments and loans. Financial panic hit Europe in May 1931 when Austria's largest bank nearly went under. That started a run on Austrian and German banks and then spread as it had in the United States to other sectors of the economy and to other nations.

The late 1920s had been years of boom in the United States and of general prosperity in Europe, but the Great Depression exposed deep-seated problems. Not all industries had recovered after the war. Coal and textile industries had long been sliding toward chronic depression. Former trade patterns had not revived, especially among the underdeveloped new countries of Eastern Europe, and economic difficulties were increased by Germany's inflation and Russia's withdrawal from commerce. Europe, which lost huge amounts of foreign investments during the war, had not regained its prewar percentage of world trade (about half), and American investments in Europe increased dramatically throughout the 1920s. Too much of the international economy rested on the unproductive passing of paper from the United States to Germany as loans, from Germany to the Allies as reparations, and from the Allies to the United States as payment of war debts; and the United States raised tariffs in 1922 and again in 1930 to levels that made it nearly impossible for Europeans to earn dollars by selling to Americans. Much of the prosperity of the 1920s rested on new processes and on new products, such as automobiles and synthetic fabrics, which proved vulnerable to the withdrawal of American investment and the decline in consumer confidence. The Great Depression underscored how uneven and artificial much of the preceding prosperity had been and showed that for Europe ten years had not been long enough to overcome the effects of World War I.

The Repercussions   By 1932 the world's industrial production was two-thirds of what it had been in 1929. Unemployment climbed to more than 13 million in the United States, 6 million in Germany, and nearly 3 million in Great Britain. Among leading industrial nations, only France, with its balanced economy and lower fertility rate, escaped a crisis of unemployment. Since the war,

and especially in democracies, governments were expected to provide solutions to economic problems. They looked first for international help. Because the reparations system had broken down amid the world economic crisis, European nations declared that they could no longer make debt payments to the United States. The United States refused to acknowledge the connection. Instead, President Hoover proposed that all intergovernment payments be suspended; his proposal, quickly accepted in 1932, was supposed to be temporary but in fact marked the end of both kinds of payments.

Other crises loomed. Austria's banking system had been saved from bankruptcy with British loans; but the deepening depression and other financial burdens forced Great Britain to abandon

▼ **Unemployed workers from Glasgow set out for London on a "famine march" in 1934.**
Mary Evans Picture Library.

the gold standard, which meant it no longer guaranteed the value of the pound sterling. The important bloc of countries that traded in sterling followed suit. Tantamount to devaluation, these moves threatened chaos for international monetary exchanges and trade; and so the League of Nations sponsored a World Economic Conference that met in London in 1933. Begun with visions of high statesmanship, it ended in failure. When the United States also went off the gold standard, the structure of credit and exchange that had been one of the signal achievements of liberal finance fell apart. For a century nations, like so many bankers, had supported international financial stability by honoring these rules of liberal economics, and that historic era had ended.[7]

National Responses In this crisis democracies responded first to domestic pressures. Austria and Germany sought a customs union, which was opposed by France and rejected by the World Court. Nearly everyone raised tariffs and import quotas, further reducing trade, while domestic programs protected political interests. Liberals were at a loss as to what else to do, and socialists were no better prepared to solve the problems of declining commerce, insufficient capital, and—most pressing of all—unemployment. Socialists could find some vindication in the evident weakness of capitalism, but their favorite nostrum, the nationalization of industry, was barely relevant. In practice, they adopted rather orthodox measures of budget reduction while supporting whatever palliatives for unemployment could be suggested, though the dole, the most common one, strained the budgets they wanted to balance.

Most government policies, then, did little to help and may have made the situation worse; bankers and financiers, desperate to stem their losses, gave little attention to the international or social effects of their actions. And the millions of unemployed were more helpless still, standing in line for the dole, eating whatever they could get, taking any bits of work available. Growing communist parties let no one forget that while a whole

international system had been collapsing, Soviet production advanced at a steady pace.

Gradually, economic conditions did improve; and by 1937, production in Germany, Britain, and Sweden was well above the 1929 level, though below that in the United States, Italy, Belgium, and France. Subsequent government intervention to shore up industries and provide employment did alleviate distress and improve morale. It also hanged economic and political life and, at least in democracies, was often as socially divisive as the Depression itself. Democracies faced the dual threat of communism and fascism with a heavy burden of economic and social failure.

IV. The Rise of Totalitarianism

Dictatorship has been recognized since ancient times as a specific political form. The most important dictatorships of this century, however, were different enough from previous examples to merit a separate term. They relied on a single political party, absolute devotion to a leader, domination of mass communications, direction of the economy, and the ruthless use of force—all in the name of an explicit, official ideology asserting that society must be transformed. The term *totalitarianism* refers to the combination of these characteristics and describes a system of rule more than specific policies, a system inclined to use oppression and terror to force citizens to participate in the regime's activities and ideology. In principle totalitarianism seeks to shape every aspect of life and to crush "enemies" identified by their race, occupation, region, or religion. Such a vision and the institutions that would attempt to carry it out did not develop all at once but evolved, primarily in Communist Russia, Fascist Italy, and Nazi Germany.

Useful as the concept of totalitarianism is, it has also come under heavy criticism for a number of reasons. In practice, none of the totalitarian regimes achieved total control. Authorities often bent to customs and institutions they could not afford to offend and negotiated with entrenched interests. Inefficiency and duplication were characteristic, even endemic, for these regimes were not monolithic. Officials and party members often bickered among themselves. No totalitarian

---

[7] Karl Polanyi elaborated on the significance of the abandonment of the gold standard in a famous essay, *The Great Transformation: The Political and Economic Origins of Our Time*.

ideology was entirely coherent or unanimously embraced, and there were important differences among totalitarian systems. The values promulgated in Soviet Russia were not at all the same as those of Nazi Germany. Italy's claim to be totalitarian was largely propaganda, and that is the point. *Totalitarianism* is a useful term not for describing how these regimes actually functioned but rather for describing the ambitions and techniques that made Europe's leading twentieth-century tyrannies a fundamentally new political form.

HITLER'S GERMANY

The Nazi regime won power in a democracy with an advanced economy and a strong administrative tradition. It took advantage of selected elements of German history, from militarism and nationalism to the weakness of the Weimar Republic, much as it played upon the social shocks Germany had recently suffered, including defeat in war, failed revolutions, clashing ideologies, and a depression that brought the most extensive unemployment in Europe.

The Rise of Hitler   As a young man, Adolf Hitler was undistinguished, his ambition to be an artist thwarted when the Academy in Vienna rejected his application. Service in World War I had been a kind of salvation, providing comradeship and some accomplishment: He was promoted in the field. In Munich after the war, he found brief employment spying on the small German Worker's party, which the army considered dangerous, and took to addressing political rallies in the beer halls, where he learned the potential of a movement that combined the personal loyalty of a paramilitary core with mass appeal and where he molded the speaking style that would him make the most powerful figure in Germany.

His speeches combined crude accusations, a messianic tone, and simple themes repeated in a spiraling frenzy. Race and universal struggle were the core of his message. Germans were victims of vast conspiracies mounted by foreign powers, capitalists, Marxists, Freemasons, and (above all) Jews—the gutter antisemitism that Hitler had absorbed in Vienna. Jews were behind war profits, reparations, inflation, and depression; but Marx-

ism was also Jewish, and Communists were agents of the Jewish conspiracy. Internationalism and pacifism were Jewish ideas intended to destroy Germany as the bastion of Western (Aryan) civilization. Life was a desperate struggle won by the ruthless, and Germany's destiny was victory over these enemies, who attacked the nation with the Versailles Treaty, economic disasters, Communists, Jews, moral decay, and abstract art. These diverse attacks had a common target, the German *Volk*, the German people whose primitive virtues must be welded into an irresistible force.

The Growth of the Nazi Party   Hitler had named his party the National Socialist German Workers' party, and the Nazis were one of many such nationalist movements when in 1923 Hitler led them in the Munich *Putsch*, or rising. After it failed and Hitler was sent to prison, the book he wrote there, *Mein Kampf*, won little notice, for it was a turbulent, repetitive outpouring of his political views interlarded with demoniac statements about how human beings are manipulated by fear, big lies, and simplistic explanations. In prison and after his release in 1925, Hitler worked to reorganize and strengthen the party. To the SA, his street army of brown-shirted storm troopers, he added the SS, an elite corps in black uniforms who served as his bodyguards and special police. The party picked up some ideas and useful phrases from Moeller van den Bruck, a literary figure respected in conservative circles, whose book *The Third Reich* advocated a corporative and nationalist regime. And the party established its own newspaper, edited by Alfred Rosenberg, who expanded Hitler's racist ideas in *The Myth of the Twentieth Century*, published in 1930, a work that despite its turgidity was significant as part of the effort to establish an official ideology.

Even with an ideology and with organizations in place, the Nazis had limited success. The party's membership of 60,000 in 1928 was not enough to have much weight in German politics. It had some notable assets, however. General Ludendorff had joined Hitler in the 1923 *Putsch*, and other officers might be expected to lend support. Some circles of Bavarian conservatives and Rhineland industrialists showed interest in the movement, and in 1929 the Nazis gained national prominence with a petition against the Young

Plan. The Plan's aim was to put a final limit on reparations, but the Nazis opposed all reparations and declared it high treason not to renounce the war-guilt clause of the Versailles Treaty. Four million Germans signed. If Hitler's intensity and bad manners offended many, others felt the fascination of a personality that radiated power; and he soon gathered a group of absolutely loyal men: Hermann Göring, an air ace; Joseph Goebbels, journalist and party propagandist; and Heinrich Himmler. They worked ceaselessly to enlarge the party, orchestrate the impressive rallies, and terrorize their opponents. The Nazis were gaining attention and support. In 1930 they became the second-largest party in the Reichstag, and the following year a group of Rhineland industrialists promised the Nazis financial support.

By the 1930s, the party was broadly based, and the question of what groups were first drawn to the Nazis has been the subject of historical controversy, because different interpretations of Nazism follow from the answer. Workers were probably the biggest single group of members, but most workers continued to favor socialists and communists. Disproportionately large numbers of Nazi supporters were small-business people and tradespeople, civil service employees, and (to a lesser extent) farmers—all groups fearful of losing income and status. In the Depression, promises of recovery, higher agricultural prices, and more employment (tens of thousands found jobs in the SA and SS) had concrete appeal. Many people were drawn to the call to rebuild the army and to save society from socialism. In 1931 an array of right-wing nationalists joined the Nazis in a manifesto denouncing the "cultural Bolshevism" of the Weimar Republic and hinting that, once they seized power, the Nazis would protect only those who had joined them now. The Nazis spoke simultaneously like a government in office and like an underworld gang, and they demonstrated their seriousness by beating up Jews and socialists.

Collapse of the Weimar Republic   The Social Democrats led the government that faced the Great Depression and did the best they could with a shaky parliamentary majority and an uncooperative president. In 1930 the government resigned, to be replaced by the Center party and Heinrich

Brüning, a cautious man with little popular appeal. President von Hindenburg allowed this government to enact measures by decree, something he had denied the Social Democrats. But a nation in crisis was in political stalemate, with an unalert, reactionary president and a Reichstag incapable of producing a stable majority; like the country, it was divided among multiple parties, each with its own agenda of outrage. Hindenburg's sporadic interventions only made the situation worse; repeated elections raised the heat but brought no resolution.

The elections of 1930 gave Nazis more than a hundred new seats from which they contemptuously disrupted parliamentary proceedings. His confidence growing, Hitler became a candidate for president in 1932, when Hindenburg's term expired. Worried politicians persuaded the nearly senile field marshal to run for reelection. Ludicrously cast as the defender of the constitution, the eighty-four-year-old Hindenburg won handily; but Hitler got more than 13 million votes. When Brüning proposed a financial reform that included expropriation of some East Prussian estates, Hindenburg dismissed him and turned to Franz von Papen, a friend of important army officers and Junkers.

Hoping to create a right-wing coalition, von Papen lifted Brüning's ban on the SA and SS, named four barons and a count to his cabinet, and declared martial law in Prussia to unseat the socialist government there. The outcry led Hindenburg to call another election. It resulted in a Nazi landslide. With 40 percent of the Reichstag's seats, it was by far its largest party. Hindenburg avoided naming Hitler chancellor by refusing to grant him the full decree powers he insisted on. The nation was sent to the polls again, and although the Nazis lost a little, they remained the largest party.

Hitler Takes Office   Hindenburg then named another chancellor, General Kurt von Schleicher, a conventional army officer. He made an easy target for the Communists, the disgruntled von Papen, who thought he saw his chance to regain power, and the Nazis. Von Papen, confident he could use Hitler but contain him, persuaded the men around Hindenburg to appoint Hitler the head of a coalition government. In fact Hitler was the only leader acceptable to the right who could command a popular following. Of the twelve men in Hitler's cabinet, only two others were Nazis. Hitler, the leader of an unsuccessful *Putsch* only ten years before, took office late in January 1933. As the anti-Weimar parties of left and right gained ground, the political system lost its flexibility. The number of votes for Marxist parties remained nearly constant, but the Communist share of them grew; and the Nazis increasingly garnered the votes of the right.

Hitler almost immediately called another election. Previous campaigns had been ugly, but this one was marked by systematic terror, especially in Prussia, where Hermann Göring was now minister-president and the police acted like electoral agents. The climax came with the burning of parliament, the Reichstag fire that the Nazis loudly blamed on the Communists. Hindenburg agreed to issue special laws—Ordinances for the Protection of the German State and Nation—that ended most civil liberties, including freedom of the press and assembly. The voters gave the Nazis 44 per-

cent of the seats, enough, with the Nazis' nationalist allies, for a bare majority. Hitler pressed on. Communists were expelled from the Reichstag, conservatives wooed with calls to nationalism, and the Center party enticed with promises to respect the privileges of the Catholic Church. By March Hitler dared demand a special enabling act that gave him, as chancellor, the right to enact all laws and treaties independent of constitutional restraints for four years. Of the 566 deputies left in the Reichstag, only 94 Social Democrats (out of 121) voted no. Blandishment and terror had done their work, but the tragedy went deeper: German politics offered no clear alternative to Hitler.

Consolidating Nazi Rule Hitler's regime moved quickly to destroy the potential for opposition. It established concentration camps, first on private estates and then in larger and more permanent institutions. A campaign to boycott Jewish businesses was followed in April by laws eliminating most Jews from public service and limiting Jews

▼ Nazi party troops march out of the rally on Nuremberg Party Day, 1933, carrying victory banners proclaiming "Germany Awake."
Archiv für Kunst und Geschichte.

to 1.5 percent and women to 10 percent of university enrollment. By July all parties except the National Socialist had been outlawed, and soon all competing political organizations disappeared. In the elections of November 1933, the Nazis won more than 90 percent of the vote. They restructured government, purged the civil service and judiciary, outlawed strikes, and clamped stricter controls on the press. In a few months Hitler had achieved fuller power than Mussolini had managed in years, and in the next few years Nazi policies on racial purity would be extended step by step throughout public life by ordinances, official policies, and police brutality.

Hitler's most serious potential rivals were within his own party, and his solution was barbarically simple. On a long weekend in June 1934, leaders of the Nazi left wing were shot or stabbed. So, among hundreds of others, were General von Schleicher and his wife, some Catholic leaders, some socialists, and some taken by mistake. Hitler admitted to seventy-four deaths; subsequent estimates raise the figure to as many as a thousand. The Night of the Long Knives proved that any horror was possible; and the purge, like the noisy accusations of homosexuality that accompanied it, established the tone of Germany's new order. When Hindenburg died in August, Germans voted overwhelmingly to unite presidency and chancellorship in the person of Adolf Hitler, who took the official title of *Führer* ("Leader").

Administrative and Economic Policies The federal states lost their autonomy through a policy of *Gleichschaltung,* or coordination, and all government employees were made appointees of the Führer. New people's courts heard secret trials for treason, now very broadly defined, and rewritten statutes allowed prosecution for intent as well as for overt acts. Arrest and detention without charge or trial became a regular practice. At the same time, the Nazi party was restructured to parallel the state, with administrative *Gaue* ("regions") headed by a party Gauleiter. The party also had its own office of foreign affairs and its own secret police, the Gestapo, which infiltrated both the bureaucracy and the army.

Economic policies scored impressive successes. Unemployment dropped steadily thanks to great public works projects—government offices, high-

▲ Under Hitler, labor battalions also marched. By 1938 this "shovel brigade" could parade through the streets of Eger, a German town near the Czech border, on its way to extend the road from the newly annexed Sudetenland.
UPI/Bettmann.

ways, public housing, reclamation and reforestation. Many of these projects used special labor battalions, in which one year's service was soon compulsory. Later the burgeoning armaments industry and growing armed forces eliminated the problem of joblessness entirely. By spending money when more traditional governments thought it essential to balance their budgets, the Nazis reduced unemployment more effectively than any other Western nation.

Paying the Cost   Such programs were expensive, and they were paid for in several ways. A currency scheme largely designed by Hjalmar Schacht, a brilliant economist, required that payments for foreign trade be made with special marks whose value changed according to the products and the nations involved. Goods that Germany bought were paid for in marks redeemable only through purchases in Germany. Tantamount to barter, this system increased Germany's self-sufficiency and its influence in countries that depended on German markets. Additional revenues came from property confiscated from Jews, high taxes, forced loans, and carefully staged campaigns urging patriotic Germans to contribute their personal jewelry to the state. Ultimately, costs would be covered by printing paper currency, with effects long hidden by a war economy and the exploitation of conquered lands. By 1945 the mark had fallen to about 1 percent of its 1933 value.

Labor policies met related goals. Strikes were outlawed and the mobility of workers regulated. The National Labor Front, which represented all workers and management, froze wages and directed personnel in the interests of business and government. Industrialists were relieved of the uncertainties of the Weimar years.

Winning Approval   At the same time, government propaganda advertised the new benefits provided workers, including the summer camps and special cruises that were part of the Nazi program of Strength Through Joy. Nazi propaganda offered comfort for those ordinary people fearful of contemporary trends by denouncing modern art, the decadence of Berlin nightlife (and especially of homosexuality), and new roles for women. Initially, women were discouraged from working outside the home as a means to reduce unemployment among men, but the concern with women went far deeper than that. Wifely subordination was presented as a principle of social order and the foundation of the family. Women were

also at the center of the Nazi obsession with biology. Social policies, schools, and clinics reinforced propaganda praising the role of Aryan women as breeders of a pure race. It is hard to know how successful such propaganda was. There is evidence that poor pay and lack of freedom were resented despite the insistent propaganda but evidence, too, of an oppressive enthusiasm for a great leader who brought order and hope.

The military had clear reasons for gratitude. Disregarding the disarmament clauses of the Treaty of Versailles (which Germany formally repudiated in 1935), Hitler pushed rearmament from the first. With the return of universal compulsory service in 1935 and the creation of an air force, Germany was soon spending several times as much on arms as Britain and France combined. If regular officers resented Nazi paramilitary organizations and looked down on the Nazis as their social inferiors, they nevertheless accepted the oath of personal loyalty Hitler required. Strengthened by his diplomatic successes, Hitler asserted control more directly in 1938, removing the minister of war, the chief of staff, and more than a dozen generals amid public tales of private vice. At the same time the foreign minister, an old-style nationalist who had served since 1933, was replaced by Joachim von Ribbentrop, a good Nazi and no aristocrat at all. The army and foreign service, strongholds of traditional conservatives, were under the Nazi thumb.

The Nazis and the Churches   The churches presented a different challenge. A concordat with the Vatican in 1933 gave the state some voice in the appointment of bishops while assuring the Church of its authority over Catholic orders and schools. Protestant denominations agreed to form a new body, the Evangelical Church, under a national bishop whom Hitler named; but when the bishop declared a need to "Aryanize" the church, dissidents formed the separate Confessional Church. The minister for Church Affairs was authorized to confiscate ecclesiastical property, withhold funds, and have pastors arrested; but in practice the state kept religion in line more through the local harassment of individual clergy. Some priests and ministers cooperated with the regime—enthusiastically supporting war, race, and Reich. Most resisted at least the more outrageous demands made of them, and some individuals spoke out courageously. In 1937 Martin Niemoeller, the leader of the Confessional Church, was arrested for his opposition to Nazism; and Pope Pius XI condemned both the deification of the state and Nazi racial doctrine. In the following years some Catholic churches were burned, and members of religious orders were frequently tried on morals charges.

Antisemitism   Nazism had always made much of its antisemitism, and the Nuremberg laws of 1935 codified and extended previous regulations. Jews (anyone with one or more Jewish grandparents was considered a Jew) were declared to be mere subjects but no longer citizens. The Law for the Protection of German Blood and Honor prohibited marriage or sexual intercourse between Aryans and Jews, "Gypsies, negroes or their bastards." Subsequently, Jews were expelled from one activity after another, required to register with the state, and ordered to give their children identifiably Jewish names.

In 1938 the murder of a German diplomat by a young Jewish boy touched off a new round of terror. Many Jews were arrested, and the SS led an orgy of violence (named *Kristallnacht*, the "night of broken glass") in which Jews were beaten and murdered, their homes and businesses smashed, and synagogues burned. A fine of 1 billion marks was levied on the Jews of Germany, and they were barred from the theater and concerts, forbidden to buy jewelry, forced to sell their businesses or property, denied access to certain streets, and made to wear a yellow star. Worse would come.

For most Germans, life went on much as before but a little better, and there was a new excitement in the air. From the beginning, the Nazis' publicity had been flamboyant, their posters striking, and their rallies well staged; after the movement came to power, propaganda became a way of life. Torchlight parades, chorused shouts of *Sieg Heil!*

▼ The six-pointed star and the word *Jude* scrawled on this Berlin department store in 1938 were a warning to good Aryans not to shop there.
UPI/Bettmann.

("Hail to victory!"), book burnings, the evocation of Norse gods, schoolyard calisthenics, the return to Gothic script—a thousand occasions offered Germans a feeling of participating, of being swept up and implicated in some great historical transformation. At the Reich Chamber of Culture, Joseph Goebbels saw to it that cinema, theater, literature, art, and music all promoted Nazism (see "Goebbels' Populist View of German Culture," p. 1021). Things primitive and brutal were praised as Aryan; any who opposed or even doubted the Führer ceased to be German. Warfare was for this new regime its natural condition.

STALIN'S SOVIET UNION

Although Mussolini had learned much from the Soviet example of a revolutionary movement with dictatorial powers, communists held that in the Soviet Union dictatorship was incidental and supposedly temporary. The reality proved different. Communist rule became more systematically brutal and bloody after Lenin's death, but in the last decade historians have uncovered substantial evidence in newly opened Russian archives that Lenin had already laid the groundwork for such policies.

The Succession to Lenin No one knew who Lenin's successors would be when he died in 1924 or even how the succession would be determined. For more than a year, Lenin had been ill and nearly incapacitated, but his prestige had precluded any public scramble for power, and many expected a more relaxed government by committee to follow. In a famous letter, Lenin had assessed two likely successors: Trotsky, whom he called overconfident but the best man in the Politburo, and Stalin, whom Lenin found "too rude" though an able organizer.

Over the next three years, Russia's leaders publicly debated complex issues of Communist theory and practical policy. Trotsky led those who clung to the traditional vision that revolution would spread across Europe, and he favored an uncompromisingly radical program at home and abroad. Stalin declared that the Soviet Revolution must survive alone, a "revolution in one country." No theoretician, and little informed about the world outside Russia, Stalin was not wholly at ease in these debates with more intellectual and experienced opponents. But they, in turn, underestimated his single-minded determination. When the Politburo formally adopted his position in December 1925, his victory rested on more than ideas.

The Rise of Stalin As general secretary of the party's Central Committee, Stalin was the link between the Politburo and the party organization below it, and he could count on the loyalty of party officials, many of whom he had appointed. He played effectively on personal antagonisms and on resentment of Trotsky's tactless arrogance. When the Politburo elected three new members at that December meeting, all were Stalin's associates. He then effectively eliminated his opponents. When leading figures publicly sided with Trotsky, Stalin labeled the break in party solidarity a threat to Communism. Trotsky and Grigori Zinoviev—the head of the Comintern, the organization of the Third International intended to lead communists around the world, whose prominence made him dangerous—were expelled from the Politburo in 1926 and from the party in 1927.

The left was broken, and the following year Zinoviev recanted his "mistake" in having supported Trotsky. Nikolai Bukharin, perhaps the party's subtlest theoretician and a leader of the right, recanted too. Trotsky, who refused to change his mind, was exiled and then deported, continuing from abroad his criticism of Stalin's growing dictatorship. None of these veterans of the October Revolution had attempted to oust Stalin; even Trotsky, who built the Red Army, never tried to use it against him. Old Bolsheviks fervently accepted the need for party loyalty, and Stalin made sure that the open debates of those early years would not recur.

The First Five-Year Plan: Agriculture In aims and enforcement, the First Five-Year Plan reflected some of the qualities that had brought Stalin to the top. It shamelessly incorporated ideas Stalin had denounced just months before, but it was thoroughly his in the bold assumption that Russia could be transformed into an industrial power by mobilizing every resource. By 1928, when the plan was launched, Russian production had regained prewar levels in most sectors.

Goebbels' Populist View of German Culture

◀◉▶

As minister of propaganda in the German government, Joseph Goebbels was also president of the Reich Chamber of Culture, an organization divided into separate sections for the various arts and for film, radio, and the press. Artists had to belong in order to exhibit, perform, or be published. The speech quoted here was an address given by Goebbels to the annual Congress of the Chamber and of the Strength Through Joy organization held in Berlin in November 1937. Goebbels' efforts were at their peak, and he reported proudly on the campaign against decadent art (which included much of the modern art most admired today), on the abolition of art criticism, and on the new recreation homes for veterans and the elderly, saying, "Nothing similar has even been tried ever or anywhere else in the world."

"My Führer! Your excellencies!

"My racial comrades!

"Organization plays a decisive role in the lives of people. . . . For every organization must demand that its members surrender certain individual private rights for the benefit of a greater and more comprehensive law of life. . . .

"The purging of the cultural field has been accomplished with the least amount of legislation. The social estate of creative artists took this cleansing into its own hands. Nowhere did any serious obstructions emerge. Today we can assert with joy and satisfaction that the great development is once again set in motion. Everywhere people are painting, building, writing poetry, singing, and acting. The German artist has his feet on the ground. Art, taken out of its narrow and isolated circle, again stands in the midst of the people and from there exerts its strong influences on the whole nation.

". . . . True culture is not bound up with wealth. On the contrary, wealth often makes one bored and decadent. It is frequently the cause of uncertainty in matters of the mind and of taste. Only in this way can we explain the terrible devastations of the degeneration of German art in the past. Had the representatives of decadence and decline turned their attention to the masses of the people, they would have come up against icy contempt and cold mockery. For the people have no fear of being scorned as out of step with the times and as reactionary by enraged Jewish literati. Only the wealthy classes have this fear. . . . These defects are familiar to us under the label "snobbism." The snob is an empty and hollow culture lackey. . . . He goes in black tie and tails to the theater in order to breathe the fragrance of

poor people. He must see suffering, which he shudderingly and shiveringly enjoys. This is the final degeneration of the rabble-like amusement industry. . . . The Volk visits the theater, concerts, museums, and galleries for other reasons. It wants to see and enjoy the beautiful and the lofty. That which life so often and stubbornly withholds from the people . . . here ought to unfold before their eyes gleaming with astonishment. The people approach the illusions of art with a naïve and unbroken joyousness and imagine themselves to be in an enchanted world of the Ideal. . . . The people seek joy. They have a right to it.

". . . 'Hence bread and circuses!' croak the wiseacres. No: 'Strength Through Joy!' we reply to them.

"This is why we have thus named the movement for the organization of optimism. It has led all strata of the people by the million to the beauties of our country, to the treasures of our culture, our art, and our life. . . . The German artist of today feels himself freer and more untrammeled than ever before. With joy he serves the people and the state. . . . National Socialism has wholly won over German creative artists. They belong to us and we to them.

". . . In this hour, we all look reverently upon you, Führer, you who do not regard art as a ceremonial duty but as a sacred mission and a lofty task, the ultimate and mightiest documentation of human life."

From Salvator Attanasio and others (trans.), Speech of Goebbels, in George L. Moesse, *Nazi Culture: Intellectual, Cultural, and Social Life in the Third Reich,* University of Wisconsin Press, 1966.

▲ **Farmers, women as well as men, drive imported tractors out of one of the Soviet Union's Machine Tractor Stations to work fields in which such mechanization had been rare.**
Sovfoto.

Lenin's New Economic Policy had depended heavily on private entrepreneurs in commerce and peasant owners in agriculture. The task now was to create a socialist economy, and the first step was to collectivize agriculture.

Using the improved techniques and the mechanization that peasants had on the whole resisted, Soviet agriculture could produce enough both to feed industrial workers and to export grain that in turn would pay for importing the machinery that industrialization required. The problem was that Russian peasants continued to withhold their goods from market when agricultural prices fell. Some 4 or 5 percent of them had the means to hire labor and lend money within their villages, which gave them a further hold over the local economy.

As famine threatened, the government mounted a sweeping campaign of propaganda and police action against these wealthier peasants, calling them kulaks—the old, pejorative term for grasping merchants and usurers. Their grain was seized (informers were given a quarter of any hoard uncovered), hundreds of thousands of people killed, and untold numbers deported to till the unbroken soil of Siberia. Peasants destroyed crops and animals rather than let the government have them.

The explosive antagonisms of rural society raged out of control, and Stalin had to intervene in 1930 to halt a virtual civil war. By then, more than half the peasants belonged to collective farms, but the strife had badly hurt production, which contributed to serious famine in 1932–1933. A kind of compromise followed. Even on collective farms peasants were permitted individual plots and privately owned tools. Larger machinery was concentrated at Machine Tractor Stations, which became the rural base for agricultural agents and party officials. By 1933 output was sufficiently reliable to permit the state to concentrate on the most massive and rapid industrialization in history.

The First Five-Year Plan: Industry According to the five-year forecast, industrial production was to double in less than five years, and in some critical areas, such as electrical power, it was to increase sixfold. More than 1,500 new factories were to be put into operation, including large automobile and tractor plants. Projects on a still grander scale included a Dnieper River power station and a great coal and iron complex in a whole new city, Magnitogorsk. These goals were met somewhat ahead of schedule, and there was only slight exaggeration in the government's proud claim to have made Russia an industrial nation almost overnight.

To pay for that achievement, indirect taxes were levied, wages allowed to increase only slightly, planned improvements postponed, peasants displaced, and peasant land collectivized. Food and most consumer items were rationed, with allotments varying according to one's contribution to the plan. Success required much more than money. Unskilled or poorly trained, laborers were unaccustomed to the pace now required: Turnover was high; output and quality, low. The state resorted to a continuous work week and moved special "shock brigades" of abler workers from plant to plant. Women and young people were urged into industrial jobs. "Socialist competition" pitted groups of workers and whole factories against each other for bonuses and prizes; piecework payment, once a hated symbol of capitalism, became increasingly common. Violators of shop rules were fined; malingering, pilfering, and sabotage (often loosely defined) became crimes against the state. "Corrective" labor camps, initially a mode of prison reform, became another way to get more work done. Special courses within factories and enlarged technical schools trained new managers and engineers to replace the foreigners who were still essential to efficient industrial production.

In effect, an entire nation was mobilized, and the need for social discipline replaced an earlier emphasis on revolutionary enthusiasm. In schools, the formal examinations, homework, and academic degrees, recently abolished, began to return; and classroom democracy gave way to greater authority for the teacher. The state stressed the importance of the family and praised the virtues of marriage; and the earlier emphasis on freedom for women gradually gave way to an emphasis on their contribution to Soviet productivity. Divorce was discouraged and regulations on abortion, which had been legalized in 1920, be-

came increasingly restrictive. Associations of writers, musicians, and artists worked on propaganda for the plan. Mass organizations of youth and workers met for indoctrination, and within the party, criticism or even skepticism was akin to treason. Hundreds of thousands of party members were expelled, and new recruits were carefully screened. "Overfulfillment" was triumphantly announced in 1932; the miracle of industrialization came with creation of a Russian totalitarianism.

Growth in the 1930s The Second (1933–1937) and Third (1938–1942) Five-Year Plans continued the push for industrialization at somewhat lower pressure. Consumer goods were more available, and rationing was eliminated by 1936. Standards of quality rose, and dramatic improvement in

▼ Villagers watch with anticipation for the first light bulb in Bryansk Province to be switched on, an achievement of the First Five-Year Plan.
Novosti/Sovfoto.

▲ **This Soviet poster of 1930 hails the International Day of Women Workers, part of the government's extended campaign to encourage women to work in factories.**
Edimedia.

transportation, especially domestic aviation, made previously remote territories accessible. By 1939 Soviet Russia ranked third among the world's industrial producers behind only the United States and Germany, producing twenty-four times more electrical power and five times more coal and steel than in 1913. Literacy among people older than school age rose from below 50 percent in 1926 to more than 80 percent in 1939. As millions moved to cities, the number of higher schools, libraries, and hospitals doubled or tripled. In these years one-seventh of the popula-

tion moved to the cities, making the country more urban than ever before. More than 90 percent of peasant households were on collective farms serviced by the Machine Tractor Stations.

Announcing that the stage of socialism had been reached, the Soviet Union adopted a new constitution in 1936. The changes it made were mainly formal. Direct voting by secret ballot replaced the cumbersome indirect elections for the Soviet of the Union. The other house, the Soviet of the Nationalities, represented the republics, which on paper had considerable autonomy. The two houses together elected the Council of Ministers (the term *Commissars* thus passed away) as well as the Presidium, which legislated and whose chairman was head of state. The constitution recognized the Communist party as "the vanguard of the working people" and provided social and political guarantees that Communists hailed as the most democratic in the world. Ninety-six percent of the population voted in the next elections, 98 percent of them for the list the party presented.

Stalinism A more confident government showed signs of relaxing its campaigns against potential enemies. Some political prisoners were amnestied in 1935, and a more controlled political police, the NKVD, replaced the sinister secret police. The campaign against religion abated. Opportunities for advancement in this expanding economy were great. White-collar classes got more respect, officers were restored to the army and navy, and supervisors were reinstalled in factories. Expression of opinion remained tightly controlled, however. Writers, Stalin commented ominously, were "engineers of human souls." Although harassed less than during the First Five-Year Plan, intellectuals had long since learned the necessity of caution. The Russian Academy of Science, an important source of money and prestige, was never far from politics.

At the center of Soviet society stood Stalin, adulated as leader in every activity. Works of art were dedicated to him, factories named after him. His picture was everywhere. Patriotism overshadowed the socialist internationalism of an earlier generation, and Stalin was placed with Ivan the Terrible and Peter the Great as one of the molders of Russia. Although he held no official position other than party secretary, he demonstrated his awful power in the great purges of the late 1930s. Directed against engineers, Ukrainian separatists, former Mensheviks, and party members accused of being counterrevolutionaries, the purges were touched off by the assassination in 1934 of Sergei Kirov, a member of the Politburo who had been a close associate of Stalin's (in fact Stalin himself was probably behind the assassination). Party and state mobilized to root out a great conspiracy. Zinoviev and members of the "left opposition" were twice tried for treason and were executed in 1937.

Other public trials followed: party leaders and army officers in 1937, members of the "right opposition," Nikolai Bukharin and other old Bolsheviks, in 1939. To the outside world, the indictments seemed vague and the evidence unconvincing. Yet the accused consistently confessed—the effect of torture perhaps, or the wish to protect their families, or maybe the final act of faith by men who were convinced of the inevitable course of history and believed that anyone resisting it was "objectively" a traitor. A reign of terror swept the country, feeding local vendettas until Stalin called a halt in 1939. The dead were countless; jails and labor camps were bursting with prisoners, perhaps 10 million. More than twice that many had gone into exile. Soviet totalitarianism had grown to be ominously like that of Germany and Italy, except for the values it professed.

V. Democracies' Weak Response

Confident Communist, Fascist, and Nazi regimes had moved dramatically to meet the challenge of the Depression and to forge social unity while tightening their hold on power. Europe's democracies responded more uncertainly, forever compromising and unable to disguise the social and ideological dissension that politics could not overcome.

DIVISIVE SOCIAL CHANGE

The Economy Economic recovery by the mid-1930s did not lessen these divisions, even though standards of living were rising again. Agriculture became more productive by becoming more mechanized and scientific, but those changes required increased capital (thus favoring larger holdings) and employed fewer laborers. Workers benefited from better transportation, mechanical refrigeration, cheaper clothes, and more leisure; but it took organized conflict for them to pry better wages from employers.

Many employees now enjoyed a shorter work week, but work itself was more subject to "American" efficiency on speeded-up assembly lines, forcing workers to repeat the same tasks at a pace set by factory managers (and known as Fordism, after the production methods of Henry Ford in Detroit). This form of production and the use of elaborate time and motion studies intended to reorganize work in ways that would further increase productivity (called Taylorism, after studies by the American efficiency expert, Frederick W. Taylor) seemed to suggest that efficiency meant treating human beings like machines.

The middle classes recouped much that inflation and depression had undermined, but not their former confidence. While small businesses and craft industries remained insecure, larger corporations benefited first from the economic upturn and tended to form more powerful cartels, combining many firms within a single field so as to gain control of the entire production process from raw materials to marketing. And businesses large and small feared labor unions and socialist parties that were sounding increasingly militant.

Cultural Life Even cultural life lacked the healing qualities once expected of it. Easier communication, increased mobility, and exile brought the achievements of Russian ballet, Bauhaus architecture, and Russian, German, and Italian scientists and scholars to Paris, London, and, most of all, the United States. New cultural movements seemed all the more foreign, politicized, and ideological. Although the new media did much to bridge the chasm between rural and urban life, mass entertainment was not given to thoughtful discourse and moral uplift. The distinction between high and popular culture sharpened, and to many intellectuals culture itself was threatened as never before by the frothy commercialism of talking motion pictures and radio. Social scientists, poets, and novelists probed the theme of

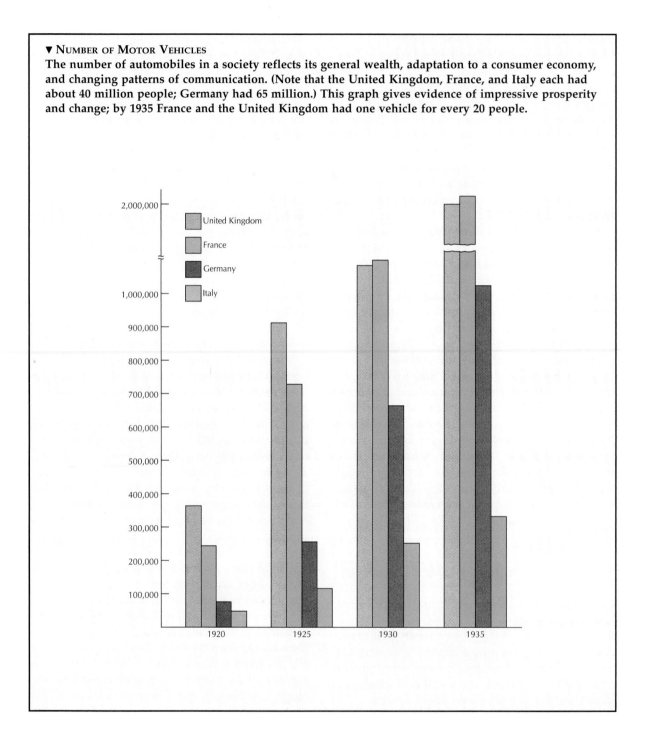

▼ Number of Motor Vehicles

The number of automobiles in a society reflects its general wealth, adaptation to a consumer economy, and changing patterns of communication. (Note that the United Kingdom, France, and Italy each had about 40 million people; Germany had 65 million.) This graph gives evidence of impressive prosperity and change; by 1935 France and the United Kingdom had one vehicle for every 20 people.

▼ Approximate Number of Radios Licensed for Every 100 People in 20 Selected Countries (1938)
Radio was an important new instrument of communication and propaganda. These statistics suggest that most families in the United Kingdom had a radio, that nearly everyone could sometimes listen to the radio in Finland and Austria, and that from Italy to Portugal, millions of people heard the radio only on special occasions when speakers blared in public places.

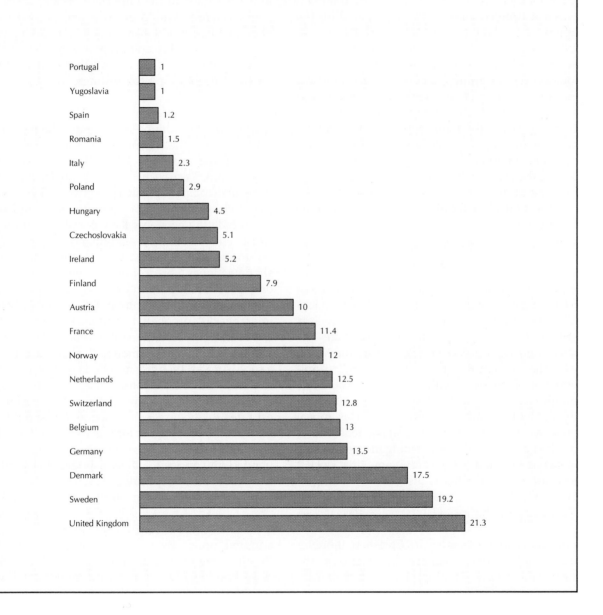

Country	Radios per 100 people
Portugal	1
Yugoslavia	1
Spain	1.2
Romania	1.5
Italy	2.3
Poland	2.9
Hungary	4.5
Czechoslovakia	5.1
Ireland	5.2
Finland	7.9
Austria	10
France	11.4
Norway	12
Netherlands	12.5
Switzerland	12.8
Belgium	13
Germany	13.5
Denmark	17.5
Sweden	19.2
United Kingdom	21.3

alienation, denounced faceless mass society, and engaged in radical politics.

In Paris, the Spanish painter Pablo Picasso became the dominant figure of twentieth-century art, restlessly experimenting with one new style after another. His most political work, *Guernica*, was a searing comment on war prepared for the Spanish pavilion at the Paris World's Fair of 1937(see p. 1032). Some artists defended the "experiments" of Hitler and Mussolini; far more joined Marxist groups, convinced that only socialism could create an acceptable society and preserve culture. The energy of the propaganda that advertised the transformation of Soviet society or the happy order, well-lit factories, and vacation resorts of Germany and Italy underscored the contrast between the ideologically coherent and purposeful societies of a single party and the aimless dislocation and dissension in the democracies.

THE ARGUMENT FOR LIBERTY

Against the strident claims of radicals and fascists, four major groups of intellectuals—Marxists, Christian thinkers, liberals, and economists—expressed a revived commitment to freedom. The most prominent of these thinkers were the Marxists. The Russian Revolution had enthralled millions of Europeans with visions of economic progress in a backward nation and of social equality and high culture in a mass society. This appeal grew as capitalist economies staggered, and it reached a peak with the promulgation of the Soviet constitution of 1936. At the same time, socialists and even communists insisted on the importance of justice, equality, and liberty, asserting that dictatorship in the Soviet Union was a special case.

Christians and Liberals In Christian thought, traditional arguments against the idolatry of the state gained new meaning. The Protestant Karl Barth and the Catholic Jacques Maritain built on firm theological orthodoxy to stress the importance of individual freedom and social justice. Similar concerns emerged in the influential work of the Russian Orthodox Nikolai Berdyaev and the Jewish scholar Martin Buber.

From a more secular perspective, noted poets and novelists such as W. H. Auden, Thomas Mann, and André Malraux wrote powerfully in behalf of human dignity and social justice, warning of the dangers of power and the evils of war. Most vigorous in the politics and universities of Britain and France, liberals were also heard even in Fascist Italy. In his important *History of European Liberalism*, Guido de Ruggiero argued that liberal values, modified yet again, offered a practical path to stability and progress; and Benedetto Croce made liberty the central theme of his historical and philosophical writings.

Keynesian Economics Economic theory also contributed to the argument for political freedom through the work of John Maynard Keynes, whose book *The General Theory of Employment, Interest and Money* appeared in 1936. Keynes rejected classical views of economic man and the self-regulating economy. Few people, he argued, consistently act in their own financial interest, for no one is free of ideas, values, and tastes that shape actions. Nor do iron economic laws inexorably dictate a pattern of booms and busts. To Keynes, massive unemployment was not only intolerable but proof that capitalism must not be left to its own devices. At the same time, he dismissed Marxism as outmoded. Instead he offered a sophisticated theory that called on governments to smooth out the economic cycle. When the economy lagged, the government should lower interest rates to encourage production and should finance public works and social welfare to stimulate consumption. As the economy expanded, the opposite policies should check inflation and excessive speculation. Keynes advocated granting government a more active role while preserving free markets. In effect he gave a theoretical foundation for practices already partially adopted under Swedish socialism, the French Popular Front (see later in this chapter), and the American New Deal, President Franklin D. Roosevelt's program of social and economic reform inaugurated in 1933. An advocate of capitalism, Keynes defended it by denying that its social evils were inevitable; most capitalists denounced him as a socialist.

Few thinkers were neutral. With socialist anger, Auden, the British poet who chose to live in America, warned capitalists that "the game is up for you and for the others."[8] T. S. Eliot, the American poet who chose to live in Britain, proposed still tougher choices in a voice of Christian outrage: "The term 'democracy' . . . does not contain enough positive content to stand alone. . . . If you will not have God (and He is a jealous God) you should pay your respects to Hitler or Stalin."[9]

DOMESTIC POLITICS

The Great Depression and rising international dangers undermined the traditional programs of democratic parties, left and right. Conservative parties pursued balanced budgets with results that embittered the unemployed. Liberals reluctantly accepted tariffs and subsidies that had few positive results. Socialists, weakened by competition from communists, antagonized workers by accepting weak welfare measures in the interest of better-balanced budgets. Issues of foreign policy had an even more paradoxical effect. Conservatives, historically supporters of military strength, were now inclined to downplay the dangers arising from Italy and Germany. Parties of the left, arguing that fascism must be resisted, tended to abandon their antimilitary rhetoric. As Finland and Czechoslovakia, whose economic growth and political freedom had made them models of the new postwar nations, felt the pressure of their stronger neighbors, the cause of democracy increasingly depended on Britain and France.

Great Britain Ramsay MacDonald became the British prime minister after a Labour victory in 1929. Following the advice of experts, he made drastic cuts in welfare and unemployment payments, measures that divided his own party. He then formed a national government with members from all three parties, in effect a conservative government in disguise, and was expelled from the Labour party amid bitter recriminations. His government then adopted controls on foreign ex-

change and increased tariffs, policies that split the Liberals. When MacDonald resigned in 1935, tired and unloved, his coalition government had overseen a slow recovery of the British economy, redefined imperial relations, and initiated some cautious steps toward government planning. But it had done so by pursuing conservative policies, and it had devastated the proletarian movement to which MacDonald had devoted his life.

He was succeeded by Stanley Baldwin's Conservative government, his third time as prime minister. Baldwin campaigned as a strong supporter of the League of Nations, in which he actually had little interest, and with a complacency that masked indecision, he steered clear of political extremes. The parliament elected with him, which would continue to sit through 1945 as the longest-lived in modern history, would later reveal a wealth of talent, testimony to the continued vitality of British political life.

In retrospect even the crisis of 1936 could be seen as a comforting assertion of tradition. King Edward VIII, who had acceded to the throne, insisted on marrying an American divorcée. He was forced to abdicate, and the transition to George VI went smoothly, quelling talk of the end of the monarchy. At the time, however, British institutions appeared weak. As international affairs grew more ominous, Britain's uncertain foreign policy further undermined the capacity of continental states to resist the expansionist policies of Germany and Italy. Doubts about Britain's role increased in 1937 when Baldwin turned the prime ministership over to his earnest Chancellor of the Exchequer, Neville Chamberlain, who was convinced he could avoid the danger of war through caution and compromise.

France France experienced the Depression later and less severely than other highly industrialized countries; but when the decline came, it lasted. The left won the legislative elections of 1932 as the economic slump began to be felt but found it difficult to construct a reliable majority, for the Socialists refused to participate in bourgeois governments. The result was unstable governments committed to reducing expenditures and protecting established interests. Outside parliament, rightist factions, including the fascist Croix de Feu (Cross of Fire), grew increasingly noisy. On

---

[8] W. H. Auden, "Consider This" and "In Our Time," in *A Little Treasury of Great Poetry,* Oscar Williams (ed.) (New York: Charles Scribner's Sons, 1947), p. 689.

[9] T. S. Eliot, *The Idea of a Christian Society* (New York: Harcourt Brace, 1960).

February 6, 1934, their uniformed militants led demonstrations against parliament that resulted in more bloodshed than Paris had seen since the Commune of 1870; and many believe that the Third Republic nearly died that day. France seemed more bitterly divided than at any time since the Dreyfus affair at the turn of the century.

The exposure of a gigantic investment swindle perpetrated by one Serge Stavisky, who had important political connections, became the basis for a strident campaign against the republic by proto-fascist groups using the now familiar devices of uniforms, antisemitism, propaganda, and demonstrations. To meet the emergency, a former president of the republic, Gaston Doumergue, was recalled from retirement to take the premiership and empowered to govern by decree. The sober old man, supported by every party except the royalists and the Marxists, held office for nine calming months before giving way to a parliament that insisted on its prerogatives but little else.

The elections of 1936 brought a dramatic change. Moderate republicans, Socialists, and Communists formed an antifascist Popular Front (cooperation made possible by the decision of the Comintern and directed from the Soviet Union to permit Communist alliances with other parties). Such rare solidarity brought the three parties a resounding victory and France its first Socialist premier, Léon Blum. He was a learned, humane intellectual and a Jew—attributes his enemies distrusted. Even as it took office, the new government faced a wave of strikes by workers determined to collect the fruits of their victory. They occupied factories, and many conservatives took that to be the revolution they dreaded. Eventually the strikes ended as the government pushed through legislation that provided for a general 12 percent increase in wages, two-week paid vacations, a forty-hour work week, and compulsory arbitration. Other reforms were soon added. Public works were launched, the Bank of France (long distrusted by the left) restructured, the arms industry nationalized, veterans given increased pensions, and small businesses offered subsidies. Each of these measures, like the devaluation of the franc, which in 1937 could no longer be avoided, frightened the business classes. New programs were hard to finance, and the economy proved more accessible to regulation than to stimulation. Blum's government—one of the Third Re-

public's most admired and most hated—had hardly begun the tax reforms its plans required when, after a year in office, it was defeated in the conservative senate. The Popular Front itself soon broke up. Subsequent governments were less daring amidst political feuds and public slander. Meanwhile, France's carefully constructed international position was collapsing.

THE FAILURES OF DIPLOMACY

The internationalism of the twenties had faded, and the sense of unreality in international affairs was underscored by the absence of the Soviet Union, which was effectively ostracized, and by the limited participation of the United States, which was absorbed in domestic affairs.

Efforts at Cooperation The League of Nations had little independent authority. China protested to the League when Japanese troops occupied the major cities of southern Manchuria in 1931; and after two years of deliberations a league committee recommended that Japan be ordered to withdraw. Japan withdrew from the League instead and in 1933 renounced the limitations on its naval strength that were part of the international agreements that had seemed so promising a decade earlier. Then Germany withdrew from the London conference on disarmament and from the League of Nations as well.

To counterbalance the threat of Germany's rapid rearmament, the Little Entente—an alliance of Czechoslovakia, Yugoslavia, and Romania, each also allied to France—drew closer together, and Greece and Turkey joined this French sphere in 1934. But Hungary and Bulgaria, authoritarian states attracted to Italy and impressed by Germany's resurgence, did not. For a while, Italy seemed the key to the balance of power in Europe. When Italian troops were rushed to the border in 1934, Austrian Nazis abandoned their attempt to force the unification of Austria and Germany through a coup d'état; and in 1935, after Germany publicly renounced the disarmament clauses of the Versailles Treaty, Mussolini used his heightened prestige to form the so-called Stresa Front with France and Great Britain.

But in fact the great powers quickly went their separate ways. France signed a mutual assistance pact with the Soviet Union, which was loudly opposed by many at home, worried Britain, and frightened Poland. Britain and Germany negotiated an agreement that the German navy, excluding submarines, should not exceed 35 percent of the British fleet—dealings that outraged France. Italy and Germany meanwhile prepared to take advantage of these international differences.

Italy and Germany Test Their Strength   In October 1935 Italy invaded Ethiopia, seemingly an old-fashioned imperialistic venture preceded by carefully arranged understandings with Britain and France. But the racist propaganda and enthusiastic bombing of defenseless populations signaled something new. Europeans were shocked, and the League of Nations labeled Italy an aggressor and banned the sale to Italy of essential war materials. Most of Europe seemed united in this crucial test of the League's peacekeeping powers. Although the embargo angered Italy and caused some hardship, it did not stop the war, partly because the most important commodity of all, oil, was not included.

More important, some leaders in France and Britain considered Italy's friendship more important than the League, including the two foreign ministers: Pierre Laval, a slippery politician who had drifted steadily to the right, and Sir Samuel Hoare, an experienced conservative diplomat. Secretly, they arranged a settlement that would, in effect, give Italy most of Ethiopia. When the plan leaked to the press, public outrage forced both men to resign; but they had delayed efforts to add oil to the list of sanctions and undermined confidence in the two democracies. By May 1936, Ethiopia had capitulated, Italy could celebrate the lifting of the embargo, and all could see the ineffectiveness of the League of Nations.

Germany then began to exploit its opportunities. Everyone knew that Germany was rebuilding its fighting forces; and when German troops marched into the demilitarized Rhineland in 1936, there was no compelling international response. Italy this time did nothing. France, unwilling to act alone as it had in 1923, consulted the British, who urged acquiescence. The German troops were cheered by their countrymen in the Rhineland just as they had been the year before when France had turned over the Saar following

a plebiscite overwhelmingly in favor of German rule. The fascist powers wanted radical changes in the international balance, and they had the initiative. Britain and France were internally divided, their leaders kept off balance by Germany's protests against the Versailles Treaty, by exuberant propaganda, and by shifting demands. Eastern European nations were torn between fear of the Soviet Union and fear of Germany.

The Spanish Civil War   Civil war in Spain drove home the sense that all of Europe was divided between the fascist right and the Marxist left, destined for a life-and-death struggle. In 1936 the army's best units, stationed in Spanish Morocco, rose up against the Spanish republic; and General Francisco Franco soon emerged as their leader. The insurgent officers counted on support from Italy, Germany, and Portugal, where Antonio de Oliveira Salazar had already established his dominance over a single-party, corporative, conservative, and Catholic state. Little interested in doctrines or ideologies, Franco recognized the utility of a modern mass appeal and a disciplined movement. His supporters were called the Nationalists. Dominated by the army, they appealed to the monarchists and fascistic Falangists (while somewhat aloof from both), to most of the clergy, and to all who favored desperate measures to escape from anarchy and communism. Italy and Germany quickly proffered their support and formed the Rome-Berlin Axis. Germany and Japan asserted their mutual sympathy and opposition to communism in the Anti-Comintern Pact. The Nationalist cause had become ideological and international.

The Spanish government's supporters included republicans, socialists, communists, anarchists, labor groups, and Catalan and Basque nationalists, a loose and badly split coalition. Known as the Loyalists, they saw themselves as the defenders of democracy against fascist aggression and of social justice against reaction; and they looked to the democracies for support. They received little except from the thousands of idealistic young men who went to Spain to fight as volunteers in national units like the Lincoln Brigade and the Garibaldi Brigade (which had its greatest moment when it defeated troops of the regular Italian army sent by Mussolini).

The Course of the Conflict Most of the Spanish navy remained loyal to the republic, and one of the insurgents' first problems was to get their armies from Spanish Morocco to the mainland, where many garrisons had risen in support of the Nationalists. Italian and German planes soon provided the needed transport, and the help of the fascist powers—in the form of military advisers, planes, tanks, and ammunition as well as significant numbers of Italian troops—remained essential. Mussolini welcomed the chance to enhance Italian prestige, and Hitler used the opportunity to test new German military technology.

Only the Soviet Union gave reliable if limited aid to the Loyalists—until 1938, when Stalin decided to cut his losses. Blum's government in France favored the Loyalists but feared the domestic and international consequences of openly aiding them; Britain's Conservative government shared France's caution, but with a deeper distaste for the radicals of Madrid and a greater hope for good relations with Italy. The democracies thus chose neutrality; and under pressure, Germany and Italy pretended to as well. All joined in an international commission to prevent foreign intervention. It merely sustained the legalisms that starved the republic, honoring international law while undermining it. As aid to the Nationalists flowed in from the fascist powers, Britain and France looked the other way.

Foreign aid, trained troops, better military organization, and modern weapons made the victory of Franco's forces almost inevitable. They nearly won Madrid and the war itself in the summer of 1936, but the Loyalists held on and in a last-minute counterattack broke the Nationalists' assault. For more than two years, despite poor equipment and internal conflict, the republicans fought on, heartened by occasional victories. As the war progressed, the Loyalists became increasingly dependent on the Soviet Union for supplies, and that dependency plus the Communists' organizational skills made them increasingly influential.

To the disgust of his Axis supporters, Franco conducted a war of attrition. Not until the spring of 1939, when Soviet supplies had ceased to come and Britain had signed special treaties of friend-

▼ *Pablo Picasso*
GUERNICA
Pablo Picasso used the still stylistic techniques he had mastered to protest the bombing of the Spanish town of Guernica by German planes in 1937. The huge, dark canvas, a political act in opposition to Franco and the Spanish Nationalists, foreshadowed modern warfare's brutal impact on civilian life. Kept in the United States for nearly fifty years, the painting can now be exhibited in a democratic Spain.
©2000 The Estate of Pablo Picasso/Artists Rights Society (ARS), New York.

▲ **A French gendarme leads members of the International Brigade who, with the fall of the Spanish republic, made their way across the French border to safety.**
Robert Capa/Magnum.

ship with Italy, did the Spanish republic finally fall. Thousands of refugees wearily crossed into France while Franco filled Spain's capacious prisons with potential enemies, undid the republic's social measures, and restored the power of the Church over education. Franco then joined the Anti-Comintern Pact and took Spain out of the League of Nations. The civil war had taken more than a million Spanish lives, many at the hands of firing squads and mobs. The bombing of the town of Guernica by German aircraft in 1937 made people shudder before the vision of what war now meant for civilians, and the tales of atrocities on both sides fed the angry arguments between left and right throughout Europe and the United States. The one clear lesson was that the Western democracies, fearful and divided, had accepted defeat while the Axis acted.

European society in the 1920s and 30s had shown itself remarkably innovative in cultural expression, social organization, and political mobilization. Where economic disaster, social failure, and political conflict were greatest, the response brought more coherent and simpler ideologies, more systematically enforced and apparently more deeply believed. Using skillful mass propaganda disseminated on an unprecedented scale, governments found new ways to organize whole societies in the name of unanimity and efficiency, exercising powers rarely equaled even in wartime. That organization of society made the vague decencies of democracy with its social and ideological conflicts and the hypothetical opportunities of free markets seem limp in comparison. Clearly the anger, intolerance, and raw violence in European domestic life and international relations could not last. Optimists hoped that these crises might dissipate; pessimists could only wait for them to explode as states increased their military strength.

Recommended Reading

Sources

Ciano, Count Galiazzo. *Diary, 1937–1938.* 1952. *Diary, 1939–1943.* 1947. The diaries of Mussolini's son-in-law and, eventually, foreign minister are often self-serving; but they give a vivid picture of the intrigue and confusion at the center of the Fascist regime.

Engel, Barbara Alpern, and Anastasia Posadskaya-Vanderbeck (eds.). *A Revolution of Their Own: Voices of Soviet Women in Soviet History.* 1997. Interviews with eight women born before the Russian revolution reveal the difficulties and gains experienced by women from different backgrounds under Russian communism.

Ortega y Gasset, José. *The Revolt of the Masses.* 1957. First published in 1932, this essay by one of Spain's leading philosophers and historians, an important work in its own right, is also a significant document of the disquiet that intellectual elites felt over the effects that increased specialization and mass society were having on the traditional culture of the West.

Reed, John. *Ten Days That Shook the World.* Available in many editions, this classic account of the Russian revolution was first published in 1922. John Reed went to Russia as a journalist and radical. His enthusiastic and perceptive report on the revolution captures both the excitement of the moment and the communist revolution's dramatic and international appeal.

Studies

*Allen, William S. *The Nazi Seizure of Power: The Experience of a Single German Town, 1930–1935.* 1965. A much-used microcosmic study.

*Arendt, Hannah. *The Origins of Totalitarianism.* 1958. This important study begins with a profoundly pessimistic application of hindsight to the imperialism and antisemitism of the late nineteenth century to make the case for Nazi totalitarianism as a phenomenon rooted in Western history.

Bessel, Richard. *Life in the Third Reich.* 1987. Essays by leading historians using recent research to provide fresh interpretations of various aspects of Nazi rule.

*Bracher, Karl D. *The German Dictatorship.* Jean Steinberg (tr.). 1970. A major synthesis of work on the origins, structure, and impact of the Nazi movement.

Broszat, Martin. *The Hitler State: The Foundation and Internal Structure of the Third Reich.* 1981. Uses the methods of social history to show the complexity and confusion of Nazi rule, emphasizing its operation in daily life.

*Bullock, Alan. *Hitler: A Study in Tyranny.* 1971. The best biography of Hitler and one that gives an effective picture of Nazi society.

Carsten, F. L. *The Rise of Fascism.* 1967. The careful synthesis of a distinguished scholar that looks at the varieties of fascist regimes.

*De Felice, Renzo. *Interpretations of Fascism.* Brenda Huff Evertt (tr.). 1977. A very thoughtful review of the interpretations of Italian Fascism.

Fitzpatrick, Sheila. *The Russian Revolution, 1917–1932.* 1982. A valuable, fresh overview that emphasizes social conditions.

*———(ed.). *The Cultural Revolution in Russia.* 1978. Essays treating varied aspects of the effort to create a new culture.

Gay, Peter. *Weimar Culture: The Outsider as Insider.* 1968. A wide-ranging essay arguing that the vigorous cultural life of Weimar Germany was shaped by those viewed as marginal to Germany's traditional culture.

Kater, Michael H. *The Nazi Party. A Social Profile of Members and Leaders, 1919–1945.* 1984. An impressive analysis of the relevant statistical data on the social origins of Nazi party members.

Kershaw, Ian. *The Nazi Dictatorship: Problems and Perspectives of Interpretation.* 1985. A significant assessment that provides an excellent introduction to and interpretation of a vast literature.

*Kershaw, Ian, and Moshe Lewin (eds.). *Stalinism and Nazism: Dictatorships in Comparison.* 1997.

Kindleberger, Charles P. *The World in Depression, 1929–1939.* 1973. A study of the origins of the Depression and of responses to it in different countries.

*Kolb, Eberhard. *The Weimar Republic.* P. S. Falla (tr.). 1988. A comprehensive account of the difficulties and failures of Germany's experiment with democracy.

Koonz, Claudia. *Mothers in the Fatherland: Women, the Family, and Nazi Politics.* 1987. Shows the importance of gender policies to Nazi ideology and rule.

Lebovics, Herman. *Social Conservatism and the Middle Classes in Germany, 1914–1933.* 1969. Looks at individual figures to explore the development of an ideology of conservatism that prepared many members of the middle class to be sympathetic to the Nazi movement.

Lee, Stephen J. *The European Dictatorships: 1918–1945.* 1987. A comprehensive and systematic comparison of Communist Russia, Fascist Italy, and Nazi Germany.

Lewin, Mosche. *The Making of the Soviet System: Essays in the Social History of Interwar Russia.* 1985. Explores the complex roots and real limitations of the regime in a period of revolutionary change.

Mack Smith, Denis. *Mussolini.* 1981. An informed, skeptical account by the leading English scholar of modern Italy.

*Nettl, J. P. *The Soviet Achievement.* 1967. Effectively tackles the difficult task of assessing both the economic development of the USSR and its social cost.

*Nolte, Ernst. *Three Faces of Fascism.* Leila Vennewitz (tr.). 1965. A learned effort to place the intellectual history of fascism in France, Germany, and Italy in the mainstream of European thought.

*Nove, Alec. *An Economic History of the USSR.* 1982. A compact survey through the Brezhnev years, which concentrates on the formation of economic policies.

Peukert, Detlev J. K. *Inside Nazi Germany: Conformity, Opposition, and Racism in Everyday Life.* 1987. Makes use of a great deal of recent research to explore the effects of Nazi tyranny on ordinary life and the difficulties of opposition to it.

*Pipes, Richard. *The Formation of the Soviet Union.* 1964. A clear, comprehensive, and very critical treatment of Soviet rule.

*Schoenbaum, David. *Hitler's Social Revolution: Class and Status in Nazi Germany.* 1933–1939. 1966. A topical discussion contrasting theory and practice in the social policies of the Third Reich.

Tannenbaum, Edward R. *The Fascist Experience: Italian Society and Culture, 1922–1945.* 1972. A wide-ranging effort to recapture the meaning in practice of Fascist rule.

Thompson, John M. *Revolutionary Russia, 1917.* 1989. A good overview of what the revolution meant for ordinary life throughout the country.

*Tucker, Robert C. *Stalin as Revolutionary, 1879–1929: A Study in History and Personality.* 1973. Sensitively explores the shaping of Stalin's character as a key to his use of power.

*Ulam, Adam B. *Lenin and the Bolsheviks.* 1969. Combines the study of ideas and of policy to explain Lenin's triumph.

Weinberg, Gerhard L. *The Foreign Policy of Hitler's Germany.* 1970. A major study by a leading American diplomatic historian that helps explain Hitler's early successes.

*Woolf, S. J. (ed.). *Fascism in Europe.* 1981. Essays on the countries that offer major examples of fascist movements.

▲ A women's unit pulls in one of the barrage balloons used for defense in the Battle of Britain. The weighted cables dangling beneath the balloons prevented low-level flights by German bombers.
Imperial War Museum.

Chapter 29

THE NIGHTMARE: WORLD WAR II

orld War II was the centerpiece of a long trial of European civilization. The outbreak of war followed a series of international crises, but in a larger sense it resulted from the kinds of governments produced by the social tensions of the era. For more than a decade Europe had experienced a kind of ideological civil war that undermined established institutions and exposed every weakness in the social fabric. Communism, Fascism, and Nazism fed those conflicts abroad while boasting that they had overcome them at home; democracy clearly had not. When war broke out, it rewarded organization, technology, and ruthlessness; and the terrors of the battlefield were exceeded by the deliberate, systematic horrors of genocide, torture, and concentration camps. After the war, a devastated continent filled with millions who had lost homes, family, health, and hope struggled just to make society function. The achievement of stability and prosperity by the 1950s was a European miracle.

I. The Years of Axis Victory

The civil war in Spain made the international situation frighteningly clear. Germany and Italy were allied, rearming, and aggressive. France and Britain, more dependent on each other than allied, were reluctantly rearming while hoping to avoid war. The countries of Eastern Europe were effectively paralyzed, and the Soviet Union was an enigma, for no one knew whether it would eventually take sides or could fight effectively if it did.

THE PATH TO WAR

For eighteen months Hitler orchestrated a series of escalating demands that culminated in the outbreak of World War II in September 1939.

The Anschluss In February 1938, with the outcome of civil war in Spain still uncertain, Hitler began to pressure Austria. He summoned the Austrian chancellor, Kurt von Schuschnigg, to the Führer's secluded mountain retreat at Berchtesgaden and subjected him to a humiliating harangue. Schuschnigg promised to include Austrian Nazis in his cabinet. On returning home, he felt braver and decided to hold a plebiscite in the hope that public opinion would rally to save Austria's independence. Hitler, furious, massed the German army on the Austrian border, and Schuschnigg realized his position was hopeless. He had previously disbanded the Socialist party, the strongest opponent of union with Germany, and Italy warned that this time it would not oppose the German moves as it had a few years earlier. The friendless Austrian chancellor was replaced by Artur von Seyss-Inquart, a Nazi, who invited German troops to restore order. They did so on March 13, and Nazis indulged in the vulgar, public humiliation of Viennese Jews and intellectuals. Within a month Austria's annexation to Germany was almost unanimously approved in a plebiscite run by the Nazis. The dream of union with Germany, *Anschluss*, had been fulfilled; Hitler's popularity at home rose still higher, and German influence spread more deeply into the Balkans. Britain and France merely protested.

Czechoslovakia Two weeks after the Austrian plebiscite, Hitler demanded autonomy for the Su-

detenland, an overwhelmingly German-speaking section of Czechoslovakia. Once again, the claims that the Versailles settlement had been unfair and that Germans were being abused rallied support at home and weakened opposition abroad. Although this challenge to the Czech republic was far more daring—Czechoslovakia was a prosperous industrial state protected by a respectable army, well-fortified frontiers, and mutual-aid treaties with both France and Russia—the parallel with Austria was lost on no one. Supported by its allies, Czechoslovakia mobilized, and Hitler ordered the Sudeten Nazis to quiet down. But Czechoslovakia was vulnerable, and Hitler was adept at fanning ethnic resentments. The republic, dominated by the more prosperous Czech region, was barely able to maintain the loyalty of the Slovaks; a pro-Nazi party had won more votes than any other in the 1935 elections, and the great powers remained divided. Britain's prime minister Neville Chamberlain wanted to parlay directly with Germany, believing that no nonnegotiable British interest was at stake in the Sudetenland, and he rejected suggestions from the United States and the Soviet Union that they meet to consider ways of restraining the Nazi dictator. Many in France and England, deeply alarmed at how close to war they were, doubted that fighting for Czechoslovakia's sovereignty over a German population was worth the risk. Throughout the summer, Sudeten Nazi leaders negotiated with the Czech state in an atmosphere heated by demonstrations there and in Germany.

In August, Chamberlain, with French concurrence, sent his own emissary to mediate while German troops held maneuvers on the Czech border, and Hitler pointedly toured Germany's fortifications in the west. Hitler's speeches became more bellicose, and Chamberlain decided, once again with French support, to visit the Führer at Berchtesgaden. When they met on September 15, Hitler raised the stakes, demanding that Germany annex the Sudetenland. Britain and France advised Czechoslovakia to submit. Desperately, the Czechs sought some escape, but only the Soviet Union was ready to support Czech resistance. In a week Chamberlain flew back to Germany with the good news that Czechoslovakia had agreed to Hitler's terms, only to find them changed again: German troops must occupy the ceded territory immediately. The Czechs would have no time to move factories and military supplies or provide for citizens who wished to evacuate. A shocked Chamberlain said no, and for five days the world listened for war.

The Munich Agreement Then, persuaded by Mussolini, Hitler agreed to a meeting with the Duce and the prime ministers of Britain and France. They met on September 29, 1938, in Munich, where just fifteen years earlier Hitler had failed to capture the town hall. Now he dealt in terms of nations. During an afternoon and evening of discussions, Hitler was granted all he asked. Neither the Soviet Union nor Czechoslovakia was consulted. The next day Czechoslovakia submitted to Hitler's terms and accepted last-minute demands from Poland and Hungary for

additional pieces of Czechoslovak territory that they had long coveted. At a single stroke, Czechoslovakia surrendered one-third of its population, its best military defenses, and much of its economic strength. Central Europe's strongest democracy was reduced to a German dependency, and a keystone of France's continental security was shattered. As the French prime minister's plane circled the Paris airport on his return from Munich, he watched with dread the crowd below. But it cheered him, and in Britain, Chamberlain became a hero. Peace, the papers echoed, had been preserved.

Poland and the Hitler-Stalin Pact German might, Hitler's speeches, virulent antisemitism, goose-stepping troops marching through central Europe, and news of what life was like in the newly

▼ Hitler and Mussolini on the way to the train station after the Munich conference. Count Galeazzo Ciano, the Italian foreign minister, is on Hitler's left; Hermann Göring is on Mussolini's right; and General William Keitel, Rudolf Hess, and Heinrich Himmler are among those behind them.
Ullstein.

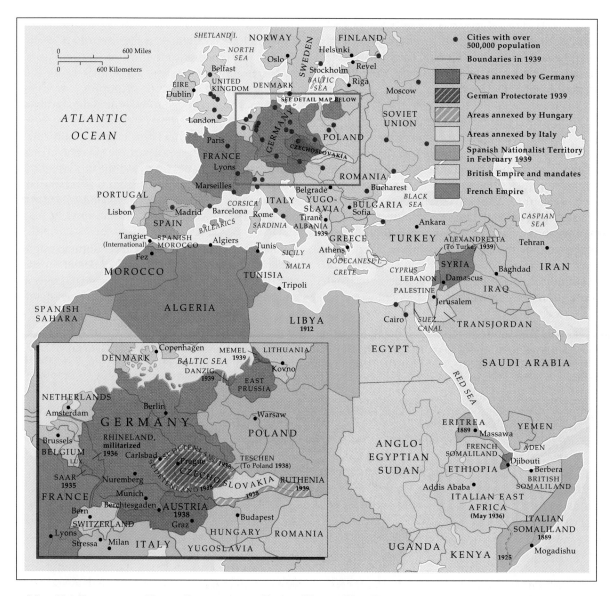

▲ MAP 29.1 EUROPE AND NORTH AFRICA ON THE EVE OF WORLD WAR II

annexed lands and in Germany itself—all gave Jews, ethnic groups the Nazis labeled inferior, peoples living along the German borders, and whole nations reason to be terrified. Early in 1939 German troops occupied all of Czechoslovakia (except for an additional piece taken by Hungary) and annexed the seaport of Memel from a frightened Lithuania. The pretext of absorbing only German peoples had now been abandoned.

Chamberlain, believing that not even Nazis could want world war, was one of many in Europe who hoped concessions would appease Hitler; but most people in England and France were resigned to the fact that Germany could only be stopped by force. Italy, inspired by Hitler's success, began a noisy campaign to get Nice and Corsica from France and in the summer of 1939 invaded and annexed Albania. The Rome-Berlin Axis was formally tightened into the "Pact of Steel," and Germany kept European chancelleries quaking with demands for nonaggression pacts. Late in August the leader of the Nazi party in German-speaking Danzig declared that his city, which the Versailles treaties had carved from Polish territory and made a free city, must be returned to the fatherland. The denunciations of the Versailles boundaries that poured from Germany, along with claims that Germans living within the Polish corridor were being persecuted, made it clear that Poland was next. As they had all summer, Britain and France renewed their pledges to protect Poland.

The summer's most important contest was for some alliance with the Soviet Union, and Hitler won that, too. Germany and the Soviet Union announced a nonaggression pact. The USSR had made overtures to Britain and France, suggesting that the territorial integrity of all the states between the Baltic and Black seas be guaranteed. The Western powers, reluctant to grant a Communist nation such extensive influence, had responded weakly. Since 1935 the Soviet Union had advocated disarmament, supported the League of Nations, supplied Loyalist Spain, and offered support to Czechoslovakia; but Stalin feared that the democracies would welcome a war between Germany and Russia. In May 1939, he replaced his foreign minister, Maxim Litvinov, the eloquent spokesman for a pro-Western policy, with Vyacheslav Molotov, a tougher and less cosmopolitan old ally. Hitler readily offered the Soviet Union a free hand in Finland, Estonia, Latvia, eastern Poland, and part of Romania, in the event that Germany sought any changes in its own eastern border. The nonagression pact between the international sponsor of antifascist fronts and the creators of the Anti-Comintern Pact was a masterpiece of cynicism (and very old-fashioned diplomacy) that shocked a world still unaccustomed to totalitarian flexibility.

The last days of August resounded with formal warnings and clarifications from the major powers. On September 1, Germany invaded Poland. Britain and France mobilized, sent Germany an ultimatum, and declared war on September 3, 1939. One year after surrendering democratic Czechoslovakia, they would fight for authoritarian Poland.

THE COURSE OF THE WAR, 1939–1941

One argument for the policy of appeasement was that it enabled Britain and France to buy time. They had been vigorously strengthening their armed forces, and the domestic consensus that war required was slowly taking shape. But much remained to be done; Germany had gained, too, in territory and power, and now there was no time left.

Blitzkrieg and Phony War For two years the Axis scored one victory after another. Having carefully prepared the invasion, Germany attacked Poland with overwhelming force in September 1939, the first blitzkrieg, or "lightning war." Poland fell in less than a month, and Hitler suggested that the war could now end. Few were tempted by his hints of peace. Concerned to strengthen its frontiers against Germany, the Soviet Union attacked Finland in November and met such fierce resistance that the war lasted until the following spring. Having regained boundaries close to those of the last tsars, Russia could afford to wait. The Western powers had been waiting, too. Hitler refrained from attacking along the French border, and the Allied commanders resolved not to risk precious planes too soon or to repeat the pointless assaults of World War I. This was the period of the so-called phony war, during which arms production and mobilization speeded up, the world waited, and little happened. The strain was bad for morale.

With the Soviet Union standing aside from the conflict, French Communists now said the war was a mistake; their party was suppressed. Paul Reynaud, energetic and determined, replaced Daladier as premier, and the Allies prepared to defend Norway, an obvious German target. But on April 9, 1940 Germany attacked Denmark, taking it in a day, and captured Norway's most important strategic points in short order, giving Germany bases for numerous assaults on British ships and cities. Chamberlain resigned in May, after a wide-ranging and often angry parliamentary debate, and Winston Churchill became prime minister of an all-party government on the day the Germans opened their attack on the Western front. A Conservative who believed in empire and an opponent of appeasement, Churchill was a political maverick given his chance in the face of disaster. His decisiveness and eloquence made him one of England's greatest leaders.

The Fall of France On May 10, and without warning, German troops flooded the Netherlands and Belgium. The Dutch, who had expected to escape this war as they had all others since the Napoleonic

▲ **Warsaw, October 5, 1939: German tanks, fresh from their lightning destruction of the Polish army, pass in review before Adolf Hitler.**
AP/Wide World.

wars, surrendered in five days. The better-prepared and larger Belgian army held out for eighteen days. On May 14 a skillfully executed German offensive broke through the Ardennes forest, thought to be impervious to tanks, reached Sedan, and drove to the channel, trapping the Belgian and British forces fighting there along with much of the French army. The German air force, the Luftwaffe, controlled the skies, and the Allies' proudest achievement in the battle for France was the evacuation from the port town of Dunkirk of 340,000 troops pinned against the sea. They left for Britain in a motley flotilla of naval vessels, commercial ferries, and private sailboats, a symbol of heroism and inferior preparation.

The Allied defense of France was broken. German forces renewed the attack on June 5 and took Paris in a week. Anxious lest he miss the war entirely, Mussolini attacked France on the tenth, and France surrendered on June 16, 1940. The armistice was signed in the railway car used for Germany's surrender in 1918. More ironic still, the man who chose to sign for France was the World War I hero of Verdun, Marshal Henri Philippe Pétain.

Germany's Victory over France Hitler seemed invincible and the blitzkrieg some terrible new Teutonic force, a totalitarian achievement other societies could not hope to equal. In fact, however, many of the tactical ideas on which it rested were first put forward by British and French experts, including a French officer, Charles de Gaulle. The blitzkrieg was the result not so much of new technology as new strategy. It combined air attacks with rapid movements of motorized columns to overcome the advantages that defensive positions had previously enjoyed. Tanks roared through and behind enemy lines, a maneuver requiring speed and precision that were nearly forbidden in older theories. In the flat terrain of Poland, Germany's panzer tank divisions quickly encircled the enemy; in France, they often assaulted troops so far in the rear that they were not yet prepared for battle. The aim was less to capture ground than to break up communications, using air power to disorient and terrify the retreating army. Even the machine-gunning of French roads clogged with civilian refugees and the bombing of Rotterdam had their place in the campaign to demoralize.

French strategy had relied too much on the defensive strength of the Maginot Line, a system of fortifications extending from the Belgian border to Switzerland, and on the assumption that Germany would respect the neutrality of Belgium and the Netherlands. The French had powerful tanks of their own but had been slow to deploy them; their air force was momentarily weakened because it was changing models. During the phony war, morale sagged with memories of the previous war and policy was undermined by politics rife with suspicion of the British, of the army, of the politicians, and of the left. Pétain, who believed France must now make its way in Hitler's Europe, blamed the Third Republic, and for a moment the nation turned to the octogenarian marshal with stunned unanimity.

He accepted terms of surrender that put three-fifths of the country under Nazi occupation and allowed French prisoners of war to be kept in Germany. The unoccupied southeastern part of France was allowed its own government, and that was established at Vichy. There a reconvened parliament maneuvered by Pierre Laval named Pétain chief of state. The new regime, known as Vichy France, relied on a confused coalition of militant fascists and the traditional right and would never really be independent of Germany. After adopting bits of corporatism and some fascist trappings, it settled into a lethargy of its own, an often willing collaborator in Hitler's new order, ruling a truncated state as rife with intrigue, personal ambition, and shifting alliances as the Third Republic it so heartily denounced.

The Battle of Britain Great Britain now stood alone. Unprepared for such enormous victories so soon, German officers planned their invasion of Britain while, beginning in June 1940, their bombers roared over England in sustained attacks that many believed would be enough to force surrender. Instead, in September the projected invasion was postponed, while the air attacks continued. The

▲ French refugees with all the possessions they can carry clog the roads, expecting to be able to escape the German armies in 1940 as their parents had twenty-five years before.
Lapi-Viollet.

German navy had suffered enough damage in encounters with the British to favor caution, and by the spring even the air raids were letting up.

The waves of German planes flying across the channel sustained losses far greater than those of Britain's Royal Air Force. British fighter planes, particularly the newer designs, proved at least the

▲ **In the hopfields of Kent in southeastern England, the pickers and their families took refuge in trenches during the air raids.**
Topham/The Image Works.

equal of the German; and they were aided by new techniques of antiaircraft defense, including radar, an English development that was the most critical addition to military technology in these years. At first the air raids concentrated on ports and shipping, then on airfields, and finally on cities, leaving great burning holes in London and completely destroying the industrial city of Coventry. But the diversity of targets dissipated the economic and military effects of the bombing, and the terror from the skies seemed to raise morale in a nation ever better organized and more fiercely determined to carry on. Merely to survive from June 1940 to June 1941 was a kind of victory in what Churchill memorably called Britain's "finest hour."

The Balkans With all the continent from Norway to Sicily and the Atlantic in their own hands or under friendly dictators in Spain and Portugal, the Axis powers looked eastward. In October 1940, Italian forces moved from Albania into Greece only to be pushed back, and Hitler had to bail out Mussolini by sending in German troops and further squeezing the Balkan States, which were rapidly losing their independence. In June 1940, the Soviet Union, stretching the terms of its pact with Germany, took Bessarabia from Romania. Hungary and Bulgaria then took some of Romania for themselves, and Hitler announced that he would protect the rest of the country. In fact all three Eastern European nations, already implicated in Hitler's mapmaking, were closely tied to Germany. It was no great step for them to join the Axis, welcome German troops in March 1941, and cooperate with Germany in invading Yugoslavia, which had hesitated too long over whether to join the Axis, and in attacking Greece, which had fought Mussolini too well.

The invasion was launched in April 1941 and swept through both countries within the month. Some Greek and British forces pulled back to Crete, only to be forced out almost immediately by German gliders and paratroops, the first time those forces had been used in war. The Allies retreated to Egypt, where British forces had held off an attack from Italy's neighboring colony of Libya. The Axis now threatened to dominate the Mediterranean, too.

The Invasion of the Soviet Union Having conquered so much, Hitler decided to complete his domination of the continent. On June 22 German forces attacked the Soviet Union. The Soviets had long feared such a move; yet they appeared genuinely surprised, at least by the timing and the size of the German invasion (see "Stalin Appeals to Patriotism," p. 1045). The assault, in three broad

Stalin Appeals to Patriotism

Stalin, apparently in a state of shock, was silent for the first week after German forces invaded the Soviet Union. Finally, on July 3, 1941, he spoke by radio to the Soviet people. His address acknowledged initial defeats, invoked the example of Russian victories over invaders in the past, and emphasized that the Allies were fighting together against Nazi tyranny. But he also called in striking detail for ordinary citizens to continue the fight by destroying anything that might be helpful to the invader (which became known as the "scorched earth" policy) and by constant sabotage.

"Comrades! Citizens! Brothers and Sisters! Men of our Army and Navy!

"I am addressing you, my friends!

"The perfidious military attack on our fatherland, begun on 22 June by Hitler's Germany is continuing.

"In spite of heroic resistance of the Red Army, and although the enemy's finest divisions and finest air-force units have already been smashed and have met their doom on the field of battle, the enemy continues to push forward, hurling fresh forces into the attack.

"Hitler's troops have succeeded in capturing Lithuania, a considerable part of Latvia, the western part of White Russia, and a part of the western Ukraine.

" . . . A grave danger hangs over our country.

"How could it have happened that our glorious Red Army surrendered a number of cities and districts to the Fascist armies?

"Is it really true that German Fascist troops are invincible, as is ceaselessly trumpeted by boastful Fascist propagandists? Of course not!

"History shows that there are no invincible armies, and never have been. Napoleon's army was considered invincible, but it was beaten successively by Russian, English, and German armies. Kaiser Wilhelm's German army in the period of the first imperialist war was also considered invincible, but it was beaten several times by Russian and Anglo-French forces.

"The same must be said of Hitler's German Fascist army today. This army has not yet met with serious resistance on the Continent of Europe. Only on our territory has it met serious resistance, and if as a result of this resistance the finest divisions of Hitler's German Fascist army have been defeated by our Red Army, it means that this army, too, can be smashed and will be smashed as were the armies of Napoleon and Wilhelm.

"There can be no doubt that this short-lived military gain for Germany is only an episode . . . , while the tremendous political gain of the USSR is a serious and lasting factor that is bound to form the basis for development of decisive military successes . . . .

"In case of a forced retreat of Red Army units, all rolling stock must be evacuated, to the enemy must not be left a single engine, a single railway car, nor a single pound of grain or a gallon of fuel.

"Collective farmers must drive off all their cattle and turn over their grain to the safekeeping of state authorities for transportation to the rear. All valuable property including nonferrous metals, grain, and fuel which cannot be withdrawn must without fail be destroyed.

"In areas occupied by the enemy, guerrilla units, mounted and foot, must be formed, diversionist groups must be organized to combat enemy troops, to foment guerrilla warfare everywhere, to blow up bridges, roads, damage telephone and telegraph lines, and to set fire to forests, stores, and transports.

"In occupied regions [the Germans] must be hounded and annihilated at every step and all their measures frustrated.

"This war with Fascist Germany cannot be considered an ordinary war. It is not only a war between two armies, it is also a great war of the entire Soviet people against the German Fascist forces.

"The aim of this national war in defense of our country against the Fascist oppressors is . . . aid to all European peoples groaning under the yoke of German Fascism.

"In this war of liberation we shall not be alone.

"In this great war we shall have loyal allies in the peoples of Europe and America, including German people who are enslaved by Hitlerite despots.

"Our war for the freedom of our country will merge with the struggle of the peoples of Europe and America for their independence, democratic liberties. It will be a united front of peoples standing for freedom and against enslavement."

Speech of Joseph Stalin on July 3, 1941, quoted in Brian MacArthur (ed.), *The Penguin Book of Twentieth-Century Speeches* (New York: Viking, 1992).

sectors, was the largest concentration of military power that had ever been assembled, and once more the blitzkrieg worked its magic. Germany's armored divisions ripped through Russian lines and encircled astonishing numbers of troops. It looked to many observers as if the Soviet Union might collapse. German armies crossed the vast lands Russia had acquired since 1939, taking Riga and Smolensk in July, reaching the Dnieper in August, claiming Kiev and the whole Ukraine in September. Then the pace slowed; but while one German force lay siege to Leningrad in the north, a second hit Sevastopol in the south and moved into the Crimea. By December still another had penetrated to the suburbs of Moscow. There the German advance stopped temporarily, halted by an early and severe winter, by strained supply lines, and (at last) by sharp Russian counterattacks. The territory now held by Germany had accounted for nearly two-thirds of Russia's production of coal, iron, steel, and aluminum, as well as 40 percent of its grain and hogs.

As the war engulfed all of Europe,[1] German power at the end of 1941 was at its height, encompassing between 7 and 10 million soldiers, a superb air force, and a navy that included more than 150 submarines, which would sink nearly 400 Allied ships in the summer of 1942. Italy added sizable forces that were especially important in Africa. And yet Axis dominance was short-lived.

II. The Global War, 1942–1945

From the 1930s on, the fascist powers had held the initiative in politics, international relations, and war. Germany's invasion of the Soviet Union extended the war across Europe to Asia (after the Allied retreat had carried it to North Africa). Japan's attack on the United States in 1941 continued the pattern of Axis surprises, but it also marked the beginning of a significant change. War in the Pacific made this a truly global war—involving Asia, the Middle East, and North Africa—and the addition of American power helped tip the balance toward the Allies, whose industrial capacity was far greater than their enemies'. Axis

---

[1] Only Sweden, Spain, Portugal, Switzerland, and Eire remained even technically neutral by grace of geography.

Chronology

MAJOR MOMENTS OF WORLD WAR II

March 1938	*Anschluss:* Germany annexes Austria
September 1938	Munich Agreement, Germany takes Sudetenland
May 1939	Hitler-Stalin Pact
September 1939	Germany invades Poland, beginning of World War II
April 1940	Germany invades Denmark, Norway
May 1940	Germany invades Belgium, France, Netherlands
June 1940	France surrenders
October 1940	Italy invades Albania and Greece
April 1941	Romania, Bulgaria, Hungary, and Germany invade Yugoslavia
June 1941	Germany invades the U.S.S.R.
August 1941	Atlantic Charter
December 1941	Japan attacks Pearl Harbor
August 1942– February 1943	Battle of Stalingrad
November 1942	Allies land in North Africa
January 1943	Casablanca Conference
July 1943	Allies land in Sicily, Mussolini ousted
November– December 1943	Teheran Conference
June 1944	Allies land in Normandy
February 1945	Yalta Conference
May 1945	Germany surrenders
July–August 1945	Potsdam Conference

propaganda was losing effect in the face of the realities of German rule, which gave some weight to Allied claims that they were fighting for civilization as Russia, the Americas, and the British Empire set out to reconquer Europe.

▲ MAP 29.2 THE HEIGHT OF AXIS POWER, 1942

THE TURN OF THE TIDE

The United States Enters the War Despite its deep partisanship for France and Britain, the United States had remained technically at peace, even as the American government sold weapons to private firms for transfer to Great Britain and traded fifty old American destroyers for the lease of British bases in the western Atlantic. The United States, which Roosevelt called "the arsenal of democracy," also extended loans to Britain and then the Soviet Union. In August, Churchill and Roosevelt met at sea to draft the Atlantic Charter, which envisioned a world "after the destruction of the Nazi tyranny" that included collective security and self-determination for all nations, a world in which "all the men of all the lands may live out their lives in freedom from fear and want."

Ideological commitment, however, did not bring the United States into the war. Japan did that. Its attack on Manchuria in 1931 had been followed by a series of aggressive actions, from war with China starting in 1937 to the conquest of French Indochina in 1941. Tension between the United States and Japan increased with each new act of Japanese aggression, and America replied to the assault on Indochina with sanctions. Anticipating more, Japan gambled that the United States could be rendered nearly harmless in one blow, an attack on the American Pacific fleet at Pearl Harbor. The raid, on December 7, was devastating, and the United States declared it an act of war. All sides immediately recognized that the wars in Asia, Europe, and North Africa were one. Germany and Italy declared war on the United States three days later. Unless the Allies were driven from the seas, the industrial and military power of the United States might make a decisive difference in a war fought around the world.

Stalingrad   Winter snows raised the specter of a continuing two-front war, which Hitler had sworn to avoid. For all its losses, Russia's Red Army was intact; and its scorched-earth policy in retreat left the German army little to live on. To secure its massive victories, Germany had to knock Russia out of the war. But the siege of Leningrad, the attacks on Moscow, and even a drive into southern Russia in the summer of 1942 that took Sevastopol (and desperately needed grain) did not accomplish that goal. The crucial battle of the Eastern front took place at Stalingrad (now Volgograd) from August to October 1942. A breakthrough for the Germans at that strategic center would open the way to the oilfields of southern Russia.

By September the Germans had penetrated the city and fighting continued from building to building. The heroic defense gave Russia time to amass more troops than the Germans thought

▼ **American servicemen survey the ruins on an airfield at Pearl Harbor; the United States had entered the war.**
Navy Department/National Archives.

were available, and in the meantime Germany's own supplies dwindled. A Russian counterattack encircled the German army, which Hitler frantically ordered to stand its ground. When it finally surrendered, in February 1943, less than one-third of its 300,000 men were left. The giant Russian pincers had cost the Germans more than half a million casualties. Stalingrad was the turning point of the war on the Eastern front.

Air Power and the Invasion of North Africa In the West, too, the Axis position was eroding. The losses that German submarines inflicted were less crippling after 1942, and Allied air supremacy extended to the continent, where thousands of tons of explosives were dropped on Germany each month in 1942, a rate that would increase fivefold in 1943. The Americans bombed strategic targets during the day; the British preferred nighttime area bombing, with a city itself as the target. The inferno created by the firebombing of Hamburg in 1943 was a horror to be exceeded two years later in a yet more massive raid that leveled Dresden, a cultural center without important industry. The Germans were unaware, of course, that the secret codes they believed unbreakable had been cracked in London as early as 1940, giving the Allies an advantage that would be more important as the war progressed.[2]

The Allies also regained control of the Mediterranean. The battle lines in North Africa had ebbed and flowed, as General Erwin Rommel, the German "desert fox," and Britain's General Bernard Montgomery parried each other's thrusts in the deserts between Libya and Egypt. In October 1942 the German *Afrikakorps* drove to El Alamein in Egypt but were defeated there. Then in November British and American forces conducted the largest amphibious action yet attempted, landing in Morocco and Algeria to attack the *Afrikakorps* from the west. The campaign was an important test of green American troops and of Allied coordination under an American commander, General Dwight D. Eisenhower. It succeeded, and by May 1943 and after heavy losses, the Axis powers had been pushed out of Africa.

After costly stands at Bataan and Corregidor, the United States lost the Philippine Islands early in 1942. Japan had the upper hand, but the situation in the Pacific began to stabilize in the course of the year. Although a naval engagement in the Coral Sea in May brought no clear-cut victory to either side, it reduced the immediate threat of further Japanese gains. A Japanese attempt to invade Midway Island in June was driven off. Shortly after the Japanese attack on Pearl Harbor, Roosevelt and Churchill had agreed to give priority to the war in Europe. Their decision acknowledged the fear that the Soviet Union might not survive without massive help, the importance of European industrial power, and the bonds of Western culture.

COMPETING POLITICAL SYSTEMS

War on this scale required the coordination of entire economies and cooperation from every sector of society. After their slow start, Britain and the United States achieved that with impressive effect. The Soviet Union proved far stronger than expected, and Germany, the state that in theory was most devoted to militarism, managed in practice less well than its enemies.

The Allied Effort at Home As bombs rained down on Britain, support for the war effort was more nearly unanimous than in any other country in the world. Civilians accepted sacrifice and welcomed the end of unemployment, and the government commanded national resources as effectively as any in the world. The United States also mobilized its full economic resources and by the end of 1942 was producing more war matériel than all its enemies combined. Ships, planes, arms, and munitions from American factories and food from American farms flowed across the oceans to Britain and the Soviet Union. In both Britain and the United States more women were employed in industry than ever before; wives and mothers were hailed as heroines supporting their men (and some women) in the armed forces, and even children and the elderly

---

[2] The code was cracked in a project named Ultra, using devices that foreshadowed the computer. The secret of Ultra was not revealed until long after the war, and historians are still assessing its impact. The information that the Allies gained through Ultra appears to have been especially important in the Battle of Britain, the protection of Atlantic shipping, later in the war in Egypt, and (above all) in the Normandy landing.

took part in volunteer activities to aid the war effort.

Even before 1939 Stalin had adopted the policy of industrializing the more backward regions east of the Urals, a safe distance from Russia's western border, and in the months preceding Hitler's attack in 1941 hundreds of factories were moved there piece by piece. Despite its enormous losses of productive capacity, the Soviet Union was able throughout the war to produce most of the military supplies it needed. Central planning, rationing, military discipline, and the employment of women were not such a dramatic change in this communist regime, but the acceptance of rationing, the increased hours of labor, the destruction of homes, the death of loved ones, and the loss of men and territory required patriotism of a rather old-fashioned and bourgeois sort. Patriotism became the dominant theme of Soviet public life.

Nazi Rule   Until 1943 German civilians did not experience hardships comparable to the sacrifices of the Soviets or the lowered standard of living of the British. Nor was German output much greater than at the war's outset. The illusion, fed by military success and propaganda, that the war would soon be over encouraged interim measures. Competing elements of the Nazi party worked at cross purposes with each other and the government. Mutual distrust made it difficult for the Nazis to cooperate consistently with science and industry. Only when Albert Speer was given increased powers over the economy did coordination improve. In mid-July 1943 German production was twice what it had been in 1939, despite Allied bombing. A year later it was three times the prewar level.

Germany certainly benefited from its vast gains of territory rich in resources, industry, and personnel; but the system that took so naturally to ruthless conquest was less well adapted to ordinary life. The Nazis alienated those they conquered with their labor conscription, racial policies, and oppressive brutality. A high percentage of Ukrainians, for example, had welcomed liberation from Russian rule, but brief acquaintance with Nazi treatment of the "racially inferior" Slavs discouraged their cooperation. Nazi rule was most severe and most destructive in Eastern Europe, and less harsh among the "Aryan" populations of the Nordic lands. In France food rations provided only about half the minimum that decent health requires. Germany's most crucial need was for workers, and slave labor was an answer in accord with Nazi racial theory. About 1 million French workers and eventually some 5 million Slavs were shipped like cattle to labor in Germany. By 1944 the 8 million foreign workers in Germany constituted one-fifth of the workforce.

Genocide   The hysteria of racial hatred dominated rational planning. Brutalized and starving workers could hardly be efficient. Transporting and guarding slave laborers became an enormous, corrupting, and expensive enterprise. Many millions of people died in forced labor, perhaps 3 million Soviet prisoners of war were killed, and millions more Slavs in occupied territory were starved to death. These deaths, evidence of massive brutality and consonant with Nazi ideas about inferior races, could be said to have had some connection with the exigencies of war, as could the German practice of killing large numbers of civilian hostages in occupied lands as a means of demoralizing resistance while reducing unworthy populations. Hounding Jews and Gypsies, cramming them into concentration camps, and killing them had less to do with the brutality of war (the massacre of prisoners taken on the Eastern front may have been a precedent) than with the implementation of Nazi racial theory. Throughout the fall of 1941 mobile SS squads executed Jews who had been rounded up on the Eastern front. Men and women, old and young were lined up, made to undress, and marched toward ditches to be shot by the SS (one squad reported having killed more than 200,000 people). The orders, equipment, and reports this slaughter required establish that many people had to have known about it.

The Holocaust   Then, in January 1942, at a secret meeting of high officials held just outside Berlin, it was agreed that the systematic and efficient extermination of Jews should be made a general policy, "the final solution of the Jewish question" (see "A Crematorium," p. 1052). By 1945, nearly 6 million Jews and as many other people (Poles,

▲ The laborers' barracks at Buchenwald at the end of the war.
Bettmann.

Gypsies, and Magyars especially) had died in concentration camps like Buchenwald and Dachau and the more recently constructed death camps like Auschwitz. Some of these camps were also supposed to be centers of production: A Krupp arms factory, an I. G. Farben chemical plant, and a coal mine were part of the Auschwitz complex. But the chief product of Auschwitz was corpses, at a rate that reached 12,000 a day.

The extermination camps remain the ultimate nightmare of modern history. Beating and torturing prisoners of war was not new, though rarely so common as under the Nazis, but the industrial organization of death in Nazi camps raises terrifying questions about modern civilization. Hundreds of thousands of people were involved in operating those camps and in rounding up men, women, and children to be shipped to them. At first, the victims were primarily Slavs and Jews from the conquered lands of Eastern Europe; then Jews from Western Europe were hunted down and added to the flow. They came by trainload, huddled in boxcars, hungry, thirsty, frightened, and confused. Upon arrival at the camps, the weakest and least "useful" (the ill, the elderly, children, and often women) were sent to showers that proved to be gas chambers. The others were given uniforms, often with patches that distinguished into neat categories the common criminals, political prisoners, homosexuals, communists, Jehovah's Witnesses, Slavs, and Jews.

A CREMATORIUM

At a meeting of high Nazi officials on January 20, 1942, Reinard Heydrich, Plenipotentiary for the Preparation of the Final Solution of the European Jewish Question, spoke proudly of the liquidation of the Jews already accomplished and of the concentration camps already established but called for a further step. "We have the means, the methods, the organization, experience, and people. And we have the will. This is a historic moment in the struggle against Jewry. The Führer has declared his determination . . . [and sees destruction of the Jews] as exterminating fatal bacteria to save the organism. . . . We will work effectively but silently." Nazi extermination camps indeed followed strikingly similar procedures, and the following description of the Birkenau camp is typical of hundreds of survivors' testimonies. It was written by a French doctor, André Lettich, who was a member of the "special commando" squad, whose job it was to empty the crematoria of corpses and make them ready for the next round.

"Until the end of January 1943, there were no crematoria in Birkenau. In the middle of a small birch forest, about two kilometres from the camp, was a peaceful looking house, where a Polish family had once lived before it had been either murdered or expelled. This cottage had been equipped as a gas chamber for a long time.

"More than five hundred metres further on were two barracks: the men stood on one side, the women on the other. They were addressed in a very polite and friendly way: 'You have been on a journey. You are dirty. You will take a bath. Get undressed quickly.' Towels and soap were handed out, and then suddenly the brutes woke up and showed their true faces: this horde of people, these men and women were driven outside with hard blows and forced both summer and winter to go the few hundred metres to the 'Shower Room'. Above the entry door was the word 'Shower'. One could even see shower heads on the ceiling which were cemented in but never had water flowing through them.

"These poor innocents were crammed together, pressed against each other. Then panic broke out, for at last they realised the fate in store for them. But blows with rifle butts and revolver shots soon restored order and finally they all entered the death chamber. The doors were shut and, ten minutes later, the temperature was high enough to facilitate the condensation of the hydrogen cyanide, for the condemned were gassed with hydrogen cyanide. This was the so-called 'Zyklon B', gravel pellets saturated with twenty per cent of hydrogen cyanide which was used by the German barbarians.

"Then, *SS Unterscharführer* Moll threw the gas in through a little vent. One could hear fearful screams, but a few moments later there was complete silence. Twenty to twenty-five minutes later, the doors and windows were opened to ventilate the rooms and the corpses were thrown at once into pits to be burnt. But, beforehand the dentists had searched every mouth to pull out the gold teeth. The women were also searched to see if they had not hidden jewelry in the intimate parts of their bodies, and their hair was cut off and methodically placed in sacks for industrial purposes."

From J. Noakes and G. Pridham (eds.), *Nazism, 1919–1945: A Documentary Reader,* Volume 3, *Foreign Policy, War and Racial Extermination*, University of Exeter Press.

Many were literally worked to death or were killed when they could work no longer. The prisoners themselves, reduced to blind survival, were caught up in this dehumanized world of beatings, limited rations, constant abuse, and contempt. Neither submission nor animal cunning guaranteed another day of life. Many inmates nevertheless managed haunting gestures of human feeling through a story told, a song sung, a bit of food shared.

German clerks and bureaucrats kept elaborate records of names, stolen possessions, and corpses, which were efficiently stripped of gold fillings and useful hair before being turned to ashes that could be used as fertilizer. Doctors invented new tortures under the guise of medical experiments to benefit the Aryan race. The sadistic pseudoscience of these doctors elaborated on the paranoid dream of purifying the Aryan race. Forced sterilization and euthanasia of the chronically ill, the physically handicapped, and the mentally retarded had been advocated and practiced by Nazis since they first came to power. In *Mein Kampf* Hitler had referred to Jews as a plague and like a bacillus weakening the Aryan race. Racial laws had extended that point to all aspects of social life, and brutal treatment helped to make prisoners seem inferior, even subhuman. Organized killing carried this denial of humanity one step further.

Yet even the SS guards—like the camp commandants, the people who arranged for trains, and the business people who bid for contracts to build gas ovens—employed euphemisms rather than acknowledge what was really happening. The residents of nearby towns rarely discussed what was carried in the trains rumbling by or asked about the odor that settled over the countryside from crematoria smokestacks. Nor did the Allies quite believe or choose to act on the stories that filtered out of Germany about atrocities on a scale too terrible to comprehend.

Resistance Movements Millions of Europeans came to rely on the British Broadcasting Corporation for news and for encouragement in occupied lands, where every act of opposition—a speech not applauded, a whispered joke—took on symbolic significance. Gradually, against great odds, organized resistance movements formed. Some developed around neighborhood groups; many were connected to prewar political parties. Always composed of a small minority, these partisan movements achieved particular strength in Denmark and Norway, the Netherlands, France, and Yugoslavia. Many of them received material aid and guidance from governments-in-exile operating from London, the most notable being the Free French, headed by General De Gaulle.

Nazi reprisals for acts of resistance were meant to be horrible. When Czechs assassinated the new Reich Protector of Bohemia and Moravia in June 1942, the Germans retaliated by wiping out the village of Lidice, which they suspected of hiding the murderers: Every man was killed; every woman and child deported. On a single day in 1943, the Germans put 1,400 men to death in a Greek village. Hundreds of towns across occupied Europe had their memorials, a burned-out building or a ditch where clusters of civilians had been massacred.

▲ The scene that greeted the Allies on entering Lansberg concentration camp. American forces required several hundred German civilians in the area to come look at it as well.
UPI/Bettmann.

Yet the underground movements continued to grow, and their actions became a barometer of the course of the war. In France, partisan activities expanded from single exploits—smuggling Allied airmen out of the country, dynamiting a bridge, or attacking individual German officers—to large-scale operations closely coordinated from London. Norway's resistance helped force the Germans to keep 300,000 troops there and away from more

The Historians' Debate on German Genocide

◆

Over the past decade historians of Germany, particularly in Germany itself, have sustained a heated debate about the ways of understanding Nazi genocide. Among the issues in this debate, known as the Historikerstreit, *are the role of racial theories, the example of the Soviet Union, and whether genocide had distinctly German roots. The citations here, from three well-known scholars, illustrate these positions.*

From Henry Friedlander, "Step by Step: The Expansion of Murder, 1939–1941," *German Studies Review, XVII*, October 1994.

"Historians investigating Nazi genocide have long debated who gave the order to commit mass murder, when it was issued, and how it was transmitted. Although the specific mechanism has been a matter of contention between rival groups of historians . . . , there now appears to be a general agreement that Hitler had a deciding voice, although no one has ever discovered, or is likely to discover, a smoking gun. Recently historians have focused on the specific dates when the idea to launch the physical annihilation of the European Jews was first advanced and when the decision to do so became irrevocable . . . My own approach is somewhat different. I am not particularly interested in exact dates. Instead, I want to trace the sequential development of mass murder.

"I define Nazi genocide, what is now commonly called the Holocaust, as the mass murder of human beings because they belonged to a biologically defined group. Heredity determined the selection of victims. Although the regime persecuted and often killed men and women for their politics, nationality, religion, behavior, or activities, the Nazis applied a consistent and inclusive policy of extermination only against three groups of human beings: the handicapped, Jews, and Gypsies.

"The attack on these targeted groups drew on more than fifty years of political and scientific arguments hostile to the belief in the equality of man. Since the turn of the century, the German elite, that is the members of the educated professional classes, had increasingly accepted an ideology based on human inequality. Geneticists, anthropologists, and psychiatrists had advanced a theory of human heredity that had merged with the racist doctrine of *völkisch* nationalists to form a political ideology of a nation based on race. The Nazi movement both absorbed and advanced this ideology. After 1933 they created the political famework that made it possible to translate this ideology of inequality into a policy of exclusion, while the German bureaucratic, professional, and scientific elite provided the legitimacy the regime needed for the smooth implementation of this policy."

From Ernst Nolte, "Between Historical Myth and Revisionism," *Yad Vashem Studies XIX* 1988.

"Auschwitz is not primarily a result of traditional antiSemitism and was not, in its essential core, mere 'genocide'; rather, it was, above all, a reaction—born out of anxiety—to the annihilations which occurred during the Russian Revolution. This copy was far more irrational than the earlier original (because it was simply an absurd notion to imagine that 'the Jews' had ever wished to annihilate the German bourgeoisie or even the German people), and it is difficult to attribute to it even a perverted ethos. It was more horrifying than the original because it carried out the annihilation of human beings in a quasi-industrial manner. It was more repulsive than the original because it was based on mere suppositions, and was almost completely free of that mass hatred which, within the midst of horror, remains nonetheless an understandable—and thus, to a limited extent, reconciling—element. All this supports the notion of singularity, yet does not alter the fact that the so-called annihilation of the Jews during the Third Reich was a reaction or a distorted copy—and not a first act, not the original."

From Hans-Ulrich Wehler, "Unburdening the German Past? A Preliminary Assessment," in Peter Baldwin (ed.), *Reworking the Past: Hitler, the Holocaust and the Historians Debate,* Beacon Press, 1990.

"Nolte's thesis concerning the fatal consequences of the Bolsheviks' anxiety-producing class warfare is directed above all against a well-grounded interpretation: that Hitler and National Socialism were products of German and Austrian history. Only after factors rooted in that past have been assessed should the broader European context be considered. Nolte has sought to undermine this hard-won insight by displacing the "primary historical guilt" onto Marx, the Russian Revolution, and the extermination policy of the Bolsheviks. I shall emphasize below the main points of the opposing view—a view that is better grounded empirically and more convincing in its interpretive approach than Nolte's theory:

"—Hitler and countless other National Socialists had internalized a fanatical anti-Marxism long before the First World War: that is, before the Russian Revolution, the civil war, and class warfare in the new Soviet Union could confirm and strengthen their hatred of the 'Reds.'

"—Social Darwinism in its vulgar (racist) form was one of the strongest forces driving the highly ideological "worldview" of Hitler and many other Nazis well before 1917. Contemporary developments thereafter only served as confirmation to these confused minds.

"—The poisonous morass of German and Austrian anti-Semitism was the source of the crazed ideas associated with the Nazi hatred of the Jews. The new racist, political anti-Semitism that flourished in the late 1870s quickly led to the explicit idea of extermination. For example, in its Hamburg resolutions of September 1899, the German Social Reform Party claimed publicly and without any embarrassment that 'in the course of the twentieth century, the Jewish question must be solved . . . once and for all by the complete separation and (if necessary for defensive purposes) the definitive exter-

mination of the Jewish people.' What was new in the 1930s was 'only' that Hitler and his cohorts took this program literally—and brought with them the will to carry out the deed itself.

"—The Nazis effortlessly adopted the widespread, fully developed antidemocratic, antiliberal, and antiparliamentary political ideology that had already been fully developed by the German Right before 1917/18.

"—The Nazis were able to exploit the deeply corrosive anticapitalist resentments of the Protestant, provincial bourgeoisie and of peasant society. They were also able to counter the difficult conflicts of a modern class society with the hypertrophied idealization of an oft-evoked *Volksgemeinschaft* (national community).

"—National Socialism benefitted from long-term conditions in Germany: the antagonisms of Germany's social structure, an authoritarian mentality, the peculiarities of Prussian militarism, the Protestant subservience to the state, the national susceptibility to charismatic leaders, a particular kind of political philosophy, etc. Hitler's regime also profited from more recent conditions that stemmed from the experiences of the period 1914–33. Among these were 'the experience of war,' 'the nation in arms,' the 'total war' of 1916–18, the beginning of the defeat, the renunciation of all war aims, the stab-in-the-back myth, the 'disgraceful peace' at Versailles, the war reparations and postwar hyperinflation, and the destructive force of the Depression. These events belong to a long list of favorable factors with fatal consequences.

"Above all, the traditions and burdens of Germany's past influenced the course of National Socialism. Only after these have been identified should historians proceed to analyze the influence of the wider European and world-historical context."

active fronts. In Yugoslavia, two groups of partisans maintained an active guerrilla war, although the British decision to support the group led by Tito all but ensured his control of the country at the end of the war. After the Allied invasion of Italy, partisan groups there maintained an unnerving harassment of Fascist and Nazi forces.

Even in Germany itself some members of the army and the old aristocracy began to plot against Hitler, and in July 1944 a group of conspirators planted a bomb under the table as the Führer conducted a conference with his staff. Hitler escaped serious injury, but the sense that he was doomed had spread to the heart of Germany.

These partisan movements were important for more than their immediate contribution to the war. The memory of their bravery eased the painful reality of defeat, and in countries like France, Italy, and Norway, where many had acquiesced in fascist regimes, the militant opposition of the resistance could be taken to express the real will of the people. In fact many of the major political parties of the postwar era were formed in the resistance, and the ideas of democracy, freedom, and equality that circulated so passionately then would be repeated in constitutions and party platforms later. Most resistance fighters were young men, but many women, too, experienced the camaraderie of activism as secret couriers, provisioners, and occasionally group commanders. By joining in the resistance, women were being drawn into the rudimentary renewal of national political life.

ALLIED STRATEGY

By 1943 the Axis was on the defensive but had the advantage of holding contiguous territory with shorter, direct lines of supply. While Hitler continued to imagine that some daring thrust or miracle weapon would bring him victory, the Allies continued to disagree as to how they should attack Hitler's "fortress Europe."

A Second Front   The Soviet Union had repeatedly urged opening a second front on the continent, and most of the American military command favored an immediate invasion. The British warned against the high cost of such an invasion, and with Roosevelt's support, Churchill prevailed. Instead, the Allies successfully invaded North Africa, ending the threat to Egypt. When that move was not followed by landings on the continent, the Soviets suspected that they and the Germans were being left to annihilate each other. The Americans, too, now favored an attack on the mainland, but the British argued for tightening the blockade of Germany and for making more limited assaults in the eastern Mediterranean and on what Churchill called the "soft underbelly" of southern Europe.

More than military strategy was at stake. The Allies, who said less about their long-range goals than they had during World War I, were divided.

Stalin looked forward to regaining the Polish territory lost in 1939 (Poland could be compensated with territory taken from a defeated Germany). The British correctly warned that Soviet expansion into Poland would be unacceptable to the Americans and recalled the earlier communist aim of revolution across the continent (and the aim of imperial Russia before that for expansion into Eastern Europe). The British hoped to place Anglo-American troops in such a way that, after the war, they could have a voice in the disposition of Eastern Europe. In London the exiled leaders of the Eastern European countries agitated for their own nationalist goals, alarmed by Stalin's references to the need for "friendly" governments along Russia's borders.

The Casablanca Conference   With such issues before them, Roosevelt and Churchill met at Casablanca in January 1943. There they decided (to the Soviets' disgust) to invade Sicily and agreed to demand the unconditional surrender of Italy, Germany, and Japan, an expression of moral outrage against fascism that was also meant to prevent the Soviet Union and the Western Allies from making any separate deals with the enemy. Welcomed by Allied public opinion at the time, the refusal to negotiate with the Axis was subsequently criticized for strengthening their desperate defense after defeat was inevitable.

The Invasion of Italy   In July a mammoth amphibious assault carried Anglo-American forces into Sicily. A victim of his own propaganda, Mussolini had consistently overestimated Italian strength. As the invaders advanced, the Fascist Grand Council in a secret session voted Mussolini out of office. The Duce was arrested, and Marshal Pietro Badoglio was named prime minister. A coalition of monarchists and moderate Fascists then sought an armistice. But Committees of National Liberation had sprung up throughout Italy; composed of anti-Fascists from liberals to Communists, these Committees wanted nothing to do with Badoglio, a Fascist hero of the campaign in Ethiopia, or with the king, who had bowed to Mussolini for twenty years. Again the Allies were divided. Britain favored the monarchy and feared leftist influence in the Committees. The Americans leaned toward the Committees but agreed that representatives of the Soviet Union should be excluded from the Allied military government that would be installed in Italy. Stalin accepted that decision, knowing that arguments about spheres of influence would be useful elsewhere; and he encouraged Italy's Communists to be flexible in cooperating with the arrangements the Anglo-Americans preferred.

In September Allied forces landed in southern Italy, where they were well dug in by the end of the month. The German army, however, had snatched control of the rest of the peninsula. Although the Allies captured Naples in October, their campaign in Italy soon bogged down in difficult terrain and in the face of fierce German resistance. In a daring rescue, German paratroops snatched Mussolini from prison and took him to northern Italy, where he proclaimed a Fascist republic that was blatantly a German puppet. At the same time, Italy's antifascist partisans were becoming increasingly effective. Italians, their country a battleground for foreign armies, were caught in civil war.

The Free French   Italy was not the first place in which the Allies indicated they might compromise with tainted regimes. At the moment of the North African invasion, Admiral Jean François Darlan, a former vice premier of Vichy France and commander of its armed forces, happened to be in Algiers. Eisenhower's staff had quickly agreed to make him governor-general of French Africa provided his forces would not resist the Allied invasion. De Gaulle was outraged. He had claimed to represent a free France since his first call for continued resistance in 1940 when, from London, he organized French forces that fought with the Allies. His hauteur, his insistence on a voice in Allied policy, and his success in winning support in the French colonies had made his relations with Britain and the United States difficult at best. The assassination of Darlan in December 1942 eased the situation, and Germany's decision to occupy all of France in response to the Allied invasion of North Africa reduced De Gaulle's fears that the Allies might choose to deal with the Vichy regime. Watching events in Italy, Europe's governments-in-exile shared Stalin's concerns about the consistency and true aims of Allied policy.

The Teheran Conference   Finally, at the end of November 1943, Roosevelt, Churchill, and Stalin met for the first time, at Teheran. The conversations were not easy. Previously, the British had mediated between the United States and the Soviet Union, but now the Americans took a middle position. They reached a tentative understanding that the Soviet Union would accept a border with Poland similar to the one proposed in 1919, and they left open the question of what kind of government a liberated Poland might have. Their unity thus preserved by postponing the most difficult issues, the Allies could plan vigorous prosecution of the war. Stalin promised to declare war on Japan as soon as Germany surrendered, and Churchill's proposal for an invasion of the Dardanelles was rejected. The British and Americans agreed instead to land in France in the following year.

THE ROAD TO VICTORY

Italy   The Allies progressed slowly in Italy, taking five months to fight their way past a costly new beachhead at Anzio. In December 1943, King Victor Emmanuel III announced that he would abdicate in favor of his son, and Badoglio gave way to a cabinet drawn from members of the Committees of National Liberation. Italy then officially joined the Allies. The Germans held the advantage of entrenched positions on one mountain ridge after another, and the slow push northward, while the main Allied forces were held aside for the invasion of France, was aided by partisan risings. Only in May 1944 did Allied armies finally seize the old Benedictine abbey of Monte Cassino, north of Naples, after a destructive bombardment. Rome, the first European capital to be liberated, was taken in June. German resistance converged on the so-called Gothic Line, running from Pisa to Rimini. Not until it was pierced in September 1944, after months of bloody fighting, could further drives lead to the capture of Ravenna (in December) and Bologna, Verona, and Genoa (in April 1945). By then German resistance had ceased.

The Soviet Union   Soviet successes were more spectacular. In the spring of 1943 the Germans could still launch an offensive of their own, but it slowed within weeks. In July the Soviet army

▲ Stalin, Roosevelt, and Churchill, meeting for the first time at Teheran, reached an understanding that laid the groundwork for Allied cooperation in pursuing the war. UPI/Bettmann.

began a relentless advance that continued, with few setbacks, for almost two years. With armies now superior in numbers and matériel, Soviet forces reached the Dnieper and Kiev by November. In February 1944 they were at the Polish border. They retook the Crimea in the spring, Romania surrendered in August, and Finland and Bulgaria fell a few weeks later. Soviet power loomed over Eastern Europe.

The Western Front For months Germany was subjected to constant pounding from the air, and the Germans knew an invasion across the English Channel was imminent. They believed it would come in the area around Calais, the shore closest to England, as a series of calculated feints seemed to indicate. Instead, on June 6, 1944, the Allies landed in Normandy. The largest amphibious landing in history, it put 150,000 men

ashore within two days, supported by 5,000 ships and 1,500 tanks. In a complex series of landings Eisenhower's Allied force poured onto the French beaches. Made possible by overwhelming control of the air and helped by a poorly coordinated German defense, the landings cost heavy losses. Within a few months, more than a million men disembarked. In July they broke through the German defense and began a series of rapid drives through France. A second amphibious attack, in southern France in mid-August, led to swift advances inland that were greatly aided by well-organized French resistance groups. On August 24 the Parisian underground rose against the Germans, and French forces under Charles de Gaulle quickly entered the cheering city. Brussels fell a week later, and ten days after that, American troops crossed the German frontier.

▲ MAP 29.3 THE ALLIED VICTORY IN WORLD WAR II

Germany had launched its "miracle" weapon in June, the relatively ineffective V-1 pilotless plane, which was followed in September by the far more dangerous V-2 rocket. Had the Nazis recognized its potential earlier, the effects might have been devastating. The V-2 flew faster than the speed of sound and was almost impossible to intercept; but these rockets were hard to aim and too few and too late to be decisive. More threatening was a counterstroke through the Ardennes in December that rocked the Allied line back. The Battle of the Bulge, the last offensive the Germans would mount, cost about 70,000 men on each side before the Allies regained the initiative in January 1945.

The Yalta Conference When Allied leaders held their last wartime meeting, at Yalta in February 1945, Russian troops occupied part of Czechoslovakia and stood on the German frontier of Poland. The decisions of the Big Three at Yalta, which were widely hailed at the time, later became the most controversial of World War II. The hurried meet-

▲ In February 1944 an American sergeant who spoke German, believing he faced six or seven Germans, called on them to surrender—fifty-six came forward.
UPI/Bettmann.

ing dealt with four broad issues, each a measure of the Allies' mutual distrust. They agreed to the creation of a United Nations Organization. The Soviet Union asked for sixteen votes, one for each of its republics, to counterbalance the votes of the British Commonwealth and of Latin America, which the United States was expected to dominate. That request was reduced to three, and the Soviet Union got the veto it demanded but with some slight restrictions on its use. The USSR promised to declare war against Japan within ninety days of Germany's defeat in return for the territories Russia had surrendered to Japan in 1905 and for a sphere of influence in Manchuria.

A more contentious issue was the treatment of Germany. Each of the Big Three was assigned a zone of occupation, and Russia reluctantly agreed to the American and British plan to carve a zone for France from the areas under their control. Russia's demands for huge reparations and "labor services" were so troubling that specific terms had to be postponed. The form of Italy's government was in fact now largely set, as was De Gaulle's ascendance in an independent France. The main issue was Soviet dominance in Eastern Europe. The creation of new governments for the liberated nations, the most difficult issue of all, could not be postponed much longer; yet every proposal ex-

▲ **Charles de Gaulle, the epitome of French resistance, greeted by Parisians on the day of the city's liberation in August 1944.**
Robert Capa/Magnum.

posed fundamental differences between the Soviet Union and the Western powers.

In most of the countries they occupied, the Soviets were tolerating broad coalitions that included all the old antifascist parties, but they would not allow a role for the Western powers, even restricting Allied observers. When Churchill visited Moscow four months earlier, he had proposed a division of interests: The Soviet Union would have predominance in Romania and the largest influence in Bulgaria, Britain would have a free hand in Greece, and the two powers would recognize their equal interests in Yugoslavia and Hungary. Such crude understandings offered few guarantees, however, though Stalin remained silent when Britain intervened in the civil war raging in Greece in order to rout the leftists.

Stalin in turn exercised a free hand in Poland after the Polish underground arose against the Germans in August 1944. As Soviet troops approached Warsaw, the Russians simply halted their advance until the Germans had wiped out the resistance fighters, who were closely tied to the anticommunist Polish government in London. The Yalta Conference did not in fact adopt cynically drawn spheres of influence; but the Conference's formulas, with their references to democratic governments and free elections, would in the end be interpreted by those with guns.

The Final Months As the Allies pushed into Germany from all sides, it became clear that Berlin would be the final battleground. Fearing that Hitler planned a last desperate stand at his retreat at Berchtesgaden in the south German mountains, Eisenhower halted the eastward advance of American and British armies at the Elbe River. The Russians took Berlin, where Hitler had ensured the maximum destruction by ordering a defense to the death. The Führer committed suicide on April 30, 1945, and his aides burned his body,

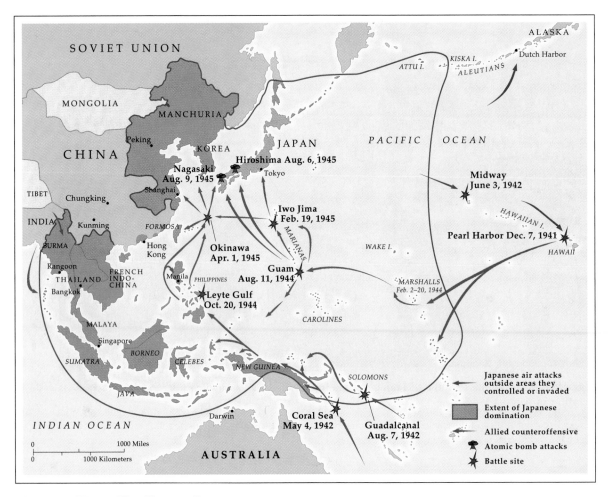

▲ Map 29.4 World War II in the Pacific

which has never been found. Four days later a group of German officers signed the final unconditional surrender. The war in Europe was over.

World conflict would continue in Asia for four months more. It was expected to last much longer, even with the Russian help that had seemed so necessary when promised at Yalta. Despite massive bombing and repeated naval victories, Allied progress through the islands and jungles of the Pacific toward Japan had been laborious and bloody. During the three months following Germany's surrender, air raids obliterated Japan's navy, industrial plants, and large parts of its cities: Nearly 200,000 people were killed in Tokyo in just one week. But still the Japanese would not surrender.

On August 6 the new president of the United States, Harry Truman (Roosevelt had died in April), authorized the use of a new weapon that had been developed after years of secret research, the atomic bomb. In one blow, half of the city of Hiroshima disappeared from the face of the earth. A quarter of its 320,000 inhabitants were killed. On August 9 the Americans dropped an even more powerful atomic bomb on the city of Nagasaki. The Soviet Union declared war in Japan on August 8; and on September 2, 1945, Japan surrendered unconditionally. The atomic bomb, an extraordinary achievement of science and technology made possible by great wealth and scores of European scientists driven to sanctuary in the United States, permitted a great democracy to end

▲ **Hiroshima, the victim of one of science's great achievements. The world had entered a new era of warfare, and for a generation the Japanese would suffer from the environmental destruction and the effects of radiation.** AP/Wide World.

World War II by unleashing a new order of terror upon humanity. Later, many people would question the morality of using so terrible a weapon. Even in the jubilation of victory, leaders reordering a shattered world now knew that another war might bring the end of civilization.

III. Building on the Ruins

For years Europeans would have to deal with the effects of death, destruction, and the displacement of millions of people. Overcoming such fundamental problems on so vast a scale was the central achievement of the next decade and the sober preoccupation of individuals, institutions, and governments. Even among the victors and the newly liberated, euphoria was brief as people set about their daily tasks in an uncertain world of economic hardship, social dislocation, and political division.

IMMEDIATE CRISES

The Devastation In contrast to World War I, a majority of the fatalities in World War II were civilian. About 4 million men died on battlefields; and for every soldier killed, two more were either wounded or taken captive. Civilian losses are harder to categorize, and often there was no one to do the counting. The Germans killed between 12 and 20 million people in occupied countries and concentration camps, and across Europe millions more civilians died just for being where armies chose to bomb or shell or shoot. In all, the European casualties in World War II were five or six times greater than in World War I (only for Britain and France were they lower). The Soviet Union lost some 27 million people; Poland, about 6 million (including 3 million Jews); Germany, nearly 5 million. So the total European casualties of World War II—dead, wounded, or crippled by inhumane treatment—remain an estimate, a number hard to comprehend in its gruesome total or ghostly imprecision: some 45 to 55 million people.

Europe's industrial capability in 1945 was perhaps half what it had been in 1939; and only parts of such major cities as Frankfurt, Dresden, Brest, and Toulon were still standing. The continent's most important ports, bridges, and rail lines had been all but destroyed. Agriculture was also hard hit. Large areas of farmland in France, Italy, and Germany could not be cultivated; the number of cattle in France had been reduced by half. In the winter of 1945–1946, starvation was a threat in many places, and in some, such as Vienna, thousands died of famine. Disease was an ever-present danger, too, although penicillin helped limit the epidemics that erupted. The rationing of food and clothes (and illegal black markets) continued in many countries into the 1950s, and Europeans looked to the United States and the Soviet Union for relief as Allied troops occupied the continent.

Refugees   In addition to the millions without jobs or housing, there were more refugees in Europe than ever before in history. Some 8 million slave laborers in the Third Reich and millions in concentration camps were put on trains headed back to where their homes had been. There were German prisoners of war and Allied prisoners in Germany. More than 7 million Soviet citizens in Germany, including defectors, had no place to go. Some 2 million Poles and Czechs returning from prison in the Soviet Union joined millions of Ukrainians and Poles who moved west to stay on the other side of the shifting border with the USSR. Romanians drove out Hungarians; Czechs expelled Hungarians and Germans. Millions of Germans whom the Nazis had transplanted to Poland in the interests of Germanization were forced to leave, and many of the 1.5 million Poles the Nazis had evicted wanted to go back home. The question of where national boundaries should be drawn, which had so troubled the peacemakers of Versailles, was settled now by first drawing the lines and then pushing inconvenient nationalities across them.

Most of the refugees who carried their few belongings along unfamiliar roads were civilians, perhaps 60 million in all, a majority of them women and children who had lost their homes and livelihood. Separated from kin and possessions, they struggled to survive in strange lands that were impoverished by war. We will never know how many died or were abused or robbed. Governments tried to make nice distinctions between the homeless (those in or near their own country) and displaced persons (who were mostly stateless—some 12 million were so registered in 1945), and they tried to separate criminals from others. Abandoned factories and warehouses, even former concentration camps, were used to house refugees. When facilities were specially built, they were usually crude barracks without plumbing or electricity and were meant to be temporary. Bit by bit the fortunate were assigned a destination, but "unaccompanied children," the disabled, and the aged were harder to place. In 1960, fifteen years after the war had ended, there were still 32,000 refugees in 107 camps in Europe, sharing tiny quarters and communal toilets.

The Terms of Peace: Potsdam   No great peace conference took place after World War II. When the leaders of the Soviet Union, Great Britain, and the United States met at Potsdam for two weeks in July 1945, they hardly knew each other. President Harry Truman had been in office only three months following the death of Roosevelt, and in the midst of the meeting Clement Attlee replaced Churchill, who had been defeated in the British elections.

The Potsdam meeting outlined the future of Germany but left details for the future. The Allies readily agreed that all Nazi institutions must be abolished, German arms production prohibited, and German industry controlled. Democracy and free speech were to be restored. In the meantime Germany was divided into four zones of occupation, and so was Berlin, isolated in the Soviet zone. Germany's eastern border was moved westward to the Oder and Neisse rivers, enlarging Poland. During the next year, the foreign ministers of the four principal Allies (now including France)

▲ Citizens of Dresden, nearly a year after the war ended, making their way through the rubble from Allied saturation bombing.
UPI/Corbis-Bettmann.

drafted treaties for the other defeated states, but their meetings soon became a forum for quarrels between the Soviets and the other three. Italy, Romania, Hungary, Bulgaria, and Finland each ceded minor territories to its neighbors. Austria, like Germany, remained divided into four occupied zones and without a formal treaty.

The Potsdam Conference had also laid down the terms for peace with Japan. The Soviet Union would get some territory, and the European nations would regain their Asian colonies. But the prime beneficiaries were China and, above all, the United States, whose troops were to occupy Japan and which already held most of the strategic islands in the Pacific.

War Crimes Trials Within Europe, the first concern was to root out fascism. In countries the Nazis had occupied, there were summary executions of collaborators and some public prosecutions, notably in France, where Pierre Laval and Marshal Pétain were tried. In Germany itself,

▲ **Göring, Hess, and von Ribbentrop (the first three on the left in the prison's dock) listen to the proceedings at the beginning of the Nuremberg trial for war crimes.**
Bettmann.

however, the numbers involved made denazification difficult. Millions of forms were filled out and hundreds of trials held, but the drive against former Nazis soon waned. Determined to establish some lasting standard, the Allies created an international tribunal to try Hitler's closest associates for crimes against humanity. The trials, held in Nuremberg in 1945 and 1946, were also intended to inform the German people of the full horror of Nazi rule. The appalling revelations of those solemn hearings were followed by restrained judgments—only twelve of the twenty-two prime defendants were condemned to death, and three were acquitted.

International Agencies The belief in international law that underlay the Nuremberg trials and the United Nations Organization was tempered by a determination to learn from the past. This peace would not be punitive; and devastated nations, defeated enemies as well as those liberated from German rule, must be helped. Even before the UN had its charter, its first agency, the United Nations Relief and Rehabilitation Administration, (UNRRA), had been created late in 1943. UNRRA played a major role in the reconstruction of postwar Europe, organizing relief of food and medical supplies and coordinating international loans. To avoid the dangerous inflation that had followed World War I, a conference at Bretton Woods, New Hampshire, in 1944 created the International Monetary Fund and an International Bank for Reconstruction and Development (later the World Bank). Those institutions, with nearly $20 billion in assets, furthered reconstruction and capital investment by supporting stable currencies. They would become influential mechanisms for shaping the international capitalist economy.

But the main instrument of peace was to be the United Nations, and a few months after the Yalta meeting, fifty-one countries approved the United Nations Charter at a special conference held in San Francisco. The charter established a General Assembly of all members to determine policy; a decision-making Security Council of eleven nations to supervise "the maintenance of international peace"; and various economic, social, and legal agencies. Permanent Security Council seats were reserved for the United States, the Soviet Union, China, Great Britain, and France, each with a right to veto any council action; the remaining six seats were filled by election from among the other member states.

Although Britain and France were on the Security Council and Scandinavians served as the UN's general secretaries until 1961, the United Nations reflected a redistribution of international power in which Europe was no longer dominant. The presence of the United States and the Soviet Union in the UN was a promising contrast to the League of Nations; but their conflicts soon dominated international relations, and within the UN they competed for the support of Asian, African, and Latin American nations not yet formally tied to one of the two major blocs.

THE DIVISION BETWEEN EAST AND WEST

Everywhere, liberation opened a battle for domestic power. Communists had played a leading part in resistance movements, and their prestige was high. Initially they joined in the general demand for democracy and social justice. On one issue after another, however, communists and socialists soon found themselves in bitter conflict with the center and the right. As each side fought for power, the lines between them hardened, and their conflicts became part of the larger competition between the Soviet Union and the United States.

Eastern Europe: Puppet Regimes Soviet troops occupied Eastern Europe from the Adriatic to the Baltic. The three formerly independent states of Estonia, Latvia, and Lithuania became Soviet re-

publics; and Russia annexed territory from East Prussia, Poland, Hungary, and Romania. In the ostensibly autonomous nations of Eastern Europe, the Soviets discouraged independent revolutions like those that followed World War I but skillfully used social issues and crude coercion to establish friendly governments. Leading anticommunists would be excluded from the governing coalition; and later a campaign of propaganda, pressure, and sudden arrests would eliminate the noncommunist parties from power until a single-party dictatorship on the Soviet model had consolidated its position with purge trials and secret police (see "Churchill Sees an Iron Curtain," p. 1068).

With Soviet production at less than two-thirds of its prewar level, the Five-Year Plan announced in 1946 openly depended on the ransacking of East Germany and other occupied areas. In the eastern zone of Germany, the Soviet Union followed the same techniques that had proved effective elsewhere. Early in 1946 the Russians forced a merger of East Germany's Social Democratic party with the smaller Communist party, and Soviet control was soon complete. After expropriating much of German industry and restricting trade with the West, the Russians gradually allowed the eastern zone to increase its industrial activity and granted it independent status in 1949 as the German Democratic Republic. Germany had in effect been divided in two.

In Romania the communists forced King Michael into exile late in 1947. Poland, where the Communists were weakest, had been promised free elections; but when these were held in 1947, repressive measures against the minority Peasant party left the Independent Socialists with an overwhelming majority. In a few months the Peasant party was purged, the Catholic Church persecuted, the Independent Socialist party subordinated to the communist Workers' party, and a Russian placed in command of the army.

The president and the foreign minister of Czechoslovakia, Eduard Beneš and Jan Masaryk, were the heirs of a notable democratic tradition. But in 1948, the Communists, the largest party, threatened to take over the country with Russian support. Beneš gave way, and Masaryk died in a mysterious fall from a window. Hungary's coalition government had an anti-Communist majority until a dubious election in 1949 gave the

CHURCHILL SEES AN IRON CURTAIN

On March 5, 1946, Winston Churchill gave a speech at Westminster College in Fulton, Missouri, that immediately received worldwide attention. After years of official emphasis on the cooperation among the wartime Allies, its directness was shocking. In effect, it announced the Cold War.

"A shadow has fallen upon the scenes so lately lighted by the Allied victory. Nobody knows what Soviet Russia and its Communist international organization intends to do in the immediate future, or what are the limits, if any, to their expansive and proselytizing tendencies. I have a strong admiration and regard for the valiant Russian people and for my wartime comrade, Marshal Stalin. There is deep sympathy and goodwill in Britain—and I doubt not here also—towards the peoples of all the Russias and a resolve to persevere through many differences and rebuffs in establishing lasting friendships. We understand the Russian need to be secure on her western frontiers by the removal of all possibility of German aggression. We welcome Russia to her rightful place among the leading nations of the world. We welcome her flag upon the seas. Above all, we welcome constant, frequent and growing contacts between the Russian people and our own people on both sides of the Atlantic. It is my duty, however, for I am sure you would wish me to state the facts as I see them to you, to place before you certain facts about the present position in Europe.

"From Stettin in the Baltic to Trieste in the Adriatic, an iron curtain has descended across the Continent. Behind that line lie all the capitals of the ancient states of Central and Eastern Europe. Warsaw, Berlin, Prague, Vienna, Budapest, Belgrade, Bucharest and Sofia, all these famous cities and the populations around them lie in what I must call the Soviet sphere, and all are subject in one form or another, not only to Soviet influence but to a very high and, in many cases, increasing measure of control from Moscow.

" . . . An attempt is being made by the Russians in Berlin to build up a quasi-Communist party in their zone of Occupied Germany by showing special favours to groups of left-wing German leaders. At the end of the fighting last June, the American and British Armies withdrew westwards, in accordance with an earlier agreement, to a depth at some points of one hundred and fifty miles upon a front of nearly four hundred miles, in order to allow our Russian allies to occupy this vast expanse of territory which the Western Democracies had conquered.

"If now the Soviet Government tries, by separate action, to build up a pro-Communist Germany in their areas, this will cause new serious difficulties in the British and American zones, and will give the defeated Germans the power of putting themselves up to auction between the Soviets and the Western Democracies. Whatever conclusions may be drawn from these facts—and facts they are—this is certainly not the Liberated Europe we fought to build up. Nor is it one which contains the essentials of permanent peace."

Reprinted in Brian MacArthur, *The Penguin Book of Twentieth-Century Speeches* (New York: Viking, 1992) and available in many other places.

Communists control. In each case Britain and the United States protested, with little effect, and the new regimes established close links with the Soviet Union. Albania and Bulgaria became solid members of the communist bloc by 1950.

Only Yugoslavia followed a different course. Marshal Tito easily won the 1945 national election, and communists dominated the government; but Tito resisted Soviet efforts to influence his foreign and domestic policies. After having joined the Cominform, which had replaced the Comintern and was similarly designed to coordinate international communist activity, Yugoslavia broke with its neighbors in 1948, using ties with the West to resist economic and political pressure from the East—an example to others of how small states could use the tense balance between the superpowers.

Western Europe: The Politics of the Past Despite their altered circumstances, most Western countries returned to prewar patterns of parliamentary life, although Spain and Portugal remained defiant dictatorships. The governments of the Low Countries and Scandinavia established much-admired social programs. The new constitutions of France and Italy, which spoke of the right to work and of social in addition to civil rights, at last granted women the vote. Few delegates opposed the change; and the new left, in which communists were prominent, did not share the old fear that priests would influence the way women voted.

Generally, reconstruction took precedence over reform. West Germany's federal structure and two dominant parties, the Christian Democrats and the Social Democrats, recalled the pre-Nazi Weimar Republic. Ironically, at war's end Germany's industry was in better shape than that of any other European nation, and the Allies soon relaxed restrictions on its economic activity. Early in 1949 they acknowledged the ad hoc division of Germany and recognized the western sections that had been occupied by Britain, France, and the United States as the Federal Republic of Germany. For the next fourteen years, West Germany's chancellor was Konrad Adenauer, the head of the Christian Democrats. Mayor of Cologne from 1917 to 1933, he was seventy-three years old in 1949, a firm and conservative leader closely allied with the United States, who promoted an atmosphere of efficient calm.

In France, the new Fourth Republic looked much like the Third. Politics was dominated by three large parties—the Communists, the Socialists, and a new Catholic party of the left, the MRP (Popular Republican Movement). The constitution they wrote kept the president subordinate to the legislature as he had been in the past and soon pushed the domineering De Gaulle from his office as provisional president. Although the nation was effectively engaged in the enormous effort of reconstruction, popular attention emphasized unstable governments, Communist intransigence, and labor agitation. Disillusionment with the Fourth Republic and the popularity of De Gaulle rose in tandem.

Italy, too, became a republic, when more than 54 percent of the electorate voted in 1946 to replace a monarchy tainted by Fascism. The Christian Democrats were by far the largest party, in themselves a coalition held together primarily by opposition to the Communists. The party's leader

from 1945 to 1953, Alcide De Gasperi, was prime minister during most of this time. A wily politician, he ostracized the Communists—the largest Communist party in the West—and took advantage of a split among Socialists to bring Italy into close alliance with the United States. His party won the crucial elections of 1948, aided by extensive American pressure, and launched a program of moderate reform, including efforts to revitalize the economy of southern Italy and to stimulate industry in the north. Italian politics had returned to the unheroic tradition of parliamentary maneuver that the Fascists had overturned, setting a pattern that would last for nearly fifty years.

In many respects, postwar politics brought greater change to Great Britain than to these new governments on the continent. Churchill's defeat in the elections of 1945 was a turning away from wartime unity and sacrifice. With an enormous majority, the Labour party under Clement Attlee launched a massive program of nationalization, taking over the Bank of England and a wide range of major industries, including coal, transportation, electricity, and iron and steel. It also instituted extensive welfare programs and established public housing, national insurance, and free medical care for all. True to its principles, the Labour government also began Britain's withdrawal from the empire to which men like Churchill had been so attached.

The Cold War   In 1947 distrust between the Soviet Union and the United States hardened into a worldwide military, political, and ideological conflict quickly dubbed the Cold War. As Russia tightened its grip on Eastern Europe, the American president announced the Truman Doctrine, promising military and economic aid to nations in danger of communist takeover. His immediate concern was civil war in Greece, where local communists were aided by neighboring Yugoslavia, and gaining American bases in Turkey. Britain, which up to that point had provided the countervailing force against the communists, could no longer sustain its military power and influence in the eastern Mediterranean, and announced that the United States was taking over that role. Money and supplies poured into Greece, and this American response, combined with Yugoslavia's break with Russia, enabled the Greek government to

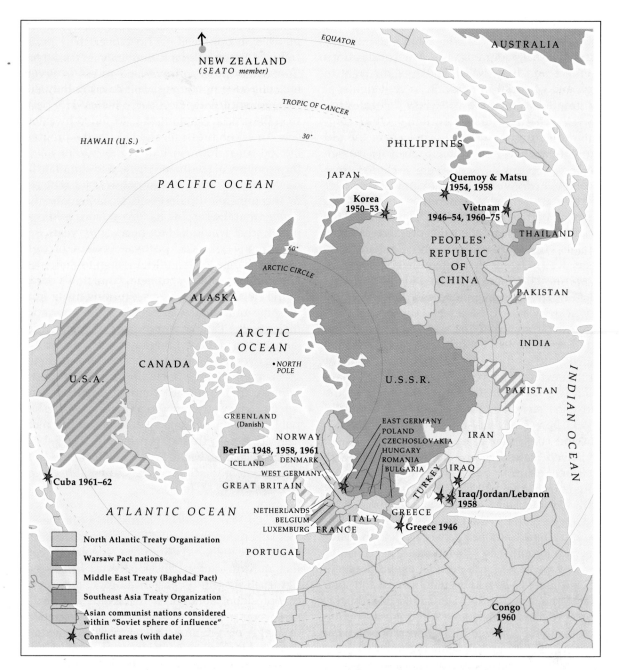

▲ Map 29.5 Cold War Alliances and Conflict

crush the opposition by 1949. Turkey, slowly moving toward democracy, received similar assistance. Opposition to communism and Soviet influence, believed to operate through international subversion, had become the focus of American policy.

A few months after the announcement of the Truman Doctrine, Secretary of State George Marshall unveiled an imaginative plan to stimulate European recovery—and overcome the European economic crisis in which communism was likely to prosper. The United States would offer massive economic aid to all nations still recovering from the war, and aid, too, became a battlefront in the Cold War. Russia forbade the participation of Eastern European governments in the American program and established its own Council of Mutual Economic Assistance (Comecon) instead. In the West, Communist parties opposed the Marshall Plan despite its obvious benefits, and the United States used its growing influence to isolate the communists, who were excluded from coalition governments in France and Italy in 1947 and from all government positions in Switzerland in 1950. West Germany banned the party itself in 1956. The two halves of Europe followed the lead of their powerful patrons.

Escalating Confrontation Fearful of the growing German economy and America's support for anticommunist movements everywhere, the Soviet Union tightened its hold over the satellite states of Eastern Europe. Suddenly, in June 1948, the Soviets closed off overland access to Berlin, believing that the former capital was becoming a dangerous outpost of Western power. War seemed imminent. The United States responded with an extraordinary airlift: For nearly a year, until the Soviets backed down, a steady stream of flights ferried in all of West Berlin's supplies.

The United States saw the Soviet Union's test of its own atomic bomb in 1949 as a direct challenge, and Truman announced that work was under way on the even more devastating hydrogen bomb. But the loss of a monopoly on atomic weapons made ground forces that did not depend on using atom bombs seem essential as a deterrent to Soviet aggression. Consequently, in 1949

▼ **The world was as impressed as the children of Berlin by the airlift that carried supplies to the city and completed 277,264 flights in a year.**
Fenno Jacobs/Black Star

the North Atlantic Treaty Organization (NATO) was created to coordinate the military planning of the United States, Canada, and ten Western European nations,[3] which now received U.S. military aid. The Russians replied with the Warsaw Pact of Communist states in 1955.

At first, the Cold War had been primarily a conflict over Europe, waged as a competition for public opinion as well as international power. Even domestic issues formed along pro-American or pro-Soviet positions. But with Eastern Europe isolated behind what Churchill called the "iron curtain" and communists excluded from political power in the West, the focus of the Cold War shifted. When the communist North Koreans invaded South Korea in 1950, the United States at once asked the United Nations to intervene, and the UN (with Russia temporarily absent) called for an international army to stop the North Koreans. The Cold War was now worldwide. Having marked the lessened autonomy of the European nations, it spread to colonial issues and conflicts in the Middle East and Asia (see "The Soviet Union Denounces the United States While Calling for Arms Reduction," p. 1073).

The Loss of Empire From a global perspective, the collapse of European empires was one of the great changes of the postwar era. It should not have been a surprise. During the war, Japan had taken Indonesia from the Dutch, Indochina from France, and much of Malaysia from Britain; and restoring empire was different from sustaining it. Neither of the superpowers wished to be of much help. The United States was traditionally unsympathetic to European empires, and opposition to imperialism was part of the Soviet Union's official stance. It supported local communist risings against imperialism. The Vichy government had lost touch with much of France's empire during the war, and both Stalin and President Roosevelt let De Gaulle know they did not favor France's return to Vietnam.

Anticolonialism Anticolonial and nationalist movements had been building since before World War I, especially in Algeria, India, Indonesia, and Vietnam. That opposition had only gained strength from familiarity with European ideologies, experience in combat, the displacement of foreign rule, anti-imperialist propaganda, and the disruption of capitalist ties. European-educated statesmen and intellectuals—like Jawaharlal Nehru in India, Léopold Sedar Senghor in Senegal, Sékou Touré in Guinea, and Franz Fanon and Aimé Césaire from the West Indies—could, while building a powerful following at home, also skillfully negotiate with European officials and win the support of European intellectuals through essays and poems that explored the profound destructiveness of imperialism. Opposition to imperialism within the Netherlands, France, and Britain came from parties (usually on the left) that favored independence and demanded that promised concessions be granted, an opposition reinforced by the public's greater interest in seeing money spent on reconstruction at home.

For all that, Europe's leaders were reluctant to let go. Lebanon and Syria had been promised independence during the war, but Britain and France briefly renewed some of their old rivalries in the Middle East before withdrawing in 1946. Trans-Jordan became independent, foreign troops left Iraq and Iran, and negotiations began for British forces to depart from Egypt and the Sudan. Despite Arab hostility, Great Britain undertook the creation of separate Jewish and Muslim states in Palestine. Mounting terror campaigns from both sides notwithstanding, the British decided to remove all their troops in May 1948, and the United Nations, eager to give Jews a refuge following Hitler's persecutions, endorsed the creation of the state of Israel. The Arabs invaded the day the British left but were driven back despite numerical superiority, and UN mediators were able to bring about a shaky truce that confirmed Israel's existence.

European Efforts to Hold On Colonial officials operated in a state of high frustration. The concessions they granted always came a little too late or led to demands for more. The use of force tended to increase opposition on the scene and around the world. By the 1940s the news of

---

[3] Great Britain, France, Belgium, the Netherlands, Luxemburg, Italy, Portugal, Denmark, Norway, and Iceland were the European members. Greece and Turkey would be added in 1952; West Germany, in 1955.

The Soviet Union Denounces the United States While Calling for Arms Reduction

Andrei Vishinsky, the Russian delegate to the United Nations, spoke to the General Assembly on November 1, 1948, proposing steps toward arms reduction and control of atomic weapons. The address was testimony, however, to the global range of the Cold War. Most of it consisted of a lengthy denunciation of the policies of the United States, which was accused of undermining the United Nations; of intervening against democracy and peace in Korea, Greece, Indonesia, and Palestine; and of harming Europe's economy with the Marshall Plan while forming a military alliance with the nations of Western Europe aimed at the "freedom-loving" states of Eastern Europe.

"The policy of the USSR is a consistent and constant policy of expanding and strengthening international cooperation. This follows from the very nature of the Soviet State. A socialist State of workers and peasants deeply interested—a State, I repeat, which is deeply interested in the establishment of the most favorable conditions for peaceful creative work in the building of a socialist society. The foreign policy of the Soviet Union pursues the course of co-operation among all countries prepared for peaceful cooperation. The USSR consistently fights against any plan and measures and designs intended to create a gap, a cleavage, among peoples. It fights for the realization and implementation of democratic principles which were born out of the war.

"Such is not the case with the present foreign policy of the United States. After the termination of the recent war, the Government of the United States has changed its foreign policy: from a policy of fighting against aggressive forces, the United States has passed over to a policy of expansion. It is now attempting to realize plans for world domination. It is in open support in various countries of the most reactionary and monarchofascist regimes and groups and rendering to them systematic aid with money and armaments for the suppression of democratic national liberation movements in these countries; organization of military alliances or blocs, the construction of new military air and naval bases as well as the expansion and reconstruction in accordance with the newest military technical requirements of old bases established during the war with Germany, Japan, and Italy; furthermore, unchecked propaganda of a new war against the Soviet Union and the new democracies of Eastern Europe; a wild race of armaments; a true worship of the cult of the atomic bomb and allegedly a means of escape from all the dangers and misfortunes threatening the capitalistic world: these are the principal aspects, the characteristic features, of the foreign policy of the United States of America at present.

"Such a policy is inciting the psychosis of war, sowing restlessness and fear among the broad masses which strive for peace and peaceful creative labor. Such a policy has nothing in common whatsoever with a policy of peace.

"[A] . . . map by the ESSO Company of New York is of the same insolently arrogant and war-inciting nature. This map is published by the Standard Oil Company of New Jersey. It is called, quite provocatively, 'The Map of the Third World War.' That is what they are publishing in the United States—the Map of the Third World War! They are handing them out to motorists. This map, with provocatively militant appeals, carries the heading: 'Pacific Theatre of Military Operations.' The map is an example of the malicious war propaganda against the Soviet Union and the new democracies of East Europe.

" . . . The reactionary circles of the United States and the United Kingdom as well as of countries such as France, Belgium, and others, do not confine themselves to slander and abuse alone. This campaign is now being headed not only by amateurs from the family of retired politicians, statesmen, Senators and Members of Parliament, but also by persons now holding high official posts in the Governments of the United States, the United Kingdom, France and some other countries.

" . . . On the instructions of the Soviet Union Government the delegation of the USSR proposes to the General Assembly, for the purpose of strengthening the cause of peace and removing the menace of a new war which is being fomented by expansionists and other reactionary elements, the adoption of the following resolution:

" . . . as the first step in the reduction of armaments and armed forces to reduce by one-third during one year all present land, naval, and air forces. . . .

" . . . to prohibit atomic weapons as weapons intended for aims of aggression and not for those of defense;

" . . . to establish within the framework of the Security Council an international control body for the purpose of the supervision and control of the implementation of . . . [these] measures. . . . "

Speech by Andrei Y. Vishinsky to the United Nations, November 1, 1948, from *Vital Speeches of the Day*, (New York: The City News Pub. Co., 1949), Vol. 15, No. 2, New York.

effective resistance spread quickly, as it had not done in the past, stimulating new protests and risings from Asia to the Middle East to Africa and the Caribbean. Administrators tried to censor the news and renewed their searches for the subversives whom they were sure must be the source of such discontent but found, most disheartening of all perhaps, the loss of support from local elites. India, where the spiritual message and personal qualities of Mohandas K. Gandhi won worldwide admiration and vast support, was granted independence from Britain in 1947. Violent conflict between Hindus and Muslims then led to recognition of an independent Pakistan.

Pulling out of empire was not easy. Sri Lanka (Ceylon) and Burma gained their independence from Great Britain in the following year; yet the conflict in Malaya, which led the British government to declare a state of emergency in 1947, did not end until 1960. France had officially recognized Vietnam as a free state in 1945, but the French continued to fight for dominance over Indochina for a decade, and war over Algeria would be even more costly. The Dutch, too, tried to reimpose their rule over Indonesia, which won its freedom in 1949 but only after years of combat. Nearly everyone came to understand that once fighting broke out, politics had failed. And on every continent formerly subject peoples demonstrated a greater willingness than their former rulers to risk everything in these struggles.

Internal conflicts in the newly established nations tended in fact to draw European states back into the political life of their former colonies. Local leaders often issued appeals to old interests, and their calls for assistance resonated in Britain and France, especially with conservatives and military officers, for whom the presence of communist movements triggered Cold War concerns.

Liberation Movements and the Cold War Although Pakistan committed itself to the West and India tried to steer a middle course, a major communist revolt broke out in Burma immediately after independence. In Vietnam the French-educated communist leader Ho Chi Minh organized a brilliant guerrilla campaign to unify the nation, and so the United States encouraged France in its fight against him. That costly war in Indochina ended only with the capture of a major French base at Dien Bien Phu in 1954 and French withdrawal from Vietnam. The Vietnamese communists were strongly supported by Russia and by China, the most formidable of the newly communist states, where after long civil conflict the communists under Mao Zedong consolidated power in 1949.

As a counterweight to communist gains in Asia, the United States promoted the economic revival of a now democratic Japan and gave strong economic and military support to Taiwan (a large island off China still held by the Chinese nationalists). The Americans also promoted a Pacific equivalent to NATO in the Southeast Asia Treaty Organization (SEATO), in which Britain, Pakistan, Australia, New Zealand, and various Asian states joined with the United States in common defense.

Following World War II, European states lacked the wealth and military might (or the confidence in their colonial mission) that empire required, and the resolution of these struggles was outside European control. Although increasingly tempered by local traditions and indigenous forms of organization, a European heritage left ties to international capitalism or international communism, to bureaucracies and parties organized on Western models, and to nationalist and socialist ideas. Great Britain sustained the Commonwealth of Nations, binding former colonies in a sometimes influential international club that often could not resolve conflicts between its members. On formally gaining independence in 1949, the fiercely anti-British republic of Eire rejected the Commonwealth. The *Union Française* gave French-speaking former colonies a voice in France's domestic politics and offered France valuable connections with the elites of the new nations, but it hardly functioned as an empire. Cold War competition, however, increased great power support for one side or the other in Asia, Africa, and the Middle East, where Soviet influence rapidly waned as American economic aid rose. In some respects this competition benefited independence movements in Africa, which could play the superpowers against each other. Foreign intervention did not end with the passing of European empires.

IV. European Recovery

Europe's economy depended as heavily on the Soviet Union and the United States as did its political divisions; yet from 1947 to 1957 economic growth was extraordinary. With rising prosperity, governments developed social policies that set new standards for equity and well-being. Even so, European states could not successfully challenge the hegemony of the superpowers.

ECONOMIC GROWTH

For all the shortages of capital and supplies, the homeland of the industrial revolution had important resources in its skilled population and infrastructure. The need to rebuild factories and transportation networks offered the chance to adopt the most efficient machinery and methods, and the millions of displaced people added to a skilled labor force as rates of employment slowly increased. European nations also had access to a backlog of unexploited technology; and as these new techniques became more important, European societies were well placed to take advantage of atomic power, the jet engine, the rocket engine, television, computers, antibiotics, and frozen foods.

This remarkable resilience was reflected in demography. In contrast to World War I, birthrates actually increased during World War II in non-belligerent nations and in England and France as well. In Germany they declined by less than they had in the previous war. This European "baby boom," though not so large as the simultaneous one in the United States, lasted until 1963, helping to replace some of the losses of war and to expand domestic markets.

Stimulus from the Soviet Union and the United States The recovery of Eastern Europe depended heavily on the Soviet Union, which through strenuous efforts had, by 1953, exceeded prewar industrial output. The USSR, its leaders confidently predicted, would surpass America. As the economy expanded, however, the costs of administration increased disproportionately, and the inefficiencies of centralized management became more pronounced. Without a free market, plan-

ners had difficulty judging costs and performance. Agriculture was a major disappointment, and the cereal harvest in 1953 was only slightly larger than in 1913.

The Soviet Union nevertheless provided an important market and economic stimulus for the countries of the Communist bloc, which organized their economies along the Russian model. All but Poland collectivized farmlands, and all instituted five-year plans to achieve rapid industrialization. In varying degrees, these governments adopted some elements of a mixed economic system—"goulash socialism," as Hungary's compromise has been called. The state retained ownership of most means of production, but managers operated within the structure of a largely free market and increased the production of consumer goods. The formula first proved most successful in the already advanced economies of Czechoslovakia and East Germany. Though dramatically less prosperous than the West, Eastern Europe had the highest rate of economic growth in its history by the 1950s.

The Western European nations looked for help to the United States, which in 1946 extended $4.4 billion in long-term credit to Great Britain and, subsequently, $1.2 billion to France. Only with the Marshall Plan in 1947 did the United States acknowledge the scale of Europe's economic problems as depleted currency reserves and inflation threatened to undermine recovery. Over the next four years, more than $15 billion was channeled into Europe under the direction of the Organization for European Economic Cooperation (OEEC), which eighteen Western states established for this purpose. Subsequently, the European Payments Union (1950–1958) was created to regulate currency exchanges. Europe's rapid recovery was made possible by this financial stability, by the planning the Marshall Plan required, and by the importation of goods from the United States the Plan provided for (which also benefited the American economy). In the three years from 1948 to 1950, the combined gross national product of the OEEC participants increased at an astonishing annual rate of 25 percent. By 1952 it was approximately half again as large as it had been in 1938, and per capita income was a third higher. Western Europe had never been wealthier.

The Economic Role of the State Throughout Western Europe the economic importance of the public sector greatly increased. In part this increase was an extension of wartime measures and a result of immediate postwar social needs. In part it was also a new attitude toward public policy. Immediately after the war, Britain and France had nationalized much of their heavy industry and banking system, and in Italy the Fascist regime had bequeathed to the state huge publicly owned conglomerates that directed hundreds of firms in some of the critical sections of industry and energy. West Germany alone made no effort to expand the number of state-owned industries, but there, too, the government had an important role (as it had during the war) in coordinating economic growth. State ownership gave no assurance of efficient management, good labor relations, or a high return on capital; but it encouraged governments to develop economic policies to guide both public and private enterprises in the interests of overall growth.

With the Monnet Plan (1946–1950), France set the model of loose but effective control (building on policies developed under the Vichy regime) by relying on refined methods of national accounting and highly trained "technocrats." Comparable plans were devised from Britain to Israel, especially in Scandinavian and Mediterranean countries. In West Germany the largest banks and a private trade association played a somewhat similar role through their close ties to government.

Nearly all European governments established programs to protect ordinary citizens and their families against sickness, impoverished old age, and unemployment. Great Britain provided the earliest and (Sweden excepted) probably the most complete example of what has come to be called the welfare state. Its cornerstone was the National Health Service, inaugurated in 1948, which assumed nearly the total cost of medical, dental, and hospital care for all. Although they structured it differently, continental governments also provided universal health care, family allowances with payments for minor children, housing programs, and a growing array of social services. By reducing insecurity, these measures also stimulated consumption. To meet their cost, states raised taxes and became more efficient in collecting them, in the process accumulating large re-serves that they used for investment according to their economic plans.

THE POLITICS OF MODERATION

By the early 1950s, European society had taken on a new look of health and stability. Not surprisingly, the political balance shifted. A notable easing of international tension permitted the Allies to agree on a peace treaty for Austria and the withdrawal of their occupation forces in 1955, and USSR granted diplomatic recognition to West Germany despite its having joined NATO. Only in Scandinavia did socialists continue in office. In Britain the Conservatives regained power in 1951 and held it for the next thirteen years, ending rationing and lowering taxes but not undoing most of the Labour program. The coronation of Queen Elizabeth II in 1953 was celebrated as the symbol of a new era of prosperity. Italy's Christian Democrats turned more to the right while keeping the Communists isolated, and West Germany under Adenauer became a model of stable prosperity.

The Crisis of France's Fourth Republic Similar trends in France, however, brought down the Fourth Republic. The government had in many respects performed very well, though just how well would become clearer in the prosperity of the 1960s. In 1954 an able prime minister of the center-left, Pierre Mendès-France, seemed about to make the political system work well despite the weaknesses of coalition governments. He announced a dynamic program of political reform and social modernization and set about concluding the negotiations that would extricate France from Indochina. He accomplished the latter, but the rest was stalled by party bickering as the political center was weakened from both right and left. An angry movement of small shopkeepers and farmers—people bypassed by the benefits of modernization—along with supporters of Charles de Gaulle gained in the elections of 1956. So did the Communists.

Given these social strains, the colonial crisis in Algeria proved fatal. A revolt against French rule was growing there, and from 1954 to 1958 the Algerian question brought down more French governments than any other issue. A French colony since 1830, Algeria had a sizable French population that had lived there for generations, and they won the support of many people in France by emphasizing their loyalty and telling of atrocities committed by Algerian nationalists. French army officers who had been fighting colonial uprisings in Africa and Asia since 1945 saw themselves, in the spirit of the Cold War, holding the line alone against communist plots around the world. They demanded that their sacrifices not be scuttled by treacherous "politicians" ready to concede autonomy or independence to Algeria, and the army redoubled repression. At the same time, leftists and intellectuals expressed outrage at the atrocities committed by the French army and at the kind of democracy that would wage war against Algerians seeking to govern themselves.

The Fifth Republic   As these tensions reached a peak in 1958, a group of French army officers seized political control in Algeria and threatened to move against the government of France. Faced with that challenge, a majority of the National Assembly turned to De Gaulle to unify the country and pacify the military insurgents. He declared that he would once again serve the nation and was invested with extraordinary powers for six years. He led France for the next ten. Although De Gaulle had been shrewdly ambiguous in his pronouncements on Algeria, the army, the center, and the right all found him acceptable. He used that strength to win support for a new constitution that was overwhelmingly approved by popular referendum in September 1958. It established the Fifth Republic as a presidential regime with a chief executive indirectly elected for a seven-year term. De Gaulle was chosen president two months later, and Gaullists became by far the largest party in parliament, where the Communists were reduced to a handful.

The president moved cautiously on the Algerian question, quietly weakening and dispersing the leaders of the military revolt. Only gradually did it become clear that De Gaulle would accept Algerian self-determination, a proposal approved by three-quarters of the voters in a referendum held in January 1961. Effectively isolated, the most intransigent of the officers formed a secret army and for eighteen months indulged in terrorism in France and Algeria. But the French president, having arranged peace with the Algerian rebels, declared war on the army rebels. By the end of 1962, they had disbanded, Algeria was independent, and France enjoyed the stability its voters had wanted.

The Soviet Union   After thirty years of dictatorship, Joseph Stalin died of a stroke in 1953. The shock and sense of loss in the Soviet Union was compounded by the problem of succession, something its communist government had faced only once before. It went surprisingly smoothly, and a form of collective leadership emerged. Only in 1956–1957 did it become clear that Nikita Khrushchev was the dominant figure. The competition for leadership involved two principal issues. Stalin's last years had brought heavy repression (with terror), ugly antisemitism, and a party line enforced on everything from socialist realism in the arts to the fallacious genetic theories of Trofim Lysenko. Many Russians wanted an end to such policies. The second issue was the standard of living, which had been sacrificed to the demanding goals of the latest five-year plan. Even Stalin had hinted that it might be time to increase consumption as well as build industry. Khrushchev had seemed conservative on the need for change, and his triumph showed again that control of the Communist party remained the key to power. Still, the infighting that brought him to the top, which included sudden dismissals and even executions, was followed not by purges but by the reassignment of his opponents to less prominent positions.

With a speech to the Twentieth Party Congress in 1956, Khrushchev established his new direction. He attacked the "cult of personality" under Stalin, naming many of Stalin's excesses, his paranoid distrust, his interference in the conduct of war, and his responsibility for the purge trials of the 1930s. Nothing like it had occurred before. Myths that for a generation had been central to the nation's enormous sacrifices were suddenly unmasked. The charges circulated widely in secret and then more openly, with unsettling effects in the Soviet Union, Eastern Europe, and communist movements everywhere. Streets and squares were renamed; statues and pictures disappeared. With

▲ **In January 1957 French paratroopers, searching for terrorists on the outskirts of Algiers, frisk a civilian in Arab clothing.**
UPI/Corbis-Bettmann.

the thaw[4] following Stalin's death, a freer and more open society appeared in prospect. Although Khrushchev quickly clamped down on criticism amid rising complaints about domestic problems and rumblings from within the Soviet bloc, restraints were never again so rigid or arbitrary as they had been under Stalin. When the Soviet Union celebrated the fortieth anniversary of the Russian Revolution in 1957 by launching the world's first space satellite, Sputnik, the USSR's status as a state both powerful and stable seemed to be dramatically confirmed.

---

[4] The metaphor of the thaw, which has come to be generally applied to these changes in domestic and foreign policy, is derived from a novel of that title written by the noted Russian fiction writer and journalist Ilya Ehrenburg.

FORAYS AT INDEPENDENCE

In their relative prosperity and stability, European nations East and West displayed some restiveness at their subordination to the superpowers. Britain and France attempted an independent foreign venture, and Eastern European nations tried more independent domestic policies. Neither was successful.

Britain and France The United States wanted to strengthen European defenses by rearming Germany, a measure the French could hardly welcome and one that Russia was determined to prevent. As a safeguard, in 1952 France had proposed the creation of a European Defense Community (EDC), in effect, a European army that would benefit from German strength without facing the risks of a separate German army. The proposal was accepted by most of the European members of NATO and pushed by the United States, but its implication of permanent continental engagement was distasteful to the British; and growing doubts in France, increased by resentment of extraordinary American pressure, led the French parliament to reject the EDC in 1954 in the last years of the Fourth Republic. Europeans were asserting their independence.

The British did so again during a crisis in relations with Egypt, a former colony in which they continued to have special knowledge and strong ties. Gamal Abdel Nasser's government was distrusted in the West for its nationalism, its radical domestic program, and its willingness to accept aid from nations in the Communist bloc. When the Western powers, following the United States, refused aid for the construction of a high dam across the Nile at Aswan, Nasser nationalized the Suez Canal, which was still owned by a British-controlled company. Britain responded strongly and, after international efforts at compromise broke down, conspired with Israel and France to take military action.

Israel attacked Egypt in October 1956, an act immediately followed by an Anglo-French bombardment and the occupation of the canal banks. Both the Soviet Union and the United States opposed the entire venture, and so the United Nations was able to force a ceasefire within a week and the withdrawal of foreign troops shortly afterward. Nothing had been gained by this return to old tactics that aroused anti-imperialist sentiment everywhere while demonstrating England and France's continuing dependence on American approval. That subordination remained even though Britain soon became the third nation to possess a hydrogen bomb and France would later be the fourth.

The Soviet Bloc The Communist governments of Eastern Europe closely mimicked Soviet rule in the ruthless use of secret police and internment camps, in the idolization of Stalin, and in general policy. But resentments at the Soviet Union's exploitation of its neighbors emerged publicly after Stalin's death. Within three months, the workers of East Berlin were in the streets proclaiming a general strike to protest increased production quotas that they blamed on the Soviet Union. Russian tanks rushed in to put down the revolt,

but it had long-lasting effects. Walter Ulbricht became the new leader of East Germany and offered a program of higher wages and better living conditions even while strengthening the dictatorship. Still tightly tied to the Soviet Union and limited in its autonomy, East Germany expanded its trade with West Germany and developed a voice of its own in the councils of Communist countries.

A workers' protest in Poland in 1956 even won support from within the Communist party among nationalists critical of Russian policies. Again Soviet forces intervened. They were jeered, and the Polish party elected Wladyslaw Gomulka its party secretary in preference to the pro-Russian candidate. Gomulka, a firm Communist, dominated the government until 1970 by convincing the Soviets of his loyalty while arguing that socialist states needed to follow national paths different from the Soviet Union's. Poland demanded and got a share of the war reparations that Germany paid, negotiated economic aid from the United States, and mitigated its repression of the Catholic Church and of Polish intellectuals.

Risings in Hungary ended more tragically. Riots in October 1956 were fiercely anti-Russian; and the Soviet troops at first withdrew from Budapest, seemingly disposed to accept Hungary's increased autonomy. Then Imre Nagy, who had been arrested the year before for "right-wing deviationism," became premier. Bowing to popular pressure, he agreed to replace the alliance with Russia with a policy of neutrality. The Soviet leaders pressured, threatened, and finally sent their army in force to crush the revolution. It did so in ten days of bitter fighting while rebel radio stations pleaded for the Western aid that many Hungarians expected. None came. Hungary suffered a heavy-handed Soviet occupation and harsh repression. Nagy himself was eventually executed, and a new wave of refugees left the country; yet his successor, Janos Kadar, slowly led the country on a more national course.

Washington denounced Russian imperialism but remained preoccupied with the crisis over Suez within its own alliance, in effect acknowledging a Soviet sphere of influence, and the USSR made it clear that satellite regimes could not break with Soviet policy. No other Communist nation was able to follow the example of independent Yugoslavia, where reconciliations with Khrushchev in 1954 and 1957 did not affect Yugoslavia's

▲ **Soviet tanks occupy the streets of Budapest; the uprising of October 1956 had been crushed.**
UPI/Bettmann.

trade with the West nor its experiments at decentralization. Albania, isolated from the Soviet sphere by geography and the most backward country on the continent, formed closer ties to mainland China in diplomatic and dogmatic opposition to Russia. Romania, like Bulgaria among the most Stalinist of the satellite regimes, distanced itself slightly by seeking better relations with the West. Little more was possible.

Europe's war, like its ideological divisions, had spread around the world; and it had taken a worldwide mobilization to defeat the Axis. The exhausting triumph over fascism and Nazism was a costly victory for European societies. Afterward, European nations recovered with astonishing speed and on the whole adjusted realistically to the loss of empire and of their former international preeminence. The Cold War's ideological and geographical division of Europe became a familiar if often uncomfortable fact of life. Neither communism nor democratic capitalism managed in power to create the societies they promised, and neither prosperity nor carefully contrived political stability necessarily resolved old conflicts. Europe had recovered from the war, but its economic, social, and cultural place in the modern world remained unclear.

Recommended Reading

Sources

*Churchill, Sir Winston S. *The Second World War* 6 vols. 1948–1954. Each volume of Churchill's detailed account can be read singly, and all are rich in documents and his masterly prose (he was awarded the Nobel prize for literature in 1953), which recapture the drama and meaning of the century's greatest war.

*Frank, Anne. *Diary of a Young Girl.* 1947. The unvarnished thoughts of a Jewish girl in hiding in Amsterdam during the Nazi occupation, valuable as historical evidence and as a moving expression of human dignity.

Hitler's Table-Talk. Hugh Trevor-Roper (ed.). 1988. Isolated in his headquarters, Hitler liked at mealtime to discourse on all sorts of topics with his closest aides. From 1941 to 1944 he allowed notes to be taken on these discussions, and this book is a translation of the transcript, edited by his secretary, Martin Bormann. Hitler's opinionated ramblings and reminiscences have a chilling fascination.

Monnet, Jean. *Memoires.* 1978. The chief architect of the European Community here reveals the intellectual roots of his vision and the personal style that made him so effective.

Studies

Adamson, Walter. *Avant-Garde Florence: From Modernism to Fascism.* 1993. An insightful and provocative assessment of the links between prewar avant-garde literary movements and fascism.

Allsop, Kenneth. *The Angry Decade: A Survey of the Cultural Revolt of the 1950s.* 1969. Captures very well the postwar disillusionment that undermined political and social consensus.

*Aron, Raymond. *The Imperial Republic: The United States and the World, 1945–1973.* 1974. A leading French thinker of the time analyzes the period of American dominance.

Brown, Colin, and Peter J. Mooney. *Cold War to Détente, 1945–1980.* 1981. A largely narrative account of relations between the superpowers.

Calvocaressi, Peter. *The British Experience 1945–1975.* 1978. A comprehensive study of British life in a period of imperial decline and economic difficulty.

Carr, Raymond. *The Civil War in Spain.* 1986. A comprehensive and unusually balanced study that effectively uses recent research to put the events of the war in the context of Spanish history and international relations.

Colton, Joel C. *Léon Blum: Humanist in Politics.* 1966. The biography of this appealing figure is particularly useful for the period of the Popular Front.

*Crossman, Richard H. (ed.). *The God That Failed.* 1950. The moving testimony of former Marxists about their lost faith during the era of Stalin; in itself a document of the Cold War.

*Crouzet, Maurice. *The European Renaissance since 1945.* 1971. An optimistic essay on the politics, society, and culture of postwar Europe reflecting the hopes that underlay the years of prosperity and the growth of the European Community.

*Dahrendorf, Ralf. *Society and Democracy in Germany.* 1969. A German sociologist assesses the special qualities of German society and its implications for the postwar West German republic.

Dawidowicz, Lucy S. *The War against the Jews, 1933–1945.* 1976. An extensive and thoughtful consideration of the twentieth century's greatest horror.

*DePorte, A. W. *Europe between the Superpowers.* 1979. A stimulating assessment of Europe's place in the postwar bipolar system.

Fejto, François. *A History of the People's Democracies: Eastern Europe since Stalin.* 1971. A careful study of the conflicts and variety among Eastern European states under Soviet dominance.

Geyer, Michael, and John Boyer (eds.). *Resistance against the Third Reich, 1933–1990.* 1994. Sober assessments of the strengths and limits of German opposition to Nazism.

Grosser, Alfred. *The Western Alliance: European-American Relations since 1945.* 1983. A clear-headed account of how international relations have worked in practice.

*Hoffman, Stanley, et al. *In Search of France.* 1965. A group of distinguished scholars attempt to define the unique patterns of French political and social life and to explain the significance of the Fifth Republic.

Iriye, Akira. *Cultural Internationalism and World Order.* 1997. Thoughtfully surveys efforts to foster international cooperation from the nineteenth century to the present that adds to the understanding of the world wars, the international agencies founded after each, and the Cold War.

Knox, MacGregor. *Mussolini Unleashed, 1939–41: Politics and Strategy in Fascist Italy's Last War.* 1982. A thorough and insightful analysis of Fascist foreign policy and strategic aims as well as of the regime's many weaknesses in pursuing them.

La Feber, Walter. *America, Russia, and the Cold War.* 1967. Consistently argues for the responsibility of the United States in creating the Cold War.

*Laqueur, Walter. *Europe since Hitler.* 1982. One of the ablest of the surveys of contemporary Europe that sees Europe as a whole.

*Liddell-Hart, Basil H. *History of the Second World War.* 1980. The crowning work of this renowned strategist and military historian.

*Maier, Charles S. *In Search of Stability: Explorations in Historical Political Economy.* 1987. Essays relating economic interests to the ambitions, limitations, and bitter divisions of European politics between the wars.

*———(ed.). *The Origins of the Cold War and Contemporary Europe.* 1978. Essays by leading scholars seeking not so much to lay blame for the Cold War but to study its connection to domestic societies.

*Mason, Tim, and Jane Caplan (eds.). *Nazism, Fascism, and the Working Class.* 1995. Ten essays engage leading historical interpretations on fascism and social class.

Michel, Henri. *The Shadow War: The European Resistance, 1939–1945.* 1972. Combines recent scholarship in a solid study of the most attractive (and romanticized) aspect of world war.

Middlemas, Keith. *Power, Competition and State.* Vol. 1: *Britain in Search of Balance, 1940–1961.* 1986. A clear assessment of the pressures that shaped British society and politics.

Milward, Alan S. *The Reconstruction of Western Europe, 1945–1951.* 1984. Concludes that the economic boom of the 1950s and 1960s began as early as 1945, through the role of government policy in establishing international economic interdependence.

*———. *War, Economy, and Society 1939–1945.* 1977. Examines the interdependence of economic planning and military strategy and its implications for the postwar period.

*Neff, Donal. *Warriors at Suez.* 1981. Well-researched and comprehensive, this dramatic account by a journalist focuses on the political leaders of the nations involved in the highly significant crisis of 1956.

*Paxton, Robert. *Vichy France: Old Guard and New Order, 1940–1944.* 1972. Stresses the continuity and lasting significance for French society and institutions of this twilight period.

*Payne, Stanley G. *The Franco Regime, 1936–1975.* 1987. A fair-minded account that sees the bases of Spain's subsequent transformation in Franco's later years.

Postan, Michael M. *An Economic History of Western Europe, 1945–1964.* 1967. A noted economic historian analyzes the roots of European recovery.

Rioux, Jean-Pierre. *The Fourth Republic, 1945–1958.* 1987. A close look at and a critical assessment of the politics of the period.

Sherwin, M. J. A. *A World Destroyed: The Atomic Bomb and the Grand Alliance.* 1975. A scholarly and balanced account of this controversial and complicated subject.

*Ulam, Adam B. *Expansion and Coexistence: The History of Soviet Foreign Policy, 1917–1973.* 1974. An expert appraisal of the consistent patterns and political pressures underlying Soviet policy.

Weinberg, Gerhard. *A World at Arms: A Global History of World War II.* 1994. Remarkably balanced and learned synthesis, attentive to political and economic as well as military aspects of the war.

Wilkinson, James D. *The Intellectual Resistance in Europe.* 1981. A wide-ranging and sensitive assessment of the content and legacy of the resistance and its place in contemporary thought.

*Available in paperback.

▲ **In November 1989 the East German government suddenly granted free access to West Berlin; the spontaneous celebrations that followed became the symbol of one of history's great turning points. The breach of the Berlin wall seemed a victory as great as any commemorated by the Brandenburg gate in the background.**
D. Aubert/Sygma.

Chapter 30

THE NEW EUROPE

In several respects 1956–1957 marked a turning point in European affairs. Postwar recovery had been accomplished. The Soviet Union's achievement in launching *Sputnik,* the first human-made satellite, implied a new equilibrium between the two superpowers. Each had its established spheres of dominance reinforced by a network of alliances. Khrushchev's policies and the reception in Eastern Europe indicated that communist regimes might become less rigidly authoritarian but also defined limits to the changes that would be allowed. In Western Europe the struggles over Algeria and Egypt were a costly last flurry of old imperial dreams. Failure brought a new constitution in France and new policies and leaders in Britain. In retrospect, however, the event of 1957 that would have the greatest effect on the future was the treaty of Rome signed by Belgium, the Netherlands, Luxemburg, France, Germany, and Italy. It created the European Economic Community, which went into effect on January 1, 1958.

Increasing prosperity in the next decade facilitated Europe's adaptation to far-reaching social changes that included greater independence for women, expanded access to advanced education, and a transformation of the urban landscape as immigrants streamed to cities from rural areas and from foreign lands. In the late 1960s, however, waves of protest challenged social and political systems across Europe. For the most part, these protests did not succeed in overturning the establishment, but attitudes and policies changed as each European society sought ways to preserve order while adapting to new economic and social pressures. It had been possible in the 1950s to imagine that the industrial societies of Eastern and Western Europe would become more alike as time passed, but by the 1970s it was clear that they were moving in different directions. In Eastern Europe entrenched one-party systems and directed economies could not keep pace with Western Europe's higher standard of living. As the European Community moved toward creating a closer knit European Union, the communist regimes of Eastern Europe suddenly and unexpectedly collapsed. At the same time, a popular culture once associated primarily with the United States and then Western Europe swept across Europe to become truly international, even global. Energetic, brash, and focused on youth, it was accompanied by intellectual movements that fostered new and critical ways of understanding culture itself.

I. Europe's Place in the World

Europe's position in world affairs was largely shaped by the effects of decolonization, the Cold War, and Western Europe's great wealth in a global economy. Decolonization, which seemed to follow from defeat and weakness, became a source of strength. The Cold War, while establishing the limitations of European power, encouraged a broad movement for increased cooperation among European nations. A divided Europe's subordination to the two superpowers brought the benefits of peace, and Western Europe's wealth pushed it toward a larger role in international relations.

THE LIMITS OF EUROPEAN POWER

Decolonization in Africa After having given up their protectorates in the Middle East and been driven out of their colonies in Asia, the imperial powers still held most of Africa. Europeans on the scene—officials, business people, and residents—did what they could to prolong European rule with grants of autonomy and promises of aid. But even they now knew that the age of empire was over. This second wave of decolonization proved less disruptive and less costly for European states than the first wave a decade earlier. Most African states won formal independence by the 1960s. Seen from Africa, the struggle was often bitter. In Europe the loss of empire no longer carried the kind of trauma that had marked the "fall" of India, Indonesia, Indochina, and Algeria; and negotiated settlements made it easier to preserve other relationships.

Britain acceded to Ghana's independence in 1957 but found it harder to deal with East Africa, in which there were many settlers of British descent (on a smaller scale, the problem was similar to the one France had faced in Algeria). After years of costly warfare, Kenya won independence in 1963, but Britain had to use force in 1979 to overturn white-supremacist rule in Rhodesia, which the new rulers renamed Zimbabwe. Portugal held on to its African empire the longest of any European nation and made the fewest concessions. The price was a decade of fighting that ended only in 1974 when a military coup at home forced Portugal to abandon its empire. Its prize colony, Angola, was almost immediately caught up in a civil war in which one side was supported by the United States and the other by the Soviet Union. African nations that wanted to avoid becoming pawns in the Cold War often found it preferable to work with the European countries whose rule they had overturned. Through diplomacy, economic interests, common languages, and similar educational, legal, and administrative institutions, Britain and France continued to influence African affairs. Internal conflicts in the new African states would sometimes bring more direct European intervention in the future.

Bipolar Stability The Warsaw Pact and the NATO alliance institutionalized the armed confrontation between the superpowers in Europe. In 1961 East-West tension was literally cast in stone when East Germany built a long gray wall across the center of Berlin, eventually extending it along East Germany's entire western border. That determination to keep East Germans from leaving, and the need to use such measures, heightened distrust and presented the division of Germany as permanent. There was a still more ominous crisis in 1961, when the United States sponsored an invasion of Cuba aimed at the overthrow of Fidel Castro. It failed, and in the following year the Russians began to base missiles on Cuba. War seemed imminent until, as the Americans massed their fleet, the Soviets withdrew their missiles. There was, after all, a mutual interest in not disturbing the balance of power, and the Soviet Union was facing a growing rift with China that made diplomatic exchanges with the United States more attractive.

Literally in the middle, European governments used their influence to favor East-West negotiations at summit conferences and on specific issues. They promoted agreements on space exploration in 1967, the beginning of the Strategic Arms Limitation Talks in 1969, and the extension of such agreements to issues of human rights at the Helsinki Conference in 1975, attended by nearly all the European states in addition to the United States and Canada. Through trades, loans, and technical agreements, the governments of Western Europe encouraged those of Eastern Europe toward whatever autonomy from the Soviet Union they were willing to attempt.

▲ **MAP 30.1 EUROPE SINCE WORLD WAR II**

National Interests As European international relations stabilized, European states developed distinctive policies to serve their interests. West Germany gradually asserted some of the political weight that its wealth implied. Less committed to the Cold War than Adenauer had been, Willy Brandt skillfully negotiated a new opening to the East. The resulting treaty between West Germany and the Soviet Union, signed in 1970, was a milestone that earned Brandt the Nobel peace prize. Although the treaty left open the possibility of a peaceful reunification of Germany, it accepted West Germany's eastern boundary, pointed to a normalization of the status of Berlin, which was still divided between Soviet and Western occupation, and paved the way for extensive relations between West Germany and the governments of Eastern Europe. By 1981–1982 this increased trade culminated in the agreement to build a natural gas pipeline from Russia to Germany, Italy, and France.

Great Britain emphasized its close ties to the United States rather than to Europe; and in the United Nations, the Scandinavian countries positioned themselves as friends of nonaligned countries and mediators between the superpowers. The most flamboyant search for an independent policy was De Gaulle's. France had been the fourth nation to become a nuclear power, and De Gaulle continued that buildup. Resentful of American policy toward France, he set upon a course that by 1966 led to the withdrawal of French forces from NATO command (and of NATO forces from French soil), although France remained a member of the alliance. France also strengthened its relations with Eastern Europe and increased its aid to developing nations. France's policies grew less assertive after De Gaulle left office in 1969, but greater independence from American policy appealed to many others in the West, especially on the left. In 1981 nearly half a million young people in Bonn and perhaps another million in other capitals marched to demand that Europe be freed of the nuclear weapons of either side.

Economic strength has also made Western European nations prominent in world affairs, from competition in arms sales to playing a crucial role in such important international economic organizations as the International Monetary Fund and the Organization for Economic Cooperation and Development (OEEC). From 1948 on, governments participating in the OEEC had recognized that the free movement of capital and labor as well as of finished products was beneficial to economic growth. But efforts to create a tariff union had failed except for agreements among Belgium, the Netherlands, and Luxemburg (the Benelux countries).

EUROPEAN COOPERATION

Western Europeans had increasingly come to see themselves as belonging to a region of shared values and culture. The experience of World War II, the Marshall Plan, and the Cold War and NATO had all strengthened this sense of a shared interest.[1] Idealism, facilitated by prosperity, contributed too.

The Council of Europe The advantages of some form of political integration had been discussed in 1948 at a meeting in The Hague, chaired by Winston Churchill, a meeting that led to the formation in the following year of a Council of Europe. Member states send delegates to the Council of Ministers and Consultative Assembly, which has its headquarters at Strasbourg. The Council has no binding powers over member states, because at its founding few governments, least of all Great Britain's, were willing to surrender any sovereignty or significant decision-making power to a supranational authority. Member states must nevertheless be committed to upholding individual freedom and the rule of law—a requirement that excluded Spain, Portugal, and Greece when they were ruled by dictators as well as all the nations of Eastern Europe.

In practice, the decisions of the Council and its Court of Justice have often been obeyed by member states (Britain, for example, abolished corpo-

---

[1] Geographers list nineteen nations as belonging to Western Europe: Austria, Belgium, Denmark, Finland, France, Greece, Iceland, Ireland, Italy, Lichtenstein, Luxemburg, the Netherlands, Norway, Portugal, Spain, Sweden, Switzerland, the United Kingdom, and West Germany. All of these countries save Finland now belong to the Council of Europe, which also includes Cyprus, Malta, and Turkey.

Belgium, Denmark, Iceland, West Germany, Italy, Luxemburg, the Netherlands, Norway, Portugal, Turkey, the United Kingdom, Canada, and the United States belong to NATO, as do France and Greece, although their armed forces no longer are under NATO command.

real punishment in schools as the result of a Council judgment), particularly on matters of human rights, for which it was given increased authority in 1997. Some forty nations, stretching from Russia to the Atlantic, now belong to the Council, and its committees and assembly regularly meet in Strasbourg to establish general policies and adjudicate complaints against any member state. The aspirations it represents (the Council's anthem is Beethoven's "Ode to Joy") have made its flag a popular symbol on buildings and private automobiles across the continent.

The European Economic Community Further European integration proved difficult to achieve, however, and so two of its principal advocates decided that it was necessary to begin with small steps. A leading French economist, Jean Monnet, and France's foreign minister, Robert Schuman, proposed an imaginative solution: the French-German Coal and Steel Authority, established in 1950. French was rich in iron ore and Germany in coal, and for nearly a century the desire to control both had been a source of conflict between the two countries. The Authority guaranteed each of them access to these resources. A year later, propelled by the euphoria of recovery, Italy and the three Benelux countries joined to establish the European Coal and Steel Community (ECSC), which was given the power to coordinate the production and distribution of the coal and steel critical to industrial growth. These organizations were the kernel of a common market.

As the ECSC demonstrated its economic value and as its authority increased, further steps became possible as Monnet and Schuman had hoped. The 1957 Treaty of Rome establishing the European Community (EC) was the result. This agreement, too, was limited. It created a new agency to coordinate the development of atomic energy and stipulated that the six member nations would eliminate tariffs between each other in gradual steps and establish a common tariff toward all other nations. The prospects for this arrangement were anything but certain; Britain refused to take part and De Gaulle was less internationalist than his predecessors. Nevertheless, six nations that had often been at war now agreed that they were "determined to lay the foundations of ever-closer union among the peoples of Europe

. . . and to ensure economic and social progress by common action. "

EC vs. EFTA Reluctant to accept permanent political ties to the continent or to loosen its Commonwealth connections, Great Britain instead fostered the creation of the European Free Trade Association (EFTA). This looser association, which set more limited goals (free trade among its members, for example, but not a common tariff) and had very limited powers of enforcement, was joined by Sweden, Norway, Denmark, Austria, Switzerland, and Portugal. The ensuing competition between the two groups was closely watched. Sweden, with the most socialist economic system, and Switzerland, with the most thoroughly free market system, already had the highest per capita incomes in the industrial world. In rate of growth, however, the United Kingdom remained last among major European countries while the states of the European Community enjoyed the highest increase in per capita productivity, more than 4 percent a year.

By 1968 (sooner than its organizers had expected) all tariffs had been abolished within the EC, and continued economic growth made it ever more attractive. After extended negotiations, Great Britain, Ireland, and Denmark joined the EC in 1973.[2] Twice before, Britain had sought membership but with special concessions (to protect it from the Community's agricultural policies and to preserve its Commonwealth interests) only to be blocked by De Gaulle's opposition and by a general concern that separate arrangements could undermine the EC's coherence. Together the nine members of the European Community surpassed the United States in the production of automobiles and steel, and by 1979, in total gross national product (GNP) as well.

Integrating the Community Fuller economic integration among the nine members came slowly, however. In 1972 the heads of government of the EC countries had begun meeting several times a

---

[2] In a surprising referendum, Norwegians voted not to join the European Community, one of many signs of resistance to the EC's centralizing tendencies and to its domination by France and Germany—concerns that have been strongest in the Scandinavian countries and in Britain.

year, an important step toward more coordinated policies, and every six months a different one of them serves as the president. That practice in itself has created some momentum for growth, for the presidents often make it a point of pride to push for some new accomplishment during their term. Routine matters are handled by the EC's permanent Council, which has a representative from each member state, and by a large bureaucracy with headquarters in Brussels, which is directed by a Commission to which each state appoints a member who is then independent of any government.

In 1979 a mechanism was created for regulating exchange rates, and the citizens of each member nation began voting directly for delegates to the Community's parliament, where the representatives sit according to political party rather than nationality.[3] Although its powers remained restricted, an elected parliament could be hailed as "the birth of the European citizen." The process of greater integration has continued through the rulings of the EC's court, creating uniform regulations (on standards of product quality, insurance, and environmental issues, for instance) and common legal rights (in the case, for example, of migrant workers). In the 1980s the Council was empowered to set some policies by majority vote rather than unanimity.

Agricultural policy was especially controversial. The EC's subsidies, which had strong domestic support from farmers, resulted in costly stockpiles of unsold produce. Because Britain imports most of its food and has a smaller farm population, it contributed far more toward these costs than the EC spent in Britain. Its vigorous protests forced adjustments and then some reform of agricultural policies in 1981; but the issue was complicated by the further enlargement of the Com-

---

[3] The complexities of representation are exemplified by the fact that France, Great Britain, Italy, and West Germany were given 81 representatives each (a large enough number to ensure that Scotland and Wales had more representatives than did Denmark or Ireland). The Netherlands and Belgium were each allotted 25, but Belgium preferred 24 (so that the Flemings and Walloons would have equal representation), which meant a gift of 1 representative to Denmark, which has 16. Ireland has 15 representatives; Luxemburg, 6; Greece, 24; Portugal, 24; and Spain, 60.

Chronology

THE MAKING OF THE EUROPEAN UNION

1950 Germany and France form the Coal and Steel Authority.

1951 Italy and the Benelux nations join.

1957 The Treaty of Rome creates the European Community of six nations.

1973 Great Britain, Ireland, and Denmark join the EC.

1979 Citizens elect the EC parliament.

1981 Greece joins the EC.

1986 Spain and Portugal join the EC, which forms the Single Market.

1992 Maastricht Treaty calls for European Union, common currency.

1995 Austria, Finland, and Sweden join the EU.

1999 Common currency, central bank takes effect.

---

munity to include Greece in 1981 and Spain and Portugal in 1986, all countries with strong and competing agricultural interests. Special grants to poorer regions—including the northwestern part of the British Isles, southern Italy, and the poorer members generally (Ireland, Portugal, Spain, and Greece)—have helped to bring those regions closer to the EC's general level of prosperity. As the Community gained a voice in matters traditionally considered the exclusive concern of national governments, especially social issues, domestic opposition to the EC tended to become more vocal.

Toward European Union   The record of small steps and acrimonious debate even on minor issues contrasted with the lofty rhetoric of the EC's supporters, and the Community's intangible impact was frequently ignored by politicians and dismissed by journalists. There was thus some surprise when Jacques Delors, the unusually effective president of the Commission, the EC's ex-

▲ **Map 30.2A European Economic Community and European Free Trade Association, 1960**

▲ Map 30.2B European Union and European Free Trade Association, 1996

ecutive body, succeeded in winning support in 1986 for the Single European Act, an agreement to create a single market. It declared that by the end of 1992 there would no longer be any restrictions within the Community on the movement of goods, services, workers, or capital. With minor exceptions, these terms were met, which brought striking changes in the lives of ordinary people. Most of the border checkpoints between member states on the continent have disappeared, and all citizens of the member states carry a community passport and cross national boundaries without restriction. Any of them could open a bank account, take out a mortgage, receive medical care, or practice a profession anywhere in the EC, for in principle at least the licenses and university degrees of one country are recognized in all the others. Such measures gave added strength to established programs for educational exchange (hundreds of thousands of students now regularly study in another European country), research, and environmental protection.

The Single European Act required that vast arrays of national regulations be made uniform. Social practice was an important as any new directives, however. Anticipating European integration, businesses, government agencies, and schools set about on their own to bring their practices in line with those of the EC, forming ties with colleagues in other countries. Organizations and individuals begin to think and operate in terms of the Community as a whole; and sensing this momentum, the leaders of the EC pressed for more. The Maastricht Treaty of 1992 changed the name of the EC to the European Union (EU) to indicate its greater integration, enlarged the powers of its parliament, and called for a coordinated foreign policy and the adoption of a common European currency by 1999. Starting in that year, all those distinctive coins and bills carrying proud national symbols will slowly

▼ Flags of the member states fly outside the Brussels headquarters of the European Union.
Steve Vidler/Leo de Wys.

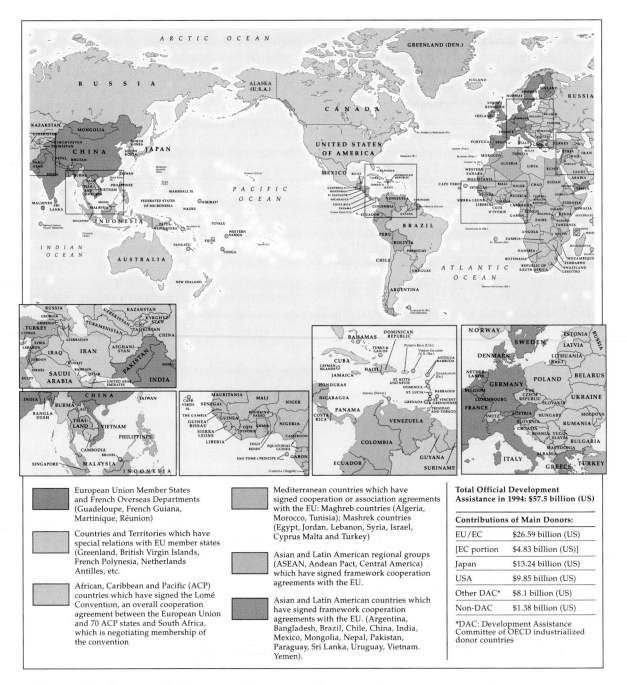

Legend

■ European Union Member States and French Overseas Departments (Guadeloupe, French Guiana, Martinique, Réunion)

□ Countries and Territories which have special relations with EU member states (Greenland, British Virgin Islands, French Polynesia, Netherlands Antilles, etc.)

□ African, Caribbean and Pacific (ACP) countries which have signed the Lomé Convention, an overall cooperation agreement between the European Union and 70 ACP states and South Africa, which is negotiating membership of the convention

□ Mediterranean countries which have signed cooperation or association agreements with the EU: Maghreb countries (Algeria, Morocco, Tunisia); Mashrek countries (Egypt, Jordan, Lebanon, Syria, Israel, Cyprus Malta and Turkey)

□ Asian and Latin American regional groups (ASEAN, Andean Pact, Central America) which have signed framework cooperation agreements with the EU.

■ Asian and Latin American countries which have signed framework cooperation agreements with the EU. (Argentina, Bangladesh, Brazil, Chile, China, India, Mexico, Mongolia, Nepal, Pakistan, Paraguay, Sri Lanka, Uruguay, Vietnam. Yemen).

Total Official Development Assistance in 1994: $57.5 billion (US)

Contributions of Main Donors:

EU/EC	$26.59 billion (US)
[EC portion	$4.83 billion (US)]
Japan	$13.24 billion (US)
USA	$9.85 billion (US)
Other DAC*	$8.1 billion (US)
Non-DAC	$1.38 billion (US)

*DAC: Development Assistance Committee of OECD industrialized donor countries

▲ MAP 30.3 THE EUROPEAN UNION AND THE DEVELOPING WORLD

give way to a uniform currency (with national emblems on one side), destined to bring more uniform prices and marketing.

The public found all these changes and requirements a little overwhelming. Attitudes toward the EC changed as domestic economies faltered, and in nation after nation the votes were so close and the treaty passed with so many conditions that its larger significance was called into question. Rising resentments of the EC's bureaucratic regulations and the complexity of the treaty itself made it an easy target for opponents. In each country strong, organized opposition formed as national coalitions brought together all the interests that feared they had something to lose. Despite the hesitance and complications, on January 1, 1994, the European Union came into being, and Austria, Finland, and Sweden joined the EU in the following year. Additionally, ten former communist states plus Greek Cyprus began the lengthy process of qualifying for membership, while the application of Turkey was postponed over such thorny issues as migration and civil rights states. Remarkably, all of the current member states accepted, and all but Greece met, the severe limits set by the Maastricht Treaty on the size of annual deficits and the rate of inflation, although three— Great Britain, Denmark, and Sweden—chose not to join the common currency on the first wave. The willingness to undertake such unpopular measures as raising taxes and cutting budgets is impressive evidence of a widespread faith in the future of the EU. Underneath all the technical language and regulations, the European Union also represents a continuing and ambitious idealism, however general. Such idealism can be seen in the EU's efforts to have all its trading partners agree to its declarations on human rights, which include opposition to racism, protection of children, and "the full participation of women in civic, political, social, and economic life."

II. Postindustrial Society

From the 1950s on, Europe's economic growth continued with only brief setbacks. Standards of living rose, and every nation became richer than it had ever been before. As the ways of creating wealth changed, so did lifestyles. Industrial production no longer dominated the economy, for the service sector employed more and more people in office work, sales, and personal services. Societies structured in this way have come to be called, a little misleadingly, *postindustrial,* to indicate that factory production and the organization of work it entails is no longer the primary source of wealth. The changes postindustrial society implies were exuberantly embraced in North America and Western Europe, while in Eastern Europe

they occurred more slowly and with greater difficulty. Everywhere, however, they brought new problems as well as clear benefits.

EUROPE'S ADVANTAGE

Historically, much of Europe outside the Soviet Union had been economically handicapped by limited natural resources and sources of energy. Once critical to industrialization, the coal fields of Britain, West Germany, and Eastern Europe and the iron ore fields of France and Sweden have been supplemented by the exploitation of other sources of energy such as natural gas and oilfields in the North Sea. More important, such resources have become less crucial. Economies today create wealth primarily through the efficient transformation of raw materials, which can be imported, and through services. And Europe, like the United States, excels in the attributes that now matter most: great amounts of capital and institutions to facilitate its rapid investment, advanced technology, experienced managers, skilled and willing workers, efficient marketing, rapid communication, high levels of education, adaptable societies, and high consumption.

Infrastructure During the 1960s every European nation launched new roadbuilding projects, and by 1980 the most important of them had been completed. Superhighways now run from Stockholm to south of Valencia and from Naples to Hamburg. Railroads, valued for passenger travel as well as for transport (and usually considered a service to be provided by the state) have been extensively modernized. In 1981 French trains, which hold world speed records, began to carry passengers from Paris to Lyons at 165 miles per hour. A tunnel under the English Channel, a project considered for centuries, opened in 1994 to provide direct automobile and rail links between Britain and the continent. Water transport along Europe's coasts, rivers, and canals is relatively inexpensive; and air travel, dense throughout the continent, is especially important across the expanses of Russia. In the face of American and Japanese competition, Western European nations have been among the technological leaders in electronic communication and have adapted, somewhat more unevenly, to computer technology.

▲ **High-speed electric trains poised for their dash from Paris to Lyons.**
Peter Beattie/Gamma/Liaison.

Increasing productivity requires high rates of investment in new technologies, and in Western Europe governments, banks, insurance companies, and stock markets have been eager to support the employment of industrial robots, microchips, and satellite communication. Until the 1980s, economic growth was often greatest in mixed economies that combined private enterprise with state planning. Since then, a strong trend toward privatization has required still further social adjustments to cost cutting, rising unemployment and international competition. The emphasis on productive efficiency, new products, marketing, and personal consumption that once seemed characteristically American has been adopted in most of Europe.

In the West agricultural productivity has increased as well, although the number of people who work the land has continued to decline (in Ireland, one of the West's least developed nations, 60 percent of the workforce was employed in agriculture in 1960 but only 20 percent in 1980). By the 1980s, nearly one-half the tractors in the world were used in Europe. With only about 3 percent of the world's farmland, Western Europe produced nearly one-third of the world's dairy products and 15 percent of the world's eggs, potatoes, and wheat (of which France alone was the fifth largest producer and the former Soviet Union was the largest, followed by the United States, China, and India).

Education Modern society requires that more of the population be more highly educated than in the past. In the late 1960s and early 1970s the necessary changes in European educational systems led to controversial reforms that caused angry demonstrations and even riots. Traditionally in Europe, secondary education has been the great mark of social difference. A small fraction of students went to secondary schools noted for their demanding and usually classical curriculums. These schools were the gateway to a university. A larger proportion of students went to vocational secondary schools, and half or more of the youths beyond the ages of twelve or fourteen went directly to work. Despite efforts to make this segregation a matter of academic performance, in practice social class made a critical difference.

The reforms that sought to make the system more democratic, while offensive to defenders of the older curriculum, did not go far enough to satisfy student radicals, but the reforms did incorporate important changes. In the West enrollments in the more prestigious forms of secondary education doubled and trebled, and a trend toward "comprehensive" schools more like the American high school allowed many of the graduates of those schools to go on to higher education. In the communist societies the children of workers and party members had priority for admission to such schools, but total enrollments increased more slowly than in the West. Expanding the years of schooling requires that society have the wealth to fund more schools and to support children for a longer period before they begin to work. Social mobility became a more universal goal, challenging but not eliminating the advantages that middle-class children enjoyed. Whenever governments reduced spending (cutbacks were especially severe in Great Britain but occurred everywhere in the 1980s), intense debate was reopened on issues of fair access, quality, general culture, and prospects for employment.

Educational systems have tended to become more similar across Western Europe, although important differences in national traditions remain. Despite creation of hundreds of new institutions of higher education, often with American-style campuses, enrollments in many countries have swollen beyond capacity. Among European nations, the Netherlands, Sweden, Denmark, France, Italy, and Norway have the highest proportion; roughly one-fifth to one-third of young adults between twenty and twenty-four years old are enrolled in universities (about one-half of American high school graduates enroll in some form of post-secondary education). The European countries with the lowest proportion (less than 10 percent)—Yugoslavia, Spain, and Portugal—are poorer ones; and nearly all the rest of Europe falls in between.

Changes Affecting Women Women's lives changed even more than men's. In most of Western Europe the proportion of women in higher education was approaching that of men by the 1980s. Women have become more prominent in all the professions and in politics. In Britain, France, and Germany, women make up some 40 percent of the workforce; and as their numbers increased, labor unions paid more attention to their needs. Thus in Italy, for example, labor unions pressed employers to grant released time with pay to allow working women to take special courses. European governments and employers have made child care available to most women, in effect, encouraging mothers to have careers. On the average, however, women workers continue to earn less than men (between two-thirds as much in Britain and four-fifths as much in France).

Young women expected to have a freedom of movement that their mothers did not as they traveled, worked, and socialized outside their families. The availability of contraception and, by the 1970s, abortion (changes that were less controversial in Europe than in the United States) added to this sense that women had the right to plan their life course. Domestic appliances in every home made it easier to keep house and hold a job, but women also suffered the pressure of multiple responsibilities set against the picture of the ideal home promulgated through consumer advertising.

Urban Planning Postindustrial society is heavily urban, and Europe has long experience in making its well-organized cities function well. The threat was clear: As urban agglomerations expanded across the surrounding suburbs, the inner

▲ The skyscrapers of Frankfurt, one of Europe's greatest commercial centers, loom over the statue of Schiller, Germany's great eighteenth-century playwright.
Luc Novovitch/Gamma/Liaison.

core of older cities tended to lose population as people with greater wealth and leisure sought more space and privacy. The new highways, extended subways, and bus lines that push the cities outward rarely keep pace with the congestion of traffic at their heart. As similar-looking skyscrapers rise in the city centers and in new business centers around what had been the periphery, similar residential districts sprawl across the outskirts. One-fifth of the population of France lives within an hour's drive of Paris, and nearly that proportion of Britain's population is similarly close to London. Volgograd stretches for forty-five miles along the river after which it was named, and some fourteen cities of the former Soviet Union have a population of more than a million.

European states were accustomed to spending money to maintain city services, but governments were unsure how best to build. In the 1950s new housing tended, East and West, to look like dreary concrete barracks and often provided few of the services necessary to create a sense of community. In nearly every country, whole new cities, often bleak and artificial, surround the metropolis: Five towns of 24,000 people each were placed around Paris; twenty-four such towns surround Moscow. Since the 1970s the trend has shifted to new urban hubs on a smaller scale, carefully planned to have shopping, recreational, and cultural centers of their own as well as some light industry so that much of the working population need not commute. Many of these ventures—those in Scandinavia were among the first—have proved to be attractive models, widely imitated, mixing large and small modern buildings, pleasant streets, and restful green spaces. War damage forced German governments into expensive projects of urban renewal, and from the 1960s on governments across much of Western Europe have invested in refurbishing urban centers and creating some of the world's most interesting experiments in urban planning, often with stunning effects.

Cities like Rome and Vienna found that banning traffic from the narrow, medieval streets of their

▼ The glass structures that replaced Paris' central market evoke the iron and glass pavilions built a century earlier but now contain shops, museums, and a media center. New apartment buildings stand in the background. Leveling the crowded old mercantile buildings surrounding the market also provided a view of the gothic church of St. Eustache that had not been seen for centuries.
Charles Graham/Leo de Wys.

old centers made them more attractive (and expensive) for shops and housing. Loud laments were heard at the razing of Les Halles in Paris, handsome wrought iron sheds built in the Second Empire to provision the capital with food, but the gains in efficiency and improved traffic were undeniable. The exciting new cultural center built in the 1970s as part of the area's renewal has become the most visited site in Paris. In London, the produce sellers of Covent Garden also had to give way to a cultural center; and Billingsgate, the fishmarket that gave the language a word for verbal abuse, closed in 1981. Europe's great cities remain among the most livable and attractive in the world.

Social Welfare By every measure, the standard of living of the working classes has risen impressively, but the gap between wage earners and the very rich has narrowed only slightly in the West (income distribution is least uneven in Sweden and the Netherlands). In communist Europe professional people and officials lived at a much higher standard and with far greater freedom of choice than workers or peasants, an important element in the unpopularity and ultimate downfall of those governments. Throughout Europe, in contrast to the United States, the full impact of these inequalities has been softened by complex provisions for social security, minimal fees for education, universal medical care, many provisions for the elderly, and a wide variety of family benefits and services. Not surprisingly, rates of infant mortality have declined and longevity rates have improved in Western Europe to be among the most favorable in the world. The elderly are an ever-increasing proportion of the population as people live longer and families have fewer children. Birthrates in Europe are now generally the lowest in the world.

The social effects of public housing have been more mixed. Housing and transport were kept relatively cheap in communist Europe, but good housing remained scarce, leading to long waiting lists for cramped apartments. In the West, too, governments extensively subsidized low-income housing (in the 1980s about one-third of new housing in Germany was government sponsored, one-half in Great Britain, two-thirds in Sweden and France). The disadvantages came from the effects of segregating the poor.

Social differences are more acceptable in periods of rapid economic growth. In the 1970s unemployment had begun to rise, depressing whole regions that had never enjoyed industrial prosperity (such as Ireland, large parts of Spain and Portugal, and southern Italy), as well as areas dependent on declining industries. On the whole, programs of special subsidies and tax incentives, meant to ease conditions in these areas, have had disappointing results; and the cost of social programs began to weigh more heavily as economic growth slowed in the 1980s. By the 1990s, endemic unemployment had become one of Europe's most pressing social problems, averaging more than 10 percent on most of the continent and hitting young people and immigrants the hardest. Governments, however, had little to offer. Taxes were already relatively high in Western Europe, absorbing between 21 and 24 percent of the GNP, and demands that they be lowered became a mainstay of the political center and right.

New Issues: Foreign Workers A massive movement of people began to alter European society in the 1960s. With jobs available in the industrial zones, many men and somewhat fewer women moved from the less developed to the more prosperous regions. At first, it seemed a continuation of older patterns, but the new migrants crossed national boundaries more freely than did their predecessors. Southern Italians went to northern Italy but also to Switzerland and Germany; Spaniards, Portuguese, and North Africans to France; Yugoslavs and Turks to Germany; African and Caribbean blacks, Indians, and Pakistanis to England. These people, too, contributed to Europe's economic miracle although they were most often employed as domestic servants, street sweepers, and the least skilled industrial workers. By the 1970s foreign immigrants made up 17 percent of the workforce in Switzerland, some 8 percent in Germany, and only slightly less than that in France.

Often different in physical appearance, language, and culture from the majority of those around them, immigrants were drawn together and forced by poverty to live in slums that quickly became ghetto subcultures resistant to and misunderstood by the larger society. Lacking the full protection of citizenship, resented by native

▲ **Many German cities have districts, like this one in Cologne, that almost look as if they were in Turkey.**
Regis Bossu/Sygma.

workers competing for jobs and higher pay, despised as sources of crime and heavy welfare costs, these migrants re-created some of the gravest social problems of the early nineteenth century, now exacerbated by prejudices of race and color. Many gradually came to see themselves as permanent residents, and many acquired citizenship, as their children automatically did (except in Germany). This second generation went to local schools and for the most part adopted local ways; yet these families often remained partially dependent on government programs and were the first to feel the effects of any economic downturn. Their plight and the prejudice against them were problems for which most European societies were ill prepared (see "A Turkish Girl Arrives in Germany," p. 1101).

New Issues: The Environment Economic growth also brought pollution that contaminated the air, waterways, and countryside as it poured from factories and automobiles and littered the landscape. Monuments and scenic places revered for centuries came to be seriously threatened; yet Western Europe was slow to respond, and in Eastern Europe the problem was ruthlessly ignored. The Rhine became one of the most polluted international waterways, and high concentrations of mercury were recorded in Geneva's Lac Leman. Escaped industrial gases caused illness and death in the outskirts of Milan, and the magnificent palaces of Venice were discovered to be slowly sinking, apparently because the earth beneath their pilings gives way as underground water is pumped up on the mainland for industrial use. Acid rain is destroying Germany's black forest, and it is now dangerous to bathe in or eat fish from much of the Baltic and Mediterranean seas. The remaining monuments of ancient Greece and Rome and the ornate facades of Gothic churches in city after city crumble and crack from the vibrations and fumes of modern traffic.

Governments intent upon stimulating growth were reluctant to impose the restrictions and to undertake the expense that protecting the environment required until strong ecology movements in Germany, Britain, the Low Countries, and France forced their hand. Political parties, known everywhere as the Greens, focused on these environmental issues, and several international agencies now enforce European standards against pollution. Although much more remains to be done, the gains have been impressive. Stern regulations eliminated the smog that had plagued

A Turkish Girl Arrives in Germany

◆◈◆

Aynur, a young Turkish girl, published in a Turkish newspaper a very personal and frank account of her life in Germany. She had gone to Germany with her mother to live with her father, who had worked there several years. Leaving her village elementary school behind, she went to a Turkish school in Germany and lived there into her teens. As she adopted new ways, she became alienated from her family, found German friends only among groups of homosexuals and drug addicts, and eventually made several visits to Turkey in search of old ties to her extended family and native culture. She ends her account with the comment, "On my birth certificate it is written that I am a 'Turk.' But in the full sense, more correctly, with my thinking, I am not completely a Turk. I do not want to be a German either." In the passage quoted here, she describes her first days in Germany.

"A bustle of activity commenced as soon as the plane landed in Berlin. Everyone wanted to disembark. I looked for the sun as soon as we went out, but it wasn't to be seen. I thought I was before a gray wall. The weather was cloudy and rainy. Later on I started looking for blond people. I always thought that all Germans were blond.

"We took a taxi. I was watching out of the window. I was trying to see the white houses which I had dreamed about. All around were large brick buildings. There were no people in sight on the wide boulevards. I was constantly asking my father, 'Which one looks like our house?'

"Finally we got out of the taxi. I was looking around to find the house that they lived in. My father, pointing to a somewhat larger door, said, 'You enter here.' An old door, all the edges of which were broken, and a somewhat large building from which the plaster was falling. After we entered through the large door and went through the small concrete courtyard, we started climbing the stairs. The holding-on places were broken.

"Suddenly all of my illusions were shattered. Pessimism and dejection overcame me. We climbed until the fourth floor. My father opened the door. A small hallway, a living room, and a kitchen. That was all there was to the home. The toilet was outside, they said.

"I asked myself, 'Is this our house?' I withdrew to a corner and started to investigate the living room. In the middle a faded rug was laid. Around it stood a few old armchairs. The only new thing was a fairly large television that stood in the corner. Forgetting everything, we started playing with the television. At each press of a button, a different film appeared.

"Six of us started to live together in the one-room house. This situation did not strike me as odd. In our village, too, we used to live all together. Since I had not had any different living experience, this did not seem unusual.

"My older sister and I did not get out of the room for a period of three months. We were afraid, and moreover, our father was not giving us permission. Our only tie to the outside was a window facing the courtyard. Children were playing in the courtyard. My only wish was to play with them. From time to time I was able to talk through the kitchen window with our neighbor's daughter, who was a year older than I. I was impatiently waiting for her return from school. My first friend in Germany was this girl.

"Her hair was cut very short. She looked like a very modern girl. We went down together to the courtyard entrance to play. I gained a little courage. After that I started going to their home.

"We used to wear skirts over pajamas in our village. My father had bought slacks for us in Istanbul. From then on we wore slacks under our skirts instead of pajamas. Slowly I began to imitate my friend. When no one was at home, I would take off my skirt and walk around in my slacks. At other times, I would take off my slacks and walk around in just my skirt. My older sister was not able to dare to do this. She would sit at the window as my lookout.

"For a long time when we went outside, we wore slacks under our skirts."

From Akural Aynur, (trans.), in Ilhan Basgöz and Norman Furniss (eds.), *Turkish Workers in Europe*, Turkish Studies Publications, 1985.

London since the sixteenth century, killing thousands of people as recently as 1952. The Thames has become a clean river for the first time in centuries. In the 1960s and 1970s, nearly every build-ing in Paris was stripped of the somber, dark patina of soot accumulated through 150 years of industrialization (to begin darkening anew from automotive exhaust). By the 1980s, citizens' movements, well-organized programs for recycling, and strict regulations were changing the landscape across Europe; and European states had become leaders in international measures to protect the environment. Green parties have remained small, even in Germany, which has the strongest green movement, but the larger parties have adopted much of their program.

III. The Politics of Prosperity

Although Western Europe's social policies were those of social democrats, capitalism and confidence in free trade were cornerstones of the European Community. Politics reflected the tension between these two emphases, pushed toward one or the other with changes in the economy or international relations. In Eastern Europe the tension was between allowing greater freedom of expression and preserving the apparatus of the single-party state loyal to the Soviet Union.

WAVES OF PROTEST

Greater well-being seemed to strengthen moral outrage. Many Western Europeans were appalled by the rising commercialism and inequality that accompanied prosperity. Many Eastern Europeans were determined to win some of the advantages that their western neighbors enjoyed. In the 1960s and 1970s a number of otherwise very different movements fought for an alternative society, less dependent on established elites and consumerism.

The Revolutions of 1968 For a few weeks in May 1968 the students of Paris seemed to recapture the revolutionary spirit of 1848, with their barricades of paving stones and trees, imaginative posters, and mocking slogans. In Germany, Italy, Great Britain, and the United States as well, students briefly acted as an independent political force in 1968 and 1969. Inspired by the movements of national liberation in Africa and Asia and outraged by the war in Vietnam, they denounced imperialism as a product of capitalist societies that used consumer goods to mask inequality and injustice. More specifically, they excoriated the rigidities and inadequacies of the educational system to

which they were subject. Their elders noted with surprise that these angry protesters were the beneficiaries of expanded educational opportunities and postindustrial prosperity. As revolutions, these movements failed. Labor unions and the traditional left were suspicious of privileged college students; liberals and conservatives were offended by rudeness and violence. In elections following these upheavals, the majority of voters turned to parties that emphasized order. These protest movements nevertheless stimulated important reforms, especially of education; and their style of protest, their challenges to middle-class values, and their questioning of authority have remained important elements in public discourse and in a distinctive youth culture. Ever since, movements of social criticism have used the organizing skills and tactics of satire and street theater that worked so well in 1968 to win the attention of a complacent society. The Greens are very much the heirs of those student activists.

In Czechoslovakia the optimism of 1968, when Alexander Dubček came to power, was short-lived. As Communist party secretary, he was able to adopt a program of liberalization calling for greater autonomy for Slovakia and for freedom of speech, assembly, and religion. Students were noisily enthusiastic for this "communism with a human face"; but Moscow saw it as an intolerable danger. In the largest military operation in Europe since World War II, troops from the Soviet Union, East Germany, Hungary, and Poland invaded Czechoslovakia in August. Dubček was soon ousted; and of his springtime program, only Slovakian autonomy was allowed to stand.

The Women's Movement Women were prominent in the student demonstrations across Europe and the United States, but many discovered that male radicals, despite their rhetoric of equality in matters of race and class, tended to allocate subordinate roles to women. Simone de Beauvoir's *The Second Sex* and Betty Friedan's *The Feminine Mystique* helped women identify the problem.

When her book first appeared in 1949, Beauvoir was well established in French intellectual circles but best known as the intimate friend of Sartre, the most admired intellectual of the day. *The Second Sex*, a memoir of her own experiences, made her famous. The book gained power in the context of the 1960s, for it reflected on the ways in which society tends to make women ancillary to others (institutions, families, husbands). Beauvoir wondered whether equality for women, even if possible, would be enough to overcome this subordination to other interests or whether women did not need to establish their own distinctive voice. Her questions and her candor pushed the women's movement in new directions.

The Feminine Mystique appeared in 1963. Betty Friedan, an experienced American journalist and mother of three, wrote about what she saw as the split between the idealized vision of the perfect homemaker and the reality of women's lives. In the years after World War II, women were expected to find personal fulfillment as wives and mothers. Instead, Friedan identified women as suffering from "the problem that has no name" and a profound crisis in identity. Along with *The Second Sex, The Feminine Mystique* became a handbook of the women's movement in the 1960s and 1970s. The new politics centering on women's needs and women's rights became one of the important developments of the latter half of the twentieth century.

Terrorism Rather than abandon fading hope for revolution, some radical groups turned to terrorism. The skills and equipment necessary for a terrorist campaign were not hard to come by in the semisecret world of international crime, espionage, and arms deals that prospered during the Cold War. Although terrorists were few in number, terrorism's complexity and anonymity made modern urban society vulnerable. These small groups did not aim to capture power but rather to provoke the authorities into repressive acts that would alienate the public. German terrorists shot at business leaders as well as politicians until caught by severely efficient police. Basque terrorists shook several Spanish governments with their bombs and murders but accomplished little more.

In Italy, Marxist and neo-Fascist underground bands competed in kidnappings and bombings accompanied by revolutionary proclamations. In 1978 the best-known of the radical groups, the Red Brigades, climaxed a series of attention-getting exploits by kidnapping Aldo Moro, a prominent politician. Police searched for him in vain as the nation held its breath until his bullet-riddled body was found in an abandoned car. Across the political spectrum, the public responded with outrage against terrorism rather than anger at the state.

▲ **After weeks of student demonstrations in Paris, police used buses to cordon off the Sorbonne shortly before storming the university and evicting the students in June 1968.**
UPI/Bettmann.

Although the Red Brigades remained active, they were on the wane by the time their leaders were arrested a few years later. Such incidents, like the shooting of Pope John Paul II by a Turkish terrorist in 1981, provoked outcries about the alienation and violence of modern society but did little to change it.

Terrorism was more effective where local hatreds gave it a popular base. Irish Protestants,

▲ **A local sign warns residents of sniper attacks in this Northern Ireland town where IRA sharpshooters had killed seven soldiers.**
MacBride/Corbis.

determined to maintain British rule in Northern Ireland, had long clashed with their Catholic neighbors who wanted Northern Ireland to be part of the Irish Republic. Neither side had much faith in the British government's proposed compromises permitting local rule, but those were never tested because terrorism reached the level of continuous war. Underground organizations on each side killed hundreds of innocent people. Although a majority of people said they favored some workable solution, loyalty to neighbors, nationalism, and recollections of past injustice, discrimination, and repression permitted violence to prevent a resolution. More distant religious strife brought terrorists to the continent, too. Supporters of the Palestine Liberation Organization, seeking a Palestinian state, killed Israeli athletes at the Munich Olympic Games in 1972, and in the 1970s Muslim terrorists placed bombs in Paris stores. Terrorists gained little for their various causes, but

heightened urban fear made tough security measures and heavily armed police a prominent part of European city life.

Eurocommunism By the 1980s, communist parties in Western Europe realized that they had to broaden their appeal; and Italy's Communist party, the largest outside the Soviet bloc, was especially innovative. It sponsored dozens of publications aimed at women, students, and intellectuals as well as at workers and held great public celebrations that had elements of an industrial exhibit and a rock concert with lectures and seminars on the side. The spectacle and the content were impressive, and the party grew less inclined to hold up the Soviet Union as the model of the future. Throughout Western Europe years of electoral and union activity had led communist parties to form coalitions and take positions on scores of practical issues. Arguing for social justice and political freedom invited commitment to pluralism and democracy. The French and Italian parties had objected to the Soviet invasion of Czechoslovakia in 1968, and the Italian party even accepted NATO. Criticizing Soviet policies in Eastern Europe opened prospects for an alternative program.

That alternative came to be known as Eurocommunism; and Italy's Communist party was its model and major proponent.[4] It proclaimed its commitment to civil rights, multiple parties, and free elections. Electoral successes increased its influence among other communist parties, so that the French Communist party, traditionally among Europe's most rigid, and a newly revived Spanish Communist party adopted Eurocommunist positions despite pressure from the Soviet Union to preserve the unity of communism and remain loyal to Soviet leadership. By the sixtieth anniversary of the Russian Revolution in 1977, Eurocommunism marked a new schism in communist ranks. But suspicion of communist parties ran

---

[4] Communist parties had traditionally attracted nearly one-third of the electorate in Italy, one-fifth in France and Finland, one-eighth in Spain, and much less elsewhere: about 5 percent in Sweden, 4 percent in Denmark, 3 percent in Belgium, 2 percent in Greece and the Netherlands, and less than 1 percent in West Germany and Great Britain. The parties in Portugal, briefly powerful after the revolution there, and in Finland were the two least inclined to Eurocommunism.

deep, and Eurocommunism's appeal to noncommunists proved limited. The weakening of radical alternatives left politics across Western Europe appearing more alike from country to country and made it easier to build toward a European Union.

The End of Dictatorship in Greece   Despite the power concentrated in the modern state, revolutions remained possible. In Greece they came primarily as military coups. Army officers had overthrown the unstable parliamentary system and eventually the monarchy itself in 1967, but in 1973, civilian leaders were able to force the military dictatorship to restore democracy. The failure of military rule was part of a larger lesson. To strengthen a fragile but modernizing economy, Greece's repressive military rulers had needed to draw closer to Western Europe where they found little inclination to deal with dictators. Weakened at home by conflict with Turkey over control of Cyprus, the military regime gradually increased freedom as it recognized its own unpopularity. Conflict between left and right remained strident in Greece, but the country was clearly on a course leading toward democracy and economic growth. That was confirmed by the acceptance of Greece as a member of the European Community in 1981.

The End of Dictatorship in Portugal   Portugal and Spain had been ruled by dictators since the 1930s. In Portugal the Salazar regime, which had paralleled Franco's long period of rule in Spain, continued in milder form even after Salazar became incapacitated in 1968. While opposition remained stymied at home, it grew stronger in Portuguese Guinea, Angola, and Mozambique, where Portugal relied on brute force to hold on to its empire. Condemned in the United Nations, by African states, and by most European nations, the overtaxed government was suddenly seized in April 1974 by a group of army officers promising full freedom and civil rights for Portugal and self-determination for the colonies. The response was overwhelming. Crowds danced in the streets and cheered smiling soldiers whose rifles were decorated with flowers.

The euphoria could not last. A poor and backward country, Portugal faced raging inflation and declining production. While peasants claimed the land they had long coveted, socialist and communist unions competed for support among the

workers, business groups struggled to defend their interests, and many prominent business people left the country. The army leaders themselves were ideologically divided, and for two years cabinets were formed and fell after a few months in the face of revolts from left and right. Nevertheless, the nationalization of banks and industry was followed by free elections in 1975 and 1976 and relatively moderate socialist governments that brought Portugal closer to other countries in Western Europe. With elections that gave Portugal its first democratically elected civilian president in sixty years, Portugal was able to join the European Community in 1986.

The End of Dictatorship in Spain   The political transformation in Spain was more gradual. Franco retired in 1973 but skillfully kept his influence until his death two years later. In 1969 he had called on Juan Carlos, the grandson of Spain's last king, to take the empty throne, in effect as Franco's heir. Juan Carlos showed himself more committed to democracy and more adept than expected. Increased freedom of speech did not lead to a recurrence of the civil war that so many people feared, and the voters approved a new constitution in 1978. Many dangers remained, but an attempted military coup failed, and greater regional autonomy reduced agitation from separatists. Suddenly, a society long dormant economically and politically came alive. A stagnant economy caught fire in the 1970s and 1980s under the premiership of the extremely popular socialist Felipe Gonzales. Although his decision to join NATO was not popular, his success in joining the European Community in 1986 and ending Spain's fifty years of relative isolation was widely cheered. The prosperous democracies of Western Europe, capitalist but committed to programs of social welfare, were the models that the rest of Europe wanted to follow.

CAPITALIST COUNTRIES: THE CHALLENGE OF RECESSION

Western democracies had grown accustomed to economic growth, which promised gains for all. When growth slowed, political conflict sharpened; and new issues came to the fore. Ecological movements gained at the polls, and regional movements acquired new strength. The traditional programs of left and right lost relevance, while weakened governments grappled with problems deeply embedded in their social and economic systems.

The Energy Crisis   European economies were instantly vulnerable when in October 1973 the oil-exporting nations (mainly in the Middle East) banded together in a cartel to raise international prices. Europe imported nearly two-thirds of its energy in the form of petroleum, and only the Soviet Union could meet its own energy needs through domestic production. In response to higher prices, Western nations redoubled efforts to develop domestic sources of energy. Over the next decade the exploitation of North Sea oilfields made Norway self-sufficient and Britain nearly so, and the Netherlands developed Europe's largest fields of natural gas. But Europe's energy consumption continued to rise, and greater self-sufficiency depended heavily on nuclear energy. By 1976 more than half the world's nuclear power plants operating or under construction were in Europe, where France became the world leader. These measures and the collapse of oil prices in 1986 eased the immediate economic crisis, but its effects remained.

Opposition to reliance on nuclear power, which had been led by the Greens, increased after the meltdown of a nuclear reactor at Chernobyl in the Soviet Union in 1986. Radioactive clouds swept over much of central Europe, creating concern for safety everywhere (the full extent of the deaths and injuries from radiation within the Soviet Union only came to be known years later).

Stagflation   The high cost of energy added to inflationary pressures. Among major capitalist nations, only West Germany consistently managed to hold the rate of inflation below 5 percent a year.

▼ France invested more heavily in nuclear energy than did any other country. Well run and efficient, the French plants provoked little public opposition, but not even a mural of a child at the beach could make the giant stacks seem to belong in their bucolic surroundings.
Philippe Psaila/Gamma/Liaison.

It rose to more than 20 percent in Britain and Italy in 1975–1976 (30 percent in Portugal) and undermined planning, savings, and trade, while squeezing salaried employees and many workers. This widespread inflation called into question practices on which prosperity had seemed to rest: deficit financing by governments, increased imports, and businesses' reliance on raising prices to maintain profits. Efforts to change these policies initiated debates that threatened to become class conflicts about social programs, especially in Britain and Italy. Economists worried about *stagflation,* the paradoxical combination of economic stagnation and rising prices, and then about a more familiar condition, recession.

Where strong anti-inflationary measures were imposed, as in Britain, unemployment rose, and in Europe generally became higher in the 1980s than at any time since World War II (although it would rise higher still a decade later). Europe was undergoing a major and painful economic transition as its now-aging industries faced increased competition from the Japanese and from new plants in other parts of the world. And the state's capacity to respond was limited. Campaigns against high taxes plus public support for social programs left little room for maneuver. An unexpected rise in regionalism led to new accusations that central governments disadvantaged local interests. Thus long-accepted national policies were called into question. Contrasting national responses—a shift to the left in France and Italy and a strengthening of the right in Germany and Britain—masked significant similarities.

Opening to the Left: France   The student revolt in May 1968 toppled De Gaulle's government. The storm was weathered with firmness and promises of reform and because student radicals frightened French voters, but the Fifth Republic was never the same. The government passed education reforms, broadened social programs, and made the civil service more responsive; but when a referendum on De Gaulle's vague but far-reaching plans for decentralizing the state was defeated in 1969, he resigned. The next two presidents differed from him more in style than policy, winning close elections with promises of stability and moderation, while the opposition criticized the political system as isolated from public opinion in its reliance on highly trained experts, however brilliant. Although most French voters were centrist, the division between a more or less Marxist left and a technocratic right dominated politics.

In 1981 the socialist leader of that opposition, François Mitterrand, won the presidential election by attempting to bridge that divide. He promised new emphasis on issues of culture, leisure, and urban life but maintained his alliance with the Communists and supported the traditional demands of the left for the nationalization of many industries and for a more equitable distribution of income. On election night there was dancing in the streets and optimistic talk of a post-Gaullist era. The new government began with dramatic measures, nationalizing many heavy industries and most banks, raising wages and benefits, and increasing social expenditures. The daring gamble failed to stimulate an economy hurt by business distrust, the fall of the franc, and an unfavorable international economy. Within a few years, separated from the Communists, Mitterrand adopted policies of austerity, deflation, and investment in high technology that were more like those of his predecessors than his own platform. As the right gained in elections, France found a socialist president leading a government of the center that was concerned with economic modernization, military strength, and support of the European Community. As to the new social problems—large pockets of endemic unemployment, drug addiction, and racial conflict—politicians had few solutions.

Opening to the Left: Italy   In 1983 Bettino Craxi became Italy's first Socialist prime minister. A wily politician who had rebuilt the Socialist party, his arrival in power was the culmination of two long-term political trends. The Christian Democrats had dominated Italian politics since the founding of the republic in 1946 by a system of semisecret negotiations and labyrinthine deals with the smaller parties but excluding the Socialists until 1963 and always excluding the Communists. While the economy boomed—Italy had enjoyed the longest period of economic growth of any European nation—this domination was acceptable. As restiveness increased, so did the search for an alternative. The other trend was the growing respectability of the Communist party.

▲ The bicentennial of the French Revolution, which had once divided all of Europe, was the occasion in 1989 for celebrations of partriotism and the importance of human rights.
D. Aubert/Sygma.

As they won local offices in much of the north, especially in the newly established regional administrations and in most of Italy's largest cities, the Communists enhanced their reputation for popular programs administered with probity and efficiency. The time had come, they argued as good Eurocommunists, for a "historic compromise," in which Communists and Christian Democrats would govern together in the interests of social and political reform. Some such solution seemed all but inevitable until Craxi set the Socialists on the opposite course, breaking away from the Communists and making his party indispensable to a governing coalition. In office Craxi brought a new decisiveness to government, but the hoped-for reforms were subordinated to more immediate economic issues. His government sustained reasonable political and economic stability, an impressive achievement in a tension-filled nation undergoing rapid social change, but one that fell far short of the reforms that the parties of the left had promised.

A Shift to the Right: West Germany In West Germany political issues tended to be overshadowed by the satisfying fact of prosperity as the Federal Republic surpassed the United States in world trade. Even the significant change in 1969 to a government led by the Social Democrats did not lessen the commitment to encouraging investment, expanding trade, and preventing inflation. Often surprisingly conservative in their economic policies, the Social Democrats pursued democratization in other ways, carrying through educational reforms, expanding social services, and requiring large firms to have elected labor representatives on a central board of directors. An unfavorable economic climate helped the Christian Democrats in 1982 to regain office under Helmut Kohl. He would be prime minister for longer than anyone since Bismarck. Kohl's government was more closely tied to the United States and friendlier to business but almost as eager as its predecessors to maintain good relations with the East. Germany, like France and Italy, looked more and more to the European Community to provide a program for the future and to shape its international role.

A Shift to the Right: Great Britain Continuity had characterized British policy for thirty years until Margaret Thatcher became prime minister in 1979. When the Conservatives were in power, they favored the private sector but largely accepted the extensive welfare programs and mixed economy they inherited. Constrained by the plight of the British economy, Labour governments in their turn reduced public expenditures and pressured trade unions to accept wage limits, while improving transport and expanding higher education.

Britain's overwhelming problem was the economy, and neither North Sea oil nor membership in the European Community solved it. Businesses failed to modernize plants or raise productivity at the pace of other industrial nations. Inflation depressed the rate of investment. Analysts found it easier to lay the blame—on the enormous cost to Britain of World War II, unimaginative and weak business managers, an inadequate educational system, the selfish conservatism of labor unions,

the high costs of welfare and defense—than to prescribe remedies. In office as the recession got worse, the Labour party lost the 1979 election.

Margaret Thatcher A doctrinaire advocate of free enterprise, Mrs. Thatcher reversed the course of British domestic policy, and the two major parties became more ideological. Out of power, Labour was dominated by its left wing, a fact that divided opposition, helping the Conservatives to stay in office. The results of Thatcher's decisive policies were impressive. The British economy restructured, and productivity rose in the late 1980s, increasing prosperity and reducing still high unemployment. That restructing, combined with reductions in social services including education, also increased social inequality.

Even her opponents—and she was widely disliked—grudgingly admired her outspokenness and fearless consistency, and there was no arguing with the economic growth. She strengthened her position by appealing to nationalist fervor in 1983 when Argentina suddenly attacked the Falkland Islands (which Britain had held and Argentina had claimed for more than a century), and she took much of the credit for Britain's victory. In 1990 she won her third consecutive election, something no prime minister had done for 160 years. But her unbending defense of unrestrained capitalism and what she considered Britain's national interest made for abrasive relations with the European Community and many politicians at home, factors that contributed to a revolt in her own party that forced her to resign soon after her last electoral victory. Her less divisive successor kept his party in power until Labour's overwhelming victory in the elections of 1997, but the Thatcher years remain a turning point in modern British history.

COMMUNIST RULE: THE PROBLEM OF RIGIDITY

Khrushchev's Effort The Soviet Union's most impressive achievement, admired throughout the world, had been its industrial growth. By the 1960s its economy was second in overall production and wealth only to that of the United States. It sent the first man into orbit around the earth in 1961; and as the world's largest producer of steel, iron, and more recently, oil, the USSR was

▲ Soviet science and industry gained enormous prestige with the first successful orbit of a space vehicle in 1957; and later, the atmosphere of détente made it possible to hold exhibits like this one in Los Angeles in 1977.
AP/Wide World.

apparently gaining in the economic competition with the West. Brashly confident, Khrushchev, who declared that the Soviet Union "would bury" the United States, promised that his government was now able to give more attention to consumer products and adequate housing. Like his campaign of de-Stalinization, such policies opened the possibility of a new evolution in Soviet rule, but it proved difficult to accomplish.

Khrushchev's plans to increase agricultural production failed, and the issue of whether to invest in consumer goods or heavy industry reopened long-standing conflicts within the highest circles. Many Kremlin leaders worried as well about the growing restiveness in Eastern Europe and the rift with China, which since 1956 had con-

sistently denounced the Soviet Union's international policies as a betrayal of communism. When, in the process of solidifying his authority, Khrushchev antagonized the military, they and his opponents in the Politburo and the Central Committee felt strong enough to speak against him. He was voted out of office in 1964 and sent into quiet retirement.

Signs of Failure The orderly transition was promising in itself, but Khrushchev's successors, led by Leonid Brezhnev, were tough party technicians who held a firm grip on power and offered no fresh solutions. The cold-blooded invasion of Czechoslovakia, the continuing agricultural crisis (which required the purchase of American grain in 1972 and 1975), and the need to import industrial technology, particularly from Italy and France, were all signs of a system failing to adapt to change.

Evidence of arbitrary repression continued to tarnish the country's international image. Throughout the West the press revealed the plight of Soviet Jews, subject to discrimination and attack and then intermittently permitted to emigrate. When Boris Pasternak's novel *Doctor Zhivago*, exposed the seamy aspects of Soviet life and earned him the Nobel prize for literature in 1958, Pasternak was not permitted to go to Stockholm to receive it. Significantly, the case of Alexander Solzhenitsyn in 1970 caused still greater international furor. He, too, was prevented from receiving the Nobel prize he won that year for his story of the *Gulag Archipelago*, a haunting account of the terrors of Soviet concentration camps. Four years later he was arrested and deported, joining a chorus of Russian writers and scientists whose criticisms were widely published outside the USSR and increasingly well known at home.

Gorbachev's Gamble When Brezhnev died in 1982, he was succeeded by elderly and ailing party figures who exemplified the bureaucratic grayness of Soviet rule. Thus the appointment in 1985 of Mikhail Gorbachev to be general secretary of the Communist party marked a new era. At fifty-four, the youngest man to lead the Soviet Union since Stalin, Gorbachev gradually revealed a personality and daring that led him in startling new directions. He spoke openly about problems of inefficiency and alienation (absenteeism and alcoholism among the workforce reached alarming levels), and he recognized the importance of radical reform in order to meet the growing demand for consumer goods and sustain the arms race with the United States. The cost, and risk, of that competition went up as the president of the United States, Ronald Reagan, poured more money into new weapons. Meanwhile, the contrast between East and West in both agricultural and industrial production had grown more striking, and the USSR's earlier achievements in heavy industry now counted for less economically than the newer technologies and services in which it lagged.

Gorbachev confronted these problems on three fronts. He set about to restructure Soviet society by decentralizing decision making, which required more open communication, greater authority for local managers, and a reduction in the role of the Communist party. Gorbachev had to overcome entrenched resistance at all levels, but his efforts made *perestroika* (political and economic restructuring) and *glasnost* (greater openness) international words and won him admirers around the world.

Internationally, his foreign policy made him the most popular figure in Soviet history. He campaigned against the threat of nuclear war; and at a summit meeting with Reagan in 1986 Gorbachev suddenly proposed breathtaking reductions in nuclear arms that nearly won Reagan's acquiescence before aides hurriedly dissuaded him. Gorbachev also knew that he must end the war in Afghanistan. Soviet troops had gone there in 1979 to support a Communist government entangled in a bloody guerrilla war against rebels heavily supported by the United States. The war was a dangerous drain on Soviet lives, wealth, and morale, and in 1987 Gorbachev began a staged withdrawal.

Remarkably, he also extended glasnost to Eastern Europe. Gorbachev realized that those governments, too, needed to restructure; and he was glad to end costly barter arrangements with the Comecon nations, which permitted them to buy Soviet oil at prices below the world market in exchange for Eastern European products that the Soviet Union did not want. But once launched, glasnost was hard to contain. When some of the East European nations began to request that Soviet troops leave their territory and then began to replace their Communist regimes, Gorbachev accepted those changes, too. However necessary, such concessions troubled already hostile hardliners at home, for each step toward reform revealed the need for more; each gesture toward glasnost increased the criticism from those people insistent on greater change and the resistance from those opposed to any.

Ethnic Conflict in the USSR A still greater danger to Soviet stability arose from the explosion of nationalist unrest that in 1988 produced demonstrations and violent clashes around the perimeter of the Soviet Union: on the Eastern frontier (in

▲ For years Gorbachev was mobbed by enthusiastic well-wishers whenever he visited Western Europe and the United States; his trip to West Germany in 1990, where he was accompanied by Chancellor Kohl, was one of his last triumphal tours.
R. Bossu/Sygma.

Georgia, Moldavia, and the Ukraine), among the Baltic republics (Latvia, Lithuania, and Estonia), and in the southern republics. Created at the end of World War I, the Baltic States lost their independence in World War II, becoming part of the Soviet Union by war's end. Demonstrations there revived passionate memories of independence, and rubber stamp representative bodies began to act like parliaments, writing new laws and constitutions. Gorbachev offered general promises, argued for the benefits of belonging to the USSR, restrained his own army, and delayed any final stand on their status.

In the southern republics, Azerbaijanis and Armenians engaged in open war, inflamed by conflicts that were ethnic (Azeri and Armenians had fought for centuries), religious (Shia Muslims and Armenian Orthodox Christians), social (the Armenians had generally been wealthier and better ed-

ucated), political (involving territorial claims and relations with Moscow), and economic (Azerbaijan's oil industry, its principal source of wealth, was declining). Eventually, Soviet troops attempted to separate the combatants but did not try to exercise sovereign authority over them. Russians constituted the largest ethnic group in the multinational USSR, and theirs was the largest republic. They had long enjoyed privileged status throughout the federation. Now, Russian nationalists fanned the fears of losing that status with a campaign in the name of culture (with appeals to the Orthodox Church), order (attractive to the military and some party members), and race (including virulent antisemitism). Nationalism was as grave a challenge to Gorbachev as bloated bureaucracy and stores with empty shelves. The bonds of ideology, institutions, and custom that had held a great state together were beginning to look weak.

Eastern Europe In 1968 the "Brezhnev doctrine" had declared that a "threat to socialism" in one country was a threat to all, and he followed the invasion of Czechoslovakia with efforts to strengthen the economic ties binding the Comecon countries, but the nations of Eastern Europe were looking westward for increased trade and badly needed loans. Romania, not content with its allotted role as a Soviet granary, had launched its own course of industrialization and an independent foreign policy that made its brutal dictator, Nicolae Ceaușescu, welcome in the West. East Germany, the second industrial power among communist states (and the seventh in Europe), oscillated between friendly overtures toward and suspicious rejection of West Germany much as it alternated between concessions and repression at home, where there were riots against the government in the early 1970s.

The pressures for change were stronger in Czechoslovakia, Hungary, and Poland, where cultural ties to Western Europe remained strong, and in the latter two countries especially the Catholic Church was an outlet for a growing restiveness. Riots against the police took place in Hungary, which had one of the strongest and most consumer-oriented economies of Eastern Europe. Riots in Poland in 1976 forced postponement of a projected rise in food prices, and four years later strikes led to the recognition of Solidarity, an organization of independent trade unions, whose leader, Lech Walesa, became a national hero. With support from the Catholic Church, the Solidarity movement grew strong enough to prompt a change of government. In a world in which public protest was dangerous and rare, events in Poland gained significance. But there was no telling where they would lead. The new head of the Polish Communist party, General Wojciech Jaruzelski, resorted to martial law and clamped down on Solidarity. East European governments continued to rely on force in the face of rising public resentment.

Yugoslavia was the maverick among communist states. Its limited market economy and its independence from the Soviet Union had once seemed to offer another kind of communism. Weakened by Tito's death in 1980 and by contention among its member republics, it could not manage the reforms necessary to shake the economy out of a prolonged economic downturn. There was, in fact, no model of how to make desired changes and preserve communist rule. Soviet presence remained the central fact of life in Eastern Europe.

IV. The End of an Era

THE MIRACLES OF 1989

The contradictions of communist rule were clear, but no one expected communism to collapse completely. For years, Eastern Europe governments had loosened controls and lessened repression as popular feeling and the need for greater efficiency seemed to require it. When those steps exposed additional institutional blockage and more threatening dissent, governments used their power to stifle reform and silence dissent. When they did not, in 1989, an unprecedented revolution followed.

Poland In Poland, despite martial law, Solidarity continued its underground propaganda with wit and daring. It turned the visit of the Polish pope into the occasion for more demonstrations. Placards and pamphlets were everywhere, and rumors and clandestine radio broadcasts nourished the rising agitation. And the government did not call out the army. Gorbachev had told the United Nations in 1988 that the Soviet Union would allow its allies to go their own way, and now that policy was tested. Sensing Walesa's popularity and the power of Solidarity, Jaruzelski decided to relax martial law and release some political prisoners. It was not enough. Public anger and frustration increased, and the economy worsened. By February 1989 the government was willing to acknowledge Solidarity's legitimacy, a major concession, but Solidarity demanded free elections. The government hesitated, and Gorbachev signaled that Poland was on its own. In April Solidarity got most of its demands; and when elections took place, Solidarity won almost all the seats in the parliament. Communist party members, stunned and frightened, did not know what to do. After various formulas for compromise failed, Solidarity took over the cabinet in August, the first noncommunist government in what for forty years had been called the Soviet bloc.

▲ Lech Walesa addressed workers outside a factory in Zyrardow, not far from Warsaw, in October 1981. The scene, reminiscent of the long history of labor movements except for the television cameras, marked the rising power of the Solidarity movement.
Giansanti/Sygma.

Hungary   Hungarians were well aware of events in Poland, for the irrepressible flow of information was an important factor in the events of 1989. Political discussion, like economic activity, was freer in Hungary than in other Communist countries, and by April even some party officials joined in public discussions of the need for free speech, civil rights, and the protection of private property. At the annual May Day celebrations, international communism's grandest occasion, opponents dwarfed the official celebration, and a huge demonstration in June dared to honor the uprising of 1956. Even some members of the government chose to attend. In October the Hungarian Communist party flexibly changed its name to the Socialist party and promised free elections for the following year. The power of people aroused seemed irresistible.

East Germany   Many old-line Communist leaders were convinced that a good show of force would restore order and keep the Communist party in power. In October Erich Honecker, the head of East Germany's party and its prime minister, took that tack. His soldiers beat and arrested demonstrators in East Berlin. A week later, however, he resigned, for Gorbachev announced that he disapproved such use of force, and the East German republic was walking away. Every day hundreds of people, especially the young and those with marketable skills, abandoned their country. Most went to Hungary, where they mobbed the West German embassy, seeking visas. Embarrassed Hungarian and West German governments arranged for special trains to carry them west, and more people came, pushing and shouting and climbing over embassy walls.

On November 9, 1989, Honecker's successor announced that East Germany's border with West Berlin would be opened that very day. The guards could not believe their orders. Then late that night they shrugged and stepped aside as hoards of people pushed through the gates of the Berlin wall. Hundreds, then thousands, cheered and waved from atop that symbol of oppression before strolling past the well-stocked shops of West Berlin. The celebrations continued in front of the television cameras for days, even after work crews began dismantling the wall. Thousands continued to come each day, some just testing what it felt like to be that free and looking in shop windows; others seeking a different life in West Germany. Throughout East Germany, meetings that would have been illegal a few weeks earlier took place in churches and public squares as the police watched and then withdrew. The government's promises for reform and official pleas for order were drowned in revelations of past corruption and talk of uniting the two Germanies.

The Final Round in Eastern Europe For a while the harsher East European governments—in Czechoslovakia, Bulgaria, and Romania—remained unscathed by the changes around them, but that isolation did not last. Crowds of protesters were filling Wenceslas Square in Prague, 40,000 people in October, then 200,000 after riot police beat up demonstrating students, and a few days later 300,000 came to shout and sing and jingle keys as a good-humored suggestion that it was time for the Communists to leave. In now familiar rites, slogans were written everywhere, posters covered the walls, and new political groups formed. By December 1989 the best organized of these, Civic Forum, had won power and elected as president of Czechoslovakia its leader, Vaclav Havel, the popular playwright whose plays had long been banned (see "Havel's Inaugural Address," p. 1116).

Even Bulgaria and Romania, with less-developed economies and weaker traditions of political participation, could not escape the historic pressure. They met it very differently. Bulgaria's Communist party took its cues from the Soviet Union and in November forced Todor Zhivkov, party secretary for thirty-five years and head of state for twenty-seven, from office. He was jailed and plans for free elections announced. Romania in contrast suffered weeks of bloodshed. When in December crowds gathered in Bucarest, the government gave the order to shoot. Still the crowds formed and violence increased. Romania's dictator, Ceauşescu, tried to make his escape but was caught and executed by firing squad on Christmas day. Fighting between the army and special police loyal to Ceauşescu continued for a week. Everywhere Romanian flags waved, a conspicuous hole in their center where the Communist hammer and cycle had been. The last communist government west of the Soviet Union (except for Albania) had fallen.

Rarely does politics produce collapse so sudden and on such a scale. Economic failure and resentment of Soviet dominance explain a good deal. Workers and Catholics in Poland, party members and entrepreneurs in Hungary, students and intellectuals in Czechoslovakia mobilized their fellow citizens with surprising speed and skill. For years radio and television had conveyed the knowledge that life was better in the West, despite all the efforts at censorship; and in the fall of 1989 images of cheering or rioting crowds spread the contagion of revolt. In the face of such diffuse anger, officials remarkably ready to quit and citizens determined to push on showed a shocking cynicism about the regimes that had ruled for more than forty years. The frequent comparisons to the revolutions across Europe in 1848 made good sense. Young men and women, especially students, were prominent in all these events, echoing in their slogans, sense of theater, and mockery as well as their clothes and music the events of 1968 and revealing the impact of an international youth culture. As crowds lost their fear, a universal hunger for freedom and a massive contempt washed away the pomp of officialdom, the claims of party ideology, and the power of the police.

Freedom illumined not only the appalling failures and corruption of the fallen regimes but also the problems still to be faced. Within months, unaccustomed freedoms resurrected old divisions—ethnic, social, and ideological. All at once, the Eastern Europe of 1990 looked much like that of the 1920s. Moderate conservatives gained the lead among Hungary's multiple parties and expressed nationalist resentment at the treatment Romania accorded Hungarians living in its territory. Czechoslovakia was soon debating yet again the relations of Czechs and Slovaks. As Poland risked the drastic medicine of sudden conversion to a market economy, rifts appeared within Solidarity. In Bulgaria, Communist party members won most of the seats in free elections, and in Romania leaders who claimed no longer to be Communists showed little

HAVEL'S INAUGURAL ADDRESS
◈

Vaclav Havel is perhaps the most widely admired of the new leaders of Eastern Europe, and his literary skill and philosophic bent made him a particularly effective spokesperson. In his inaugural address on January 1, 1990, as president of the Czech Republic, he commented on the historical meaning of the dramatic changes that brought him to office.

"My dear fellow citizens, for forty years you heard from my predecessors on this day different variations of the same theme: how our country flourished, how many million tons of steel we produced, how happy we all were, how we trusted our government, and what bright perspectives were unfolding in front of us.

"I assume you did not propose me for this office so that I, too, would lie to you.

"Our country is not flourishing. The enormous creative and spiritual potential of our nation is not being used sensibly. Entire branches of industry are producing goods which are of no interest to anyone, while we are lacking the things we need. A state which calls itself a workers' state humiliates and exploits workers. Our obsolete economy is wasting the little energy we have available. A country that once could be proud of the educational level of its citizens spends so little on education that it ranks today as seventy-second in the world. We have polluted our soil, our rivers and forests, bequeathed to us by our ancestors, and we have today the most contaminated environment in Europe. Adult people in our country die earlier than in most other European countries. . . .

"But all this is still not the main problem. The worst thing is that we live in a contaminated moral environment. We fell morally ill because we became used to saying something different from what we thought. We learned not to believe in anything, to ignore each other, to care only about ourselves. Concepts such as love, friendship, compassion, humility, or forgiveness lost their depth and dimensions, and for many of us they represented only psychological peculiarities, or they resembled gone-astray greetings from ancient times, a little ridiculous in the era of computers and spaceships. Only a few of us were able to cry out loud that the powers that be should not be all-powerful, and that special farms, which produce ecologically pure and top-quality food just for them, should send their produce to schools, children's homes, and hospitals if our agriculture was unable to offer them to all. The previous regime—armed with its arrogant and intolerant ideology—reduced man to a force of production and nature to a tool of production. In this it attacked both their very substance and their mutual relationship. It reduced gifted and autonomous people, skillfully working in their own country, to nuts and bolts of some monstrously huge, noisy, and stinking machine, whose real meaning is not clear to anyone. It cannot do more than slowly but inexorably wear down itself and all its nuts and bolts."

From Brian MacArthur (ed.), *The Penguin Book of Twentieth-Century Speeches* (New York: Viking, 1992).

willingness to allow real democracy. East Germans voted for those who promised the most rapid assimilation into the German Federal Republic.

THE DISINTEGRATION OF THE USSR

A hero in Western Europe and the United States, Gorbachev was never so popular at home. Efforts to create more of a market economy threatened jobs. Attempts to make one sector more efficient were stymied by related sectors that operated in the old ways. The new price structure increased inflation, uncertainty, and hoarding. Many party members and the army resented the erosion of their own authority and the weakening of the Soviet Union's international position.

The Opposition to Gorbachev Seeking a strong political base, Gorbachev called for a huge Congress of People's Deputies as a step toward greater democracy. It met in 1989 and elected Gorbachev president of the Soviet Union, and it rejected the constitution's assertion that the Communist party must be preeminent (like all Soviet leaders since Stalin, Gorbachev's power had previously come from his position as party secretary). Discussions were more open than ever before. Deputies attacked old abuses, denounced the KGB, and gave vent to a rising chorus of competing ethnic demands. Solzhenitsyn warned against allowing Western decadence to infiltrate Russian society. Caught in the middle, Gorbachev clamped down on the media and allowed the army to threaten that it might restore order in the Baltic republics.

Among the opponents of this authoritarian turn, Boris Yeltsin, the head of the Communist party in Moscow, stood out. An outspoken populist, he reached ordinary people as Gorbachev never had; and in 1991 he was elected by popular vote president of the Russian republic, the largest in the Soviet Union. Other enemies of Gorbachev were active, too. When Gorbachev took his August vacation in the Crimea, hard-liners in his own government, the military, and the KGB staged a coup. Tanks filled the streets, and the coup leaders announced that Gorbachev had been replaced. Beyond that, they seemed to have no plan. Yeltsin held firm against the coup with remarkable support from public opinion. Crowds pleaded with the soldiers not to act, miners in Siberia went on a strike, demonstrators marched in city after city, and some army officers declared their support of Yeltsin.

Within two days, the leaders of the coup were in prison and Gorbachev was back in Moscow, but he was now overshadowed by Yeltsin. He had no party, for across the nation, people pulled down the symbols of communism, closed and sometimes looted Communist party offices. Only eight of the fifteen Soviet republics responded to his call for a meeting. In October 1991 Russia, Ukraine, Belarus, and Kazakhstan declared that the Soviet Union had ceased to exist. No significant group fought to save it, and it was replaced by the looser Confederation of Independent States. Gorbachev resigned, a victim of the revolution he had unleashed.

EUROPE WITHOUT COLD WAR

The fall of communism and the collapse of the Soviet Union meant the end of the Cold War. The policies of fifty years had to be rethought as did the hard-headed assumptions on which they had rested. No one could know the implications of such fundamental changes, but it was clear that domestic politics, economic policies, and international relations would all now be different.

German Unification The fall of communism affected Germany right away. Chancellor Kohl pushed for the immediate unification of East and West Germany, moving faster than many Germans thought wise, outmaneuvering the opposition parties, and capturing popular enthusiasm. By the end of 1989, he had gained the support of the United States and then of France, in effect, forcing a reluctant Britain to join in negotiations aimed at winning Soviet acceptance of German unification. Many were frightened at the prospect, but Kohl reassured the West with the promise that an enlarged Germany would be fully integrated into the European Community. The Soviet Union feared the increase in NATO's strength, but such concerns were rooted in an era quickly passing.

▼ **May 1990: Having pulled a statue of Lenin to the ground, Romanian workers remove the cable from his neck.**
Reuters/Bettmann.

▲ Lithuanian crowds hold up a banner that says "Ivan Go Home" and cheer as a Soviet soldier is burned in effigy. This demonstration in April 1990 followed two years of similar agitation.
Reuters Bettmann.

In August 1990 the victors of World War II—the Soviet Union, the United States, Britain, and France—signed a treaty with the two Germanies. In return for the promise to respect its boundary with Poland and to limit the size of its combined army, Germany could unify and remain in NATO as Europe's richest and most powerful state.

For Germans, however, the benefits were not immediate. The East German economy, which had been the most productive in Eastern Europe, revealed enormous weakness. Its outmoded and inefficient industry could not compete in the dynamic economy of the West, and unemployment rose. East Germans resented what felt like subordinate status, and West Germans struggled with the unexpectedly high cost of unification as well as a flood of German immigrants.

Domestic Politics and Immigration The collapse of communist regimes had important repercussions elsewhere, too. Italian politics since World War II had been shaped by the presence of a powerful Communist party that was excluded from power. Increasingly moderate, it responded to the events of 1989 by making a final break with old-line communism and changing its name. The Christian Democrats, however, lost their principal reason for being, which had been to keep the Communists out of power. When charges of corruption uncovered a vast network of graft, the Christian

Democratic party and their Socialist allies both simply disintegrated. In the next parliament, two-thirds of the deputies had never held any elective office and most belonged to new parties with new leaders. Public contempt for the old political class and a new electoral system (reducing the effects of proportional representation) opened the way for a restructuring of the political system.

Throughout Europe, politics was altered by the weakening of the traditional left, its Marxism now suspect, by the weakening of the anticommunist right, and by the resentment of foreigners. Heightened primarily by unemployment but also by a rise in numbers as immigrants from Eastern Europe joined those from Turkey, the Middle East, and Africa, anti-foreign feeling reflected the competition for space and ill-paying jobs. In Italy a new party, the Northern League, gained ground in the prosperous north by combining in one program opposition to immigration and the denunciation of government corruption and high taxes. In France, unemployed industrial workers who had voted communist in the past were often sympathetic to the xenophobic but influential campaigns of the National Front. Aimed especially at Muslims from North Africa, these campaigns made immigration a national issue that influenced governmental policies. And in Germany, where hundreds of thousands of people made their way from the faltering economies of Eastern Europe, incidents in which gangs of skinheads and neo-Nazis burned immigrant housing were an ominous reminder of Germany's past.

The Transition from Communism

The governments of Eastern Europe turned out to have heavier debts and more outmoded industries than even the critics of communism had suspected, and industrial pollution on an enormous, sometimes life-threatening, scale was a difficult problem for new governments in strapped economies. Unsure of the loyalty or competence of their own administrations, they had to attempt painful reforms while subject to unfamiliar public criticism. The capitalism suddenly unleashed was often socially disruptive, and the need to quickly re-create a sense of community encouraged appeals to ethnic identity.

Poland undertook the most radical shift to a market economy, and economic indicators showed dramatic improvement. Ordinary citizens often suffered, however, and former Communists gained in the elections of 1993 by promising to slow the transition. Russia, Hungary, Poland, and the Czech Republic pleaded for more foreign aid and foreign investment. Economic strains reinforced ethnic and religious conflict. The relentless drive to capitalism in prosperous Czech regions and the cynical ambitions of Slovak politicians forced the breakup of Czechoslovakia broke into the Czech Republic and Slovakia, although opinion polls indicated a majority in each country would have preferred to stay together.

Yugoslavia

Former Communists, in fact, proved particularly adept at stirring ethnic resentments, especially in the former Soviet Union and, most tragically of all, in Yugoslavia. Ethnic differences had not prevented Yugoslavia's six republics from effectively functioning together even after the death of Tito. Croatia and Slovenia, the economically most developed Yugoslav republics, began to criticize the economic and political policies of the Serbian-dominated Yugoslav government in the 1980s. Those policies, they argued, were unfair to them, and their demands for reform grew stronger with the fall of communism all around them. The Serbian Communists resisted calls for reform by raising support at home with appeals to Serbian nationalism. Tensions reached the point that four of Yugoslavia's republics declared their independence in 1990–1991. Serbia and Montenegro stayed together and called themselves Yugoslavia. Two, Slovenia and Macedonia, managed to secede relatively unscathed.

But the independence of Croatia and Bosnia-Herzegovina was opposed by large numbers of Serbs living within their borders, and the Yugoslav government under Slobodan Milosevic supported their armed resistance. Ideological, economic, and regional differences were thus transmuted into ethnic civil war in which each side, recalling past injustices, committed new atrocities. Truces were signed and then broken, and uncontrolled local units knew their ethnic brothers would support them no matter what horrors they committed. Slaughter and rape destroyed whole villages. By 1993 the Serb forces had recaptured about one-third of Croatia and nearly two-thirds of Bosnia-Herzegovina, a republic in which Serbs, Croatians,

BOUNDARY CHANGES SINCE 1989

——— Former boundary of Soviet Union

▨ Former area of Soviet Union

——— Former boundary of Czechoslovakia

——— Former boundary of Yugoslavia

- - - - - Former boundary between East & West Germany

All other boundaries as of 1998

⚡ **SIGNIFICANT NATIONALIST MOVEMENTS**

1 France (Brittany)

2 France (Corsica)

3 Great Britain (Scotland)

4 Great Britain (Wales)

5 Italy (Sardinia)

6 Italy (Tyrol)

7 Spain (Basque Region)

8 Spain (Catalonia)

✦ AREAS OF VIOLENT CONFLICT OR OPEN WAR

1 Armenia-Azerbaijan

2 Georgia-Abkhazia

3 Moldova

4 Bosnia-Herzegovina, former Yugoslavia

5 Northern Ireland

6 Persian Gulf War

7 Israeli-Palestinian conflict

8 Kurdish-Turkish-Iraqi conflict

9 Chechnya

⬡ ETHNIC-BASED DISPUTES

1 Hungarian populations in Slovakia

2 Hungarian poulations in Romania

3 Russian populations in Crimea (Ukraine)

4 Russian populations in Georgia

5 Russian populations in Azerbaijan

6 Russian populations in Baltic States

▲ **MAP 30.4 ETHNIC AND TERRITORIAL CONFLICT IN EUROPE AND THE MIDDLE EAST**

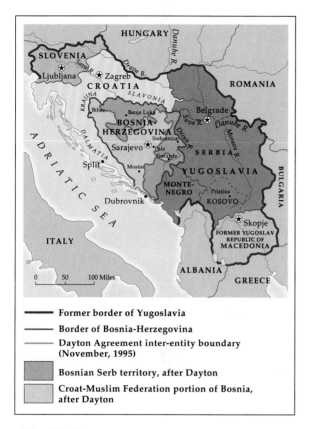

Former border of Yugoslavia

Border of Bosnia-Herzegovina

Dayton Agreement inter-entity boundary (November, 1995)

Bosnian Serb territory, after Dayton

Croat-Muslim Federation portion of Bosnia, after Dayton

▲ Map 30.4 Inset

and Muslims had once been proud of peacefully living together.

The European Union and NATO responded weakly. They denounced ethnic violence but did not hide their fear of being drawn into a Balkan war. Almost by default, the United States assumed a cautious leadership, pressuring the contending parties to accept a truce in 1995. American and even some Russian troops then joined European and UN forces as peacekeepers with limited roles. There were signs of rising opposition to Milosevic within Serbia and Montenegro, but voices of moderation tended to be squelched by the militant nationalists who profited from war. Consistent pressure did have some effect, and a few of the people accused of war crimes were brought to trial; but ethnic separation seemed about the most that could be hoped for.

Yeltsin Holds On Yeltsin was president of Russia when the Soviet Union had ceased to exist. Only

Yugoslavia had more serious ethnic conflicts than Russia, and no former communist country found the transition to free markets more difficult. Yeltsin postponed as much as he could and tried to moderate disputes within the new Confederation of Independent States while he pushed for drastic economic reform. The effects, though limited, were painful. Unemployment rose, the ruble all but collapsed, and production fell to about half what it had been a few years before. Managers did not know how to adjust to a market economy; many officials resisted change altogether; and as repression eased, criminal gangs flourished and ugly groups of nationalists and neo-Nazis grew louder.

When free elections in 1991 produced a Congress of People's Deputies in which Yeltsin's opponents—communists, nationalists, members of the military, and representatives of regional movements—outnumbered his supporters, he compromised when possible and ignored the congress when he could. As parliamentary resistance stiffened and his own popularity declined, Yeltsin risked a national presidential election in the spring of 1993 and won. A few months later Yeltsin declared the parliament dissolved. Several hundred delegates refused to obey. Holed up in their skyscraper, they collected arms and called on the people and the army for support. The army remained silent, but the delegates were heartened when groups of Yeltsin's opponents gathered outside parliament. Amid calls to bring the government down, shots were fired from within the parliament, and finally, the army bombarded and then stormed the parliament building. A hundred or more people died, more bloodshed than Moscow had seen since 1917.

The need to rely on the military, like Yeltsin's measures against parliament and his indifference to the rulings of the supreme court, was troubling proof that Russia had not achieved a constitutional system or the rule of law. Although seemingly rather indifferent, the public was prepared to support Yeltsin when forced to choose, and he surprised pollsters by winning reelection in 1996. By then the economy was improving, and Russia could take its place in meetings of the nations with the largest economies.

International Implications The end of the Cold War affected international affairs around the world. The United Nations, no longer hobbled by

▲ **The Soviet army surveys the streets of Moscow in October 1993 after having preserved Yeltsin's hold on power by storming the parliament's White House, where opposition leaders had barricaded themselves.** Anthony Suau/Gamma/Liaison.

a Security Council in which the United States and Russia nearly always disagreed, began to function more in the way envisioned at its founding, pacifying local conflicts and providing humanitarian aid. When Iraq invaded Kuwait in 1991, Russia supported the American-led attack on Iraq in response. Once the superpowers ceased to compete, all sides in the Middle East had to reassess their positions. Without Soviet support, the Muslim states could only lose by diplomatic intransigence, and once Israel was no longer a Cold War bastion, it could no longer be so certain of unending American aid. After decades of stalemate, Palestinians and Israelis agreed in 1993 to negotiate on limited autonomy for Palestine.

Ironically, the diplomatic implications of the Cold War's end were less clear in Europe, where that confrontation had begun. The future of NATO was a major issue, and its failure to act in Yugoslavia increased public doubts about its continued usefulness. The United States, with British support, insisted it was still needed; Germany and France appeared tempted by the idea of a more autonomous European force. Ultimately it was agreed that NATO should expand to include nations once in the Soviet bloc (Hungary, Poland, and the Czech Republic were expected to be the first to join and others indicated they would also want to). That agreement guaranteed continued American involvement on the continent and assured East European nations protection from Russia. It might also prevent those nations from fighting each other over boundaries that had changed many times and been a cause of war in the past. The risks were in the reactions that might eventually come from isolating Russia, selecting which states could become NATO members, and requiring those countries to invest in the modern arms that NATO membership required. Meanwhile, although negotiations to have nuclear warheads dismantled went slowly in the three former Soviet republics that harbored them, the topic itself was encouraging.

V. Contemporary Culture

◆

The burst of artistic creativity that followed World War II embraced new trends and styles in all the arts. At the same time, the global expansion of a dynamic popular culture is one of the hallmarks of the second half of the twentieth century. Gradually interwoven into modern social thought, these developments have contributed to new ideas about culture that have spread through the humanities and social sciences and influenced modern social movements.

POSTWAR CREATIVITY

With the end of the war European artists could reflect more freely on the searing experiences of repression and bloodshed that had darkened the previous decade. They could take part in artistic movements that had been banned under fascist governments, and they could catch up on the new ideas and styles coming from America, where the many European artists and intellectuals who fled the continent had helped to make New York the cultural capital of the Western world. Figures already famous in the 1930s, like the painter Pablo Picasso and the poet T. S. Eliot, could now be simultaneously honored as founders of modern art and savored with a freshness usually reserved for the newly discovered, for the works most admired in the 1950s and 1960s showed considerable continuity with the avant-garde works of the prewar period.

Authors wanting to show how ordinary people had experienced dictatorship, war, and postwar dislocation favored a style noted for its directness and telling detail. Called neorealism, this style flourished especially in Italy, where the novels of Ignazio Silone and Alberto Moravia gave incisive, often bitter, yet affectionate accounts of the daily struggles of people buffeted by movements and events beyond their control, and where the films of Roberto Rossellini and Vittorio de Sica combined the harsh eye of the candid camera with sympathy for the minor characters who are society's victims and its strength.

These forms gradually gave way to ones that built on more radical prewar art and presented several points of view simultaneously, challenging any assumption of a single reality. In Germany the plays of Bertolt Brecht used such devices for a firm Marxist purpose (in 1949 Brecht left the West to live in East Berlin), and the savagely satirical novels of Heinrich Böll extended the once-shocking surrealism of Franz Kafka to convey central Europe's experience of the twentieth century. Stimulus from outside Europe was also important. The most admired sculptor, the English artist Henry Moore, was directly influenced by African art in designing huge reclining figures that combined clean lines, solid masses, and provocative empty spaces.

Adapting Traditional Values The arguments for human decency needed restatement following the horrors of genocide, totalitarianism, and war. Existentialism, one of the most influential movements of the postwar period, offered a radical solution to the problem of ethics. Life may be absurd and meaningless, the French philosopher Jean-Paul Sartre reasoned, but to take any action is to make a decision, and that is to make a personal moral choice. Building on the prewar work of Karl Jaspers and Martin Heidegger in Germany, Sartre constructed a radical individualism that centered on moral responsibility. Even in the worst of circumstances, human beings were free to make some choices; and the sum of the choices made gave each life its moral meaning. The soldier could refuse to torture; the civilian could choose to resist custom or authority. Underneath its relentless pessimism, Sartre's existentialism—set forth in essays, dramas, and criticism—held out the possibility of moral heroism.

Christian voices shared in the public anguish over values that marked the postwar period. Leading theologians—also mainly men of an older generation, like Jaspers, Karl Barth, and Jacques Maritain—were studied with renewed interest. The Protestant Paul Tillich and the Catholic Pierre Teilhard de Chardin achieved a large following with their systematic claims for Christianity's relevance to modern life. This confidence, reflected in the postwar vigor of Christian political parties, illuminated the papacy (1958–1963) of Pope John XXIII. He was extraordinarily popular, admired by Protestants as well as Catholics and by peasants and workers as well as intellectuals. Determined to recast the Church's position in the modern world, he called the Vatican Council known as Vatican II which opened in 1962. Devoted to *aggiornamento*, the Council sought to bring the Catholic Church

▲ **Prelates from around the world stand as Pope Paul VI is carried on his throne into St. Peter's during the Vatican Council. Amid Renaissance splendor the leaders of the Catholic Church set about the task of** *aggiornamento.*
AP/Wide World.

up to date not just organizationally but in social policy as well. It made the leadership of the Church far more international, directed attention to the concerns of developing nations, made respect for Jews a formal policy, and expressed belief in religious liberty. Putting more emphasis on individual understanding than institutional uniformity, it ordered that Masses be conducted in the vernacular instead of Latin. These changes encountered resis-

tance, and with Pope John's death before the Council was completed, the Church turned to more cautious consolidation of doctrine and structure.

THE EXPLOSION OF POPULAR CULTURE

American Influence   A very large part of the commercial entertainment that Europeans watch and listen to comes from the United States. American dominance in the motion picture industry, apparent in the 1930s, has grown since World War II. Although European governments have tried a variety of measures to reduce the proportion of American productions in their movie theaters and on television, all have failed. In the 1950s well more than half of the movies that Europeans attended were from the United States, and by the 1990s the figure was more than 80 percent. American films had some commercial advantages. They could be offered cheaply because a large domestic market had already covered most of their production costs. American movie companies were masters at distribution, and the American government was willing to pressure other countries to provide access to American films. American productions have had similar success on European television, as privately owned television networks compete with those that governments run by filling a majority of their airtime with inexpensive American reruns.

In fact, American television productions have demonstrated remarkably wide appeal. The television series *Dallas* was as popular and well known in Europe as in the United States, and Italian judges have found themselves explaining to defendants more familiar with *Perry Mason* than with their own justice system that "your honor" is not a term used in Italian courts. By the 1990s, soap operas from Brazil (especially popular in Portugal and Spain) and Australia (especially popular in Great Britain) were added to American shows as regular fare on European television networks owned by Italian, French, and German media tycoons. Theme parks, too, have spread from the United States to Europe. Denmark has its Legoland; and *Parc Asterix*, based on a series of French comic books, is located on the outskirts of Paris, not far from the European Disneyland.

An International Youth Culture   Much criticized on both sides of the Atlantic, such commercial entertainment had been especially troubling to many European intellectuals who were used to seeing the United States as an example of what the future would be like everywhere. Conservatives worried that American-style democracy led to cultural decline, Marxists believed that ruthless capitalism created that decline by making culture a commodity. The signs that something more was

▲ **In Poland in 1987, fans at a rock concert celebrate in international style.**
Christophe Kazor/Sygma.

at stake—the creation of an international youth culture—became clearer in the 1950s with the international appeal of American rock and roll and the fashions that went with it.

American jazz had been popular in Europe since the 1920s, especially in France; and after the war, the presence of American troops and the programs of Armed Forces Radio did much to disseminate American popular music. The new musical culture did not come exclusively from the United States, however. The Beatles, who combined American influences with those of the British music hall, were by far the most influential popular music group of the 1960s and, along with the Rolling Stones, helped to create a transatlantic style that was at home on the continent and in Latin America as well as in Britain and the United States. By the 1980s an international tour was a normal part of star status in pop music. In each country, performances were usually preceded by local groups, adding to the sense of a single culture with national variants. When in 1997 the Irish band U2 performed in Rome and Sarajevo, or when Bob Dylan and gospel singers appeared with the Pope at a eucharistic congress, national origin hardly seemed to matter.

New Directions   The arts had never been more international than after World War II, and they were necessarily affected by the energy of new forms of popular culture. One response was to turn away from the fast-paced plots of American cinema in favor of a more reflective mood. The novels of Alain Robbe-Grillet and the films of Jean François Truffaut and Ingmar Bergman were contemplative personal essays, held together by the sensitivity and imagination of a single creator and by images simultaneously surreal and real. Identified in France as the *nouvelle vague* of the 1960s, this style had its counterpart in all the arts.

Experiment and Shock　The desire to convey individual and fleeting perceptions encouraged further experimentation with varied forms of narrative in literature and a freer use of surrealistic images in the visual media. The highly personal and even autobiographical films of Federico Fellini incorporated swirling images of circus-like fantasy. In painting, highly disciplined abstract Expressionism gave way to a great variety of styles that often made use of popular culture and referred to urban consumerism. New styles, such as Pop Art and Op Art, returned to the representation of recognizable objects but treated them satirically and were deliberately garish and disturbing. Younger artists found original ways to transform the familiar into something new, using common objects and materials of every sort to produce strange forms and creating gigantic "environmental" sculptures consisting of lines traced across deserts or plastic wrapping stretched around whole buildings.

At the same time that popular music tended to become more complex and artistically serious, noted composers of classical, or so-called serious, music were drawn to experiments using everyday noises and musical sounds carefully arranged on spliced tapes, a form known as *musique concrète,* and with electronic music in the manner of the American John Cage and the German Karlheinz Stockhausen. Even when it employed traditional instruments, the dissonances and strange rhythms of avant-garde music won only a tiny audience, but it was closer to the mainstream in the determination to breach artistic conventions. In their need to stimulate a public already bombarded by images and sensations, artists used technology for aesthetic purposes. Taking advantage of the ambiguity of random noise, flashing lights, plastics forms, and mechanical motion, they further eroded the distinctions between art and advertising.

Postmodernism　The change of attitude as the arts tended to become less austere and less con-

▲ The Monument of a postmodern and international age, this Guggenheim museum was designed by the American architect Frank Gehry and opened in 1997 in Bilbao, Spain, a city once known primarily as a grimly, industrial town.
J. Pavlovsky/Sygma.

cerned with the principles that academies taught and critics adhered to, was particularly clear in architecture. Modern architecture, influenced by the Bauhaus school (see p. 992), had developed an international style that favored the pure and simple forms of cube and rectangle and the simplicity of unadorned walls of glass. By the 1970s, however, newer styles rejected that aesthetic and instead deliberately featured unexpected shapes, pitched roofs with gables, echoes of many older styles, and whimsical ornamentation. Because the element that this eclectic architecture most obviously shared was its rejection of modernism, it came to be called *postmodern,* a term soon applied to many other fields as well. A preference for playful attitudes and individualistic innovation more than a formal school of thought, postmodernism reflected important cultural tendencies. Labeling regularity, rigid logic, and the control of nature or human beings as modern made postmodernism a convenient way to describe a new direction in the arts and social sciences.

SOCIAL THOUGHT

Following World War II, the major schools of social thought generally assumed that rational analysis could explain social behavior with a certain objectivity that would lead to beneficial policies. From the 1970s on, however, students of society have been increasingly inclined to show instead how programs for social improvement, claims to objective knowledge, and the promotion of high culture may actually be exercises in dominance by those with power.

Modernization and Marxism   Social and political thought in the 1950s combined efforts to explain the recent past with prescriptions for dealing with the present. Theories of modernization traced a line of development from the era of absolute monarchy to a modern age of liberal democracy; and in doing so, they sought to explain what went wrong in nations like Germany, Italy, and Spain that had not sustained democracy. The answers to these historical questions could then be used to guide the policies of developing nations around the world, helping them achieve democratic stability. Writings on modernization, especially pervasive in the United States, influenced the social sciences throughout the West. They demonstrated the connection between political freedom and economic growth and showed that these developments were in turn intricately related to other social changes, such as literacy and urbanization. Discussions of modernization tended to advocate for all societies the values, legal systems, and social practices they saw as characteristic of Western Europe and the United States. Studies of modernization encouraged interdisciplinary research, the use of sophisticated social scientific theories and methods (including opinion surveys and quantification), and greater attention to the non-Western world. By the 1970s these theories had come under heavy attack for creating an idealized description of Western (often American) society and seeking to impose it on everyone else, for stressing consensus and compromise while largely ignoring social conflicts and glaring injustices, and

for serving as a Cold War ideology in competition with Soviet Marxism.

Marxist thought, which also incorporated ideas of progress, provided the principal alternative to theories of modernization. Varieties of Marxism less rigid than Soviet communism were influential throughout European intellectual life, especially in England and Italy in the late 1960s and 1970s. In their flexibility and subtle insights, these neo-Marxist analyses made lasting contributions to the understanding of society and culture, especially through ideas associated with the so-called Frankfurt school and with Antonio Gramsci. A group of innovative and Marxian social scientists and philosophers had flourished in Frankfurt under Germany's Weimar republic until Hitler forced its leaders into exile. Although their writings were rigorous and difficult, they gained a wide readership in the postwar period. And their analyses, whether of the arts or social structure, interlaced modern sociology and psychology (especially Freudian ideas) with a profound distaste for mass culture and contemporary society. One of their members, Herbert Marcuse, became a hero to leaders of the student revolts of 1968 because of his powerful criticism of the commercialism and the illusory freedom of modern society.

The pervasiveness of Marxist thinking also owed a great deal to the work of Antonio Gramsci. Like the more doctrinaire Hungarian Georg Lukacs, Gramsci was a communist intellectual who took culture seriously, not simply as a reflection of society's material structure but as the collection of values that held it together. One of Italy's leading Communist activists, Gramsci was imprisoned by the Fascist authorities; most of his writing consists of notebooks and letters written in prison during the 1920s and 1930s and published after the war. Pondering the importance of religion and art and wanting to explain why peasants and workers accept inequality, Gramsci developed the concept of cultural hegemony. It begins an exploration of how the values and styles that elites invent and promulgate come to be shared across social classes, shaping the thought and action of entire societies. Ideas and symbols matter, Gramsci argued, and radicals must provide an alternative culture that matches the qualities of the culture they wish to overturn.

Cultural Studies   English, French, German, and American scholars applied these ideas to their own histories and to current political debates, exposing a bias toward the status quo in liberal ideology and elitism in much current scholarship. The field of cultural studies has evolved from this line of attack on dominant ideologies while distancing itself from Marxism and gaining momentum from changes in world politics as well as culture. Decolonization invited a new look at how imperialism functions and provoked renewed interest in how non-Western societies wrestle with Western cultural and economic domination. The self-serving assumptions built into European assessments of non-European cultures (a topic that dominates anthropology today) had become easier to identify. Movements in behalf of ethnic minorities—Afro-Americans in the United States and other ethnic groups in the United States and Europe—undermined any claims that society's established institutions and authoritative voices were ever neutral. Cultural studies has also made popular culture the object of serious study, especially in Britain, welcoming its irreverence and finding within it a yearning for freedom and the creative expression of marginalized people alienated from consumer society.

Michel Foucault The methods, insights, and vocabulary of cultural studies owe a great deal to the work of the Frenchman Michel Foucault, perhaps the most influential thinker of the 1980s, particularly in the United States and England. Foucault was trained as a philosopher, and his work achieved international resonance much as Sartre's had a generation earlier. Foucault consistently acknowledged his debt to Nietzsche and was clearly influenced by Marx , the new social history,[5] and the work of the French anthropologist Claude Lévi-Strauss. Lévi-Strauss believed that every aspect of a supposedly primitive society—its kinship systems, customs, rituals, and myths—can be understood as the extension of unstated, complex, and integrated structures of thought. These hidden structures, he declared, reflect the nature of the human mind, a view that led him to an ad-

miration of premodern societies comparable to that felt by many modern artists.

All these currents were present in Foucault's thought, but most of all he built on the rising science of semiotics, the study of the signs by which human beings communicate. In Foucault's hands, semiotics provided the means for reinterpreting modern history and civilization. His periodization was conventional: Modernity emerged in the late eighteenth century and was heralded by the French Revolution. But he upended the conventional interpretations of what modernity meant. Medicine, psychology, and prison reform were not simply the progressive results of increased knowledge but instruments of a new social discipline. The scientific observation of other people, however neutral or objective it claims to be, is a means of controlling behavior through shared *discourse*—a crucial Foucauldian term. By discourse Foucault means a framework of understanding used consciously and unconsciously that automatically excludes some possibilities and urges others. To talk about certain behavior as an illness, for example, is a form of power; and power is one of Foucault's central concerns. Discourse functions within society to make power diffuse and pervasive, independent of public intent. Foucault's ideas (like his witty, perceptive, and involuted style) provided a new and effective way to challenge not just the acknowledged evils of modern society but the laws, institutions, practices, and conception of knowledge on which society rests. Without proffering solutions, Foucault's works offer an arsenal of weapons with which to unmask intellectual claims to authority or objectivity (see "Foucault on Sexual Discourse," p. 1129).

Poststructuralism A further powerful attack on the apparent neutrality of scientific categories and logical reason is heavily indebted to French intellectual Jacques Derrida. Like Foucault, Derrida uses the tools of semiotics and philosophy and has more followers in the United States than in Europe. The two have been called the philosophers of 1968 because of their ties to the student movement of those years. Derrida studies literature by concentrating on the text and subjecting it to a technique he named *deconstruction*. For deconstructionists, texts contain linguistic signs that are not straightforward—not *transparent,* to use their term—but instead carry multiple associations

---

[5] French historians centered around the journal *Annales* began before World War II to develop approaches to social history that influenced historical study around the world in the 1960s and 1970s and continue to make important contributions to the social sciences and humanities. Foucault himself was close to although not part of the *Annales* group.

Foucault on Sexual Discourse
◆

One of Michel Foucault's last major works was The History of Sexuality, *which explored the topic from ancient Greece to the present. In the selection here he touches on several of his major themes.*

"But there may be another reason that makes it so gratifying for us to define the relationship between sex and power in terms of repression: something that one might call the speaker's benefit. If sex is repressed, that is, condemned to prohibition, nonexistence, and silence, then the mere fact that one is speaking about it has the appearance of a deliberate transgression. A person who holds forth in such language places himself to a certain extent outside the reach of power; he upsets established law; he somehow anticipates the coming freedom. This explains the solemnity with which one speaks of sex nowadays. When they had to allude to it, the first demographers and psychiatrists of the nineteenth century thought it advisable to excuse themselves for asking their readers to dwell on matters so trivial and base. But for decades now, we have found it difficult to speak on the subject without striking a different pose: we are conscious of defying established power, our tone of voice shows that we know we are being subversive, and we ardently conjure away the present and appeal to the future, whose day will be hastened by the contribution we believe we are making. Something that smacks of revolt, of promised freedom, of the coming age of a different law, slips easily into this discourse on sexual oppression. Some of the ancient functions of prophecy are reactivated therein. Tomorrow sex will be good again. Because this repression is affirmed, one can discreetly bring into coexistence concepts which the fear of ridicule or the bitterness of history prevents most of us from putting side by side: revolution and happiness; or revolution and a different body, one that is newer and more beautiful; or indeed, revolution and pleasure. What sustains our eagerness to speak of sex in terms of repression is doubtless this opportunity to speak out against the powers that be, to utter truths and promise bliss, to link together enlightenment, liberation, and manifold pleasures; to pronounce a discourse that combines the fervor of knowledge, the determination to change the laws, and the longing for the garden of earthly delights. This is perhaps what also explains the market value attributed not only to what is said about sexual repression, but also to the mere fact of lending an ear to those who would eliminate the effects of repression. Ours is, after all, the only civilization in which officials are paid to listen to all and sundry impart the secrets of their sex: as if the urge to talk about it, and the interest one hopes to arouse by doing so, have far surpassed the possibilities of being heard, so that some individuals have even offered their ears for hire.

"But it appears to me that the essential thing is not this economic factor, but rather the existence in our era of a discourse in which sex, the revelation of truth, the overturning of global laws, the proclamation of a new day to come, and the promise of a certain felicity are linked together. Today it is sex that serves as a support for the ancient form—so familiar and important in the West—of preaching. A great sexual sermon—which has had its subtle theologians and its popular voices—has swept through our societies over the last decades; it has chastised the old order, denounced hypocrisy, and praised the rights of the immediate and the real; it has made people dream of a New City. The Franciscans are called to mind. And we might wonder how it is possible that the lyricism and religiosity that long accompanied the revolutionary project have, in Western industrial societies, been largely carried over to sex."

From Michel Foucault, Robert Hurley (trans.), *The History of Sexuality, Vol. 1: An Introduction,* Vintage Books, 1990.

with individual words, with style and syntax, and with all the literary, cultural, social, and personal contexts from which a given text has emerged. Necessarily, the signs on the page must be (mis)translated in the mind of the reader. Thus no text has one stable meaning but communicates differently to different people and on many levels at once. Deconstruction, the exploration of multiple and hidden signification, directly denies the existence of absolutes and any pretense to objectivity.

These currents of contemporary thought, obviously related to postmodernism, are often referred to as *poststructuralism* because they have moved beyond logical structures, scientific models, and

A REFLECTION ON CONTEMPORARY FEMINISM

Julia Kristeva arrived in Paris in 1966 as a twenty-six-year-old Bulgarian scholar trained in linguistics. She quickly became an important contributor to the semiotics movement in France, noted for her remarkable knowledge of European philosophy, Marxism, and influential Russian scholarship in semiotics. An active participant in the events of 1968, she subsequently trained in the leading French school of psychoanalysis and developed her own practice. In addition to widely acclaimed scholarly works, essays, and novels, she writes frequently on women's issues. Provocative and controversial, her studies are nevertheless representative of European feminist writings in several respects: their engagement with European philosophy from Plato through Hegel and Nietzsche; their sophisticated use of psychoanalysis and literary criticism, including deconstruction (she has been particularly close to Derrida); their analysis of the contemporary historical context; and their search for a new feminism through close attention to immediate, practical and personal issues. Following are excerpts from "Women's Time" by Julia Kristeva, an essay first published in French in 1979 and subsequently reprinted many times in many languages.

"In its beginnings, the women's movement, as the struggle of suffragists and of existential feminists, aspired to gain a place in linear time as the time of project and of history. In this sense, the movement, while immediately universalist, is also deeply rooted in the socio-political life of nations. The political demands of women; the struggles for equal pay for equal work, for taking power in social institutions on an equal footing with men; the rejection, when necessary, of the attributes traditionally considered feminine or maternal in so far as they are deemed incompatible with insertion in that history—are all part of the *logic of identification* with certain values: ... with the log-

ical and ontological values of a rationality dominant in the nation-state. Here it is unnecessary to enumerate the benefits with this logic of identification and the ensuing struggle have achieved and continue to achieve for women (abortion, contraception, equal pay, professional recognition, etc.); these have already had or will soon have effects even more important than those of the Industrial Revolution. Universalist in its approach, this current in feminism *globalizes* the problems of women of different milieux, ages, civilizations or simply of varying psychic structures, under the label 'Universal Woman.'

continues on next page

fixed categories. Under the influence of poststructuralism, the techniques of literary analysis have become important to contemporary writings about society. Social custom, forms of courtesy and dress, organizations and law, education and religion can all be studied like a text for the multiple messages they convey.

Gender Studies In no field has the large body of poststructuralist theory had greater impact than in gender studies, which looks beyond biological or sexual differences to the social construction of different roles for men and women, differences fabricated from custom, from views about the nature of women and men, and above all, from seemingly neutral dichotomies such as strength/weakness, rationality/irrationality, and public/private which when associated with male/female become constraints on the roles thought proper for women. Such studies have made it necessary to rethink and

rewrite a great deal of history, anthropology, and sociology. If the theoretical base has been heavily European, its application has been more extensive in the United States, where the structure of universities, the rapid opening of careers to women, and public preoccupation with oppressed groups has fostered the development of gender studies. In Europe, too, however, similar reinterpretations of society and culture have given new strength to feminist movements and to campaigns in behalf of groups previously marginalized (see "A Reflection on Contemporary Feminism," pp. 1130–1131). Europe's admired, established culture and the institutions that sustain it have come under attack from many quarters, and those attacks have made their own contributions to culture. That established culture, which remains at the core of education, religion, and much of public life, meanwhile draws millions of people each year to museums and concert halls.

"In a second phase, linked, on the one hand, to the younger women who came to feminism after May 1968, and, on the other, to women who had an aesthetic or psychoanalytic experience, linear temporality has been almost totally refused, and as a consequence there has arisen an exacerbated distrust of the entire political dimension. . . . Essentially interested in the specificity of female psychology and its symbolic realizations, these women seek to give a language to the intra-subjective and corporeal experiences left mute by culture in the past. Either as artists or writers, they have undertaken a veritable exploration of the *dynamic of signs,* an exploration which relates this tendency, at least at the level of its aspirations, to all major projects of aesthetic and religious upheaval. . . .

"Finally, it is the mixture of the two attitudes—*insertion* into history and the radical *refusal* of the subjective limitations imposed by this history's time . . . —that seems to have broken loose over the past few years in European feminist movements, particularly in France and Italy.

"The desire to be a mother, considered alienating and even reactionary by the preceding generation of feminists, has obviously not become a standard for the present generation. But we have seen in the past few years an increasing number of women who not only consider their maternity compatible with their professional life or their feminist involvement (certain improvements in the quality of life are also at the origin of this: an increase in the number of daycare centers and nursery schools, more active participation of men in child care and domestic life, etc.), but also find it indispensable to their discovery, not of the plenitude but of the complexity of the female experience. . . . It is [also] in the aspiration towards artistic and, in particular, literary creation that women's desire for affirmation now manifests itself. . . . These few elements of the manifestations by the new generation of women in Europe seem to me to demonstrate that, beyond the socio-political level where it is generally inscribed (or inscribes itself), the women's movement—in its present stage, less aggressive but more artful—is situated within the very framework of the religious crisis of our civilization.

"I call 'religion' this phantasmic necessity on the part of speaking beings to provide themselves with a *representation* (animal, female, male, parental, etc.) in place of what constitutes them as such, in other words, symbolization. . . . The elements of the current practice of feminism that we have just brought to light seem precisely to constitute such a representation which makes up for the frustrations imposed on women by the anterior code (Christianity or its lay humanist variant).

From Alice Jardine and Harry Blake (trans.), "Women's Time," by Julia Kristeua, in *Signs*, Vol. 7, No. 1, University of Chicago Press, August 1981, pp. 13–35.

Without the harsh simplicity of bipolar conflict, European affairs looked more complex after the collapse of the Soviet Union and the end of the Cold War, but that complexity also reflected the astounding gains of fifty years of peace. The promise of well-being was never more universal or real. To be sure, capitalism brought dangerous dislocation across the continent. Freedom allowed ethnic conflict. But political and ideological differences were less important and the distinction between Eastern and Western Europe less relevant. Intellectual creativity has generated excitement but no clear consensus. Questions of values remain painfully unresolved. Whereas social equality has yet to be achieved, increased wealth has been accompanied by the signs of alienation revealed in drug abuse and xenophobia. There are troubling indications every day of the anger, frustration, and disillusionment many people feel. Nevertheless, Eastern Europe is freer than ever before in its history and Western Europe more united than it has ever been. A half-century ago very few people expected that by the end of the twentieth century, in an increasingly global society, Europe would remain a favored continent, enviable in its wealth, liberty, and culture.

Recommended Reading

Sources

Ash, Timothy Garton. *The Magic Lantern: The Revolution of '89 Witnessed in Warsaw, Budapest, Berlin, and Prague.* 1990. An eyewitness account by a particularly keen and informed observer.

de Beauvoir, Simone. *Memoirs of a Dutiful Daughter.* James Kickup (tr.). 1959. *All Said and Done.* Patrick O'Brian (tr.). 1974. Important to the history of contemporary feminism, Beauvoir's memoirs also give a sense of the intellectual life of the times.

*Ellul, Jacques. *The Technological Society.* John Wilkinson (tr.). 1964. One of the most striking and influential of contemporary attacks on the effects of technology.

Gorbachev, Mikhail. *Perestroika: New Thinking for Our Country and the World.* 1989. This presentation of Gorbachev's vision of the future is as revealing for the issues it does not address as for its specific recommendations.

Studies

*Albertini, Rudolf von. *Decolonization. The Administration and Future of the Colonies, 1919–1960.* Francisca Garvie (tr.). 1982. A solid account that focuses on Britain and France and is especially valuable for its historical depth.

*Ardagh, John. *France in the 1980s.* 1987. A fascinating examination of the fabric of daily life, with an eye on the development of the whole period since 1945 and of France's position in Europe.

* Ash, Timothy Garton. *The Polish Revolution: Solidarity.* 1984. Rich in insights into the social roots, techniques, ideas, and effectiveness of a moment that captured worldwide attention.

Berger, Suzanne (ed.). *Organizing Interests in Western Europe: Pluralism, Corporatism, and the Transformation of Politics.* 1981. Important assessments of the political balance of power by some of the leading American social scientists.

Brown, B. E. *Protest in Paris: Anatomy of a Revolt.* 1974. The student revolt in Paris subjected to scholarly study.

*Caplan, Richard, and John Feffer. *Europe's New Nationalism: States and Minorities in Conflict.* 1996. Essays on regions from Scotland to Eastern Europe that discuss the important historical issues raised by some of the less-familiar outbursts of nationalism since the end of the Cold War.

*Craig, Gordon. *The Germans.* 1983. A noted historian's insightful, handsomely written, and critical assessment of German society.

*Heidenheimer, Arnold J., Hugh Heclo, and Carolyn Adams. *Comparative Public Policy: The Politics of Social Choice in Europe and America.* 1975. Studies the background and implications of the varied approaches to social policy, written as the limitations of these programs were becoming apparent.

*Helias, Pierre-Jakez. *The Horse of Pride: Life in a Breton Village.* June Guicharnaud (tr.). 1980. A compelling account of a preindustrial society about to be transformed.

Hennessy, Peter, and Anthony Seldons. *Ruling Performance: British Governments from Attlee to Thatcher.* 1987. Contrasting perspectives on British politics in radically different governments.

Hoffmann, Stanley, and Paschalis Kitromilides. *Culture and Society in Contemporary Europe.* 1981. An anthology of essays by leading intellectuals attempting to evaluate the condition of Europe.

*Hooper, John. *The Spaniards: A Portrait of the New Spain.* 1987. An engaging look at the European society that went through its greatest transformation in the last twenty years.

Hoskins, Geoffrey. *The Awakening of the Soviet Union.* 1990. An excellent overview of how change came to a society that had resisted it for so long.

*Hughes, H. Stuart. *The Sea Change: The Migration of Social Thought, 1930–1960.* 1977. A major study of the role of European intellectuals in the United States and their contributions to modern social thought.

*———. *Sophisticated Rebels.* 1990. An intellectual historian considers the nature of dissent in the West as well as in Eastern Europe during the critical years of 1988 and 1989.

*Hulsberg, Werner. *The German Greens: A Social and Political Profile.* 1988. A systematic treatment of the strongest of the European environmental movements.

*Jarausch, Konrad H. *The Rush to German Unity.* 1994. Uses recently opened archives to provide an historian's assessment of recent, complicated events.

*Jay, Martin. *The Dialectical Imagination. A History of the Frankfurt School and the Institute of Social Research, 1923–1950.* 1973. A rewarding study of some of the most influential thinkers of modern social science written with a keen understanding of the intellectual background and prejudices from which they wrote about modern society.

*Jenkins, Keith. *The Postmodern History Reader*. 1997. Selections from more than thirty historians suggest the variety of ways that current intellectual trends have affected the writing of history.

Katzenstein, Mary F., and Carol M. Mueller (eds.). *The Women's Movements of the United States and Western Europe*. 1987. These collected essays make for a book with wide coverage that underscores some striking national differences.

*Kavanagh, Dennis, and Anthony Seldon (eds.). *The Thatcher Effect*. 1989. A variety of critical appraisals of Thatcher's policies.

Kennedy, Paul. *Preparing for the Twenty-First Century*. 1993. A historian's skeptical look at power relations in the near future.

Keylor, William R. *The Twentieth-Century World. An International History*. 1984. A stimulating attempt to break out of the traditional national boundaries.

Lewin, Moshe. *The Gorbachev Phenomenon*. 1988. A brilliant analysis written as the phenomenon was unfolding that relates current events to the developments in Soviet society over the previous fifty years.

*Maier, Charles S. *Dissolution: The Crisis of Communism and the End of East Germany*. 1997. Connects domestic and international politics to ideology and social conditions to explain the collapse of communism and the German unification.

*Mandelbaum, Michael. *The Nuclear Revolution: International Politics before and after Hiroshima*. 1981. A thoughtful study, making good use of parallels from the diplomacy of earlier eras to assess the implications of the nuclear age for international relations.

Marrus, Michael R. *The Emergence of Leisure*. 1974. A historical study that identifies one of the important characteristics of modern life as an important historical trend.

Merkl, Peter H. *The Federal Republic at Forty*. 1989. A distinguished political scientist evaluates the German republic that has lasted far longer than the Weimar Republic.

*Parker, Geoffrey. *The Logic of Unity*. 1975. Usefully analyses the forces for European unity from a geographer's perspective.

Payne, Stanley G. *Politics and Society in Twentieth-Century Spain*. 1976. A historian's recognition that Spain's remarkable modernization had firm foundations in the past.

Poster, Mark. *Existential Marxism in Postwar France*. 1975. An able analysis of an intellectual movement that had a wide impact on its generation.

Riddle, Peter. *The Thatcher Decade: How Britain Has Changed during the 1980s*. 1989. An unusually positive assessment of the long-term effects of the Thatcher period on British society.

Silber, Laura, and Allan Little. *The Death of Yugoslavia*. 1995. A moving, penetrating, and unusually balanced account.

Williams, Raymond. *Communications*. 1976. A leading British writer and historian reflects on the role of communication in modern societies.

*Available in paperback.

EPILOGUE

To some extent we all think historically, for the history of the world in the last 200 years has made awareness of change an essential part of our outlook. We assess the present by contrasting it with the past; our fears and hopes for the future are largely based on historical trends that seem to forecast conditions to come. Publicists announce "revolutions" in everything from world politics and technology to manners and fashions. Politicians justify their decisions by confidently predicting what "history will say"; conservatives and radicals claim to know "the lessons of history." Obviously, much about the way we think about the world depends on our understanding of the past.

I. The Present and the Past

Historical understanding begins with a sense of historical perspective. When the Berlin Wall came down and Europe's communist regimes collapsed, everyone recognized in those dramas a major historical watershed. These great changes were all the more striking because they were unintended, not the aim of any policy but the effect rather of a surge of popular feeling among millions of Eastern Europeans wanting the freedom and prosperity enjoyed in Western Europe. Such sudden change, facilitated by modern mass communication and peacefully achieved, made it easy to believe, in both East and West, that a wholly new era had begun and that the world had entered an age of disarmament, liberal governments, and capitalist economies.

HISTORICAL PERSPECTIVE

Assumptions of such total change need to be tempered with historical perspective, which suggests four reasons for caution. The first is simply that great transformations are difficult, and the strains they create can have unexpected results. The Reformation, the expansion of Europe, the French Revolution, industrialization, and the revolutions of 1848 brought important changes, many of them very different from initial expectations.

Second, historical perspective tempers assumptions about sweeping change, for there is often surprising continuity in social life. Established patterns matter. Differences persist even today between those parts of Europe that belonged to the Roman Empire and those that did not, between those Christian missionaries converted in the Early Middle Ages and those converted later, between those peoples who experienced the Protestant Reformation and those who did not. If the nations of central and Eastern Europe were to be ranked today according to the relative strengths and weaknesses of their economies and political systems, they would stand in relation to each other much as they did seventy years ago, following World War I and the collapse of the Habsburg Empire.

Many observers, of course, have noticed this; and facile analogies to the past have become as common as simplistic assumptions that everything is different. Such analogies are a third reason for caution. Commentators on current events in Eastern Europe point to parallels with Russia in the nineteenth century and the arguments then between Slavophiles and Westerners, to the surge of nationalism in the nineteenth century that led to the unification of Italy and Germany, and to ethnic and religious conflicts in Europe going back to the Middle Ages. Such examples can be invaluable when used analytically to explore how contemporary issues evolved and how societies evoke the loyalties that enable them to function. The examples are inherently selective, however, and easily manipulated. Historical awareness, which should lessen surprise at the renewed vigor of nationalism in Eastern Europe, includes recognition of how readily political leaders and intellectuals reconstruct the past, how they recall past glories wrongly subverted and injuries never adequately revenged. Self-serving histories—and all societies create them—can achieve the power of founding myths that speak more to current feeling than to any past reality.

Finally, historical understanding recognizes that human history is always contingent on many elements; identifying trends does not predict outcomes. In this century the impact of individual decisions by intellectuals, demagogues, revolutionaries, popes, and political leaders has continued to be great and unpredictable. Gorbachev came to power as part of a process of adaptive reform that seemed likely to strengthen the Soviet Union. Almost no one imagined that his daring determination would have such effect that the Soviet Union would soon cease to exist. Good historical thinking leaves room for unforeseeable decisions, for unexpected results, for the interplay of multiple forces, trends, and interests, and for sheer accident.

Seeing the Past through the Present Historical understanding is constantly renewed by new research based on new methods and, even more important, on new questions. A major source of those questions is contemporary experience. The social concerns of the twentieth century stimulated new schools of social and demographic history that have fundamentally altered our vision of the European past. Decolonization and increasing international trade fostered fresh analysis of the historical relations between economies at different levels of development, from the Middle Ages to the present. That research has revised the understanding of imperialism and of capitalism in both the present and the past. From the 1950s through the 1980s, the harsh realities of the Cold War caused many commentators and politicians to look at history in terms of power politics, the rise and fall of superpowers, and the differences between East and West. The studies that followed illuminated aspects of history often overlooked and affected interpretations of the Cold War itself. With the end of the Cold War, we see more clearly the effects it had on domestic parties, social programs, and basic freedoms around the world, raising new questions about even the recent past.

Periodization   These changing views of the connection between present and past are especially clear in terms of periodization. In the 1950s and 1960s, it was common to say that the world had entered the Atomic Age, because the promise of atomic energy and the fear of atomic warfare seemed to shape an era. In the 1990s references to the Atomic Age are rare because both that promise and that fear have faded. Similarly, the promise that World War I would make the world safe for democracy is now remembered primarily as a bitter irony; but should stable democracies in fact become the European norm, the process that accomplished this might well be seen as having been at work since 1918. Some observers see 1968–1970 as a turning point, when failed revolutions, a new kind of social criticism, and the oil crisis undermined confidence in established institutions, consumerism, and perpetual economic growth.

Many historians, diplomats, and politicians once identified the decline of Europe as one of history's major trends. In that light a new era could be said to have begun with World War I or a generation later when a continent tragically dominated by the Axis plunged into a war that destroyed Europe's international power and left it subject to Soviet and American domination. In 1940 France dropped from the ranks of the world's most powerful states; Germany did so five years later; and in the 1950s even victorious Great Britain could no longer sustain an international position comparable to that of the United States and the Soviet Union. The economic crises of the postwar period and the loss of colonial empires seemed to confirm a process of relative decline in Western Europe's strength. Thus in the 1950s Arnold Toynbee's widely admired, multivolume *Study of History* echoed the earlier gloom of Oswald Spengler in proclaiming that a millennium of European preeminence in world history had come to an end.

Shifting dates just a few years, however, could produce a periodization that points to a new era in European history beginning in the 1950s and marked by rapid social change, unprecedented prosperity, and the trend toward European union. Neither periodization is wrong; each fits a different set of questions. The questions asked of historical evidence may evolve from prior research, from a body of theory, or from current concerns. The findings that result lead to new understanding and, in turn, new questions. To think about European history in terms of current issues can thus be fruitful both for historical research and for insight into the present. Many of the world's pressing problems, after all, have roots in the history of Europe; and Europe's future will be molded through its response to worldwide trends.

A Global Era   Recent research by archaeologists and historians has uncovered extensive connections of commerce and culture even in the ancient world and in the Early Middle Ages. There is now impressive evidence that metals, olive oil, wine, and new technologies moved along routes that reached from Asia to Europe. Nevertheless, the extent of communication, technology, and trade at the end of the twentieth century seems to be creating a new kind of global society, accelerating a pattern that goes back to a restless Europe's expansion through the crusades, the voyages of discovery, the conquest of the New World, the spread of Dutch and British trade in the seventeenth century, the building of empires in North America and India a century later, direct rule in the age of imperialism, and the extension of Western interests in the competition of the Cold War. This expansion involved knowledge of the world and its peoples, bloodshed, idealism, and greed. There is no reason to think that the process of building a global society will be simpler or have political and cultural effects that are any less mixed.

EUROPE AND THE WORLD

Despite its great wealth, Europe will not again dominate the world as it once did. At the most, it will be one of many poles of wealth and power. Having learned to exercise their diplomatic influence in the interstices of Cold War competition, European nations have become accustomed to limited influence in circumstances like those in which many states of the former Soviet Union now find themselves.

Cultural Exchanges　In part because Europeans have been more consistently interested in other societies—as objects of exploration, study, conversion, and exploitation—than people from any other region, European ideas, institutions, and techniques have spread around the world and are so much a part of local history that in many places they are no longer merely European. In the last fifty years European societies have become far more open to extra-European influences through commerce, mass communications, and formal study but also through the massive presence of Americans, Asian tourists, and immigrants from the Middle East, Africa, and the Caribbean.

These enriching cultural encounters have produced a long history of misunderstandings, abuse, and resentment that is part of world politics today. They have also led to concern everywhere that local ways will be overcome by the homogenizing impact of global contact. While it is true, for example, that urban life around the world has become more similar (from its conveniences to its problems of traffic and pollution), it is also true that Western influence, even when reinforced by brute force, the power of wealth, and new technologies, has not obliterated cultural differences. Within Europe itself local cultures have often found ways to preserve much of their identity while adapting to outside pressures; regional differences have survived the laws, armies, and roads of ancient Rome; the demands of national states; the intrusion of railroads, newspapers, and universal schooling; and the impact of telephones, television, and computers. European cities may be crowded with restaurants that offer American fast food in addition to Chinese, North African, Middle Eastern, Indian, and Vietnamese foods, and eating habits do seem to be changing. Yet national and regional cuisines have lost neither their identity nor their popularity.

II. The Modern Economy

Economic growth, once primarily a Western preoccupation, is now a universal goal. The power of the Japanese economy and the extraordinary growth of other Asian economies may be as significant for Europe (and as great a competitive challenge) as the economic expansion of the United States has been. Many experts expect this pattern of growth to extend through much of the rest of Asia, including the giant economies of China and India, and to much of Latin America and the Middle East. Development on this scale would have enormous implications for Europe, implications unlikely to be contained by Europe's high productivity, its historic ties to the non-Western world, its investments there, or its role as the principal source of economic and technological assistance.

NATIONAL STANDING

As the pioneer of an expansive capitalism, Europe has long experience of the fact that comparative economic advantages rarely last. The decline of the great commercial centers of the Middle Ages was followed by the relative decline of Renaissance Italy, then Spain, and then the Netherlands as the centers of shipping, banking, and textile production moved north. Shifts in relative economic strength speeded up with industrialization. England had the world's most productive economy and was the world's greatest trader for much of the nineteenth century, only to be overtaken by Germany and the United States.

Recent Developments　Such trends are sometimes reversible, however. As late as 1960 almost no one expected France and then Italy to surpass Britain, nor would anyone have anticipated the recent rapid growth of Spain. Sudden economic transformations remain possible despite the advantages that accrue from tradition, capital, technology, infrastructure, and education—advantages demonstrated in Germany's impressive recovery from defeat in two world wars.

Although the resources and technologies that matter most today are far different from those that were important in the past, Europe's wealthiest regions at the end of the twentieth century include many that were the wealthiest centuries ago. If, as some predict will happen, information replaces production as the principal source of wealth, European societies may be well situated for future growth. Certainly all nations now hope to take part. In Eastern Europe the collapse of communism left room for the kind of speculation and raw entrepreneurship associated with the American wild west. Disastrous pyramid investment schemes that shocked society in Romania and brought down the government of Albania were also touching evidence of how far ahead of harsh reality the myths of capitalist wealth had spread.

Trade and Wages   A more immediate challenge arises from the tendency of international corporations to shift production from older centers to developing countries in which wages are lower. Even if neoliberal theories are correct in predicting benefits for all in the long term, the immediate social impact is serious. High and seemingly permanent unemployment is already a major problem across the continent. The historic pattern that led to higher wages and increased consumption may have been broken, for labor unions were weakened by changes in the workforce and by international competition that favors low-wage areas. The policies traditionally favored by the left to raise workers' incomes become less relevant when governments declare their helplessness before the pressures of global trade. The balance of power among capital, labor, and the state seems to have shifted.

While the majority of Western Europeans have enjoyed increased freedom and a rising standard of living, a significant minority suffers unemployment, segregation, and discrimination. Thus many Europeans worry about the creation of a permanent underclass and what some have called "the two-thirds society," societies in which two-thirds of the population continues to prosper, enjoying increased wealth and leisure, while a bottom third is left out forever. Even mild economic downturns in a world in which economic growth is expected to continue can have serious social and political consequences. The revolutions of 1848, the political crises at the end of the nineteenth century, the revolutions in Russia, the rise of fascism, and the fall of communism were all related to economic crises. Thus the concern that a downturn,

especially when large segments of the population are already hard-pressed, would challenge the social principles and the political stability of modern Europe as seriously as industrialization and the Great Depression did in the past.

The Limits of Growth   In fact, perpetual growth may be doomed by demographic and ecological constraints. Industrial expansion in nineteenth-century Europe benefited from growing populations, but now demographic factors are more likely to have a negative economic effect. In Europe, as people live longer and families are smaller, the population grows older; and an aging population requires more services and produces less. The still graver issue is how much growth the environment can sustain. Italy suffered for centuries from the erosion of a mountainous terrain that had been stripped of trees in order to supply the shipbuilders of ancient Rome and of the medieval maritime republics. In the seventeenth century the Spanish economy was severely harmed by the effects of overgrazing. Since the Renaissance, cities have tried to regulate pollution, and in the sixteenth and seventeenth centuries states tried to control practices likely to cause flooding or threaten the animals that nobles liked to hunt. Until the end of the eighteenth century, however, Europeans usually understood environmental disaster as an act of God, like epidemics and natural catastrophes such as earthquakes and volcanic eruptions.

Europe was fortunate in the nineteenth century that, as its supply of timber or grain or other critical resources seemed about to run short, unexploited sources of energy, new agricultural techniques, and the expansion of trade permitted a timely readjustment. The rest of the world may not be so lucky in the future, and predictions of environmental catastrophes no longer seem so exaggerated. Western European societies today spend a great deal of money to combat the pollution they create. The far graver effects of pollution in Eastern Europe, still being discovered, will be a burden at least through the next generation. Environmental issues challenge the status quo and suggest policies that run counter to the immediate interests of specific groups and sometimes of whole regions. They divide traditional political parties and push governments into new areas of activity, and they are often so international that responsibility is diffused and responses are necessarily complicated. The many important environmental movements in Europe have enjoyed only limited political success, despite their strong appeal, especially to young people; but they offer added reasons for a distrust of politics, formal institutions, and established interests.

III. The Functions of the State

The modern state is a European invention that has spread around the world. From the Carolingian and Norman monarchies of the Middle Ages and the city-states of Renaissance Italy to the present, the steady growth of the state has shaped European history. The national monarchies of Spain, France, and England made the state an instrument for creating military might, dispensing uniform justice, and supporting a national culture. With the French Revolution and Napoleonic rule, the role of the state increased enormously, its intrusive efficiency expanding as it more fully engaged the entire citizenry. The demands of nationalism, democracy, and two world wars added still more to the state's power and the range of its activities. So did fascism, communism, and programs of social welfare. International organizations have also proliferated in this century, but in all of them, member states have tenaciously defended their individual sovereignty. Yet many thoughtful observers now suggest that the state may be losing some of its functions and much of its autonomy.

ECONOMIC POLICIES

Modern economic life has added to the responsibilities of the state, which is expected to provide a stable currency and banking system, an environment favorable to investments and trade, and the education, detailed statistical information, and means of communication that postindustrial societies require. These demands of course are not entirely new.

Directed Economies   The city-states and monarchies of the Middle Ages sponsored guilds and free cities, where duties and taxes were reduced, in order to stimulate the economy. The fact that the states of the early modern period adhered to theories of mercantilism, restricting imports and encouraging exports through regulation, is a reminder of how ideological economic policy often is.

The last twenty years have seen an enormous growth in the power of international corporations eager to shift capital and plants for economic advantage, independent of national states. The governments themselves, especially those in the most developed economies, have tended to accept the argument that reducing trade barriers is beneficial to all. In the early phases of industrialization, governments abolished guilds as organizations that stifled competition and protected the privileged and inefficient; but those same ordinances also made labor organizations illegal, a situation rectified only after generations of conflict. Today the free movement of goods and capital tends also to create an international labor market, undermining the state's role as protector of employment and wages.

By the 1970s most informed observers outside the communist world suspected that Soviet-style planning was not working well. A very different kind of planning, looser, more general, and reliant on free markets was very much in favor, however. In France, a planning office with a large staff of experts and a consultative assembly representing business, labor, and governmental agencies created long-range programs and drafted legislation for parliamentary action. Most other European countries had, and to a large extent still have, comparably comprehensive arrangements. Nearly all sought to manage their economies, indirectly through tax and fiscal policies and sometimes directly through nationalized industries and subsidies.

Now the trend is away from such intervention. Members of the European Union are prepared to surrender much of their fiscal sovereignty to a new central European bank at the same time that they are abandoning many older policies intended to give direction to the economy. West Germany's economy became Europe's largest while limiting the government's direct role in economic affairs. In England the Conservative party under Margaret Thatcher launched a systematic campaign to limit the government's economic role and to dis-

and Italy are selling off government-owned industries; and the nations of Eastern Europe are, to varying degrees and often at great social pain, allowing prices, wages, production, and distribution to be largely determined by the free market.

Social Policies When socialist parties first gained power during the Great Depression, they found themselves applying the policies of economic liberalism, balancing budgets and reducing deficits. In 1996 and 1997, parties that were once socialist won elections in many European countries, including Britain, France, and Italy. Concerned to stimulate competition and contain social expenditures, they have followed budgetary policies not very different from those of their opponents.

The social activism of European governments was aimed at much more than the economy, for it sought to create a more just and egalitarian society. Large-scale programs for housing, welfare, health, and education implied some reallocation of wealth from the well-to-do to the less fortunate. In practice, the middle of society probably benefits as much as the poor, and the accompanying tax burden is in fact too great to fall on the rich alone.

Now, both the cost and many of specific policies of the welfare state have come under attack; yet few Europeans seem to favor reducing social programs to the level of such programs in the United States. Unemployment is lower in the United States and in Britain than on the continent, but the disparity between rich and poor is also much greater in America, and Britain has a higher proportion of the population at or below the poverty level than do continental nations. Thus the tension between the goal of social equity and the desire to encourage investment and to meet international competition remains unresolved, the fault line of contemporary politics.

DIMINISHING THE STATE

Arguably, these debates about what functions the state should perform are beginning to undermine the state's position as the dominant social organization.

Bureaucracy The state, and its bureaucratic mode of organization, became a pervasive model adopted throughout society. Expected in principle to be efficiently organized for well-defined tasks, bureaucracy was expected to deal with specific problems rationally and objectively and was supposed to be managed by people selected for their talent and technical training. Each nation developed its distinctive bureaucratic style reflecting its own history—the independent role of the aristocracy in England, the service tradition of the Junkers in Prussia, the centralized expertise of royal and Napoleonic government in France, which was adopted in many other countries.

The institutions with which governments deal—political parties, businesses, unions, education systems, hospitals—have tended to be organized in similar bureaucracies, in theory, maintaining similar standards of fairness and expertise. In practice, of course, no government agency is removed from special interests and political prejudices. This bias makes bureaucracy itself a central issue in modern society. Bureaucratic organization can subvert official policies and inhibit social flexibility. Its procedures tend to be especially resented in democracies and its cost unpopularly tangible in the tax rate.

In the past decade many Europeans, finding fault with bureaucracy, have become increasingly critical of the state's prominence. The state has become an object of suspicion, not so much for being the captive agent of the ruling class (the classic Marxist reason) or as a threat to individual liberty (the traditional liberal fear) but simply as a concentration of power dedicated to its own interests. To some extent a similar criticism is applied to other large organizations—business corporations, political parties, and universities. A distrust of institutions is an important element in what are known collectively as the New Social Movements. Like environmentalism and feminism, NSMs that have had the greatest effect operate beyond ordinary politics and look beyond the state, preferring to found new groups, influence public opinion, and affect individual lives.

Federalism Criticism of the state has strengthened the call for increased federalism. Regional movements appeal to traditional differences in customs and dialects and at the same time make very modern arguments about their distinctive and neglected economic needs and about the obtuseness of distant officials. Even in effective democracies, the political process often seems far removed from the people, a sort of private game of interests. The breakup of the Soviet Union was a criticism of centralized communist rule as well as an expression of local nationalisms. Though not so thoroughly federal as Germany, France has created regional governments, and Spain has granted increased regional autonomy. In 1997 an Italian assembly worked on creating a federal structure, and the Scots voted for devolution granting increased local rule and a parliament of their own (which they had rejected a few years before). In accepting the advantages of smallness, national governments shed some of their historic functions (especially in areas such as urban planning, cultural subsidies, social services, adult education, recreation, programs to attract investment, and tourism).

The Military While the economic and social roles of the modern state are being challenged, so is its most traditional function as the locus of military power. With war in Europe unlikely and the Cold War ended, European states have reduced their military budgets. British and French forces played an active if subordinate role in the Gulf War against Iraq, but it may be that in the future national pride in the military can be satisfactorily expressed through limited peacekeeping missions. The major European nations have joined other countries in these missions, and the pressure they applied in local conflicts helped to undermine the white government of South Africa and to bring about conversations between Catholics and Protestants in Northern Ireland and negotiations between Palestinians and Israelis. But European democracies have clearly not been eager to take major risks to quell brutal fighting in Rwanda and Burundi or Bosnia. Although a strong army and participation in NATO remain significant, military strength may be less important to the European state than ever before.

The European Union In this light the European Union takes on considerable historical interest. There are many reasons for the remarkable momentum behind its growth. The most recognized, of course, is its impressive economic success. A reason often overlooked is its moral and social appeal as the embodiment of a new kind of polity, socially progressive and antinationalist. Ireland elected its second consecutive woman president in 1997; and of the five candidates, four were women. When asked why women had such prominence, the influence of the European Union on Irish culture was one of the first explanations the candidates gave. As the former communist states of Eastern Europe prepare to make their case for membership in the EU, they seek to establish that they meet the unstated standard of modern democracy that the EU is thought to represent, including free speech, civil rights, and equality for women and minorities.

In some respects the European Union is absorbing many of the traditional functions of the state. National governments are making wrenching sacrifices that might well be politically impossible without the EU in order to meet the criteria for joining the European single currency, the Euro. Adopting the Euro, however, means that each nation surrenders control over its own currency, a sovereign power that states have manipulated for millennia and a symbol of authority from the ancient world to the present. Great Britain, without a written constitution, now has in effect a written bill of rights, the result of decisions by the European court. A great deal of the legislation that issues from Brussels on everything from insurance to safety in the workplace and standards for food is adopted by national legislatures with minimum review.

Perhaps, then, the European Union will replace the national state in many realms. On the other hand, the fear that it might do so was one of the principal objections to the Maastricht treaties heard throughout the member countries. Denunciations of EU bureaucracy and its voluminous rulings are even louder, especially when established practices are criticized from abroad, as when the farmers of Normandy are told they must make Camembert cheese with pasteurized milk or British companies are told that chocolate bars should not contain vegetable oils. Not having found a way to make its institutions democratic, the EU does not yet have the legitimacy of the democratic state.

IV. Questions of Values

◆

Ironically, at the very time that certain values seem to be widely accepted as human rights that are applicable everywhere, intellectuals have launched powerful criticisms of the assumptions on which those ideals rest. They question whether one society or group has the right to impose its standards on another, and their research undermines the belief that European values have timeless and universal meaning. Issues of values become more pressing as individuals find that their greater liberty, knowledge, and prosperity broadens the burden of the difficult choices they must make.

HUMAN RIGHTS

The belief that its principles should be universal has been characteristic of Western thought. Greek philosophy searched for truths applicable to everyone, and Roman law was extended wherever Roman civilization could reach. Christian belief always emphasized the need to carry Christian teachings to all peoples, and in the last two centuries Europeans have variously but confidently proposed capitalism, liberalism, Marxism, and democracy as ideals to be universally embraced.

Specific Issues   Within the European Union and among nations that aspire to join it is effective unanimity on the importance of human rights and their content, ranging from freedom of speech and religion to opposition to the rights of labor and opposition to the death penalty. The Council of Europe and its Court of Justice have set very explicit standards so that, for example, Croatia began in 1996 to remove restraints on a free press in order to be allowed to join the Council.

Many people in Europe (and many more in the United States) criticize Eurocentrism and emphasize cultural diversity as an important value in itself. Such concerns induce self-consciousness about advocating human rights around the world. The very conception of such rights may be "fundamentally a product of the liberal imagination,

reflecting the complacent cultural imperialism of the modern Western world."[1]

In 1989 Salman Rushdie, an Indian Muslim educated in England, published *Satanic Verses,* a novel that the Ayatollah Khomeini considered blasphemous in its references to Muhammad. To Khomeini the book was the latest of many assaults from Western culture on an Islamic way of life. Supported by the other leaders of Iran, he pronounced a death sentence on Rushdie and on all who, knowing the book's contents, participated in its publication. Rushdie was forced into hiding. Western intellectuals and political leaders expressed outrage and reaffirmed their commitment to freedom of expression. Crowds of militant Muslims demonstrated in the streets of England, India, Pakistan, the Middle East, and North Africa to protest against insults to Islam and the imposition of Western values. Rushdie lives in guarded seclusion.

The Problem of Choice   These issues are not just differences between East and West, for there is conflict within Europe and America between those who give absolute priority to individual rights and those who place social values first, between those who insist on the right of individuals to make moral choices, even wrong ones, and those who insist that society and the state must embody and enforce some absolute truths. The movement to accord to women all the opportunities for education, careers, and independent activity permitted to men can thus be seen as a logical extension of individual rights. To some it will mean the dangerous destruction of a tradition that built the family around the distinctive domestic role of women. Such conflicts between social needs and personal aims were explored in Classical Greek drama, wrestled with by the Church fathers, and recast during the Renaissance and the Reformation. The great intellectual battles of the Enlightenment were often fought on just these issues, and they have remained divisive ever since.

Several factors, however, have made these disputes especially difficult at the end of the twentieth century. Mobility, education, science, and

---

[1] Stephen Shute and Susan Hurley (eds.), *On Human Rights: The Oxford Amnesty Lectures. 1993,* (New York; Basic Books, 1993).

▲ **Burning a poster of the cover of Salman Rushdie's** *Satanic Verses*, **Kuala Lumpur, March, 1989.** Reuters/Bettmann.

market economies have broadened the range of personal choices. Matters such as diet and dress that were once simply determined by custom have become personal statements, and people are expected to make wise choices about their lifestyle and their occupation, about where they live and how they spend their leisure. Furthermore, decisions about even such intimate choices as marriage and divorce, contraception, and abortion are surrounded by public discussion and debate—in which religious leaders, moralists, and feminists disagree because these are issues of personal identity and of social ethics at the same time. In practice the wide availability of contraception has made possible vast changes in human relations and has allowed women a freedom that seemed impossible at the beginning of the century. Many people are also convinced, however, that these changes have devalued human life and the sanctity of marriage.

The Family That concern is one of the reasons for widespread fear that the institution of the family is being undermined, despite the likelihood that belief in the importance of the family may be as high as it has ever been. There is little reassurance in the fact that alarm over threats to the family has been heard from thousands of pulpits for centuries; that serfdom, slavery, and poverty have also endangered the family; and that the Christian view of human nature and the Freudian view of the human psyche both acknowledge that the constraints of family life are difficult to accept. Despite all the pessimistic predictions, the family has survived. It has survived the effects of industrialization, which separated household members for nearly all their waking hours, moved millions of people to new places, and deprived the family of the traditional social support of relatives and village custom. Indeed, the expectations of the family have steadily increased since the eighteenth century. The Victorian conception of the Christian family raised the norms for loyalty and comity, and they have risen higher since then. Marriage in the twentieth century is expected to be a mutual choice and a delightful partnership in which child rearing lasts longer and is more intensive than ever before.

Warnings that society is losing its ethical compass are difficult to assess in historical terms. For some commentators, the spread of acquired immunodeficiency syndrome (AIDS) became the basis for denunciations of sexual promiscuity, homosexuality, and the ease with which people and disease now move across continents. A quite different assessment of modern values follows from those observers who emphasize instead the extensive scientific research on AIDS in Europe and the United States and the widespread determination that the victims of this disease should not be treated the way lepers were for centuries.

Social Responsibility Many people now argue that feelings of alienation, which Marx attributed primarily to the faulty organization of production, have become more general, affecting not just craftsmanship but attitudes toward society and work in general, taste in entertainment, and the prevalence in modern Western societies of crime and drug addiction. Or perhaps this behavior is not so different from the alcoholism of Hogarth's

London or the centuries of peasant revolts, highway robbery, cockfighting, prostitution, and public hangings in the past.

Critics often assert that the contemporary world has experienced a sharp decline in civic responsibility, and they point to examples like weak neighborhood ties and gratuitous vandalism. This tension between individualism and social responsibility, familiar in the United States, is at the center of intense public concern in Europe and underlies the debate between neoliberal advocates of free markets and defenders of the welfare state. The issue is particularly acute in former communist societies. There, individualism is for many a new battle cry that is especially attractive to the young, but can be used to excuse racketeering and worse. A poll of teenagers in Russia in 1997 asked them to list the careers that most attracted them. Of the thirty-six choices, contract killer finished in the middle, cosmonaut dead last. Understandably, the press worried about a return of the nihilism that was strong in Russia exactly a century earlier.

A generalized sense of responsibility may be growing, nevertheless. Environmentalism asks individuals to sacrifice some personal convenience for a larger good; and from France to Finland half to two-thirds of all glass is recycled, which means that every day millions of people make an extra effort in behalf of a social benefit they never see. Similarly the spreading ordinances against smoking or boycotts against manufacturers who hire underpaid workers in developing countries all give more weight to a social good than to individual pleasure.

No question has raised the issue of social responsibility more dramatically than the Holocaust, a source of continuing anguish. In 1997, more than fifty years after the event, a court trial in France hammered home the fact that many French people had cooperated with the Nazis in rounding up Jews to be sent to concentration

▼ *Anselm Kiefer*
Burning Rods
Anselm Kiefer, "Burning Rods." 1984–87. Mixed media on canvas. The St. Louis Art Museum. Purchase: Gift to Mr. and Mrs. Joseph Pulitzer, Jr., by exchange.

camps, and official organizations of French police and attorneys apologized for having once acquiesced in antisemitism. Swiss banks confessed to still holding the funds that Jews had deposited on their way to death or exile. Fresh accounts appeared about the profits that Swiss interests had garnered from cooperation with Nazi Germany, and in Sweden newly published documents revealed that major firms had carefully assured their German contractors that they employed no Jews. The Roman Catholic Church apologized for the indifference of many Catholics to the plight of the Jews, and the pope appointed a commission to study anti-Judaic prejudice in the Church. Memories that whole societies had conspired to repress have become the occasion for wrestling with the nature of moral responsibility.

Communists, too, have found soul searching necessary, and many of them took the occasion to praise a book written by a group of French historians, most of them Marxists, attempting to assess how many human beings communism had killed around the world. On the eightieth anniversary of the Russian revolution, the European press was filled with comment on its estimates: 85 million people killed (half of them in China), including 15 million killed in the Soviet Union between 1917 and 1953. The commentators could all remember, and many had marched in, earlier commemorations of the Russian revolution when across Europe thousands sang songs and carried banners expressing their hope in revolution.

V. The Nature of Community
◆

Conflicts over social justice, moral values, and culture make for great disagreements over what a social contract might contain or whether society rests at all on the kinds of principles that Locke and Rousseau described and on which liberalism was founded.

COHESION AND CONFLICT

Freedom, some people argue, has gone too far, and prosperity has proved to be morally dangerous. Yet highly organized societies leave individuals feeling powerless and manipulated despite the apparent array of choices before them. Signif-

icantly, social control, a central concern in the writings of the Frankfurt school and Michel Foucault, has become a favorite subject for social research, which finds it operating through advertising and education as well as through religion and custom, laws and institutions. The effect, these critics argue, is to keep the disadvantaged docile and to obscure issues of social justice. Suddenly, the question of what kind of social contract should be extended to foreign immigrants or to citizens who merely lack the skills most in demand has become one of the burning issues of modern Europe.

Religion Around the world, nationalism and vibrant religious movements demonstrate the power of community feeling, raising the question of whether Europeans will once again turn to such movements as they have in the past and whether postindustrial societies can satisfy the desire for social solidarity. Although fundamentalist religious movements remain weak in most of Europe, there is a significant Catholic fundamentalist movement in Italy; a Protestant one in Northern Ireland; Muslim ones in Britain, France, and Russia; and Orthodox ones in the former Soviet Union. Religious clashes have been endemic in Europe—part of medieval battles against heretics and Muslims, warfare between Protestants and Catholics, and modern conflicts between church and state.

Religion can mobilize opposition to current social trends, as in the frequent campaigns against immoral ways, whether of dress or drugs; opposition to the state, as in the Solidarity movement in Poland; and opposition to other social groups, as in the enduring conflict in Ireland. Under John Paul II, elected pope in 1978 (and the first non-Italian pope in 455 years), the Roman Catholic Church has become more resolutely conservative and outspoken on theological, institutional, and moral issues while remaining a vigorous critic of modern materialism and the injustices of capitalism. Conceivably, religious issues could heighten some of the conflicts in contemporary European society as they did in the 1920s and 1930s.

Identity Ethnic conflict, too, has rarely been absent in European history, and Yugoslavia in the 1990s provided frightening proof that it remains possible for political leaders to inflame ethnic hatreds for their own purposes. Such efforts are in fact under way in much of Eastern Europe, and parties opposed to foreigners have gained attention and votes in France, Germany, and Italy. Western societies, which have generated the most powerful ideas and most effective movements opposed to racism, have also spawned virulent racist movements. The memory of Nazi genocide must affect any assessment of Western civilization and any evaluation of modern history, and nationalist movements anywhere in Europe are bound to evoke that fear. Nazism did strengthen the sense of German national identity, and national sentiment remains strong throughout Europe. As the Falkland war, the union of East and West Germany, and bloodshed in the Balkans show, political leaders can play no stronger card than an appeal to national loyalty.

In the last half century, Western Europeans have been drawn closer together and gotten to know each other better than ever before. The question is whether a fulfilling sense of community can come either from pride in a more integrated Europe or from regional loyalties that encourage a symbolic nationalism without a state. Polls indicate that 51 percent of the people living in EU countries feel that being European is part of their identity (men more than women, the young more than those older, and citizens of the founding six nations more than those in countries that have joined more recently).

SPLINTERED CULTURES

Sharing culture once implied proximity; now it occurs among people similar in class or age more readily than place. Eurovision allows national networks to participate in Europe-wide transmissions; and styles in music and dress have become more global than European. Formal or high culture has also become more international than in the nineteenth century, in part because exiles from Hitler's Europe and Stalin's Russia made cultural life more international and transatlantic.

Whose Culture? Nevertheless, at negotiations on the General Agreement on Tariff and Trade in 1994, the countries of the European Union supported France in insisting that their mass media must reserve some support for European productions. That argument was not about the content or function of popular culture but where it originated and who profited.

Research in the sciences and humanities conducted in Europe now often has a distinctively and perhaps increasingly European rather than national flavor. Scholars from one part of Europe teach and work in another, and research teams include people from several European countries. In the arts individual performers, orchestras, and works of art move freely across Europe's national borders, and student exchanges within the European Union have become the norm. No previous civilization supported so much scholarship, so many centers of learning, or so many artists.

Contemporary observers are less confident, however, than those Enlightenment thinkers who more than two centuries ago compared ancient and modern culture and decided that the moderns had the advantage. At the end of the twentieth century, the proportion of Europeans certain of modern progress is probably lower than a century earlier. Instead, revelations of mass murder under a Soviet regime that proclaimed humane values and sustained an admirable high culture serves as a reminder that the expanded capacities of modern society include the ability to kill. The role of culture is much clearer as a basis for opposition than as an expression of commitment. It was in the euphoria of liberation that Czechoslovakia picked a playwright as president.

Popular and High Culture Part of this unease about the role of culture stems from the troubling separation nowadays between popular and formal culture. The great literary works of all ages continue to be taught in schools and universities and are still read with pleasure. More people than ever before hear classical music and visit museums and art galleries. Yet commercial entertainment, ubiquitous and international, conveys quite a different set of values; and the morally earnest culture of the nineteenth century, of which so much was expected, threatens to become merely academic, a matter for special study by experts. The very forms that defined that culture—long novels and epic poems, symphonies, operas, impressive museums—are, by current standards, discouragingly demanding of attention, time, and money. Ironically, this older bourgeois culture was lavishly supported under communism; but now state subsidies for elite culture, though far more common in Europe than in the United States, are questioned everywhere.

The music, art, and literature that the twentieth-century avant-garde proudly called modern and that it used to attack the established high culture from which it grew never achieved a broad popularity. Doubt about human rationality and disdain for elites have made anti-intellectualism respectable, and there has been a remarkable revival of interest in the occult. Computers, after all, can also be used to plot astrological charts. For centuries, Europeans have taken culture to be the most significant expression of society, and we tend to identify historical eras by their characteristic cultural achievements. If that is done in the future, what will be said of this era?

The Consolation of History   Because every era tends narcissistically to believe that its problems are unique, that very assumption deserves to be doubted. Europe today faces no threat comparable to the barbarian invasions of ancient Rome or the Black Death. If social change now is rapid, we have learned to expect and even anticipate it; the changes that followed the fifteenth century or those in the hundred years after 1780 may well have been more shocking and harder to absorb. We should not let nostalgia make it seem that earlier ages enjoyed a confidence and comforting unanimity denied to us. Rarely in Western history has a single philosophy or set of values enjoyed undisputed hegemony. The view that other eras were informed by a single spirit is largely the product of distance, which makes outlines clearer and fissures more obscure. The competing claims of throne and altar and the disputes about forms of transubstantiation were once as socially shattering as issues about public and private ownership, ethnic minorities, or abortion and euthanasia are today.

And there are encouraging lessons to be learned. Good causes can be served by ordinary people with all the normal human flaws. The resistance movements that fought fascism and are rightly honored throughout Western Europe were often formed around old conflicts and resentments. If the future is uncertain, as futures always are, that is partly because what human beings choose to do does make a difference. History takes a turn at the intersection of long-term trends and accident, where personalities interact within larger frameworks of ideas and social structures. European history demonstrates that the past is inescapable but also that memory is malleable, that radical transformations can be consonant with great continuity. That being so, the western tip of the Eurasian peninsula can be expected to generate in the future the conflicts, dangers, discoveries, institutions, customs, ideas, and dreams that have made the Western experience such a compelling experiment.

Appendix

Recommended Films

Chapter 19

Amadeus. 158 min. Color. 1984. Spectacular presentation of Mozart's life and times.

Civilization: The Pursuit of Happiness. 52 min. Color. Time-Life Films. Kenneth Clark on eighteenth-century music and art.

Civilization: The Smile of Reason. 52 min. Color. Time-Life Films. Kenneth Clark on the Enlightenment.

Ridicule. 102 min. Set in the eighteenth-century court of Versailles.

Chapter 20

Danton. 135 min. Color. 1992. Powerful film by Polish director Andrzej Wajda on the personality and political differences between Danton and Robespierre; Gerard Depardieu as Danton.

La Marseillese. 130 min. B/W. 1937. French with English subtitles. A celebration of the revolutionary spirit in 1792.

The Battle of Cholet: 1794. 30 min. Color. Films for the Humanities. Revolt in the Vendée.

Chapter 21

The Battle of Austerlitz; The Battle of Trafalgar; The Battle of Waterloo. 30 min. each. Color. Films for the Humanities. Probably the single most important battles of the era.

The Hundred Days: Napoleon from Elba to Waterloo. 53 min. Color. 1969. Time-Life Films. Filmed on location.

Chapter 22

The Crystal Year. 30 min. B/W. 1965. National Educational Television. England in 1851.

Pride and Prejudice. 226 min. Color. BBC. An effective adaptation of Jane Austen's famous novel that gives a good picture of genteel village life in England.

Silas Marner. 100 min. Color. BBC. Country village relations during the early industrial revolution.

Chapter 23

Civilization: The Worship of Nature. 52 min. Color. 1969. BBC. Kenneth Clark on the nineteenth-century belief in the divinity of nature.

Great Expectations. 124 min. Color. 1974. BBC. A somewhat condensed version of Dickens' classic novel that captures the bustle of industrial England.

When Ireland Starved. Four 26-min. episodes. Color. Films for the Humanities. The Irish famine, why it occurred, what was done, and what resulted; uses contemporary reports and illustrations.

Chapter 24

1848. 22 min. B/W. 1949. Radim Films. Daumier graphics show Paris in 1848.

Bismarck: Germany from Blood and Iron. 30 min. Color. 1976. Learning Corporation of America. Bismarck's word to describe German unification.

The Leopard. 205 min. 1963. A superb adaptation of Lampedusa's great novel of nineteenth-century Sicily.

Chapter 25

Europe, the Mighty Continent: Hey-Day Fever and *A World to Win*. 52 min. each. Color. 1976. Time-Life Films. Europe in 1900 and in the decade before the First World War.

Zulu. 138 min. Color. 1964. Classic account of battle between Zulu army and a small group of British soldiers; filmed on location in South Africa.

Chapter 26

Art of the Western World. Vol. III, 7. *A Fresh View of Impressionism and Post-Impressionism*. 56 min. Color. 1989. Educational Broadcasting Corporation, funded by Annenberg Project CPB.

The Battleship Potemkin. 75 min. B/W. 1925. Eissenstein's classic film study of the Odessa Mutiny of 1903 is also an important document of early Soviet propaganda that captures the enthusiasm of the revolution.

La Belle Epoque: 1840–1914. 60 min. Color. ABC Video in association with the Metropolitan Museum of Art. Evokes this time of wealth and pleasure for the upper classes.

Chapter 27

All Quiet on the Western Front. 130 min. B/W. 1930. Beautiful film from the novel.

The Grand Illusion. 95 min. B/W. 1937. Jean Renoir's magnificent essay against the Great War that portrays differences of social class among the French and sympathetically suggests differences in cultural attitudes between the French and Germans.

Verdun. 30 min. B/W. 1965. Indiana University. The battle.

Chapter 28

Between the Wars. Eight 60-min. episodes. Color. 1978. Anthony Potter Production. Different aspects of these two decades.

Triumph of the Will. 110 min. B/W. 1935. Leni Riefenstahl's powerful film of the 1934 Nuremberg rally.

The Twisted Cross. 53 min. B/W. 1956. NBC. Study of Hitler's rise to power. Includes newsreel film.

Chapter 29

The Bicycle Thief. 90 min. B/W. 1949. A classic neorealist film about the postwar struggle for survival in Rome

D-Day. 50 min. B/W. 1962. Films, Inc. German and Allied footage of the landings.

Open City. 103 min. B/W. 1945. The beginning of the great wave of Italian postwar films; work on this film began as the Germans were evacuating the city. A moving presentation of the official myth of the resistance: supported by the honest poor and led by a heroic communist and a heroic priest.

Shoah. 570 min. Color. 1985. Claude Lanzmann's stunning documentary, based on interviews with people involved in rounding up Jews and sending them to the death camps and with survivors.

*Stalingrad. 135 min. 1993. German antiwar film that traces the WWII Stalingrad campaign. Follows structure of *All Quiet on the Western Front*.

Chapter 30

The Battle of Algiers. 135 min. B/W. 1965. Casbah. An important film of the revolt against French colonial rule.

Europe on the Brink. 1992. CNN. The fall of the Berlin Wall and the Soviet Union, and the changes in Eastern Europe.

Frontline: The Struggle for Russia. 1992. PBS. Documentary exploring Boris Yeltsin's presidency.

Gandhi. 188 min. Color. 1982. The struggle for Indian independence from colonialism.

Text Credits

Chapter 19

Page 662 Specified excerpts from *The Habsburg and Hohenzollern Dynasties in the 17th and 18th Centuries* by C. A. Macartney. Copyright © 1970 by C. A. Macartney. Reprinted by permission of HarperCollins Publishers, Inc. **Page 668** Excerpt from *The Norton Anthology of Literature by Women: The Tradition in English*, edited by Sandra M. Gilbert and Susan Gubar, 1985. Reprinted by permission of W. W. Norton & Company. **Page 670** Excerpt from Jean-Jacques Rousseau, *The Social Contract*, Book I, David Campbell Publishers. Reprinted by permission.

Chapter 20

Page 697 From R. R. Palmer (trans.), *The Coming of the Revolution*. © 1989 by Princeton University Press. Reprinted by permission of Princeton University Press. **Page 697** Excerpt from *Origins of the French Revolution* by William Doyle, 1988. Reprinted by permission of Oxford University Press.

Chapter 21

Page 749 From James B. Tueller, (trans.), *Political Constitution of the Spanish Monarchy*, proclaimed in Cadiz, March 19, 1812. Copyright James B. Tueller 1993. Reprinted by permission.

Chapter 22

Page 766 From Mrs. Alexander Napier, (trans.), Prince Richard Metternich (ed.), *Memoirs of Prince Metternich, 1815–1829*, Scribners Sons Publishers, 1970. **Page 770** Excerpt from Louis L. Snyder (ed.), *Documents of German History*, Rutgers University Press, 1958, pp. 158–159. **Page 779** From *European Historical Statistics, 1750–1970* by B. R. Mitchell. Copyright © 1979, Columbia University Press. Reprinted with permission of the publisher. **Page 786** Excerpt from *Documents of European Economic History, Vol. 1*, edited by Sidney Pollard and Colin Holmes, pp. 494–495, 497–498. Copyright © 1968 Sidney Pollard and Colin Holmes. Reprinted with permission of St. Martin's Press, Incorporated. **Page 789** From Thomas S. Ashton, "The Standard of Life of the Workers in England, 1790–1830," *Journal of Economic History*, Vol. 9, (1949). Reprinted by permission of Cambridge University Press. **Page 789** From Eric J. Hobsbawm, "The British Standard of Living, 1790–1850," *Economic History Review*, 1957. **Page 790** From Ronald M. Hartwell, "The Rising Standard of Living in England 1800–1850," *Economic History Review*, 1961. Reprinted by permission of the author. **Page 790** From *The Birth of a New Europe, State and Society in the Nineteenth Century* by Theodore S. Hamerow. Copyright © 1983 by the University of North Carolina Press. Used by permission of the publisher. **Page 791** From Philip A. M. Taylor (ed.), *The Industrial Revolution in Britain: Triumph or Disaster?* D. C. Heath, 1970.

Chapter 23

Page 798 From William Wordsworth, "Preface to the Second Edition of *Lyrical Ballads*" in *William Wordsworth: Selected Poems and Prefaces*, edited by Jack Stillinger. Copyright © 1965 by D. C. Heath and Company. **Page 807** From Oakley C. Johnson (ed.), *Robert Owen in the United States*, Humanities Press, 1970. **Page 814** From *The Working Population and its Structure* by P. Bairoch et al., 1968. Reprinted by permission of Gordon & Breach Science Publishers Inc.

Chapter 24

Page 843 From Louis L. Snyder (ed.), *The Documents of German History*, Rutgers University Press, 1958. **Page 850** From Giuseppe Mazzini, *On the Duties of Man*, Greenwood Publishing Group. **Page 861** From Louis L. Snyder (ed.), *The Documents of German History*, Rutgers University Press, 1958.

Chapter 25

Page 876 From P. Bairoch et al., *The Working Population and Its Structure*, Gordon & Breach, 1968, p. 119. **Page 890** From *European Historical Statistics, 1750–1970* by B. R. Mitchell. Copyright © 1979, Columbia University Press. Reprinted with permission of the publisher. **Page 894** From Heinz Norden (trans.), *Two Es-*

says by Joseph Schumpeter: Social Classes, Imperialism, A. M. Kelly Publishers, 1951, pp. 97–98. **Page 894** Extract taken from *Theories of Imperialism* by Wolfgang J. Mommesen, P. S. Fall (trans.), published by Weidenfeld & Nicolson Ltd., London, 1980. Reprinted by permission.

Chapter 26

Page 920 From Robert M. Cutler (trans. and ed.), *Mikhail Bakunin: From Out of the Dustbin: Bakunin's Basic Writings, 1869–1871*, Ardis Publishers, 1985. Reprinted by permission. **Page 925** From Richard Levy, (editor), *Antisemitism in the Modern World*. Copyright © 1991 by D. C. Heath and Company. Used with permission of Houghton Mifflin Company. **Page 930** From Emmeline Pankhurst, "The Last Fight for Human Freedom," speech given in Canada in 1912, in *Twentieth-Century Speeches*, edited by Brian MacArthur, Viking Penguin, 1992.

Chapter 27

Page 946 Reprinted with the permission of Simon & Schuster from *The Origins of the World War* by Sidney B. Fay. Copyright (1930 by Macmillan Publishing Company; copyright renewed © 1958 by Sidney Bradshaw Fay. **Page 960** From Brenda Girvin and Monica Coxens, "Meet the 'Khaki Girls'," *The Englishwoman*, 1917. **Page 962** Reprinted from Harold Owen and John Bell, (eds.), *Wilfred Owen: The Collected Letters*, © Oxford University Press 1967, by permission of Oxford University Press. **Page 975** Copyright © Sidney Pollard and Colin Holmes. From *Documents of European Economic History, Vol. 3* by Sidney Pollard and Colin Holmes. Reprinted with permission of St. Martin's Press, Incorporated.

Chapter 28

Page 987 Excerpt from "Manifesto of Futurism" from *Marinetti: Selected Writings* by F. T. Marinetti, edited by R. W. Flint, translated by R. W. Flint and Arthur A. Coppotelli. Translation copyright © 1972 by Farrar, Straus & Giroux, Inc. Reprinted by permission of Farrar, Straus and Giroux, Inc. **Page 989** From *The Decline of the West* by Oswald Spengler, Charles Francis Atkinson, trans. Copyright 1928 and renewed 1956 by Alfred A. Knopf, Inc. Reprinted by permission of the publisher. **Page 997** From *Leaves from a Russian Diary*. E. P. Dutton, 1920. Expanded

edition Beacon Press, 1950. **Page 1005** From S. William Halperin (ed.), *Mussolini and Italian Fascism*, Van Nostrand, 1964. **Page 1021** From Salvator Attansio and others (trans.), Speech of Goebbels, in *Nazi Culture: Intellectual, Cultural and Social Life in the Third Reich* by George L. Mosse, University of Wisconsin Press, 1996. Reprinted by permission.

Chapter 29

Page 1045 From Joseph Stalin, speech given July 3, 1941, in *The Penguin Book of Twentieth-Century Speeches* edited by Brian MacArthur, Viking Penguin, 1992. **Page 1052** From *Nazism 1919–1945: A Documentary Reader*, Volume 3, *Foreign Policy, War and Racial Extermination*, edited by J. Noakes and G. Pridham, University of Exeter Press. Reprinted by permission. **Page 1054** From Henry Friedlander, "Step by Step: The Expansion of Murder, 1939–1941," *German Studies Review*, XVII, October 1994. Reprinted with permission from the German Studies Association. **Page 1054** From Ernst Nolte, "Between Historical Myth and Revisionism," *Yad Vashem Studies*, XIX, 1988. **Page 1054** From *Reworking the Past* edited by Peter Baldwin. © 1990 by Peter Baldwin. Reprinted by permission of Beacon Press, Boston. **Page 1068** From Winston Churchill, speech given at Westminster College, March 5, 1946, in *The Penguin book of Twentieth-Century Speeches*, edited by Brian MacArthur, Penguin, 1992. Copyright the Estate of Sir Winston S. Churchill. Reproduced with permission of Curtis Brown Ltd., London, on behalf of the Estate of Sir Winston S. Churchill.

Chapter 30

Page 1101 From *Turkish Workers in Europe* edited by Ilhan Basgoz and Norman Furniss, Akural Aynu translator, 1985. Reprinted by permission of Indiana University Turkish Studies Publications. **Page 1116** From Vaclav Havel, inaugural address, January 1, 1990, in *The Penguin Book of Twentieth-Century Speeches*, edited by Brian MacArthur, Penguin, 1992. **Page 1129** From *The History of Sexuality, Vol. 1: An Introduction* by Michel Foucault, Robert Hurley, Jr. (trans.). Copyright © 1976 by Gallinard. Reprinted by permission of Georges Borchardt, Inc. **Page 1130** Excerpt from Alice Jardine and Harry Blake (trans.), "Women's Time," by Julia Kristeva, in *Signs*, Vol. 7, No. 1, August 1981, pp. 13–35. Copyright © 1981. Reprinted by permission of Chicago University Press.

Index notes: Main themes are indicated in **bold type**. Page numbers in *italics* indicate illustrations and their captions; page numbers followed by *M* indicate maps; page numbers followed by *t* indicate tables; page numbers followed by *n* indicate notes.